CPA Exam Study Manual

Business Environment & Concepts

2007/2008

Kaplan CPA Review

This publication is designed to provide accurate and authoritative information in regard to the subject matter covered. It is sold with the understanding that the publisher is not engaged in rendering legal, accounting, or other professional service. If legal advice or other expert assistance is required, the services of a competent professional should be sought.

President: Andrew Temte
Vice President: Dave Wiley
CPA Content Manager: Teresa Coile Anderson

© 2007 by Kaplan CPA Review, a division of Kaplan Professional Companies

Published by Kaplan CPA Review

1905 Palace Street
La Crosse, WI 54603
(608) 779-5599
www.kaplanCPAreview.com

All rights reserved. The text of this publication, or any part thereof, may not be reproduced in any manner whatsoever without permission in writing from the publisher.

Printed in the United States of America

CONTENTS

Introduction 4

Frequently Asked Questions 5

Ch. 1 Business Structures: Corporations 8

Ch. 2 Business Structures: Partnerships 51

Ch. 3 Finance: Ratio Analysis 92

Ch. 4 Finance: Working Capital Management & Long-term Financing 131

Ch. 5 Finance: Capital Budgeting 164

Ch. 6 Finance: Risk 198

Ch. 7 Finance: Financial Models Valuation 204

Ch. 8 Finance: Derivatives 221

Ch. 9 Planning and Measurement: Cost Volume Profit Analysis 255

Ch. 10 Planning and Measurement: Cost Accounting 290

Ch. 11 Planning and Measurement: Cost Accounting—Other Areas 326

Ch. 12 Planning and Measurement: Variance Analysis 385

Ch. 13 Information Technology: IT Fundamentals 422

Ch. 14 Information Technology: Business Information Systems 439

Ch. 15 Information Technology: System Operation 449

Ch. 16 Information Technology: IT Roles & Responsibilities 457

Ch. 17 Information Technology: Disaster Recovery & Business Continuity 469

Ch. 18 Information Technology: Business Implications 474

Ch. 19 Information Technology: IT Control Issues 479

Ch. 20 Information Technology: Flowcharts 504

Ch. 21 Economics: Economics of the Firm 509

Ch. 22 Economics: Competitive Environment of the Firm 550

Ch. 23 Economics: Sensitivity of the Firm to the Macroeconomy 585

Ch. 24 Economics: Government Policies 619

Ch. 25 Economics: Global Currency Risk and Hedging 648

Cram Essentials 676

Exam Strategies 773

Index 809

©2007 Kaplan CPA Review

INTRODUCTION

Thank you for choosing Kaplan CPA Review to guide your preparation for the CPA exam. You are about to embark on a journey that is unparalleled in your academic and professional training until now. Success on the CPA exam requires your total commitment of focus, discipline, time, and energy. We are here to guide you to those all-important words: "I passed!"

Kaplan, the leader in standardized test preparation for nearly 70 years, is dedicated to helping you pass the CPA exam the first time. Inside this book, you will find study notes and outlines as well as comprehensive questions and answers for the Business Environment & Concepts section of the CPA exam. Other volumes published by Kaplan CPA Review cover the remaining three sections of the exam. We realize you have a very busy life, and we have structured this volume to include only the topics you need to know for the exam. We do not include a lot of extra material that is unlikely to be tested. You do not have time for that!

We realize that everyone's needs are different when it comes to preparing for an important exam. Some people require only a brief refresher of well-known concepts; others look for a more in-depth review. Our Kaplan CPA Review Learning System is designed to provide you with the level of preparation *you* need. In addition to this Kaplan CPA Review Study Manual, the following companion products in our Learning System include study tools that are geared to all learning styles and that provide the flexibility today's busy professionals require:

- Kaplan Activity Planners to provide day-by-day guidance.
- Lesson and Problems Videos (available online or on optional CDs) providing more than 100 hours of instruction across all four sections.
- Online CPA QBank containing 3,000 T/F and 2,200 M/C questions, Testlets, and Simulations.
- Audio CDs presented as a series of Q&As providing more than 22 hours of strategic retention exercises.
- 2,100 Flashcards for hours of critical topic review.
- E-mail an Instructor and E-mail Lessons provide additional assistance.

We appreciate the opportunity to guide your study for the CPA exam. We wish you the best of success. Check our Web site at *www.kaplanCPAreview.com* for free resources to help you get ready for the exam, and practice with sample exam-like questions. Call us today at 800-CPA-2DAY (800-272-2329) or e-mail us at *cpainfo@kaplan.com* to take the first step towards passing the exam and getting on with the beginning of the rest of your life.

We're Kaplan. We build futures one success story at a time. Let yours be our next one.

FREQUENTLY ASKED QUESTIONS

ABOUT THE BUSINESS ENVIRONMENT & CONCEPTS SECTION OF THE CPA EXAM

Q: When should I start the application process to take the CPA exam?

A: First, you need to be certain that you have all education and other requirements fulfilled for the state where you want to have your scores reported. Go to www.cpa-exam.org and click on "Apply Now" and then follow the links to find your state. Be positive that you have (or will have) the hours and the courses that are required. Laws vary considerably by state and tend to change over time. Do not take the requirements for granted; check on the rules of your state. Second, keep in mind that the approval process can take up to six or seven weeks. You probably need to send in your application at least two months prior to when you want to sit for one or more parts of the exam.

Q: Can I begin the application process prior to completing all requirements so that I can sit for the exam as soon as I am qualified?

A: Check your state requirements. However, most states specify that the requirements have to be completed prior to beginning the application process.

Q: What is an NTS?

A: The NTS is your "notice to schedule," which indicates that your application has been approved. At that point, you can contact Prometric at *www.prometric.com/CPA* to find a test center and schedule an exam. Prometric is the company that administers the CPA exam. Make sure that you carefully read the NTS; it contains a lot of helpful information.

Q: Do I have to take the CPA exam in a particular state?

A: No, as long as you are properly approved and scheduled, you can take the CPA exam in any Prometric Center regardless of its location. For example, you can take the exam as an Iowa candidate but sit in a testing center in Hawaii.

Q: How long do I have to pass all four parts of the CPA exam?

A: That depends entirely on the law of the state where you are having your scores reported. Be certain to check by reading the rules of your state when you go to *www.cpa-exam.org*. The time can vary considerably by state.

Q: When is the CPA exam offered?

A: The CPA exam is given in four windows during the year: January–February, April–May, July–August, and October–November. Each section of the exam can be taken

---

©2007 Kaplan CPA Review

Page 5

STUDY MANUAL – BUSINESS ENVIRONMENT & CONCEPTS
FREQUENTLY ASKED QUESTIONS

once in each window. Thus, you could potentially sit for Business Environment & Concepts (as well as all other sections) a maximum of four times in any calendar year.

Q: Should I take all four parts of the CPA exam in one window?

A: That depends almost entirely on your ability to prepare for the exam. Most experts feel that a total of 250–400 hours is needed to prepare properly for all four sections of the exam. Many individuals take one or two parts per window unless they have a sufficient amount of time available to prepare for more. It is not unusual, though, for a candidate to take one part at the beginning of a window and a second part toward the end of that same window.

Q: Which part of the CPA exam should I take first?

A: There are a lot of different theories about which part should be taken first. One theory holds that you should take the part that you feel most positive about at the beginning so that you increase the chances of getting off to a good start. Other theories, though, do exist.

Q: Is the CPA exam only given by computer?

A: Correct. Starting back in 2004, the CPA exam was switched from a paper and pencil exam to a computerized exam. A multitude of changes in the exam took place at that time.

Q: What does the Business Environment & Concepts exam look like?

A: Business Environment & Concepts opens with 24 multiple-choice questions. When those 24 are submitted by the candidate as being complete, a second testlet of 24 more questions are given and then a final 24 appear. For Business Environment & Concepts, there are a total of 72 multiple-choice questions that make up the first portion of the exam.

Q: Should I guess if I do not know an answer?

A: The grade is computed based on the questions that you get correct. Therefore, you should answer all questions even if you must guess.

Q: After I answer a question can I go back and change my answer?

A: Each of the three testlets in Business Environment & Concepts has 24 multiple-choice questions. Until you finish a testlet, you can always change your answers. Once a testlet has been submitted, you cannot go back and change those answers.

Q: Are all of those multiple-choice questions in Business Environment & Concepts actually graded?

A: Of the 72 multiple-choice questions, 60 are graded while the other 12 are being tested for future use and do not affect the candidate's grade. However, you cannot tell which ones are graded. Unfortunately, it is possible to spend a long time attempting to answer a question that is not even graded.

Page 6 ©2007 Kaplan CPA Review

STUDY MANUAL – BUSINESS ENVIRONMENT & CONCEPTS
FREQUENTLY ASKED QUESTIONS

Q: Do all of those multiple-choice questions have the same value?

A: No, each question is individually weighted through a complicated mathematical process. In simple terms, answering a complex question correctly is worth more than answering an easy question correctly.

Q: After finishing the multiple-choice questions, what happens next in Business Environment & Concepts?

A: In all parts of the CPA exam other than Business Environment & Concepts (BEC), there are also two simulation questions. On BEC, however, there are currently no simulations. The AICPA will inform us, and we will inform you, if they ever decide to include simulations on BEC.

Q: What is a passing score?

A: A candidate must make a score of 75 to pass. However, because of the complex weighting system, that does not equate to getting 75% of the questions correct.

Q: How long are the exams?

A: Regulation is 3 hours, Auditing and Attestation is 4.5 hours, Financial Accounting & Reporting is 4 hours, and Business Environment & Concepts is 2.5 hours.

Q: How difficult are the questions on the CPA exam?

A: Not surprisingly, the complexity of the questions tends to vary significantly. However, almost anyone who has been around the CPA exam will assert that the breadth of the questions is more challenging than the depth. In other words, most questions are not extremely difficult but the exam tends to cover every possible topic. You have to move your thinking from one topic to another very quickly. The first question might be on itemized deduction while the second is on dividend income and the third on the taxation of partnerships. Few questions are necessarily difficult but that constant movement of topics from one to another poses a challenge.

Q: What is the pass rate on Business Environment & Concepts?

A: The pass rate on each of the four parts is roughly in the 40% to 44% range. It is a difficult exam but it is certainly not impossible. People who put in enough hours tend to pass.

Q: Where can I get more information on Kaplan CPA Review?

A: Go to *www.kaplanCPAreview.com* or send an e-mail to *CPAinfo@kaplan.com*.

©2007 Kaplan CPA Review

BUSINESS STRUCTURES: CORPORATIONS

STUDY MANUAL – BUSINESS ENVIRONMENT & CONCEPTS
CHAPTER 1

Study Tip: Almost every person has some habit or fondness that eats up a lot of their time. For some, it is television, while for others it is card playing, going to the movies, or the like. When you first begin to study for the CPA exam, determine what activity you use to waste time. Do not avoid this activity completely, but work to reduce that time to a specific but reasonable amount each week. That helps you take control over your time and find the time needed to prepare properly.

OVERVIEW OF THE BUSINESS STRUCTURES COVERAGE ON THE CPA EXAM

Business Structures is a topic previously entitled Business Organizations and was included in the Business Law and Professional Responsibilities section of the exam. In the revised exam format, Business Structures is included in the Business Environment and Concepts section. This topic accounts for approximately 17 percent to 23 percent of BEC and consists of multiple-choice questions only—no simulations, essays, or other question formats.

According to the American Institute of Certified Public Accountants (AICPA) Content Specification Outline, the candidate should be aware of the following aspects of Business Structures:

- Advantages, implications, and constraints of legal structures for business
- Formation, operation, and termination of businesses
- Financial structure, capitalization, profit and loss allocation, and distributions
- Rights, duties, legal obligations, and authority of owners and management

Business Structures will be divided into sole proprietorships and general partnerships, two types of business organizations that do not provide limited liability protection for owners, and corporations and other types of entities, such as limited liability companies, limited liability partnerships, and limited partnerships, that do provide some form of limited liability protection for their owners. The concept of limited liability is an important difference affecting a variety of business structure issues. Each type of business structure will be discussed in terms of the four specific areas listed above and identified by the AICPA.

CORPORATIONS

A. Unlike a sole proprietorship or a partnership, a corporation is a legal entity created under the authority of a statute to carry out the purposes permitted by that statute and the articles of incorporation. The corporation is treated as a legal entity with rights and obligations separate from its owners and managers. Corporations are governed by shareholders (owners), who elect a board of directors. Directors establish corporate policies and elect or appoint corporate officers who carry out the policies in the day-to-day management of the organization.

1. A corporation is formed under a state statute when persons, called incorporators, file articles of incorporation and, upon approval, receive a certificate of incorporation (a corporate charter) from the state.

   a. A private corporation is organized to earn profits for its owners (for-profit corporation) or for charitable purposes (not-for-profit corporation). A close (or closely held) corporation has the following features:

      • It is owned by a relatively small number of shareholders.
      • It does not sell its stock to the public.
      • It need not have officers and directors.
      • Shareholders are active in management and control.

   b. Quasi-public corporations owe a duty to the public (e.g., utility).

   c. A public corporation is organized for public purposes related to the administration of government (e.g., an incorporated municipality). It is formed by specific legislation that defines its purpose and powers. It may be funded by local taxes.

   d. A corporation is classified as domestic in the state in which it is organized (i.e., where its articles of incorporation are filed).

   e. A corporation is foreign in every other state. A certificate of authority required to do business within the borders of another state is obtained by:

      • Filing appropriate documents with the Secretary of State
      • Paying required fees
      • Designating a resident agent

   f. A corporation organized in another country is classified as alien. It must obtain a certificate of authority to do business from each host state.

   g. The S corporation is a close corporation that has made an election under federal law to be taxed similarly to a partnership. Hence, an S corporation does not usually pay income tax. It should be distinguished from a C corporation (i.e., an entity subject to the corporate income tax). The S corporation shareholders report their proportionate shares of the entity's income, losses, deductions, and credits, regardless of whether they have received distributions. S corporation status is terminated immediately when any one of the following eligibility requirements is no longer met:

- The corporation may have only one class of stock.
- The number of shareholders is limited to 100.
- The corporation must be incorporated in the United States.
- An S corporation should not have excessive net passive investment income.
- Shareholders are limited to individuals, estates, qualified trusts, and certain others.
- Nonresident aliens may not own shares.

h. Professional corporations arise when state statutes allow accountants, lawyers, and other professionals to incorporate. The statutes typically restrict stock ownership to specific professionals licensed within that state.

2. Advantages of incorporation include:

a. Limited liability. A shareholder owns a property interest in the underlying net assets of the corporation and is entitled to share in its profits, while his or her personal assets are not subject to corporate liabilities. The shareholder's exposure is limited to the investment in the corporation.

b. Separation of ownership from management. Shareholders have no inherent right to participate directly in management. They elect a board that sets corporate policy and appoints officers to conduct operations. A shareholder may be an officer or a director.

c. Free transferability of interests. Assuming no contractual or legal restriction, shares in a corporation may be freely transferred.

- A shareholder has no interest in specific corporate property. He or she owns a proportional, intangible property interest in the entire corporation.
- Traditionally, the shareholder's ownership interest was represented by a stock certificate. The interest was usually transferred by endorsing the certificate. Securities of publicly traded corporations are now customarily held indirectly (indirect holding) in order to facilitate trading. Thus, certificates are held by a depository institution on behalf of securities intermediaries (brokers or banks), which represent the owners. Trades are reflected in accounting entries made by the securities intermediaries, rather than with the physical transfer of a certificate.

d. Perpetual life. A corporation has perpetual existence unless the articles provide for a shorter life or it is dissolved by the state. Death, withdrawal, or addition of a shareholder, director, or officer does not end its existence.

e. Ease of raising capital. A corporation raises capital (to start or expand the business) by selling stock or issuing bonds. The sale of stock is governed by state corporate securities laws called *blue-sky laws,* as well as federal securities laws.

    f.   Constitutional rights. A corporation is a "person" for most purposes under the U.S. Constitution. Thus, it has the right to equal protection, due process, freedom from unreasonable searches and seizures, and freedom of speech.

3. The disadvantages of incorporation include:

    a.   Reduced individual control of the business

    b.   Income taxed to both the corporation and the shareholder (unless the entity qualifies for and elects S corporation status)

    c.   Substantial costs of meeting the requirements of corporate formation and operation

    d.   Possible hostile takeover of a publicly traded corporation

    e.   Transfer of unrestricted shares in a close corporation to unknown parties

    f.   The inability of a minority shareholder in a close corporation to liquidate his or her interest or to influence the conduct of the business

4. Pre-incorporation issues are handled by a promoter. A promoter arranges for formation of the corporation, provides for the capital structure and financing of the corporation, and assures compliance with any relevant securities laws. The promoter may also arrange for procurement of necessary personnel, services, assets, licenses, equipment, and leases.

    a.   Prior to incorporation, the promoter enters into ordinary and necessary contracts required for the initial operation of the business. If the contracts are executed in the promoter's name and there is no further action, the promoter is personally liable for them.

         • The corporation is not liable because a promoter cannot be an agent of a nonexistent corporation. Prior to formation, a corporation has no capacity to enter into contracts or employ agents.
         • A pre-incorporation contract made by promoters in the name of a corporation and on its behalf may bind the corporation if so provided by statute.

    b.   The corporation may adopt contracts formed by a promoter. Adoption is the acceptance of assignment of rights and delegation of duties that are contained in the contracts.

         • Adoption may be implied by accepting the benefits of a contract.
         • The contract, by its terms, may provide that the promoter is released from liability upon adoption of the contract by the corporation.

c. A promoter may avoid liability by acquiring an option (assignable to the corporation) to bind the third party to a contract.

d. If the promoter has no liability by the terms of an agreement, and the agreement is not an option, it may be treated as a continuing offer until revoked or accepted by the corporation.

e. If the promoter (the third party) and the corporation enter into a *novation*, substituting the corporation for the promoter, only the corporation is liable and the promoter is released. A *novation* is defined as the substitution of a new contract for an old one, where the rights under the old one are terminated.

f. Promoters owe a fiduciary duty to each other, to the corporation, and to stock subscribers and shareholders. This fiduciary duty requires good faith, fair dealing, and full disclosure of all material facts concerning transactions on behalf of the soon-to-be-formed corporation. Promoters have a duty to account for any secret profits earned when dealing with the corporation.

g. The promoter secures potential investors using stock subscription agreements. Each subscriber agrees to purchase a certain amount of stock at a specified price, payable at an agreed future time. However, a publicly traded corporation cannot use this device because of how its stock is traded and held and the requirements of the securities laws.

   - Technically, the subscriber is an offeror—offers to enter into a contract to purchase the stock.
   - The Revised Model Business Corporation Act (RMBCA) provides that a pre-incorporation subscription agreement is irrevocable for six months, unless otherwise provided for in the subscription agreement or unless all of the subscribers consent to the revocation.

5. Incorporation technicalities: Articles need only be executed in one state, although each state requires that a copy of the articles of incorporation be filed with the Secretary of State or another designated official for a corporation to do business there. (A corporation may incorporate in one state but have its principal place of business or conduct its business operations in another state or states.)

a. Incorporators are the persons who sign the articles. Typically, an incorporator may not be a minor. Modern statutes require only one incorporator and permit the incorporator to be a corporation.

b. Under the RMBCA, the content of the articles includes the following:

   - Corporation's name
   - Number of authorized shares of stock
   - Street address of the corporation's initial registered office
   - Name of the registered agent at that office
   - Name and address of each incorporator

c. Under the RMBCA, a corporation is first recognized as a legal entity when the articles are filed with the Secretary of State. However, some states may also require filings in designated counties. In other states, issuance of a certificate of incorporation commences corporate existence. *Filing* is a technical term, generally meaning state approval of the documents evidenced by all three of the following actions:

- Affixing an official stamp to the documents
- Issuing a formal charter
- Issuing a dated receipt for the filing fee

d. After filing, the incorporators elect the members of the initial board of directors if they have not been named in the articles. The incorporators then resign.

e. The board of directors holds an organizational meeting to take all steps needed to complete the organizational structure. The new board:

- Adopts bylaws to govern the internal management of the corporation. The power to change bylaws is vested in the board unless specifically reserved to the shareholders in the articles.
- Elects officers, typically a president, treasurer, and secretary.
- Considers other transactions appropriate for furthering the business purposes of the corporation, such as:
    - Adopting or rejecting pre-incorporation contracts of promoters
    - Adopting the form of certificate representing shares of the company's stock
    - Accepting or rejecting stock subscriptions
    - Complying with requirements for doing business in other states

6. De jure versus defective incorporation: A corporation incorporated in strict compliance with applicable state statutes is called a *de jure corporation* (de jure means "according to the law"). A *defective incorporation* is one that does not follow the strict requirements of applicable laws. However, a defective incorporation may still result in the existence of a corporation.

a. A *de facto corporation* (de facto means "in reality, in actuality") is recognized when the following conditions exist:

- A statute exists under which the business could have been incorporated, even though it was not.
- A good-faith but unsuccessful attempt was made to comply with the statute.
- There was an actual or attempted exercise of corporate powers.

b. Under the RMBCA, the legal existence of a de facto corporation can be challenged only by the state, not by a creditor of the corporation.

c. The RMBCA establishes a conclusive presumption that, when the articles have been filed, the corporation exists even if the filing was defective.

- The effect is to treat a corporation as de jure once the Secretary of State has filed the articles, even though the filing may not have complied with a certain mandatory legal provision.
- If the entity is so defectively formed that it does not even qualify as a de facto corporation, the RMBCA imposes liability on all persons purporting to act on behalf of a corporation, knowing that there was no incorporation under this act. The RMBCA therefore excuses inactive parties and those not knowing of the defective incorporation.

    d.   Corporation by estoppel occurs when an organization that is neither a de jure nor a de facto corporation is treated as a corporation in a suit by a third party. Thus, it may be *prevented* (or *estopped*) from denying corporate status if:

- The organization has represented itself as a corporation.
- The representation is followed by reasonable reliance and material alteration of position by a third party based on that representation.
- The third party demonstrates fair and equitable conduct.
- Injustice can be avoided only by treating the business as a corporation.

7.   Courts disregard the separate corporate entity when the corporate form is used merely to commit wrongdoing, shield its shareholders from fraud, or otherwise circumvent the law. This is called *piercing the corporate veil*. In this situation, shareholders are personally liable for corporate acts (as is a general partner in a partnership). A court might disregard a corporate entity if it finds any of the following:

    a.   The corporation is merely the alter ego of a shareholder. This may occur, for example, if the

- Assets of the corporation and the shareholders are commingled
- Corporate formalities are ignored
- Corporation was established for a sham purpose

    b.   Two or more business enterprises are related corporations (such as parent-subsidiary or brother-sister corporations) and, in practice, do not maintain sufficiently independent existence.

    c.   A corporation is inadequately capitalized to carry on its intended business.

8.   A state may exercise personal jurisdiction (authority) over a foreign corporation, for example, to require registration with the state or to allow service of process (giving valid notice to a defendant corporation) in another state. A corporation is considered *foreign* in all states *other* than the state in which it is incorporated. In its state of incorporation, it is called a *domestic* corporation.

However, a state has personal jurisdiction *only* if the corporation has at least minimum contact with the state.

    a.   *Minimum contact* consists of activity that is significant.

b. A *state long-arm statute* may authorize general jurisdiction over a foreign corporation based on an active business office or substantial activity in the state. Such activity might include maintaining inventory and records.

c. Mere solicitation of offers to be accepted out of state, to be delivered by interstate carrier from out of state, and to be paid for by mail is *not* considered "doing business" sufficiently to constitute minimum contacts.

d. State long-arm statutes also authorize jurisdiction over foreign corporations that perform isolated or single acts in the state, or whose conduct directly affects the state, but only for claims arising from those acts.

B. Following are the statutory, express, and implied powers of incorporation.

1. Authority for corporate action derives from the state law and/or the articles of incorporation. The RMBCA grants a corporation the "same powers as an individual to do all things necessary or convenient to carry out its business and affairs." Thus, it may engage in any lawful business unless a more limited purpose is stated in the articles. These rights are called statutory powers. These powers include the right to:

a. Sue, be sued, complain, and defend in the corporate name

b. Exist perpetually

c. Acquire and dispose of real or personal property, or any legal or equitable interest, wherever it may be located

d. Elect directors, appoint officers and agents, hire employees, set their compensation, and lend them money or credit

e. Operate within or outside the state of incorporation

f. Engage in any transactions involving interests in, or obligations of, any other entity

g. Make contracts, give guarantees, incur liabilities, issue debt instruments (whether or not convertible or containing options to purchase other securities), and give security interests

h. Be a partner, promoter, manager, or associate of a partnership, joint venture, trust, or other entity

i. Lend money, invest funds, and hold collateral

j. Have a corporate seal

k. Make and amend bylaws

l. Dispose of all or part of its property by any proper means

©2007 Kaplan CPA Review

m. Make donations for the public welfare or for charitable, scientific, or educational purposes

n. Pay pensions and establish profit-sharing and other benefit or incentive plans for corporate officers, directors, employees, and agents

o. Transact any lawful business in aid of governmental policy

p. Make payments or donations or do any other lawful act in the furtherance of the business of the corporation

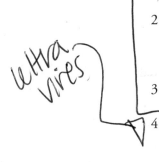
ultra vires

2. Express powers are specifically granted to a particular corporation by the articles of incorporation. They describe ownership, control, and overall operational structure.

3. Implied powers are necessary and appropriate to carry out express powers.

4. Acts beyond the corporation's express or implied powers are said to be *ultra vires*.

   a. Generally, if a corporation acts ultra vires, shareholders (or the state's attorney general) may institute a legal proceeding to enjoin (prohibit) the act.

   b. The corporation (or the shareholders on its behalf) may sue the directors or officers responsible for the act for damages.

   c. However, articles of incorporation authorizing any lawful business transaction are now common. The effect is to eliminate the *availability* of the doctrine of ultra vires.

C. Capitalization: By definition, every corporation issues or offers to issue equity securities. It may or may not issue debt securities.

1. Debt

   a. Short-term debt financing may consist of obtaining short-term bank credit, assigning accounts receivable, pledging some or all of the corporation's properties, and issuing short-term notes.

   b. A corporation accomplishes long-term debt financing primarily by issuing bonds. These debt securities represent a debtor-creditor relationship between the corporation and the holders.

   - A bond is a negotiable security expressing the corporation's promise to pay:
     - The face, contract, or principal amount of the bond at a future date
     - Interest, which is typically paid semiannually at a fixed rate
   - The board of directors may issue bonds without shareholder authorization.

- Secured bonds (also called *mortgage bonds*) represent creditors' claims that are enforceable against specific corporate property. If the collateral is insufficient, the bondholder becomes a general unsecured creditor of the corporation for the amount of the deficiency.
- Unsecured bonds (also called *debentures*) are backed only by the general credit of the corporation. No property is pledged as security. Debenture holders are unsecured creditors and rank equally with other general creditors.

2. Shareholders' equity represents ownership interest in the corporation; however, a share of stock does not confer title to any specific property owned by the corporation.

   a. Priority. In the event of bankruptcy or liquidation, creditors, including bondholders, have first claim on corporate assets. Any surplus is distributed to the shareholders. Hence, shareholders have greater potential risks and rewards than bondholders.

   b. Most state incorporation statutes require that the articles of incorporation specify the number of authorized shares and the classes of stock.

      - Authorized capital stock cannot be increased or decreased without amending the articles of incorporation.
      - The board may choose to issue all, part, or none of the authorized shares.

   c. Shares are issued in exchange for consideration. Subject to state and federal securities regulation, shares may be issued for cash, property (tangible or intangible), or past services rendered.

      - The RMBCA provides that consideration may consist of any tangible or intangible property or benefit to the corporation, including cash, promissory notes, services performed, contracts for services to be performed, or other securities of the corporation. However, the RMBCA also provides for placing shares in escrow or making other restrictive arrangements until "the services are performed, the note is paid, or the benefits are received." Usually, the state statute does not permit shares to be issued in exchange for unspecified obligations that may or may not ever be performed.
      - Shares may be issued without certificates.
      - Watered stock is stock not issued for full and adequate consideration.

   d. Until shares of stock have been issued, they are considered authorized but unissued. Afterward, they are considered issued and outstanding.

   e. Any issuance of stock in violation of state corporate law is voidable (not void) at the option of the recipient shareholder.

   f. Par value, if set by the promoters or the board, is a dollar amount below which the shares may not be initially sold without future assessment against

©2007 Kaplan CPA Review

STUDY MANUAL – BUSINESS ENVIRONMENT & CONCEPTS
CHAPTER 1

the shareholders. However, the RMBCA has abolished the par value requirement.

    g.   All states do (and the articles may) authorize issuance of no-par stock. It is sold by the issuing corporation at whatever price the board of directors determines is reasonable. This decision will be upheld in the absence of fraud or self-dealing.

    h.   Treasury stock is stock issued and later reacquired by the corporation. Under the RMBCA, repurchased shares are restored to authorized but unissued status. The shares may be held indefinitely, resold, issued as a stock dividend, or retired. The corporation may not pay dividends on Treasury stock, and the shares may not be voted.

    i.   The most widely used classes of stock are *common* and *preferred*. Common shareholders are entitled to receive liquidating distributions only after all other claims have been satisfied, including those of preferred shareholders.

- Common shareholders are not entitled to dividends. A corporation may choose not to declare dividends.
- State statutes typically permit different classes of common stock with different rights or privileges (e.g., class A common with voting rights and class B common with no voting rights).
- If only one class of stock is issued, it is treated as common, and each shareholder must be treated equally.
- Common shareholders elect directors to the board.

    j.   Preferred shareholders have an intermediate position between common shareholders and debt holders. They have the right to receive dividends at a specified rate stated on the face of the shares (before common shareholders may receive any) and the right to receive distributions before common shareholders (but after creditors) upon liquidation or bankruptcy. But they tend not to enjoy the same level of capital gains as the common shareholders when the entity is successful.

- The articles must designate which shares are preferred.
- If a board issues preferred stock, it may establish different classes or series. Each may be assigned independent rights, dividend rates, and redemption prices.
- Cumulative preferred stock gives the holder the right to receive the stated dividend in full each year. If payment is not made in any year, the unpaid dividends accumulate and must be paid in full before any dividends are paid to common shareholders.
    - A dividend may be cumulative to the extent earned. Hence, preferred dividends may accumulate in a given year only if the corporation had sufficient earnings to pay them.
    - If the nature of preferred stock is unclear, most courts have ruled that preferred stock is impliedly cumulative.

- Holders of participating preferred stock, in addition to being entitled to the stated dividend before any dividend can be paid to common shareholders, participate with the common shareholders in any remaining funds allocated for dividend payments.
- When shareholders have the option to convert the stock into shares of another class (at a predetermined ratio set forth in the articles or bylaws), they hold convertible preferred stock. Moreover, some types of preferred stock may be convertible into shares of another entity.
- Preferred stock is issued with the condition that it may be "called" (redeemed or repurchased) by the issuer at a stated price and time. Issuers may establish a sinking fund for redemption purposes. Preferred stock may also be redeemable at the option of the shareholder.

3. With respect to dividends and distributions, the board has the discretion to determine the time and amount of dividends to be paid.

   a. Persons who invest in corporate stock are motivated in part by the expectation of receiving dividends. Two general prerequisites to the declaration of a dividend are corporate profits and a resolution by the directors to declare a dividend.

      - To ensure the corporation's financial health and growth, profits (or some portion) can be reinvested in the corporation.
      - The corporation's directors determine the time and amount of dividends, if any. However, if the directors refuse to declare a dividend, and they have clearly abused their discretion, a court may require payment of a dividend.

   b. All states impose the equity insolvency test. Thus, payment of a dividend is prohibited if, as a result of paying the dividend, the corporation could not pay its debts as they become due in the usual course of business.

      - The RMBCA also prohibits a distribution if the result would be that total assets are less than the sum of liabilities and liquidation preferences.
      - Moreover, it permits the board to determine the acceptability of a distribution based on either of the following:
        - Financial statements prepared using accounting principles reasonable under the circumstances
        - A fair valuation or other method that is reasonable under the circumstances
      - The majority of states require that dividends be paid out of earned surplus and not stated capital. However, the RMBCA and many states have abolished the concepts of stated capital and surplus because they provide no genuine protection to investors.
        - Stated capital is the par value of par-value stock (or the stated value of no-par stock).
        - Capital surplus is the excess of the selling price over the par or stated value.
          - Earned surplus is retained earnings.

STUDY MANUAL – BUSINESS ENVIRONMENT & CONCEPTS
CHAPTER 1

- Some state laws provide that dividends may be paid out of current earnings if sufficient capital exists to pay the liquidation preference of all shares, even if the corporation has a negative surplus.
- Directors who approve a dividend declared in violation of the applicable state test have abused their discretion. They are jointly and severally liable to the corporation for the amount. Shareholders who know a dividend is illegal must repay it. Those who do not know must repay it only if the corporation is insolvent or made insolvent by payment of the dividend.
- The declaration date is the date the board of directors, by vote, approves a resolution to declare a dividend. The vote is irrevocable. Once declared, payment of the dividend is a legal obligation of the corporation.
- The directors fix a record date. The registered holder on the record date is sent the payment on the payment date.
  - If the record holder receives payment but has transferred the stock, the corporation is not liable to the transferee, provided it (the corporation) was unaware of the transfer. The transferee must sue the transferor (not the corporation) for the amount.
  - Absent an agreement with the transferee to the contrary, the transferor is entitled to all dividends declared prior to the transfer.
  - However, stock traded on an organized exchange and purchased during the settlement period is ex dividend (without dividend) to the buyer.
  - If a record date is not set, the declaration date is treated as the record date.
- The payment date is the date that the corporation will actually tender payment of the dividend to the shareholders of record.
- Dividends are usually paid in cash, stock, stock rights, or other property (called a *dividend in kind*).
- A stock dividend is payable in the stock of the dividend-paying corporation.
- A stock split is an issuance of shares for the purpose of reducing the unit value of each share. Accordingly, the par or stated value, if any, is also reduced. The ratio at which shares are exchanged is arbitrary. Shares may be split one-and-a-half to one, two to one, or in any other way.
  - A stock split does not increase a shareholder's proportionate ownership.
  - A stock split does not require that a corporation possess retained earnings or meet any statutory dividend requirements.

D. Governance includes the rights and obligations of shareholders, board of directors, and officers of the corporation, as well as the basic requirements of the Sarbanes-Oxley Act of 2002.

1. Acquisition of a share of stock makes a person an owner of the corporation issuing the stock. However, a shareholder has no right to manage the corporation directly.

   a. The shareholders' primary participation in corporate policy and management is by meeting annually and electing directors by majority vote.

Page 20   ©2007 Kaplan CPA Review

- By their power to remove any and all directors, shareholders indirectly control the actions of the corporation.
- In addition to electing directors, shareholders must approve fundamental corporate changes.

b. The articles may provide for more or less than one vote per share.

- Usually, each shareholder is entitled to one vote for each share owned for each new director to be elected (i.e., straight voting). Election is by a plurality.
- Cumulative voting for directors is mandatory in some states, but the RMBCA allows cumulative voting only if it is provided for in the articles. Cumulative voting entitles shareholders to accumulate votes. The shareholder can do either of the following:
    - Give one candidate as many votes as the number of directors to be elected multiplied by the number of shares owned
    - Distribute that number of votes among as many candidates as he or she wishes, thereby increasing minority shareholder power
- Shareholders entitled to vote are those who are identified on a voting list prepared by the corporation for the purpose of giving notice of a meeting.
- The RMBCA permits different voting rights for different classes of shares. For example, each class may have the right to elect one director. The result is class voting. Thus, even a closely held corporation may have two or more classes of common shares with different voting rights.
- The RMBCA specifically permits a *voting agreement,* a signed contract in which shareholders specify how they will vote their shares. It is specifically enforceable; that is, a party who breaches the contract may be legally compelled to vote the shares as agreed rather than pay damages.
- Shareholders may transfer their shares to one or more voting trustees in exchange for voting trust certificates. The trustees must comply with the voting trust agreement, which may or may not grant them considerable discretion.
- A proxy is an appointment by a shareholder for someone else to vote on his or her behalf. Usually, a proxy must be in writing or in an authorized electronic transmission. It is revocable at any time.
    - Under the RMBCA, a proxy is effective for no more than 11 months, unless another time period is specifically included in the appointment.
    - A general proxy permits a holder to vote on all corporate proposals other than fundamental corporate changes. A limited proxy permits a holder to vote only on matters specified in the proxy.

c. Preemptive rights are important to owners of a close corporation. They give a shareholder an option to subscribe to a new issuance of shares in proportion to the shareholder's current interest in the corporation. Thus, they limit dilution of equity in the corporation. Almost all states recognize preemptive rights. However, preemptive rights may not exist unless they are specifically reserved in the articles of incorporation.

STUDY MANUAL – BUSINESS ENVIRONMENT & CONCEPTS
CHAPTER 1

    d. Under the RMBCA, shareholders have a fundamental right to inspect the corporation's books and records that may not be limited by the articles or bylaws.

- Inspection must be at the corporation's principal office during regular business hours. The shareholders must give five business days' written notice that states the purpose of the demand and the records to be inspected. The records must be directly related to the purpose.
- Inspection must be in good faith and for a proper purpose, for example, to determine the following:
  - Corporate financial condition.
  - The propriety of dividends.
  - Mismanagement of the corporation.
  - The names and addresses of other shareholders.
- An improper purpose includes an ulterior motive to:
  - Harass management.
  - Discover trade secrets.
  - Gain a competitive advantage.
  - Develop a mailing list for sale or for similar use.
- Courts have permitted a shareholder to obtain a copy of a shareholder list, even when the only purpose was to engage in a takeover battle.
- Shareholders have an unconditional right to inspect records such as the articles, bylaws, minutes of shareholder meetings, and the annual report.

    e. Generally, shareholders may act only at a meeting.

- Annual meetings are required and must be held at a time fixed in the bylaws. The purpose is to elect new directors and to conduct other necessary business. Notice of any meeting must be in writing, and defective notice or lack of notice voids action taken at the meeting.
- Special meetings (e.g., to approve a merger) may be called by the board of directors, the owner(s) of at least 10 percent of the issued and outstanding common stock, or any other persons authorized in the articles of incorporation (RMBCA). Special meetings require both written notice and a description of purpose.
- A *quorum* must be represented in person or by proxy to conduct business at a shareholders' meeting. The RMBCA defines a quorum as a majority of shares outstanding.
- The RMBCA permits shareholders to act without a meeting if all shareholders entitled to vote consent in writing to the action.

    f. An individual shareholder may sue a corporation to preclude ultra vires acts, to recover improper dividends, to obtain a remedy for management's breach of duty, etc. A shareholder may also enforce preemptive, inspection, dividend, or other rights of shareholders. These rights may have been created by statute, the articles, the bylaws, or common law.

- Direct suits occur when shareholders sue on their own behalf, either individually or as members of a class. In a class action, the plaintiffs represent not only themselves but "all others similarly situated."
- A shareholder may also file a shareholder derivative suit to recover for wrongs done to the corporation. The action is for the benefit of the corporation, and any recovery belongs to it, not to the shareholder. The corporation is the true plaintiff.
  - A shareholder must first demand that the corporation bring suit unless it is obvious that demand would be futile (e.g., the action is against corporate officers or directors).
  - Most states require that the shareholder prove the following:
    - He or she owned shares at the time of wrongdoing.
    - A written demand was made on the directors.
    - The directors refused to sue.
    - The refusal was in bad faith.
  - A shareholder can generally recover reasonable litigation expenses from the corporation but no compensation for his or her time.

2. Shareholder liability is limited to his or her capital contribution except in certain instances (e.g., if the corporate veil is pierced or the corporation was defectively formed).

   a. Stock subscription agreements. The subscriber remains liable to the corporation for any unpaid installment balance, even if the corporation becomes insolvent or declares bankruptcy. If the subscriber dies, his or her estate may be liable for any balance due.

   b. Par or stated value. If stock is authorized with a par or stated value and is originally issued (sold) for less, the purchasing shareholder is, and remains, liable (to the corporation) for the deficiency.

   - A person who subsequently purchases the stock is subject to the liability if he or she knows the stock was issued for less than par or stated value.
   - The RMBCA has eliminated the requirement of par value. However, if stock was issued with a par value before this change, the par value and rules related to par value remain in effect. The only way for a corporation to "eliminate" par value under the RMBCA revised rules is to issue new stock that does not have a par.

   c. Watered stock. If stock is *not* issued in exchange for full and adequate consideration, and the facts indicate fraud or bad faith by the shareholders, they (and probably the directors) will be personally liable for any amount underpaid.

   d. Illegal dividends. Some states permit a corporation to recover damages from shareholders who receive a dividend or other corporate distribution when the shareholder knows that the distribution is wrong. A shareholder may be held liable for unpaid debts of the corporation up to the amount received as an illegal dividend or distribution.

e. A seller of a controlling block of shares may be liable to nonselling minority shareholders if the seller has or should have had a reasonable suspicion that the purchaser would mismanage or loot the corporation, unless investigation shows no basis for it. A court also may compel the seller of a controlling interest to distribute ratably to all shareholders any control premium received in excess of the fair value.

f. Usurpation. If a purchaser wishes to buy the corporation's assets and the controlling shareholder proposes that the purchaser buy his or her stock instead, the controlling shareholder may be liable for usurping a corporate opportunity.

g. A breach of the fiduciary duty of utmost good faith, loyalty, and impartiality, owed by the majority to the minority (in a closely held corporation), gives rise to liability for oppressive conduct. Controlling shareholders must:

  • *Not* cause the corporation to purchase their shares at a price unavailable to the minority
  • Act in good faith regarding payment of salaries and dividends

3. Shareholder agreements: One of the notable features of the RMBCA is that it permits the shareholders to change, by unanimous agreement, the provisions otherwise applicable to corporate governance. This flexibility may allow a close corporation to function more nearly as a partnership without loss of corporate status.

a. The RMBCA provides for a shareholder agreement set forth in the articles of incorporation, bylaws, or a separate signed agreement that is approved by all shareholders.

b. This agreement governs the exercise of corporate powers, management of the business and affairs of the corporation, and the relationship between shareholders, directors, and the corporation, and must not be contrary to public policy.

4. Specifics regarding the board of directors:

a. Each state has a specific requirement with respect to the number of directors elected to sit on the board. Many states require a minimum of three. Under the provisions of the RMBCA, a minimum of one director is usually required. However, the RMBCA permits a corporation to remove/replace a board of directors pursuant to a unanimous shareholder agreement.

b. The initial board of directors is usually appointed by the incorporators or named in the articles of incorporation, and this board serves until the first meeting of the shareholders. Subsequent directors are elected by a vote of the shareholders at the annual meeting.

c. Most publicly held corporations have two types of directors. *Inside directors* are officers of the corporation and full-time employees, and *outside directors* may be unaffiliated with the corporation except for stock ownership.

d. Generally, a director serves a three-year term. The charter or bylaws may provide for a longer term. Directors on a board of nine or more are often *classified*. This arrangement permits staggering of terms by creating separate classes of directors. The members of one class will then be elected at each annual meeting.

e. Power authorizing the board to increase its size without shareholder approval may be reserved in the articles or bylaws.

f. Normally, a director is elected by a plurality (rather than a majority) of shareholder votes. Cumulative voting may be permitted or mandatory.

g. Typically, if a director dies or resigns, or if the size of the board has been increased, the remaining directors may elect a director to fill the vacancy until the next shareholders' meeting.

h. In most states, shareholders may, by a majority vote, remove with or without cause, any director or the entire board.

i. Statutes usually permit the board to remove a director who has been declared insane or convicted of a felony. Rarely would a board be permitted to remove a director for any other reason.

j. The RMBCA authorizes a court to issue an order to remove a director in a proceeding brought by or on behalf of the corporation if the court finds both of the following:

- The director engaged in fraudulent conduct regarding the corporation or the shareholders, intentionally harmed the corporation, or grossly abused his or her authority.
- Removal is in the best interest of the corporation.

5. Director's authority: Although the directors formulate overall corporate policy, they are neither trustees nor agents of the corporation. A director cannot act individually to bind the corporation.

a. The board establishes and implements corporate policy including:

- Selection and removal of officers
- Determination of capital structure
- Adding, amending, or repealing bylaws
  - Bylaws govern the internal structure and operation of the corporation.
  - Initial bylaws are adopted by the incorporators or the board.

    - Initiation of fundamental changes

- Declaration of dividends
- Setting of management compensation

b. Directors owe a fiduciary duty to the shareholders and to the corporation. Thus, express agreement is necessary to authorize compensation. It is common to compensate outside directors.

c. Directors have power to bind the corporation only when acting as a board.

d. The board may act only at a formal meeting of directors or by duly executed written consent, if authorized by statute, unless contrary to the articles or bylaws.

e. Many statutes, articles, and bylaws permit boards to act:

- By simultaneous telephone conference call
- By video conference
- Without a meeting by unanimous written consent

f. Formal meetings are held at fixed intervals established in the bylaws.

g. Special meetings may be held after proper notice has been given to all directors. A director's attendance at any meeting is a waiver of notice, unless the director attends for the express purpose of objecting to the transaction on the grounds that the meeting is not lawfully convened.

h. Unless required by statute or bylaws, the board need not meet at the corporate offices or even in the state of incorporation. Most modern statutes allow meetings outside the United States.

i. Actions taken by a board are expressed in formal resolutions adopted by a majority of the board during a meeting at which a quorum is present. Directors have the right to inspect corporate books and records so they can perform their duties.

fiduciary duty

6. Directors have a fiduciary relationship to the corporation and its shareholders. They can be held personally liable for failure to be informed of matters internal to, and external but relevant to, the corporation. A director's conduct is tested objectively.

a. The RMBCA requires that a director discharge his or her duties:

- In good faith
- With reasonable care
- In a manner he or she reasonably believes to be in the best interests of the corporation

b. Reasonable care is the care an ordinarily prudent person in a similar position would exercise under similar circumstances. Thus, a director must not be negligent.

c. In exercising reasonable care, a director may rely on information, reports, opinions, and statements prepared or presented by officers or employees whom the director reasonably believes to be competent in the matters presented. A director may also rely on the specialized knowledge of lawyers, accountants, investment bankers, and board committees.

d. Directors are expected to be informed about and conversant with pertinent corporate information when rendering advice to the board. A director has not exercised the required care if he or she does not:

- Attend meetings of the board
- Analyze corporate financial statements
- Review pertinent legal opinions
- Become conversant with the available relevant information

7. Directors of a corporation owe a duty of loyalty to the corporation and its shareholders.

duty of loyalty

a. Conflicting interest transactions: To protect the corporation against self-dealing, a director is required to make full disclosure of any financial interest in any transaction to which both the director and the corporation may be party. Unanimous approval of a self-dealing transaction by disinterested, informed shareholders may release an interested director from liability for self-dealing, even if the transaction is unfair to the corporation.

b. Under the RMBCA, a transaction is not voidable merely on the grounds of a director's conflict of interest if the transaction is fair to the corporation or has been approved by a majority of informed, disinterested directors or shareholders. This rule applies even if the director was counted for the quorum and voted to approve the transaction.

- A transaction is fair if reasonable persons, bargaining at arm's length (independently), would have entered into the transaction if they had been in the same circumstances as the corporation.
- A contract between a director and the corporation that is neither fair nor approved by disinterested directors or shareholders may be rescinded or upheld by the corporation, and the director may be required to pay damages.

c. Directors may not usurp any corporate opportunity. A director must give the corporation the right of first refusal.

8. Business judgment rule: Courts avoid substituting their business judgment for that of the corporation's officers or directors.

a. The rule protects a director from personal liability if he or she:

- Acted in good faith
- Was not motivated by fraud, conflict of interest, or illegality
- Was not guilty of gross negligence

STUDY MANUAL – BUSINESS ENVIRONMENT & CONCEPTS
CHAPTER 1

    b.   To avoid personal liability, directors and officers must:

- Make informed decisions (educate themselves about the issues)
- Be free from conflicts of interest
- Have a rational basis to support their position

    c.   Some decisions concern incumbent management's opposition to tender offers to shareholders made by a third party to buy the shareholders' stock at a price above the market price. Directors may be liable to shareholders; that is, the business judgment rule may *not* apply if either of the following situations exist:

- The directors make a decision to oppose a tender offer before they have carefully studied it.
- The directors' actions indicate that they are opposing the tender offer in order to preserve their jobs.

    d.   Most states permit corporations to indemnify directors and officers for expenses of litigation concerning business judgments, subject to some exceptions.

9.   Officers are elected or appointed by the board and generally serve at the will of the board, which may remove any officer at any time. However, the board may not remove an officer elected or employed by the shareholders without cause.

    a.   Typically, state statutes set a minimum number of officers, but not a maximum. Under the RMBCA, the corporation has the officers stated in the bylaws or appointed by the board pursuant to the bylaws. One officer must be delegated the responsibility for:

- Preparing the minutes of directors' meetings
- Authenticating records of the corporation

    b.   Officers typically appointed are president, vice president, secretary, and treasurer. One person may hold more than one office. Many states require that the same person not hold the offices of president and secretary simultaneously.

    c.   The officers are agents of the corporation. They have express authority conferred by the bylaws or the board. They have implied authority to do things that are reasonably necessary to accomplish their express duties. Courts have held that official titles confer limited inherent authority on officers.

- The president supervises and controls all the business and affairs of the corporation, subject to the discretion of the board.
  - He or she presides at board and shareholders' meetings.

STUDY MANUAL – BUSINESS ENVIRONMENT & CONCEPTS
CHAPTER 1

- ◆ Traditionally, the president had no inherent authority. However, the trend is that he or she can bind the corporation in the ordinary course of its business.
- The general manager or chief executive officer holds broad implied authority to conduct the corporation's business.
- The vice president traditionally performs the duties of the president if the president is unable to perform them.
- The secretary is the custodian of the corporate seal and records.
  - ◆ The secretary notifies participants of shareholders' and board meetings and maintains the minutes (records).
  - ◆ The secretary maintains the stock transfer ledgers and, along with the president, signs for the issuance of stock certificates.
  - ◆ The secretary certifies the authenticity of the president's signature and corporate records when necessary.
- The treasurer maintains the financial accounts and records. Typically, the treasurer signs all checks and gives receipts for, and deposits money due and payable to, the corporation.

d. Officers, like directors, owe fiduciary duties to the corporation.

- As an agent, an officer has a duty to act within the authority granted by the articles, the bylaws, and the board.
- Like directors, officers are subject to the same duties of care and loyalty to the corporation.
- Likewise, absent bad faith, fraud, or breach of a fiduciary duty, the business judgment rule applies to officers. Like a director, the officer is insulated by the business judgment rule if the management decision is informed, conflict-free, and rational. Officers may be indemnified to the extent, consistent with public policy, as provided by the articles of incorporation, bylaws, actions of the board, or contract.

10. The Sarbanes-Oxley Act of 2002: The federal response to numerous financial reporting scandals involving large public companies contains provisions relating to corporate governance. The act applies to issuers of publicly traded securities subject to federal securities laws.

a. It requires that each member of the audit committee, including at least one who is a financial expert, be an independent member of the issuer's board of directors.

- An independent director is not affiliated with and receives no compensation (other than for service on the board) from the issuer.
- The audit committee must be directly responsible for appointing, compensating, and overseeing the work of the public accounting firm employed by the issuer. In addition, this firm must report directly to the audit committee, not to management.
- Another function of the audit committee is to implement procedures for the receipt, retention, and treatment of complaints about accounting and auditing matters.

STUDY MANUAL – BUSINESS ENVIRONMENT & CONCEPTS
CHAPTER 1

- The audit committee also must be appropriately funded by the issuer and may hire independent counselors or other advisors.

b. The chief executive officer and chief financial officer of the issuer must certify that the issuer's financial statements and disclosures "present fairly, in all material respects, the operation and financial condition of the issuer." This statement must accompany the audit report. A CEO or CFO will be liable only if he or she knowingly and intentionally violates this part of the act. The maximum penalty for a violation is a fine of $500,000 and imprisonment for five years.

c. It is also illegal for an officer or director to exert improper influence on the conduct of an audit with the intent to make financial statements materially misleading.

d. If an issuer materially restates its financial statements as a result of material noncompliance with reporting requirements, the CEO and CFO must return to the issuer any amounts received within 12 months after the issuance or filing in the form of both of the following:

- Incentive-based or equity-based compensation
- Profits from the sale of the issuer's securities

e. The Securities and Exchange Commission (SEC) may freeze extraordinary payments to directors, officers, and others during an investigation of securities law violations.

f. The SEC may prohibit anyone convicted of securities fraud from serving as an officer or director of a publicly traded firm.

E. Fundamental changes in structure may be beyond the authority of the board of directors.

1. Some changes affect a corporation in such a fundamental manner that they are beyond the authority of the board and require shareholder approval. Shareholder approval of fundamental changes does not usually require unanimity. In some instances, minority shareholders have the right to dissent and recover the fair value of their shares after appraisal.

2. Shareholders who disagree with fundamental corporate changes may have dissenters' (appraisal) rights. The corporation must pay dissenting shareholders the fair value of their stock in cash within 30 days after the appraisal form is submitted by dissenting shareholders.

a. Under the RMBCA, fair value is the value immediately before the corporation acts on the proposed fundamental change. Fair value is determined using current valuation techniques without discounting for lack of marketability or minority status.

b. The RMBCA requires that a shareholder asserting appraisal rights:

- Not vote in favor of the transaction
- Make written demand before the vote that the corporation purchase his or her stock if the action is approved

c. Under the RMBCA, the right to dissent covers:

- A disposition of assets that leaves the corporation without a significant continuing business activity
- Mergers and share exchanges
- Certain amendments to the articles of incorporation, for example, when the right is provided in the articles, bylaws, or a board resolution. However, other statutes provide a broad right to dissent when an amendment materially and adversely affects shareholder rights.

d. Most state statutes (including the RMBCA) exclude shares that are publicly traded from being subject to appraisal rights.

3. Amendments to the articles: Modern corporation statutes permit the articles of incorporation to be freely amended.

a. Generally, the board adopts a resolution setting forth, in writing, the proposed amendment. The resolution must be approved in a meeting at which a quorum is present (i.e., a majority of the shareholder votes entitled to be cast).

- Some statutes require a supermajority (a specified majority percentage, such as "at least 80 percent") shareholder vote.
- A class of shareholders may be entitled to vote as a class.

b. After shareholder approval, articles of amendment are filed with the Secretary of State. The amendment is effective when a certificate of amendment is issued.

c. The RMBCA permits the board to adopt certain de minimis amendments (e.g., changing the corporation's registered agent) without shareholder action, unless the articles of incorporation provide otherwise.

4. Sale of corporate assets: If a sale or lease of all or substantially all corporate assets is not in the regular course of business, approval of the board and shareholders is required if the corporation is left without a significant continuing business activity.

a. In most states, dissenting shareholders have appraisal rights.

b. A mortgage or pledge of any or all of the property and assets of a corporation, whether or not in the regular course of business, does not require shareholder approval (absent a contrary provision in the articles).

c. The acquirer does not ordinarily become liable for the acquiree's obligations. Exceptions are made for express or implied assumptions of liability, when

STUDY MANUAL – BUSINESS ENVIRONMENT & CONCEPTS
CHAPTER 1

business is continued, when the transaction was effectively a merger or consolidation, and in certain other cases.

5. A merger is the combination of all the assets of two or more corporations (A + B = A). In a merger, one corporation is absorbed by another corporation and ceases to exist. State statutes set forth specific procedures for mergers.

    a. The shareholders of a merged corporation may receive stock or other securities issued by the surviving corporation.

    b. Stock of the merged (acquired) corporation is canceled.

    c. A merger requires the approval of each board and of shareholders entitled to vote for each corporation. Under the RMBCA, shareholder approval must be given at a meeting at which a majority of votes entitled to be cast is represented (but the articles of incorporation or the board may require a greater vote or a greater number of votes to be represented).

        *   Other statutes require a supermajority to approve the merger.
        *   Shareholders of each corporation must be provided a copy of the plan of merger to enable informed voting.

    d. The surviving corporation succeeds to the rights, duties, liabilities, and assets of the merged corporation.

    e. Shareholders of each corporation have appraisal rights.

    f. Under the RMBCA, no shareholder approval is required in a short-form merger. In a short-form merger, a corporation that owns at least 90 percent of the outstanding shares of a subsidiary merges the subsidiary into itself.

        *   The parent must give ten days' notice to the subsidiary's shareholders.
        *   Shareholders of the subsidiary have appraisal rights.

    g. The RMBCA requires that articles of merger be filed with the Secretary of State.

    h. The RMBCA provisions for share exchanges are similar to those for mergers.

        *   A share exchange occurs when one corporation acquires all of the shares of one or more classes or series of shares of another in exchange for shares, securities, cash, or other property.
        *   A share exchange maintains the separate corporate existence of both entities.

6. In a consolidation, a new corporation is formed where A + B = C, and the two or more consolidating corporations cease operating as separate entities.

    a. The requirements and effects of the combination are similar to those for a merger.

Page 32   ©2007 Kaplan CPA Review

STUDY MANUAL – BUSINESS ENVIRONMENT & CONCEPTS
CHAPTER 1

    b.   The shareholders receive stock or other securities issued by the new corporation.

    c.   The term *statutory merger* applies to combinations involving merger or consolidation as described here.

7.   Tender offers: A merger, consolidation, or purchase of substantially all of a corporation's assets requires approval of the board of directors of the corporation whose shares or assets are acquired. An acquiring corporation may bypass board approval by extending a tender offer of cash or shares, usually at a higher than market price, directly to shareholders to purchase a certain number of the outstanding shares.

    a.   After obtaining control of the target corporation, the tender offeror may effect a merger or consolidation.

    b.   Managements of target corporations have implemented diverse strategies to counter hostile tender offers. Courts apply the business judgment rule when such strategies are challenged. They have generally upheld the strategies.

    c.   States regulate tender offers by statute or administrative regulation to protect interests other than those of a would-be raider.

    d.   The Williams Act of 1968 extended reporting and disclosure requirements of federal securities regulation to tender offers.

8.   Dissolution: The RMBCA permits voluntary dissolution of a corporation that has not commenced business or issued stock. The dissolution requires a majority vote of its incorporators or directors.

    a.   A corporation that has issued stock and commenced business may be voluntarily dissolved by a shareholder vote at a special meeting called for the purpose, if the directors have adopted a resolution of dissolution. Unless the board or the articles require otherwise, a majority of the votes entitled to be cast must be represented at the meeting. The corporation files articles of dissolution with the Secretary of State to petition for a voluntary dissolution. Dissolution is effective when filed.

    b.   The Secretary of State may proceed administratively to dissolve a corporation that fails to file its annual report, pay any franchise tax or penalty, or maintain a resident agent or office in the state. Typically, the Secretary of State gives written notice to the corporation to correct the default or demonstrate that none exists.

    c.   Expiration of the period of duration stated in the articles is another basis for administrative dissolution.

    d.   Under the RMBCA, shareholders may seek a judicial dissolution if any of the following situations occur:

STUDY MANUAL – BUSINESS ENVIRONMENT & CONCEPTS
CHAPTER 1

- A corporate deadlock develops.
- Those in control have acted, are acting, or will act, illegally, oppressively, or fraudulently.
- Assets are being misapplied or wasted.

 e. The attorney general may seek judicial dissolution of a corporation if it is proved that a corporation obtained its articles of incorporation by fraud or that it exceeded or abused its legal authority.

 f. A creditor may seek judicial dissolution of an insolvent corporation if either of the following situations exists:

- The creditor has an unsatisfied judgment against the debtor.
- The debtor has admitted the claim in writing.

9. Liquidation: After dissolution, the corporate business and affairs must be wound up and liquidated.

 a. The directors have a duty to "discharge or make reasonable provision" for claims. They must then distribute assets to shareholders.

 b. Directors will not be liable to claimants with regard to claims barred or satisfied if they have complied with the RMBCA's statutory procedures for:

- Giving notice to known claimants
- Publishing notice of dissolution
- Requesting that other claimants present their claims
- Obtaining appropriate judicial determinations (e.g., of the amount of collateral needed for payment of contingent claims, claims reasonably expected to arise after dissolution, or claims not yet made)

Page 34   ©2007 Kaplan CPA Review

STUDY MANUAL – BUSINESS ENVIRONMENT & CONCEPTS
CHAPTER 1

QUESTIONS: BUSINESS STRUCTURES: CORPORATIONS

1. Knox, president of Quick Corp., contracted with Tine Office Supplies, Inc., to supply Quick's stationery on customary terms and at a cost less than that charged by any other suppliers. Knox later informed Quick's board of directors that Knox was a majority stockholder in Tine. Quick's contract with Tine is:
   A. valid because the contract is fair to Quick.
   B. void because of Knox's self-dealing.
   C. void because the disclosure was made after execution of the contract.
   D. valid because of Knox's full disclosure.

2. Under the Revised Model Business Corporation Act, a merger of two public corporations usually requires all of the following EXCEPT:
   A. approval by the board of directors of each corporation.
   B. receipt of voting stock by all stockholders of the original corporations.
   C. a formal plan of merger.
   D. an affirmative vote by the holders of a majority of each corporation's voting shares.

3. The limited liability of a stockholder in a closely held corporation may be challenged successfully if the stockholder:
   A. sold property to the corporation.
   B. was a corporate officer, director, or employee.
   C. undercapitalized the corporation when it was formed.
   D. formed the corporation solely to have limited personal liability.

4. The corporate veil is most likely to be pierced and the shareholders held personally liable if:
   A. the corporation has elected S corporation status under the Internal Revenue Code.
   B. an ultra vires act has been committed.
   C. a partnership incorporates its business solely to limit the liability of its partners.
   D. the shareholders have commingled their personal funds with those of the corporation.

5. Which of the following actions may be taken by a corporation's board of directors without stockholder approval?
   A. Dissolving the corporation.
   B. Amending the articles of incorporation.
   C. Purchasing substantially all of the assets of another corporation.
   D. Selling substantially all of the corporation's assets.

©2007 Kaplan CPA Review

6. Under the Revised Model Business Corporation Act, which of the following actions by a corporation would entitle a stockholder to dissent from the action and obtain payment of the fair value of his/her shares?

   I. An amendment to the articles of incorporation that materially and adversely affects rights in respect of a dissenter's shares because it alters or abolishes a preferential right of the shares.
   II. Consummation of a plan of share exchange to which the corporation is a party as the corporation whose shares will be acquired, if the stockholder is entitled to vote on the plan.

   A. Both I and II.
   B. Neither I nor II.
   C. I only.
   D. II only.

7. Johns owns 400 shares of Abco Corp. cumulative preferred stock. In the absence of any specific contrary provisions in Abco's articles of incorporation, which of the following statements is TRUE?
   A. Johns will be entitled to vote if dividend payments are in arrears.
   B. If Abco declares a cash dividend on its preferred stock, Johns becomes an unsecured creditor of Abco.
   C. Johns is entitled to convert the 400 shares of preferred stock to a like number of shares of common stock.
   D. If Abco declares a dividend on its common stock, Johns will be entitled to participate with the common stock shareholders in any dividend distribution made after preferred dividends are paid.

8. Jane Cox, a shareholder of Mix Corp., has properly commenced a derivative action against Mix's Board of Directors. Cox alleges that the Board breached its fiduciary duty and was negligent by failing to independently verify the financial statements prepared by management upon which Smart & Co., CPAs, issued an unqualified opinion. The financial statements contained inaccurate information which the Board relied upon in committing large sums of money to capital expansion. This resulted in Mix having to borrow money at extremely high interest rates to meet current cash needs. Within a short period of time, the price of Mix Corp. stock declined drastically. Which of the following statements is correct?
   A. The Board may avoid liability if it acted in good faith and in a reasonable manner.
   B. The Board may avoid liability in all cases where it can show that it lacked scienter.
   C. The Board is strictly liable, regardless of fault, since it owes a fiduciary duty to both the corporation and the shareholders.
   D. The Board is liable since any negligence of Smart is automatically imputed to the Board.

9. Rice is a promoter of a corporation to be known as Dex Corp. On January 1, Rice signed a nine-month contract with Roe, a CPA, which provided that Roe would perform certain accounting services for Dex. Rice did not disclose to Roe that

Dex had not been formed. Prior to the incorporation of Dex on February 1, Roe rendered accounting services pursuant to the contract. After rendering accounting services for an additional period of six months pursuant to the contract, Roe was discharged without cause by the board of directors of Dex. In the absence of any agreements to the contrary, who will be liable to Roe for breach of contract?

A. Both Rice and Dex.
B. Rice only.
C. Dex only.
D. Neither Rice nor Dex.

10. Which of the following provisions must a for-profit-corporation include in its Articles of Incorporation to obtain a corporate charter?

    I.   Provision for issuance of voting stock.
    II. Name of the corporation.

    A. I only.
    B. II only.
    C. Both I and II.
    D. Neither I nor II.

11. Under the Revised Model Business Corporation Act, which of the following must be contained in a corporation's articles of incorporation?
    A. Quorum voting requirements.
    B. Names of stockholders.
    C. Provisions for issuance of par and non-par shares.
    D. The number of shares the corporation is authorized to issue.

12. Absent a specific provision in its articles of incorporation, a corporation's board of directors has the power to do all of the following, except:
    A. Repeal the bylaws.
    B. Declare dividends.
    C. Fix compensation of directors.
    D. Amend the articles of incorporation.

13. Which of the following facts is (are) generally included in a corporation's articles of incorporation?

	Name of registered agent	Number of authorized shares
A.	Yes	Yes
B.	Yes	No
C.	No	Yes
D.	No	No

©2007 Kaplan CPA Review

14. Under the Revised Model Business Corporation Act, which of the following statements regarding a corporation's bylaws is (are) correct?

   I. A corporation's initial bylaws shall be adopted by either the incorporators or the board of directors.
   II. A corporation's bylaws are contained in the articles of incorporation.

   A. I only
   B. II only.
   C. Both I and II.
   D. Neither I nor II.

15. Which of the following statements best describes an advantage of the corporate form of doing business?
   A. Day to day management is strictly the responsibility of the directors.
   B. Ownership is contractually restricted and is not transferable.
   C. The operation of the business may continue indefinitely.
   D. The business is free from state regulation.

16. Destiny Manufacturing, Inc., is incorporated under the laws of Nevada. Its principal place of business is in California and it has permanent sales offices in several other states. Under the circumstances, which of the following is correct?
   A. California may validly demand that Destiny incorporate under the laws of the state of California.
   B. Destiny must obtain a certificate of authority to transact business in California and the other states in which it does business.
   C. Destiny is a foreign corporation in California, but not in the other states.
   D. California may prevent Destiny from operating as a corporation if the laws of California differ regarding organization and conduct of the corporation's internal affairs.

17. Which of the following statements is a general requirement for the merger of two corporations?
   A. The merger plan must be approved unanimously by the stockholders of both corporations.
   B. The merger plan must be approved unanimously by the boards of both corporations
   C. The absorbed corporation must amend its articles of incorporation.
   D. The stockholders of both corporations must be given due notice of a special meeting, including a copy or summary of the merger plan.

18. A corporate stockholder is entitled to which of the following rights?
   A. Elect officers.
   B. Receive annual dividends.
   C. Approve dissolution.
   D. Prevent corporate borrowing.

19. A parent corporation owned more than 90% of each class of the outstanding stock issued by a subsidiary corporation and decided to merge that subsidiary into itself. Under the Revised Model Business Corporation Act, which of the following actions must be taken?
    A. The subsidiary corporation's board of directors must pass a merger resolution.
    B. The subsidiary corporation's dissenting stockholders must be given an appraisal remedy.
    C. The parent corporation's stockholders must approve the merger.
    D. The parent corporation's dissenting stockholders must be given an appraisal remedy.

20. A stockholder's right to inspect books and records of a corporation will be properly denied if the stockholder:
    A. Wants to use corporate stockholder records for a personal business.
    B. Employs an agent to inspect the books and records.
    C. Intends to commence a stockholder's derivative suit.
    D. Is investigating management misconduct.

21. To which of the following rights is a stockholder of a public corporation entitled?
    A. The right to have annual dividends declared.
    B. The right to vote for the election of officers.
    C. The right to a reasonable inspection of corporate records.
    D. The right to have the corporation issue a new class of stock.

22. Under the Revised Model Business Corporation Act, when a corporation's bylaws grant stockholders preemptive rights, which of the following rights is (are) included in that grant?

	The right to purchase a proportionate share of newly-issued stock	The right to a proportionate share of corporate assets remaining on corporate dissolution
A.	Yes	Yes
B.	Yes	No
C.	No	Yes
D.	No	No

23. For what purpose will a stockholder of a publicly held corporation be permitted to file a stockholders' derivative suit in the name of the corporation?
    A. To compel payment of a properly declared dividend.
    B. To enforce a right to inspect corporate records.
    C. To compel dissolution of the corporation.
    D. To recover damages from corporate management for an ultra vires management act.

STUDY MANUAL – BUSINESS ENVIRONMENT & CONCEPTS
CHAPTER 1

24. Which of the following statements is correct regarding the fiduciary duty?
   A. A director's fiduciary duty to the corporation may be discharged by merely disclosing his self-interest.
   B. A director owes a fiduciary duty to the shareholders but not to the corporation.
   C. A promoter of a corporation to be formed owes no fiduciary duty to anyone, unless the contract engaging the promoter so provides.
   D. A majority shareholder as such may owe a fiduciary duty to fellow shareholders.

25. Which of the following securities are corporate debt securities?

	Convertible bonds	Debenture bonds	Warrants
A.	Yes	Yes	Yes
B.	Yes	No	Yes
C.	Yes	Yes	No
D.	No	Yes	Yes

26. An owner of common stock will not have any liability beyond actual investment if the owner:
   A. Paid less than par value for stock purchased in connection with an original issue of shares.
   B. Agreed to perform future services for the corporation in exchange for original issue par value shares.
   C. Purchased treasury shares for less than par value.
   D. Failed to pay the full amount owed on a subscription contract for no-par shares.

27. In general, which of the following statements concerning treasury stock is correct?
   A. A corporation may not reacquire its own stock unless specifically authorized by its articles of incorporation.
   B. On issuance of new stock, a corporation has preemptive rights with regard to its treasury stock.
   C. Treasury stock may be distributed as a stock dividend.
   D. A corporation is entitled to receive cash dividends on its treasury stock.

28. Ambrose purchased 400 shares of $100 par value original issue common stock from Minor Corporation for $25 a share. Ambrose subsequently sold 200 of the shares to Harris at $25 a share. Harris did not have knowledge or notice that Ambrose had not paid par. Ambrose also sold 100 shares of this stock to Gable for $25 a share. At the time of this sale, Gable knew that Ambrose had not paid par for the stock. Minor Corporation became insolvent and the creditors sought to hold all the above parties liable for the $75 unpaid on each of the 400 shares. Under these circumstances:
   A. The creditors can hold Ambrose liable for $30,000.
   B. If $25 a share was a fair value for the stock at the time of issuance, Ambrose will have no liability to the creditors.
   C. Since Harris acquired the shares by purchase, he is not liable to the creditors, and his lack of knowledge or notice that Ambrose paid less than par is immaterial.
   D. Since Gable acquired the shares by purchase, he is not liable to the creditors, and the fact that he knew Ambrose paid less than par is immaterial.

29. Which of the following rights is a holder of a public corporation's cumulative preferred stock always entitled to?
   A. Conversion of the preferred stock into common stock.
   B. Voting rights.
   C. Dividend carryovers from years in which dividends were not paid, to future years.
   D. Guaranteed dividends.

30. West owns 5,000 shares of $7 cumulative preferred stock of Sky Corp. During the first year of operations, cash dividends of $7 per share were declared on Sky's preferred stock but were never paid. In the second year of operations, dividends on Sky's preferred stock were neither declared nor paid. If Sky is dissolved, which of the following statements is correct?
   A. West will have priority over the claims of Sky's debenture bond owners.
   B. West will have priority over the claims of Sky's unsecured judgment creditors.
   C. Sky will be liable to West as an unsecured creditor for $35,000.
   D. Sky will be liable to West as an unsecured creditor for $70,000.

31. Price owns 2,000 shares of Universal Corp.'s $10 cumulative preferred stock. During its first year of operations, cash dividends of $5 per share were declared on the preferred stock but were never paid. In the second year, dividends on the preferred stock were neither declared nor paid. If Universal is dissolved, which of the following statements is correct?
   A. Universal will be liable to Price as an unsecured creditor for $10,000.
   B. Universal will be liable to Price as a secured creditor for $20,000.
   C. Price will have priority over the claims of Universal's bond owners.
   D. Price will have priority over the claims of Universal's unsecured judgment creditors.

STUDY MANUAL – BUSINESS ENVIRONMENT & CONCEPTS
CHAPTER 1

32.   Carr Corp. declared a 7% stock dividend on its common stock. The dividend:
    A.   Must be registered with the SEC pursuant to the Securities Act of 1933.
    B.   Is includable in the gross income of the recipient taxpayers in the year of receipt.
    C.   Has no effect on Carr's earnings and profits for federal income tax purposes.
    D.   Requires a vote of Carr's stockholders.

33.   All of the following distributions to stockholders are considered asset or capital distributions, except:
    A.   Liquidating dividends.
    B.   Stock splits.
    C.   Property distributions.
    D.   Cash dividends.

34.   Generally, officers of a corporation:
    A.   Are elected by the shareholders.
    B.   Are agents and fiduciaries of the corporation, having actual and apparent authority to manage the business.
    C.   May be removed by the board of directors without cause only if the removal is approved by a majority vote of the shareholders.
    D.   May declare dividends or other distributions to shareholders as they deem appropriate.

35.   Under the Revised Model Business Corporation Act, a corporate director is authorized to:
    A.   Rely on information provided by the appropriate corporate officer.
    B.   Serve on the board of directors of a competing business.
    C.   Sell control of the corporation.
    D.   Profit from insider information.

36.   Under the Revised Model Business Corporation Act, which of the following statements is correct regarding corporate officers of a public corporation?
    A.   An officer may not simultaneously serve as a director.
    B.   A corporation may be authorized to indemnify its officers for liability incurred in a suit by stockholders.
    C.   Stockholders always have the right to elect a corporation's officers.
    D.   An officer of a corporation is required to own at least one share of the corporation's stock.

37.   Which of the following must take place for a corporation to be voluntarily dissolved?
    A.   Passage by the board of directors of a resolution to dissolve.
    B.   Approval by the officers of a resolution to dissolve.
    C.   Amendment of the certificate of incorporation.
    D.   Unanimous vote of the stockholders.

38. Which of the following would be grounds for the judicial dissolution of a corporation on the petition of a shareholder?
    A. Refusal of the board of directors to declare a dividend.
    B. Waste of corporate assets by the board of directors.
    C. Loss operations of the corporation for three years.
    D. Failure by the corporation to file its federal income tax returns.

39. Which one of the following will render a corporation ineligible for S corporation status?
    A. One of the stockholders is a decedent's estate.
    B. One of the stockholders is a bankruptcy estate.
    C. The corporation has both voting and nonvoting common stock issued and outstanding.
    D. The corporation has 105 stockholders.

40. Which of the following conditions will prevent a corporation from qualifying as an S Corporation?
    A. The corporation has both common and preferred stock.
    B. The corporation has one class of stock with different voting rights.
    C. One shareholder is an estate.
    D. One shareholder is a grantor trust.

41. Village Corp., a calendar year corporation, began business in 20X0. Village made a valid S Corporation election on December 5, 20X3, with the unanimous consent of its shareholders. The eligibility requirements for S status continued to be met throughout 20X4. On what date did Village's S status become effective?
    A. January 1, 20X3.
    B. January 1, 20X4.
    C. December 5, 20X3.
    D. December 5, 20X4.

42. On February 10, 20X3, Ace Corp., a calendar year corporation, elected S corporation status and all shareholders consented to the election. There was no change in shareholders in 20X3. Ace met all eligibility requirements for S status during the preelection portion of the year. What is the earliest date on which Ace can be recognized as an S corporation?
    A. February 10, 20X4.
    B. February 10, 20X3.
    C. January 1, 20X4.
    D. January 1, 20X3.

43. An S corporation has 30,000 shares of voting common stock and 20,000 shares of non-voting common stock issued and outstanding. The S election can be revoked voluntarily with the consent of the shareholders holding, on the day of the revocation:

	Shares of voting stock	Shares of nonvoting stock
A.	0	20,000
B.	7,500	5,000
C.	10,000	16,000
D.	20,000	0

©2007 Kaplan CPA Review

STUDY MANUAL – BUSINESS ENVIRONMENT & CONCEPTS
CHAPTER 1

44. After a corporation's status as an S corporation is revoked or terminated, how many years is the corporation generally required to wait before making a new S election, in the absence of IRS consent to an earlier election?
    A. 1
    B. 3
    C. 5
    D. 10

45. An S corporation may:
    A. Have both common and preferred stock.
    B. Have a corporation as a shareholder.
    C. Be a member of an affiliated group.
    D. Have as many as 100 shareholders.

46. Under the Revised Model Business Corporation Act, which of the following conditions is necessary for a corporation to achieve a successful voluntary dissolution?
    A. Successful application to the secretary of state in which the corporation holds its primary place of business.
    B. A recommendation of dissolution by the board of directors and approval by a majority of all shareholders entitled to vote.
    C. Approval by the board of directors of an amendment to the certificate of incorporation calling for the dissolution of the corporation.
    D. Unanimous approval of the board of directors and two-thirds vote of all shareholders entitled to vote on a resolution of voluntary dissolution.

Study Manual – Business Environment & Concepts
Chapter 1

ANSWERS: BUSINESS STRUCTURES: CORPORATIONS

1. **A** An officer or director may make a personal profit on a contract with their own corporation if they make a full disclosure and do not participate in the approval process. Absent pre-approval, they may do so only if the contract is fair and reasonable to the corporation. Knox did not receive pre-approval for the stationery contract. However, since the price charged by Knox was less than any other supplier, the contract was fair to Quick and would be valid. The contract was valid and the disclosure was only made after the contract. Without pre-approval the contract could only be valid if it was fair and reasonable.

2. **B** A merger of two corporations requires the approval of a majority of both boards of directors and the approval of a majority of the voting stockholders of both corporations. The corporations must submit a copy of the merger plan to all stockholders and provide notice of the time and the place of the meeting at which the vote will occur. A formal plan of merger is required; it must be submitted to the stockholders and receive approval of the majority of those voting and it must receive the approval of a majority of the board of directors. Receipt of voting stock by all stockholders of both corporations is not required.

3. **C** A stockholder may be held personally liable for corporate debts (piercing the corporate veil). Specifically this may be done by a showing of fraud, undercapitalization of the corporation and commingling of corporate and personal funds by the stockholder. Thus, the corporate veil may be pierced if the stockholder undercapitalized the corporation when it was formed. Forming the corporation solely to have limited personal liability is incorrect because one of the principal reasons for choosing the corporate form over others is to obtain limited personal liability. It is not grounds to pierce the corporate veil. The mere fact that a stockholder sold property to the corporation or was an officer, director, or employee is insufficient grounds to pierce the corporate veil.

4. **D** A stockholder may be held personally liable for corporate debts (piercing the corporate veil). Specifically this may be done by a showing of fraud, undercapitalization of the corporation and commingling of corporate and personal funds by the stockholder. Thus, the corporate veil may be pierced if the stockholder commingled their personal funds with those of the corporation. Choosing S corporation status, commission of an ultra vires act, and incorporation to obtain limited personal liability are all insufficient grounds to pierce the corporate veil.

5. **C** Stockholders get to vote on fundamental changes in the corporation. This specifically includes the right to vote on mergers, consolidations, compulsory share exchanges, sale of substantially all of the corporation's assets (but not buying all of another corporation's assets), dissolutions and amending the articles of incorporation. Selling substantially all of the corporation's assets, dissolving the corporation and amending the articles of incorporation are all examples of fundamental changes that would require stockholder approval. Purchasing substantially all of the assets of another corporation may be a minor matter to the acquiring corporation and thus not constitute a fundamental change requiring a stockholder vote.

6. **A** Stockholders have dissenters' rights or a right of appraisal for certain fundamental changes in the corporation. Such changes include mergers, consolidations, compulsory share exchanges, sale of substantially all of the corporation's assets (but not buying all of another corporation's assets) and any amendment to the articles of incorporation that materially and adversely affects stockholders' rights concerning their shares. I is a correct statement because dissenters' rights would be available for an amendment that materially

©2007 Kaplan CPA Review

Page 45

STUDY MANUAL – BUSINESS ENVIRONMENT & CONCEPTS
CHAPTER 1

and adversely affected a preferential right of the stockholders' shares. II is a correct statement because dissenters' rights are available for mergers and consolidations and would thus be available if a corporation's shares were being acquired by another business.

7. **B**   Once a dividend is duly declared by the board of directors, the stockholders become unsecured creditors of the corporation. Thus, once Abco declares a cash dividend, Johns became an unsecured creditor of Abco. A preferred stockholder is not entitled to convert preferred stock into common stock unless this right is specifically authorized. Johns is a holder of cumulative preferred stock, not participating preferred stock. Only participating preferred stock shareholders may participate with common stock shareholders on dividend distributions. Cumulative preferred stock is usually non-voting stock. Whether voting or non-voting depends on the stock, not whether dividend payments are in arrears.

8. **A**   Under the business judgment rule, directors and officers are not liable if they acted reasonably and in good faith. Thus, the Mix's board may avoid liability by showing that it acted in good faith and in a reasonable manner. A director is not strictly liable. The negligence of the CPA firm is not automatically imputed to the board. The board may usually rely on the reports of officers and agents (like a CPA firm's report). The board can be liable without proof of scienter (intent to deceive). A director is liable for negligence, which does not require proof of scienter.

9. **A**   Promoters are primarily liable on pre-incorporation contracts they make. They remain primarily liable, even if the corporation accepts the contract. Rice (the promoter) is primarily liable for the contract made with Roe. The corporation, by using Roe's services for six months after incorporation, had impliedly accepted the contract and would be liable also. The only answer that indicates that both Rice and Dix are liable is (a).

10. **C**   The articles of incorporation must contain provisions as to stock to specifically include the amount of authorized shares, the par value of the stock and the classes of the stock to include which stock has voting rights. It must also contain the names of the corporation, its registered agent, and all incorporators. Only answer (c) reflects that both provisions as to the issuance of voting stock and the name of the corporation must be included.

11. **D**   The articles of incorporation must contain provisions as to stock to specifically include the amount of authorized shares, the par value of the stock and the classes of the stock to include which stock has voting rights. Answers (a) and (b) are incorrect because the articles of incorporation need not contain quorum voting requirements or the names of stockholders. Answer (c) is incorrect because although the par value of stock will be listed if there is par value stock, there is no requirement that there be par value stock or no par value stock.

12. **D**   Stockholders get to vote on fundamental changes in the corporation. This specifically includes the right to vote on mergers and consolidations, dissolution and amending the articles of incorporation. Thus, the board of directors would not have the power to amend the articles of incorporation because it would require stockholder approval. Answers (a), (b) and (c) are incorrect because directors do have the power to repeal the bylaws, declare dividends and fix their own compensation.

13. **A**   The articles of incorporation must contain provisions as to stock to specifically include the amount of authorized shares. It must also contain the names of the corporation, its registered agent, and all incorporators. Only answer (a) states that the articles of incorporation must contain the name of the registered agent and the number of authorized shares.

STUDY MANUAL – BUSINESS ENVIRONMENT & CONCEPTS
CHAPTER 1

14. **A** The bylaws of a corporation govern the corporation's internal management. The bylaws may be adopted by either the incorporators or the board of directors; thus I is a correct statement. The bylaws are not filed with the state as are the articles of incorporation. Thus, II is not a correct statement because the bylaws are not contained in the articles of incorporation.

15. **C** One of the advantages of the corporate form is that a corporation has perpetual existence and therefore may continue to do business indefinitely. Answer (a) is incorrect because it is the officers, not the directors, that are responsible for day to day management. Answer (b) is incorrect because another advantage of the corporation is that shares of a corporation are freely transferable, unless specifically restricted by contract. Answer (d) is incorrect because a disadvantage of the corporate form is a greater degree of governmental supervision.

16. **B** A foreign corporation is one doing business in any state other than their state of incorporation. A foreign corporation must obtain a certificate of authority from each state in which they do business. Thus, Destiny is a foreign corporation in California because they were incorporated in Nevada and they were doing business in California. Destiny must obtain a certificate of authority from California and all other states in which it does business. Answer (a) is incorrect because incorporation is not required merely because a corporation is doing business in a state. Answer (c) is incorrect because Destiny is a foreign corporation in any state in which it does business. Answer (d) is incorrect because Destiny as a Nevada corporation is only required to comply with Nevada's requirements for incorporation and not California's requirements.

17. **D** A merger of two corporations requires the approval of a majority of both boards of directors and the approval of a majority of the voting stockholders of both corporations. The corporations must submit a copy of the merger plan to all stockholders and provide notice of the time and the place of the meeting at which the vote will occur. Answers (a) and (b) are incorrect because unanimous approval is not required by either the stockholders or the directors. Answer (c) is incorrect because the absorbed corporation no longer exists and, thus, has no articles of incorporation to amend.

18. **C** Stockholders get to vote on fundamental changes in the corporation. This specifically includes the right to vote on mergers, consolidations, compulsory share exchanges, sale of substantially all of the corporation's assets (but not buying all of another corporation's assets), dissolutions and amending the articles of incorporation. Answer (a) is incorrect because stockholders do not get to elect officers. They elect directors. Answer (b) is incorrect because there is no inherent right to receive dividends. Answer (d) is incorrect because stockholders cannot prevent corporate borrowing. Corporate borrowing need not involve a fundamental change in the corporation and stockholders may only vote on fundamental changes.

19. **B** When a corporation owns 90% or more of the shares of a subsidiary corporation, the subsidiary may be merged into the parent corporation without the approval of the stockholders of either the parent corporation or the subsidiary corporation and without the approval of the subsidiary corporations board of directors. This is called a short-form merger. Thus, answers (a) and (c) are incorrect. In a short-form merger stockholders of the subsidiary corporation have dissenters' rights, but the stockholders of the parent corporation do not. Thus, answer (b) is correct and answer (d) is incorrect.

20. **A** A stockholder has the right to inspect books and records of the corporation at reasonable times and upon written demand. They lose this right if they have an improper motive. Obtaining corporate information for use in a personal business would be an improper motive. Answer (b) is incorrect because the stockholder may use an agent to inspect.

©2007 Kaplan CPA Review
Page 47

STUDY MANUAL – BUSINESS ENVIRONMENT & CONCEPTS
CHAPTER 1

Answers (c) and (d) are incorrect because commencing a derivative suit on behalf of the corporation and investigating management misconduct both have the proper motive of attempting to protect their investment.

21. **C** A stockholder has the right to inspect books and records of the corporation at reasonable times and upon written demand. Answer (a) is incorrect because there is no inherent right to dividends for stockholders. Answer (b) is incorrect because stockholders elect directors, not officers. Officers are appointed by the directors. Answer (d) is incorrect because stockholders do not generally have the right to participate in management. They have only two management rights: electing directors and voting on fundamental changes in the corporation. They do not have the right to have the corporation issue a new class of stock as this is not a fundamental change in the corporation.

22. **B** By definition, preemptive rights are the right of a stockholder to purchase a proportionate amount of a new issue equal to his/her percentage of ownership. Although stockholders have the right upon dissolution to a proportionate share of corporate assets after all creditors have been paid, this is not preemptive rights.

23. **D** A derivative suit is a law suit brought by a large group of stockholders on behalf of the corporation to enforce a corporate right. Derivative suits may specifically be brought to recover damages for management's ultra vires acts. A derivative suit must be brought for a corporate harm and cannot be brought to enforce personal stockholder rights. Answers (a), (b) and (c) are incorrect because compelling payment of a properly declared dividend, inspecting corporate records and compelling dissolution of the corporation are personal rights of stockholders and not a harm to the corporation itself.

24. **D** Although stockholders usually do not owe a fiduciary duty to others, a majority stockholder may owe a fiduciary duty to fellow stockholders. This is due to the fact that a majority stockholder is in a position of control. Answer (b) is incorrect because a director owes a fiduciary duty of loyalty to the corporation and to the stockholders. Answer (a) is incorrect because disclosure by itself will not discharge a director's fiduciary duty of loyalty. Answer (c) is incorrect because a promoter owes a duty of loyalty to subscribers, future stockholders and the corporation.

25. **C** Debt securities or bonds create a creditor-debtor relationship between the bondholder and the corporation and are not an ownership interest in the corporation. Convertible bonds can be exchanged for other corporate securities. Debenture bonds are unsecured bonds. Since both convertible bonds and debenture bonds are types of bonds, they are debt securities. Warrants are stock options that are evidenced by a certificate. Stock options are equity securities and are not debt securities.

26. **C** Treasury stock can be sold by the corporation at a price that is less than par value. Thus, one who purchased treasury stock for less than par value would not be liable. If par value stock was purchased at less than par in connection with an original issue, it would be watered stock and the purchaser would be liable or the difference in price. Thus, (a) is incorrect. Answer (b) is incorrect because a stockholder must pay present value for stock. An agreement to perform future services in exchange for stock would leave the stockholder liable until the future services were performed. Answer (d) is incorrect because a stockholder must pay present value for stock. Failure to pay the full amount owed on a subscription contract leaves the stockholder liable for the amount unpaid.

27. **C** Treasury stock may be distributed as a stock dividend. Answer (a) is incorrect because a corporation may purchase treasury stock as long as it has the surplus funds to do so. The power to purchase does not require specific authorization by the articles of incorporation. Answer (b) is incorrect because there are no preemptive rights with treasury stock. Answer (d) is incorrect because there are no cash dividends paid on treasury stock.

STUDY MANUAL – BUSINESS ENVIRONMENT & CONCEPTS
CHAPTER 1

28. **A**   If par value stock is sold at less than par in an original issue, the stock is watered stock and the purchaser is liable for the difference between the amount paid and the par value. All other purchasers with notice that the stock was being sold for less than par value would also be liable for the difference in price. Ambrose purchased 400 shares of $100 par value stock in an original issue for $25 a share. Ambrose is therefore liable for $75 per share, the difference between the $25 per share paid and $100 par value. The total amount of Ambrose's liability would be $75 times the 400 shares purchased, or $30,000. Thus, answer (a) is correct and (b) is incorrect. Answer (c) is incorrect because subsequent purchasers are only liable if they had notice that the stock was being sold for less than par. The lack of notice by Harris would be material. Answer (d) is incorrect because Gable's purchase with knowledge that the stock was sold at less than par would make Gable liable.

29. **C**   Cumulative preferred stock entitles the holder to a dividend carryover to future years if the dividend is not paid in any given year. Answer (a) is incorrect because it does not permit the holder to convert preferred stock into common stock. Answer (b) is incorrect because cumulative preferred stock is usually non-voting. Answer (d) is incorrect because no stockholder has an inherent or guaranteed right to dividends.

30. **C**   Once a dividend is duly declared by the board of directors, the stockholders become unsecured creditors of the corporation. Since $7 per share dividend on Sky's preferred stock was declared and West owned 5,000 shares, Sky is liable to West as an unsecured creditor for $35,000 ($7 times 5,000 shares). Answers (a) and (b) are incorrect because West as an unsecured creditor does not have a priority over any other creditor. Answer (d) is incorrect because no other dividends were declared on the preferred stock. Thus, West is only entitled to $35,000, not $70,000.

31. **A**   Once a dividend is duly declared by the board of directors, the stockholders become unsecured creditors of the corporation. Since Universal declared a $5 per share dividend on their preferred stock and Price owned 2,000 shares, Universal would be liable to Price as an unsecured creditor for $10,000 ($5 per share times 2,000 shares). Answer (b) is incorrect because Price is not a secured creditor. Additionally, Price is not entitled to $20,000 because no other dividends were declared. Answers (c) and (d) are incorrect because Price is an unsecured creditor and does not have a priority over any other creditor.

32. **C**   Stock dividends have no effect on earnings or profits of a corporation for federal income tax purposes. Answer (a) is incorrect because a stock dividend is a "no sale transaction" wherein a corporation is dealing exclusively with existing shareholders without payment of a commission. No sale transactions are exempt from registration under the Securities Act of 1933. Answer (b) is incorrect because stock dividends are not usually treated as gross income for federal tax purposes. Answer (d) is incorrect because dividends are declared by the board and do not require stockholder approval. Stockholders may only vote to elect directors and on fundamental changes in the corporation.

33. **B**   A stock split is a type of stock dividend and neither reduces the assets of a corporation nor increases the stockholder's percentage of ownership. It is not considered a distribution and does not distribute assets. Thus, it cannot be considered an asset or capital distribution. Answer (a) is incorrect because a liquidating dividend is a distribution of capital assets to stockholders. Answer (c) and (d) are incorrect because both property distributions and cash distributions involve distribution of assets to stockholders. One distributes the assets in property and the other in cash.

34. **B**   Officers are agents of the corporation and are therefore fiduciaries. All agents can have actual and apparent authority. Answer (a) is incorrect because stockholders elect directors, not the officers. Answer (c) is incorrect because stockholders do not have the right to vote

---

©2007 Kaplan CPA Review

Page 49

STUDY MANUAL – BUSINESS ENVIRONMENT & CONCEPTS
CHAPTER 1

on removal of officers. They may only vote on the election of directors and on fundamental matters. Answer (d) is incorrect because directors declare dividends, not officers.

35. A Directors may rely on reports of officers or agents. Answers (b) and (d) are incorrect because a director is a fiduciary and must act solely in the corporation's best interest. Serving on the board of a competing company and profiting from insider information would be a breach of a director's fiduciary duty of loyalty. Answer (c) is incorrect because a director does not own control of the corporation, the majority stockholders do. Since the director does not own control of the corporation, the director can not sell control of the corporation

36. B Under the Revised Model Business Corporation Act a corporation may indemnify an officer or director for liability incurred in a suit by stockholders if they acted in good faith in the best interests of the corporation. Answer (a) is incorrect because an officer may also be a director. This is a common occurrence in business. Answer (c) is incorrect because stockholders elect directors, not officers. Answer (d) is incorrect because an officer is not required to own stock.

37. A Voluntary dissolution requires both a resolution to dissolve by the board of directors and approval by a majority of the stockholders. Answer (b) is incorrect because dissolution does not require approval by the officers. Answer (c) is incorrect because dissolution does not require an amendment to the articles of incorporation. Once the corporation is dissolved there is no need for the articles of incorporation. Answer (d) is incorrect because dissolution requires approval by a majority of the stockholders, not a unanimous vote.

38. B An involuntary dissolution may be forced by stockholders for waste of corporate assets. Answers (a), (c) and (d) are incorrect because refusal of a board to declare dividends, loss operations for three years, and failure to file federal income tax are insufficient grounds for an involuntary dissolution.

39. D The maximum number of shareholders allowed in an S Corporation is 100.

40. A An S Corporation is allowed only one class of stock. That stock may, however, have different voting rights.

41. B Since the shareholders of Village Corporation did not make the consent by March 15, 20X3, the election takes effect on January 1, 20X4 (the next year).

42. D Since the shareholders of Ace Corporation made the consent by March 15, 20X3, the election takes effect on January 1, 20X3 (the current year).

43. C 10,000 and 16,000. What is needed is a majority of the voting and nonvoting shares to revoke the election. In this problem the total number of shares is 50,000, therefore more than 25,000 is needed. Only answer (c) with 26,000 shares qualifies.

44. C 5 years. Once an S Corporation is revoked or terminated, the corporation generally may not re-elect for five years without IRS consent to an earlier election.

45. D A S Corporation may have up to 100 shareholders. However, it may not have both common and preferred stock; have a corporation as a shareholder; or be a member of an affiliated group (at least 80%).

46. B Corporations require a recommendation by the board of directors and approval by a majority of all shareholders entitled to vote. Contrast this with a partnership, which requires the unanimous consent of all partners.

BUSINESS STRUCTURES: PARTNERSHIPS

STUDY MANUAL – BUSINESS ENVIRONMENT & CONCEPTS
CHAPTER 2

Study Tip: Decide how many days you will be able to use to prepare for each section of the CPA exam. Divide that number of days into three equal periods of time. During the first third, focus 100% of your time on learning new material. In the second third, allocate 60–70% of your time to new subjects with the remainder for reviewing previously covered topics. For the final days, 30–40% of the coverage should be new areas with the rest for review. When taking the exam, all topics need to be kept fresh in your memory until you walk in to take *and pass* the CPA exam.

SOLE PROPRIETORSHIPS

FORMATION

A. By definition, a sole proprietorship is a business with only one owner.

B. Legal requirements of a sole proprietorship are few.

1. Formation is subject to only a few legal requirements (e.g., licensing laws, zoning laws), compared to other business structures.

2. State law usually requires a proprietor doing business under a fictitious name to make a d/b/a (or *doing business as*) filing.

C. The advantages of forming a business as a sole proprietorship include the following:

1. Of all business structures, a sole proprietorship is the easiest and cheapest to create.

2. Formation of a sole proprietorship does not require formal filings with the state.

3. The owner has complete control of, and can make all decisions for, the business.

D. The primary disadvantage of formation as a sole proprietorship is the unlimited personal liability that puts the personal assets of the sole proprietor (and community property of the spouse) at risk.

©2007 Kaplan CPA Review

Page 51

STUDY MANUAL – BUSINESS ENVIRONMENT & CONCEPTS
CHAPTER 2

CAPITALIZATION

A. The primary sources of capital for a sole proprietorship are the personal resources and personal borrowing capacity of the owner. Generally, a bank loan to the proprietor is the major source of financing.

B. The primary advantage of organizing as a sole proprietorship is the minimal capital needed to start up and maintain the business.

C. Disadvantages include:

   1. Debt financing is necessary to obtain working capital for the ongoing operations of the business.

   2. Business expansion may require additional borrowings by the owner.

   3. If financing needs outpace the borrowing capacity of the owner, equity financing is an alternative. However, bringing in a partner or issuing an ownership interest will change the business structure from sole proprietorship to some other entity.

PROFITS AND LOSSES

A. Advantage: all profits are received by the sole proprietor.

B. Disadvantage: all losses are incurred by the sole proprietor.

C. Risk: unlimited personal liability for all torts and contracts puts the proprietor's nonbusiness-related assets at risk.

TAXATION

A. Since the sole proprietorship is not a separate legal or taxable entity, the profit or loss of the business flows directly to the proprietor's tax return.

B. Benefits of this tax structure include the following:

   1. The proprietor receives the tax benefits of all business deductions and losses.

   2. A proprietorship avoids potential double taxation, which occurs with the corporate form.

   3. The proprietor files only one tax return, rather than both personal and business returns.

OPERATION

A. Advantages of sole proprietor management include the following:

   1. The sole proprietor has the flexibility to act quickly and make changes as needed.

Page 52   ©2007 Kaplan CPA Review

2. A sole proprietorship has the simplest management structure of all business organizations.

3. A sole proprietorship ordinarily can do business in any state without having to file, register, or otherwise qualify to do business in that state.

4. The owner does not report to, or need permission from, other executives, directors, or owners.

B. Disadvantages of sole proprietor management include the following:

1. Control is concentrated in one person, and the sole proprietor may lack the expertise and experience that a group of decision makers would bring to an organization.

2. A sole proprietorship may lack checks and balances relative to the decision-making process that would be found in more complex organizations.

3. The sole proprietor has unlimited personal liability for all contracts, torts, and other liabilities of the business. The owner may mitigate losses for torts through insurance, but not for contracts and other debts.

TERMINATION

A. The duration of the sole proprietorship is at the proprietor's discretion.

1. The interest of the proprietor may be transferred during his or her life, but the sole proprietorship is then dissolved.

2. An advantage of a sole proprietorship is that a change in control of the enterprise can occur only with the proprietor's consent.

B. The sole proprietorship is automatically terminated upon the proprietor's death; thus, it lacks perpetual existence.

GENERAL PARTNERSHIPS

DEFINITIONS

A. According to the Revised Uniform Partnership Act (RUPA), a partnership is "an association of two or more persons to carry on as co-owners of a business for profit."

1. The general partnership is the oldest, simplest, and most common form of business organization other than the sole proprietorship.

2. It differs from other partnerships in that each partner has unlimited personal liability for all losses and debts of the business. This distinction is a major disadvantage of the general partnership.

©2007 Kaplan CPA Review

STUDY MANUAL – BUSINESS ENVIRONMENT & CONCEPTS
CHAPTER 2

3. A key legal issue is whether a partnership is an entity separate from its owners. The RUPA states that a partnership is an entity distinct from the partners (owners) in some cases.

   a. The assets of a partnership are treated as those of the business unit.

   b. Title to real property may be acquired in the partnership's name.

   c. Each partner is considered a fiduciary of the partnership.

   d. Each partner is considered an agent of the partnership.

   e. The partnership may sue and be sued in its own name. Thus, a judgment against the partnership is not a judgment against the partner.

4. In other ways, a partnership is treated as an aggregate of the individual partners.

   a. Unlike a corporation, a partnership lacks continuity of existence.

   b. No person can become a partner without consent of all the partners. Therefore, the transferee of a partnership interest, unlike the transferee of shares in a corporation, does not become an owner.

   c. Debts of a partnership are ultimately the debts of the individual partners.

   d. A partnership is not subject to regular federal income tax. Instead, taxable income is determined at the individual level.

5. The partnership may be for a term, open-ended, or at will. Since no fixed or specified duration of partnership existence must be stated, the partnership can be dissolved at any time by any partner giving notice of his or her express will to withdraw as a partner.

B. Each partner must consent to being both a principal and an agent of the partnership.

1. A principal is a person who permits or directs another to act on his or her behalf.

2. An agent is a person who agrees to act on the principal's behalf.

   a. An agent has actual or apparent authority to take actions that obligate the partnership. Thus, the personal liability incurred by one partner as a principal may result from conduct of another partner as an agent.

   b. Such liability may arise without the partner's fault, authorization, or knowledge.

C. Under the law of agency, the partnership (principal) can be bound by the acts of the partner (agent) if the partner acts with either actual or apparent authority.

1. Actual authority is that which the partnership explicitly grants to the partner, plus any authority that could reasonably be implied from that explicit grant of authority. For example, if a partner is explicitly granted the authority to operate a car wash, the authority to hire employees would be implied.

2. Apparent authority is that which a party outside of the principal/agent relationship prudently believes that the agent possesses, merely because the agent is held out by the principal as an agent.

    a. Apparent authority is very broad.

    b. Any actions taken by the partners in the ordinary course of conducting partnership business will legally bind the partnership through apparent authority.

    c. However, actions taken by partners that are outside the scope of the ordinary course of business will not bind the partnership.

FORMATION

A. A general partnership can be created without any formalities. Since no filings are required, the existence of the partnership may arise from a written or oral agreement. An agreement also may be implied by the conduct of the parties. If the partnership is to exist for a definite period of time, exceeding one year, the statute of frauds requires the partnership agreement to be in writing.

1. A formal partnership agreement should specify:

    a. Who contributes capital, how much should be contributed (now or later), and any limitations on capital contributions

    b. The rights and responsibilities of each partner

    c. How profits and losses are to be divided

    d. How assets should be divided in the event of dissolution

2. A partnership agreement cannot:

    a. Unreasonably restrict access to books and records

    b. Eliminate the duty of loyalty or the obligation of good faith and fair dealing

    c. Unreasonably reduce the duty of care

    d. Vary the power to dissociate

    e. Waive or vary the right to seek court expulsion of another partner

f. Vary the law applying to a limited liability partnership

g. Vary the right to dissolution and winding up

h. Restrict third-party rights

3. The law recognizes the supremacy of the partnership agreement in most situations, giving advantage to the partners, who may, by contract, establish relationships among themselves. Therefore, the RUPA is largely a series of default rules that govern matters not addressed by the partners in their agreement.

B. If the elements stated in the definition of a partnership are present, a partnership may be formed even if the parties do not intend to become partners. Conversely, a partnership is not formed in the absence of one of the elements in the definition even if the parties intend to be partners. Consequently, parties may disagree about whether their business arrangement is a partnership, especially in the absence of a written agreement.

C. Any person with the legal capacity to enter into a contract may enter into a partnership agreement. Persons include individuals, partnerships, corporations, estates, trusts, joint ventures, and other associations. Under the RUPA, persons include any legal or commercial entity.

1. Each of the parties must be a co-owner.

2. They must share profits and losses and management authority (unless otherwise agreed upon).

D. A partnership must carry on a business, which is any trade, occupation, or profession. The co-owners must also intend that their business make a profit, even if no profit is earned. Thus, religious, patriotic, and educational organizations that are not-for-profit cannot be considered partnerships.

1. A person who receives a share of the profits of a business is generally presumed to be a partner. Profit sharing by itself does not necessarily signify the existence of a partnership. The presumption is overcome if the profit share is merely payment of, or for, any of the following:

a. Debt or interest on a loan

b. Compensation to an employee or independent contractor

c. Rent to a landlord

d. A health or retirement benefit to the beneficiary or a representative of a deceased or retired partner

2. A joint interest in (co-ownership of) property or the sharing of gross returns does not by itself establish a partnership.

E. A partnership by estoppel may be recognized when an actual partnership does not exist. The duties and liabilities of a partner may be imposed on a nonpartner who has represented his or her interest as that of a partner.

1. A third party who has reasonably relied on the representation and suffered harm as a result may assert the existence of a partnership. The purported partner then will be prevented (estopped) from denying the existence of a partnership.

   For example, Lawyer A falsely represented to Client that Lawyer A and Lawyer B were partners. Client, in reasonable reliance on this statement, sought legal services from Lawyer B. Because these services were performed without due care, Client suffered harm. Lawyer A (as well as Lawyer B) was liable as a partner, despite the absence of an actual partnership.

CAPITALIZATION

A. In a general partnership, two or more persons may contribute cash, property, or services to the business.

1. Combining the resources of two or more persons may improve the credit standing of the business.

2. A general partnership cannot raise equity capital by selling shares.

3. The partnership agreement should state the nature and amounts of initial and subsequent contributions by partners.

   a. It should address whether withdrawals are restricted.

   b. It should also address whether individual partner capital, income, and drawing accounts are to be maintained.

4. A person may become a partner even though he or she only contributes services.

PROFITS AND LOSSES

A. A partner's interest is determined by the degree to which the partner shares in profits, losses, and distributions.

1. Unless otherwise agreed, profits and losses are shared equally, regardless of the amount each partner contributed to the partnership. Also, unless otherwise agreed, each partner must contribute, in proportion to his or her share of profits, toward any losses sustained by the partnership.

2. A partner also has the right to distributions. A distribution is a transfer of partnership property from the partnership to a partner. A distribution may result from:

   a. A share of profits

STUDY MANUAL – BUSINESS ENVIRONMENT & CONCEPTS
CHAPTER 2

  b. Compensation for services

  c. Reimbursement for payments made, and indemnification for liabilities incurred in the ordinary course of business or to preserve the business or its property

  d. Reimbursement for advances (loans) in excess of agreed-upon capital contributions

   (The payments made and liabilities incurred are loans that accrue interest.)

 3. Generally, the right to compensation for services is the right to receive a share of the profits. A partner is not generally entitled to be paid for services rendered for the partnership, except for winding up its business. However, a partnership agreement can, and often does, provide for additional compensation to a partner for performing additional duties, such as personnel management or general office management.

B. A partner's transferable interest consists of a partner's share of partnership profits and losses and the right to receive distributions.

 1. Partners may sell or otherwise transfer (assign) their interest to the partnership, another partner, or a third party, without the loss of the rights and duties of a partner (except the interest transferred). Moreover, unless all other partners agree to accept the assignee as a new partner, the assignee does not become a partner in the firm.

  The ability to transfer the financial interest in the firm but not ownership status is a disadvantage of the partnership form. For example, a partner cannot transfer ownership status to a family member, either during his or her life or through inheritance.

 2. When a partner dies, his or her partnership interest is considered part of the estate. The interest is personal property and may be inherited according to the provisions of the deceased partner's will. Heirs of the partnership interest are assignees, not partners.

  Many partnership agreements provide that the surviving partners or the partnership itself will have a right of first refusal to purchase the interest. A partnership agreement may incorporate a provision to fund the purchase of the interest using life insurance proceeds.

 3. A creditor who has obtained a judgment against a partner may attach the partner's transferable interest in the partnership only by securing, from a proper court, a charging order. A charging order is a lien on the transferable interest.

  a. The court may order foreclosure of the interest at any time.

  b. After the order, the debtor partner's interest is sold at a judicial sale.

Page 58   ©2007 Kaplan CPA Review

c. Before the sale, the debtor, the other partners, or the partnership itself may redeem the interest by paying the debt.

d. The purchaser of a partnership interest at a judicial sale does not become a partner unless all partners consent.

TAXATION

A principal advantage of the partnership is that it is not a federally taxable entity. The partnership files only an information return on Form 1065. The partnership's profits and losses are instead passed through to the partners, who report their share of profits and losses on their individual income tax returns.

RIGHTS

The law of agency largely defines the rights, duties, and powers between and among partners. However, partners may agree to limit rights to which individual partners may otherwise be entitled by law. Nevertheless, neither the partners nor the partnership can modify obligations to third parties imposed by law.

A. Each partner has a right to equal participation in partnership management.

1. The general rule for ordinary matters is majority rule.

2. Issues not ordinarily connected with day-to-day partnership business (such as amending a partnership agreement or admitting a new partner) require a unanimous decision.

3. Different classes of partners may be formed with different management rights.

4. A disadvantage of a partnership is that a decision-making deadlock may develop when partners have equal management rights.

5. As a result, partnership agreements commonly restrict management rights to a few or even one partner.

B. A partner's right of access to partnership information is the right to access, inspect, and copy the partnership's books and records.

1. Books and records, if any, must be maintained at the partnership's chief executive office.

2. Each partner and the partnership must provide a partner with information "reasonably required for the proper exercise of the partner's rights and duties" under the partnership agreement or the RUPA.

3. A reasonable demand for any other information about the partnership must also be honored.

STUDY MANUAL – BUSINESS ENVIRONMENT & CONCEPTS
CHAPTER 2

C. The right to use or possess partnership property may only be exercised on behalf of the partnership. The RUPA states, "Property acquired by a partnership is property of the partnership and not of the partners individually."

   1. Property is partnership property when it is acquired in the name of the partnership. It is also deemed partnership property when it is acquired in the name of a partner, provided the instrument of transfer indicated partner status or the existence of a partnership.

   2. Furthermore, property purchased with partnership assets is presumed to be partnership property.

   3. Partners do not own any specific partnership property directly or individually. It is owned by the partnership as a legal entity.

      a. Likewise, the creditors and heirs of an individual partner have no right to specific partnership property. A partner's interest in specific partnership property is a joint right to possess partnership property for partnership purposes only. The partner's interest in a specific item of such property is not transferable and cannot be attached by personal creditors or pass through a decreased partner's estate.

      b. Whether property belongs to the partnership or a partner also determines who has the power to transfer it, who receives the proceeds (or bears the loss) from its disposal, and how it will be disposed of upon termination of the firm.

D. The right to choose associates means that no partner may be forced to accept any person as a partner. The RUPA states, "A person may become a partner only with the consent of all of the partners." When a partner transfers his or her interest to another, the purchaser or other transferee is entitled only to receive the share of profits and losses and the right to distributions allocated to the interest he or she has acquired.

E. The right to an *accounting* may be invoked by a partner. An accounting is a judicial proceeding to provide a comprehensive and effective settlement of all partnership affairs.

   1. An auditor or other court appointee conducts the accounting with oversight by the court.

   2. The accounting makes a final determination of the monetary value of each partnership interest.

   3. In addition, the RUPA provides a broad right to sue the partnership or other partners for any form of relief available from a court, with or without an accounting.

      a. A suit may be brought to enforce rights under the partnership agreement or the RUPA, or to protect interest arising independently of the partnership.

b. The RUPA also allows the partnership to sue a partner for breaching the partnership agreement or violating a duty to the partnership.

F. Each partner is assumed to have an account that is credited with his or her contributions and share of profits, and debited for his or her share of losses and distributions.

DUTIES

A partner has the actual or apparent authority under the principles of agency law to take actions that impose personal liability on other partners without their knowledge and consent. Hence, a partner is in a fiduciary position (i.e., a position involving trust and confidence). He or she has a duty to act primarily for the benefit of the other partners in partnership affairs.

A. Duties imposed upon partners include the fiduciary duties of loyalty and care.

1. The duty of loyalty is limited to:

a. Not competing with the partnership

b. Not dealing with the partnership on the conduct or winding up of the partnership business as (or for) a party with an adverse interest

c. Accounting to the partnership and holding for it in trust any benefit resulting from either of the following:

- The conduct or winding up of the partnership business
- The use of partnership property

d. Accordingly, a partner cannot, for personal gain, exploit a partnership opportunity or secretly use partnership assets.

2. The duty of care in the conduct or winding up of the partnership business is not to engage in knowing violations of the law, international wrongdoing, gross negligence, or reckless behavior.

B. A partner is also obligated to act in good faith and fair dealing. A partner therefore must be honest in dealing with factual information and meet reasonable (objective) standards of fair dealing. However, no duty is violated solely because the partner acts in his or her own interest.

C. A partner may lend money to, or otherwise do business with, the partnership on the same basis as a nonpartner.

POWERS

A. The actual powers granted to each partner are governed by law and by the specific terms contained in the partnership agreement.

B. A partner's status grants him or her apparent authority to act as an agent of the partnership in any legal transaction that is apparently for "carrying on in the ordinary course the partnership business or business of the kind carried on by the partnership" (business that is normal for the partnership or for a similar partnership).

1. Apparent authority is derived from words or conduct of the principal (the partnership) that reasonably induce a third party to rely on the agent's (partner's) authority. The partnership is bound even if the partner had no actual authority in the matter, unless the third party knew or had received notification of the lack of actual authority.

2. However, if a partner acts without actual authority on a matter not within the apparent scope of partnership business, neither the partnership nor the other partners are bound by the act, unless the other partners ratify the transaction.

C. The RUPA provides for filing a statement of partnership authority that may give notice of limitations on the authority of a partner.

1. A statement of denial may also be filed by a person named in a statement of authority. It states the fact being denied (e.g., partner authority or status).

2. The extent of authority described in the statement of authority may be relied upon by a person dealing with a partner if that person gives value in a transaction without knowledge to the contrary (assuming no other filing cancels the authority).

3. A stronger safeguard against unauthorized transfers is provided for real property. If the filing limits a partner's authority to transfer the partnership's real property, and filing is in the public real property records, any person is assumed to know of the limitation. However, except in this case and in the cases of filed statements of dissociation or dissolution, a person who is not a partner is not assumed to know of a limitation on authority solely because of a filing.

D. Transfer of partnership property requires the following:

1. Subject to a filed statement of authority, property in the name of the partnership may be transferred, in the partnership name, by any partner name.

2. Property in the name of a partner(s) or in the name of another person(s) may be transferred by the named person(s).

3. Recovery of partnership property requires the partnership to prove that:

   a. The transferor partner(s) had no authority (actual or apparent).

   b. The transferee had notice of these facts.

LIABILITIES

A. The liabilities of a partner and the partnership are based on the principles of agency.

   1. A partner acts concurrently as a principal and an agent for the partnership, and also acts as an agent for his or her copartners.

   2. When an actual partner appears to a third party to be carrying on the business of a partnership in the usual manner, or when a partner is authorized by the other partners to take an unusual action, he or she has the power to obligate the partnership and his or her copartners.

   3. Accordingly, a partnership is liable for loss or injury caused by the actionable conduct (wrongful acts or omissions) of any partner while the partner is acting within the ordinary course of the partnership business or with its authority.

B. Joint and several liability allow either joint suits or separate actions (and separate judgments) at the plaintiff's option.

   1. Each general partner has joint and several liability for any partnership obligation.

   2. Thus, the partners are each individually liable for the full amount of a partnership obligation and also liable together as a group.

C. A partner may obligate the partnership and partners by contract when he or she is:

   1. Specifically authorized by the partnership agreement

   2. Apparently carrying on the business of a partnership in the usual manner

   3. Acting with the actual or implicit consent of the other partners

      Furthermore, when partners agree to limit the authority of a partner to act on behalf of the partnership, a third party who has no notice of the limitation of authority is not bound by it.

D. Admission into an existing partnership results in liability for partnership obligations.

   1. A new partner is liable for preadmission obligations of the partnership only to the extent of his or her investment.

   2. An incoming partner may expressly or implicitly assume personal liability for existing partnership debt, and he or she has unlimited liability for partnership obligations arising subsequent to admission.

E. Criminal liability is not ordinarily imposed on partners as a result of a copartner's criminal conduct unless they were involved.

©2007 Kaplan CPA Review

F. A partner's knowledge or receipt of notice of a fact relating to the partnership is ascribed to the partnership.

TERMINATION

The process to end a partnership may be governed by the partnership agreement. If it is not, the RUPA provides a scheme that consists of dissociation, dissolution, and winding up (also known as liquidation). The partner's management rights (except with regard to winding up) will terminate at the end of the partnership.

A. Dissociation is the legal effect of a partner's ceasing to be associated with the conduct of the business of the partnership. A partner has the power (if not the right) to dissociate at any time, subject to payment of damages if the dissociation is wrongful. Note: this does not have to result in ultimate dissolution, winding up, and termination of the partnership.

1. Dissociation results from:

   a. Notice of a partner's express will to withdraw

   b. An event stipulated in the agreement

   c. Expulsion of a partner under the terms of the partnership agreement

   d. Expulsion by a unanimous vote of the other partners on the grounds that:

   - The partnership business cannot legally be conducted with that partner.
   - The partner is a dissolving corporation or partnership.
   - The partner has transferred substantially all of his or her interest.
   - The partner's interest is subject to a charging order.

   e. A court order on the grounds of a material breach of the partnership agreement or a duty, misconduct materially affecting the business, or conduct making continuation of the business with the partner impracticable (e.g., a deadlock between partners)

   f. A partner's incapacity

   g. A partner's death

   h. A partner's insolvency

   i. Distribution by a trust or estate of its entire transferable interest

2. After dissociation, the business either continues after purchase of the dissociated partner's interest, or dissolution begins.

3. The dissociation of a partner terminates the duty not to compete. The other aspects of the duties of loyalty and care continue, but only with regard to predissociation matters, unless the partner participates in winding up.

4. The partnership is not necessarily dissolved by dissociation unless it occurs by express will of the partner.

5. A statement of dissociation may be filed by the partnership or a dissociated partner. It is deemed to provide notice of dissociation 90 days after filing.

   a. Such notice terminates the partner's apparent authority and his or her liability for the partnership's postdissociation obligation.

   b. Without this statement or some other form of notice, the dissociated partner will have apparent authority for two years to bind the partnership to contracts with third parties who reasonably believe the person is a partner. (Thus, the partnership remains liable for what the partner does.)

   c. A dissociated partner may also be liable on postdissociation contracts for up to two years if third parties reasonably believe that he or she is still a partner. Thus, the partner is highly motivated to file the statement. (Here, as compared to "b" just above, the partner would remain individually liable without the statement.)

   d. A dissociated partner remains liable to creditors for predissociation obligations even if the other partners agreed to assume the debts.

6. If the business is not wound up, the partnership must purchase the dissociated partner's interest. The price is determined based on a hypothetical sale of the partnership at the dissociation date.

   a. The buyout price is the amount of the distribution receivable by the partner if the partnership were sold for the greater of:

   • Liquidation value
   • The sales value of the entire going concern without the partner

   b. The buyout price is offset by damages for wrongful dissociation and other amounts owed to the partnership.

7. The dissociation provision assures greater continuity of partnerships and supports the view that a partnership is to be treated as an entity whenever possible.

B. Dissolution and winding up is the alternative to dissociation and continuation of the partnership. However, although dissolution changes the working relationships of the partners, it is distinct from winding up.

   1. Dissolution results from notice of a partner's express will to withdraw.

2. In a partnership for a definite term or specific undertaking, dissolution also results from:

   a. Expiration of the term or completion of the undertaking

   b. Unanimous agreement of the partners

   c. Wrongful dissociation or death of a partner, unless a majority in interest of the other partners agrees to continue

   d. An event designated in the partnership agreement as causing winding up

   e. An illegality of business

   f. A judicial determination of:

      - Frustration of the economic purpose of the partnership
      - Impracticability of doing business with a particular partner
      - Impracticability of doing business under the partnership agreement

   g. A judicial determination made at the request of a transferee of a transferable interest that winding up is equitable

3. A partnership continues until the winding up of partnership affairs is complete. All partners are entitled to participate in the winding up (liquidation) process except a partner who has wrongfully dissociated.

   a. However, before winding up is complete, the partners (excluding a partner who wrongfully dissociated) may unanimously agree to continue the business as if dissolution had not occurred.

   b. This provision furnishes another opportunity to compensate for the continuity (going concern) problems faced by partnerships.

4. The actual authority of a partner to act on behalf of the partnership terminates upon dissolution except as necessary to wind up partnership affairs.

5. Apparent authority of a partner may continue to exist throughout the winding up process unless notice of the dissolution has been communicated to the other party to the transaction.

6. The fiduciary duties of the partners also remain in effect, with the exception of the duty not to compete, which ceases to exist after dissolution.

7. A statement of dissolution may be filed by any partner who has not wrongfully dissociated. It is deemed to provide notice to nonpartners, 90 days after the filing, regarding dissolution and the limitation of the partner's authority.

C. Winding up is the administrative process of settling partnership affairs, including the use of partnership assets and any required contributions by partners to pay creditors.

1. The RUPA states that the person winding up may:

   a. Continue the business as a going concern for a reasonable amount of time

   b. Take judicial actions

   c. Settle and close the business

   d. Dispose of and transfer property

   e. Discharge liabilities

   f. Distribute assets

   g. Settle disputes by mediation or arbitration

   h. Perform any other necessary acts

2. Creditors are paid in full before any distributions are made to partners. However, partners who are creditors share equally with nonpartner creditors under the RUPA. In practice, because partners are liable for all partnership debts, partnership creditors are paid first.

3. After payment of creditors, any surplus is paid in cash to the partners. A partner has no right to a distribution in kind nor is a partner required to accept a distribution in kind.

4. To settle partnership accounts with credit balances, each partner receives a distribution equal to the excess of credits over debits to his or her account. Thus, no distinction is made between distributions of capital and of profits.

   a. Profits and losses from liquidation of assets are credits and debits, respectively.

   b. Prior credits to an account include contributions made and the partner's share of profits.

   c. Prior debits include distributions received and the partner's share of losses.

5. If the account has a debit balance, the partner is liable to contribute the amount of the balance.

   a. If a partner does not make a required contribution, the other partners must pay the difference in the same proportion in which they share losses.

   b. A partner making an excess contribution may recover the excess from the other partners.

STUDY MANUAL – BUSINESS ENVIRONMENT & CONCEPTS
CHAPTER 2

    c.   Moreover, the representative of creditors of the partnership or of a partner (e.g., a trustee in bankruptcy) may enforce the obligation to contribute to the partnership.

    d.   One effect of these rules is that, consistent with the federal Bankruptcy Code, partnership creditors:

- Have priority in partnership assets
- Share equally with creditors of partners in the partner's separate assets

OTHER BUSINESS STRUCTURES: JOINT VENTURES

Note to Student: The joint venture is the association; the joint venturer is one of the members of the joint venture. Compare "joint venture" to "partnership"; compare "joint venturer" to "partner."

A.   A joint venture is a business structure that is an association of individual members to accomplish a specific business purpose or objective. It has the advantage of ease of formation and is often organized for a single transaction. The individual members of a joint venture may be persons or business entities.

B.   A joint venture is similar to a partnership in some respects, but a joint venture is NOT a partnership. However, most rules governing general partnerships apply to joint ventures, including those related to formation.

C.   The rights and duties of joint venturers are generally governed by the RUPA.

    1.   A joint venturer, like a partner, is entitled to an accounting.

    2.   Joint venturers owe each other the same fiduciary duties as do partners.

    3.   The most significant difference between joint venturers and partners is that joint venturers typically have less implied and apparent authority to bind their associates due to the limited scope of the joint venture. Thus, an advantage of the joint venture is that no joint venturer is liable for similar activities of other joint venturers outside the scope of the venture.

    4.   Each joint venturer has the disadvantage of being personally liable for debts of the venture.

    5.   Each joint venturer is liable for negligence of another, acting within the scope and course of the business venture.

    6.   Joint ventures are treated as partnerships (nontaxable entities) for federal income tax purposes. Hence, joint venturers have the advantage of avoiding double taxation.

    7.   Barring a contrary agreement, joint ventures share profits and losses equally.

Page 68   ©2007 Kaplan CPA Review

8. Joint venturers may be sued; however, the joint venture is usually not a legal entity and therefore cannot be sued.

9. Antitrust laws apply to joint ventures that are competitors. However, less stringent rules are applied to international joint ventures.

10. Not-for-profit entities cannot be joint ventures.

LIMITED PARTNERSHIPS (LPs)

A. A limited partnership has characteristics of both an unlimited liability structure (i.e., general partnership) and a limited liability structure (i.e., corporation). It was developed to facilitate investments by those who want to make a financial investment in a business activity without facing unlimited liability.

1. The limited partnership is a separate legal entity.

2. It is a partnership formed by two or more persons under a state statute. These statutes are based on the Revised Uniform Limited Partnership Act (RULPA). A limited partnership has one or more general partners and one or more limited partners.

   a. The term person includes a natural person or business entity, such as a general partnership, limited partnership, or corporation.

   b. A general partner is responsible for management of the partnership and has full personal liability for debts of the partnership. In the majority of states, a general partner may be another partnership or a corporation.

   d. A person can be both a general partner and a limited partner with the rights and liabilities of each. These interests are separately accounted for in the books of the limited partnership.

B. Compared to the general partnership, the limited partnership has the disadvantage of requiring significant legal formalities for its creation.

1. The RULPA requires that a written certificate of limited partnership (a document similar to a corporation's articles of incorporation) be filed as a public record with the Secretary of State in the state in which it is organized, and that an organizational fee be paid. The certificate gives potential creditors notice of the partner's limited liability.

   a. If a certificate is not filed, the organization is treated as a general partnership.

   b. A certificate of amendment may be filed for "any proper purpose" determined by the general partners. A certificate of amendment must be filed within 30 days of certain fundamental changes, which might include:

   • Admission of a general partner

©2007 Kaplan CPA Review

Page 69

- Withdrawal of a general partner
- Continuation of the business after an event of withdrawal of a general partner (any of various events that result in voluntary or involuntary withdrawal, such as death, dissolution of a corporate general partner, incapacity, or transfer of all of the partner's interest)

c. A certificate of cancellation is filed, either after dissolution and at the beginning of winding up, or at any time when there are no limited partners.

d. A limited partnership agreement, although not legally required, is also commonly executed by the partners. The agreement sets forth the rights and duties of the general and limited partners and the terms and conditions of operation, dissolution, and termination. Absent a separate agreement, the certificate of limited partnership serves as the articles of limited partnership, and state law (the RULPA) fills in omissions in the agreement.

2. The limited partnership certificate must be signed by all general partners and contains:

   a. The name of the limited partnership

   b. The address of its office

   c. The name and address of its agent for service of process

   d. The name and business address of each general partner (but not of each limited partner)

   e. The latest date upon which the limited partnership is to dissolve

   f. Any other matters the general partners determine should be included

3. A limited partnership comes into existence when the certificate of limited partnership is filed, or at a later date as specified in the certificate. Substantial compliance with the filing requirements suffices for creation of the limited partnership.

4. A limited partnership may carry on any business that a general partnership may conduct, with some statutory exceptions. (It is not necessary to know the specific statutory exceptions for the CPA Exam.)

5. To protect creditors, the name must include the words "limited partnership."

   a. The name may not include the name of a limited partner.

   b. The name may not be deceptively similar to that of a corporation or another limited partnership doing business in the state.

6. The LP must agree to submit to jurisdiction in the state, so it can sue and/or be sued.

C. A limited partnership may be capitalized by the partners' contributions of cash, property, services, or promises to make such contributions. An advantage of the limited partnership compared with the general partnership is that it can attract greater financing because of the limited liability enjoyed by the limited partners.

D. Partnership interest refers to the rights of the partners to share in profits and losses.

1. The written partnership agreement controls the sharing of profits, losses, and distributions. In the absence of such an agreement, profits and losses are shared in proportion to the relative value of each partner's capital account balance.

2. A partnership interest is considered personal property and is assignable.

a. The assignment of a partnership interest does not dissolve the limited partnership or entitle the assignee to become a partner. Although unlimited right to assignment may enhance the ability of this business form to raise capital, restraints on assignment are often imposed by the partnership.

- A limited partnership interest is a security, and it is subject to registration under federal securities laws. If the partners wish to sell these interests under an exemption from registration, assignability may prevent these interests from qualifying for such an exemption. An exemption may require restrictions on resale.
- Ready assignability of a limited partnership interest may also cause the Internal Revenue Service (IRS) to view the partnership as a corporation for tax purposes.
- Consequently, the partnership agreement may restrict assignment.

b. The assignee of a partnership interest is only entitled to receive the distributions owed to the assignor-partner. However, the assignee of a partnership interest (limited or general) may become a limited partner if either of the following situations exist:

- All partners agree.
- The partnership agreement gives the assignor the right to confer limited partner status on the assignee.

c. The interest of a limited partner is subject to a charging order, which may be obtained by a creditor (from a court) for payment of an unpaid judgment. The judgment creditor does not become a limited partner as a result of obtaining a charging order.

E. The limited partnership is a pass-through (conduit) entity for federal income tax purposes. Hence, partners report their share of all limited partnership revenue, expense, gain, and loss on their personal income tax returns.

1. The limited partnership files only an informational return.

STUDY MANUAL – BUSINESS ENVIRONMENT & CONCEPTS
CHAPTER 2

    2. A limited partner not only enjoys limited liability, but avoids the double taxation to which corporate earnings are subject.

    3. The IRS considers whether a limited partnership is, in substance, a corporation. It evaluates factors such as the transferability of interests, as well as the assets and net worth of the general partners, to determine whether the limited partnership form should be disregarded for tax purposes.

F. The rights of partners:

    1. The general partner in a limited partnership has the same rights, duties, liabilities, and authority as a partner in a general partnership.

    2. A limited partner, under the RULPA, now has the authority to participate in management and control of the business, as noted below.

    3. Without loss of limited liability status, a limited partner has always had the right to do the following:

        a. Vote on any matter, if granted by the partnership agreement.

        b. Inspect and copy the partnership records.

        c. Obtain financial information, tax returns, and other partnership information if just and reasonable.

        d. Assign his, her, or its partnership interest.

        e. Receive the fair value of the partnership interest upon withdrawal

    4. A limited partner would have lost limited liability status by engaging in the following acts; however, now under the RULPA he or she may do all of these without losing limited liability protection:

        a. Allow use of name in LP name.

        b. Acting as a consultant to a general partner.

        c. Acting as a guarantor of an obligation of the limited partnership.

        d. Requesting or attending a partners' meeting.

        e. Making proposals and approving or disapproving certain matters.

G. Typically, the financial risk (liability) of a limited partner who does not participate in management and control of the business is limited to the partner's investment in the

Page 72   ©2007 Kaplan CPA Review

partnership. However, a limited partner may incur personal liability for the firm's debts if:

1. No limited partnership certificate was filed.

2. The certificate contained a false statement.

H. A limited partnership goes through dissolution and winding up before it is terminated.

1. A limited partnership can be dissolved upon occurrence of any of the following events:

   a. The time or event specified in the limited partnership agreement occurs.

   b. All partners agree, in writing, to dissolve.

   c. An event of withdrawal of a general partner occurs, unless:

      • The written terms of the agreement provide that the business may be carried on by the remaining general partners (if any).
      • All partners agree in writing to continue the business, and appoint one or more new general partners if necessary or desired.

   d. The limited partnership is dissolved by a court order.

2. After dissolution, winding up is done by a general partner who has not caused the dissolution. If there is no general partner to conduct the winding up, it may be performed by the limited partners or by some person designated by a court.

3. Remaining assets, if any, are distributed as follows:

   a. To creditors, including creditors who are partners

   b. To current and former partners for distributions previously due to them and unpaid, except as otherwise provided in the limited partnership agreement

   c. To the partners as a return of their contributions, except as otherwise provided in the limited partnership agreement

   d. To the partners for their partnership interests, in the proportions in which they share distributions, except as otherwise provided in the limited partnership agreement (to the extent of any remaining assets)

4. The final distribution terminates the limited partnership.

©2007 Kaplan CPA Review

STUDY MANUAL – BUSINESS ENVIRONMENT & CONCEPTS
CHAPTER 2

LIMITED LIABILITY NONCORPORATE ENTITIES

A. Limited liability partnerships (LLPs) are relatively new in the business structures area, but are now available in the majority of states. The LLP is a structure combining the attributes of a general partnership (GP) and a limited partnership (LP). It is a business form frequently used by professionals, such as law firms, accounting firms, and other similar industries.

1. Formation of an LLP requires more formality than a GP, similar to an LP. An LLP:

   a. Must file articles of formation with the Secretary of State and pay a formation fee.

   b. Must use LLP in the name.

   c. May be formed as a transition from a GP.

2. As with an LP, LLPs can raise capital through debt financing or taking on new partners.

3. LLPs are taxed in the same method as GPs and LPs, with flow-through to the partners.

4. The biggest difference between LLPs and GPs is liability. All partners have unlimited personal liability in a GP, whereas all partners have limited liability in an LLP, generally speaking.

   a. Most states allow limited liability for contracts (debts) and general torts.

   b. Partners cannot limit their liability for their own malpractice, but they do not have unlimited personal liability for other partners' malpractice.

5. The biggest difference between LLPs and LPs has to do with management. Whereas in an LP limited partners cannot participate in management, in an LLP partners can do anything that a partner in a GP can do, including:

   a. Using the LLP name.

   b. Voting on all LLP matters.

   c. Owning/managing LLP assets.

6. Partners in an LLP share profits and losses in the same manner as partners in a GP.

7. Termination issues are handled in the same manner as with a GP.

Page 74 ©2007 Kaplan CPA Review

B. Limited liability companies (LLCs): All states now have some form of LLC structure, a hybrid combination of a GP and a corporation.

1. Formation of an LLC requires greater formality than a GP, but generally less than a corporation. An LLC:

   a. Must file articles of organization with the Secretary of State and pay formation fees.

   b. Is considered a separate legal entity that must subject itself to the state's jurisdiction so that it can sue and/or be sued.

   c. Must use LLC in its name.

2. Unlike corporations, LLCs cannot issue stock to capitalize. As with partnerships, the only methods available for raising capital are to incur debt or take on new co-owners.

3. As with partnership entities, LLCs are not corporations subject to corporate income tax, but rather are taxed under the flow-through method used for all business entities other than corporations.

4. Like corporations and other limited liability entities such as LPs and LLPs, LLCs have the advantage of limited liability protection for their owners, known as members. Members have limited liability for contracts and torts, not unlike shareholders of corporations.

5. Somewhat like GPs and LLPs, LLCs are managed by vote of the members (member-managed), although the members may choose to hire a professional manager to run the business (manager-managed).

   a. Members usually have a contract between all of them, known as an operating agreement, governing the management of the business, somewhat similar to that of a partnership.

   b. All members have voting rights and can participate in management.

6. Generally, members share profits and losses in the same manner as do partners in a GP.

   a. The law always gives priority to terms of a membership operating agreement.

   b. In the absence of an operating agreement, members share profits and losses equally.

©2007 Kaplan CPA Review

7. Dissolution of an LLC will occur in the following situations:

   a. By agreement.

   b. A member withdraws, dies, or goes bankrupt. The LLC may continue if remaining members vote to continue.

8. The order of distribution of assets upon termination is as follows:

   a. Creditors.

   b. Members' unpaid distributions.

   c. Members' capital contributions.

   d. Remaining assets to members according to agreement.

STUDY MANUAL – BUSINESS ENVIRONMENT & CONCEPTS
CHAPTER 2

QUESTIONS: BUSINESS STRUCTURES: PARTNERSHIPS

1. Generally, under the Uniform Partnership Act, a partnership has which of the
    following characteristics: Unlimited duration? Obligation for payment of federal
    income tax?
    A. Yes; no.
    B. No; yes.
    C. No; no.
    D. Yes; yes

2. Which of the following statements is TRUE concerning liability when a partner
    in a general partnership commits a tort while engaged in partnership business?
    A. The partner committing the tort is the only party liable.
    B. The partnership is the only party liable.
    C. Each partner is liable to pay an equal share of any judgment.
    D. Each partner is jointly and severally liable.

3. Under the Uniform Partnership Act, which of the following statement(s)
    concerning the powers and duties of partners in a general partnership is(are)
    TRUE?

    I.   Each partner is an agent of every other partner and acts as both a principal
         and an agent in any business transaction within the scope of the partnership
         agreement.
    II. Each partner is subject to joint liability on partnership debts and contracts.

    A. I only.
    B. Both I and II.
    C. Neither I nor II.
    D. II only.

4. Locke and Vorst were general partners in a kitchen equipment business. On
    behalf of the partnership, Locke contracted to purchase 15 stoves from Gage.
    Unknown to Gage, Locke was not authorized by the partnership agreement to
    make such contracts. Vorst refused to allow the partnership to accept delivery of
    the stoves and Gage sought to enforce the contract. Gage will:
    A. win, because Locke had apparent authority to bind the partnership.
    B. lose, because Locke was not an agent of the partnership.
    C. win, because Locke had express authority to bind the partnership.
    D. lose, because Locke's action was not authorized by the partnership agreement.

5. Cass is a general partner in Omega Company general partnership. Which of the
    following unauthorized acts by Cass will bind Omega?
    A. Submitting a claim against Omega to arbitration.
    B. Selling Omega's goodwill.
    C. Leasing office space for Omega.
    D. Confessing a judgment against Omega.

STUDY MANUAL – BUSINESS ENVIRONMENT & CONCEPTS
CHAPTER 2

6. The partnership agreement for Owen Associates, a general partnership, provided that profits be paid to the partners in the ratio of their financial contribution to the partnership. Moore contributed $10,000, Noon contributed $30,000, and Kale contributed $50,000. For the year ending December 31, 20X4, Owen had losses of $180,000. What amount of the losses should be allocated to Kale?
   A. $60,000.
   B. $100,000.
   C. $90,000.
   D. $40,000.

$$\frac{5}{9} \times \frac{180}{1} = \frac{900}{9} = 10$$

7. Dowd, Elgar, Frost, and Grant formed a general partnership. Their written partnership agreement provided that the profits would be divided so that Dowd would receive 40 percent; Elgar, 30 percent; Frost, 20 percent; and Grant, 10 percent. There was no provision for allocating losses. At the end of its first year, the partnership had losses of $200,000. Before allocating losses, the partners' capital account balances were: Dowd, $120,000; Elgar, $100,000; Frost, $75,000; and Grant, $11,000. Grant refuses to make any further contributions to the partnership. Ignore the effects of federal partnership tax law.

   What would be Grant's share of the partnership losses?
   A. $50,000.
   B. $9,000. $20-11=9$
   C. $39,000.
   D. $20,000.

8. In a general partnership, a partner's interest in specific partnership property is:
   A. transferable to a partner's estate upon death.
   B. subject to a surviving partner's right of survivorship.
   C. subject to a partner's liability for alimony.
   D. transferable to a partner's individual creditors.

9. Which of the following statements best describes the effect of the assignment of an interest in a general partnership?
   A. The assignment transfers the assignor's interest in partnership profits and surplus.
   B. The assignee becomes a partner.
   C. The assignee is responsible for a proportionate share of past and future partnership debts.
   D. The assignment automatically dissolves the partnership.

10. Which of the following statement(s) are usually correct regarding general partners' liability?

I. All partners are jointly and severally liable for partnership torts.
II. All general partners are liable only for those partnership obligations they actually authorized.

A. Both I and II.
B. II only.
C. Neither I nor II.
D. I only.

11. Which of the following statements regarding a limited partner is(are) generally TRUE: The limited partner is subject to personal liability for partnership debts? The limited partner has the right to take part in the control of the partnership?

A. Yes; yes
B. No; no.
C. Yes; no.
D. No; yes.

12. Cobb, Inc., a partner in TLC Partnership, assigns its partnership interest to Bean, who is not made a partner. After the assignment, Bean asserts the rights to:

I. Participate in the management of TLC.
II. Cobb's share of TLC's partnership profits.

Bean is correct as to which of these rights?
A. I only.
B. Neither I nor II.
C. II only.
D. I and II.

13. Ted Fein, a partner in the ABC Partnership, wishes to withdraw from the partnership and sell his interest to Gold. All of the other partners in ABC have agreed to admit Gold as a partner and to hold Fein harmless for the past, present, and future liabilities of ABC. A provision in the original partnership agreement states that the partnership will continue upon the death or withdrawal of one or more of the partners. The agreement to hold Fein harmless for all past, present, and future liabilities of ABC will:

A. not affect the rights of partnership creditors to hold Fein personally liable for those liabilities of ABC existing at the time of his withdrawal.
B. prevent partnership creditors from holding Fein personally liable only as to those liabilities of ABC existing at the time of Fein's withdrawal.
C. permit Fein to recover from the other partners only amounts he has paid in excess of his proportionate share.
D. prevent partnership creditors from holding Fein personally liable for the past, present, and future liabilities of ABC.

14. Which of the following requirements must be met to have a valid partnership exist?

I. Co-ownership of all property used in a business.
II. Co-ownership of a business for profit.

A. I only.
B. II only.
C. Both I and II.
D. Neither I nor II.

15. When parties intend to create a partnership that will be recognized under the Revised Uniform Partnership Act, they must agree to:

	Conduct a business for profit	Share gross receipts from a business
A.	Yes	Yes
B.	Yes	No
C.	No	Yes
D.	No	No

16. Which of the following is not necessary to create an express partnership?
A. Execution of a written partnership agreement.
B. Agreement to share ownership of the partnership.
C. Intention to conduct a business for profit.
D. Intention to create a relationship recognized as a partnership.

17. Generally, under the Revised Uniform Partnership Act, a partnership has which of the following characteristics?

	Unlimited duration	Obligation for payment of federal income tax
A.	Yes	Yes
B.	Yes	No
C.	No	Yes
D.	No	No

18. The apparent authority of a partner to bind the partnership in dealing with third parties:
A. Must be derived from the express powers and purposes contained in the partnership agreement.
B. Will be effectively limited by a formal resolution of the partners of which third parties are unaware.
C. May allow a partner to bind the partnership to representations made in connection with the sale of goods.
D. Would permit a partner to submit a claim against the partnership to arbitration.

19. Which of the following statements is correct regarding a limited partnership?
    A. The general partner must make a capital contribution.
    B. It can only be created pursuant to a statute providing for the formation of limited partnerships.
    C. It can be created with limited liability for all partners.
    D. At least one general partner must also be a limited partner.

20. Which of the following statements is correct with respect to a limited partnership?
    A. A limited partner may not be an unsecured creditor of the limited partnership.
    B. A general partner may not also be a limited partner at the same time.
    C. A general partner may be a secured creditor of the limited partnership.
    D. A limited partnership can be formed with limited liability for all partners.

21. In general, which of the following statements is correct with respect to a limited partnership?
    A. A limited partner has the right to obtain from the general partner(s) financial information and tax returns of the limited partnership.
    B. A limited partnership can be formed with limited liability for all partners.
    C. A limited partner may not also be a general partner at the same time.
    D. A limited partner may hire employees on behalf of the partnership.

22. In general, which of the following statements is correct with respect to a limited partnership?
    A. A limited partner will be personally liable for partnership debts incurred in the ordinary course of the partnership's business.
    B. A limited partner is unable to participate in the management of the partnership in the same manner as general partners and still retain limited liability.
    C. A limited partner's death or incompetency will cause the partnership to dissolve.
    D. A limited partner is an agent of the partnership and has the authority to bind the partnership to contracts.

23. Which of the following statements is correct concerning the similarities between a limited partnership and a corporation?
    A. Each is created under a statute and must file a copy of its certificate with the proper state authorities.
    B. All corporate stockholders and all partners in a limited partnership have limited liability.
    C. Both are recognized for federal income tax purposes as taxable entities.
    D. Both are allowed statutorily to have perpetual existence.

STUDY MANUAL – BUSINESS ENVIRONMENT & CONCEPTS
CHAPTER 2

24. Which of the following statements is correct regarding the division of profits in a general partnership when the written partnership agreement only provides that losses be divided equally among the partners? Profits are to be divided:

A. Based on the partners' ratio of contribution to the partnership.
B. Based on the partners' participation in day to day management.
C. Equally among the partners.
D. Proportionately among the partners.

Question 25 is based on the following:

Dowd, Elgar, Frost, and Grant formed a general partnership. Their written partnership agreement provided that the profits would be divided so that Dowd would receive 40%; Elgar, 30%; Frost 20%; and Grant, 10%. There was no provision for allocating losses. At the end of its first year, the partnership had losses of $200,000. Before allocating losses, the partners' capital account balances were: Dowd, $120,000; Elgar, $100,000; Frost, $75,000; and Grant, $11,000. Grant refuses to make any further contributions to the partnership. Ignore the effects of federal partnership tax law.

25. After losses were allocated to the partners' capital accounts and all liabilities were paid, the partnership's sole asset was $106,000 in cash. How much would Elgar receive on dissolution of the partnership?

A. $37,000
B. $40,000
C. $47,500
D. $50,000

26. Unless the partnership agreement prohibits it, a partner in a general partnership may validly assign rights to:

	Partnership property	Partnership distributions
A.	Yes	Yes
B.	Yes	No
C.	No	Yes
D.	No	No

27. The partners of College Assoc., a general partnership, decided to dissolve the partnership and agreed that none of the partners would continue to use the partnership name. Under the Revised Uniform Partnership Act, which of the following events will occur on dissolution of the partnership?

	Each partner's existing liability would be discharged	Each partner's apparent authority would continue
A.	Yes	Yes
B.	Yes	No
C.	No	Yes
D.	No	No

Page 82   ©2007 Kaplan CPA Review

STUDY MANUAL – BUSINESS ENVIRONMENT & CONCEPTS
CHAPTER 2

Questions 28 through 30 are based on the following:

Downs, Frey, and Vick formed the DFV general partnership to act as manufacturers' representatives. The partners agreed Downs would receive 40% of any partnership profits and Frey and Vick would each receive 30% of such profits. It was also agreed that the partnership would not terminate for five years. After the fourth year, the partners agreed to terminate the partnership. At that time, the partners' capital accounts were as follows: Downs, $20,000; Frey, $15,000; and Vick, $10,000. There also were undistributed losses of $30,000.

28. Which of the following statements about the form of the DFV partnership agreement is correct?
   A. It must be in writing because the partnership was to last for longer than one year.
   B. It must be in writing because partnership profits would not be equally divided.
   C. It could be oral because the partners had explicitly agreed to do business together.
   D. It could be oral because the partnership did not deal in real estate.

29. Vick's share of the undistributed losses will be:
   A. $0
   B. $1,000
   C. $9,000
   D. $10,000

30. If Frey died before the partnership terminated:
   A. Downs and Vick, as a majority of the partners, would have been able to continue the partnership.
   B. The partnership would have continued until the five year term expired.
   C. The partnership would automatically dissolve.
   D. Downs and Vick would have Frey's interest in the partnership.

31. A joint venture is a (an):
   A. Association limited to no more than two persons in business for profit.
   B. Enterprise of numerous co-owners in a nonprofit undertaking.
   C. Corporate enterprise for a single undertaking of limited duration.
   D. Association of persons engaged as co-owners in a single undertaking for profit.

32. Unless otherwise provided in a general partnership agreement, which of the following statements is correct when a partner dies?

	The deceased partner's executor would automatically become a partner	The deceased partner's estate would be free from any partnership liabilities	The partnership would be dissolved automatically
A.	Yes	Yes	Yes
B.	Yes	No	No
C.	No	Yes	No
D.	No	No	No

©2007 Kaplan CPA Review

Page 83

33. Park and Graham entered into a written partnership agreement to operate a retail store. Their agreement was silent as to the duration of the partnership. Park wishes to dissolve the partnership. Which of the following statements is correct?
    A. Park may dissolve the partnership at any time.
    B. Unless Graham consents to a dissolution, Park must apply to a court and obtain a decree ordering the dissolution.
    C. Park may not dissolve the partnership unless Graham consents.
    D. Park may dissolve the partnership only after notice of the proposed dissolution is given to all partnership creditors.

34. Lark, a partner in DSJ, a general partnership, wishes to withdraw from the partnership and sell Lark's interest to Ward. All of the other partners in DSJ have agreed to admit Ward as a partner and to hold Lark harmless for the past, present, and future liabilities of DSJ. As a result of Lark's withdrawal and Ward's admission to the partnership, Ward:
    A. Acquired only the right to receive Ward's share of DSJ profits.
    B. Has the right to participate in DSJ's management.
    C. Is personally liable for partnership liabilities arising before and after being admitted as a partner.
    D. Must contribute cash or property to DSJ to be admitted with the same rights as the other partners.

35. Dill was properly admitted as a partner in the ABC Partnership after purchasing Ard's partnership interest. Ard immediately withdrew from the partnership. The partnership agreement states that the partnership will continue on the withdrawal or admission of a partner. Unless the partners otherwise agree:
    A. Dill's personal liability for partnership debts incurred before Dill was admitted will be limited to Dill's interest in partnership property.
    B. Ard will automatically be released from personal liability for partnership debts incurred before Dill's admission.
    C. Ard will be permitted to recover from the other partners the full amount that Ard has paid on account of partnership debts incurred before Dill's admission.
    D. Dill will be subjected to unlimited personal liability for partnership debts incurred before being admitted.

36. On dissolution of a general partnership, distributions will be made on account of:

    I. Partners' capital accounts.
    II. Amounts owed partners with respect to profits.
    III. Amounts owed partners for loans to the partnership in the following order.

    A. III, I, II.
    B. I, II, III.
    C. II, III, I.
    D. III, II, I.

37. Long, Pine, and Rice originally contributed $100,000, $60,000, and $20,000, respectively, to form the LPR Partnership. Profits and losses of LPR are to be distributed 1/2 to Long, 1/3 to Pine, and 1/6 to Rice. After operating for one year, LPR's total assets on its books are $244,000, total liabilities to outside creditors are $160,000 and total capital is $84,000. The partners made no withdrawals. LPR has decided to liquidate. If all of the partners are solvent and the assets of LPR are sold for $172,000:

A. Rice will personally have to contribute an additional $8,000.

B. Pine will personally have to contribute an additional $4,000.

C. Long, Pine, and Rice will receive $6,000, $4,000, and $2,000, respectively, as a return of capital.

D. Long and Pine will receive $28,000 and $4,000, respectively, and Rice will have to contribute an additional $20,000.

38. Eller, Fort, and Owens do business as Venture Associates, a general partnership. Trent Corp. brought a breach of contract suit against Venture and Eller individually. Trent won the suit and filed a judgment against both Venture and Eller. Trent will generally be able to collect the judgment from:

A. Partnership assets only.

B. The personal assets of Eller, Fort, and Owens only.

C. Eller's personal assets only after partnership assets are exhausted.

D. Eller's personal assets only.

STUDY MANUAL – BUSINESS ENVIRONMENT & CONCEPTS
CHAPTER 2

ANSWERS: BUSINESS STRUCTURES: PARTNERSHIPS

1. **C** A partnership is not usually considered to be a separate legal entity. Specifically, a partnership does not pay federal income tax. A partnership does not have perpetual existence like a corporation. Only C states no unlimited duration for a partnership and no obligation to pay federal income tax.

2. **D** Partners are agents of the partnership and each other. Thus, agency rules apply. If a partner commits a tort while acting in the scope of partnership business, the partner would be liable, the partnership would be liable and all other partners would be liable (respondeat superior). Partners are joint and severally liable for all partnership torts. Other choices are incorrect because the partner committing the tort, the partnership and all other partners would be liable. Also, each partner would be personally liable for the whole amount of any judgment, not just an equal share.

3. **B** Statement I is correct because partners are agents of the partnership and agents of each other. Since partners are co-owners of the business, when a partner acts on behalf of the business the partner is acting as both a principal and as an agent. Statement II is correct partners are jointly liable on all partnership debts and contract obligations. This means all partners must be sued as a group.

4. **A** Partners are agents of the partnership and each other. Thus, a partner can bind the partnership and fellow partners to a contract if the partner had actual authority or apparent authority. Although Locke exceeded Locke's actual authority, the partnership will still be liable based on Locke's apparent authority. Apparent authority depends on how things appear to third parties. It was reasonable for Gage to believe that a partner, like Locke, could purchase 15 stoves for the business. Since it appeared to Gage that Locke was authorized, Gage will win based on apparent authority. Other choices were incorrect as Locke was an agent of the partnership and did not have express authority. The partnership agreement expressly stated Locke was not authorized to make such contracts.

5. **C** It takes unanimous consent of all partners to submit a claim to arbitration, to confess a judgment (admit liability in a law suit) and to sell the partnership's goodwill. Leasing office space for the partnership by a partner would be within the partner's apparent authority. Since it would be reasonable to believe that a partner could lease space, the partnership would be bound.

6. **B** If a division of profits is specified in a partnership agreement, but not a division of losses, losses will be divided in the same manner as profits. The partnership agreement for Owen specified that profits were to split according to capital contributions (Moore, $10,000; Noon, $30,000; and Kale, $50,000). Therefore, losses must be split the same way. With losses of $180,000, Kale's share of the loss would be $100,000 (5/9 of $180,000).

7. **D** If a division of profits is specified in a partnership agreement, but not a division of losses, losses will be divided in the same manner as profits. This partnership agreement specified that profits were to be split Dowd, 40%; Elgar, 30%; Frost, 20%; and Grant, 10%. Therefore losses must be split the same way. With losses of $200,000 and Grant's share being 10%, Grant's share of the losses would be $20,000.

STUDY MANUAL – BUSINESS ENVIRONMENT & CONCEPTS

CHAPTER 2

8. **B**   Each partner is a co-owner of partnership property (called a tenancy in partnership). If a partner dies, the property goes to the surviving partners (called a right of survivorship). The other choices are incorrect because it takes unanimous consent of all partners to transfer partnership property to others. Thus, partnership property is not transferable to an individual partner's creditor, cannot be subject to a partner's liability for alimony and is not transferable to a deceased partner's estate without the unanimous consent of all other partners.

9. **A**   An assignment of a general partnership interest confers on the assignee only the right to receive the assignor's share of profits, if any. The assignee does not become a partner without the consent of all other partners. The assignor is still liable for debts and the assignee is not liable. An assignment does not dissolve the partnership.

10. **D**   Statement I is correct because partners are jointly and severally liable for all partnership torts. This is because partners are agents of the partnership and each other. If a partner commits a tort while acting in the scope of the agency, the principal is liable. Statement II is incorrect because general partners are jointly liable for all partnership debts and contract obligations whether they actually authorized them or not. Additionally, partners are agents of the partnership and each other and therefore can be liable for actions sanctioned not only by actual authority, but also by apparent authority.

11. **B**   Limited partners have no personal liability beyond their investment, thus they are not personally liable. Limited partners may not take part in the control of the partnership. If they do, they are liable like general partners to anyone reasonably believing they were a general partner.

12. **C**   An assignee of a partner's interest in a partnership does not become a substitute partner. The assignee receives no rights other than the right to receive the assignor's share of profits, if any. Thus, Bean received the right to Cobb's share of profits, but did not receive the right to participate in the management of the partnership. The correct answer is the only choice that reflects the right to profits, but not the right to participate in management.

13. **A**   A partner is personally liable for all partnership debts that occurred while he was a partner. Fein was a member of the ABC partnership and was personally liable for all debt's of ABC that occurred while he was a partner. The agreement to hold Fein harmless was made by the other partners and not by the creditors. The agreement to hold Fein harmless does not relieve Fein from liability to creditors, it merely gives Fein the right to recover any amounts he may have to pay to the creditors from the other partners. Choices regarding preventing creditors are incorrect because the creditors are not prevented from holding Fein liable for debts that occurred while Fein was a partner. The hold harmless agreement allows Fein to recover from the other partners all amounts he may have to pay to creditors, not just the amount in excess of his proportionate share.

14. **B**   A partnership is an association of two or more co-owners of a business for profit. Thus, (II) is a requirement of a partnership. It is not necessary that each piece of property used in the business be co-owned by all the partners. For example, the partnership may lease equipment from a third party or may use property that is owned by one partner and not others. Thus (I) is not a requirement of a partnership.

15. **B**   A partnership is an association of two or more co-owners of a business for profit. Thus, to create a partnership, the parties must intend to conduct a business for profit. It is not necessary to share gross receipts from a business to form a partnership. Indeed, partners share net receipts, not gross receipts.

©2007 Kaplan CPA Review

Page 87

STUDY MANUAL – BUSINESS ENVIRONMENT & CONCEPTS
CHAPTER 2

16. **A** A partnership is not one of the six types of contracts that require a writing under the statute of frauds (GRIPE + marriage). Only a partnership impossible to perform in one year and a limited partnership would require a writing. Answers (b), (c) and (d) are incorrect because co-ownership of a business for profit and with the intent to create a partnership are all necessary requirements to create an express partnership.

17. **D** A partnership is not usually considered to be a separate legal entity. Specifically, a partnership does not pay federal income tax. A partnership does not have perpetual existence like a corporation. Only answer (d) states no unlimited duration for a partnership and no obligation to pay federal income tax.

18. **C** Partners are agents of the partnership and each other. A partner acting with real or apparent authority can impose contract liability on the partnership and on their fellow partners. Thus, a partner selling goods with either real or apparent authority would bind the partnership. Answer (a) is incorrect because apparent authority depends on how things appear to third parties, not on the express provisions of the partnership agreement. Answer (b) is incorrect because if a partner's authority was expressly limited by a resolution and the third party was unaware of the resolution, it may still appear that the partner was authorized. In such a case, apparent authority would exist. Answer (d) is incorrect because partnership law requires unanimous consent of all partners to submit a claim to arbitration.

19. **B** To form a limited partnership in a state, there must be a special state statute that permits limited partnerships. The limited partnership must file a certificate of limited partnership with the state. Answer (a) is incorrect because a general partner is not required to make a capital contribution. Answer (c) is incorrect because a limited partnership must have at least one general partner and general partners are personally liable for all partnership debts. Answer (d) is incorrect because although a general partner may also be a limited partner in the same partnership at the same time, a general partner is not required to also be a limited partner.

20. **C** Both general and limited partners may be creditors of a limited partnership. A general partner may be either a secured or an unsecured creditor and so may a limited partner. Thus, (c) is correct and (a) is incorrect. Answer (b) is incorrect because a general partner may also be a limited partner in the same partnership at the same time. Answer (d) is incorrect because a limited partnership must have at least one general partner and general partners are personally liable for all partnership debts.

21. **A** The law gives to all investors the right to inspect books and records at reasonable times. Stockholders, general partners and limited partners all have this right. Thus, a limited partner may obtain financial information to include tax returns. Answer (b) is incorrect because a limited partnership must have at least one general partner and general partners are personally liable for all partnership debts. Answer (c) is incorrect because a limited partner may also be a general partner in the same partnership at the same time. Answer (d) is incorrect because a limited partner may not take part in the control of the partnership.

STUDY MANUAL – BUSINESS ENVIRONMENT & CONCEPTS

CHAPTER 2

22. **B**   Limited partners may not take part in the control of the partnership. If they do, they are liable like general partners to anyone reasonably believing they were a general partner. Thus, a limited partner may not participate in the management of the partnership in the same manner as general partners without losing their limited liability. Answer (a) is incorrect because limited partners are not personally liable for partnership debts. Answer (c) is incorrect because changes in limited partners do not dissolve the partnership. Only changes in general partners cause the dissolution of the partnership. Answer (d) is incorrect because limited partners are not agents of the partnership, only general partners are agents of the partnership.

23. **A**   Both a limited partnership and a corporation are created pursuant to state statutes and both must file with the secretary of state. Answer (b) is incorrect because a general partner in a limited partnership is personally liable for partnership debts. Equally, corporate law permits piercing of the corporate veil and holding stockholders personally liable in certain situations. Answer (c) is incorrect because a limited partnership is not recognized as a taxable entity for federal income tax purposes. Answer (d) is incorrect because only a corporation has perpetual existence.

24. **C**   Each partner has an equal right to share in profits and losses, unless otherwise agreed. Thus, profits are to be divided equally among the partners when the agreement is silent on the matter. Answers (a), (b) and (d) are incorrect because profits are not divided based on capital contributions, on management participation or proportionally. Profits are divided equally.

25. **A**   The order of distribution upon dissolution is to pay creditors, then pay back loans made by the partners, then pay back capital contributions. All liabilities have been paid and there were not any loans made by the partners. The next order of distribution is to pay back capital contributions. The partners share of losses was allocated to their capital accounts. Dowd contributed $120,000 and had a $40% share of the $200,000 loss ($80,000). Thus, Dowd is due $40,000 ($120,000 minus $80,000). Elgar contributed $100,000 and had a 30% share of a $200,000 loss ($60,000). Thus, Elgar is due $40,000 ($100,000 minus $60,000). Frost contributed $75,000 and had a 20% share of a $200,000 loss ($40,000). Thus, Frost is due $35,000 ($75,000 minus $40,000). Grant contributed $11,000 and had a 10% share of a $200,000 loss ($20,000). Thus, Grant should contribute $9,000 because of the negative balance ($11,000 minus $20,000). Grant has refused to contribute the $9,000, thus each partner must proportionately share in this shortfall. Dowd's proportionate share is 4/9 of $9,000 ($4,000), Elgar's is 1/3 of $9,000 ($3,000) and Frost's is 2/9 of $9,000 ($2,000). Final payment would be Dowd $36,000 ($40,000 minus $4,000), Elgar $37,000 ($40,000 minus $3,000) and Frost $33,000 ($35,000 minus $2,000) equaling the $106,000 available. The only answer that reflects that Elgar receives $37,000 is (a).

26. **C**   A partner may validly assign the right to receive partnership distributions. The assignee would only receive the right to receive the assignor's share of profits, if any. A partner may not validly assign rights to specific partnership property because it takes unanimous consent of all partners to transfer partnership property to others. Only answer (c) reflects the right to assign distributions, but not the right to assign partnership property.

STUDY MANUAL – BUSINESS ENVIRONMENT & CONCEPTS
CHAPTER 2

27. **C** Partners are agents of the partnership and each other. Thus, agency rules apply. If a partnership dissolves, partners must give actual notice to old customers and published notice to new ones. Failure of a partner to give proper notice would give a partner apparent authority to act on behalf of the partnership with customers who were unaware of the dissolution. Although dissolution would discharge a partner's actual authority, it does not discharge a partner's apparent authority. Only answer (c) reflects that a partner's liability is not automatically discharged by dissolution and that apparent authority would continue.

28. **A** A partnership impossible to complete in one year would require a writing under the statute of frauds. The partners agreed the partnership was not to be terminated for five years and thus, a writing was required. Answer (b) is incorrect because how profits are to be divided has no bearing on whether a writing is required. Answers (c) and (d) are incorrect because a writing was required for this partnership and thus, the partnership could not be oral.

29. **C** If a division of profits is specified in a partnership agreement, but not a division of losses, losses will be divided in the same manner as profits. This partnership agreement specified that profits were to be split Downs - 40%, Frey and Vick - 30% each. Therefore, losses will be split the same way. Vick has a 30% share of a $30,000 loss or $9,000. Only answer (c) reflects this amount.

30. **A** Under RUP, if a majority of the partners agree to continue the partnership, they may do so and the partnership is not dissolved. Answer (b) is incorrect because the partnership agreement merely states that the partnership will not end for five years, inferring that it may go beyond five years. Answer (c) is incorrect because one of the significant changes under RUPA is that a partnership is an entity in itself and the departure of a partner does not automatically dissolve the partnership. In a two-person partnership, the departure of one partner would dissolve the partnership, since a partnership must have two persons. Answer (d) is incorrect because Frey's interest becomes part of his estate; however, the estate cannot become a partner without the consent of all the other partners, which is unlikely. The estate's interest is similar to that of an assignee.

31. **D** Joint ventures are a business association of two or more co-owners acting together for profit for a limited purpose and for a limited duration. They are usually for a single undertaking. Joint ventures are treated as a partnership in most cases by the law. Answer (a) is incorrect because a joint venture may have more than two persons. Answer (b) is incorrect because the co-owners must act together for profit. Answer (c) is incorrect because a joint venture is not a corporate enterprise.

32. **D** A partner's estate does not become a partner unless agreed to by all the other partners. The estate is responsible for all partnership liabilities up until the partner's death. The partnership would not automatically dissolve if a majority of the remaining partners agree to continue.

33. **A** Park may dissolve the partnership at any time. Since there are only two partners, the departure of Park leaves only one partner. A partnership requires two partners operating a business for profit.

STUDY MANUAL – BUSINESS ENVIRONMENT & CONCEPTS

CHAPTER 2

34. **B** Everything in a partnership is equal unless otherwise agreed. This includes the right to participate in management. Since the partners agreed to admit Ward as a partner, Ward has the right to participate in management. Answer (a) is incorrect because Ward has an equal right in all partnership matters unless the partners specifically agree otherwise. An assignee acquires only the right to receive their assignor's share of profits. Ward was more than an assignee, Ward was a partner. Answer (c) is incorrect because Ward is only personally liable for partnership debts that occur after (s)he is admitted as a partner. Ward would not be personally liable for debts that occurred prior to becoming a partner. Answer (d) is incorrect because a partner is not required to contribute cash or property to become a partner. They may contribute services or they may not contribute anything.

35. **A** An incoming partner is not personally liable for partnership debts occurring prior to becoming a partner. However, an incoming partner's interest in partnership property can be attached by creditors. Thus, the liability of Dill (the incoming partner) would be limited to Dill's interest in partnership property. Answer (b) is incorrect because a departing partner is personally liable for all partnership debts that occurred while (s)he was a partner. Answer (c) is incorrect because Ard cannot recover from the other partners the full amount that Ard paid creditors unless the other partners specifically agreed to hold Ard harmless. There was no hold harmless agreement given to Ard. Answer (d) is incorrect because Dill is only personally liable for partnership debts that occur after (s)he is admitted as a partner. Dill would not be personally liable for debts that occurred prior to becoming a partner.

36. **A** Upon dissolution of a general partnership the following order of distribution occurs: first creditors are paid, second partners are repaid for any loans or advances made to the partnership, third capital contributions are paid and lastly profits are split. Only answer (a) reflects this order of distribution.

37. **A** Upon dissolution of a general partnership the following order of distribution occurs: first creditors are paid, second partners are repaid for any loans or advances made to the partnership, third capital contributions are paid and lastly profits are split. Creditors are owed $160,000, there are no loans made by partners and a total of $180,000 is due for capital contributions (Long - $100,000, Pine - $60,000 and Rice-$20,000). Thus, $340,000 is needed to pay creditors and capital contributions ($180,000 + $160,000). Of the $340,000 needed, only $172,000 is available from the sale of assets. This leaves a shortfall of $168,000 ($340,000 minus $172,000 = $168,000). Long's share of the shortfall is 1/2 of $168,000 or $84,000. Thus, Long will receive his capital contribution ($100,000) minus his share of the shortfall ($84,000), or $16,000. Pine's share of the shortfall is 1/3 of $168,000 or $56,000. Thus Pine will receive his capital contribution ($60,000) minus his share of the shortfall ($56,000), or $4,000. Rice's share of the shortfall is 1/6 of $168,000 or $28,000. Rice will receive his capital contribution ($20,000) minus his share of the shortfall ($28,000) leaving a negative balance of $8,000. Thus, Rice will have to contribute an additional $8,000. The only answer that reflects this distribution is (a).

38. **C** Partnership creditors can only go after a partner personally after all partnership assets are first exhausted. Thus, Trent can only go after the personal assets of Eller after the partnership assets are exhausted. Answer (a) and (b) are incorrect because a creditor can collect a judgment from both partnership assets and from partners personally. Answer (d) is incorrect because partnership creditors must first exhaust partnership assets before they can go after a partner personally.

©2007 Kaplan CPA Review

Page 91

FINANCE: RATIO ANALYSIS

STUDY MANUAL – BUSINESS ENVIRONMENT & CONCEPTS
CHAPTER 3

Study Tip: No matter how busy you get preparing for the CPA exam, make time to exercise several times each week. Even 15 minutes of walking around your neighborhood every other day will help you release tension and keep your mind clear. Candidates often try to study every minute they are awake and then do not understand why they make careless mistakes and cannot concentrate. Get enough exercise so you can maximize the efficiency of your study time.

FINANCIAL STATEMENT ANALYSIS

INTRODUCTION TO FINANCIAL STATEMENT ANALYSIS

Financial statement analysis can seem like an overwhelming task. There are so many different factors and sources of information to consider that a beginning analyst cannot help but feel uncertain of where to begin. The purpose of this section is to relieve that uncertainty and provide clear direction in how to proceed with financial statement analysis.

Before we can discuss where to begin the financial statement analysis process, we must have a clear understanding of where we are going. Figure 1 is a map for financial statement analysis. The purpose of the map is to give the analyst a clear sense of direction in the journey. First, let us focus on our destination or goals of financial statement analysis.

Figure 1: Map of Financial Statement Analysis

Step 1	Step 2	Step 3	Step 4	Step 5
Audience	*Goals or Objectives*	*Sources of Information*	*Analytical Tools*	*Financial Position*
Investors	Valuation	Financial statements (annual report or 10-K)	Common-size financial statements	Valuation
Creditors	Ability to pay debt	Footnotes	Ratio analysis	Liquidity
Management	Efficiency	Management discussion	Cash flow projections	Profitability
		Other industry data		Solvency

Upon beginning financial statement analysis, the first step for an analyst is to determine the user of the analysis. As illustrated in Figure 1, the user may be management, investors, or creditors. It is key to assess the users up front, so their goals or objectives can be established. Investors are most commonly interested in the valuation and profitability of a firm, while creditors are concerned with ability to repay debt, and management is interested in assessing the overall efficiency of the firm (from operations, to use of assets and debt, to increasing shareholder value).

As indicated in Figure 1, once the audience and their objectives are determined, the analyst can move on to the various sources of information available for analysis. The next step is translating the information into useful analytical tools such as ratios and cash flow projections. Finally, these analytical tools are used to assess the financial position of the firm and, ultimately, answer the concern of the audience.

Next we will elaborate on each step of the financial statement analysis process, beginning with the goals and objectives of financial statement analysis.

As previously discussed, investors, creditors, and company management use financial statements with different goals in mind. Figure 2 is an overall summary of the users, their primary goals, and the underlying objectives they are seeking to accomplish in order to meet those goals.

Figure 2: Users of Financial Statements

User of Financial Statement Analysis	Primary Goal	Objectives
Equity investors	Valuation	Profitability Risk analysis Growth analysis
Creditors	Ability to repay debt	Liquidity Solvency
Management	Efficiency	Profitability Solvency Operating performance

A. Equity investors.

  1. Equity investors use financial statement analysis to estimate the value of the corporation. These investors can purchase ownership in the corporation through common stock, merger, or acquisition. An investor could also purchase the corporation with the intention of liquidating it.

  2. Companies with many outside owners who are not usually involved with business operations are known as publicly traded corporations. Publicly traded corporations are required by the Securities and Exchange Commission (SEC) in the United States to disclose information publicly so all outside creditors and equity holders have access to the same information.

  3. The equity investors of publicly traded firms are subject to moral hazard. Therefore, equity owners of publicly traded corporations are at a disadvantage in

©2007 Kaplan CPA Review

gathering information. They must rely on management to provide the necessary information to make decisions. In contrast, majority owners of private firms have access to all information.

4. The profitability of a firm and its ability to generate a return on its investment (dividends, or capital gains) are of particular interest to equity investors.

5. Equity investors may analyze the financial statements themselves; however, they often rely on analysis by third-party researchers. Most brokerage houses employ an equity research staff. There are also companies whose only business is to provide research to either institutional or individual investors.

B. Creditors.

1. Creditors are most concerned with the corporation's ability to repay principal and interest on debt. Corporate bankers, bondholders, and trade creditors focus on the cash flow of the organization over the life of the debt.

2. Third-party researchers specialize in credit analysis. The best known of these researchers are credit-rating companies such as Moody's and Standard & Poor's (S&P). Brokerage houses and insurance companies also employ credit analysts.

3. Fixed income investors rely on the expertise of credit-rating agencies to determine the amount of risk and appropriate required return for their debt investments.

   a. Short-term credit ratings indicate the ability of an organization to meet liquidity needs.

   b. Long-term bond ratings indicate an organization's ability to remain solvent and repay debt over longer periods of time.

4. The higher the rating, the less uncertainty there is regarding the ability of the organization to meet future financial obligations.

C. Management.

1. Management's use of financial statements focuses on the overall profitability, efficiency, and direction of the firm. Additionally, the financial statements are prepared for and used to analyze specific segments, product lines, and divisions of the organization.

2. Management is the primary user of financial statements and employs the information to make strategic and operating decisions.

3. Management is the driver of the decisions that will ultimately increase shareholder value.

D. The basic financial statements used for financial analysis include:

1. The income statement, which reflects the corporation's operating results over a period of time.

2. The balance sheet, which provides a snapshot of the assets, liabilities, and owner's equity of the corporation at a point in time.

3. The statement of owner's equity, which summarizes the activity within the equity accounts from the balance sheet.

4. The statement of cash flows, which reflects information from both the balance sheet and income statement. It summarizes the changes in the firm's cash account and shows the cash flow changes as a result of operating, investing, and financing activities.

    a. Operating cash flows are those that result from the operations of the business. Positive cash flow from operations is essential for every organization's longevity. If an organization is unable to generate positive cash flows from operations, it will eventually be forced to shut down either voluntarily or involuntarily through bankruptcy.

    b. Investing cash flows are those resulting from the purchase or sale of long-term assets.

    c. Financing cash flows are those resulting from increased borrowing, the reduction of existing debt, the sale or repurchase of equity, and cash dividends paid by the firm to its shareholders.

E. Other information in annual reports.

In addition to the three financial statements, an annual 10-K, filed with the SEC, is required for publicly traded corporations and includes other valuable information regarding the operations of the corporation.

1. The annual report typically has a section entitled management discussion of operations. In this section, the analyst is able to gain insights regarding historical and future operations. In addition to this report, management will often make new information available to investors and analysts regarding their expectations of quarterly revenues, earnings, and major events.

2. Footnotes to the financial statements provide valuable information regarding the depreciation method, inventory methods, and other key financial information that is necessary in the analysis.

3. There are other sources of information in addition to the financial statements and footnotes available to analysts. The Internet and other technological advances have greatly enhanced the availability of information. Even small individual investors now have the ability to gather a great deal of information at relatively nominal cost.

©2007 Kaplan CPA Review

STUDY MANUAL – BUSINESS ENVIRONMENT & CONCEPTS
CHAPTER 3

TOOLS OF FINANCIAL STATEMENT ANALYSIS

A. Common-size analysis converts balance sheet and income statement data into relative measures. For example, when analyzing the balance sheet, each balance sheet item is divided by the amount of total assets. For the income statement, each income statement item is divided by total sales. The following example (see Figure 3) illustrates why relative measures are necessary for comparison purposes:

Figure 3: Relative Measures

Company A		Company B	
Accounts receivable	$125,000	Accounts receivable	$250,000
Total assets	$1,250,000	Total assets	$3,000,000
% of total assets	10%	% of total assets	8.3%

1. Company A and Company B have accounts receivable of $125,000 and $250,000, respectively. However, an analyst cannot conclude that since Company B's accounts receivable are greater, B is more liquid. It is necessary to know the percentage of accounts receivable to total assets. Since Company B is larger ($3,000,000 in total assets) than Company A ($1,250,000 in total assets), the relative percentage of accounts receivable is actually smaller for Company B at 8.3 percent versus Company A at 10 percent.

2. Relative measures make it easier to compare companies of different sizes, as well as companies to the industry. Relative measures enable the analyst to identify strengths and weaknesses and track historical trends.

RATIO ANALYSIS

A. Financial statement analysis regularly relies on financial ratios to assess a firm's financial position. These ratios are calculated from a company's income statement and balance sheet for a wide variety of items. Financial ratios are one of an analyst's most powerful tools—converting financial statement information into a form that is easier to analyze.

B. The examination of financial ratios provides insights into how a firm has performed historically and how it is performing relative to its competitors and its industry. Financial ratios can be viewed as equalizers, allowing for relative comparisons to be made. For instance, via ratio analysis, current year ratios can be compared with the ratios from previous years to assess trends in the performance of the company. Financial ratios can also be compared to those of other firms as well as the overall industry and economy-wide averages to assess the relative performance of a company. These comparisons are critical for analysts who are evaluating a company's common stock or creditworthiness.

C. Trend analysis is a valuable planning tool. Historical financial statements will reflect peak and trough periods of operations based on seasonality or some other relevant factor. These seasonal factors will help management determine staffing and inventory needs and then allow them to deal with the financing impacts of those needs.

D. Trend analysis is also of value to prospective buyers of the company. Potential buyers may be willing to pay top dollar for a business that shows an upward trend in operating performance, which indicates an efficiently run business that may be capable of even better results in the future. Flat trends, however, typically indicate one of two things: a business that has not been efficiently managed or a business that is in a mature market. If a business has been inefficiently managed, new management may be able to increase revenues and profits by making improvements to the business.

E. It is not necessarily valid to compare common-size financial statements and ratios for two firms. As the old saying goes, it is important to compare "apples to apples and oranges to oranges." Analysts generally try to make comparisons based on similar industries. However, even within the same industry, the acceptable norms may be different for large and small firms. It is highly unlikely to find two firms that are exactly alike. Firms often try to find unique niches for competitive advantages and may or may not be more diversified across different industry segments.

F. The key financial variable that investors care most about is cash flow. It is cash that pays creditors and creates value for shareholders. Therefore, a thorough understanding of historical and projected cash flows is essential for analysis from the investors' perspective.

G. Management of the firm is concerned not only with the perspectives of investors and creditors, but they must also focus on allocating resources, controlling growth, and managing key areas of the firm to maximize the value of the organization. An understanding of the state of the economy and industry is essential for making wise decisions for the future.

PERFORMING FINANCIAL STATEMENT ANALYSIS

A. The appropriate steps for financial statement analysis are summarized as follows:

Step 1: Identify the goals and objectives of the analysis.

    a.   Valuation of the firm.

    b.   Ability to repay debt.

    c.   Overall management of the firm.

Step 2: Gather appropriate information for analysis.

Step 3: Use appropriate tools to prepare common-size statements and ratio analysis to look for historical trends, and compare the firm to competitors and the industry.

STUDY MANUAL – BUSINESS ENVIRONMENT & CONCEPTS
CHAPTER 3

Step 4: Identify the risks and conditions of the firm based on evaluations using the appropriate financial statement analysis tools.

Step 5: Use knowledge of key ratios, trends, industry, and economic data to prepare pro forma financial statements.

Step 6: Summarize findings based on analysis and make appropriate recommendations related to the overall objectives.

While income statement analysis provides an indication about the financial health (profitability) of a company, using cash flow analysis along with the income statement can provide even more useful information about the firm.

LIQUIDITY ANALYSIS

A. Companies can be quite profitable and still have difficulty with liquidity or long-term solvency. If the cash required for working capital and fixed-asset investments is continually higher than the income produced by the company, the firm will eventually become insolvent. Review of cash flow information should indicate whether a firm has the ability to finance its growth from internal operations. Operating cash flow tells an analyst how much cash is generated by the sales activity of the company. It is the most important component of cash flow analysis.

1. The cash flow statement will show problems with liquidity and solvency. Negative operating cash flows indicate that the company will have to rely on external sources of financing to fund operations. This might be expected from a company experiencing high growth, but would be a problem for a stable, mature company.

2. Trends in cash flows can be extrapolated to estimate how the company will be performing over the next few years. Trend analysis is particularly useful when compared to the trend of income over time. Discrepancies between the trends in income and cash flow can suggest that earnings trends are not reliable.

3. Interrelationships between cash flow components (e.g., cash inputs and cash collections) provide insight similar to ratio analysis with income statement figures.

4. Positive cash flows are desired, particularly with respect to operating cash flow. Analysts should, however, view a company's continual reliance on investing and financing activities to generate positive cash flows as a red flag.

B. Keep in mind, while cash flows show whether a firm is generating a positive or negative cash flow, when analyzed alone, an analyst cannot make judgments on the firm's ability to continue and be profitable. The cash flow statement must be reviewed in combination with the balance sheet and income statement.

C. Free cash flow is a calculation analysts often use to predict future cash flows. Since net income is subject to varying accounting methods, free cash flow is less subjective and more useful when analyzing a firm. Free cash flow attempts to measure the cash

Page 98   ©2007 Kaplan CPA Review

available for discretionary purposes. The result is the firm's cash available for creditors and owners.

D. Formally, it should be the operating cash flow minus those cash flows necessary to maintain the firm's productive capacity. The analyst must use discretion in determining which capital expenditures are necessary to maintain capacity. If the analyst has no additional information available to make such a determination, it might be prudent to assume all capital expenditures are necessary to maintain capacity. In that case, free cash flow is measured by:

Free cash flow = Operating cash flow – Net capital expenditures

E. When used for valuation purposes, some adjustments to free cash flow must be made. If the analyst is interested in free cash flow to all investors, after-tax interest expense must be added back [I × (1 - t)]. If the analyst is interested in free cash flow to shareholders, debt repayments may be subtracted.

THE DuPont System

A. The DuPont system is an approach that can be used to analyze return on equity (ROE). It uses basic algebra to breakdown ROE into a function of different ratios, so an analyst can see the impact of leverage, profit margins, and turnover on shareholder returns. There are two variants of the DuPont system, the traditional approach and the extended system.

1. For the traditional approach, we start with ROE defined as:

$$ROE = \frac{\text{net income}}{\text{equity}}$$

2. The common equity figure that is used is not average equity, but simply end-of-year equity. For the algebra of the DuPont system to work, only end-of-year balance sheet figures can be used.

3. Multiplying ROE by sales/sales and rearranging terms produces:

$$ROE = \left(\frac{\text{net income}}{\text{sales}} \right) \times \left(\frac{\text{sales}}{\text{equity}} \right)$$

4. The first term in this expression of ROE is the profit margin and the second term is the equity turnover. Thus, we have:

ROE = Net profit margin × Equity turnover

5. We can expand this further by multiplying these terms by assets/assets and rearranging terms:

$$ROE = \left(\frac{\text{net income}}{\text{sales}} \right) \times \left(\frac{\text{sales}}{\text{assets}} \right) \times \left(\frac{\text{assets}}{\text{equity}} \right)$$

6. The first term is still the profit margin, the second term is now asset turnover, and the third term is an equity multiplier that will increase as the use of debt financing increases. Here, we can state:

   ROE = Net profit margin × Total asset turnover × Equity multiplier

7. This is the traditional DuPont equation. It is arguably the most important equation in ratio analysis, since it breaks down a very important ratio (ROE) into three key components. If ROE is too low, at least one of the following must be true:

   a. The company has a poor profit margin.

   b. The company has poor asset turnover.

   c. The firm is not highly leveraged.

Example: Traditional DuPont analysis

Explain how an Internet-based car dealer and a traditional car dealership might differ in terms of asset turnover and gross profit margin and how those differences may impact ROE.

Answer

One would expect that the traditional car dealership would have much lower asset turnover than the Internet-based dealership. The regular dealer has to have a large amount of capital tied up in its physical facility. Also, most dealers have repair facilities that require a lot of equipment. An Internet dealership will not have the same investment needs.

Conversely, the traditional dealership would likely have a higher gross profit margin than the Internet dealer. Selling a commodity over the Internet is very competitive, and price pressures would likely drive the sales price to slightly above cost. Traditional dealers attempt to keep margins higher by differentiation—offering various services—and through salesmanship.

Assume the asset turnover of the Internet-based car dealership is twice as much as the asset turnover of the traditional dealership. Further assume the profit margin of the traditional dealership is twice as high as the profit margin for the Internet-based dealership. If the amount of leverage employed for the two dealerships were the same, their ROE would be identical, albeit for very different reasons. This example illustrates the importance of the DuPont equation—an analyst is able to attribute the

STUDY MANUAL – BUSINESS ENVIRONMENT & CONCEPTS

CHAPTER 3

sources of ROE, making the information provided by the ratio much more meaningful.

Example: Traditional DuPont analysis

A company has a profit margin of 4 percent, asset turnover of 2.0, and a debt-to-assets ratio of 60 percent. What is the ROE?

Answer

Debt to assets is 60 percent, which means equity to assets is 40 percent; this implies assets over equity of 1/0.4 = 2.5.

$$\text{ROE} = \text{net profit margin} \times \text{total asset turnover} \times \frac{\text{assets}}{\text{equity}} = 0.04 \times 2.0 \times 2.5 = 0.20,$$

or 20%

The extended DuPont equation takes the net profit margin and breaks it down further. The numerator of the net profit margin is net income. Since net income is equal to earnings before taxes multiplied by 1 minus the tax rate $(1 - t)$, the DuPont equation can be written as:

$$\text{ROE} = \left(\frac{\text{earnings before tax}}{\text{sales}}\right) \times \left(\frac{\text{sales}}{\text{assets}}\right) \times \left(\frac{\text{assets}}{\text{equity}}\right) \times (1 - t)$$

Earnings before tax is simply EBIT minus interest expense. If this substitution is made, the equation becomes (after some fancy algebra):

$$\text{ROE} = \left[\left(\frac{\text{EBIT}}{\text{sales}}\right) \times \left(\frac{\text{sales}}{\text{assets}}\right) - \left(\frac{\text{interest expense}}{\text{assets}}\right)\right] \times \left(\frac{\text{assets}}{\text{equity}}\right) \times (1 - t)$$

The first term is the operating profit margin. The second term is the asset turnover. The third term is new and is called the interest expense rate. The fourth term is the same leverage multiplier defined in the traditional DuPont equation; and the fifth term, $(1 - t)$, is called the tax retention rate. The equation can now be stated as:

ROE = (operating profit margin × asset turnover − interest expense rate)
× leverage multiplier × tax retention rate

Note that in general, high profit margins, leverage, and asset turnover will lead to high levels of ROE. However, this version of the formula shows that more leverage does not always lead to higher ROE. As leverage rises, so does the interest expense rate. Hence, the positive effects of leverage can be mitigated by the higher interest payments that accompany more debt. Note that higher taxes will always lead to lower levels of ROE.

©2007 Kaplan CPA Review

Page 101

STUDY MANUAL – BUSINESS ENVIRONMENT & CONCEPTS
CHAPTER 3

Example: Extended DuPont analysis

An analyst has gathered data presented in Figure 4 for two companies in the same industry. Calculate the ROE for both companies, and explain the critical factors that can lead to a higher ROE.

Figure 4: Company Data

	Company A	Company B
Revenues	500	900
Operating income	35	100
Interest expense	5	0
Income before taxes	30	100
Taxes	10	40
Net income	20	60
Total assets	250	300
Total debt	100	50
Owner's equity	150	250

Answer

$$\text{operating margin} = \frac{\text{operating income}}{\text{sales}}$$

$$\text{Company A: operating margin} = \frac{35}{500} = 7.0\%$$

$$\text{Company B: operating margin} = \frac{100}{900} = 11.1\%$$

$$\text{asset turnover} = \frac{\text{sales}}{\text{assets}}$$

$$\text{Company A: asset turnover} = \frac{500}{250} = 2.0$$

$$\text{Company B: asset turnover} = \frac{900}{300} = 3.0$$

$$\text{interest expense rate} = \frac{\text{interest expense}}{\text{assets}}$$

$$\text{Company A: interest expense rate} = \frac{5}{250} = 2.0\%$$

Company B: interest expense rate $= \dfrac{0}{300} = 0.0\%$

$$\text{financial leverage} = \dfrac{\text{assets}}{\text{equity}}$$

Company A: financial leverage $= \dfrac{250}{150} = 1.67$

Company B: financial leverage $= \dfrac{300}{250} = 1.2$

$$\text{financial leverage} = \dfrac{\text{assets}}{\text{equity}}$$

Company A: income tax rate $= \dfrac{10}{30} = 33.3\%$

Company B: income tax rate $= \dfrac{40}{100} = 40.0\%$

ROE = (operating margin × asset turnover - interest expense rate) × leverage × (1 – tax rate).

Company A: ROE = (7.0% × 2.0 – 2.0%) × 1.67 × (1 – 33.3%) = 13.3%.

Company B: ROE = (11.1% × 3.0 – 0%) × 1.2 × (1 – 40%) = 24.0%.

Asset turnover for Company B is much higher, which is the main reason its ROE is higher. Profit margin is also a contributing factor. Company B's ROE is higher despite the fact that it is using less leverage.

8. A single value of a financial ratio is not meaningful by itself, but must be examined relative to industry norms and the company's own historical performance.

    a. Comparison to industry norms is the most common type of comparison. Industry comparisons are particularly valid when the products generated by the industry are similar.

    b. Primarily, comparisons are made to industry averages. However, if there are wide variations within the industry, it may be more appropriate not to use all of the firms in the industry, but to use a subset of firms with similar size and characteristics. Using a subset of firms with similar characteristics relative to the firm being analyzed is called cross-sectional analysis.

    c. For firms that operate in multiple industries, an analyst can calculate composite industry averages by using a weighted-average based on the proportion of the company's sales in each industry segment.

STUDY MANUAL – BUSINESS ENVIRONMENT & CONCEPTS
CHAPTER 3

    d.   Comparing a firm with its own history is very common. Analysts often conduct time-series analysis, which considers the trend in a ratio. Indeed, it is problematic to simply consider long-term averages of ratios without taking their trend into account. It is particularly useful to look at trends in a company's ratios in relation to trends in the industry's average ratios.

    e.   When analyzing trends in a company's ratios, an analyst should consider the condition of the overall economy—this is particularly important when overall business conditions are changing. For example, a stable profit margin might be considered good if the economy is in recession and the economy-wide average profit margin is declining. On the other hand, it might be considered problematic if a stable profit margin occurs during an economic expansion, when overall average profit margins are increasing.

    f.   In most ratio comparisons, it is considered desirable to be near the industry (or economy) average. For example, in all turnover ratios, a value could be considered too high or too low if it differs widely from the industry average. However, for some ratios, simply being high is considered good, even if it deviates from the industry average. This is true for most ratios involving income or cash flow. For example, most analysts would agree that having a high return on assets or high profit margin is good. An analyst would not suggest that a company with a return on assets of 15 percent had an ROA that was too high when the industry average was 10 percent.

    g.   Sometimes the goodness of a ratio depends on the context. A high ROE that results from high profit margins or asset turnover is typically looked upon favorably. However, high ROEs that result from high levels of leverage are typically met with a great deal of skepticism.

Example: Trend analysis and industry comparison

The following is a company's balance sheet for 20X3 and 20X4 and its income statement for 20X4. Using the company information presented in Figure 5 and Figure 6, calculate the ratios listed in Figure 7, and discuss how these ratios compare with the company's performance last year and with the industry's performance.

STUDY MANUAL – BUSINESS ENVIRONMENT & CONCEPTS
CHAPTER 3

Figure 5: Balance Sheets

	20X4	20X3
Assets		
Cash	$105	95
Receivables	205	195
Inventories	310	290
Total current assets	620	580
Gross property, plant, and equipment	1,800	1,700
Accumulated depreciation	360	340
Net property, plant, and equipment	1,440	1,360
Total assets	$2,060	1,940
Liabilities and Equity		
Payables	$110	90
Short-term debt	160	140
Current portion of long-term debt	55	45
Current liabilities	325	275
Long-term debt	610	690
Deferred taxes	105	95
Common stock	300	300
Additional paid-in capital	400	400
Retained earnings	320	180
Common shareholders equity	1,020	880
Total liabilities and equity	$2,060	1,940

Figure 6: Income Statements

20X4	
Sales	$4,000
COGS	3,000
Gross profit	1,000
Operating expenses	650
Operating profit	350
Interest expense	50
Earnings before taxes	300
Taxes	100
Net income	$200
Common dividends	$60

©2007 Kaplan CPA Review

STUDY MANUAL – BUSINESS ENVIRONMENT & CONCEPTS
CHAPTER 3

Figure 7: Company and Industry Ratios

	Company	Last Year	Industry
Current ratio	?	2.1	1.5
Quick ratio	?	1.0	0.9
Receivables collection period	?	18.9	18.0
Inventory turnover	?	10.7	12.0
Total asset turnover	?	2.3	2.4
Equity turnover	?	4.8	4.0
Gross profit margin	?	27.4%	29.3%
Net profit margin	?	5.8%	6.5%
Return on capital	?	13.3%	15.6%
Return on equity	?	24.1%	19.8%
Debt-to-equity	?	78.4%	35.7%
Interest coverage	?	5.9	9.2
Retention rate	?	50.0%	43.6%
Sustainable growth rate	?	12.0%	8.6%

Answer

$$\text{current ratio} = \frac{\text{current assets}}{\text{current liabilities}}$$

$$= \frac{620}{325} = 1.9$$

The current ratio indicates lower liquidity levels when compared to last year and more liquidity than the industry average.

$$\text{quick ratio} = \frac{\text{cash} + \text{receivables}}{\text{current liabilities}}$$

$$= \frac{105 + 205}{325} = 0.95$$

The quick ratio is lower than last year, indicating liquidity has slightly declined but is higher than the industry average.

$$\text{average collection period} = \frac{365}{\text{sales/average receivables}}$$

$$= \frac{365}{\dfrac{4,000}{\left(\dfrac{205 + 195}{2}\right)}} = 18.2$$

Page 106   ©2007 Kaplan CPA Review

The average collection period is a bit lower relative to the company's past performance, but slightly higher than the industry average. This suggests that customers are paying their bills more quickly than they did in the prior year, but not as quickly as customers of other firms in the industry.

$$\text{inventory turnover} = \frac{\text{COGS}}{\text{average inventories}}$$

$$= \frac{3,000}{\left(\frac{310 + 290}{2}\right)} = 10.0$$

The inventory turnover is lower than last year and the industry average. This suggests that the company is not managing inventory efficiently and may have obsolete stock.

$$\text{total asset turnover} = \frac{\text{sales}}{\text{average assets}}$$

$$= \frac{4,000}{\left(\frac{2,060 + 1,940}{2}\right)} 2.0$$

The total asset turnover is slightly lower than last year and the industry average.

$$\text{equity turnover} = \frac{\text{sales}}{\text{average equity}}$$

$$= \frac{4,000}{\left(\frac{1,020 + 880}{2}\right)} = 4.2$$

The equity turnover is lower than last year but still above the industry average.

$$\text{gross profit margin} = \frac{\text{gross profit}}{\text{net sales}}$$

$$= \frac{1,000}{4,000} = 25.0\%$$

The gross profit margin is lower than last year and much lower than the industry average. This suggests that the firm has a high cost structure relative to the industry, and is a reason for concern.

$$\text{net profit margin} = \frac{\text{net income}}{\text{net sales}}$$

$$= \frac{200}{4,000} = 5.0\%$$

©2007 Kaplan CPA Review

The net profit margin is lower than last year and much lower than the industry average. Again, this suggests higher costs and/or expenses compared to other firms in the industry and is a cause for concern on the part of the analyst.

$$\text{return on capital} = \frac{\text{net income} + \text{interest expense}}{\text{average total capital}}$$

$$= \frac{200 + 50}{\left(\dfrac{2,060 + 1,940}{2}\right)} = 12.5\%$$

The return on capital is below last year and the industry average. This suggests a problem stemming from the low asset turnover and low profit margin.

$$\text{return on common equity} = \frac{\text{net income} - \text{preferred dividends}}{\text{average owners equity}}$$

$$= \frac{200}{\left(\dfrac{1,020 + 880}{2}\right)} = 21.1\%$$

The return on common equity is below last year but better than the industry average. The reason it is higher than the industry average is probably because of greater use of leverage.

$$\text{debt-to-equity ratio} = \frac{\text{long-term debt (not including deferred taxes)}}{\text{total equity}}$$

$$= \frac{610}{1,020} = 59.8\%$$

Note: This calculation assumes that deferred taxes are not a part of long-term debt.

The debt-to-equity ratio is lower than last year but still much higher than the industry average. This suggests the company is trying to get its debt level more in line with the industry.

$$\text{interest coverage} = \frac{\text{net income} + \text{income taxes} + \text{interest expense}}{\text{interest expense}}$$

$$= \frac{200 + 100 + 50}{50} = 7.0$$

The interest coverage is better than last year but still worse than the industry average. This, along with the slip in profit margin and return on assets, might cause some concern.

$$\text{retention rate} = 1 - \left(\frac{\text{dividends}}{\text{earnings}} \right)$$

$$= 1 - \left(\frac{60}{200} \right) = 7.0\%$$

The retention rate is much higher than last year and much higher than the industry. This might suggest that the company is aware of its cash flow and earnings issues and is reinvesting cash into the company to improve the ratios.

$$\text{ROE} = \frac{\text{net income}}{\text{equity}}$$

$$= \frac{200}{1,020} = 19.6\%$$

sustainable growth rate, g = retention rate × ROE = 0.7 × 0.196 = 13.7%.

With the high retention rate and good ROE, the company is positioned to grow at a faster rate than last year and faster than the rest of the industry.

The company has average liquidity. However, performance figures suggest that earnings have declined, and turnover has worsened. Coverage ratios are worse than the industry average, which might cause some concern, particularly for lenders.

9. There are several limitations of analyzing a company using financial ratios.

    a. Financial ratios are not useful when viewed in isolation. They are only valid when compared to other firms or the company's historical performance.

    b. Comparisons with other companies are made more difficult because of different accounting treatments. This is particularly important when analyzing foreign-owned companies.

    c. It is difficult to find comparable industry ratios when analyzing companies that operate in multiple industries.

    d. Conclusions cannot be made from viewing one set of ratios. All ratios must be viewed relative to one another.

    e. Determining the appropriate target or comparison value for a ratio is difficult. There might be cases in which the industry average is not the optimal target to which a firm should be compared.

STUDY MANUAL – BUSINESS ENVIRONMENT & CONCEPTS
CHAPTER 3

EFFECTS OF USING DIFFERENT INVENTORY METHODS

A. As you learned in early accounting courses, FIFO, LIFO, weighted-average, and specific identification methods result in different inventory valuations. It is important to understand these differences and their implications to the financial statements.

B. First, let's look at how rising or declining costs affect the financial statements. During periods of increasing or stable inventory quantities and rising costs:

1. The FIFO cost flow assumption will result in the lowest COGS because the costs that are first in go to COGS and are lowest. Because of low COGS, FIFO produces the highest net income. The lower the COGS, the higher the ending inventory that appears on the balance sheet (under FIFO, recently incurred costs remain in inventory, which are the highest).

2. LIFO will result in the highest COGS (because the last costs incurred are the highest) and lowest income. The higher the COGS, the lower the ending inventory on the balance sheet (under LIFO, the earliest costs incurred remain in inventory, which are the lowest).

3. Income taxes will be lower with LIFO, if LIFO is used for tax-reporting purposes. If income taxes are lower, net cash flow will be higher under LIFO. Although COGS and inventory are both factored into the cash flow from operations (CFO) calculation, increases in one account are offset by decreases in the other, so the only effect on CFO is the lower tax payment.

4. Figure 8 can help you visualize the FIFO-LIFO difference during periods of rising costs and increasing inventory levels:

Figure 8: LIFO and FIFO Comparison: Rising Prices and Increasing Inventories

LIFO results in...	FIFO results in...
higher COGS	lower COGS
lower net income	higher net income
lower taxes	higher taxes
lower inventory balances	higher inventory balances
lower working capital	higher working capital
higher net cash flow	lower net cash flow

5. During periods of rising costs, LIFO results in higher COGS, lower net income, and lower inventory levels. This decreases the current ratio (CA/CL) and increases inventory turnover (COGS/average inventory).

6. If costs do not change, the different inventory valuation methods do not affect the financial statements.

7. By decreasing inventory to levels below the normal level and allowing old, lower costs to flow to COGS, a firm's management can manipulate profits with LIFO. In this case, COGS under LIFO will be low, and profit will be high. This is called a LIFO liquidation.

8. With LIFO liquidation (e.g., the firm sells more items than purchased during the period), LIFO COGS and net income are distorted.

9. Weighted-average, being an average, is in between the FIFO and LIFO valuations.

10. Specific identification cannot be generalized because it depends upon the particular situation.

   Figure 8 summarizes the results of LIFO and FIFO in periods of rising prices and stable or increasing inventory quantities.

11. The opposite relationships hold for falling prices, assuming level or increasing inventory quantities.

EFFECTS OF INVENTORY MISSTATEMENTS

A. Misstatement of inventory balances has a direct effect on net income and other financial results. An analyst should understand how a misstatement (overstatement or understatement) of inventories affects the financial statements, particularly the income statement. Misstatements can occur (1) accidentally by miscalculation or (2) intentionally via fraudulent accounting.

1. The effect that overstating or understating inventories has on a company's financial statements is measured by using the basic inventory equation:

   Ending inventory = Beginning inventory + Purchases – COGS

   COGS = Beginning inventory + Purchases – Ending inventory

2. Figure 9 summarizes the effect overstatement and understatement of ending inventory has on the balance sheet (total assets) and income statement (COGS and net income).

   Figure 9: Effect of Overstating/Understating Ending Inventory

Ending Inventory	Effect on Total Assets	Effect on COGS	Effect on Net Income
Overstated	Overstated	Understated	Overstated
Understated	Understated	Overstated	Understated

3. As an example, let's assume a company's ending inventory in Year 1 was overstated by $1,000. As a result, in Year 1 COGS will be understated, net income (before taxes) will be overstated, and ending inventory will be overstated, all by $1,000.

©2007 Kaplan CPA Review

STUDY MANUAL – BUSINESS ENVIRONMENT & CONCEPTS
CHAPTER 3

4. If ending inventory is correctly measured at the end of Year 2, the balance sheet at the end of Year 2 will be correct. However, the overstatement of beginning inventory in Year 2 (which is ending inventory in Year 1) will cause the Year 2 COGS to be overstated by $1,000 and the Year 2 net income to be understated by $1,000.

5. Figure 10 illustrates how an ending inventory valuation error in year 1 is resolved by the end of Year 2 if ending inventory is corrected by the end of Year 2.

Figure 10: Correlation of ending inventory valuation error

	Year 1	Year 2
Beginning Inventory	—	(O) 1,000
Plus: Purchases	—	—
Less: Ending Inventory	(O) $1,000	—
COGS	(U) 1,000	(O) 1,000
Net Income	(O) $1,000	(U) 1,000

6. Because the choice of inventory accounting method impacts income statement and balance sheet items, it also affects financial indicators such as profitability and asset ratios. In general, an analyst should use LIFO values when examining profitability or cost ratios and FIFO values when examining asset or equity ratios.

EFFECTS ON PROFITABILITY OF DIFFERENT INVENTORY METHODS

A. As we have seen, when prices are rising, COGS reported under LIFO will be higher, and net income reported under LIFO will be lower than that reported under FIFO because the prices used to compute costs are more recent.

1. As a result of the lower income under LIFO, all profitability ratios, such as gross margin and net margin, will be lower under LIFO.

2. Because costs under LIFO are higher, and therefore a more accurate reflection of economic costs, analysts evaluating firms that use FIFO should recompute all of the firm's profitability ratios using values adjusted to LIFO.

EFFECTS ON LIQUIDITY ANALYSIS OF DIFFERENT INVENTORY METHODS

A. Compared to LIFO, FIFO produces ending inventory figures that are higher and are a better measure of economic value. LIFO inventory figures use prices that are outdated and have less relevance to the economic value of ending inventory.

1. Because ending inventory values are higher under FIFO, measures of liquidity (e.g., the current ratio) are higher under FIFO than under LIFO, and ratios calculated using FIFO are more accurate for comparison purposes.

Page 112 ©2007 Kaplan CPA Review

STUDY MANUAL – BUSINESS ENVIRONMENT & CONCEPTS
CHAPTER 3

2. Looking back, the current ratio is the best known measure of liquidity: Current ratio = Current assets/Current liabilities. The higher the current ratio, the more likely it is the company will be able to pay its short-term bills.

3. For firms using FIFO, because COGS under LIFO is higher, and therefore a more accurate reflection of economic costs, analysts should recompute all of the firms, profitability ratios using values adjusted to LIFO.

4. For firms that use LIFO, liquidity ratios should be recalculated using ending inventory balances that have been restated to FIFO by adding the LIFO reserve to LIFO ending inventory.

EFFECT ON INVENTORY TURNOVER OF DIFFERENT INVENTORY METHODS

A. The key activity ratio that is affected by the choice of accounting method is inventory turnover, which is computed by dividing COGS by average inventory.

1. Because COGS is higher under LIFO, and inventory is lower under LIFO, the inventory turnover ratio is always higher when using LIFO than when using FIFO.

2. Looking back, inventory turnover measures a firm's efficiency with respect to its processing and inventory management: Inventory turnover = COGS/Average inventory.

3. Given that LIFO produces a better current estimate of COGS, while FIFO produces a better current estimate of ending inventory, analysts prefer to compute inventory turnover on a current cost basis, by dividing COGS under LIFO by average inventory measured using FIFO.

EFFECT ON LEVERAGE OF DIFFERENT INVENTORY METHODS

A. The use of FIFO produces higher inventory and higher income versus LIFO. Leverage ratios such as the total debt ratio and debt-to-equity ratio will be lower under FIFO because the denominators under FIFO are higher. Equity is higher due to the higher income that comes through via the change in retained earnings.

1. Because FIFO is a more accurate measure of ending inventory, analysts should adjust stockholders' equity as well as inventory by adding the LIFO reserve (net of any income tax adjustment) to stockholders' equity.

EFFECT ON CASH FLOW OF DIFFERENT INVENTORY METHODS

A. Cash flow will be higher under LIFO than cash flow under FIFO solely because taxable income is lower under LIFO, which means the company will pay less taxes.

©2007 Kaplan CPA Review

Page 113

STUDY MANUAL – BUSINESS ENVIRONMENT & CONCEPTS
CHAPTER 3

Except for the tax effect, there are no cash flow implications of the inventory accounting method chosen. (See Figure 11 for a LIFO/FIFO recap.)

Figure 11: LIFO and FIFO: Comparison and Suitability

Financial Indicator	LIFO	FIFO	Ideal Choice
Profitability	Lower	Higher	LIFO
Liquidity	Lower	Higher	FIFO
Turnover	Higher	Lower	LIFO for COGS, FIFO for inventory
Leverage	Higher	Lower	FIFO
Cash flow	Higher	Lower	Method the company is using

SOLVENCY AND OFF-BALANCE-SHEET FINANCING

A. An important aspect of financial statement analysis is understanding a company's solvency, or the company's ability to pay its liabilities when due and continue as a going concern (going concern is an accounting term referring to a company's ability to continue in the future). A company's use of debt is a key component in assessing solvency by determining whether the company is overleveraged. Companies issue debt via mortgages, loans, and bonds to finance growth, versus using existing equity. It is important to understand the basics of debt and how it affects the financial statements and related financial indicators.

1. Off-balance-sheet accounting refers to the methods a company can use to keep certain assets and liabilities off its balance sheet. Often the motivation for off-balance-sheet accounting is to improve solvency and other debt-related financial risk ratios by transferring business risk from the parent company onto unconsolidated businesses.

2. The following are primary ways to move assets and liabilities "off the balance sheet."

   a. Joint ventures, subsidiaries, or partnerships that do not meet requirements for consolidation.

   b. Leasing or other financing agreements.

3. Typically, off-balance-sheet companies are separate legal entities that are jointly financed by the parent company and independent outside investors. The Financial Accounting Standards Board (FASB) refers to these relationships as variable interest entities (VIE), although they are also called special purpose entities. Generally, these arrangements are legitimate and considered by both Generally Accepted Accounting Principles (GAAP) and the Internal Revenue Service (IRS) as valid methods to finance high-risk business investments—for

Page 114   ©2007 Kaplan CPA Review

instance, investing in a line of business substantially different from the parent company.

4. Since the Enron scandal, off-balance-sheet accounting has received much negative attention. In response, the FASB issued *Interpretation No. 46*, "Consolidation of Variable Interest Entities." The objective of this interpretation was not to restrict the use of VIE but to improve financial reporting by the enterprise involved with the VIE. The FASB believes that if a business has a controlling financial interest (regardless of the percentage of ownership), the assets, liabilities, and results of activities should be included in the company's financial statements.

EFFECT OF LEASING ALTERNATIVES

A. If the lease is classified as an operating lease, no entry is made at the inception of the lease. The payments made by the lessee are treated as rent expense and charged to income and operating cash flow.

Example: Operating lease

Timber, Inc., leases a saw from ABC Leasing for $85,000 per year. Assume the lease is an operating lease. How will Timber account for the first year of the lease?

Answer

The accounting entry will be to decrease (credit) cash and increase (debit) an expense account, equipment lease expense, for the full amount of the $85,000 in rent paid by Timber.

A lease classified as a capital lease for accounting purposes is reported as a depreciable asset, which is financed by debt. The transactions to record a capital lease impact both sides of the balance sheet.

At the inception of the lease, the lessee creates a leasehold asset and a leasehold liability in the amount of the present value of the lease payments.

The interest expense portion of the lease payment is calculated each year by multiplying the year's beginning value of the leasehold liability by the discount rate on the lease.

The leasehold liability at the end of each year is calculated by subtracting the principal portion of the lease payment (the difference between the lease payment and interest expense) from the beginning liability balance.

The principal repayment is not charged against income or operating cash flow. It is considered a financing cash flow.

The asset is depreciated over the life of the lease when no transfer or bargain purchase exists, or over the life of the asset otherwise. Depreciation is charged to income, but does not affect operating cash flow.

STUDY MANUAL – BUSINESS ENVIRONMENT & CONCEPTS
CHAPTER 3

Example: Capital lease

Affordable Products Company leases a machine. The following are the terms of the lease:

- Four years with annual, end-of-year payments of $10,000.
- At the end of the lease, the lessor regains possession, and the asset is expected to be sold for scrap value.
- The discount rate on the lease is 6 percent.
- Affordable's incremental borrowing rate is 7 percent.

Calculate the immediate impact of the lease on Affordable's balance sheet and the impact on Affordable's income statement and balance sheet for each of the next four years. Affordable depreciates all of its assets on a straight-line basis.

Answer

- The lease is classified as a capital lease, because the asset is being leased for at least 75 percent of its useful life (we know this because at the end of the lease term the asset will be sold for scrap).
- The lease should be capitalized at 6 percent, the lower of the discount rate on the lease and Affordable's incremental borrowing rate.
- The present value of the lease payments at 6 percent is $34,651.

$$N = 4; \quad I/Y = 6; \quad PMT = 10,000; \quad FV = 0; \quad CPT \rightarrow PV = \$34,651$$

This $34,651 is immediately recorded on the balance sheet as both an asset (leasehold asset) and a liability (leasehold liability).

Straight-line depreciation will reduce income ($34,651/4) $8,663 per year and reduce the value of the leasehold asset account on the balance sheet by the same amount. The leasehold asset will be $25,988; $17,325; $8,662; and $0 at the end of each of the next four years, respectively.

Interest expense will reduce income in each year by the beginning leasehold liability in column 1 (see Figure 12) multiplied by the interest rate of 6 percent. The leasehold liability account on the balance sheet will have the values shown in column 4.

Figure 12: Leasehold Liability Computations

Year	(1) Beginning Leasehold Liability	(2) Interest Expense (1) × 6% on Income Stmt.	(3) Lease Payment	(4) Ending Leasehold Liability (1) + (2) - (3) on Balance Sheet
0				$34,651
1	$34,651	$2,079	$10,000	$26,730
2	$26,730	$1,604	$10,000	$18,334
3	$18,334	$1,100	$10,000	$9,434
4	$9,434	$566	$10,000	$0

Figures 13 and 14 summarize the differences between the effects of capital leases and operating leases on the financial statements (in general):

Figure 13: Financial Statement Impact of Leasing Decisions

Financial Statement Totals	Capital Lease	Operating Lease
Assets	Higher	Lower
Liabilities	Higher	Lower
Operating income	Higher	Lower
Net income (in the early years)	Lower	Higher
Cash flow from operations	Higher	Lower
Cash flow from financing	Lower	Higher
Total cash flow	Same	Same

Figure 14: Ratio Impact of Leasing Decisions

Ratios	Capital Lease	Operating Lease
Asset turnover	Lower	Higher
Return on assets	Lower	Higher
Return on equity	Lower	Higher
Debt-to-equity	Higher	Lower

B. Balance sheet effects.

1. Because capital leases increase recorded assets and liabilities:

   a. Turnover ratios that use total or fixed assets in their denominators will appear lower for capital leases relative to operating leases.

   b. Return on assets will be lower for capital leases.

   c. Leverage ratios (e.g., total debt ratio and debt-to-equity ratio) will be higher with capital leases because of the larger amount of liabilities.

STUDY MANUAL – BUSINESS ENVIRONMENT & CONCEPTS
CHAPTER 3

Example: Balance sheet effects of leasing

Let's compare two companies.

Figure 15: Selected Financial Data for Knotting Corp. and Lace Inc.

	Knotting Corp.	Lace Inc.
Assets at beginning of year	$45,000	$45,000
Capital leasehold asset	7,500	0
Assets at end of year	52,500	45,000
Liabilities at beginning of year	23,000	23,000
Capital leasehold liability	7,500	0
Liabilities at end of year	30,500	23,000
Equity	22,000	22,000
Sales	295,000	295,000

The Knotting Corp. leased a machine in 20X5 and classified it as a capital lease. Knotting recorded a leasehold asset of $7,500. Lace uses operating leases and has no capital leases. Calculate the asset turnover and debt-to-equity ratios for 20X5. Note: Assume the beginning of the year liabilities include no long-term debt.

Answer

Knotting's asset turnover is 6.05 ($295,000/$48,750), while Lace's is 6.56 ($295,000/$45,000). Knotting's average assets are higher, since the lease was capitalized, resulting in a lower asset turnover ratio. Note: $48,750 represents Knotting's *average assets* for 20X5.

Knotting's debt-to-equity ratio is 1.39 ($30,500/$22,000), compared to Lace's 1.05 ($23,000/$22,000).

C. Income statement effects.

1. Operating income is higher for capital leases than for operating leases, because the depreciation expense for a capital lease is always less than the lease payments, which are expenses under an operating lease.

2. From the Affordable Products example, note that depreciation expense is $8,663 for a capital lease, while lease expense of $10,000 would be subtracted in calculating operating income if the lease were treated as an operating lease.

3. Net income. Although the lease payments and depreciation are constant, interest expense is higher in the first few years of the lease (typical of an amortizing loan). Consequently, net income in the first few years of the lease will be lower for capital leases because the sum of depreciation and interest expense exceeds the lease payment early in the lease's life.

4. This is illustrated in the Affordable Products example and is summarized in Figure 16. The depreciation expense of $8,663 plus the interest expense of $2,079 (see column 2 of Figure 16) in the first year reduces net income by a total

Page 118   ©2007 Kaplan CPA Review

STUDY MANUAL – BUSINESS ENVIRONMENT & CONCEPTS
CHAPTER 3

of $10,742. In the fourth year, interest expense is only $566, so the net income reduction is $9,228. In each of the four years of the Affordable Products example, if the lease had been classified as an operating lease, the reduction in net income would have been $10,000 in lease expense.

Figure 16: Expense Items

Expense	Capital	Operating	Difference
Year 1	$10,742	$10,000	$742
Year 2	10,267	10,000	267
Year 3	9,763	10,000	-237
Year 4	9,228	10,000	-772
Cumulative	40,000	40,000	0

As Figure 16 illustrates, measured over the entire lease term, total income will be the same for operating and capital leases. This is because the sum of the depreciation plus the interest expense will equal the total of the lease payments over the life of the lease. In the Affordable Products example, depreciation expense ($8,663 multiplied by three years and $8,662 in the last year) plus interest expense ($2,079 + $1,604 + $1,100 + $566) total $40,000 over four years, the same as the sum of the four $10,000 lease expense entries that would be made for an operating lease.

D. Cash flow effects.

1. Capital lease.

   a. Cash flow from operations (CFO). The interest expense portion of the lease payment is treated as an operating cash flow.

   b. Cash flow from financing (CFF). The principal portion of the lease payment is treated as a financing cash flow.

   c. Depreciation. Under a capital lease depreciation does not affect cash flows.

2. Although CFO is higher, CFF is lower for a capital lease. Note that net cash flow is the same under both methods.

3. Operating lease:

   a. CFO. The entire lease payment is expensed on the income statement and treated as a CFO. Thus, CFO is lower for operating leases.

   b. CFF. An operating lease does not affect CFF.

Example: Lease comparison

Referring back to the Affordable Products Company example, calculate the differences between the lease being classified as an operating lease and a capital lease on the following income statement, balance sheet, and cash flow items:

©2007 Kaplan CPA Review

Page 119

STUDY MANUAL – BUSINESS ENVIRONMENT & CONCEPTS
CHAPTER 3

1. Total assets at the beginning of year 1

2. Total debt at the beginning of year 1

3. Shareholders' equity at the beginning of year 1

4. Operating income

5. Net income

6. CFO

7. CFF

8. Net cash flow

Answer

Figure 17: Differences Between Capital and Operating Leases for Affordable Products

Year 1	Capital	Operating	Difference
Total assets	$34,651	0	Higher by $34,651
Total debt	$34,651	0	Higher by $34,651
Shareholders' equity	0	0	No difference
Operating income	Decrease by $8,663	Decrease by $10,000	Higher by $1,337
Net income	Decrease by $10,742	Decrease by $10,000	Lower by $742
CFO	Decrease by $2,079	Decrease by $10,000	Higher by $7,921
CFF	Decrease by $7,921	No effect	Lower by $7,921
Net cash flow	Decrease by $10,000	Decrease by $10,000	No difference

1.&2.   Assets and total debt will be $34,651 higher for the capital lease than for the operating lease because the present value of the lease payments is recorded on the financial statements under a capital lease.

3.   There will be no difference in shareholders' equity at the beginning of the year.

4.   The depreciation expense of $8,663 for the capital lease is the only deduction in calculating operating income (interest expense is typically not shown as an operating income item on the income statement). The deduction in calculating operating income for the operating lease is the $10,000 lease payment. Operating income will be $10,000 - $8,663 = $1,337 higher for the capital lease.

5.   The deductions in calculating net income for the capital lease are the interest expense of $2,079 and the depreciation expense of $8,663, for a total of $10,742.

Page 120   ©2007 Kaplan CPA Review

The deduction in calculating net income for the operating lease is the $10,000 lease payment. Net income will be $10,742 - $10,000 = $742 lower for the capital lease.

6. The only deduction from CFO for the capital lease is the interest expense of $2,079. The deduction from CFO for the operating lease is the $10,000 lease payment. CFO will be $10,000 - $2,079 = $7,921 higher for the capital lease.

7. The principal reduction (lease payment of $10,000 less interest expense of $2,079) of $7,921 in year 1 under the capital lease is a reduction in CFF. There is no CFF effect from an operating lease.

8. Net cash flow is a decrease of $10,000 under either method.

Now let's proceed to make the same calculations for year 2:

1. Total assets at the beginning of year 2

2. Total debt at the beginning of year 2

3. Shareholders' equity at the beginning of year 2

4. Operating income

5. Net income

6. CFO

7. CFF

8. Net cash flow

STUDY MANUAL – BUSINESS ENVIRONMENT & CONCEPTS
CHAPTER 3

Answer

Figure 18: Year 2 Differences Between Capital and Operating Leases for Affordable Products Company

Year 2	Capital	Operating	Difference
Total assets	$25,988	0	Higher by $25,988
Total debt	$26,730	0	Higher by $26,730
Shareholders' equity	Lower by $742	0	Lower by $742
Operating income	Decrease by $8,663	Decrease by $10,000	Higher by $1,337
Net income	Decrease by $10,267	Decrease by $10,000	Lower by $267
CFO	Decrease by $1,604	Decrease by $10,000	Higher by $8,396
CFF	Decrease by $8,396	No effect	Lower by $8,396
Net cash flow	Decrease by $10,000	Decrease by $10,000	No difference

1. Assets will be $25,988 ($34,651 - $8,663 depreciation in year 1) higher for the capital lease than for the operating lease.

2. Debt will be $26,730 higher for the capital lease.

3. Shareholders' equity will be $742 lower at the beginning of the year for the capital lease due to the lower net income in year 1 for the capital lease. Note that the balance sheet balances. Assets are higher by $25,988 and liabilities and owner's equity is higher by the same amount ($26,730 - $742).

4. Just as in year 1, the only deduction in year 2 in calculating operating income for the capital lease is the depreciation expense of $8,663 (interest expense is listed below the operating income line on the income statement). The deduction in calculating operating income for the operating lease is the $10,000 lease payment. Operating income will again be $10,000 - $8,663 = $1,337 higher for the capital lease.

5. The deductions in calculating net income for the capital lease are the interest expense of $1,604 and the depreciation expense of $8,663, for a total of $10,267. The deduction in calculating net income for the operating lease is the $10,000 lease payment. Net income will be $10,267 - $10,000 = $267 lower for the capital lease.

Page 122   ©2007 Kaplan CPA Review

STUDY MANUAL – BUSINESS ENVIRONMENT & CONCEPTS
CHAPTER 3

6. The only deduction from cash flow from operations for the capital lease is the interest expense of $1,604. The deduction from cash flow from operations for the operating lease is the $10,000 lease payment. CFO will be $10,000 - $1,604 = $8,396 higher for the capital lease.

7. The principal reduction (lease payment of $10,000 less interest expense of $1,604) of $8,396 in year 2 under the capital lease is a reduction in CFF. There is no CFF effect from an operating lease.

8. Net cash flow in year 2 is a decrease of $10,000 under either method.

ADVANTAGES AND DISADVANTAGES OF THE DIFFERENT LEASE CLASSIFICATIONS

Companies consider many issues when negotiating a lease. Some issues relate to the accounting classification (operating or capital) that will apply to their leased assets.

A. Advantages of operating leases to a lessee

1. General advantages:

a. The period of use may be short compared to the economic life of the asset.

b. Bond covenants may restrict the addition of debt to a company's financial picture (an operating lease does not affect the amount of debt reported).

c. Lessee may be in a worse position than lessor to resell the asset on favorable terms upon lease termination.

2. Financial reporting advantages:

a. The lessee's net income is higher in the early years than it is with a capital lease.

b. The lessee's assets and debt are lower, making leverage ratios appear lower, and turnover ratios and return on assets appear higher.

B. Advantages of capital leases to the lessee

1. General advantages:

a. The period of use is similar to or longer than the economic life of the asset.

b. Lessee may be able to resell the asset favorably after a long period of use.

2. Financial reporting advantages:

a. Lessee shows higher asset levels (but also higher debt levels).

b. Lessee CFO appears higher with a capital lease than with an operating lease.

©2007 Kaplan CPA Review

Page 123

STUDY MANUAL – BUSINESS ENVIRONMENT & CONCEPTS
CHAPTER 3

QUESTIONS: FINANCE: RATIO ANALYSIS

1. Which of the following is a key determinant of operating leverage?
   A. The firm's beta.
   B. The trade-off between fixed and variable costs.
   C. Level and cost of debt.
   D. The competitive nature of business.

2. Following is an income statement for year X. Assume variable costs will remain the same percentage of sales, fixed costs will remain the same, and the corporate tax rate remains constant. Use this information to determine the financial leverage of the company.

Revenue	$1,000
Variable costs of sales	400
Fixed costs	300
EBIT	300
Interest expense	100
Taxable income	200
Tax	80
Net income after tax	$120

   The financial leverage (degree of financial leverage) for the company is
   A. 1.10.
   B. 1.80.
   C. 2.00.
   D. 1.50.

3. An analyst has gathered the following expenditure information for four different firms, each of which has a sales level of $4 million.

   Costs for firms under construction. All values in millions of dollars

	Firm			
	A	B	C	D
Variable costs	$2.40	$2.00	$0.80	$2.80
Fixed costs	$1.20	$1.00	$2.80	$1.40
Interest expense	$0.00	$0.20	$0.00	$0.20

   Which firm has the highest level of operating leverage?
   A. Firm A.
   B. Firm B.
   C. Firm C.
   D. Firm D.

STUDY MANUAL – BUSINESS ENVIRONMENT & CONCEPTS
CHAPTER 3

4. Successful use of financial leverage is evidenced by a:
   A. rate of return on sales greater than the cost of debt.
   B. rate of return on sales greater than the rate of return on stockholders' equity.
   C. rate of return on investment greater than the rate of return on stockholders' equity.
   D. rate of return on investment greater than the cost of debt.

5. All else equal, a firm's sensitivity to swings in the business cycle is higher when:
   A. fixed costs are the highest portion of its expense.
   B. variable costs are the highest portion of its expense.
   C. variable and fixed costs are roughly in the same proportion.
   D. the firm has low operating leverage.

6. On December 31, year 7, North Park Co. collected a receivable due from a major customer. Which of the following ratios would be increased by this transaction?
   A. Current ratio.
   B. Receivable turnover ratio.
   C. Quick ratio.
   D. Inventory turnover ratio.

7. North Bank is analyzing Belle Corp.'s financial statements for a possible extension of credit. Belle's quick ratio is significantly better than the industry average. Which of the following factors should North Bank consider as a possible limitation of using this ratio when evaluating Belle's creditworthiness?
   A. Belle may need to sell its available-for-sale investments to meet its current obligations.
   B. Belle may need to liquidate its inventory to meet its long-term obligations.
   C. Fluctuating market prices of short-term investments may adversely affect the ratio.
   D. Increasing market prices for Belle's inventory may adversely affect the ratio.

8. Are the following ratios useful in assessing the liquidity position of a company: Defensive-interval ratio? Return on stockholders' equity?
   A. Yes; no.
   B. No; yes.
   C. Yes; yes.
   D. No; no.

9. Which of the following is a measure of a firm's liquidity?
   A. ROE.
   B. Cash ratio.
   C. Net profit margin.
   D. Equity turnover.

©2007 Kaplan CPA Review

Page 125

STUDY MANUAL – BUSINESS ENVIRONMENT & CONCEPTS
CHAPTER 3

10. Assume a firm with a debt-to-equity ratio of 0.50 and debt equal to $35 million makes a commitment to acquire raw materials with a present value of $12 million over the next three years. For purposes of analysis, the best estimate of the debt-to-equity ratio should be:
   A. 0.573.
   B. 0.500.
   C. 0.343.
   D. 0.671.

11. Cash that normally would have been used to pay the company's accounts payable is used instead to pay off some of the company's long-term debt. This will cause the company's:
   A. current ratio to rise.
   B. payables turnover to rise.
   C. quick ratio to fall.
   D. cash conversion cycle to lengthen.

12. If the inventory turnover ratio is seven, what is the average number of days the inventory is in stock?
   A. 25 days.
   B. 36 days.
   C. 52 days.
   D. 70 days.

13. Which of the following financial ratios is NOT used to gauge a firm's internal liquidity?
   A. Cash ratio.
   B. Quick ratio.
   C. Current ratio.
   D. Gross profit margin ratio.

14. If a company has a great deal of inventory built up, which of the following ratios would be the largest?
   A. Cash ratio.
   B. Quick ratio.
   C. Current ratio.
   D. Gross profit margin ratio.

15. Given the following information about a company:
   - Net sales = $1,000.
   - Cost of goods sold = $600.
   - Operating expenses = $200.
   - Interest expenses = $50.
   - Tax rate = 34%.

   What are the gross and operating profit margins, respectively?
   A. 20%; 10%
   B. 40%; 10%
   C. 20%; 15%
   D. 40%; 20%

Page 126   ©2007 Kaplan CPA Review

STUDY MANUAL – BUSINESS ENVIRONMENT & CONCEPTS

CHAPTER 3

16. An analyst gathered the following data about a company:
*   Current liabilities are $300.
*   Total debt is $900.
*   Working capital is $200.
*   Capital expenditures are $250.
*   Total assets are $2,000.
*   Cash flow from operations is $400.

If the company would like a current ratio of 2, it could:
A. increase current assets by 100 or decrease current liabilities by 50.
B. decrease current assets by 100 or increase current liabilities by 50.
C. decrease current assets by 100 or decrease current liabilities by 50.
D. increase current assets by 100 or increase current liabilities by 50.

17. Skipper Enterprises runs half-day yacht tours off the coast of Oahu. To meet borrowing covenants in the operating line of credit, accountant Gilligan Whitecap must somehow increase the current ratio above the current level of 1.4. Of the following options, Whitecap is most likely to:
A. purchase supplies on credit.
B. use cash to retire a short-term note payable to creditor Thurston.
C. sell two of the company's marketable securities (price equal to book value).
D. ask employees Hinkley, Summer, and Grant to go an extra week without being paid.

18. Which of the following ratios would NOT be useful to evaluate a company's operating efficiency?
A. Equity turnover.
B. Total asset turnover.
C. Fixed asset turnover.
D. Quick ratio.

19. All else equal, which of the following will help decrease a company's total debt-to-equity ratio?
A. Buying Treasury stock.
B. Lowering the dividend payout ratio.
C. Paying cash dividends to stockholders.
D. Converting long-term debt to short-term debt.

20. The cash conversion cycle is the:
A. length of time it takes to sell inventory.
B. length of time it takes the firm to pay the credit extended to it for purchases.
C. sum of the time it takes to sell inventory and collect on accounts receivable, less the time it takes to pay for credit purchases.
D. sum of the time it takes to sell inventory and the time it takes to collect accounts receivable.

©2007 Kaplan CPA Review

Page 127

ANSWERS: FINANCE: RATIO ANALYSIS

1. **B** Operating leverage can be defined as the trade-off between variable and fixed costs. Beta is a measure of the relationship between an investment's returns and the market's returns. This is a measure of the investment's nondiversifiable risk.

2. **D** The degree of financial leverage is defined as the change in the net income relative to the change in the EBIT.

    If EBIT is increased and the remainder of the income statement is calculated, the relationship between the change in EBIT and the change in income can be determined. Any percentage change in EBIT can be used, and 10 percent is used here.

EBIT	$300	$300
(increase EBIT by 10%, to $330) Interest expense	100	100
Taxable income	200	230
Tax (revised due to increase in EBIT)	80	92
Net income after tax	$120	$138

    The change in EBIT was 10%. ($330/$300) − 1 = 0.10 or 10%.

    The change in net income was ($138/$120) −1 = 0.15 or 15%.

    $$\text{The degree of financial leverage} = \frac{15\%}{10\%} = 1.50.$$

    At this level of sales, for every 1 percent change in EBIT, net income will change by 1.50 percent. This relationship will be different at different levels of EBIT.

3. **C.** Operating leverage is a function of the relationship between fixed and variable costs. The higher the percentage of fixed costs, the higher the operating leverage. The percentage of total costs that are fixed for the four companies is as follows:

    Firm A: $1.20/($2.40 + $1.20)
          = $1.20/$3.60
          = 0.33

    Firm B: $1.00/($2.00 + $1.00)
          = $1.00/$3.00
          = 0.33

    Firm C: $2.80/($0.80 + $2.80)
          = $2.80/$3.60
          = 0.78

Firm D: $1.40/($1.40 + $2.80)$
= $1.40/$4.20$
= 0.33

Note: Interest expense does not play a role in this analysis.

4. **D** Financial leverage results from the use of fixed cost debt securities in the capital structure of an entity. Successful use of leverage (favorable leverage) results when invested funds earn more than the cost of borrowing the funds.

5. **A** The higher the percentage of a firm's costs that are fixed, the higher its operating leverage; therefore, the greater the firm's business risk and the more susceptible it is to business cycle fluctuations.

6. **B** Receivable turnover ratio

   Accounts receivable turnover = Sales/Average accounts receivable

   Collection of accounts receivable would reduce the accounts receivable balance and resulting average accounts receivable. This reduction in the denominator of the AR turnover ratio would result in an increase in the whole fraction.

7. **C** The quick ratio includes the current assets that can be "quickly" converted to cash such as cash, marketable securities, and receivables. Therefore, fluctuating market prices for short-term investments (marketable securities) may adversely affect the ratio.

8. **A** The defensive-interval ratio is a measure of liquidity, which is the company's ability to meet operating cash needs without external cash flows.

$$\text{defensive interval ratio} = \frac{\text{cash + ST mk. sec. + ST sec.}}{\text{av. daily expenditures for operations}}$$

   ST = short term

   The rate of return on stockholders' equity is a measure of profitability (to the owners).

9. **B** Equity turnover, ROE, and net profit margin are all measures of a company's operating performance. The cash ratio is (cash + marketable securities) divided by current liabilities. It is a measure of how fast a company can pay off current liabilities.

10. **D** The original debt-to-equity ratio = $35/70 = 0.5$. Now adjust the numerator but not the denominator. Why? You have commitments (liabilities) but no new equity.
    Debt-to-equity = $(35 + 12)/70 = 0.671$.

11. **C** The quick ratio = (Cash + Receivables)/Current liabilities. Therefore, if cash is reduced, the numerator will decrease, which will cause the ratio to decrease.

12. **C** Average inventory processing period = 365/Inventory turnover = $365/7 = 52$ days.

13. **D** The gross profit margin ratio is a measure of a firm's operating performance. The other three ratios measure liquidity.

©2007 Kaplan CPA Review

STUDY MANUAL – BUSINESS ENVIRONMENT & CONCEPTS
CHAPTER 3

14. **C** The current ratio is the only one out of the current, cash, and quick ratios that has total current assets (thus inventory) in the numerator, making it the largest of the three ratios. Gross profit margin ratio measures gross profit as a percentage of sales, and is not a balance sheet ratio.

15. **D** Gross profit margin = ($1000 net sales - $600 COGS)/$1000 net sales = 400/1000 = 0.4

   Operating profit margin = ($1000 net sales – $600 COGS – $200 operating expenses) / $1,000 net sales

   = $200 / $1,000

   = 0.2

16. **A** First, calculate the current ratio based on the above information. Remember that CA – CL = working capital, and working capital + CL = current assets, so current assets = $500, or $200 + $300 = $500. The current ratio is Current assets/Current liabilities, or $500 / $300 = 1.67.

   For the current ratio to equal 2.0, current assets would need to move to $600 (or up by $100) or current liabilities would need to decrease to $250 (or down by $50).

17. **B** Since the current ratio is greater than one, decreasing a current asset to decrease a current liability will increase the current ratio. The other statements describe actions that will decrease the current ratio. Delaying payment to employees will result in an increase in accounts payable (current liability) with no corresponding increase in current assets. Since the current ratio is greater than one, increasing a current asset to increase a current liability (purchasing supplies on account) by the same amount will decrease the current ratio. Selling marketable securities with price equal to book value will not affect the current ratio.

18. **D** The quick ratio = (Cash + Marketable securities + Receivables)/ Current liabilities is used to evaluate a company's internal liquidity. The other three ratios are measures of operating efficiency (i.e., measures of how the company is using fixed assets, total assets, and equity).

19. **B** Buying Treasury stock and paying cash dividends will decrease stockholders' equity, and thus increase the debt/equity ratio. Converting long-term debt to short-term will have no effect on total debt or stockholders' equity. Lowering the dividend payout ratio will increase retained earnings, thus increasing stockholders' equity and decreasing debt-to-equity ratio.

20. **C** Cash conversion cycle = Average receivables collection period + Average inventory processing period – Payables payment period.

FINANCE: WORKING CAPITAL MANAGEMENT & LONG-TERM FINANCING

STUDY MANUAL – BUSINESS ENVIRONMENT & CONCEPTS
CHAPTER 4

Study Tip: Before you get too involved in studying for the CPA exam, make sure you know exactly why you want to pass this exam. It is much easier to do the necessary work if you have a clear understanding of why you want pass.

CAPITAL STRUCTURES: STRATEGIES FOR LONG- AND SHORT-TERM FINANCING

A. Working capital management (WCM) refers to managing a company's current assets and current liabilities. Net working capital (NWC) = CA - CL. The higher the level of NWC, the greater the firm's liquidity and the safer the position of the firm's creditors.

1. Managing current assets. Current assets generally consist of cash, marketable securities, accounts receivable, and inventory. CAs provide liquidity. However, most firms face a sharply upward sloping yield curve for the asset side of their balance sheet (it is harder to make additional profits as the amount of current assets continues to rise). Fixed assets generally earn a substantially higher return than current assets. For that reason, increased liquidity comes at the cost of reduced profitability. Firms, therefore, generally try to minimize their current assets without jeopardizing their ability to pay their bills on a timely basis or adversely impacting their credit rating.

   a. Cash. There are a number of reasons to hold cash:

      • Transactions balance (bill payments).
      • Compensating balance (balances required by a bank in order to grant a loan).
      • Precautionary balance (unexpected expenses).
      • Speculative balance (provides the ability to take advantage of opportunities).
      • Firms want to generate positive cash flow but then want to invest as much of that cash as possible in income-generating assets because cash is an idle asset (non income- producing).

©2007 Kaplan CPA Review

Page 131

STUDY MANUAL – BUSINESS ENVIRONMENT & CONCEPTS
CHAPTER 4

- Consequently, companies attempt to keep low cash balances. Cash can be replaced by lines of credit—prearranged borrowing levels from a bank.
- Generally if a line of credit is not utilized, then there is no cost to the firm.

2. Calculation of minimum cash balance.

   a. Cash conversion cycle is the time between the payment for raw materials and receiving cash for your finished goods. Computed as the average age of inventory (assume 80 days) + average age of accounts receivable (40 days) minus average age of accounts payable (30 days). Therefore, 90 days is the cash conversion cycle in this example. Goal is to shorten the cycle.

   b. Cash turnover = 365 days/Cash cycle. 365/90 = 4.06 times.

   c. Minimum cash balance (MCB) = Annual cash expenditures (assume $10m)/ Cash turnover. $10m/4.06 = $2,463,054.

   d. Opportunity cost. Determined as the MCB × Opportunity cost or Cost of capital. Assume a 10 percent opportunity cost. Then, there is $2,463,054 (0.10) or $246,305 in forgone revenue by holding $2,463,054 in a nonrevenue-producing asset.

3. Cash management techniques.

   a. Float is the difference between the balance shown in a checkbook and the balance on the bank's records. Net float is equal to disbursement float (the time between when you make a payment and your bank account is reduced) minus collections float (the time between when you make a collection and the bank account is increased). The goal is to improve your collection and clearing process so that you limit the time when cash is not available to be used in generating revenues. Float has three components:

      - Mail float (the time the money being paid or received takes to get to or from the other party).
      - Processing float (the time the company takes to process payments and collections).
      - Clearing (banking system) float (the time that it takes for money to get through the banking system). Methods available to speed up the process:
        - A lockbox plan speeds up collections and reduces float by having customers send their payments to local area post office boxes. Several times a day a bank (for a fee) opens the lockbox and deposits the checks in the bank. Lockboxes can make funds available two to five days faster.
        - Concentration banking. Customers send their payment to a local branch office rather than to headquarters. This reduces float. For example, Sears would have customers send their payment to the closest office rather than to its headquarters in Chicago.

Page 132   ©2007 Kaplan CPA Review

- Wire payments or automatic debit. Funds are automatically deducted from one account and deposited into another. (Electronic debits)
- Depository transfer checks (official bank check). Used to move funds from one account to another account of the same company without a signature being required.
- Zero balance account. A disbursement account on which a company writes checks, even though the balance is maintained at zero. When a check is written on the account, funds are automatically transferred into it by the bank from a master account held by the same company.

4. Marketable securities. Short-term (less than one year, mostly less than 270 days), highly liquid (easily converted into cash) securities that provide a positive (although usually low) rate of return. Treasury bills (U.S. government bonds), commercial paper (large corporate bonds), Certificates of Deposit (bank), Bankers Acceptance (international trade) are examples of marketable securities. Marketable securities are sometimes referred to as *money market securities*.

5. Inventory. The rate of return on inventory is negative. Costs such as insurance, taxes, and rent must be paid while inventory is held but do not increase the inventory's value. In addition, funds must be borrowed to finance these assets with a resulting interest cost. Inventory, although necessary to generate sales, can also be costly. Holding too little inventory may result in customer dissatisfaction and lost revenue. Holding too much inventory can result in increased carrying cost. Inventory costs fall into fixed (order costs) and variable (handling, insurance, storage) components. The goal is to minimize the total cost.

    a. Economic order quantity (EOQ) point. The formula to determine how many orders to place and how many units to order each time. EOQ is a function of order cost, the annual usage, and the variable cost of carrying a unit in inventory.

    b. Reorder point. The formula to determine when to place an order. Assume it takes a supplier five days to fill an order, the company uses 1,600 units per day, and works 365 days per year. Lead time (the number of days it takes the supplier to fill your order) multiplied by daily usage gives the numbers of units used while waiting for the order to be filled. Therefore, at 1,600 units per day for five days, the company should place an order when (1,600 × 5) = 8,000 units remain.

    c. Safety stock. The pure reorder point computed above assumes the new order arrives just as inventory levels reach zero. A safety stock provides a cushion if shipment is delayed. In the above example, if a safety stock of 100 is chosen, a new order should be placed when current level drops to 8,100 units.

    d. Just-in-time (JIT). An attempt to keep inventory levels close to zero. Suppliers arrive each day with sufficient raw materials to complete the day's scheduled production needs. JIT lowers the firm's cost of carrying inventory. JIT requires reliable suppliers and defect-free raw materials. It also leaves the company vulnerable to a supply disruption (strike).

STUDY MANUAL – BUSINESS ENVIRONMENT & CONCEPTS
CHAPTER 4

6. Accounts receivable management. Competitive forces require most firms to offer credit. Days sales outstanding (average collection period) is equal to annual sales/ 365. This measures collection performance and should be compared to the credit terms offered by the firm. An aging schedule breaks down the receivables by age of account. Credit terms involve stating the credit period and any discounts offered. The terms, 2/10 net 30, offer the buyer a 2 percent discount if the invoice is paid by the 10th day. If not, the balance is due in 30-days. Credit standards determine the criteria for determining who gets credit and how much. Collection policy is the procedures the firm uses to collect its receivables. Accounts receivable can be used to obtain financing for the firm. Pledging involves using the firm's accounts receivable as collateral for a loan. Factoring is the sale of accounts receivable at a discount from face value.

7. Managing current liabilities. There are three advantages to using short-term liabilities rather than long-term liabilities: (1) lower cost, (2) flexibility, and (3) ease of acquisition. The disadvantages are that the rates can change quickly, the debt must be periodically refinanced, and too much reliance on current liabilities may adversely impact liquidity and credit rating.

8. Financing current and fixed assets. Most businesses experience seasonal or cyclical variations in asset size. Several methods exist to finance a firm's assets. A matching maturity approach finances current assets with current liabilities and fixed assets with long-term funds. The advantage is that current liabilities are cheaper than long-term funds and the cost would be lower. In an exact match there would be zero net working capital (NWC), which would adversely impact liquidity. A conservative approach would finance all anticipated assets with long-term liabilities leaving current liabilities to cover unexpected financing needs. This policy results in maximum NWC and liquidity, but with a higher financing cost.

9. Bank loans and interest notes.

   a. Short-term bank loans.

      - A promissory note is a document that specifies the terms and conditions of a loan, the amount, interest rate, and repayment schedule.
      - A compensating balance is a minimum amount the borrower must maintain in a checking account at the bank, usually a percentage of the loan amount.
      - Line of credit is an agreement where the bank pre-approves the borrower up to a stated maximum debt level.
      - A revolving credit agreement is similar to a line of credit but the bank has a legal obligation to make the funds available to the borrower in exchange for a commitment fee. Interest rates tend to be variable and tied to the prime rate (the rate the banks charge their best business customers).
      - The prime rate plus points is the standard format where 100 basis points = 1%. Prime plus 150 basis points is Prime + 1.5%. Loans can be secured (with collateral) or unsecured.
      - LIBOR (London Interbank Offered Rate) is often used to price loans outside the United States; increasingly domestic loans are being priced at LIBOR plus points rather than prime plus points.

b. Commercial paper (CP). An unsecured, short-term (less than 270 days) promissory note of a large corporation with a very strong credit rating. Denominations are for $100,000 and up. CP is sold at a discount from face value and pays face value at maturity. The discount equates to the interest earned/paid. The commercial paper interest rate tends to be below the prime rate but above the Treasury bill rate.

c. Loan covenants. Requirements that the borrower must maintain (affirmative) or things they cannot do (negative) as a condition of the loan. Covenants are designed to protect the lender and ensure repayment of the loan. Common covenants include minimum levels of NWC as well as maintaining certain ratios such as the current ratio. There can also be limits on taking on additional debt without the permission of the existing debt holders. If a covenant is breached, the borrower is technically in default and the entire loan amount becomes due immediately.

d. Letter of credit (LOC). A document issued by a bank (for a fee) guaranteeing the payment of a customer's draft up to a stated amount and for a specified period. An LOC substitutes a bank's credit for that of the buyer, eliminating credit risk to the seller. LOCs are widely used in international trade transactions.

10. Interest on loans. Interest payments are tax-deductible expenses to a business. The after-tax cost of debt to a firm is the interest rate × (1 - tax rate). Dividends are not deductible as expenses so debt tends to have a lower after-tax cost than equity to the firm. Debt holders are paid before equity holders so debt has less risk than equity. Other advantages of debt are the fact that it does not involve dilution in ownership, and that debt can create beneficial leverage if the company can make a higher return on the money borrowed than it cost.

a. Fixed versus variable rates. Variable rate debt has its interest rate tied to an index (such as the prime rate) and fluctuates over time. Generally, variable rate debt has a lower rate than fixed rate debt for the same maturity. Variable rate debt is riskier to the borrower because the rate can escalate. Similarly, short-term debt costs less than long-term debt but is also riskier in regards to interest, since rates can increase and the debt must be regularly refinanced when it comes due in a short period of time.

Interest rates are expressed in nominal (stated rate to be paid on the contract) and real terms. Real interest rates are the rates being charged by lenders adjusted for inflation. If the bank charges 7 percent and inflation is 2 percent, the real interest rate is 5 percent. Historically, long-term real interest rates in the United States average around 4 percent. The Fisher effect states that nominal rates are comprised of the real rate demanded by investors increased by the expected rate of inflation.

Figure 1: Yield Curve

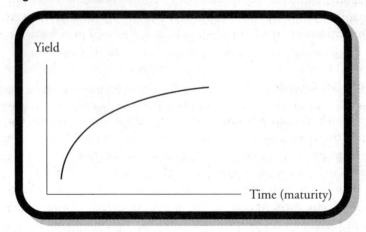

b. Term structure of interest rates. The yield curve (see Figure 1) diagrams the relationship between yields and maturity on U.S. government securities. Yields on government bills (a term of less than one year), notes (one to ten years), and bonds (greater than ten years) are plotted on this curve. The normal yield curve is upward sloping as shown above. Longer-term debt typically has higher risk than short-term debt because so many circumstances can change over time. A normal yield curve offers investors a trade-off between risk and return. Longer-term debt offers a higher return to offset the increased risk.

Three theories exist to explain the shape(s) of the yield curve:

- Liquidity preference theory. Investors prefer less risk to more and will only take an additional risk (longer maturity) if they are compensated with the additional return. Under this theory, the yield curve will always be upward sloping.
- Market segmentation theory. The term structure consists of multiple markets rather than a single market. There is a short-term, intermediate-term and long-term market for government securities. Supply and demand in each market determines the shape of the yield curve.
- Expectations theory. Investors' expectations about future interest rates determine the shape of the yield curve. When rates are expected to rise, the yield curve is upward sloping. If rates are expected to decline, the curve will be inverted. When investors are undecided as to the direction of interest rates it will be flat.

c. Stated (nominal) versus effective interest rates. The nominal rate is the rate stated on the loan, while the effective rate includes the effects of compounding.

d. Discount interest. A company borrows $10,000 for one year at 10 percent and makes only one payment at the end of the year of $11,000 ($10,000 principal + $1,000 interest). This is simple interest and the loan cost is 10 percent. However, if the bank requires the debtor to pay the interest in advance (discount interest), the interest payment is still $1,000 but the debtor only has $9,000 left to use after paying the interest. The effective cost is the interest paid divided by the money used or $1,000/$9,000 which is 11.11 percent even though the stated rate was 10 percent.

e.   Compensating balance. The bank charges 10 percent interest on a $10,000 loan at the end of the year but requires the debtor to keep a compensating balance of 15 percent ($1,500). The debtor cannot use the $1,500 so the effective cost is $1,000/$8,500 or 11.76 percent. If the bank asks for interest in advance ($1,000) and a 15 percent compensating balance ($1,500), the effective cost is $1,000/$7,500 or 13.33 percent.

f.   Add-on interest (installment loans). A debtor borrows $5,000 for 1 year at 10 percent to buy a used car. The 10 percent interest is add-on interest. You will make 12 equal monthly payments. Interest charged is $5,000 (original loan) multiplied by 10 percent (interest rate) or $500. $5,000 + $500 = $5,500 to be repaid divided by 12 gives a monthly payment of $458.33. However, the effective interest rate is 20 percent. The only time the debt was $5,000 was on day 1. On the last day of the year the debt was zero. The average loan balance was $2,500 but the debtor paid $500 in interest so that the rate is 20 percent ($500/$2,500).

g.   Annual percentage rate (APR). Rate reported by lenders when the effective rate exceeds the nominal rate of interest. The reporting of this rate is required by the Truth in Lending Laws. APR = Periods per year × Rate per period

CAPITAL STRUCTURE AND LEVERAGE

A.   Capital structure refers to the relative proportions of debt and equity the owners of a firm have used to finance operations. We can observe a firm's capital structure by examining its balance sheet. In Figure 2, we have reproduced the balance sheet for J&J Dogs. Capital structure gives information about the firm's long-term or permanent sources of capital. In the following balance sheet, we see the relationship between the long-term liabilities and the equity accounts.

Figure 2: J&J Dogs Balance Sheet, July 31, 200X

Current assets		Current liabilities	
Cash	$2,434	Accounts payable	$850
Inventory	1,150		
Supplies	750	Long-term liabilities	
Prepaid rent	1,000	Note payable	4,000
Prepaid insurance	3,000	Total liabilities	$4,850
Total current assets	$8,334		

Fixed assets

STUDY MANUAL – BUSINESS ENVIRONMENT & CONCEPTS
CHAPTER 4

Figure 2: J&J Dogs Balance Sheet, July 31, 200X

Equipment	3,100		
Less acc. depreciation	36		
Net fixed assets	3,064	Owner's equity	6,548
Total assets	$11,398	Total liabilities	
		plus owners' equity	$11,398

1. The typical large corporation has several different issues of long-term debt (bonds) outstanding, as well as a great deal of common stock and retained earnings. It is the relative proportions of these sources of financing that represent the capital structure of the firm.

2. If a firm with $1,000,000 in total assets is financed with $500,000 long-term debt (usually referred to simply as debt) and $500,000 common equity, we say the firm's debt ratio is 50 percent (i.e., $500,000/$1,000,000 = 0.50). Notice its equity ratio, the ratio of equity to total assets, is also 50 percent and its debt-to-equity ratio is $500,000/$500,000 = 1.0.

3. Capital structure will affect the rate at which the firm can borrow and the rate required by its equity holders. Management's choices for funding can affect not only the firm's cost of capital but the value of the firm as well.

4. A firm's target capital structure is the debt ratio that the firm tries to maintain over time and is typically similar to the average for the industry in which the firm operates. Should the firm's debt ratio fall below the target level, new capital needs will be satisfied by issuing debt. On the other hand, if the debt ratio is greater than the target level, the firm will raise new capital by retaining earnings or issuing new equity.

5. When setting its target capital structure, management must weigh the trade-off between risk and return associated with the use of debt, since the use of debt increases the risk borne by both shareholders and bondholders. However, using debt also leads to higher expected rates of return for stockholders. The higher risk associated with debt may depress stock prices, while the higher expected return may increase stock prices. Thus, the firm's optimal capital structure is the one that balances the influence of risk and return and maximizes the firm's stock price. The optimal debt ratio will be the firm's target capital structure.

CONSIDERATIONS IN DEFINING A COMPANY'S CAPITAL STRUCTURE

A. Four factors influence the firm's capital structure decision.

1. Business risk. This is the risk that is inherent to the firm's basic operations in the absence of debt. The greater the firm's business risk, the lower its optimal debt ratio.

a. For example, a public utility could be viewed as fairly low risk. Compared to most industrial firms, a public utility firm's demand is fairly predictable. Therefore, it is uncommon for utilities to face financial difficulties. On the other hand, a deep-sea exploration firm might be considered very risky. Not only does the ship and crew continually face the perils of the open sea, the probability of finding anything of value is remote.

b. Firms that face a high degree of business risk will typically maintain a larger proportion of equity in their capital structure.

2. Tax exposure. One of the reasons for using debt is the tax deductibility of interest payments. The tax deductibility of interest lowers the effective cost of using debt. You should note, however, that when a firm already has a low tax rate because its income is sheltered from taxes by depreciation, interest on current debt, or tax loss carry-forwards, additional debt will not be as advantageous as it would be for firms with higher effective tax rates.

3. Financial flexibility. This refers to a firm's ability to go to the capital markets during adverse times and raise funds at reasonable terms. If the firm already employs a good deal of debt, management might find it nearly impossible to sell new debt (i.e., the firm's capacity to hold debt has already been reached). Lower debt levels provide more financial flexibility.

4. The conservatism or aggressiveness of management. Firms with aggressive managers are more inclined to use debt in an effort to boost profits.

BUSINESS RISK AND FINANCIAL RISK

A. Business risk is the uncertainty inherent to a firm's return on assets (ROA). It is the most important consideration when a firm determines its capital structure. The following are the main factors affecting business risk:

1. Demand (unit sales) variability. The more variable a firm's sales, the higher the firm's business risk.

2. Sales (output) price variability. Volatile market prices will expose a firm to more business risk than that experienced by firms whose output prices are stable.

3. Input price variability. Firms have high business risk if their input costs, including product development costs, are uncertain.

4. Ability to adjust output prices as input prices change. A firm has low business risk if it can quickly raise the selling price to cover an increase in input costs.

5. Operating leverage (the extent to which costs are fixed relative to variable). The higher the percentage of a firm's costs that are fixed, the greater the firm's business risk.

STUDY MANUAL – BUSINESS ENVIRONMENT & CONCEPTS
CHAPTER 4

B. Financial risk refers to the additional risk common stockholders have to bear as the firm increases the use of debt and preferred stock as a source of financing. The degree to which a firm uses fixed income financing is measured using a concept referred to as financial leverage. As a firm's financial leverage increases, earnings per share become more sensitive to changes in sales.

THE RELATIONSHIP BETWEEN DEBT FINANCING AND EARNINGS PER SHARE

A. EBIT/EPS analysis. Changes in the use of debt will cause changes in the EPS and consequently in the stock's price. To understand this relationship you should work through the following example.

Example: Debt versus EPS

Suppose Jayco, Inc., has total assets of $200,000. The table in Figure 3 contains the cost of debt for Jayco.

Note that the higher the percentage of debt in the capital structure, the higher the interest rate.

Figure 3: Cost of Debt for Jayco, Inc.

Amount Borrowed	Debt/Assets Ratio	Interest Rate, k_d, on All Debt
$20,000	10%	8.0%
$40,000	20%	8.3%
$80,000	40%	10.0%
$100,000	50%	12.0%

Figure 4

	Project Atom	Project Beta
Price	$4.00	$4.00
Variable costs	$3.00	$2.00
Fixed costs	$40,000	$120,000
Assets	$400,000	$400,000
Tax rate	40%	40%

Suppose that Jayco has fixed costs of $40,000, variable costs are 60 percent of sales, and the tax rate is 40 percent. The total number of shares outstanding for Jayco at zero debt is 10,000. Assume that next period the firm's expected sales will be

$200,000. Given this level of sales, determine how different levels of debt will affect EPS.

Answer

You can calculate EPS with the following equations:

$$EPS = \frac{(\text{sales} - \text{fixed costs} - \text{variable costs} - \text{interest})(1 - \text{tax rate})}{\text{shares outstanding}}$$

$$EPS = \frac{(EBIT - 1)(1 - t)}{\text{shares outstanding}}$$

If debt-to-assets (D/A) = 0

$$EPS = \frac{(\$200,000 - \$40,000 - \$120,000 - 0)(0.6)}{10,000} = \$2.40$$

If D/A = 50%, then equity = 50%, implying 5,000 shares and debt = $100,000

$$EPS = \frac{(\$200,000 - \$40,000 - \$120,000 - \$12,000)(0.6)}{5,000} = \$3.36$$

Note that as Jayco issues debt to finance its assets, its EPS increases.

LEVERAGE

A. Operating leverage is the trade-off between variable costs and fixed costs. High operating leverage generally produces a higher expected rate of return. A firm is said to have high operating leverage if a high percentage of its total costs are fixed. Holding all else constant, high operating leverage indicates that a small change in sales will cause a large change in operating income.

B. The degree of operating leverage (DOL) is defined as the percentage change in operating income (EBIT) that results from a given percentage change in sales:

$$DOL = \frac{\text{percentage change in EBIT}}{\text{percentage change in sales}} = \frac{\frac{\Delta EBIT}{EBIT}}{\frac{\Delta Q}{Q}}$$

1. Another way to estimate DOL is:

$$DOL_Q = \text{degree of operating leverage in output units, } Q = \frac{Q(P - V)}{Q(P - V) - F}$$

STUDY MANUAL – BUSINESS ENVIRONMENT & CONCEPTS
CHAPTER 4

Alternatively, based on dollar sales rather than units, $DOL_S = \dfrac{S - VC}{S - VC - F}$

Example: Degree of operating leverage

Assume the quantity produced in the previous example was 100,000 units. **Calculate the degree of operating leverage (DOL) for projects Atom and Beta (see Figure 4).**

Answer

For Project Atom:

$$DOL_Q\,(Atom) = \frac{Q(P-V)}{[Q(P-V)-F]} = \frac{100,000(4-3)}{[100,000(4-3)-40,000]}$$

$$DOL_Q = (Atom) = \frac{100,000}{60,000} = 1.67$$

For Project Beta:

$$DOL_Q\,(Beta) = \frac{Q(P-V)}{[Q(P-V)-F]} = \frac{[100,000(4-2)]}{[100,000(4-2)-120,000]}$$

$$DOL_Q\,(Beta) = \frac{200,000}{80,000} = 2.5$$

The results suggest that if Project Beta has a 10 percent increase in sales, its EBIT will increase by 2.5 × 10% = 25%, while for Project Atom, the increase in EBIT will be 1.67 × 10% = 16.7%.

C. Financial leverage refers to the use of fixed-income securities, like debt and preferred stock.

1. As mentioned earlier, financial risk refers to the additional risk common stockholders have to bear because of financial leverage.

2. Financial leverage magnifies the variability of earnings per share due to the existence of the required interest payments.

Page 142   ©2007 Kaplan CPA Review

STUDY MANUAL – BUSINESS ENVIRONMENT & CONCEPTS
CHAPTER 4

D. The degree of financial leverage (DFL) measures the percentage change in earnings per share for a given percentage change in earnings before interest and taxes (EBIT). DFL is calculated as:

$$DFL = \frac{\text{percentage change in EPS}}{\text{percentage change in EBIT}}$$

$$DFL = \frac{EBIT}{EBIT - 1}$$

Example: Degree of Financial Leverage

Assume that Jayco, Inc., has $2 million in sales, variable costs of 70 percent of sales, fixed costs of $100,000, and annual interest expense of $50,000. If Jayco's EBIT increases by 10 percent, by how much will its earnings per share increase?

Sales	$2,000,000
Operating cost	-1,400,000
Fixed cost	−100,000
EBIT	$500,000

Answer

$$DFL = \frac{EBIT}{EBIT - 1} = \frac{\$500,000}{\$500,000 - \$50,000} = 1.111$$

$$\%\varDelta EPS = DFL \times \%\varDelta EBIT$$

Hence, earnings per share will increase by:

1.11 × 10% = 11.1%

1. As financial leverage increases, the expected rate of return will increase, but at the cost of increased risk. This trade-off in using debt raises two related questions.

   a. First, is the higher expected rate of return associated with debt sufficient to compensate for the increased risk?

   b. Secondly, what is the optimal amount of debt?

   c. The answer to both questions is essentially the same. That is, if the issuance of debt increases the value of the firm, debt should be used, and the debt ratio that maximizes the firm's value is the optimal capital structure.

©2007 Kaplan CPA Review
Page 143

STUDY MANUAL – BUSINESS ENVIRONMENT & CONCEPTS
CHAPTER 4

Example: Degree of Total Leverage

Continuing with our previous example, how much will Jayco's EPS increase if the company's sales increase by 10 percent?

Answer

$$DOL = \frac{S - VC}{S - VC - F}$$

$$DOL = \frac{\$2,000,000 - \$1,400,000}{\$2,000,000 - \$1,400,000 - \$100,000}$$

$$DOL = \frac{\$600,000}{\$500,000} = 1.2$$

Thus, $DTL = (DOL)(DFL) = (1.2)(1.111) = 1.333$

$\%DEPS = (DTL)(\%DSales)$

EPS will increase by: $(1.333)(0.10) = 0.1333$ or 13.33%

2.   In an earlier example, EPS is maximized at 50 percent debt. Should the firm then issue 50 percent debt? The answer is NO! The optimal capital structure is the one that maximizes the firm's stock price and not the one that maximizes the firm's EPS.

3.   Notice that with the increased use of debt, the cost of debt increases. This is because lenders recognize that with other factors held constant, firms with higher debt levels are more likely to experience financial distress, so they require higher rates of return. Now you are going to have to investigate what the stockholders want.

THE DIVIDEND POLICY

A.   Company earnings may be reinvested in the firm or distributed to stockholders. This topic review deals with the questions that arise when a firm decides to distribute its income to its common stockholders. There are three key issues:

1.   Determining the percentage of earnings that should be distributed as dividends

2.   The form of the dividend (i.e., cash distribution or a share repurchase)

3.   The growth rate of dividends

B.   When deciding on the size of a cash distribution to stockholders, managers must bear in mind that the objective of the firm is to maximize shareholder value. Therefore, *the*

Page 144   ©2007 Kaplan CPA Review

target payout ratio (dividends per share/earnings per share) should be based on whether investors prefer cash dividends or capital gains.

C. Factors influencing dividend policy are: legal constraints such as bond indentures, preferred stock restrictions, state restrictions of dividends to retained earnings, and the government tax on improperly accumulated earnings.

D. Corporate constraints, like the firm's investment opportunity schedule, the nature of the firm's investment projects, flotation costs, and the firm's ability to substitute debt for equity can also have an impact.

E. The dividend policy decision must be made in conjunction with the firm's capital structure and investment goals. Dividend policy may influence the firm's cost of equity for the following reasons:

1. Stockholders may have a preference for current over future income.

2. Stockholders may perceive capital gains to be riskier than dividends.

3. Because of taxes, some stockholders may prefer capital gains to cash dividends.

4. Stockholders may perceive dividends as conveying information.

STUDY MANUAL – BUSINESS ENVIRONMENT & CONCEPTS
CHAPTER 4

QUESTIONS: FINANCE: WORKING CAPITAL MANAGEMENT & LONG-TERM FINANCING

1. If a bank wants to increase the promised return from a loan, without raising the interest rate charged, it can:
   A. increase the compensating balance.
   B. decrease the reserve requirement.
   C. increase the risk premium.
   D. raise the prime rate.

2. Traditional credit enhancements (a benefit to the creditor) include each of the following EXCEPT:
   A. letters of credit.
   B. callable bond provisions.
   C. collateral.
   D. bond insurance.

3. Which of the following is the most correct statement about stated and effective annual interest rates?
   A. The stated rate adjusts for frequency of compounding.
   B. As long as interest is compounded more than once a year, the effective rate will always be more than the stated rate.
   C. The periodic interest rate is used to find the effective annual rate, and as long as interest is compounded more than once a year, the effective rate will always be more than the stated rate.
   D. The stated rate adjusts for frequency of compounding, and the periodic interest rate is used to find the effective annual rate.

4. A local bank offers an account that pays 8 percent, compounded quarterly, for any deposits of $10,000 or more that are left in the account for a period of five years. The effective annual rate of interest on this account is:
   A. 2.00 percent.
   B. 4.65 percent.
   C. 8.24 percent.
   D. 9.01 percent.

5. When calculating the weighted-average cost of capital (WACC), an adjustment is made for taxes because:
   A. equity is risky.
   B. the interest cost of debt is tax deductible.
   C. preferred stock is involved.
   D. equity earns higher return than debt.

Page 146   ©2007 Kaplan CPA Review

STUDY MANUAL – BUSINESS ENVIRONMENT & CONCEPTS
CHAPTER 4

Questions 6 through 8 are based on the following:

The Frame Supply Company has just acquired a large account and needs to increase its working capital by $100,000. The controller of the company has identified four alternative sources of funds which are given below.

- Alternative A: Pay a factor to buy the company's receivables, which average $125,000 per month and have an average collection period of 30 days. The factor will advance up to 80 percent of the face value of receivables at 10 percent and charge a fee of 2 percent on all receivables purchased. The controller estimates that the firm would save $24,000 in collection expenses over the year. Assume the fee and interest are not deductible in advance.
- Alternative B: Borrow $110,000 from a bank at 12 percent interest. A 9 percent compensating balance would be required.
- Alternative C: Issue $110,000 of six-month commercial paper to net $100,000. (New paper would be issued every 6 months.)
- Alternative D: Borrow $125,000 From a bank on a discount basis at 20 percent. No compensating balance would be required.

Assume a 360-day year in all of your calculations.

6.　　The cost of Alternative B is
  A. 9.0 percent.
  B. 10.5 percent.
  C. 12.0 percent.
  D. 13.2 percent.

7.　　The cost of Alternative C is:
  A. 20.0 percent.
  B. 10.0 percent.
  C. 11.1 percent.
  D. 18.2 percent.

8.　　The cost of Alternative D is:
  A. 10.0 percent.
  B. 20.0 percent.
  C. 25.0 percent.
  D. 40.0 percent.

9.　　A company obtained a short-term bank loan of $500,000 at an annual interest rate of eight percent. As a condition of the loan, the company is required to maintain a compensating balance of $100,000 in its checking account. The checking account earns interest at an annual rate of three percent. Ordinarily, the company maintains a balance of $50,000 in its account for transaction purposes. What is the effective interest rate of the loan?
  A. 7.77 percent.
  B. 8.50 percent.
  C. 9.44 percent.
  D. 8.56 percent.

©2007 Kaplan CPA Review　　　　　　　　　　　　　　　　Page 147

STUDY MANUAL – BUSINESS ENVIRONMENT & CONCEPTS
CHAPTER 4

10. If a firm borrows $500,000 at 10 percent and is required to maintain $50,000 as a minimum compensating balance at the bank, what is the effective interest rate on the loan?
A. 10.0 percent.
B. 11.1 percent.
C. 9.1 percent.
D. 12.2 percent.

11. Elan Corporation is considering borrowing $100,000 from a bank for one year at a stated interest rate of 9 percent. What is the effective interest rate to Elan if this borrowing is in the form of a discounted note?
A. 8.10 percent.
B. 9.00 percent.
C. 9.81 percent.
D. 9.89 percent.

12. The Dixon Corporation has an outstanding one-year bank loan of $300,000 at a stated interest rate of 8 percent. In addition, Dixon is required to maintain a 20 percent compensating balance in its checking account. Assuming the company would normally maintain a zero balance in its checking account, the effective interest rate on the loan is:
A. 6.4 percent.
B. 8.0 percent.
D. 9.6 percent.
D. 10.9 percent.

13. A company obtained a short-term bank loan of $250,000 at an annual interest rate of 6 percent. As a condition of the loan, the company is required to maintain a compensating balance of $50,000 in its checking account. The company's checking account earns interest at an annual rate of 2 percent. Ordinarily, the company maintains a balance of $25,000 in its checking account for transaction purposes. What is the effective interest rate of the loan?
A. 6.44 percent.
B. 7.11 percent.
C. 5.80 percent.
D. 6.66 percent.

14. When purchasing temporary investments, which one of the following BEST describes the risk associated with the ability to sell the investment in a short period of time without significant price concessions?
A. Investment risk.
B. Interest rate risk.
C. Purchasing power risk.
D. Liquidity risk.

15. A firm's target or optimal capital structure is consistent with which one of the following?
    A. Maximum earnings per share.
    B. Minimum cost of debt.
    C. Minimum risk.
    D. Minimum weighted average cost of capital.

16. Which one of the following factors might cause a firm to increase the debt in its financial structure?
    A. An increase in the corporate income tax rate.
    B. Increased economic uncertainty.
    C. An increase in the Federal funds rate.
    D. An increase in the price/earnings ratio.

17. DQZ Telecom is considering a project for the coming year which will cost $50 million. DQZ plans to use the following combination of debt and equity to finance the investment.
    • Issue $15 million of 20-year bonds at a price of 101, with a coupon rate of 8 percent, and flotation costs of 2 percent of par.
    • Use $35 million of funds generated from earnings.

    The equity market is expected to earn 12 percent. U.S. treasury bonds are currently yielding 5 percent. The beta coefficient for DQZ is estimated to be 0.60. DQZ is subject to an effective corporate income tax rate of 40 percent.

    Assume that the after-tax cost of debt is 7 percent and the cost of equity is 12 percent. Determine the weighted average cost of capital.
    A. 10.50 percent.
    B. 8.50 percent.
    C. 9.50 percent.
    D. 6.30 percent.

18. Which one of a firm's sources of new capital usually has the lowest after-tax cost?
    A. Retained earnings.
    B. Bonds.
    C. Preferred stock.
    D. Common stock.

19. A preferred stock is sold for $101 per share, has a face value of $100 per share, underwriting fees of $5 per share, and annual dividends of $10 per share. If the tax rate is 40 percent, the cost of funds (capital) for the preferred stock is:
    A. 4.2 percent.
    B. 6.2 percent.
    C. 10.0 percent.
    D. 10.4 percent.

STUDY MANUAL – BUSINESS ENVIRONMENT & CONCEPTS
CHAPTER 4

20. The theory underlying the cost of capital is primarily concerned with the cost of:
    A. long-term funds and old funds.
    B. short-term funds and new funds.
    C. long-term funds and new funds.
    D. short-term funds and old funds.

21. If Brewer Corporation's bonds are currently yielding 8 percent in the marketplace, why would the firm's cost of debt be lower?
    A. Market interest rates have increased.
    B. Additional debt can be issued more cheaply than the original debt.
    C. There should be no difference; cost of debt is the same as the bonds' market yield.
    D. Interest is deductible for tax purposes.

22. The overall cost of capital is the:
    A. rate of return on assets that covers the costs associated with the funds employed.
    B. average rate of return a firm earns on its assets.
    C. minimum rate a firm must earn on high risk projects.
    D. cost of the firm's equity capital at which the market value of the firm will remain unchanged.

23. Debentures are:
    A. income bonds that require interest payments only when earnings permit.
    B. subordinated debt and rank behind convertible bonds.
    C. bonds secured by the full faith and credit of the issuing firm.
    D. a form of lease financing similar to equipment trust certificates.

Questions 24 through 26 are based on the following:

Williams Inc. is interested in measuring its overall cost of capital and has gathered the following data. Under the terms described below, the company can sell unlimited amounts of all instruments.

- Williams can raise cash by selling $1,000, 8 percent, 20-year bonds with annual interest payments. In selling the issue, an average premium of $30 per bond would be received, and the firm must pay flotation costs of $30 per bond. The after-tax cost of funds is estimated to be 4.8 percent.
- Williams can sell 8 percent preferred stock at par value, $105 per share. The cost of issuing and selling the preferred stock is expected to be $5 per share.
- Williams' common stock is currently selling for $100 per share. The firm expects to pay cash dividends of $7 per share next year, and the dividends are expected to remain constant. The stock will have to be underpriced by $3 per share, and flotation costs are expected to amount to $5 per share.
- Williams expects to have available $100,000 of retained earnings in the coming year; once these retained earnings are exhausted, the firm will use new common stock as the form of common stock equity financing.

Page 150   ©2007 Kaplan CPA Review

STUDY MANUAL – BUSINESS ENVIRONMENT & CONCEPTS
CHAPTER 4

- Williams' preferred capital structure is:
  Long-term debt   30%
  Preferred stock   20
  Common stock   50

24.   The cost of funds from the sale of common stock for Williams Inc. is:
        A. 7.0 percent.
        B. 7.6 percent.
        C. 7.4 percent.
        D. 8.1 percent.

25.   The cost of funds from retained earnings for Williams Inc. is:
        A. 7.0 percent.
        B. 7.6 percent.
        C. 7.4 percent.
        D. 8.1 percent.

26.   If Williams Inc. needs a total of $200,000, the firm's weighted average cost of capital would be:
        A. 19.8 percent.
        B. 4.8 percent.
        C. 6.5 percent.
        D. 6.8 percent.

27.   The firm's marginal cost of capital:
        A. should be the same as the firm's rate of return on equity.
        B. is unaffected by the firm's capital structure.
        C. is inversely related to the firm's required rate of return used in capital budgeting.
        D. is a weighted average of the investor's required returns on debt and equity.

28.   Short-term interest rates are:
        A. generally lower than long-term rates.
        B. generally higher than long-term rates.
        C. lower than long-term rates during periods of high inflation only.
        D. not significantly related to long-term rates.

29.   The marketable securities with the *least* amount of default risk are:
        A. federal government agency securities.
        B. US treasury securities.
        C. repurchase agreements.
        D. commercial paper.

30.   Commercial paper:
        A. has a maturity date greater than one year.
        B. is generally sold only through investment banking dealers.
        C. generally does not have an active secondary market.
        D. has an interest rate lower than treasury bills.

©2007 Kaplan CPA Review
Page 151

STUDY MANUAL – BUSINESS ENVIRONMENT & CONCEPTS
CHAPTER 4

31. The working capital financing policy that subjects the firm to the *greatest* risk of being unable to meet the firm's maturing obligations is the policy that finances:
A. fluctuating current assets with long-term debt.
B. permanent current assets with long-term debt.
C. permanent current assets with short-term debt.
D. all current assets with long-term debt.

32. Which one of the following financial instruments generally provides the largest source of short-term credit for small firms?
A. Installment loans.
B. Commercial paper.
C. Trade credit.
D. Mortgage bonds.

33. Which one of the following provides a spontaneous source of financing for a firm?
A. Accounts payable.
B. Mortgage bonds.
C. Accounts receivable.
D. Debentures.

34. Which one of the following responses is NOT an advantage to a corporation that uses the commercial paper market for short-term financing?
A. This market provides more funds at lower rates than other methods provide.
B. The borrower avoids the expense of maintaining a compensating balance with a commercial bank.
C. There are no restrictions as to the type of corporation that can enter into this market.
D. This market provides a broad distribution for borrowing.

35. Which one of the following statements about trade credit is correct? Trade credit is:
A. not an important source of financing for small firms.
B. a source of long-term financing to the seller.
C. subject to risk of buyer default.
D. usually an inexpensive source of external financing.

Page 152 ©2007 Kaplan CPA Review

36. The treasury analyst for Garth Manufacturing has estimated the cash flows for the first half of next year (ignoring any short-term borrowings) as follows.

	Cash (millions)	
	Inflows	Outflows
January	$2	$1
February	$2	$4
March	$2	$5
April	$2	$3
May	$4	$2
June	$5	$3

Garth has a line of credit of up to $4 million on which it pays interest monthly at a rate of 1 percent of the amount utilized. Garth is expected to have a cash balance of $2 million on January 1 and no amount utilized on its line of credit. Assuming all cash flows occur at the end of the month, approximately how much will Garth pay in interest during the first half of the year?

A. Zero.
B. $61,000.
C. $80,000.
D. $132,000.

37. An automated clearinghouse (ACH) electronic transfer is a(n):
A. electronic payment to a company's account at a concentration bank.
B. check that must be immediately cleared by the Federal Reserve Bank.
C. computer-generated deposit ticket verifying deposit of funds.
D. check-like instrument drawn against the payor and not against the bank.

38. A lock-box system:
A. accelerates the inflow of funds.
B. reduces the need for compensating balances.
C. provides security for late night deposits.
D. reduces the risk of having checks lost in the mail.

39. Which one of the following would increase the working capital of a firm?
A. Cash collection of accounts receivable.
B. Refinancing of accounts payable with a two-year note payable.
C. Purchase of equipment financed by a thirty-year mortgage payable.
D. Cash payment of accounts payable.

40. An organization would usually offer credit terms of 2/10, net 30 when:
A. most competitors are offering the same terms, and the organization has a shortage of cash.
B. the organization can borrow funds at a rate less than the annual interest cost.
C. the cost of capital approaches the prime rate.
D. most competitors are not offering discounts, and the organization has a surplus of cash.

STUDY MANUAL – BUSINESS ENVIRONMENT & CONCEPTS
CHAPTER 4

41. Using a 360-day year, what is the opportunity cost to a buyer of not accepting terms 3/10, net 45?
A. 55.67 percent.
B. 31.81 percent.
C. 15.43 percent.
D. 95.24 percent.

42. A company has daily cash receipts of $150,000. The treasurer of the company has investigated a lockbox service whereby the bank that offers this service will reduce the company's collection time by four days at a monthly fee of $2,500. If money market rates average four percent during the year, the additional annual income (loss) from using the lockbox service would be:
A. $6,000.
B. $(6,000).
C. $18,000.
D. $12,000.

43. Starrs Company has current assets of $300,000 and current liabilities of $200,000. Starrs could increase its working capital by the:
A. prepayment of $50,000 of next year's rent.
B. refinancing of $50,000 of short-term debt with long-term debt.
C. acquisition of land valued at $50,000 through the issuance of common stock.
D. purchase of $50,000 of temporary investments for cash.

44. Shaw Corporation is considering a plant expansion that will increase its sales and net income. The following data represents management's estimate of the impact the proposal will have on the company.

	Current	Proposal
Cash	$100,000	$120,000
Accounts payable	350,000	430,000
Accounts receivable	400,000	500,000
Inventory	380,000	460,000
Marketable securities	200,000	200,000
Mortgage payable (current)	175,000	325,000
Fixed assets	2,500,000	3,500,000
Net Income	500,000	650,000

The effect of the plant expansion on Shaw's working capital would be a(n):
A. decrease of $150,000.
B. decrease of $30,000.
C. increase of $30,000.
D. increase of $120,000.

45. Net working capital is the difference between:
A. current assets and current liabilities.
B. fixed assets and fixed liabilities.
C. total assets and total liabilities.
D. shareholders' investment and cash.

STUDY MANUAL – BUSINESS ENVIRONMENT & CONCEPTS
CHAPTER 4

46. All of the following are valid reasons for a business to hold cash and marketable securities EXCEPT to:
    A. satisfy compensating balance requirements.
    B. maintain adequate cash needed for transactions.
    C. meet future needs.
    D. earn maximum returns on investment assets.

47. Which one of the following would increase the working capital of a firm?
    A. Refinancing a short-term note payable with a two-year note payable.
    B. Purchase of a new plant financed by a 20-year mortgage.
    C. Cash collection of accounts receivable.
    D. Payment of a 20-year mortgage payable with cash.

48. Foster Inc. is considering implementing a lock-box collection system at a cost of $80,000 per year. Annual sales are $90 million, and the lock-box system will reduce collection time by 3 days. If Foster can invest funds at 8 percent, should it use the lock-box system? Assume a 360-day year.
    A. Yes, producing savings of $140,000 per year.
    B. Yes, producing savings of $60,000 per year.
    C. No, producing a loss of $20,000 per year.
    D. No, producing a loss of $60,000 per year.

49. A working capital technique that increases the payable float and, therefore, delays the outflow of cash is:
    A. concentration banking.
    B. a draft.
    C. Electronic Data Interchange (EDI).
    D. a lock-box system.

STUDY MANUAL – BUSINESS ENVIRONMENT & CONCEPTS
CHAPTER 4

ANSWERS: FINANCE: WORKING CAPITAL MANAGEMENT & LONG-TERM FINANCING

1. **A** Banks can increase the promised return on a loan without increasing the rate charged by increasing the amount of compensating balance that the debtor is required to keep on deposit.

2. **B** The right to put a bond would offer the holder protection against the deteriorating credit of the issuer, but a call provision would offer no protection to the holder. The call provision would be a benefit to the issuer. All other answers would provide benefit to the creditor or purchaser of a bond.

3. **C** This statement is true because in calculating the EAR, you begin with the periodic stated rate and the EAR exceeds the stated rate when interest is compounded more often than annually because of "interest on interest." The effective annual rate, not the stated rate, adjusts for frequency of compounding.

4. **C** $(1 + \text{periodic rate})m - 1 = (1.02)4 - 1 = 8.24\%$. (Be sure to know this EAR equation.)

    M = Number of years

5. **B** Equity and preferred stock are not adjusted for taxes because dividends are not deductible for corporate taxes. Only interest expense is deductible for corporate taxes.

6. **D** Interest at 12% on $110,000 = $13,200.

    Compensating balance of 9%, which is $9900, reduces the amount available to $100,100 (110,000 – 9,900) immediately. Interest of $13,200 is paid for effectively borrowing $100,100.

$$\text{Therefore, effective interest rate} = \frac{\text{interest costs}}{\text{net usable cash}}$$

$$= \frac{13,200}{100,100} = 13.2\%$$

7. **A** $10,000 [$110,000 – $100,000] is paid as interest for 6 months.

$$\text{Therefore effective rate for 6 months} = \frac{\$10,000}{\$100,000} = 10\% \text{ for 6 months}$$

    Therefore, for 1 year = 10% × 2 = 20%

Page 156   ©2007 Kaplan CPA Review

STUDY MANUAL – BUSINESS ENVIRONMENT & CONCEPTS
CHAPTER 4

8. **C** Amount borrowed: $125,000

Discounted rate: 20%

Amount received immediately: [(125,000) − (20% × $125,000)] = $100,000

$$\text{Effective interest rate} = \frac{\text{Interest cost (discount)}}{\text{Cash received}}$$

$$= \frac{\$25,000}{100,000}$$

$$= 25\%$$

9. **D** The effective interest rate of the loan is 8.56 percent.

Annual interest expense = $500,000 × 0.08 = $40,000

Extra interest earned on second $50,000 = $50,000 × 0.03 = $1,500

Net expense = $40,000 − $1,500 = $38,500

With the company only having use of $450,000, the effective interest rate is: $38,500 / $450,000 = 8.555 percent

10. **B** The effective interest rate on the loan is 11.1 percent.

.10 × $500,000 = $50,000 annual interest

$500,000 − 50,000 = $450,000 usable funds

Therefore, the effective interest rate is: $50,000 = $\dfrac{\$50,000}{\$450,000}$ = .1111 = 11.11%

11. **D** The effective interest rate to Elan if this borrowing is in the form of a discounted note is 9.89 percent.

$$\text{The effective interest rate} = \frac{\text{yearly interest expense}}{\text{usable loan proceeds}}$$

Interest on the loan is 9% × $100,000 = $9,000.

Borrowing in the form of the discounted loan means the interest is taken out of the proceeds of the loan; thus the loan only generated $91,000 in usable cash ($100,000 − $9,000 = $91,000).

The effective interest rate = $9,000 / $91,000 = 0.0989 = 9.89%

©2007 Kaplan CPA Review

Page 157

STUDY MANUAL – BUSINESS ENVIRONMENT & CONCEPTS
CHAPTER 4

12. **D** The effective interest rate on the loan is 10.0 percent.

With a required 20% compensating balance, Dixon is only using $240,000 of the $300,000.

$300,000 × 20% = $60,000

$300,000 − $60,000 = $240,000

8% interest on the $300,000 loan = $24,000

$$\text{The effective interest rate} = \frac{\text{yearly interest expense}}{\text{usable loan proceeds}}$$

Therefore, the effective interest rate is: $24,000 / $240,000 = 0.10 = 10 percent.

13. **A** Effective rate of interest can be calculated as follows.

Loan amount 250,000 × 6%	15,000
Extra amount to be kept in the checking account 25,000 × 2%	−500
Net Interest Cost	14,500

$$\text{Effective interest} = \frac{\text{Net Interest Cost}}{\text{Loan amount available for actual utilization}} \times 100$$

$$= \frac{14,500}{225,000} \times 100 = 6.44\%$$

The company has to put an extra $25,000 into the checking account as a condition of the loan so, in effect, the amount free to be utilized out of the loan proceeds is only $225,000. Similarly, the interest is $15,000 out of which $500 is received on checking account. Net cost to the company is $14,500. Effective interest is calculated taking into account net cost and net loan proceeds.

14. **D** Liquidity risk relates to the risk of selling an investment in a short period of time without significant price concessions. Answer (a) is not correct. Investment risk relates to the investment, not the ability to sell an investment in a short period of time without significant price concessions. Answer (b) is not correct. Interest rate risks relates to the risk of interest rate changes affecting the value of the investments. Answer (c) is not correct. Purchasing power risk relates to the risk of changes in the value of the U.S. dollar.

15. **D** Answer (a) is incorrect. A firm's target or optimal capital structure is not consistent with maximum earnings per share. A firm's target or optimal capital structure minimizes the cost of capital, not the overall maximum earnings per share. Answer (b) is incorrect. A firm's target or optimal capital structure is not consistent with minimum cost of debt. A firm's target or optimal capital structure is concerned with minimizing the cost of debt and equity, not just debt. Answer (c) is incorrect. A firm's target or optimal capital structure is not consistent with minimum risk because the optimum capital structure minimizes cost, not risk.

STUDY MANUAL – BUSINESS ENVIRONMENT & CONCEPTS
CHAPTER 4

16. **A**   An increase in the corporate income tax rate might cause a firm to increase the debt in its financial structure. Answer (b) is incorrect. Increased economic uncertainty would not cause a firm to increase the debt in its financial structure. Answer (c) is incorrect. An increase in the Federal funds rate would not cause a firm to increase the debt in its financial structure. Answer (d) is incorrect. An increase in the price/earnings ratio would not cause a firm to increase the debt in its financial structure.

17. **A**   The weighted average cost of capital is 10.50 percent.

$$\frac{\$15 \text{ million}}{\$50 \text{ million}} = .30 = 30 \text{ percent debt}$$

$$\frac{\$35 \text{ million}}{\$50 \text{ million}} = .70 = 70 \text{ percent debt}$$

$$
\begin{aligned}
70\% \times 12\% &= & 0.084 \\
30\% \times 7\% &= & \underline{0.021} \\
& & 0.105 = 10.5\%
\end{aligned}
$$

18. **B**   The source of new capital that has the lowest after-tax cost is bonds because the interest is tax deductible for the organization.

19. **D**   The cost of capital for preferred stock is the dividends per year divided by the net amount received upon stock issuance. Thus, the cost of capital for the preferred stock is 10.4% ($10 / $96).

20. **C**   The theory underlying the cost of capital is primarily concerned with the cost of long-term funds and new funds. Answer (a) is incorrect because the cost of capital is primarily concerned with new funds, not old funds. Answer (b) is incorrect because the cost of capital is primarily concerned with long-term funds rather than short-term funds. Answer (d) is incorrect because short-term funds and old funds are not the primary focus of cost of capital.

21. **D**   Interest is tax deductible; therefore, the firm's cost of debt would be the percentage cost of the bonds less the tax effect.

22. **A**   The overall cost of capital is the rate of return on assets that covers the cost associated with the funds employed. The overall cost of capital is the weighted average cost of capital which includes both debt and equity. Answer (b) is incorrect because the overall cost of capital is not the average rate of return a firm earns on its assets. Hopefully, a firm earns a higher rate of return than the overall cost of capital. Answer (c) is incorrect because the minimum rate a firm must earn on any project is not related to the overall cost of capital. Answer (d) is incorrect because the overall cost of capital is not related to the cost of a firm's equity capital at which the market value of the firm will remain unchanged.

23. **C**   Debentures are bonds secured by the full faith and credit of the issuing firm. Answer (a) is incorrect because debentures are not income bonds that require interest payments only earnings permit. Answer (b) is incorrect because debentures are not subordinated debt and ranked behind convertible bonds. Answer (d) is incorrect because debentures are not a form of lease financing similar to equipment trust certificates.

©2007 Kaplan CPA Review
Page 159

STUDY MANUAL – BUSINESS ENVIRONMENT & CONCEPTS
CHAPTER 4

24. **B** $\dfrac{\text{yearly dividend}}{\text{proceeds from stock issuance}} = \dfrac{\$7}{\$100} - \dfrac{\$7}{\$3 - \$5} = \$92 = 7.6\%$

25. **A** $\dfrac{\text{yearly dividend}}{\text{current selling price of stock}} = \dfrac{\$7}{\$100} = .07 = 7\%$

26. **C** The company wishes to maintain a capital structure of 30 percent debt, 20 percent preferred stock, and 50 percent common stock (includes retained earnings).

Retained earnings	50% × 7%	= 3.50%
Preferred stock	20% × 8%	= 1.60%
Debt	30% × 4.8%	= 1.44%
		6.54%

27. **D** A firm's marginal cost of capital is a weighted average of the investor's required returns on debt and equity. The marginal cost of capital is the weighted average cost of additional debt and equity which is the return that investors in the debt and investors in the equity require. Answers (a), (b), and (c) are incorrect because the firm's marginal cost of capital is the weighted average of the investor's required returns on debt and equity.

28. **A** Short-term interest rates are generally lower than long-term interest rates. Answer (d) is incorrect because short-term interest rates are related to long-term rates.

29. **B** The marketable securities with the least amount of default risk are U.S. Treasury securities. Answer (a) is incorrect because federal government agencies securities do not have the least amount of default risk. Answer (c) is incorrect because repurchase agreements do not have the least amount of default risk. Answer (d) is incorrect because commercial paper does not have the least amount of default risk.

30. **C** Commercial paper generally does not have an active secondary market. Answer (a) is incorrect because commercial paper does not always have to have a maturity date greater than one year. Answer (b) is incorrect because commercial paper is not generally sold only through investment banking dealers. Answer (d) is incorrect because commercial paper does not have an interest rate lower than treasury bills.

31. **C** The working capital financing policy that subjects the firm to the greatest risk of being unable to meet the firm's maturing obligations is the policy that finances permanent current assets with short-term debt. Permanent current assets should be financed with long-term liabilities. Answer (a) is incorrect. The working capital financing policy that subjects the firm to the greatest risk of being unable to meet the firm's maturing obligations is not the policy that finances fluctuating current assets with long-term debt. Answer (b) is incorrect. The working capital financing policy that subjects the firm to the greatest risk of being unable to meet the firm's maturing obligations is not the policy that finances permanent current assets with long-term debt. Answer (d) is incorrect. The working capital financing policy that subjects the firm to the greatest risk of being unable to meet the firm's maturing obligations is not the policy that finances all current assets with long-term debt. This is the least risky among the alternatives.

32. **C** Trade credit generally provides the largest source of short-term credit for small firms. Answer (a) is incorrect. Installment loans do not generally provide the largest source of short-term credit for small firms although installment loans can be a source of short term credit. Answer (b) is incorrect. Commercial paper does not generally provide the largest

source of short-term credit for small firms. Large, well-known firms can find a market for their own short term unsecured notes (commercial paper) but small firms can not. Answer (d) is incorrect. Mortgage bonds do not generally provide the largest source of short-term credit for small firms. Mortgage bonds are normally long-term credit.

33. **A**   Accounts payable provides a spontaneous source of financing for a firm. Answer (b) is incorrect. Given mortgage bonds link to real estate and its long term nature, mortgage bonds do not provide a spontaneous source of financing for a firm. Answer (c) is incorrect. Accounts receivable do not provide a spontaneous source of financing for a firm. Accounts receivable is when others owe us, not a source of financing for a firm. Answer (d) is incorrect. Debentures do not provide a spontaneous source of financing for a firm. Debentures are unsecured bonds used for long-term financing.

34. **C**   The fact that "there are no restrictions as to the type of corporation who can enter the market" is not an advantage to the borrower. Answer (a) is incorrect since obtaining funds at a lower rate is one of the advantages commercial paper provides. Answer (b) is incorrect since borrowing through the commercial paper market avoids the expense of maintaining a compensating balance and is therefore an advantage. Answer (d) is incorrect since it is an advantage to have a broad distribution for borrowing.

35. **C**   Trade credit is subject to the risk of buyer default. This arises as a part of the purchase transaction on account -- seller runs risk of buyer not paying. Choice (a) is incorrect since trade credit is an important source of financing for small firms. Choice (b) is incorrect since trade credit is not long-term financing to the seller. Choice (d) is incorrect since trade credit is an expensive source of external financing.

36. **B**   The cash balances for each month are as follows:

Starting balance	2,000,000
End of January	3,000,000
End of February	1,000,000
End of March	−2,000,000
End of April	−3,000,000
End of May	−1,000,000
End of June	1,000,000

Thus, we would need to borrow 2,000,000 for one month, 3,000,000 for one month, and 1,000,000 for one month. The cost is = 1% per month; therefore, approximately $60,000 is the answer.

37. **A**   An automated clearinghouse (ACH) electronic transfer is an electric payment to a company's account at a concentration bank.

38. **A**   A lockbox system accelerates the inflow of funds. A company has numerous locations throughout their servicing area which will receive payments and are immediately deposited in the company's bank accounts, thereby speeding the availability of the funds. Answer (b) is incorrect because a lockbox system does not reduce the need for compensating balances. Answer (c) is incorrect because a lockbox system has nothing to do with security for late night deposits. Answer (d) is incorrect because a lockbox system does not reduce the risk of having checks lost in the mail. Checks are still sent in the mail to the various locations within the servicing area.

©2007 Kaplan CPA Review

STUDY MANUAL – BUSINESS ENVIRONMENT & CONCEPTS
CHAPTER 4

39. **B** Working capital would increase if a firm refinances accounts payable with a two year note payable. Answer (a) is incorrect because working capital would not change when cash collected from accounts receivable. The assets would go up and down by the same amount. Answer (c) is incorrect because working capital would not be affected by a purchase of equipment financed by 30 year mortgage payable. Answer (d) is incorrect because working capital would not increase when a firm makes a cash payment of accounts payable.

40. **A** An organization would usually offer credit terms of 2/10 net 30 when most competitors are offering the same terms, and the organization has a shortage of cash.

41. **B** Using a 360-day year, the opportunity cost to a buyer of not accepting terms 3/10, net 45 is 31.81 percent.

42. **B** If money market rates average four percent during the year, the additional annual income (loss) from using the lockbox service would be $(6,000).

Increased daily cash receipt = $150,000 × 4 days = $600,000.

Interest earned on increase = $600,000 × 0.04 = $24,000.

Annual fees = $2,500 × 12 months = $30,000.

Net loss = $24,000 – $30,000 = ($6,000).

43. **B** Working capital is equal to current assets - current liabilities. The refinancing of $50,000 of short term debt with long term debt decreases current liabilities and increases long term debt. The decrease in short term debt decreases current liabilities causing working capital to go up. Answer (a) is incorrect because the prepayment of $50,000 of next year's rent increases and decreases current assets, thus causing no change in working capital. Answer (c) is incorrect because the acquisition of land through the issuance of common stock has no effect on current assets or current liabilities, therefore no change in working capital. Answer (d) is incorrect because the purchase of temporary investments for cash increases and decreases current assets, thereby not changing working capital.

44. **B** The calculation of working capital is current assets minus current liabilities. The current assets in this question are cash, accounts receivable, inventory and marketable securities. The current liabilities are accounts payable and mortgage payable (current). Under the current situation, the total current assets equal $1,080,000 and total current liabilities equal $525,000 which calculates working capital to be $555,000. Under the proposal the current assets equal $1,280,000 and the current liabilities equal $755,000, calculating a working capital equal to $525,000. Given this, the effect of the plant expansion on Shaw's working capital is a decrease of $30,000 ($555,000 – $525,000).

45. **A** Net working capital equals current assets minus current liabilities.

46. **D** To earn maximum returns on investment assets is not a valid reason for a business to hold cash and marketable securities.

STUDY MANUAL – BUSINESS ENVIRONMENT & CONCEPTS
CHAPTER 4

47. **A** Refinancing a short-term note payable with a two-year note payable would increase the working capital of a firm.

Current Assets – Current Liabilities = Working Capital.

Assuming CA = $10 and CL = $6, WC = $4. ($10 – $6 = $4).

If a company refinances $2 worth of short-term notes payable with a two year note payable, working capital would increase. ($10 – $4 = $6).

Answer (b) is incorrect. The purchase of a new plant financed by a 20-year mortgage would not increase the working capital of a firm. WC would stay the same. Answer (c) is incorrect. A cash collection of accounts receivable would not increase the working capital of a firm. WC would stay the same. Answer (d) is incorrect. A payment of a 20-year mortgage payable with cash would not increase the working capital of a firm. WC would decrease.

48. **C** No, Foster should not use the lock-box system, producing a loss of $20,000 per year.

Daily sales = $90 million / 360 = $250,000.

Three days reduction in collection time = $250,000 × 3 = $750,000 available for investment.

At 8%, $750,000 will earn $60,000 annually.

Earned $60,000 – lockbox cost of $80,000 = ($20,000).

A $20,000 loss would be incurred if Foster implements the lockbox system. Therefore do not use the lockbox system.

49. **B** A draft delays the outflow of cash. A draft (check) is a 3-party instrument whereby the drawer orders the drawee to pay a certain sum of money to the payee. Choice (a) is incorrect since concentration banking does not delay the outflow of cash but instead regional banks may become centers for transfer of lockbox receipts. Choice (c) is incorrect since electronic data interchange does not delay the outflow of cash. Choice (d) is incorrect since a lockbox system is used to expedite the receipt of cash.

©2007 Kaplan CPA Review

FINANCE: CAPITAL BUDGETING

STUDY MANUAL – BUSINESS ENVIRONMENT & CONCEPTS
CHAPTER 5

Study Tip: After you qualify to take the CPA exam and sign up for a date, the examiners will send you all of the information they believe you need in advance. Read all of that material very carefully. They have studied the problems experienced by candidates in the past to determine what information is needed. They will expect you to have read the material and you should do so. The more you understand about the process, the more likely it is you will pass.

CAPITAL BUDGETING

A. Capital budgeting is the process of determining and selecting the most profitable long-term (greater than one year) projects.

   1. Capital budgeting may be the most important responsibility that a financial manager has.

   2. First, since a capital budgeting decision involves the purchase of a long-term asset with a life of many years, the firm sacrifices some degree of flexibility in terms of being locked in for the duration of the asset's life.

   3. Second, an acquisition of an asset to expand operations is based on its expected future revenues, so a decision to buy an asset will require forecasts of revenue over the asset's life.

   4. Finally, a firm's strategic plan is defined by its capital budgeting decisions.

B. Capital projects may be classified as follows:

   1. Replacement decisions to maintain the business are normally made without detailed analysis. The only issues here are whether or not the existing operations should continue and, if so, should the same procedures or processes be maintained.

   2. Replacement decisions for cost-reduction purposes determine whether equipment that is obsolete, but still usable, should be replaced. A fairly detailed analysis is necessary in this case.

   3. Existing product or market expansion involves a complex decision-making process since it requires an explicit forecast of future demand. A very detailed analysis is required.

Page 164 ©2007 Kaplan CPA Review

4. New products or markets development also involves a complex decision-making process that will require a detailed analysis.

5. Mandatory investments, such as safety-related and/or environmental projects, often accompany new revenue-producing projects.

6. Further distinctions among capital investment opportunities are whether the projects are mutually exclusive or independent.

7. Mutually exclusive means that only one project in a set of possible projects can be accepted.

8. Independent projects are projects that are unrelated to each other. If you have unlimited funds, you may accept or reject any combination of independent projects.

C. The payback period (PBP) is the number of years it takes to recover the initial cost of an investment.

Example: Payback period

Calculate the payback periods for the two projects that have the cash flows presented in Figure 1. Note the year 0 cash flow represents the net cost of each of the projects.

Figure 1: Expected Net After-Tax Cash Flows

Year (t)	Project A	Project B
0	-$2,000	-$2,000
1	1,000	200
2	800	600
3	600	800
4	200	1,200

Answer

Note that the cumulative net cash flow (NCF) is just the running total of the cash flows at the end of each time period. Payback will occur when the cumulative NCF equals zero. To find the payback periods construct a table like Figure 2.

Figure 2: Cumulative Net Cash Flow Table

	Year (t)	0	1	2	3	4
Project A	Net cash flow	-2,000	1,000	800	600	200
	Cumulative NCF	-2,000	-1,000	-200	400	600
Project B	Net cash flow	-2,000	200	600	800	1,200
	Cumulative NCF	-2,000	-1,800	-1,200	-400	800

STUDY MANUAL – BUSINESS ENVIRONMENT & CONCEPTS
CHAPTER 5

The payback period is determined from the cumulative net cash flow table as follows:

$$\text{payback period} = \text{years until full recovery} + \frac{\text{unrecovered cost at the beginning of the last year}}{\text{cash flow during the last year}}$$

$$\text{payback period A} = 2 + \frac{200}{600} = 2.33 \text{ years}$$

$$\text{payback period B} = 3 + \frac{400}{1,200} = 3.33 \text{ years}$$

D. Generally speaking, the shorter a project's payback, the better. To decide which project(s) to accept, the firm must first establish a benchmark payback period. Presume that the firm requires a payback period of three and a half years.

   Decision rule: payback ≤ the benchmark payback, accept the project

   payback > the benchmark payback, reject the project

   If A and B are independent, accept project A and project B.

   If A and B are mutually exclusive, then A would be accepted over B (because the payback period is shorter for A).

E. Drawbacks of payback period:

   1. The main drawback of the payback period is that it ignores the time value of money.

   2. The payback period ignores cash flows beyond the payback period.

   3. This means terminal or salvage value wouldn't be considered.

F. Benefits of payback period:

   The payback period is a good measure of project liquidity and riskiness.

G. The discounted payback method discounts the estimated cash flows by the project's cost of capital. It is the number of years it takes for a project to return its initial investment in current (present value) dollars.

Page 166   ©2007 Kaplan CPA Review

Example: Discounted payback method

Compute the discounted payback period for projects A and B described in Figure 3. Assume that the firm's cost of capital is 10 percent.

Figure 3: Cash Flows for Projects A and B

	Year (t)	0	1	2	3	4
Project A	Net cash flow	-2,000	1,000	800	600	200
	Discounted NCF	-2,000	910	661	451	137
	Cumulative DNCF	-2,000	-1,090	-429	22	159
Project B	Net cash flow	-2,000	200	600	800	1,200
	Discounted NCF	-2,000	182	496	601	820
	Cumulative DNCF	-2,000	-1,818	-1,322	-721	99

Answer

Discounted payback A = 2 + 429/451 = 2.95 years
Discounted payback B = 3 + 721/820 = 3.88 years
Decision rule: payback ≤ the benchmark payback, accept the project
              payback > the benchmark payback, reject the project

Assume the firm's maximum discounted payback period is four years.

If A and B are independent projects, accept both projects.

If A and B are mutually exclusive, accept A over B.

1. The drawback of the discounted payback is that it does not consider any cash flows beyond the payback period.

2. Both the payback and discounted payback give an indication of a project's risk and liquidity (i.e., the shorter the payback, the greater the liquidity). Payback is a measure of project risk, since distant cash flows are riskier than shorter-term cash flows.

H. The net present value (NPV) method relies on discounted cash flow (DCF) analysis.

1. The first step in NPV analysis is to find the present value of each cash flow discounted at the project's cost of capital. This assumes that the cost of capital has been adjusted for risk.

2. Next, compute the NPV, which equals the sum of these discounted cash flows (note that CF_0 is a negative cash flow, the project's initial cost).

3. The NPV is the amount of cash flow (in present value terms) that the project generated after repaying the invested capital (project cost) and paying the required rate of return on that capital. A project with a positive NPV increases shareholder wealth, while a negative NPV project decreases shareholder wealth.

STUDY MANUAL – BUSINESS ENVIRONMENT & CONCEPTS
CHAPTER 5

4. For independent projects, the NPV decision rule is to accept the project if NPV > 0. For mutually exclusive projects, choose the one with the higher NPV, as long as its NPV is greater than 0.

5. Using the information in Figure 4, focus on the Discounted NCF for each project.

Figure 4: Cash Flows for Projects A and B

		0	1	2	3	4
Year (t)						
Project A	Net cash flow	-2,000	1,000	800	600	200
	Discounted NCF	-2,000	910	661	451	137
	Cumulative DNCF	-2,000	-1,090	-429	22	159
Project B	Net cash flow	-2,000	200	600	800	1,200
	Discounted NCF	-2,000	182	496	601	820
	Cumulative DNCF	-2,000	-1,818	-1,322	-721	99

a. Project A has net present value of {-2,000 + 910 + 661 + 451 + 137}, for a total of $159, which equals the Cumulative DNCF.

b. Project B has net present value of {-2,000 + 182 + 496 + 601 + 820}, for a total of $99, equal to the Cumulative DNCF.

c. Decision rule: If projects A and B are independent, accept both. If projects A and B are mutually exclusive, A has the higher NPV and would, therefore, be accepted.

I. The internal rate of return (IRR) is the rate of return that equates the present value of a project's estimated cash inflows with the present value of the project's costs. That is, IRR is the discount rate that makes the following relationship hold:

PV (inflows) = Project cost in present value terms

1. Alternatively, the IRR may also be defined as the rate of return for which the net present value of a project is zero.

2. To calculate the IRR you may use the trial-and-error method. That is, just keep guessing IRRs until you get the right one.

3. IRR decision rule: First, define the firm's hurdle rate as the minimum rate the firm will accept for a given project.

a. This is usually the firm's cost of capital. Note that the cost of capital may be adjusted upward or downward to adjust for differences in project risk.

b. For independent projects:

IRR > the cost of capital (hurdle rate), accept the project.
IRR < the cost of capital (hurdle rate), reject the project.
For mutually exclusive projects, rank all projects for which IRR ≥ hurdle rate.

Page 168   ©2007 Kaplan CPA Review

4. A project's NPV profile is a graph that plots the project's NPV for different discount rates. Remember, when you change the discount rate you change the NPV. The NPV profiles for the two projects described in Figure 1 are presented in Figure 5. The discount rates shown in the table at the bottom of Figure 5 are located along the *x*-axis of the NPV profile, and the corresponding NPVs are plotted on the *y*-axis.

5. Note that the projects' IRRs are located where the NPV profiles intersect the *x*-axis (cost of capital), where the NPV is zero. This is because, by definition, the IRR is the discount rate that makes the NPV zero.

Figure 5: NPV Profile Graph

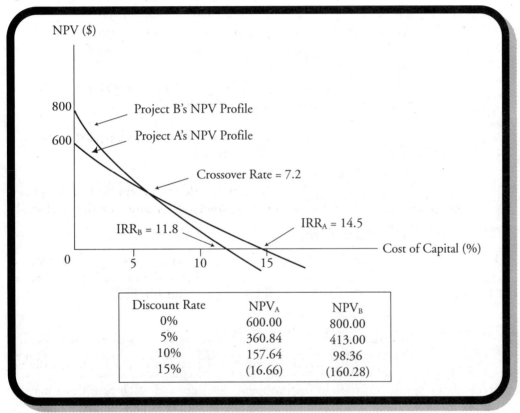

6. Also notice in Figure 5 that the NPV profiles intersect. They intersect at the discount rate that makes the NPVs of both projects equal.

7. The NPV profiles for projects A and B intersect because of a difference in the timing of the cash flows. From the cash flows for the projects (Figure 1) we see that the total cash inflows for project B are greater ($2,800) than those of project A ($2,600). Since they both have the same initial cost ($2,000), at a discount rate of zero, project B has a greater NPV (2,800 - 2,000 = 800) than project A (2,600 - 2,000 = 600).

8. We can also see from the cash flows in Figure 1 that the cash flows for project B come later in the project's life. That's why the NPV of project B falls faster than the NPV of project A as the discount rate increases, and the NPVs are eventually

equal at a discount rate of 7.2 percent. At discount rates above 7.2 percent, the fact that the total cash flows of project B are greater in nominal dollars is overridden by the fact that project B's cash flows come later in the project's life than those of project A.

J. A key advantage of NPV is that it is a direct measure of the dollar benefit of the project to shareholders. NPV is considered the best measure.

  1. The NPV method is considered the best method since it leads to theoretically correct capital budgeting decisions.

  2. Its main weakness is that it does not measure the size of the project, just the size of the return. For example, an NPV = $100 is great for a project costing $100 but very bad for a project costing $1 million.

K. A key advantage of IRR is that it measures profitability as a percentage, showing the return on each dollar invested. The IRR provides safety margin information to management. The IRR tells you how much the project return could fall (in percentage terms) before the firm's capital is at risk.

  1. The disadvantages of the IRR method are:

    a. The potentially conflicting accept or reject decisions when compared to NPV for mutually exclusive projects

    b. The multiple IRR problem

    c. *Note:* As long as a project yields a single IRR, the NPV > 0 and IRR > cost of capital decision rules give the same decision. They are mathematically identical.

  2. If a project has cash outflows during its life or at the end of its life where the sign of the net cash flow goes from minus to plus back to minus, the project is said to have a non-normal cash flow pattern. (Do not be concerned about making these calculations; just be aware of the problem.) Projects with such cash flows may have multiple IRRs. This problem doesn't exist with the NPV method.

  3. For independent projects, the IRR and NPV methods always give the same accept or reject decision. To see why, assume A and B are independent and look again at Figure 5. If the cost of capital is less than 14.5 percent, both the NPV method and the IRR method would accept project A. On the other hand, if the cost of capital is greater than 14.5 percent, both methods reject the project. Similar analysis shows that for project B both methods give similar accept/reject decisions.

  4. For mutually exclusive projects, sometimes the IRR and NPV methods give different accept or reject decisions. Referring to Figure 5, again assume A and B are mutually exclusive. As long as the cost of capital is greater than the crossover rate of 7.2 percent, both methods give the same decision, so accept A (NPVA > NPVB > 0 and IRRA > IRRB > 10.0% > 7.2%). If the cost of capital is below the

crossover rate, the NPV method ranks project B over project A, while the IRR method favors project A. When such a conflict occurs, go with the NPV method, because it selects the project that maximizes shareholders' wealth.

   a. *Note:* The NPV method implicitly assumes the reinvestment rate for the cash flows is the cost of capital, while the IRR method assumes the reinvestment rate is the IRR.

5. The reason, described earlier, that the NPV rankings switch for projects A and B in our examples is the difference in the timing of the cash flows (early in the project's life versus late in the project's life). A second reason, besides timing differences, that NPV and IRR may give conflicting project rankings is that the projects may be of different sizes. Consider an extreme (and somewhat unrealistic) example: two projects, one with an initial outlay of $100 and one with an initial outlay of $1 million. The smaller project may have higher IRR, but the increase in firm value (NPV) may be small compared to the increase in firm value (NPV) of the larger project, even though its IRR is not as high.

6. It is important to follow up all capital budgeting decisions a firm makes. An analyst should compare the actual results to the projected results. The project managers should explain why their projections did or didn't match up to actual performance. The capital budgeting process is only as good as the input estimates used to calculate the cash flows. The function of the postaudit is to improve forecasting and operations.

CASH FLOW ESTIMATION AND OTHER TOPICS IN CAPITAL BUDGETING

When estimating cash flow for capital budgeting purposes, the first thing that should be done is to identify the relevant cash flows. In this vein, capital budgeting decisions must be based on (1) cash flows (as opposed to accounting income) and (2) only *incremental cash flows*—those cash flows that are relevant to the decision to accept or reject the project under consideration.

A. Cash flows versus accounting income. In capital budgeting, we use annual net cash flows, not accounting income to make our decision.

   We can define *net cash flow* as:

   1. NCF = Net income + Depreciation = Return *on* capital + Return *of* capital

   2. Net cash flows should reflect all noncash changes, not just depreciation. Depreciation is usually the largest noncash charge for a firm.

B. Incremental cash flows are cash flows that occur if, and only if, the project is accepted. These cash flows represent the change in the total cash flow for the firm as a result of the acceptance of a project. Some issues that must be addressed when determining incremental cash flows include the following:

1. A sunk cost is a cash outflow that has been previously committed or has already occurred. Since these costs are not incremental, they should not be included in the analysis. An example of sunk costs is a consulting fee paid to a marketing research firm to estimate demand for a new product.

2. Opportunity costs are cash flows that a firm is passing up by acquiring the asset in question. In other words, these are cash flows that would have been provided from an asset the firm already owns, had that asset not been used for the project under consideration. For example, when building a plant, if the firm already owns the land, the cost of the land is an opportunity cost and should be charged to the project.

3. Externalities are the effects the acceptance of a project may have on other parts of the firm. The primary externality is referred to as *cannibalization,* which occurs when a new project takes sales from an existing product. When considering externalities, the full implication of the new project (loss in sales of existing products) should be taken into account. A good example of cannibalization is when a soft drink company introduces a diet version of an existing beverage.

4. Any costs for shipping and installing equipment must be added to the purchase price of the equipment. The depreciable basis of the asset then becomes its purchase price plus shipping and handling.

C. Changes in net working capital (NWC) must be included in the capital budgeting decision. Whenever a firm undertakes a new operation, product, or service, additional inventories are usually needed to support increased sales, and the increased additional sales lead to increases in accounts receivable. Accounts payable and accruals will probably also increase spontaneously.

1. Changes in net working capital are defined as the difference between the changes in current assets and changes in current liabilities.

   Changes in NWC = Δcurrent assets - Δcurrent liabilities

2. If the change is positive, additional financing is required and represents a cash outflow. (If negative, the project frees up cash, creating a cash inflow.) Note that at the termination of the project, the firm will receive an end-of-project cash inflow (or outflow) when the need for the additional working capital ends.

INFLATION EFFECTS ON CAPITAL BUDGETING

A. Inflation must be considered in capital budgeting.

1. Expected inflation is built into interest rates because inflation expectations are impounded in the expected returns used to calculate the weighted-average cost of capital (WACC).

2. The NPV method involves finding the PV of future cash flows. Inflation will cause the WACC to increase, which causes the PV of future cash flows to fall, which lowers the NPV. So NPV is adjusted for inflation through the WACC.

3. Since inflation is in the WACC, future cash flows *must be* adjusted upward to reflect inflation. If this adjustment is not made, the NPV will be biased downward.

B. There are three types of risk associated with a capital budgeting project:

1. Stand-alone risk is the risk that is unique to the individual project. It does not reflect the fact that a project is only one part of a firm's portfolio of assets. The variability of a project's expected returns is used to quantify stand-alone risk, which is easier to measure than corporate or beta risk.

2. Corporate risk is the project's contribution to the firm's total risk. It takes into account that the project is part of the firm's portfolio of assets. This risk is measured by the impact of the project on the uncertainty of the firm's future earnings. Corporate risk is important to undiversified stockholders, small business owners, and the firm's managers, employees, suppliers, and creditors. Empirical studies show that both corporate and market risk affect stock prices.

3. Market (beta) risk is the risk associated with a project from the perspective of a well-diversified stockholder. A project's market risk is measured by its effect on a firm's beta.

Stand-alone risk, corporate risk, and market risk are highly correlated.

TECHNIQUES FOR ANALYZING AND DEALING WITH RISK IN CAPITAL BUDGETING

A. Sensitivity analysis involves changing an input (independent) variable to see how sensitive the dependent variable is to the input variable.

1. For example, by varying sales, you could determine how sensitive a project's net present value (NPV) is to changes in sales, assuming that all other factors are held constant.

2. With sensitivity analysis, you start with the base-case scenario. Base case would be the net present value you determined by using the project's input estimates. Now you change one of the selected variables by a fixed percentage point above and below the base case, noting the effect this change has on the project's NPV. You could do this for all the variables used in the analysis.

B. Scenario analysis is a risk analysis technique that considers both the sensitivity of some key output variable (e.g., NPV) to changes in a key input variable (e.g., sales) and the likely probability distribution of these variables. In scenario analysis, we study the different possible scenarios, *worst case*, *best case*, and *base case*. With the

©2007 Kaplan CPA Review

STUDY MANUAL – BUSINESS ENVIRONMENT & CONCEPTS
CHAPTER 5

assignment of probabilities to the different cases, you can estimate the dependent variable's expected value, standard deviation, and coefficient of variation.

C. Monte Carlo simulation uses simulation techniques to tie together sensitivities and probability distributions of input variables (e.g., sales, variable cost per unit, etc.). Random values of input variables are generated, and then the NPVs are computed. This procedure may be repeated thousands of times; in this example, we assume 1,000 times. From this set of 1,000 NPV values, the mean and standard deviation of a project's NPV are computed. The mean NPV is then used as a measure of expected profitability, and risk is measured by the standard deviation or coefficient of variation.

D. Risk-adjusted discount rate approach. The risk-adjusted discount rate procedure starts with the normal cost of capital for the entire firm. The firm's cost of capital is then adjusted upward or downward to reflect an individual project's risk. Projects with greater uncertainty about after-tax incremental cash flows will be evaluated with a higher discount rate (firm WACC + risk adjustment). The size of the adjustment is a subjective judgment, but this method is used where the Capital Asset Pricing Model (CAPM) estimate of a project's beta is unavailable or believed to be unreliable. Discount rates are also adjusted downward for projects with assets (such as real estate) that provide especially good collateral and will tend to reduce the cost of debt financing.

CAPITAL RATIONING AND ITS RELATIONSHIP TO CAPITAL BUDGETING

A. Ideally, firms will continue to invest in positive NPV projects until their marginal returns equal their marginal cost of capital. Should a firm have insufficient capital to do this, it must *ration* its capital (allocate its funds) among the best possible combination of acceptable projects.

B. Capital rationing may be defined as the allocation of a fixed amount of capital among the set of available projects that will maximize shareholder wealth. A firm with less capital than profitable (positive NPV) projects should choose the combination of projects it can afford to fund that has the greatest total NPV.

Annual Percentage Yield (Effective Annual Rate)

A. In order to make good decisions about investing and borrowing opportunities, it is important to make the stated interest rates of each alternative comparable. We need to make apples-to-apples comparisons. The same rate of interest compounded differently in two different investment alternatives is not apples-to-apples. To make a logical comparison, we convert the interest rates to annual percentage yield (APY), or the effective annual rate (EAR).

B. We begin with the stated or nominal rate, which is the rate specified in the contract of the loan or the investment. For example, one investment might yield 8 percent compounded annually, whereas another might yield 7.85 percent compounded quarterly. It is never appropriate to compare stated or nominal rates unless the compounding periods are the same.

C. The APY, or EAR, is simply the annual compound rate that produces the same return as the stated or nominal rate.

D. The calculation for APY or EAR is:

APY or EAR = $(1 + \text{quoted rate}/m)^m - 1$, where m is the number of compounding periods within a year.

Example: A stated rate of 8 percent, compounded semiannually, has an APY or EAR of:

$[1 + 0.08/2]^2 - 1 = 8.16\%$ (or, 1.04 squared, minus 1)

COST OF CAPITAL

A. The capital budgeting process involves discounted cash flow analysis.

1. To conduct such analysis, you must know the firm's proper discount rate.

2. This topic review discusses how you can determine the proper rate at which to discount the cash flows associated with a capital budgeting project.

3. This discount rate is called the *cost of capital* or the firm's *weighted-average cost of capital (WACC)*.

B. Basic definitions. On the right (liability) side of a firm's balance sheet, we have debt, preferred stock, and common equity.

1. These are normally referred to as the *capital components* of the firm.

2. Any increase in a firm's total assets will have to be financed through an increase in at least one of these capital accounts.

3. The cost of each of these components is called the *component costs of capital*.

4. Throughout this review we focus on the following capital components and their component costs:

   a. k_d The rate at which the firm can issue new debt. This is the yield to maturity on existing debt. This is also called the *before-tax component cost of debt*.

   b. $k_d(1 - t)$ The after-tax cost of debt. Here t is the firm's marginal tax rate. The after-tax component cost of debt, $k_d(1 - t)$, is used to calculate the WACC.

   c. k_{ps} The cost of preferred stock.

   d. k_s The cost of retained earnings (or internal equity). It is identical to the required rate of return on common stock and is generally difficult to estimate.

STUDY MANUAL – BUSINESS ENVIRONMENT & CONCEPTS
CHAPTER 5

e. k_e The cost of external equity. This is the cost of equity obtained through the issuance of new common stock as opposed to retained earnings. As you will see, it is necessary to distinguish between the cost of equity obtained from retained earnings (k_s) and the cost of equity obtained by selling new stock (k_e). You should also know that k_e will always be greater than k_s.

WEIGHTED-AVERAGE COST OF CAPITAL (WACC)

A. How a company raises capital and how it budgets or invests the capital are considered independently.

1. Most companies have separate departments for the two tasks.

2. The financing department is responsible for keeping costs low and using a balance of funding sources: common equity, preferred stock, and debt.

3. Generally, it is necessary to raise each type of capital in large sums. The large sums may temporarily overemphasize the most recently issued capital, but in the long run, the firm will ascribe to target weights for each capital type.

4. Because of these and other financing considerations, the investment decision must be made assuming a WACC including each of the different sources of capital and using the long-run target weights.

CALCULATION OF THE COMPONENT COSTS OF (A) DEBT, (B) PREFERRED STOCK, (C) RETAINED EARNINGS, AND (D) NEWLY ISSUED STOCK

A. The after-tax cost of debt, $k_d(1 - t)$, is used in computing the WACC. It is the interest rate at which firms can issue new debt (k_d) net of the tax savings from the tax-deductibility of interest $(k_d t)$.

> After-tax cost of debt = Interest rate - Tax savings = $k_d - k_d(t) = k_d(1 - t)$
>
> After-tax cost of debt = $k_d (1 - t)$

Example: Cost of debt

Dexter, Inc., is planning to issue new debt at an interest rate of 8 percent. Dexter has a 40 percent marginal federal-plus-state tax rate. What is Dexter's cost of debt capital?

Answer

> $k_d (1 - t) = 8\% (1 - 0.4) = 4.8\%$

The cost of preferred stock (k_{ps}) is:

$k_{ps} = D_{ps}/P_{net}$

where
D_{ps} = Preferred dividends
P_{net} = Net issuing price after deducting flotation costs

Example: Cost of preferred stock

Suppose Dexter has preferred stock that pays an $8 dividend per share and sells for $100 per share. If Dexter were to issue new shares of preferred, it would incur a flotation (or underwriting) cost of 5 percent. Calculate Dexter's cost of preferred stock.

Answer

$$k_{ps} = \frac{D_{ps}}{P_{net}}$$

$$P_{net} = 100 \times (1 - 0.05) = \$95$$

$$k_{ps} = \frac{\$8}{\$95} = 0.084 = 8.4\%$$

1. Note that the equation $k_{ps} = D_{ps}/P_{net}$ is just a rearrangement of the preferred stock valuation model $P_0 = D_{ps}/k_{ps}$, where P_0 is the actual market price today. P_0 equals $100 in this example, but the cost of preferred stock will be just a bit higher than the rate required by investors because of the need to compensate for flotation costs.

2. The opportunity cost of retained earnings (k_s) is the return that a firm's stockholders require on the equity that the firm retains from its earnings. You should know that if a stock is in equilibrium, the rate of return investors require is equal to the rate of return they expect to get. In equilibrium:

    required rate of return (k_s) = expected rate of return (k_s)

    required rate of return = k_{RFR} + risk premium (RFR = risk-free rate)

    expected rate of return = (D_1/P) + growth in dividends

B. The cost of retained earnings can be estimated using one of the following three approaches:

   1. The capital asset pricing model approach

      Step 1: Estimate the risk-free rate, RFR. The short-term Treasury bill (T-bill) rate is usually used, but some analysts feel the long-term Treasury rate should be used.

Step 2: Estimate the stock's beta, *b*. This is the stock's risk measure.

Step 3: Estimate the expected rate of return on the market (R_{mkt}).

Step 4: Use the capital asset pricing model (CAPM) equation to estimate the required rate of return:

$$k_s = RFR + b\,(R_{mkt} - RFR)$$

Example: Using CAPM to estimate k_s

Suppose RFR = 6%, R_{mkt} = 11%, and Dexter has a beta of 1.1. Calculate the required rate of return on retained earnings.

Answer

The required rate of return for Dexter's stock is:

$$k_s = 6\% + (11\% - 6\%)(1.1) = 11.5\%$$

2. Bond yield plus risk premium approach. Analysts often use an ad hoc approach to estimate the required rate of return. They add a risk premium (3 to 5 percentage points) to the interest rate of the firm's long-term debt.

    $$k_s = \text{Bond yield} + \text{Risk premium}$$

Example: Estimating k_s with bond yields plus a risk premium

Dexter's interest rate on long-term debt is 8 percent. Supposed the risk premium is estimated to be 5 percent. Calculate Dexter's cost of equity.

Answer

Dexter's cost of equity estimate is:

$$k_s = 8\% + 5\% = 13\%$$

Since it is difficult to estimate the firm's risk premium, k_s will be just a ballpark estimate.

3. The discounted cash flow or dividend yield plus growth rate approach. If dividends are expected to grow at a constant rate, *g*, then the current price of the stock is given by the dividend growth model:

    $$P_o = \frac{D_1}{k_s - g}$$

    where:

D_1 = next year's dividend

k_s = the investor's required rate of return

g = the firm's expected constant growth rate

Rearranging the terms, you can solve for k_s:

$$k_s = \frac{D_1}{P_o} + g$$

In order to use $k_s = \frac{D_1}{P_o} + g$, you have to estimate the expected growth rate, g. This can be done by:

- Using the growth rate as projected by security analysts
- Using the following equation:

g = (Retention rate)(Return on equity) = (1 - Payout rate)(ROE)

The difficulty with this model is estimating the firm's future growth rate.

Example: Estimating k_s using the dividend discount model

Suppose Dexter's stock sells for $21, next year's dividend is expected to be $1, Dexter's expected ROE is 12 percent, and Dexter is expected to pay out 40 percent of its earnings. Calculate Dexter's cost of equity.

$$\frac{1}{21} + (1 - .4)(.12)$$

Answer

g = ROE × retention rate

g = 0.12 × (1 - 0.4) = 0.072 = 7.2%

$$k_s = \left(\frac{\$1}{\$21}\right) + 0.072 = 0.12 = 12\%$$

Note that the three models gave you three different estimates of k_s. The CAPM gave you 11.5 percent, the bond yield plus risk premium gave 13 percent, and the discounted cash flow model gave 12 percent. Analysts must use their judgment to decide which is most appropriate.

4. The cost of newly issued equity (k_e) will be higher than the cost of retained earnings because of the existence of flotation costs. Cost of new common equity is given by:

$$k_e = \frac{D_1}{P_o \times (1 - F)} + g$$

©2007 Kaplan CPA Review

STUDY MANUAL – BUSINESS ENVIRONMENT & CONCEPTS
CHAPTER 5

where:

F = the percentage flotation cost incurred in selling new stock

$$= \frac{\text{current stock price} - \text{funds going to company}}{\text{current stock price}}$$

Example: Cost of newly issued equity

The cost of new equity for Dexter is:

$$k_e = \frac{1}{21 \times (1 - 0.1)} + 0.072 = 0.125 = 12.5\%$$

Note that the cost of new equity (12.5 percent) is higher than the cost of retained earnings (12 percent). Remember, because of flotation costs, $k_e > k_s$.

It is also important for you to know that if the firm does not earn 12.5 percent on that portion of the investment project that is financed with the new equity capital, the firm's growth rate of 7.2 percent will not be met, and the price of the firm's stock will fall. Thus, the sale of new equity is not by itself dilutive. The dilution of earnings comes about only if the new funds are not invested in such a manner as to cover the return of new equity capital.

5. The WACC is given by:

$$\text{WACC} = [w_d \times k_d \times (1 - t)] + (w_{ps} \times k_{ps}) + (w_{ce} \times k_s)$$

where:
w_d = the weights used for debt
w_{ps} = the weights used for preferred stock
w_{ce} = the weights used for common equity

The weights are based on the firm's target (optimal) capital structure. Given such an assumption, the weights should be based on the market value of the firm's securities. However, if the firm's book value figures (accounting values shown on the balance sheet) are reasonably close to their market values, then and only then should you use book value weights to approximate market values.

Example: Computing WACC

Suppose Dexter's target capital structure is as follows:

$w_d = 0.45$, $w_{ps} = 0.05$, and $w_{ce} = 0.50$

If all new equity will come from retained earnings and k_s is calculated using the dividend yield plus growth rate approach, Dexter's WACC will be:

$$WACC = (0.45)(0.08)(0.6) + (0.05)(0.084) + (0.50)(0.12) = 0.0858 @ 8.6\%$$

On the other hand, if new equity will come from newly issued common stock, then:

$$WACC = (0.45)(0.08)(0.6) + (0.05)(0.084) + (0.50)(0.125) = 0.0883 @ 8.8\%$$

MARGINAL COST OF CAPITAL

A. The marginal cost of capital (MCC) is the cost of the last dollar of new capital the firm raises. The MCC increases as a firm increases the amount of capital it raises during a given period.

1. The WACC is the firm's average cost of funds. It differs from the marginal cost of capital (MCC) in that the MCC is the cost of the last dollar raised by the company. As the firm raises more and more capital, the MCC is likely to be higher than the WACC.

2. Referring to Figure 6, you can see that as long as Dexter keeps its capital structure on target for each dollar the firm raises (by issuing debt and preferred stock and retaining earnings), the cost of capital will be 8.6 percent. However, at some point the firm's retained earnings will be exhausted. Beyond that point, Dexter will need to issue new common stock, and its cost of capital will increase to 8.8 percent. Note that the marginal cost of capital is 8.6 percent for all capital values below $120 million and 8.8 percent for all capital raised above $120 million. It is the computation of the break point on the MCC schedule that is critical to the MCC calculation.

3. This means that after Dexter has raised total capital of $120 million, the firm will be forced to issue new common stock, and Dexter's WACC will jump to 8.8 percent.

4. There is some disagreement as to the shape of the WACC curve to the right of the break point. If the firm keeps the same capital structure and does not increase the risk level of new investments, the curve should be flat. Empirical studies, however, show that the marginal cost of capital schedule tends to curve upward to the right from the break point.

STUDY MANUAL – BUSINESS ENVIRONMENT & CONCEPTS
CHAPTER 5

Figure 6: Marginal Cost of Capital Schedule

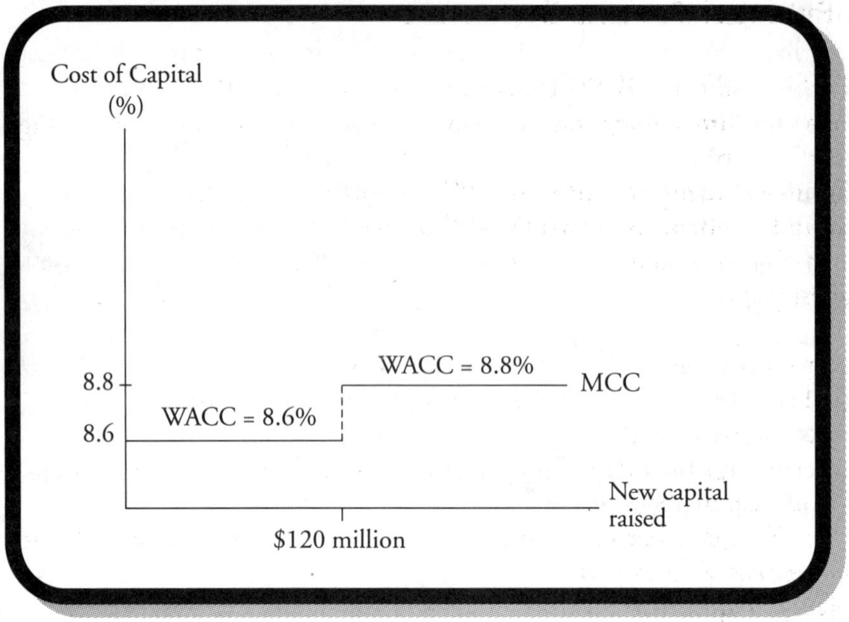

INTERNAL ISSUES THAT AFFECT THE COST OF CAPITAL

A. Factors not under the control of the firm

1. The level of interest rates. As interest rates rise, the cost of debt will certainly increase, and the cost of capital will rise. Rising interest rates will also most likely affect the cost of equity.

2. Tax rates. As tax rates change, the after-tax cost of debt will change.

3. Government action can influence the firm's WACC and thus its capital structure.

B. Factors under the control of the firm

1. Capital structure policy. The firm can alter its target capital structure. As the firm issues more and more debt, the cost of debt rises. The same argument holds true for equity. As more equity is issued, the cost of equity rises.

2. Dividend policy. The firm can change its payout ratio, thus shifting the break point of the MCC schedule. Recall that the dividend payout ratio dictates the break point between lower cost internally generated equity (retained earnings) and higher cost externally generated equity.

3. Investment policy. The major assumption is that all investments have the same degree of risk. By changing the riskiness of investments, the firm will cause the cost of both equity and debt to change.

4. The firm's actions and decisions will influence its level of business and financial risk causing the WACC to change.

Page 182   ©2007 Kaplan CPA Review

STUDY MANUAL – BUSINESS ENVIRONMENT & CONCEPTS

CHAPTER 5

QUESTIONS: FINANCE: CAPITAL BUDGETING

1. Which of the following is NOT a net present value (NPV) decision rule?
   A. When choosing among independent projects, select the one with the highest rate of return.
   B. If an independent investment's NPV is negative, reject the project.
   C. If an independent investment's NPV is positive, accept the project.
   D. When choosing among mutually exclusive projects, select the one with the highest NPV.

2. The financial manager at Johnson & Smith estimates that its required rate of return is 11 percent. Which of the following independent projects should Johnson & Smith accept?
   A. Project A requires an up-front expenditure of $1,000,000 and generates an NPV of negative $4,600.
   B. Project B requires an up-front expenditure of $800,000 and generates a positive IRR of 10.5 percent.
   C. Project C requires an up-front expenditure of $600,000 and generates a positive internal rate of return of 12.0 percent.
   D. Project D requires an up-front expenditure of $100,000 and generates a negative IRR of 3.2 percent.

3. In order to calculate the net present value (NPV) of a project, an analyst must know all of the following EXCEPT the:
   A. size of the expected cash flows from the project.
   B. internal rate of return (IRR) of the project.
   C. opportunity cost of capital for the project.
   D. timing of the expected cash flows from the project.

4. Capital budgeting is critical for all of the following reasons EXCEPT:
   A. it requires forecasts of revenues over the asset's life.
   B. a firm's assets define a firm's strategic plan.
   C. it focuses on the purchase of assets that will be sold within one year.
   D. the firm loses some flexibility in its ability to invest in other assets.

5. Which of the following statements about various capital budgeting terms is FALSE?
   A. Opportunity costs are cash flows that a firm passes up by taking a project.
   B. Sunk costs are developmental costs that should be considered in the capital budgeting decision.
   C. Shipping and installation costs are part of the depreciable basis of a project.
   D. Externalities refer to the cannibalization of sales that occurs when a new project is initiated.

©2007 Kaplan CPA Review

Page 183

STUDY MANUAL – BUSINESS ENVIRONMENT & CONCEPTS
CHAPTER 5

6. Which of the following statements about the payback period is FALSE?
    A. The payback method considers all cash flows throughout the entire life of a project.
    B. The payback period provides a rough measure of a project's liquidity and risk.
    C. The cumulative net cash flow is the running total through time of a project's cash flows.
    D. The payback period is the number of years it takes to recover the original cost of the investment.

7. A company is considering the purchase of a copier that costs $5,000. Assume a cost of capital of 10 percent and the following cash flow schedule:
    *   Year 1: $3,000
    *   Year 2: $2,000
    *   Year 3: $2,000

    What is the project's payback period?
    A. 1.5 years.
    B. 2.0 years.
    C. 2.5 years.
    D. 3.0 years.

8. Jack Smith, CPA, is analyzing independent investment projects X and Y. Smith has calculated the net present value (NPV) and internal rate of return (IRR) for each project:

    Project X: NPV = $250; IRR = 15%

    Project Y: NPV = $5,000; IRR = 8%

    Smith should make which of the following recommendations concerning the two projects:

	Project X	Project Y
A.	Accept	Accept
B.	Accept	Reject
C.	Reject	Accept
D.	Reject	Reject

9. Which of the following is NOT a net present value (NPV) decision rule?
    A. When choosing among mutually exclusive projects, select the one with the highest NPV.
    B. If an independent investment's NPV is positive, accept the project.
    C. If an independent investment's NPV is negative, reject the project.
    D. When choosing among independent projects, select the one with the highest rate of return.

10. The firm's target capital structure is consistent with which of the following?
   A. Maximum earnings per share (EPS).
   B. Minimum weighted-average cost of capital (WACC).
   C. Minimum cost of equity (k_s).
   D. Minimum risk.

11. The capital structure that:
   A. minimizes the interest rate on debt also maximizes the expected EPS.
   B. minimizes the required rate on equity maximizes the stock price.
   C. maximizes the stock price minimizes the weighted-average cost of capital.
   D. maximizes expected EPS maximizes the price per share of common stock.

12. Which of the following is likely to encourage a firm to increase the amount of debt in its capital structure?
   A. The corporate tax rate increases.
   B. The firm's assets become less liquid.
   C. The firm's earnings become more volatile.
   D. The personal tax rate increases.

13. A firm's optimal debt ratio:
   A. minimizes risk.
   B. is a value equal to 1.0.
   C. is the firm's target capital structure.
   D. maximizes return.

14. A firm's capital structure affects:
   A. default risk but not return on equity.
   B. return on equity and default risk.
   C. return on equity but not default risk.
   D. neither return on equity nor default risk.

15. Which of the following influence(s) the cost of capital?
   A. General economic conditions.
   B. Marketability of securities.
   C. Amount of financing the firm requires.
   D. All of these choices are correct.

16. Which of the following statements about the cost of capital is FALSE?
   A. If the firm needs more funding than can be supported by retained earnings, the firm's weighted-average cost of capital (WACC) will increase.
   B. As the firm raises more and more capital, market efficiency would indicate that the firm's marginal weighted-average cost of capital should fall.
   C. Assuming constant risk, the firm's marginal WACC is the correct discount rate to use in making capital budgeting decisions.
   D. If a firm earns exactly the marginal cost of capital on its new investment projects, it will satisfy the return requirements of its creditors and equity investors.

STUDY MANUAL – BUSINESS ENVIRONMENT & CONCEPTS
CHAPTER 5

17. National Auto uses debt, preferred stock, and common stock to finance operations. Calculation of the cost of capital requires identification of the:
A. company's product.
B. risk-free rate.
C. percentage of financing coming from each financing source.
D. net present value of the project to be financed.

18. American Outlook, Inc., is issuing bonds to obtain the funding necessary to acquire a major competitor. Review of the balance sheets indicates that American Outlook has also issued preferred and common stock in the past. Which component cost(s) should American Outlook use to evaluate the financial cost of acquiring the new firm?
A. The weighted-average component cost of common stock, preferred stock, and debt.
B. The cost of the new debt issue alone.
C. The price the firm paid for its assets divided by their market value.
D. Shareholders' equity.

19. Julius, Inc., is interested in calculating the weighted-average cost of capital (WACC) for the firm but must first calculate the various component costs of capital. The firm is in a 40 percent marginal tax bracket. The firm can raise as much capital as needed in the bond market at a cost of 10 percent. The preferred stock has a fixed dividend of $4. The price of preferred stock is $35, and the issue cost will equal 10 percent. The after-tax costs of debt and preferred stock are closest to:

	Debt	Preferred Stock
A.	10.0%	12.7%
B.	6.0%	11.4%
C.	10.0	11.4%
D.	6.0%	12.7%

20. The most expensive source of capital is:
A. debt.
B. preferred stock.
C. new common stock.
D. retained earnings.

21. If the Fed caused the risk-free rate to increase, we would expect the cost of capital to:
A. decrease.
B. increase.
C. remain unchanged.
D. need more information to answer the question.

Page 186   ©2007 Kaplan CPA Review

22. Ravencroft Supplies is estimating its weighted-average cost of capital (WACC). Ravencroft's optimal capital structure includes 10 percent preferred stock, 30 percent debt, and 60 percent equity. It can sell additional bonds at a rate of 8 percent. The cost of issuing new preferred stock is 12 percent. The firm can issue new shares of common stock at a cost of 14.5 percent. The firm's marginal tax rate is 35 percent. Ravencroft's WACC is closest to:
    A. 11.1 percent.
    B. 13.3 percent.
    C. 12.3 percent.
    D. 11.5 percent.

23. Assume a firm uses a constant WACC to select investment projects rather than adjusting the projects for risk. If so, the firm will tend to:
    A. accept profitable, low-risk projects and reject unprofitable, high-risk projects.
    B. accept profitable, low-risk projects and accept unprofitable, high-risk projects.
    C. reject profitable, low-risk projects and accept unprofitable, high-risk projects.
    D. reject profitable, low-risk projects and reject unprofitable, high-risk projects.

24. Which of the following statements about zero-coupon bonds is FALSE?
    A. The lower the price, the greater the return for a given maturity.
    B. A zero-coupon bond may sell at a premium to par when interest rates decline.
    C. A zero-coupon bond provides a single cash flow at maturity equal to its par value.
    D. All interest is earned at maturity.

25. Which of the following contains the overall rights of the bondholders?
    A. Indenture.
    B. Trustee.
    C. Rights offering.
    D. Covenant.

26. When calculating the weighted-average cost of capital (WACC), an adjustment is made for taxes because:
    A. equity is risky.
    B. the interest cost of debt is tax deductible.
    C. preferred stock is involved.
    D. equity earns higher return than debt.

27. The three elements needed to estimate the cost of equity capital for use in determining a firm's weighted average cost of capital are:
    A. current dividends per share, expected growth rate in dividends per share, and current book value per share of common stock.
    B. current dividends per share, expected growth rate in earnings per share, and current market price per share of common stock.
    C. current earnings per share, expected growth rate in dividends per share, and current market price per share of common stock.
    D. current dividends per share, expected growth rate in dividends per share, and current market price per share of common stock.

STUDY MANUAL – BUSINESS ENVIRONMENT & CONCEPTS
CHAPTER 5

28. When evaluating capital budgeting analysis techniques, the payback period emphasizes
   A. liquidity.
   B. profitability.
   C. cost of capital.
   D. net income.

29. If the net present value of a capital budgeting project is positive, it would indicate that the:
   A. present value of cash outflows exceeds the present value of cash inflows.
   B. payback period is less than one-half of the life of the project.
   C. internal rate of return is equal to the discount percentage rate used in the net present value computation.
   D. rate of return for this project is greater than the discount percentage rate used in the net present value computation.

30. A disadvantage of the net present value method of capital expenditure evaluation is that it:
   A. is calculated using sensitivity analysis.
   B. computes the true interest rate.
   C. does not provide the true rate of return on investment.
   D. is difficult to apply because it uses a trial and error approach.

31. The net present value of a proposed investment is negative; therefore, the discount rate used must be:
   A. greater than the project's internal rate of return.
   B. less than the project's internal rate of return.
   C. greater than the firm's cost of equity.
   D. less than the risk free rate.

32. Willis Inc. has a cost of capital of 15 percent and is considering the acquisition of a new machine which costs $400,000 and has a useful life of five years. Willis projects that earnings and cash flow will increase as follows.

Year	Net Earnings	After-Tax Cash Flow
1	$100,000	$160,000
2	100,000	140,000
3	100,000	100,000
4	200,000	100,000

15% Interest Rate Factors

Period	Future Value of $1	Future Value of an annuity of $1
1	0.87	0.87
2	0.76	1.63
3	0.66	2.29
4	0.57	2.86
5	0.50	3.36

The net present value of this investment is:
A. negative, $64,000.
B. negative, $14,000.
C. positive, $18,600.
D. positive, $200,000.

33. The net present value method of capital budgeting assumes that cash flows are reinvested at
A. the risk free rate.
B. the cost of debt.
C. the rate of return of the project.
D. the discount rate used in the analysis.

34. The method that recognizes the time value of money by discounting the after-tax cash flows over the life of a project, using the company's minimum desired rate of return is the:
A. accounting rate of return method.
B. net present value method.
C. internal rate of return method.
D. payback method.

35. The length of time required to recover the initial cash outlay of a capital project is determined by using the:
A. discounted cash flow method.
B. payback period.
C. weighted net present value method.
D. net present value method.

Questions 36 and 37 are based on the following:

The Keego Company is planning a $200,000 equipment investment which has an estimated five-year life with no estimated salvage value. The company has projected the following annual cash flows for the investment.

Year	Projected Cash Inflows	Present Value of $1
1	$120,000	.91
2	$60,000	.76
3	$40,000	.76
4	$40,000	.63
5	$40,000	.44
Totals	$300,000	3.27

36. The net present value for the investment is:
A. $18,800.
B. $218,800.
C. $196,200.
D. $(3,800).

©2007 Kaplan CPA Review

STUDY MANUAL – BUSINESS ENVIRONMENT & CONCEPTS
CHAPTER 5

37. Assuming that the estimated cash inflows occur evenly during each year, the payback period for the investment is:
    A. .75 years.
    B. 1.67 years.
    C. 4.91 years.
    D. 2.50 years.

38. A company has unlimited capital funds to invest. The decision rule for the company to follow in order to maximize shareholders' wealth is to invest in all projects having a(n):
    A. present value greater than zero.
    B. net present value greater than zero.
    C. internal rate of return greater than zero.
    D. accounting rate of return greater than the hurdle rate used in capital budgeting analyses.

39. The internal rate of return is the:
    A. rate of interest that equates the present value of cash outflows and the present value of cash inflows.
    B. minimum acceptable rate of return for a proposed investment.
    C. risk-adjusted rate of return.
    D. required rate of return.

40. An investment project requires an initial investment of $100,000. The project is expected to generate net cash inflows of $28,000 per year for the next five years. Assuming a 12 percent cost of capital, the project's payback period is:
    A. .28 years.
    B. 3.36 years.
    C. 3.57 years.
    D. 20 years.

41. Crown Corporation has agreed to sell some used computer equipment to Bob Parsons, one of the company's employees, for $5,000. Crown and Parsons have been discussing alternative financing arrangements for the sale. The following information is pertinent to these discussions.

Present Value of an Ordinary Annuity of $1

Payments	5%	6%	7%	8%
1	0.952	0.943	0.935	0.926
2	1.859	1.833	1.808	1.783
3	2.723	2.673	2.624	2.577
4	3.546	3.465	3.387	3.312
5	4.329	4.212	4.100	3.993
6	5.076	4.917	4.767	4.623
7	5.786	5.582	5.389	5.206
8	6.463	6.210	5.971	5.747

Page 190   ©2007 Kaplan CPA Review

Crown Corporation has offered to accept a $1,000 down payment and set up a note receivable for Bob Parsons that calls for four $1,000 payments at the end of each of the next four years. If Crown uses a six percent discount rate, the present value of the note receivable would be:

A. $3,960.
B. $3,168.
C. $4,212.
D. $3,465.

42. Mercken Industries is contemplating four projects, Project P, Project Q, Project R, and Project S. The capital costs and estimated after-tax net cash flows of each mutually exclusive projects are listed below. Mercken's desired after-tax opportunity cost is 12 percent, and the company has a capital budget for the year of $450,000. Idle funds cannot be reinvested at greater than 12 percent.

	Project P	Project Q	Project R	Project S
Initial cost	$200,000	$235,000	$190,000	$210,000
Annual cash flows				
Year 1	$93,000	$90,000	$45,000	$40,000
Year 2	93,000	85,000	55,000	50,000
Year 3	93,000	75,000	65,000	60,000
Year 4	-0-	55,000	70,000	65,000
Year 5	-0-	50,000	75,000	75,000
Net present value	$23,370	$29,827	$27,333	$(7,854)
Internal rate of return	18.7%	17.6%	17.2%	10.6%
Excess present value index	1.12	1.13	1.14	0.96

If Mercken was able to accept only one project, the company would choose:
A. Project P.
B. Project Q because it has the highest net present value.
C. Project P because it has the highest internal rate of return.
D. Project S.

43. Fitzgerald Company is planning to acquire a $250,000 machine that will provide increased efficiencies, thereby reducing annual operating costs by $80,000. The machine will be depreciated by the straight-line method over a five-year life with no salvage value at the end of five years. Assuming a 40 percent income tax rate, the machine's payback period is:

A. 3.13 years.
B. 3.21 years.
C. 3.68 years.
D. 4.81 years.

STUDY MANUAL – BUSINESS ENVIRONMENT & CONCEPTS
CHAPTER 5

ANSWERS: FINANCE: CAPITAL BUDGETING

1. **A** NPV focuses on dollar amounts, seeking the highest dollar amount possible. The underlying assumption is that positive NPVs add to the value of the firm and, hence, to shareholder wealth. So, the higher the dollar amount the better. The internal rate of return decision rules focus on rates of return. The highest rate of return does not necessarily mean that the dollar value of the firm will be maximized. Also, the internal rate of return must be higher than the required rate of return. If no project's return exceeds the hurdle rate, no projects should be accepted.

2. **C** When projects are independent, you can use either the NPV method or IRR method to identify the best project. Only Project C has an IRR in excess of 11%. Acceptance of Project A would reduce the firm's value by $4,600.

3. **B** The NPV is calculated using the opportunity cost, size of the expected cash flows, and timing of the expected cash flows from the project. The project's IRR is not used to calculate the NPV.

4. **C** Capital budgeting is the process of determining and selecting the most profitable long-term (> 1 year) investment projects. These investments dictate the firm's mission and strategic plan as the firm's capital is typically locked in for the duration of the asset's life. Given the importance of investment selection, accurate cash flow projections (including revenues and expenditures) are necessary.

5. **B** Sunk costs are not included in capital budgeting analysis because they will not impact the cash flows if the project is taken on or not. They are not incremental costs. An example of a sunk cost is old equipment that is fully depreciated with no salvage value.

6. **A** The payback period does not take into consideration any cash flows after the payback point.

7. **B** After one year, the amount to be recovered is $2,000 ($5,000 – $3,000). After the second year the amount is fully recovered.

8. **A** The projects are independent, meaning it does not matter if one or both projects are chosen. Both projects have a positive NPV, therefore both projects add to shareholder wealth and both projects should be accepted.

9. **D** NPV focuses on dollar amounts, seeking the highest dollar amount possible. The underlying assumption is that positive NPVs add to the value of the firm and, hence, to shareholder wealth. So, the higher the dollar amount the better. The internal rate of return decision rules focus on rates of return. The highest rate of return does not necessarily mean that the dollar value of the firm will be maximized. Also, the internal rate of return must be higher than the required rate of return. If no project's return exceeds the hurdle rate, no projects should be accepted.

10. **B** At the optimal capital structure, the firm will minimize the WACC, maximize the share price of the stock, and maximize the value of the firm.

11. **C** The firm's optimal capital structure will minimize the WACC, maximize the share price of the stock, and maximize the value of the firm.

STUDY MANUAL – BUSINESS ENVIRONMENT & CONCEPTS
CHAPTER 5

12. **A**   An increase in the corporate tax rate will increase the tax benefit to the corporation, because interest expense is deductible in calculating taxable income. An increase in the personal tax rate will not impact the firm's cost of capital. More volatile earnings and less liquidity increase the risk of the firm; therefore, the firm would not desire to increase financial risk as a result of these changes.

13. **C**   The optimal debt ratio for a firm balances the influences of risk and return, leading to a maximization of share price. As such, the optimal debt ratio serves as a target level of debt financing for the value-maximizing firm. A debt ratio of 1.0 would be possible only if 100 percent of the firm were financed with debt, eliminating equity ownership. Such a scenario is impossible.

14. **B**   A firm's capital structure affects both its return on equity and its risk of default. More equity would reduce the return on equity and more debt would increase the risk of default.

15. **D**   If the firm needs to raise additional capital through the equity or debt markets, this action typically increases the cost of capital, due to issue costs for equity and possibly higher interest rates for debt if more risk is perceived. General economic conditions impact market interest rates and therefore the cost of capital for the firm. The marketability of the securities will impact the cost of issuing new securities.

16. **B**   To be true, this statement should read "weighted-average cost of capital should rise." As the firm issues more and more debt, risk increases and therefore debt holders require a higher rate of return causing the cost of debt to rise. Due to the costs of issuing new equity, the cost of equity will also increase after all retained earnings have been used. Note: The capital structure policy is considered to be controllable by the firm.

17. **C**   The weighted-average cost of capital is a weighted-average of the marginal costs of each relevant component. The weights are based on the percentage each particular component represents in the firm's capital structure. Those sources providing more financing of firm assets have a greater weight in calculation of the firm's cost of capital. The risk-free rate only has an impact in that lenders consider it in assigning an interest rate to the firm. The net present value is used in capital budgeting decisions.

18. **A**   How a company raises capital and how it budgets or invests it are considered independently. The financing department is responsible for keeping costs low and using a balance of funding sources. The investment decision should be made assuming a weighted-average cost of capital including each of the different sources of capital.

19. **D**   After-tax cost of debt = 10% × (1 − 0.4)

   = 6% (the after-tax interest rate)

   Cost of preferred stock = $4/[$35 × (1 − 0.10)]

   = 12.7% (the dividend / the net proceeds from issuing the stock)

20. **C**   The required return to investors or cost of capital is greater for equity than for debt or preferred stock because debtors and preferred equity holders must be paid prior to common equity dividends. The cost of issuing new common equity is more than the cost of retained earnings due to issue costs.

STUDY MANUAL – BUSINESS ENVIRONMENT & CONCEPTS
CHAPTER 5

21. **B** An increase in the risk-free rate will cause the cost of equity to increase. It would also most likely cause the cost of raising new debt to increase as market rates increase based on the increase in the Fed funds rate.

22. **D** $0.10(12\%) + 0.30(8\%)(1 - 0.35) + 0.6(14.5\%) = 11.46\%$. This is the standard formula for calculating WACC. Remember that only the debt has a tax-deductible interest, so its cost is calculated on an after-tax basis.

23. **C** The firm will reject profitable, low-risk projects because it will use a hurdle rate that is too high. The firm should lower the required rate of return for lower-risk projects. The firm will accept unprofitable, high-risk projects because the hurdle rate of return used will be too low relative to the risk of the project. The firm should increase the required rate of return for high-risk projects.

24. **B** Zero-coupon bonds always sell below their par value, or at a discount, prior to maturity. "Zero coupon" means that there is no periodic interest payment, so the return to the purchaser is the appreciation to par value that takes place between the date of purchase and the date of maturity. The amount of the discount may change as market interest rates change, but a zero-coupon bond will always be priced less than par. The lower the price the greater the return is true, because the maturity value will be fixed. It is true that all interest is earned at maturity, because at that point, the bond can be cashed in for its maturity value. This describes the last remaining answer, which says that holding the bond to maturity yields a single cash flow equal to its par.

25. **A** An indenture is a bond contract. Covenants (aka agreements) are the features and conditions of the bond, and are part of the indenture. The trustee acts as a representative of the bondholders. A rights offering describes an equity offering—not a bond offering.

26. **B** Equity and preferred stock are not adjusted for taxes because dividends are not deductible for corporate taxes. Only interest expense is deductible for corporate taxes.

27. **D** The three elements needed to estimate the cost of equity capital include current dividends per share, expected growth rate in dividends per share, and current market price per share of common stock.

28. **A** The payback period emphasizes liquidity: The project with the shortest period required to recoup capital invested is preferred. Answer (b) is not correct because the payback method does not look at profitability: It focuses on cash flows, not profits. Answer (c) is not correct because the payback method does not use cost of capital or any interest rate, since it does not discount the cash flows. Answer (d) is not correct because the payback method uses cash flows, not net income.

29. **D** A rate of return greater than the discount percentage produces a positive net present value, just as a rate of return less than the discount percentage produces a negative one. Answer (a) is not correct because if the present value of the cash outflows exceeds the present value of the cash inflows, the net present value would be negative. Answer (b) is not correct the payback period, which does not use discounted cash flows, has no mathematical relation to the net present value. Answer (c) is not correct because if the internal rate of return is equal to the discount percentage used in the net present value computation, the net present value would be zero.

30. **C** The NPV method does not provide the true rate of return on an investment. Rather, it uses a company's discount rate to evaluate whether or not the investment has a positive NPV. To compute an investment's rate of return, a company should use the internal rate

Page 194
©2007 Kaplan CPA Review

of return method. Choice (a) is incorrect. The NPV is not calculated using sensitivity analysis. It is calculated using amount assumed to be accurate. However, sensitivity analysis may subsequently be used to measure the sensitivity of the NPV to changes in the assumed amounts. Choice (b) is incorrect. NPV does not compute any interest rate. It uses a company's discount rate to evaluate whether or not an investment has a positive NPV. Choice (d) is incorrect. NPV does not use a trial and error approach. It uses cash flow amounts and a discount rate assumed to be accurate and computes NPV one time.

31. **A**   The internal rate of return (IRR) of a project is that rate which discounts the future cash inflows back to an amount equal to its initial investment, or that rate which produces a zero net present value. A discount rate greater than the IRR will produce a negative NPV, suggesting that the company is requiring a higher rate of return than this project generates. Choice (b) is incorrect. If the company's discount rate is less than the project's IRR, then the project would have a relatively high IRR and would be acceptable because its NPV would be positive. Choice (c) is incorrect. The relationship between a firm's cost of equity and its discount rate has no bearing on whether any given investment is acceptable (positive NPV) or unacceptable (negative NPV). Choice (d) is incorrect. The discount rate should probably never be less than the risk-free rate (e.g., the rate that could be earned on U. S. Treasury instruments). Even if it were, it would have no bearing on whether any given investment is acceptable (positive NPV) or unacceptable (negative NPV).

32. **C**   The net present value is computed as follows:

Year	After-Tax Cash Flow	Present Value of $1	Present Value of Cash Flows
1	$160,000	0.87	$139,200
2	140,000	0.76	106,400
3	100,000	0.66	66,000
4	100,000	0.57	57,000
5	100,000	0.50	50,000

Total present value of future cash inflows	$418,600
Less initial investment	400,000
Net present value	$18,600

33. **D**   The NPV method uses the discount rate used in the analysis to bring the future cash flows back to their present value. It thus assumes that cash generated in future years earns that rate of return. Choice (a) is incorrect. The risk-free rate (e.g., the rate U. S. Treasury instruments are earning) is not used in the NPV analysis. Choice (b) is incorrect. The specific cost of debt should not be used in NPV analysis because methods of financing should not be considered until after a project has been found to be acceptable. Choice (c) is incorrect. The rate of return of the project (its internal rate of return) may be the correct answer for the internal rate of return method, but not for the NPV method.

34. **B**   The net present value method does indeed recognize the time value of money by discounting the after-tax cash flows using the company's hurdle rate. The accounting rate of return (choice a) deals with net income, not cash flows, and does not use the time value of money. The internal rate of return (choice c) does not use the company's minimum desired rate of return for discounting, but rather finds the rate of return which produces a zero net present value. The payback method (choice d) does not discount cash flows and may not even utilize all of the cash flows over the life of a project, only those flows until payback is achieved.

STUDY MANUAL – BUSINESS ENVIRONMENT & CONCEPTS
CHAPTER 5

35. **B** The payback method divides the initial cash outlay by the annual cash inflows (if equal every year) or else the method subtracts from the initial cash outlay the yearly inflows until the amount is reduced to zero. In either case, the number of years required to recover the initial cash outlay is determined. The discounted cash flow method (answer a) discounts future cash flows at a given interest rate to calculate their present value, or determines the interest rate which will discount their present value to equal the initial cash outlay. The net present value method (answer d) discounts future cash inflows at the company's hurdle rate to determine whether their sum exceeds the initial cash outlay. The weighted net present value method (answer c) is like the net present value method but management may choose to assign weights to different amounts.

36. **A** The present value of the cash inflows is computed as follows:

Year	Cash Inflows	Present Value Factor	Net Present Value
1	$120,000	0.91	$109,200
2	60,000	0.76	45,600
3	40,000	0.63	25,200
4	40,000	0.53	21,200
5	40,000	0.44	17,600

Present value of cash inflows	$218,000
Less initial outlay	200,000
Net present value	$18,800

37. **D** The payback period is determined by computing how long it would take the inflows to equal the initial outflow of $200,000. The inflows from the first two years total $180,000. Thus $20,000 is needed from the third year, or $20,000/$40,000 or .5 of the third year's cash flow is required. Thus the payback is 2.5 years.

38. **B** All projects with a net present value greater than zero will increase shareholders' wealth. Choice (a) is wrong because present value generally refers to the present value of the cash inflows, before considering reducing it by the initial cash outflow; choice (c) is wrong because an internal rate of return greater than zero does not make a project desirable unless it is also greater than the company's cost of capital; choice (d) is wrong because the accounting rate of return has several flaws, such as not considering the time value of money.

39. **A** The internal rate of return (IRR) is indeed that interest rate which yields a net present value of zero for the project. Choices (b) and (d) are wrong because it is rather the cost of capital which is usually considered the minimum acceptable, or required rate of return for a project; choice (c) is wrong because the risk-adjusted rate of return is a rate subjectively adjusted by management to require higher rates for riskier projects

40. **C** The payback period is the initial investment divided by the net annual cash inflows. Thus, $100,000 divided by $28,000 is 3.57. The cost of capital is not used in payback computations.

41. **D** The table gives the present value of an ordinary annuity factor, and payments at the end of years are ordinary annuities. Thus, the factor for 6% and 4 years is 3.465 for $1. For $1,000, the amount would be 1,000 times 3.465, or $3,465.

42. **B** Any project can be chosen, but only one. Maximizing net present value is usually considered the best criterion for ranking capital projects. Thus Project Q would be chosen.

STUDY MANUAL – BUSINESS ENVIRONMENT & CONCEPTS
CHAPTER 5

43. **C**   The payback period is computed by dividing the initial cost by the annual net after-tax cash inflows (assuming equal inflows each year).

The inflows consist of two items, the first of which is the $80,000 in cost savings. If the tax rate is 40%, the company keeps 60% of the $80,000 after tax, which is $48,000.

The second inflow is the depreciation tax shield. The company will deduct depreciation expense of $50,000 per year. At a 40% tax rate, this will save the company 40% of $50,000, which is $20,000.

Thus, the total after-tax cash inflow per year is $48,000 + $20,000, or $68,000.

Finally, then, the payback period is $250,000 divided by $68,000 savings per year, or 3.68 years.

©2007 Kaplan CPA Review

FINANCE: RISK

STUDY MANUAL – BUSINESS ENVIRONMENT & CONCEPTS
CHAPTER 6

Study Tip: The more you know about the CPA exam, the more chance you have for success. Before you get too far into your preparation, go to ww.cpa-exam.org and read the official "Candidate Bulletin."

ENTERPRISE-WIDE RISK MANAGEMENT CONCEPTS

A. Introduction to ERM.

1. Enterprise-wide risk management (ERM) is an attempt to manage all types of risk across all business units of the firm. The types of risk that must be managed include the following:

   a. Broad risk (e.g., market risk, credit risk).

   b. Instrument risk (equity, bond, or commodity risk).

   c. Risks associated with individual segments of the firm.

   d. Risks associated with the firm as a whole (e.g., legal risk and regulatory risk).

2. ERM systems can be implemented in very different ways, depending on the business needs of the firm. Characteristics that may vary across ERM systems are the level of sophistication, timeliness of information, and the level of integration of risk analysis.

3. ERM systems can range from a simple sharing of relevant information across the firm to a sophisticated centralized risk-management system. Timeliness of data and information can vary from real time to far less frequent updating. The level of integration of risk analysis can vary from little integration to a sophisticated centralized risk-assessment system.

B. The benefits of ERM.

1. The benefits of an ERM system are directly proportional to the complexity of the firm. Some of the benefits are:

   a. Major enhancements to risk-return analysis. With the improvement in risk reporting associated with an ERM system, the quality of risk-return analysis is greatly improved.

b. Improved decision making at all levels. With an ERM system, all decision makers are better informed regarding risk across other business units and at the firm level. Thus, coordination across all levels of management is more efficient.

c. Improved allocation of capital. With an ERM system, the computation of risk and, therefore, the computation of expected risk-adjusted marginal returns are improved, thus providing for better allocation decisions.

d. Enhanced data collection and analysis. An ERM system imposes discipline on the firm with respect to data collection, ensures consistency in measurement and processing, highlights gaps and other data problems, facilitates auditing and monitoring, reduces the likelihood of human error or fraud, and enhances managerial control over business units with respect to risk.

e. Enhanced information available to market participants. With an ERM system, firms are better able to communicate to the market their risk exposures and hedging status to the investing public.

C. Features of an ERM system.

1. Centralized data storage.

a. The first step in establishing an ERM system is the creation of "one-stop" shopping, i.e., a centralized storage system that allows access to all position, credit, and transactions data. This is an overwhelming job for large firms. Consider the disparate data sources, conventions, procedures, and even regulatory requirements across a large firm, and it is easy to recognize the difficulty associated with this task.

b. Once the data has been centralized, it needs to be standardized and cleaned. Keep in mind that offices across locations are likely to have different computer systems, and the information is not likely to be in the same format or entered in a similar manner. This is easily the most daunting step in developing an ERM system.

2. Data analysis

a. Once the data has been centralized, the next step is to put it to work. Management needs to be able to properly analyze the data through several value at risk (VAR) methodologies (e.g., variance-covariance, historical, and Monte Carlo simulation), sophisticated credit risk analysis, liquidity risk analysis, and even operational and legal risk analysis.

3. Continual monitoring and updating.

a. The third step is to ensure that the system output gets to the proper monitors who continually evaluate it as well as look for new or different data necessary for successful monitoring. This would include the ability to easily identify data problems, identify position limit violations, perform diagnostics on

STUDY MANUAL – BUSINESS ENVIRONMENT & CONCEPTS
CHAPTER 6

pricing and VAR measures computed by the analytics system, and allow for risk adjustments and performance evaluation.

4. Dissemination of the analysis.

   a. The system must provide the means for disseminating the analysis to the appropriate personnel. This allows the decision makers to take corrective actions where necessary or to allocate resources more efficiently.

D. Integration of risk analysis.

   1. The benefits of an integrated risk-analysis system include:

      a. Efficient use of resources. Since most risk measurement systems now use similar methods, duplicative systems make little sense.

      b. Consistent and comparable results.

      c. Consistency across different risk measures in their underlying assumptions.

      d. More easily understood cross-effects of the different risk measures (e.g., the interaction between credit and market risk).

      e. Better integration of analysis for several types of risks for hybrid securities. With the increasing number of hybrid securities in the market, an integrated risk-analysis system is required for proper risk measurement.

   2. Analyzing the risks separately makes little sense, since the value of these instruments is influenced by the interaction of several different types of risk.

STUDY MANUAL – BUSINESS ENVIRONMENT & CONCEPTS
CHAPTER 6

QUESTIONS: FINANCE: RISK

1. Invect Corporation is considering an investment that has an estimated cost of $5,000 and a single cash inflow of $9,000 in exactly two years. Of the following scenarios, which would NOT be considered risk?
    A. The possibility of receiving a cash inflow of either $12,000 or $8,500 in two years.
    B. The possibility of receiving a cash inflow of $8,000 in two years.
    C. No possibility of having a cash inflow that is either greater or less than $9,000.
    D. The possibility of the investment cost being greater than $5,000 with the cash inflow remaining at $9,000.

2. Which of the following statements about business risk and financial risk is FALSE?
    A. Financial risk is the additional risk placed on the common stockholders as a result of the decision to use debt.
    B. Factors that affect business risk are demand, sales price, and input price variability.
    C. The greater a company's business risk, the higher its optimal debt ratio.
    D. Business risk is the riskiness of the company's assets if it uses no debt.

3. Hughes Continental is assessing its business risk. Which of the following factors would NOT be considered in the analysis?
    A. Use of preferred stock instead of common stock to finance acquisitions.
    B. Unit sales levels.
    C. Unit sales trends.
    D. Input price variability.

4. The uncertainty in return on assets due to the nature of a firm's operations is known as:
    A. tax efficiency.
    B. financial leverage.
    C. financial flexibility.
    D. business risk.

5. Which of the following sources of uncertainties would be affected by the firm's debt versus equity decision?
    A. Business risk.
    B. Country risk.
    C. Financial risk.
    D. Liquidity risk.

©2007 Kaplan CPA Review   Page 201

STUDY MANUAL – BUSINESS ENVIRONMENT & CONCEPTS
CHAPTER 6

6. In order to minimize credit risk with a letter of credit:
   A. the issuer of the letter of credit should be wholly owned by the debtor.
   B. there should be a high correlation between the financial performance of the debtor and the issuer of the letter of credit.
   C. the creditor should have a financial investment in the issuer of the letter of credit.
   D. there should be a low correlation between the financial performance of the debtor and the issuer of the letter of credit.

7. Which of the following parties is least likely to benefit from risky strategies that increase risk and expected return for a company?
   A. Chief financial officers.
   B. Chief executive officers.
   C. Stockholders.
   D. Creditors.

8. Which of the following factors does NOT affect business risk?
   A. Input price variability.
   B. Demand variability.
   C. Interest rate variability.
   D. Operating leverage.

9. Which of the following is NOT an example of mechanisms used by shareholders to motivate managers to act in the stockholders' best interests?
   A. Shares of stock for achieving a benchmark increase in earnings per share.
   B. Fringe benefits, such as interest-free loans and on-site child care.
   C. Institutional investors persuasively intervening on important corporate issues.
   D. The board of directors threatening to fire current management.

10. The agency problem refers to:
    A. hiring independent agents to sell a firm's products in the wholesale market.
    B. buying insurance to protect a firm's assets through an agent who charges sales commission.
    C. selling products through an agent who has final control over the selling price and not the manufacturer.
    D. managers acting in their own best interest at the expense of stockholders.

Page 202   ©2007 Kaplan CPA Review

STUDY MANUAL – BUSINESS ENVIRONMENT & CONCEPTS
CHAPTER 6

ANSWERS: FINANCE: RISK

1. **C**   Investment risk is uncertainty about the initial or future cash flows. Even if the cash flows may be higher than expected, in a strict sense, risk appears because it results in uncertainty about what the cash flows will be. If there is no possibility that the actual cash flows will differ from the expected (forecasted) cash flows, then there is no risk.

2. **C**   The greater a company's business risk, the lower its optimal debt ratio.

3. **A**   The main factors affecting business risk are demand variability, sales price variability, input price variability, ability to adjust output prices, and operating leverage. Although preferred stock is referred to as stock, it represents a claim to the company revenues that comes prior to that of common shareholders. This claim may be in the form of annual dividends, which typically cannot be overlooked by the managers of the company. Product sales and input prices influence a company's performance regardless of whether preferred stock (or debt) is issued.

4. **D**   Business risk is a function of the firm's revenue and expenses, resulting in operating income, or earnings before interest and taxes (EBIT). The main factors affecting business risk are demand variability, sales price variability, input price variability, ability to adjust output prices, and operating leverage (use of fixed costs).

5. **C**   The firm's financial risk is the uncertainty introduced through the method by which the firm finances its investments, which includes the debt versus equity decision.

6. **D**   There should be a low correlation between the financial performance of the debtor and the letter of credit issuer in order to minimize the credit risk to the creditor. Since the creditor is exposed to the credit risk of the debtor, the creditor should not have any financial interest in the guarantor of that credit.

7. **D**   Creditors bear the responsibility for bankruptcy in that they will not receive the principal back from their investment. If the project is a great success, creditors' returns will not increase; they will only receive the money loaned plus interest. On the other hand, stockholders could see the value of their shares rise many times over, while the reputation of the managers (and their bonuses) is likely to rapidly increase.

8. **C**   Business risk can be defined as the uncertainty inherent in a firm's return on assets (ROA). While changes in interest rates may impact the demand or input prices, there is a more direct impact on business risk with the other three choices.

9. **B**   Tying compensation to performance is the key mechanism shareholders use to align management's and shareholders' interests. Threats of firing, takeover, monitoring, and direct intervention by shareholders are also mechanisms used to keep managers acting in the best interests of stockholders.

10. **D**   Managers act as agents for stockholders. When managers make decisions that benefit themselves at the cost of stockholders, the problem is referred to as an agency problem.

©2007 Kaplan CPA Review

FINANCE: FINANCIAL MODELS VALUATION

STUDY MANUAL – BUSINESS ENVIRONMENT & CONCEPTS
CHAPTER 7

Study Tip: Before you go to bed each night, write down what exam preparation you plan to accomplish the following day and when you will do it. In that way, you begin each day with an organized plan and do not have to waste time determining what to do as the day progresses.

FINANCIAL MODELING: TIME VALUE OF MONEY CONCEPTS AND APPLICATIONS

INTRODUCTION

In order for money to have time value, it must be possible to invest it at a positive rate of return. The rate of return (interest rate) that provides money with time value is composed of three components:

1. Risk-free rate. This is the rate that is earned on a riskless investment, and it represents the compensation that investors require to defer current consumption. The rate on short-term U.S. Treasury securities is typically used to represent the risk-free rate.

2. Inflation premium. This is the return that investors require to compensate them for the change of purchasing power over an investment horizon.

3. Risk premium. This is the compensation that investors require for being exposed to various types of investment risk.

The concept of compound interest and interest on interest is deeply embedded in time value of money (TVM) procedures. When an investment is subjected to compound interest, the growth in the value of the investment from period to period reflects not only the interest earned on the original principal amount but also on the interest earned on the previous period's interest earnings—the interest on interest.

TVM applications frequently call for the determination of the future value (FV) of an investment's cash flows as a result of the effects of compound interest. The process of computing FVs involves projecting the cash flows forward on the basis of an appropriate compound interest rate to the end of the investment's life.

Page 204   ©2007 Kaplan CPA Review

The computation of the present value (PV) works in the opposite direction—it brings the cash flows from an investment back to the beginning of the investment's life on the basis of an appropriate compound rate of return.

The usefulness of being able to measure the PV and/or FV of an investment's cash flows comes into play when comparing investment alternatives, because the value of the investment's cash flows must be measured at some common point in time, either at the end of the investment horizon (FV) or at the beginning of the investment horizon (PV).

It is often a good idea to draw a timeline before you start to solve a TVM problem. A **timeline** is simply a diagram of the cash flows associated with a TVM problem. A cash flow that occurs in the present (today) is put at time 0. Cash outflows (payments) are given a negative sign, and cash inflows (receipts) are given a positive sign. Once the cash flows are assigned to a timeline, they may be moved to the beginning of the investment period to calculate the PV through a process called *discounting,* or to the end of the period to calculate the FV using a compounding process.

Figure 1 illustrates a timeline for an investment that costs $1,000 today (outflow) and will return a stream of cash payments (inflows) of $300 per year at the end of each of the next five years

Figure 1: Timeline

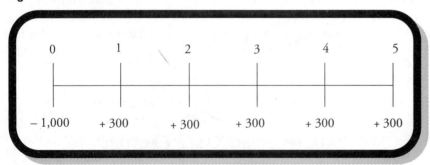

Recognize that the cash flows occur at the end of the period depicted on the timeline. Furthermore, note that the end of one period is the same as the beginning of the next period. For example, the end of $t = 2$ is the same as the beginning of $t = 3$, but the beginning of Year 3 cash flow appears at time $t = 2$ on the timeline. Keeping this convention in mind will help you keep things straight when you are setting up TVM problems.

TERMINOLOGY

A. The real risk-free rate of interest is a theoretical rate on a single-period loan that has no expectation of inflation in it.

   1. When we speak of a real rate of return, we are referring to an investor's increase in purchasing power (after adjusting for inflation).

2. Since expected inflation in future periods is not zero, the rates we observe on T-bills, for example, are risk-free rates but not real rates of return.

3. T-bill rates are nominal risk-free rates because they contain an inflation premium. The approximate relation here is:

Nominal risk-free rate = Real risk-free rate + Expected inflation rate

4. Securities may have one or more of several risks, and each added risk increases the required rate of return on the security. These types of risk are:

a. Default risk—the risk that a borrower will not make the promised payments in a timely manner.

b. Liquidity risk—the risk of receiving less than fair value for an investment if it must be sold for cash quickly.

c. Maturity risk—the prices of longer-term bonds are more volatile than those of shorter-term bonds. Longer-maturity bonds have more maturity risk than shorter-term bonds and require a maturity risk premium.

5. Each of these risk factors is associated with a risk premium that we add to the nominal risk-free rate to adjust for greater default risk, less liquidity, and longer maturity relative to a very liquid, short-term, default risk-free rate such as that on U.S. Treasury bills. We can write:

Required interest rate on a security = Nominal risk-free rate + Default risk premium + Liquidity premium + Maturity risk premium.

CALCULATIONS USING TABLE FACTORS

A. Future value is the amount to which a current deposit will grow over time when it is placed in an account paying compound interest.

Also called the *compound value,* the FV is simply an example of compound interest at work.

B. The present value of a single sum is today's value of a cash flow that is to be received at some point in the future.

1. In other words, it is the amount of money that must be invested today, at a given rate of return over a given period of time, in order to end up with a specified FV.

2. The process for finding the PV of a cash flow is known as *discounting* (i.e., future cash flows are discounted back to the present).

3. The interest rate used in the discounting process is commonly referred to as the *discount rate* but may also be referred to as the *opportunity cost, required rate of return,* and the *cost of capital.*

> 4. Whatever you want to call it, the present value represents the annual compound rate of return that can be earned on an investment. (In a later section, we will discuss cost of capital in more detail.)

C. Note that for a single future cash flow, PV is always less than the FV whenever the discount rate is positive.

D. Present and future value questions on the CPA Exam can be solved with present and future value factors, which will be provided in the question. You may be asked to select from several factors to ensure that you understand the tables.

1. Present value of an amount tables provide the number of periods and the factor for several interest rates. These factors will always be less than one, because when you take the present value of any amount, the PV will be less than the amount to be received later.

2. Future value of an amount tables also provide the number of periods and the factor for several interest rates. These factors will always be more than one, because when you calculate the future value of any amount, you are adding compound interest to the amount and it will, therefore, grow over time.

E. These calculations on the CPA Exam require you to use the following equations:

$$\$PV = \$FV \times PV \text{ factor}$$

$$\$FV = \$PV \times FV \text{ factor}$$

F. Remember the following things when using the tables and the equations:

1. The tables give "periods of time" down the left side. Periods can be years, semiannual periods (i.e., six months), quarters (i.e., three months), or months.

2. The tables give interest rates across the top. The interest rate must correspond to the periods.

3. Interest rates are always stated on an annual basis. Therefore, for quarterly compounding, the annual rate must be divided by four, with the number of periods as total quarters.

4. Example: You are determining the PV or FV of an amount in one year.

   a. If you are finding the PV or FV using 12 percent interest per year, compounded quarterly, then you would look up a table factor for 3 percent and four periods (quarters).

   b. If that interest of 12 percent per year is compounded every six months, or semiannually, your factor would be found at the intersection of 6 percent and two periods.

©2007 Kaplan CPA Review

c. If the interest is compounded annually, the factor would be found at the intersection of one period and 12 percent.

G. Below is a sample selection from PV and FV tables in the format that you might see in CPA Exam questions. Generally, you would be given several factors, and not a complete table.

Present value of 1 at 14% for 4 periods	0.59
Future amount of 1 at 14% for 4 periods	1.69
Present value of an ordinary annuity of 1 at 14% for 4 periods	2.91

ANNUITIES

H. An annuity is a stream of equal cash flows that occur at equal intervals over a given period during which the interest rate does not change. Receiving $1,000 per year at the end of each of the next eight years is an example of an annuity.

1. The ordinary annuity is the most common type of annuity. It is characterized by cash flows that occur at the end of each compounding period. This is a typical cash flow pattern for many investment and business finance applications.

2. The difference between single-sum and annuity TVM problems is that instead of solving for the PV or FV of a single cash flow, we solve for the PV or FV of a stream of equal periodic cash flows, where the size of the periodic cash flow is defined as the payment (PMT).

Example: FV of an ordinary annuity

What is the future value of an ordinary annuity that pays $150 per year at the end of each of the next 15 years given the investment is expected to earn a 7 percent rate of return? The timeline for the cash flows in this problem is depicted in Figure 2:

Figure 2: Future Value of Ordinary Annuity

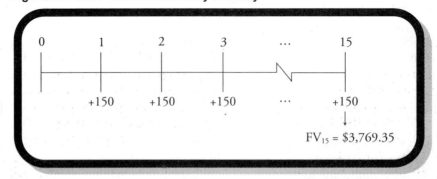

Solution:

As with present value and future value of amount questions, you will be provided factors to be used in solving annuity questions. You will be asked to select the proper factor from several, by identifying the type of problem (FV or PV of ordinary annuity

STUDY MANUAL – BUSINESS ENVIRONMENT & CONCEPTS
CHAPTER 7

or annuity due), the number of periods (number of interest compounding periods), and the appropriate interest rate that corresponds to that number of periods.

In the example above, the factor is for 7 percent interest (*note:* annual interest unless otherwise specified) and 15 periods (years, in this case.) The factor happens to be 25.129. The calculation is:

$Payment × FV annuity factor = $FV of annuity

$150.00 × 25.129 = $3,769.35

BREAKEVEN ANALYSIS

A. Breakeven analysis is a tool used by firms to quantify the effects of operating leverage on their investment projects and on the firm as a whole.

   1. Operating leverage is the trade-off between variable costs and fixed costs.

   2. Operating leverage amplifies the earnings of the firm.

   3. A firm using high operating leverage will make years of good profitability look even better.

   4. Conversely, the same firm will make years of poor profitability look even worse.

   5. These effects are created by the use of fixed costs in the operating structure.

B. Fixed costs cannot be changed in the short run. The costs must be paid no matter how many units of a particular product the firm chooses to produce.

C. Variable costs, on the other hand, are dependent on the number of units the firm produces. If no production is undertaken, no variable costs are incurred.

D. In order to make a profit, the firm must sell enough of its product to cover both the variable and fixed costs. The level of sales at which a firm covers all of its fixed and variable costs is called the *breakeven point*. The breakeven sales quantity, Q_{BE}, can be defined as follows:

Sales revenue = Operating costs

or

(Price per unit)(quantity) = (Variable cost per unit × Quantity) + Fixed costs

or

$PQ = VQ + F$

©2007 Kaplan CPA Review
Page 209

STUDY MANUAL – BUSINESS ENVIRONMENT & CONCEPTS
CHAPTER 7

E. At breakeven, $PQ - VQ - F = 0$. Therefore $Q_{BE} = F/(P - V)$. We have simply solved for Q, which leaves us with a ratio of fixed costs to what is known as the *contribution margin* (i.e., $P - V$). The breakeven quantity of sales is the point at which operating profit is equal to zero. Sales of a quantity greater than Q_{BE} will result in positive operating profit for the firm. Sales of a quantity less than Q_{BE} will result in operating losses for the firm.

Example: Breakeven quantity

Consider the costs for the projects presented in Figure 3. Compute and illustrate the breakeven point for each project.

Figure 3: Project Costs

	Project Atom	Project Beta
Price	$4.00	$4.00
Variable costs	$3.00	$2.00
Fixed costs	$40,000	$120,000
Assets	$400,000	$400,000
Tax rate	40%	40%

Answer:

For Project Atom, the breakeven quantity is:

$$Q_{BE}(\text{Atom}) = \frac{\$40,000}{\$4.00 - \$3.00} = 40,000 \text{ units}$$

The breakeven quantity and the relationship between sales revenue, total operating cost, operating profit, and operating loss are illustrated in Figure 4. (EBIT = Earnings before interest and taxes.)

Figure 4: Breakeven Analysis for Project Atom

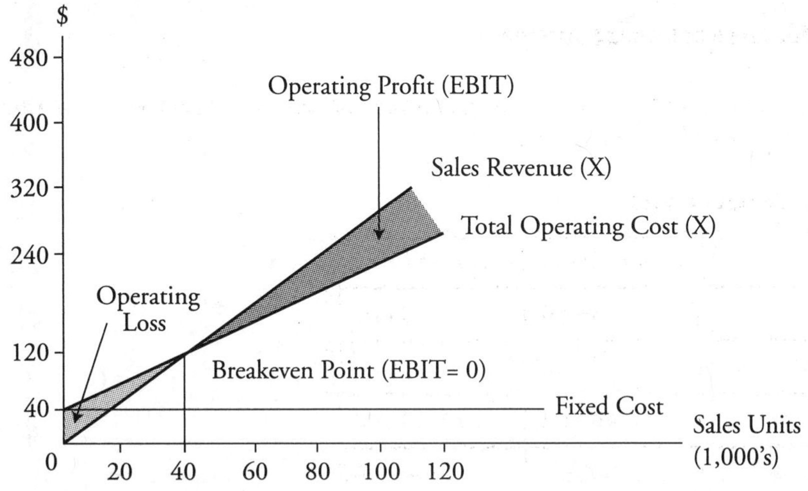

For Project X: $Q_{BE} = \$40,000 / (\$4.00 - \$3.00) = 40,000$ units

Similarly, for Project Beta, the breakeven quantity is:

$$Q_{BE}(\text{Beta}) = \frac{\$120,000}{\$4.00 - \$2.00} = 60,000 \text{ units}$$

The breakeven quantity and the relationship between sales revenue, total operating cost, operating profit, and operating loss are illustrated in Figure 5.

Figure 5: Breakeven Analysis for Project Beta

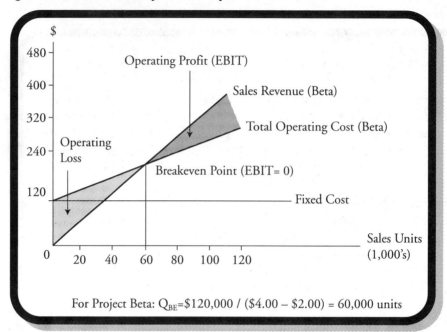

For Project Beta: $Q_{BE} = \$120,000 / (\$4.00 - \$2.00) = 60,000$ units

MEASURES OF RESIDUAL INCOME

A. Residual income (RI), or economic profit, is the net income of a firm less a charge that measures stockholders' opportunity cost of capital.

1. The rationale for the residual income approach is that it recognizes the cost of equity capital in the measurement of income. A similar measure is Economic Value Added (EVA).

2. This concept of economic income is not reflected in traditional accounting income, whereby a firm can report positive net income but not meet the return requirements of its equity investors.

   a. Accounting net income includes a cost of debt (i.e., interest expense) but does not reflect dividends or other equity capital-related funding costs.

   b. This means that accounting income may overstate returns from the perspective of equity investors. Conversely, residual income explicitly *deducts all capital costs*.

STUDY MANUAL – BUSINESS ENVIRONMENT & CONCEPTS
CHAPTER 7

Example: Calculating residual income

Figure 6: Economic Value Added and Market Value Added

Segment	1	2	3
Invested capital	$450,000	$630,000	$520,000
Operating income	$75,000	$90,000	$80,000
Capital charge @ 15%	$67,500	$94,500	$78,000
Residual income	$7,500	$(4,500)	$2,000

A. Economic value added (EVA) measures the value added to shareholders by management during a given year. A company must produce EVA in order to increase its market value. EVA can be calculated as follows:EVA = Net operating profit after tax (NOPAT) – (Weighted-average cost of capital × Invested capital). The term "EVA" is a registered trademark of Stern Stewart & Co., a consulting firm.

B. Market value added (MVA) is the difference between the market value of a firm's long-term debt and equity and the book value of invested capital supplied by investors. It measures the value created by management's decisions since the firm's inception. MVA is calculated as:

  Market value added = Firm value – Invested capital

Example: Calculating EVA and MVA

VBM Inc. reports NOPAT of $2,100, a WACC of 14.2 percent, and invested capital of $18,000. The market price of the firm's stock is $25 per share, and VBM has 800 shares outstanding. The market value of the firm's long-term debt is $4,000. Calculate VBM's economic value added (EVA) and market value added (MVA).

Answer:

First calculate EVA:

  0.142 ($WACC) × $18,000 = $2,556

  EVA = $2,100 – $2,556 = –$456

The market value of the company is the market value of the equity plus the market value of the debt:

  MV of a company = ($25 × 800) + $4,000 = $24,000

The firm's MVA is:

  MVA = $24,000 – $18,000 = $6,000

©2007 Kaplan CPA Review

STUDY MANUAL – BUSINESS ENVIRONMENT & CONCEPTS
CHAPTER 7

QUESTIONS: FINANCIAL MODELS VALUATION

1.   Jayco, Inc., has a division that makes red ink for the accounting industry. The unit has fixed costs of $10,000 per month and is expected to sell 40,000 bottles of ink per month. If the variable cost per bottle is $2, what price must the division charge in order to break even?
A. $2.25.
B. $2.50.
C. $2.75.
D. $3.25.

2.   Jarvis Co. has fixed costs of $200,000. It has two products that it can sell, Tetra and Min. Jarvis sells these products at a rate of two units of Tetra to one unit of Min. The contribution margin is $1 per unit for Tetra and $2 per unit for Min. How many units of Min would be sold at the breakeven point?
A. 44,444.
B. 50,000.
C. 88,888.
D. 100,000.

3.   Which of the following tables should be used to calculate the amount of the equal periodic payments that would be equivalent to an outlay of $3,000 at the time of the last payment?
A. Present value of $1.
B. Amount of $1.
C. Amount of an annuity of $1.
D. Present value of an annuity of $1.

4.   Which of the following tables would show the *largest* value for an interest rate of 5 percent for six periods?
A. Amount of annuity of $1 per period.
B. Present value of annuity of $1 per period.
C. Amount of $1 at compound interest.
D. Present value of $1 at compound interest.

Page 214   ©2007 Kaplan CPA Review

STUDY MANUAL – BUSINESS ENVIRONMENT & CONCEPTS

CHAPTER 7

Use the following information to answer Questions 5 through 8.

Given below are the present-value factors for $1 discounted at 8 percent for one to five periods. Each of the following items is based on 8 percent interest compounded annually from day of deposit to day of withdrawal.

Periods	PV of $1 Discounted at 8% Per Period
1	0.926
2	0.857
3	0.794
4	0.735
5	0.681

5. What amount should be deposited in a bank today to grow to $1,000 three years from today?
    A. $1,000 × 0.926 × 3.
    B. $1,000/0,794.
    C. $1,000 × 0.794.
    D. ($1,000 × 0.926) + ($1,000 × 0.8570 + ($1,000 × 0.794).

6. What amount should an individual have in his or her bank account today before withdrawal if he or she needs $2,000 each year for four years with the first withdrawal to be made today and each subsequent withdrawal at one-year intervals? The individual is supposed to have exactly a zero balance in the bank account after the fourth withdrawal.
    A. ($2,000/0.735) × 4.
    B. $2,000 + ($2,000 × 0.926) + ($2,000 × 0.857) + ($2,000 × 0.794).
    C. ($2,000/0.926) × 4.
    D. ($2,000 × 0.926) + ($2,000 × 0.857) + ($2,000 × 0.794) + ($2,000 × 0.735).

7. If an individual put $3,000 in a savings account today, what amount of cash would be available two years from today?
    A. $3,000 × 0.857 × 2.
    B. $3,000 × 0.857.
    C. ($3,000/0.926) × 2.
    D. $3,000/0.857.

8. What is the present value today of $4,000 to be received six years from today?
    A. $4,000 × 0.681 × 0.926.
    B. $4,000 × 0.794 × 2.
    C. $4,000 × 0.926 × 6.
    D. Cannot be determined from the information given.

STUDY MANUAL – BUSINESS ENVIRONMENT & CONCEPTS
CHAPTER 7

9. Jarvis wants to invest equal semiannual payments in order to have $10,000 at the end of 20 years. Assuming that Jarvis will earn interest at an annual rate of 6 percent compounded semiannually, how would the periodic payment be calculated?
    A. The present value of an ordinary annuity of 40 payments of $1 each at an interest rate of 3 percent per period divided by $10,000.
    B. The future amount of an ordinary annuity of 20 payments of $1 each at an interest rate of 6 percent per period divided by $10,000.
    C. $10,000 divided by the present value of an ordinary annuity of 40 payments of $1 each at an interest rate of 3 percent per period.
    D. $10,000 divided by the future amount of an ordinary annuity of 40 payments of $1 each at an interest rate of 3 percent per period.

10. Which of the following statements regarding market value added (MVA) and economic value added (EVA) is TRUE?
    A. Market value added equals the book value of the firm's capital minus the market value of the capital employed by the firm.
    B. Market value added equals the firm's net operating profit after tax minus the firm's weighted-average cost of capital multiplied by the total capital employed.
    C. Market value added should be equal to the present value, at the company's cost of capital, of the future levels of economic value added.
    D. For a high-growth firm, economic value added is equal to the economic profit of the firm divided by its weighted-average cost of capital.

11. For a given year, a company's economic value added will be positive if the:
    A. firm has a net operating profit after tax greater than the market value of the debt capital employed.
    B. .firm's MVA is positive.
    C. firm earns a return greater than its cost of capital.
    D. firm has a net operating profit after tax greater than the book value of the capital employed.

12. A bank is considering building a branch on a piece of property it already owns. Which of the following cash flows should NOT be considered in the capital budgeting analysis? The:
    A. $50,000 the firm will forgo in lost revenue from the sale of the property if the company decides to build.
    B. $100,000 spent to determine whether there are any environmental issues regarding the property.
    C. several hundred customers that will switch from alternative branches to the new branch if the bank makes the investment.
    D. shipping and installation charges the bank must spend to get equipment in the new branch.

STUDY MANUAL – BUSINESS ENVIRONMENT & CONCEPTS
CHAPTER 7

13. Zig Corp. provides the following information:

Pretax operating profit	$300,000,000
Tax rate	40%
Capital used to generate profits	
50%, 50% equity	$1,200,000,000
Cost of equity	15%
Cost of debt	5%

What of the following represents Zig's year-end economic value-added amount?
A. $0.
B. $60,000,000.
C. $120,000,000.
D. $180,000,000.

STUDY MANUAL – BUSINESS ENVIRONMENT & CONCEPTS
CHAPTER 7

ANSWERS: FINANCIAL MODELS VALUATION

1. **A**   The question asks for the price to charge for each bottle of ink. Let P = price per bottle.

    Remember that the formula for breakeven quantity is Fixed costs/Contribution margin per unit = BE units.

    Contribution margin per unit is price - Variable cost per unit. So, Contribution margin = P – $2.

    We can use the traditional formula to calculate price (rather than the usual breakeven units).

    40,000 bottles = $10,000/(P – $2)

    (40,000 × P) – (40,000 × $2) = $10,000

    40,000 × P = $90,000

    P = $90,000/40,000 = $2.25

2. **B**   This is a breakeven question in which there are multiple products.

    Fixed costs = $200,000.
    Contribution margin for Tetra = $1.
    Contribution margin for Min = $2.
    The sales mix is 2/3 Tetra and 1/3 Min.

    For every unit of Min sold, two units of Tetra are sold. Therefore, the combined contribution margin for each unit of Min sold would be:

    (1 unit × $2) + (2 units × $1) = $4.

    Breakeven = Fixed costs/Contribution margin

    = $200,000/$4

    = 50,000 units (Min)

    Proof: (50,000 Min × $2) + (100,000 Tetra × $1) = $200,000 (Fixed costs)

    An alternative solution is:

    Weighted-average contribution margin is ($1 × 2 units of Tetra) plus ($2 × 1 unit of Min) = $4. $4/3 = $1.33 weighted-average contribution margin.

    $200,000/$1.333 = 150,000 units in total

    2/3 × 150,000 Tetra = 100,000 units

    1/3 × 150,000 Min = 50,000 units

Page 218 ©2007 Kaplan CPA Review

STUDY MANUAL – BUSINESS ENVIRONMENT & CONCEPTS
CHAPTER 7

3. **C** The equal periodic payments are an annuity and the $3,000 is the future value of the annuity; therefore, the appropriate table of interest factors is the compound value (future value) of an annuity of $1. This is a future value problem, where you know the future value and are asked to calculate the associated payment. A common error is to say "I know the future value to be $3,000, so this must be a present value problem." Don't make that mistake!

4. **A** Compound value factors are larger than present value factors as they include principal plus interest for a given period. Annuity factors are larger than single sum factors as they represent a series of payments for a period.

5. **C** Remember: you know the future value and want to know the present value. Present value of a lump sum is defined as:

$$PV = FV \times PV \text{ Factor}$$

$$PV = 1,000 \times 0.794$$

6. **B** The present value of an annuity is equal to the sum of the present values of the individual amounts. The first annuity payment was to be made at the beginning of the first year; therefore, its present value was equal to the amount of the payment ($2,000).

7. **D** Here is a question asking for the future value, but all you have to work with is the present value table. Therefore, set up the equation below:

$$PV = FV \times PV \text{ Factor}$$

$$\$3,000 = FV \times 0.857$$

$$FV = \$3,000/0.857$$

8. **A** The problem here is that you have a question for six years, but the table only goes to five years. You should discount the $4,000 back five years, then discount that answer back one more year. So, it's a two-step problem, using both the five-year and the one-year factors. The $4,000 is first discounted for five years to determine its equivalent at the end of the first year. This amount is then discounted for one year to determine its equivalent at the beginning of the first year. Note that any combination that totaled six years could have been used.

9. **D**
    - Payments are to be semiannual for 20 years. Therefore, there will be 40 payments.
    - Because the annual interest rate is 6 percent, the semiannual rate equals 3 percent.
    - Because we are dealing with compounding, we are interested in future values.

    Period payment needed = $10,000 at the end of 20 years/40 payments at 3 percent. This is a future-value problem, where you know the future value and are asked to calculate the payment amount. You are really using the equation: FV = payment amount × FV table factor, and solving for the payment amount.

10. **C** Theoretically, market value added should be equal to the present value, at the firm's cost of capital, of the future levels of economic value added. "Net operating profit after tax minus the firm's weighted-average cost of capital multiplied by the total capital employed" is the definition of EVA.

©2007 Kaplan CPA Review

STUDY MANUAL – BUSINESS ENVIRONMENT & CONCEPTS
CHAPTER 7

11. **C** EVA is positive when a company earns a rate of return greater than its cost of capital. EVA is a financial performance measure that attempts to calculate true economic profit. The formula is net operating profit after tax reduced by a measure of the cost of all capital of the firm. Its focus is on maximizing shareholder wealth.

Market value added (MVA) is the difference between the market value of a company and the capital contributed by investors (both bondholders and shareholders). Higher MVA is better than lower MVA. A high MVA company is one that has created substantial wealth for its shareholders.

12. **B** The $100,000 spent on an environmental analysis is a sunk cost and should not be considered in the analysis. The $50,000 lost from the sale of the property is an opportunity cost and should be considered. The transferred customers result in cash flows that are externalities/cannibalization for the bank and must be considered. Also, the shipping and installation charges are added to the depreciable basis and are counted.

13. **B** Key point: EVA begins with net operating profit after taxes but before interest. This problem begins with pretax operating profit which, by definition, excludes interest. If the problem had begun with income before taxes, the candidate would have added back the interest before calculating taxes.

Solution:

Pretax operating income	$300,000,000
Less taxes at 40%	(120,000,000)
Operating income after taxes	$180,000,000
Less cost of capital charge*	
$1,200,000,000 × 10%	(120,000,000)
EVA	$ 60,000,000

*The cost of capital is calculated based on the weighted average cost of capital, which is $15\% + 5\% \div 2 = 10\%$.

Finance: Derivatives

Study Manual – Business Environment & Concepts
Chapter 8

Study Tip: Keep a diary of your study time. Each day, write down the amount of time you spend and what you get accomplished. People often tend to overestimate their study hours and, thus, quit too soon. A diary will help you monitor whether you are investing an adequate amount of time so that you can take remedial action if necessary.

Risk Management and Derivatives

A. Introduction to Risk

1. In economics, we learn how all of our personal decisions are made in terms of costs and benefits. Corporate finance is not immune to this concept. When a corporate manager makes a decision to purchase a certain piece of equipment, expand operations, or start a new product line, the manager must consider both the costs and the benefits of the decision.

2. In this section, we will study costs and benefits in the framework of risk and return. Decisions made by the corporate financial manager will usually involve money, since money is both the cost and the benefit of most financial decisions. Risk is quite important when virtually no financial decision is immune from uncertainty.

3. We will use the word *uncertainty* as a synonym for *risk*. In finance, whenever there is uncertainty about an outcome, that outcome is considered risky. Let's assume today is the day your best friend, Chris, promised to pay back the $20 he borrowed from you last week. Are you certain Chris will pay you the $20 today as promised? If Chris gives you the money today, you will have received the payment exactly as you expected. If you receive the money tomorrow or the next day, you will have received the amount expected but not at the original time expected.

4. Let's define risk as "the possibility of an unfavorable event." Is receiving the $20 late an unfavorable event? What if you needed the money today to pay your cable television bill? It doesn't matter if you receive the money late or even if you don't receive it at all, because either outcome results in discontinued cable service.

5. Since most financial decisions result in receiving (or paying) a cash flow in the future, and since the future is always uncertain, there is obviously risk associated with any future cash flow. In fact, as the cash flow occurs farther and farther into the future, the cash flow will tend to become riskier.

©2007 Kaplan CPA Review

Page 221

STUDY MANUAL – BUSINESS ENVIRONMENT & CONCEPTS
CHAPTER 8

6. Given enough time, just about anything can happen. That means that the longer the time before you expect a cash flow, the higher the possibility that something will happen to affect the way it is received or even if it is received at all. Since no one can predict the future, we must accept that some amount of risk is inevitable.

SOURCES OF RISK: A GLOSSARY

A. Business risk is the uncertainty of income flows to a firm caused by the type of business it is in. Some firms, such as retailers, experience highly seasonal cash flows, while other firms, such as automobile manufacturers, sell consumer durables and are more susceptible to business cycles.

   1. The implications of variability in revenues to the firm depend in large part on the amount and type of assets the firm owns and uses. Some firms have considerable fixed assets with high fixed costs. Downturns to these firms are much more serious than to service firms with little or no fixed costs. Business risk is a component of equity risk, and it is partly determined by operational risk.

B. Credit risk can arise if either the buyer or the seller of a financial contract defaults on its obligations. There are three main components to credit risk: default risk, credit spread risk, and downgrade risk.

   1. Default risk is the risk that the issuer will not pay interest and/or principal when due. Default risk is a huge concern for managers and can be effectively hedged by transferring credit risk through the use of credit options, forwards, and swaps.

   2. Credit spread risk is the risk that the spread on an asset (i.e., its yield premium over the relevant risk-free benchmark) will increase. Credit spread changes are often associated with macroeconomic events in either the domestic or global financial markets. An increase in the spread would cause the asset to underperform the risk-free benchmark on a relative basis.

   3. Downgrade risk reflects the possibility that the credit rating of an asset/issuer is downgraded by a major credit-rating organization, such as Moody's, Fitch's, or S&P. If the credit rating is downgraded, the price of the bond will fall and its yield will rise.

      a. Downgrade risk is an absolute measure of credit risk, while credit spread risk is a relative measure of credit risk. Downgrade risk can be managed through the use of credit options, forwards, and swaps.

C. Equity risk refers to the volatility of equity prices and returns. These prices can change from market or systematic risk factors, such as economy-wide changes in interest rates, and from firm-specific or nonsystematic risk factors including:

   1. The firm's type of business (business risk).

   2. The amount of leverage the firm uses (financial risk).

Page 222   ©2007 Kaplan CPA Review

3. How well the managers operate the business (operational risk).

D. Event Risk.

1. Event risk refers to risks that are beyond the control of management. Examples of event risk include:

   a. Legal risk, which is the risk of a regulatory change.

   b. Disaster risk, which refers to devastating acts of nature such as floods, earthquakes, and fires, as well as devastating acts of man (e.g., war and terrorism).

2. The use of insurance can help financially cover much of the impact of event risk. Contingency planning and the use of backup facilities can help reduce the resulting business disruption.

E. Financial risk or financial leverage is the additional variation of returns on the equity of a firm caused by how much leverage (debt) was used to purchase the firm's assets.

F. Foreign exchange risk results from the changes in an asset's value due to the volatility and imperfect correlations between different currencies. Although foreign exchange risk is recognized as a risk category itself, much of the differences in currency values are caused by the differences in interest rates and inflation in different countries. Fluctuations in currency values pose one of the largest risks faced by multinational firms.

G. Inflation risk or purchasing-power risk arises because of the variation in the real value of cash flows from a security or other investment. The real value refers to the amount of a given bundle of goods the cash flows will purchase (e.g., the bundle of goods in the U.S. Consumer Price Index).

H. Interest rate risk refers to the change in price of an asset or liability in response to a change in interest rates. The values of most assets, particularly fixed-income investments, fall (rise) in response to a rise (fall) in interest rates.

1. If the assets produce cash flows, such as bond interest payments, reinvestment of these cash flows will partially offset the change in price. For example, if interest rates fall, the price of a bond increases but interest payments received must be reinvested at a lower rate. If rates increase, the price falls but interest receipts are reinvested at a higher rate.

2. Changes in interest rates can cause large changes in the cash flows to banks and can affect the bank's equity value. Banks tend to hold large positions in assets producing fixed periodic inflows and liabilities that are paid at flexible rates. If rates increase, the value of the banks' assets will fall, but the values of the liabilities will not, due to their variable rates.

3. There are a variety of subcategories of interest rate risk, including:

©2007 Kaplan CPA Review

STUDY MANUAL – BUSINESS ENVIRONMENT & CONCEPTS
CHAPTER 8

   a. Yield-curve risk, which refers to relative changes in short- and long-term interest rates.

   b. Basis risk, which refers to changes in the rate spread between similar instruments of the same maturity such as Treasury bills and eurodollars.

I. Legal and regulatory risk refers to the risk of a loss in value due to legal or regulatory issues. Legal risk can come about in a number of ways. Examples of legal risk include:

   1. A counterparty sues a bank to avoid meeting its obligations.

   2. Parties unknowingly enter into unenforceable contracts.

   3. Possibility that laws will change making existing contracts unenforceable.

J. Liquidity risk includes both funding liquidity risk and trading-related liquidity risk.

   1. Funding liquidity risk refers to the risk that a financial institution will be unable to raise the cash necessary to roll over its debt; to fulfill the cash, margin, and collateral requirements of counterparties; and to meet capital withdrawals.

   2. Trading-related liquidity risk is the risk that an institution will have difficulty executing a transaction because of a temporary lack of supply or demand. Trading liquidity risk, for many financial instruments, is reflected in the dealer bid-ask spread of the instrument.

K. Market risk is caused by macroeconomic factors, and usually refers to the risk associated with financial securities such as stocks and bonds, and it encompasses several types of risk. Those types include equity, interest rate, commodity (movements in the prices of commodities such as oil and other raw materials), and foreign exchange risk, which have been described. For institutional investors and financial firms that hold large portfolios of securities and/or loans, market risk is a major source of risk. Nonfinancial firms can face varying levels of market risk exposure from the liquid assets they hold, their management of publicly traded equity, and how commodity prices and exchange rates affect their cash flows.

L. Operational risk is the risk of loss due to inadequate monitoring systems, management failure, defective controls, fraud, and human errors. It applies to both the execution of financial transactions (e.g., buying and selling derivatives) and the uncertainties associated with the activities of a nonfinancial firm. Some firms define operational risk as all risk other than financial and credit risk.

RISK AND USES OF DERIVATIVES

You do not need to be an expert on derivatives, which is a good thing, because this is a very complex topic, even for many CPAs. Spend as much time as you can on these few pages and at least develop some familiarity with the terminology. This is one of those things you might want to read shortly before you take the BEC part of the exam!

Sections A-E are background information to help you understand this topic and are not expected to be tested.

Given the many sources of risk described in this topic, there is a clear need for a variety of methods for controlling risk. The list of available methods and products for managing risk has grown dramatically over the past 30 years. Although this is by no means an exhaustive list, there have been three major reasons for this growth: (1) uncertainty of oil prices due to conflicts in the Middle East, (2) changes in the banking industry, and (3) a change in Federal Reserve policy.

A. Early Examples of Derivatives.

1. While some types of risk management derivatives are relatively new, versions of many types of instruments have existed for centuries. The use of forward contracts is very old. In the 1100s, Flemish traders, who gathered for trade fairs on land held by the counts of Champagne, used forward contracts for delivery of products. The term for these contracts was a *letter de faire*. Five centuries later in the same area, futures markets for tulip deliveries appeared. Amsterdam traders used futures on various commodities in the 1700s. Futures contracts appeared in Japan in the 1600s to manage the volatility in rice prices caused by the weather and other unpredictable occurrences. In the United States, futures contracts have traded on the Chicago Board of Trade (CBOT) since 1865.

2. Financial markets have long been creative when responding to changing conditions; and hybrid securities, or securities that are created from two or more financial assets, are not new. In 1863, the Confederate States of America issued cotton bonds, which were 20-year bonds that were convertible into cotton. In other words, the Confederate States of America issued a dual-currency cotton-indexed bond in response to conditions brought on by war.

B. The Growth of Commodities.

1. Conflicts in the Middle East and the associated oil embargoes increased the need for risk management for dealers in the oil market. Because oil is an important input into many products used in households and businesses including agriculture, the increased volatility of oil prices increased the volatility of prices of many other commodities. The increase in inflationary pressures in the 1970s was partly caused by increases in oil prices, which in turn increased the risk for firms who entered into long-term contracts of all types.

2. Since the 1970s, swap markets have begun to play an important role in managing commodity risk. For example, firms may enter into commodity swap agreements where they agree to pay a fixed rate for the multiperiod delivery of a commodity and receive a corresponding floating rate based on the average commodity spot rates at the time of delivery. Although many commodity swaps exist, the most common use is to manage the costs of purchasing energy resources such as oil and electricity.

C. The Growth of Interest Rate and Foreign Exchange Derivatives.

STUDY MANUAL – BUSINESS ENVIRONMENT & CONCEPTS
CHAPTER 8

1. Swaps originated in the market for foreign exchange. The concept of a swap began when firms were able to identify likely counterparties facing similar foreign exchange risks and began entering into parallel loans. The mechanics of such early agreements were straightforward. Firm A in Country X makes a loan to a subsidiary of Firm B that is based in Country Y, and Firm B makes an offsetting loan to a subsidiary of Firm A in Country Y.

2. Arrangements between firms in the same country, such as interest rate swaps, soon followed.

3. The growth in the use and variety of interest rate derivatives accompanied changes in the banking industry. Regulatory changes in the 1970s and 1980s allowed interest rate volatility to increase. Also, the regulatory changes affected the nature of competition in the banking industry. Bank consolidations and an increased level of competition from nonbank financial institutions made banks look for creative ways to increase profits. Swap instruments, for example, can allow banks to specialize in the types of loans for which they have a comparative advantage. Also, the customers of banks increased their demand for such products to lower the increased interest rate risk that has accompanied deregulation.

4. From 1933 to the 1970s, banks operated in a highly regulated environment that resulted from the Great Depression and World War II. Three of the most important regulations for this time period include:

    a. The Glass-Steagall Act of 1933, which effectively separated commercial banking from investment banking in the United States.

    b. Regulation Q, which limited the interest rates that banks can pay on savings deposits in the United States.

    c. The Bretton-Woods Accord of 1944, which had central banks of most nations maintaining a fixed exchange-rate system.

5. Also during this time period, the central bank of the United States, the Federal Reserve, focused on interest rate stability at the expense of monetary stability. For example, if faced with an upward pressure on interest rates, the Federal Reserve would allow the money supply to increase to reduce this pressure.

6. Many things began to change in the 1970s:

    a. By 1974, major nations began to allow exchange rates to fluctuate, and the Bretton-Woods Accord collapsed. This brought about the aforementioned development of foreign exchange swaps.

    b. The U.S. Federal Reserve changed its goals to one of steady money-supply growth.

7. Given the increased volatility in interest rates, Regulation Q was no longer enforceable, and the Depository Institutions Deregulation and Monetary Control

Page 226 ©2007 Kaplan CPA Review

Act (DIDMCA) of 1980 phased out Regulation Q. The combination of all these developments led to a dramatic increase in interest rate and exchange-rate risk.

8. Since the 1970s, there have been several interest rate cycles marked by their peaks in 1981 (United States and United Kingdom), early 1990s (United Kingdom), and 1994 (United States) among others. To hedge the risks associated with volatile interest rates, interest-sensitive derivatives were offered by exchanges, banks, and other financial intermediaries. Since 1972, a multitude of products have become available through the exchanges and the over-the-counter (OTC) markets for managing risks associated with equities, foreign exchange, and interest rates.

9. Banks have become the major players in the derivatives market. Trading revenues from derivatives transactions now represent a substantial portion of total bank revenues. Not surprisingly, the majority of this revenue comes from interest rate and foreign exchange derivatives trading activities. The following is a list of some important products and when they were introduced:

   a. Futures contracts on foreign exchange (May 1972, International Monetary Market of the Chicago Mercantile Exchange, CME).

   b. Currency swaps (August 1981, World Bank).

   c. Option contracts on British pounds (December 1982, Philadelphia Exchange), followed in early 1983 by option contracts on the Canadian dollar, the deutsche mark, the Japanese yen, and the Swiss franc.

   d. Options on foreign exchange futures in these currencies (CME): deutsche mark and French francs (January 1984); British pound and Swiss francs (February 1985); Brazilian real (November 1985); Japanese yen (March 1986); Canadian dollar (June 1986).

important derivatives products

D. The Increased Demand for Equity Derivatives.

1. The October 1987 stock market crash in the United States resulted in price declines of 23 percent, which wiped out over $1 trillion in equity value. Japan experienced a similar fate during 1989–1991, suffering equity price declines of over 50 percent, which resulted in a loss equivalent to $2.7 trillion. More recently, in 2000–2002, the drop in the U.S. equity markets led by technology firms (NASDAQ), followed by the S&P 500, are reminders of increased stock market volatility.

2. In response to these large swings in prices, investors have increased their use of derivatives to protect value (e.g., protective puts) and enhance return (e.g., covered calls). Thus, the market for equity derivatives has also increased.

E. Measuring the Growth of Derivatives.

1. Over-the-counter markets in equity and bond futures, swaps, forwards, and hybrid securities have expanded offerings to investors, presenting a vast array of

STUDY MANUAL – BUSINESS ENVIRONMENT & CONCEPTS
CHAPTER 8

methods for trading and hedging. The growth in these markets has been dramatic, but figures measuring the growth of the market for risk management products must be carefully defined. For example, since the beginning of the 1970s, derivatives trading activity had grown considerably, up to about $50 trillion by 1995.

2. The amount of $50 trillion represents the *notional amount,* which is the value of the underlying assets controlled by the derivatives. The magnitude of derivatives trading activity is better viewed in terms of its replacement cost, about $2 trillion, which is only 4 percent of the notional amount. The replacement cost refers to the price of the derivatives themselves. Even on this basis, the derivatives market has grown substantially.

F.   Interest Rate Risk.

1. Market risk is associated with the potential change in the value of an asset in response to a change in some basic source of uncertainty. In financial markets, the three main sources of uncertainty are interest rates, equity prices, and exchange rates. Because changes in any or all of these factors can significantly affect the value of an asset or portfolio, it is important for managers to know how to identify them.

2. Interest rate risk is the risk that the value of an asset may change as the result of changes in market interest rates. Market interest rates are specific to a particular term or maturity, a particular level of credit risk, and sometimes to a certain issuer.

3. Interest rate risk is most commonly associated with fixed-income instruments or bonds. Most bonds have an inverse relationship with interest rates, meaning that as interest rates rise, bond prices will fall, and vice versa.

4. Interest rate risk can also result from transaction exposure, meaning that assets and liabilities will each respond differently to a change in rates, thus causing the potential for a significant change in the value of a firm.

5. One of the most vivid examples of interest rate transaction exposures is the effect that interest rate volatility had on the U.S. savings and loan (S&L) association industry. In the 1970s, the U.S. yield curve experienced an extended period of time where the curve was upward sloping—longer-term rates were higher than shorter-term rates. To take advantage of this, S&Ls decided to make long-term, fixed-rate mortgage loans and finance them with assets in short-term deposits. The S&Ls had a huge interest rate transaction exposure, because any changes in short-term interest rates would have a direct impact on their expenses. By the 1980s, the yield curve inverted, making short-term interest rates higher than the fixed rates they were receiving on their loans to homeowners. Needless to say, the S&L industry was hit hard, which resulted in an unusually high number of industry failures.

G.   Measuring the exposure to interest rate risk is a 3-part task. Each of these items are listed here with a brief description:

Page 228   ©2007 Kaplan CPA Review

Step 1: Quantifying the value of the asset held (long or short).

    a.   This is the easiest of the three tasks, as the value of the holding is determined by reference to market prices. If the asset is common and the market is pricing the asset frequently, market prices are taken directly from the market contemporaneously. The valuing of unique or infrequently traded assets must be approximated through their price relationship with other more frequently traded assets.

Step 2: Identifying and quantifying the sensitivity of the value of the asset to the change in interest rates

In measuring the exposure to interest rate risk, researchers and practitioners have developed two concepts. Duration is defined as the sensitivity of the value of an asset to the change in interest rates, while convexity is the change in duration in response to changes in interest rates. Duration alone is often sufficient for determining the change in asset value for a very small change in interest rates; however, for larger changes both duration and convexity must be considered.

Step 3: Quantifying the volatility of interest rates.

The volatility of interest rates is often determined through historical observation. When using historical volatility, the assumption is made that the period over which the volatility estimate is being used is the same, or very similar to, the historical period from which the data is drawn. In order to improve the accuracy of our volatility estimate, as many economic factors as possible need to be identified, and historical periods where these factors are very similar need to be selected. The "market's best estimate" of the interest rate volatility could also be used by examining the implied volatility in interest rate option contracts.

H. Measuring the exposure to foreign exchange risk is a 3-step process.

Step 1: Quantifying the value of exchange risk exposure

In order to determine the current value of exposure to exchange-rate risk, first decide what currency to use. The exposure of a portfolio of assets priced in different currencies could be described in any currency. Often, the currency of choice is the one in which the financial performance of the firm is reported. For instance, a German firm that produces most of its products in Germany and sells most of its products to Japanese customers would probably describe their foreign exchange risk in euros, and the risk would be described as fluctuations in the euro/yen exchange rate. The "quantity" of exposure could be expressed as the sum of current holdings, or the total currency flows expected over a period of time.

Step 2: Identifying and quantifying the sensitivity of the value of the exposure to the change in exchange rate.

This step almost becomes invisible when the value of the exposure is expressed in currency units. If the exposure is described in any other manner (such as a percentage of cost of goods, etc.), then we have to determine the sensitivity of the exposure value to the changes in exchange-rate components.

Step 3: Quantifying the volatility of exchange rates.

Currency exchange rates are determined by many factors, including expected economic performance of the countries, differences in interest rates and/or inflation rates, differences in export and import flows, and other economic and political factors. Volatility of exchange rates can also be estimated based on historical data. Similar to the other cases, the selection of a historical period from which to draw data implicitly assumes similarity between the historical period and the future period for which the estimate is prepared. Similarly, other indicators of volatility can be used, such as the implied volatility of currency exchange options.

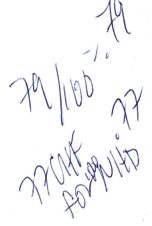

4. Exchange risk is caused by changes in currency quotes due to unexpected political and economic events.

Example: Exchange risk

A Swiss bank exposes itself to exchange-rate risk by accepting NZD (New Zealand dollar) 100,000 for CHF (Swiss franc) 79,000. How much will the bank lose or gain if exchange rates change to 0.7700 CHF/NZD before the bank can sell off the NZD?

Answer:

If exchange rates change to 0.7700 CHF/NZD, the bank will only collect (0.7700 × 100,000), or CHF 77,000. Thus, the bank could lose CHF 2,000 (CHF 79,000 − CHF 77,000) in a matter of seconds. Holding foreign currency exposes the bank to exchange-rate risk.

The greater the uncertainty and volatility in the market, the greater the expected return foreign currency dealers will demand. This increase in required return is reflected in increased bid-ask spreads. In general, the more uncertain or volatile the currency, the wider the bid-ask spread.

1. Determinants of exchange rates.

    a. The main concern here is showing how exchange rates are interpreted and how they behave given the movement in inflation and income in different countries.

    b. In a flexible exchange-rate system, exchange rates are determined by supply and demand. If there is an excess demand for dollars by Australians, Australians will sell AUD and buy dollars. This will make the dollar appreciate relative to the AUD. When would this happen? Australians would create an excess demand for dollars if they desired to increase their imports of U.S. goods. In order to buy U.S. goods, Australians need dollars. Hence, the price of the dollar would rise relative to the AUD.

2. Changes in exchange rates.

    a. There are three major factors that cause a country's currency to appreciate or depreciate:

        •   Differential income growth among nations will cause nations with the highest income growth to demand more imported goods. The heightened demand for imports will increase demand for foreign currencies, appreciating the foreign currencies relative to the domestic currency.
        •   Differential inflation rates will also cause a movement in exchange rates. If prices in the United States are rising twice as fast as in Australia, U.S. citizens will increase their demand for Australian goods (because Australian goods are now cheaper relative to domestic goods). This increased demand will cause the AUD to appreciate, making Australian goods more expensive for Americans. Hence, adjustments in the exchange rate will offset the effects of different inflation rates.
        •   Differential interest rates will cause a flow of capital into those countries with the highest available real rates of interest. Therefore, there will be an increased demand for those currencies, and they will appreciate relative to countries whose available real rate of return is low.

    b. A good way to approach answering exchange-rate questions is to ask: who has created a demand for a currency and who is supplying it? Also, think of physically going out and selling dollars for AUD. This will help in visualizing the demand (AUD) and supply ($) sides of the argument.

    c. What will cause a nation's currency to appreciate?

        •   Slow growth of income relative to one's trading partners will cause imports to lag behind exports.
        •   A rate of inflation lower than those of its trading partners.
        •   A domestic real interest rate that is greater than real interest rates abroad.

    d. What will cause a nation's currency to depreciate?

        •   Rapid growth of income relative to one's trading partners that stimulates imports relative to exports.
        •   A rate of inflation higher than those of its trading partners.
        •   A domestic real interest rate that is lower than real interest rates abroad.

I. Options. There are two basic types of options: call options and put options. The buyer of a call option has the right, but not the obligation, to purchase the underlying security, while the buyer of the put option has the right to sell the underlying security. The seller of the option is obligated to take the opposite side of the transaction. The call writer must sell the security to the call owner if the option is exercised, while the put writer must buy the security from the put owner if the option is exercised.

1. The division of rights and obligations among buyers and writers of options creates some unique characteristics. These include:

©2007 Kaplan CPA Review

a. Owner's rights. Purchasing an option contract gives the owner the right, but not the legal obligation, to conduct a transaction involving an underlying asset on or before a predetermined future date at a predetermined price (called the *exercise* or *strike price*).

b. Value. The value of an option contract cannot be less than zero. The holder of an option contract will not choose to exercise the option if, in doing so, he or she will suffer a loss. This feature is what creates the asymmetrical distribution of possible payoffs.

c. Writer's obligations. The option writer has the obligation to perform if the buyer chooses to exercise the contract. This means that the seller of a call option *must* sell the underlying asset at the exercise (strike) price if the buyer of the option contract chooses to exercise the option.

d. Trading strategies. Investors can use an option contract by itself, in combination with other option contracts, or together with long or short positions in the underlying assets in order to implement a variety of investment strategies.

2. Investors use options to speculate on price moves, to hedge the value of other positions, to reduce transaction costs, to avoid tax exposure, and to avoid market restrictions that may preclude other forms of trading.

   a. Every option contract must have two sides:

      • For every buyer of an option, there must be a seller (also called a writer).
      • Gains to one position offset losses to the other, making option trading a zero-sum game.

   b. A participant in an option contract can take one of four possible option positions:

      • The buyer of a call option.
      • The writer (seller) of a call option.
      • The buyer of a put option.
      • The writer (seller) of a put option.

3. It is important to reiterate that in these agreements, the rights lie with the buyer or owner of the option, and the obligations lie with the writer or seller. The buyer pays a premium to the writer and, in exchange, receives the right to buy or sell the underlying asset on specific terms stated in the contract. The writer or seller of the option receives the premium, obligating him or her to sell or purchase the underlying asset on specific terms at the discretion of the option buyer.

4. Many of the terms used to describe option contracts are similar to those used to describe other investment contracts; many others are unique to options.

   a. American option. An American option contract can be exercised at any time up to expiration.

b. At-the-money. An option is said to be at-the-money when the price of the underlying asset is equal to the strike price of the option contract. An option contract that is at-
the-money has no intrinsic value.

c. Buyer. The buyer of an option contract purchases from the writer the right to either purchase (call) or sell (put) the underlying asset from or to the writer, at a specified price, on or before a specified date. A buyer of the option is said to have a long position in the option.

d. Call. A call is an option contract that gives the holder the right to purchase the underlying asset at the strike price set in the contract.

e. European option. A European option contract can be exercised only at expiration.

f. Exercise. Exercising an option forces the writer to fulfill his or her contractual obligation. The writer of a put must purchase the underlying asset at the strike price set in the contract. The writer of a call must sell the underlying asset at the strike price set in the contract.

g. Strike (exercise) price. The stated price at which the underlying asset may be purchased (call) or sold (put); usually designated by X.

h. Expiration. The expiration of an option contract is the date at which the owner's option to exercise expires. After expiration, the contract is worthless, as it cannot be exercised.

i. In-the-money. A call option is said to be in-the-money when the price of the underlying asset is greater than the strike price of the option contract. A put option is said to be in-the-money when the price of the underlying asset is less than the strike price of an option contract. Any option contract that is in-the-money has an intrinsic value greater than zero.

j. Intrinsic value. This value is the amount the holder would receive if the option were exercised immediately.

Call option: $S - X$ (S = Asset price, X = Strike price)

Put option: $X - S$

Intrinsic value is the greater of: $S - X$ or zero for a call, or $X - S$ or zero for a put. Intrinsic value cannot be negative.

k. Long. A long position in an option contract is the position held by the owner or buyer of the contract.

l. Offsetting order. An order that closes an existing order is called an *offsetting order.* An investor opens a position by buying an option and may later close the position before expiration by selling a similar option. Investors can also open a position by selling (writing) an option and later close the position by buying a similar option.

    m.   Out-of-the-money. A call option is said to be out-of-the-money when the price of the underlying asset is less than the strike price of the option contract. A put option is said to be out-of-the-money when the price of the underlying asset is greater than the strike price of an option contract. Any option that is out-of-the-money has an intrinsic value of zero.

    n.   Premium. The premium of an option contract is the price paid by the buyer to the writer of the contract for the right to exercise; usually designated as C for a call option and P for a put option.

    o.   Put. A put is an option contract that gives the holder the right to sell the underlying asset at the strike price set in the contract.

    p.   Short. A short position in an option contract is the position held by the writer or seller of the contract.

    q.   Time value. Prior to expiration, all American options and some European options will have value based upon the time remaining until expiration. The time value is equal to the difference between the option contract's market price and its intrinsic value.

    r.   Writer. The seller of an option contract. The writer assumes the obligation to buy or sell the underlying asset at the discretion of the option buyer. The writer of the option is said to hold a short position in the contract.

5.   The terms *American* and *European* do not describe where options are traded, but rather, the type or style of option contracts. Although American and European options may have identical strike prices and expiration dates, they still differ in one important aspect. The owner of an American option may exercise the option at any time before or at expiration. The owner of a European option may only exercise the option at expiration.

6.   Two options, one American and one European, that are otherwise alike in every respect, may have different values because of the American option's opportunity to exercise early. At expiration, the options will have the same value, but up until this time, it is necessary to distinguish between the two styles in order to determine the option value.

7.   If an American and a European option are identical in all ways (e.g., maturity, underlying stock, strike price), the value of the American option will always equal or exceed the value of the European option. The American contract has an option to exercise early, and the value of this ability to exercise early cannot be negative. If the option owner chooses not to exercise the American option early, it will have the same value as the European option on the expiration date. In most cases, the early exercise of an option on a nondividend-paying stock cannot be economically supported. However, early exercise in order to capture dividends or to gain power or influence (through voting rights) is often enticing to the holder of the option.

8. The vast majority of options traded throughout the world are American options, but most texts and training materials use examples of European options. European options are simpler to analyze than American options and can be used to effectively demonstrate the basic characteristics of options.

9. The types of options contracts now offered include the following:

   a. Stock options. These are contracts on 100 shares of common stock issued by a corporation.

   b. Index options. These options follow the performance of a group of stocks, precious metals, or any other group of assets that can be indexed.

   c. Foreign currency options. These options use a foreign currency's value as the underlying asset.

   d. Futures options. These options use futures contracts as the underlying asset.

J. This topic introduces the terminology needed to understand futures and forward contracts as well as the basic mechanics of their use.

   1. The most basic type of futures or forward contract obligates one counterparty to buy and the other counterparty to sell a given asset at a given price. Comparing forward and futures contracts (aka forwards and futures) to spot contracts is a useful first step in understanding these derivatives.

   2. Spot contracts are used when a seller of an asset agrees to deliver the asset immediately and the buyer agrees to purchase the asset immediately.

   3. Forward contracts are contracts in which the buyer and seller agree on a price and quantity today, but delivery does not occur until some prespecified date in the future.

   4. Futures contracts are essentially forward contracts that are arranged by an organized exchange. Futures contracts usually require a margin deposit. This position is marked to market daily.

   5. Futures contracts are standardized according to the guidelines of the exchange.

   6. Forwards are bilateral contracts subject to counterparty default risk, while counterparty default risk on futures contracts is essentially eliminated, because the futures exchange clearinghouse guarantees the transaction.

   7. There is a long and growing list of variables upon which futures and forwards can be written. For example, forwards and futures can hedge interest-rate risk, foreign exchange risk, equity risk, commodity risk, and even catastrophe risk. There is also a long list of terminology associated with these markets. The following list includes the most common terms:

©2007 Kaplan CPA Review

a. Basis is the difference between the futures price and the spot price of an underlying asset.

b. Basis risk is the volatility of the basis over time.

c. Cash settlement is a procedure for settling a contract with only a transfer of cash, and there is no delivery of the underlying asset.

d. The cheapest-to-deliver bond is the bond that has the lowest price for settling a given futures contract on that type of bond.

e. Clearinghouses or clearinghouse corporations are firms that guarantee the fulfillment of contracts traded on their respective exchanges. They do this by enforcing rules that lower counterparty risk and by fulfilling a contract in the case of default.

f. Contango describes the situation where the futures price is above the expected future spot price.

g. Contract size is the amount of the underlying asset covered by the contract. For financial instruments, size is expressed in a currency such as dollars or pounds sterling. For a product like corn, for example, it would be a physical amount like the number of bushels.

h. Convenience yield is the benefit from owning (i.e., having on hand) an asset that is not earned by the holder of a long futures contract on the same asset.

i. Cost of carry refers to the financing and storage costs of holding a physical asset minus the income earned on the asset.

j. Cross hedging refers to hedging a position with a contract that has an underlying asset that is not exactly the same as the position being hedged, so that the correlation of the contract's value with that of the underlying is less than perfect.

k. A forward exchange rate is the forward price of one unit of a foreign currency.

l. A forward interest rate is a rate that applies to a period of time that begins in the future, but it is derived from the relationships of current interest rates.

m. The forward price is the delivery price in a forward contract that is specified today.

n. Futures price refers to the delivery price currently applicable to a futures contract.

o. Hedge ratio is the size of a position in a hedging instrument relative to the size of the position being hedged.

p. Index futures are contracts on a stock index or other index.

q. Initial margin is the cash that a futures trader must deposit in an account at the time the trader takes a position in the derivative.

r. Long refers to the counterparty who will be obligated to purchase the underlying asset at the maturity of a forward or futures contract.

s. Margin is the amount of cash or cash equivalents that a trader must deposit when taking a futures position.

t. Maintenance margin is the lower limit on a futures trading margin account. If the margin falls below this level, the trader must contribute cash or cash equivalents to bring the account back up to the initial margin.

u. Margin call is the request for extra margin when the balance in the margin account falls below the maintenance margin level.

v. Marking to market is the practice of revaluing an instrument to reflect the current values of the relevant underlying variable.

w. Normal backwardation describes the situation when the futures price is below the expected future spot price. This is the opposite of "contango."

x. Open interest is the total number of long positions in a futures contract. It also equals the total number of short positions in a futures contract.

y. Settlement price is the average of the prices that a contract trades for immediately before the bell signaling the close of trading for a day. It is used in mark-to-market calculations.

z. Short refers to the counterparty who will be obligated to sell the underlying asset at the maturity of a forward or futures contract.

aa. Spot price is the price of an asset for immediate delivery.

bb. Underlying variable or simply the underlying refers to the variable or asset that determines the price of a derivative such as a futures contract.

cc. Variation margin is the extra margin required to bring the balance in a margin account up to the initial margin when there is a margin call.

dd. Wild card play is the right to deliver on a futures contract at the closing price for a period of time after the close of trading.

8. Two very important terms in this list are *long* and *short*. Since most futures and forward contracts have a zero value at inception, there is no actual purchase at that time. The counterparty that has contracted to purchase the asset later has the long position, and the counterparty that has contracted to sell the asset later has the short position. At any given point in time for a given type of contract, the open interest is the number of long positions, which is equal to the number of short positions.

STUDY MANUAL – BUSINESS ENVIRONMENT & CONCEPTS
CHAPTER 8

9. It is useful to examine forward contracts before futures contracts, because the basic principles of forward contracts apply to futures contracts. Futures contracts then have added considerations such as marking to market. After the basic mechanics of contracting for transactions that take place on a future date are established, the effects of the institutional aspects of futures markets can be examined.

10. A forward contract is an over-the-counter (OTC) contract; therefore, the counterparties can negotiate the contract size, maturity, and any other details pertinent to the transaction. At its origination, the value of a forward contract is zero. As the value of the underlying changes, the value of the contract increases to one counterparty and decreases by an equal amount to the other counterparty. This scenario results in a zero-sum game—one party's gains are equally offset by the opposite party's losses. Most forward contracts are not marked to market.

11. If the forward contract has no provisions for early settlement, the counterparties can still, by mutual agreement, settle the contract if they choose to do so. When the contract expires, most contracts allow for two methods of settlement. Cash settlement is frequently used, which consists of the payment of the net difference between the contract price and the spot price on the settlement date. Physical delivery of the actual underlying asset can also occur, where the short counterparty actually delivers the underlying asset to the long counterparty at the agreed-upon price.

12. With cash settlement, one of the counterparties will pay the other an amount equal to the difference between the spot price and futures price multiplied by the contract size. Usually, the contract size is the value of some amount of an asset such as a foreign exchange or a quantity of a commodity such as an agricultural product. If we let F_0 represent the futures price at contract initiation and S_T represent the spot price at contract expiration, then if $F_0 > S_T$, the long counterparty will pay the short counterparty an amount equal to $(F_0 - S_T) \times$ (Contract size), and if $F_0 < S_T$, the short counterparty will pay the long counterparty an amount equal to $(S_T - F_0) \times$ (Contract size).

13. Theoretically, if the short counterparty delivers the asset to the long counterparty, the profits/losses to each counterparty will be the same as those for a cash settlement. The short counterparty would simply buy the asset on the open market at price S_T and then deliver it for payment at price F_0. The short counterparty would earn the same profit/loss as it would with cash settlement. The long counterparty can then sell the asset at S_T, and incur the same profit/loss it would with cash settlement. For this reason, and the fact that the vast majority of contracts are settled with a transfer of cash, the cash settlement method will be used to describe the mechanics of forward and futures contracts.

Example: Forwards

A forward contract consists of an agreement to sell 100 ounces of gold at a price of $303.85 per ounce at maturity. The spot price of gold is $305.22 per ounce at the maturity of the contract. What will be the profit/loss to each counterparty?

STUDY MANUAL – BUSINESS ENVIRONMENT & CONCEPTS

CHAPTER 8

Answer:

Since $F_0 < S_T$, then the long counterparty would benefit by buying the gold from the short counterparty at the contracted forward price, which is lower than the market price. The cash settlement would consist of the following payment from the short counterparty to the long counterparty:

($305.22 - $303.85) × 100 = $137 profit to the long position

What determined F_0 (in this example, $303.85) at the origination of the contract? For an asset like gold, which does not pay a dividend and has low storage costs, F_0 is a function of S_0, the spot price at the time of contract initiation, and the prevailing interest rate for loans where gold is collateral. If that rate is 3 percent, and the current price of gold is $295, then the following forward price that should prevail is:

1-year forward price = $295 × 1.03 = $303.85

14. This topic gives an overview of the use of futures and forwards as tools to hedge risk. Although many types of futures and forward contracts exist to hedge a wide variety of risks, some basic concepts apply in most cases. The short position of a contract locks in a selling price, and a long position locks in a purchase price. Each side eliminates uncertainty concerning the price of an asset in a future transaction. Also, the value of the contract will vary with the price of the underlying asset over the life of the contract. This variation in value can help manage the risk exposure and return of many types of portfolios.

15. Although a wide variety of contracts exist, not all assets and portfolios can be perfectly hedged with forwards and futures. Cross hedging refers to the practice of using forwards and futures to hedge positions that are not exactly the same as the underlying of the contract used in the hedge. Regression analysis can help determine the optimal use of a cross hedge, and/or if it is a worthwhile alternative to hedging risk.

16. The objective of hedging with futures contracts is to reduce or eliminate the price risk of an asset or a portfolio. For example, a farmer with a large corn crop that will be harvested in a few months could wait until the end of the growing season and sell his or her corn at the prevailing spot price, or the farmer could sell corn futures and "lock in" the price of his or her corn at a predetermined rate. By taking a short position in a corn futures contract, the farmer eliminates—or at least reduces—exposure to fluctuating corn prices. This is an example of a short hedge—the user locked in a future selling price.

17. Alternatively, a cereal company will need to purchase corn in the future. The company could wait to buy corn in the spot market and face the volatility of future corn spot prices or lock in its purchase price by buying corn futures in advance. This demonstrates an anticipatory hedge. The cereal company has an anticipated need for corn and buys corn futures to lock in the price of those future corn purchases. This is also an example of a long hedge—the user locked in a future purchasing price.

©2007 Kaplan CPA Review

STUDY MANUAL – BUSINESS ENVIRONMENT & CONCEPTS
CHAPTER 8

18. These two hedgers are natural trading partners. The farmer goes short and the cereal company goes long to reduce the uncertainty of future corn prices. Ideally, they would enter into this contract with each other. However, a liquid and efficient market for corn futures contracts exists, and there are dealers standing ready to enter into either side of the contract. Therefore, it is more likely that the farmer and cereal company would enter into these contracts independently by contacting a broker who puts in an order on the corresponding exchange. The other side of the contract may be taken by a dealer who then looks for another order to offset the risk of the first order. Also, the other side of the contract may be taken by a speculator who assumes the risk of one of the positions to make a profit.

19. Fluctuations in exchange rates increase the risk associated with doing transactions in foreign currencies. Two important exposures are transaction exposure and translation exposure.

20. In a transaction exposure, the hedger will be physically converting one currency into another and would like to eliminate the risk of fluctuating exchange rates.

21. Translation exposure relates to the accounting for foreign currency transactions. SFAS 52 outlines the procedures for foreign currency reporting under U.S. GAAP. Translation exposure hedging involves reducing the volatility in reported earnings due to changes in exchange rates.

K. A Perfect Hedge.

1. The following example of a hedging transaction exposure illustrates a case where there are contracts available that exactly match the hedge horizon. A follow-up example illustrates the potential complexities that usually exist in such a case.

Example: Hedging

Suppose that a U.S.-based manufacturer of premium sweaters wishes to hedge a purchase of wool from England. In three months, the firm will purchase £10 million of wool. The current pounds sterling exchange rate is $1.56/ and the 3-month futures rate is $1.50/. The firm's research department expects that in three months pounds sterling will appreciate to $1.60/. Calculate both the hedged and unhedged cost of wool in three months. Each futures contract controls £62,500.

Answer:

The firm should go long:

$$\frac{£10,000,000}{£62,500/contract} = 160 \text{ contracts}$$

If the firm locks in the exchange rate by going long in a pounds sterling futures contract, the cost of the wool will be:

Page 240   ©2007 Kaplan CPA Review

$$\frac{\$1.50/\text{\pounds}}{\text{\pounds}10,000,000} = \$15,000,000$$

For an unhedged position, where the forecasted move in the exchange rate is realized, the effective cost of wool to the firm will be:

($1.60/)(10,000,000) = $16,000,000

Clearly, hedging is beneficial in this case.

L. Swaps.

1. Understanding swaps is challenging because there are many types of swaps and there is a great deal of flexibility in the construction of each type. Becoming thoroughly familiar with terms such as counterparty, notional principal, and trade date as they apply to an interest rate swap, is an important first step in understanding swaps. The reason for the variety of swaps is so they can be used to hedge a variety of risks (e.g., interest rate, foreign exchange, commodity, and equity). The popularity of swaps attests to their effectiveness and cost efficiency.

2. Swaps are like forwards and futures in that they usually have no market value at origination, and they represent an obligation for both parties. In any given period, one party must pay the other a cash flow based on a change in some market variable such as an interest rate, a foreign exchange rate, a commodity price, or an equity index value. The primary difference between swaps and forwards is that swaps cover multiple settlement periods. A swap is like a forward contract in that it is an over-the-counter (OTC) agreement where the counterparties can tailor the contract to suit their particular needs. This topic will summarize the basic components of most swap contracts and discuss the determining factors of the periodic cash flows.

3. Although any one or more market variables can determine the payoff of a swap, the two most popular swaps are interest rate swaps and currency swaps.

    a. Interest rate swaps are agreements in which the counterparties exchange cash flows in a single currency tied to fixed- and/or floating-market interest rates.

    b. Currency swaps are agreements in which the counterparties exchange cash flows in two different currencies tied to fixed- and/or floating-market interest rates.

4. Swap terminology. In a basic interest rate swap, two parties agree that one party will pay the other an amount each period based upon some portfolio value and the value of some market interest rate relative to a predetermined fixed rate. The following list summarizes the important terms to know when describing an interest rate swap:

©2007 Kaplan CPA Review

STUDY MANUAL – BUSINESS ENVIRONMENT & CONCEPTS
CHAPTER 8

a. Business day conventions are rules for counting business days (e.g., what to do when a holiday falls on a Sunday). These can vary from country to country.

b. Counterparties are the two parties who agree to the terms of the swap. For most swaps and periods, in any given period one counterparty will pay the other a cash amount.

c. Day count conventions refer to whether interest accrues on a 360- or 365-day year.

d. The effective date is the day that the interest begins accruing on the notional principal.

e. The fixed rate is a predetermined interest rate that, for a plain-vanilla interest rate swap and most other cases, is constant for the life of the contract.

f. Fixed-rate payer or pay-fixed party refers to the counterparty who makes payments when the reference rate is below the fixed rate and receives payments when the reference rate is above the fixed rate. The fixed-rate payer is often said to have "bought the swap" or is "long the swap."

g. Floating-rate payer or receive-fixed party refers to the counterparty who makes payments when the reference rate exceeds the fixed rate. The floating-rate payer will receive payments from the other counterparty when the reference rate is below the fixed rate. The floating-rate payer is often said to have "sold the swap" or is "short the swap."

h. The maturity date is the date that the swap stops accruing interest.

i. Notional principal is the term that refers to the specific cash value that, with the relevant interest rates, determines the size of the cash flows between counterparties.

j. Plain-vanilla interest rate swap is the term used to describe the most basic interest rate swap, where one counterparty pays a fixed rate and the other pays a floating rate.

k. The reference rate is the variable market interest rate the value of which, on a given date and relative to a fixed rate, determines the direction of the cash flow payments. Combined with the notional principal, the reference rate and the fixed rate determine the size of the cash flows.

l. Reset frequency is the frequency with which payments are made (e.g., quarterly or semiannually).

m. The swap rate is an interest rate that when used to discount the projected cash flows based on forecasts of interest rates (often derived from spot forward rates) makes the present value of the swap equal to zero. Generally, on the trade date of a plain-vanilla swap, the swap rate is the fixed rate. As interest rates and expected interest rates change, the swap rate will change.

n. The swap spread represents the credit spread over Treasury notes that high-quality borrowers would pay in the swap market. For example, assuming that the 5-year Treasury note yields 4.75 percent and the 5-year swap spread is trading at 75 basis points, the 5-year swap rate would be quoted at 5.5 percent.

o. The tenor of a swap is its term to maturity or number of settlement periods.

p. The trade date is the date that the counterparties commit to the swap.

5. Using these terms, we might describe a particular swap contract as follows. On the trade date of January 1, 2003, Firm A agreed to be the fixed-rate payer and Firm B agreed to be the floating-rate payer for a plain-vanilla interest rate swap with an effective date of March 1, 2003, a maturity date of January 1, 2013, and a reset frequency of three months. The notional principal is $10,000,000. The reference rate is 3-month LIBOR with a fixed rate of 6 percent. In this arrangement, every three months, Firm B will pay Firm A if LIBOR is greater than 6 percent and Firm A will pay Firm B if LIBOR is less than 6 percent. The payment for a given period will be a function of the notional principal of $10,000,000 and the difference between the current LIBOR and 6 percent. The approximate payment for Firm B each quarter would be $10,000,000 × (LIBOR – 6%)/4. As will be explained shortly, the precise amount would depend upon the exact number of days in the quarter and day-count conventions for the interest rates.

6. Role of a swap dealer.

a. Swap dealers often play an important role in the creation of a swap contract. Swap dealers act as intermediaries. Prospective clients contact the swap dealer to find a counterparty to their particular needs. The swap dealer may only act as an agent and connect prospective counterparties and, for this service, charge a fee or periodic payment defined in terms of basis points and the notional principal. In acting only as an agent, the swap dealer assumes no risk. When helping facilitate a transaction, the swap dealer may, for more compensation, act as a true dealer and assume some or all of the counterparty risk of the transaction. The swap dealer may also warehouse a swap—that is, become the counterparty, with the anticipation of transferring or assigning the contract to another counterparty in the near future. The swap dealer assumes counterparty risk for the time the swap is warehoused.

7. Swaps compared to other derivatives contracts.

a. Advantages of swaps:

- Although futures contracts can hedge interest rate and foreign exchange risk, the flexibility and anonymity of the swap market have led to swaps

©2007 Kaplan CPA Review

Page 243

becoming increasingly popular. More detailed explanations of these properties follow.

- Anonymity means swaps market participants can trade without revealing their identity. In the futures pit, everyone knows who is buying and selling.
- The swaps market is virtually unregulated in most countries. By comparison, the futures market is closely regulated (e.g., Commodity Futures Trading Commission is the primary regulator in the United States).
- Expiration and payment dates are negotiable in the swaps market, so swap terms can be custom-tailored to the needs of both parties. Futures markets only offer standardized contracts with specific contract sizes and expiration dates.
- Length of maturity and multiperiod settlement are important features of swaps. Swaps generally offer much longer-term contracts than futures markets, where contract maturities beyond one year are rare. Swaps cover several settlement periods to hedge risk on several dates.
- With the exception of the multiperiod settlement, forward contracts have many of the same advantages over futures contracts. However, a borrower with a flexible-rate loan who needs to hedge a stream of periodic interest rate payments over a long horizon would have to have a portfolio of forward contracts to hedge the interest rate risk while the same task could be accomplished through a single swap contract.
- A swap can be defined as a portfolio of forward contracts. However, the popularity of swaps has led to the writing of contracts with tenors in excess of 50 years, which is much longer than the longest forward contract. Also, the popularity of swaps compared to forwards has led to swaps often having more liquidity than forward contracts.

b. Disadvantages of swaps.

- Swaps also share many of the same disadvantages of forward contracts.
- Swap participants must find counterparties with similar maturity, cash flow, and payment date needs, because swap contract terms are not standardized like futures contracts.
- Early termination (and alteration of other contract terms) of the swap contract is not possible without the agreement of both parties or a successful search for a third party willing to take on the obligations of one side of the swap. Traders can easily and quickly close their futures positions by simply taking the other side of the transaction.
- In the swaps market, there is no clearinghouse to guarantee counterparty performance under the contract, as is the case in futures markets. Therefore, swap participants face counterparty risk (i.e., the risk that the other party will not honor his or her obligations).
- Although lenders adjust lending rates to compensate for risk, they also can restrict the amount of funds that a firm can borrow. One reason a lender might restrict the supply of funds to a firm is the volatility of the borrower's earnings. Another factor that can affect credit risk is the amount of a particular type of debt a borrower carries. Examples of each

of these types of risk and how swaps can mitigate the risks to increase access to debt follow.

8. Stabilize earnings.

    a. Firms can increase their access to funds (or borrowing capacity) by using swaps to reduce the volatility of their earnings. For example, the airline industry is very capital intensive, and firms depend on large amounts of debt to finance the purchase or lease of airplanes. The earnings of airline firms are very sensitive to jet fuel costs, and commodity price swaps could be used to stabilize the future cost of a commodity like jet fuel. Commodity-producing firms can use swaps to stabilize the price of its products. A coal-mining company may have some long-term contracts to sell coal, but the terms may stipulate sales to be at spot prices. By entering into swap agreements, paying the variable spot price, and receiving a fixed price, the firm can reduce its earnings' volatility. Both buyers and suppliers of raw materials can reduce earnings volatility with swaps and improve their credit ratings to gain more access to debt.

9. Transform available debt to suit needs.

    a. Many lenders impose loan or bond covenants that restrict the activities of borrowing firms. Such covenants can restrict the types of additional debt that the firm may assume. For example, if a covenant restricts a firm from acquiring additional floating-rate debt, but allows it to borrow additional debt at a fixed rate, the firm can borrow at the fixed rate and then use a swap to effectively convert the new debt to floating-rate debt.

    b. For interest rate swaps, the cash flow process distills to a periodic payment from one counterparty to the other. The prevailing reference rate, the fixed rate, and the notional principal, determine the size and direction of the cash flow. Currency swaps differ from interest rate swaps in that there are two notional principals, which can be actually exchanged, and the cash flows can go both ways each period because the cash flows are denominated in different currencies. Interest rate swaps and currency swaps are both over-the-counter (OTC) instruments that are vulnerable to counterparty and liquidity risk. Swap dealers are active in both markets to lower these risks.

    c. Understanding interest rate and currency swaps will readily allow understanding of most other types of swaps with only a little extra effort.

    d. In a plain-vanilla interest rate swap, the counterparties are a fixed-rate payer and a floating-rate payer. Theoretically, in each period the fixed-rate payer pays a fixed interest rate and receives a floating rate based on a reference rate, usually the LIBOR rate for the reset period, from the floating-rate payer. In practice, in almost all cases the counterparties net the cash flows and whichever party owes more pays the other the net amount. For example, if LIBOR has risen above the fixed rate of the swap contract, then the floating-rate payer would owe a net cash flow to the fixed-rate payer.

STUDY MANUAL – BUSINESS ENVIRONMENT & CONCEPTS
CHAPTER 8

    e.   The following formula computes the actual payments made:

$$(\text{fixed rate payment})_t = (\text{swap fixed rate} - \text{LIBOR}_{t-1}) \times \left(\frac{\text{number of days}}{\text{360 or 365}} \right) \times \left(\begin{array}{c} \text{notional} \\ \text{principal} \end{array} \right)$$

    f.   If this number is positive, the fixed-rate payer owes a net payment to the floating-rate payer. If this number is negative, then the fixed-rate payer receives a net flow from the floating-rate payer. Note the subscript of "t – 1" on LIBOR. This indicates that the previous period's floating rate determines the payment in the current period.

M. Floating-rate securities are bonds that pay a variable rate of interest. That is, rather than being set for the life of the issue, the cash coupons on these bonds will vary period by period, depending on market interest rates. For example, if market interest rates are moving up, the coupon rate on a variable-rate bond will also increase. In essence, floating-rate bonds have coupons that are reset periodically (normally every 6 to 12 months), according to prevailing market conditions. The formula for computing the floating rate is prespecified in the bond indenture. The most prevalent types of floaters are floating-rate bonds, deleveraged floaters, inverse floaters, dual-indexed floaters, range notes, ratchet bonds, stepped-spread floaters, extendible reset bonds, and noninterest rate indexed floaters.

    1.   The most common procedure for setting coupon rates on floating-rate securities is to use a reference rate, such as the rate on a U.S. Treasury bill (T-bill) or the London Interbank Offered Rate (LIBOR). A stated margin is then added to (or subtracted from) that reference rate. The quoted margin may also vary over time according to a schedule that is stated in the indenture. To find the new coupon rate, you would use the following coupon formula:

        New coupon rate = Reference rate ± Quoted margin

        Note that the margin may be added to, or subtracted from, the reference rate.

    2.   The rate of interest is usually lower on floating-rate bonds, compared with otherwise identical fixed-rate bonds, because the issuer assumes the interest rate risk that was previously borne by the bondholder. For example, if a corporation issues a floating-rate bond, the amount of the periodic coupon payment is uncertain. If interest rates rise, the amount of the floating-rate periodic coupon payment will increase. The corporation pays a lower initial coupon, with the trade-off being the risk of paying a higher coupon in the future.

    3.   Many bank loans are now variable rate, with a reference rate of LIBOR or the prime rate. Adjustable-rate mortgages (ARMs) are a type of floating-rate security. If a bank loan is made at LIBOR plus 2 percent, and LIBOR is currently at 4.25 percent, then the rate on the loan is 6.25 percent. If LIBOR increases to 5.5 percent, the loan rate increases to 7.5 percent. In the case of an ARM, the property owner is the *issuer*. By issuing an adjustable-rate mortgage, the property owner pays a lower initial monthly payment, with the trade-off being the risk of paying a higher monthly payment if interest rates increase.

Page 246

©2007 Kaplan CPA Review

4. As the coupon rate for a floating-rate security, or floater, varies over time, it may become very high or very low, depending upon movements in the reference rate of interest. If two parties to the bond contract want to limit their exposure to such extreme fluctuations, they do so by placing upper and lower limits on the adjusted coupon rate. The upper limit, which is called the cap, limits the maximum interest paid by the borrower. The lower limit, called the floor, limits the minimum interest received by the lender. When both limits are present simultaneously, the combination is called a *collar*.

5. Some bonds have "embedded options." These options are embedded in the sense that they are an integral part of the bond contract and are not stand-alone options. For the time being, it is enough to know that an option is a right, but not an obligation, to do something. Some embedded options favor the issuer, while others favor the bondholder.

6. Embedded options favoring the issuer (borrower).

   a. Prepayment option. Amortizing securities, such as those backed by mortgages and car loans, give the borrower the right to prepay the loan balance without penalty. Loans may be prepaid for a variety of reasons, such as refinancing at a lower rate, or the sale of the home/car before it is paid off. The prepayment right is an embedded option granted to the borrower.

   b. Call provision. A call provision gives the issuer of bonds the right to redeem the entire issue prior to maturity at a predetermined price. As we have seen earlier, the call price is usually set above the par value of the bonds. An issuer will call the bonds when the cost of new debt is less than the existing debt. If the cost of new debt exceeds the cost of the existing debt, the issuer will choose not to call the bonds. That is, the issuer has the option to call the bonds under favorable circumstances, and this option is embedded in the bond.

   c. Accelerated sinking fund option. The accelerated sinking fund provision gives the issuer of bonds the right to call part of the issue at a date prior to maturity at a predetermined price. An issuer will call more of the bonds than is required under the sinking fund provision when the cost of new debt is less than the existing debt. If the cost of new debt exceeds the cost of the existing debt, the issuer will retire only what is required under the sinking fund provision. That is, the issuer has the option to call part of the remaining bonds under favorable circumstances, and this option is embedded in the bond.

N. Embedded options favoring the bondholder (investor).

1. Conversion rights. Some bonds grant the holder of a bond the right to convert the bond into common shares of the issuer. The number of shares into which each bond is convertible (the conversion ratio) is prespecified in the indenture. If the conversion price, which is found by dividing the face value of the bond by the conversion ratio, is less than the market price of the shares, the bondholder will convert the bond into common shares. That is, the bondholder has the option of

converting the bond into common shares. This option is embedded in the bond and is valuable to the bondholder.

2. Put provisions. Bondholders may also have the right to sell the bond back to the issuer on certain dates prior to maturity at what is known as the put price. The put price is generally close to par if the bonds were originally issued at or close to par. If interest rates have risen, the market price of such bonds—in the absence of the put provision—would ordinarily fall below par value. In such a case, the bondholder would exercise the option to sell the bonds back to the issuer at the put price (i.e., par value). Therefore, the put option is valuable to the bondholder.

3. We have discussed the fact that debt financing increases the expected return to stockholders, but also increases the risk to stockholders. So how much debt is optimal? Theoretically, the firm should use the amount of debt versus equity that maximizes the firm's stock price (equivalently, that which minimizes the firm's cost of capital). In practice, it is difficult, if not impossible, to determine the exact amount of leverage that maximizes the stock price. There are several guiding principles to the amount of leverage, including (in no particular order):

   leverage factors

   a. Revenue and cost stability. If revenue and input costs are more stable, the firm can take on more financial leverage, and the risk that accompanies it.

   b. Operating leverage. If the firm has a high proportion of fixed costs in the cost structure, profits are more variable and the firm should employ less debt.

   c. Taxes. Debt is tax deductible and, thus, firms in high marginal tax brackets should employ more debt.

   d. Financial flexibility. Management generally desires the ability to issue debt in the future in order to fund profitable projects. This involves maintaining adequate borrowing capacity.

   e. Management attitudes. More conservative management teams tend to employ less debt.

   f. Lender and rating agency attitudes. A firm's management may be informed from its current lenders or by a rating agency that if it issues more debt, there will be consequences (i.e., a downgrade).

   g. Market conditions. A firm may be forced to issue debt or equity because of high interest rates or low stock prices.

   h. Profitability. If the firm is more profitable (and pays a low dividend, thus increasing retained earnings), the firm has a higher internal growth rate and can avoid external financing altogether. As retained earnings grow, the firm's debt decreases relative to its equity.

   i. Signaling. If the firm has favorable information (i.e., about a new technology) that investors do not yet have, the firm would not want to issue

STUDY MANUAL – BUSINESS ENVIRONMENT & CONCEPTS
CHAPTER 8

stock at the depressed price. Instead, the firm would issue debt and lever up for the coming gains. If prospects for the firm were bad, the firm would issue stock to allow new investors to share the losses.

STUDY MANUAL – BUSINESS ENVIRONMENT & CONCEPTS
CHAPTER 8

QUESTIONS: FINANCE: DERIVATIVES

1.   The holder of a put option:
     A. will not gain from exercising if the strike price is greater than the stock price.
     B. pays the writer an amount equal to the strike price on the exercise date.
     C. has an obligation to exercise if the stock price is less than the strike price.
     D. may sell the option to another party prior to expiration.

2.   A derivative security:
     A. has a value based on stock prices.
     B. has a value based on another security or index.
     C. has a no-default risk.
     D. is traded only in the over-the-counter market.

3.   Which of the following statements regarding forward contracts is TRUE?
     A. The buyer of a forward contract gains when prices decrease, and the seller of a forward contract loses when prices increase.
     B. The buyer of a forward contract gains when prices increase, and the seller of a forward contract loses when prices decrease.
     C. When prices increase, the buyer of a forward contract gains and the seller of a forward contract loses.
     D. When prices decrease, the buyer of a forward contract gains, and the seller of a forward contract loses.

4.   A futures contract is NOT:
     A. regulated.
     B. backed by the clearinghouse.
     C. standardized.
     D. illiquid.

5.   The seller of a call option has:
     A. the right to buy an asset at a fixed price.
     B. an obligation to sell an asset at a fixed price.
     C. the obligation to buy an asset at a fixed price.
     D. the right to sell an asset at a fixed price.

6.   Some forward contracts are termed cash settlement contracts. This means:
     A. either the long or the short in the forward contract will make a cash payment at contract expiration, and the asset is not delivered.
     B. the short, at settlement, can either pay cash or deliver the asset.
     C. at contract expiration, the long can buy the asset from the short or pay the difference between the market price of the asset and the contract price.
     D. at settlement, the long purchases the asset from the short for cash.

Page 250   ©2007 Kaplan CPA Review

7. Which of the following statements regarding futures and forward contracts is FALSE?
   A. Forwards have default risk.
   B. Futures contracts are highly standardized.
   C. Both forward contracts and futures contracts trade on an organized exchange.
   D. Forwards require no cash transactions until the delivery date while futures require a margin deposit when the position is opened.

8. Madison Bailey recently purchased a futures contract. The transaction did NOT:
   A. take place through a private party.
   B. use a structured contract.
   C. require a margin deposit.
   D. include a guaranty by a clearinghouse.

9. Which is the most common method of closing a futures contract?
   A. Exchange of physicals.
   B. Physical delivery.
   C. Reversing or offsetting trade.
   D. Clearinghouse adjustment.

10. Which of the following statements regarding option buyers and option writers is FALSE?
   A. The buyer of a call option has the right to buy an asset at a specific price for a specific period of time.
   B. The writer of a put option promises to sell an asset at a specific price for a specific period of time.
   C. The buyer of a put or call option has limited loss potential (the option premium).
   D. Options are a zero-sum gain. What the writer makes, the purchaser loses and vice versa.

11. An investor owns stock and is concerned that prices may fall in the future. Which strategy could help him or her hedge against adverse market conditions?
   A. Buy a futures contract.
   B. Buy an over-the-counter forward.
   C. Buy a put option.
   D. Buy a call option.

12. Which of the following statements about futures markets is FALSE?
   A. The cost of a futures transaction is similar to an insurance premium.
   B. The futures price is an estimate of the future forward price.
   C. Delivery details are included in every contract.
   D. Speculators establish the majority of futures positions.

STUDY MANUAL – BUSINESS ENVIRONMENT & CONCEPTS
CHAPTER 8

13. Which of the following statements about European and American options is FALSE?
    A. European options are easier to analyze and value than American options.
    B. American options can be exercised at any time on or before the expiration date.
    C. American options are far more common than European options.
    D. European options offer more flexible trading opportunities for speculators.

14. Which of the following statements concerning an American-style option is FALSE?
    A. It allows the holder the right to exercise before maturity of the option.
    B. They are only traded in the United States.
    C. It must be worth at least as much as a European-style option.
    D. The predominant option type is American-style, rather than European-style.

15. A contract that involves a series of forward commitments is a:
    A. future.
    B. strap.
    C. swap.
    D. stack.

16. A financial instrument that has payoffs based on the price of an underlying physical or financial asset is a(n):
    A. derivative security.
    B. future.
    C. forward.
    D. option.

Page 252

©2007 Kaplan CPA Review

STUDY MANUAL – BUSINESS ENVIRONMENT & CONCEPTS
CHAPTER 8

ANSWERS: FINANCE: DERIVATIVES

1. **D** The holder of a put option may sell the option to another party. The other statements are false. Although it is true that a put option is in-the-money when the stock price is less than the strike price, the holder is not obligated to exercise. Instead, the holder has the right to exercise. The put writer has the obligation to honor the terms of the contract. The holder of a put option receives an amount equal to the strike price from the put writer on the exercise date. (A put is the right to sell the underlying asset at a specified price.) An option holder will exercise if it is profitable to do so. Exercising a put when the strike price exceeds the stock price is profitable, and thus the investor would gain.

2. **B** This is the definition of a derivative security. Those based on stock prices are equity derivatives.

3. **C** If the price of the underlying instrument sold forward increases, the seller of the futures contract will have to pay more than planned to deliver the product and will lose on the forward part of the transaction. For example, say that a dairy farmer contracts to sell milk for delivery three months from now at $11.80 per hundredweight. Assume that by the end of three months the spot price of milk is $13.00 per hundredweight. Because of convergence, the futures price must move closer to the spot price as delivery nears. If the farmer takes the opposite position in the futures contract (buys) to close out the contract, the farmer will lose $1.20 per hundredweight in the futures transaction (but will gain $1.20 per hundredweight from selling in the spot market).

4. **D** Futures contracts are standardized, backed by the futures clearinghouse, and subject to governmental and exchange regulation. They are actively traded in the secondary market.

5. **B** The seller of a call option has an obligation to sell an asset at a fixed price.

6. **A** In a cash settlement forward contract, there is a cash payment at settlement by either the long or the short depending on whether the market price of the asset is below or above the contract price at expiration. The underlying asset is not purchased or sold at settlement.

7. **C** Forward contracts are custom-tailored contracts and are not exchange traded while futures contracts are standardized and are traded on an organized exchange.

8. **A** A futures transaction is an exchange-traded contract. A forward contract occurs between private parties. The following table illustrates the differences between forwards and futures:

Forwards	Futures
Private contracts	Exchange-traded contracts
Unique contracts	Structured contracts
Default risk	Guaranteed by clearinghouse
No up-front cash	Margin account
Low/no regulation	Regulated

©2007 Kaplan CPA Review
Page 253

STUDY MANUAL – BUSINESS ENVIRONMENT & CONCEPTS
CHAPTER 8

9. **C**   A reverse, or offsetting, trade in the futures market is how most futures positions are settled. Since the other side of your position is held by the clearinghouse, if you make an exact opposite trade (maturity, quantity, and good) to your current position, the clearinghouse will net your positions out, leaving you with a zero balance.

There are two less common ways to get out of a futures position once you take it:

Delivery: You can satisfy the contract by delivering the goods. Depending on the wording of the contract, delivery may be made by physically delivering the goods to the designated location or by making a cash settlement of any gains or losses. Deliveries represent less than 1 percent of all settlements.

Exchange for physicals: Here, you find a trader with an opposite position to your own and deliver the goods and settle up between yourselves off the floor of the exchange (called an ex-pit transaction). This is the one exception to the federal law that requires that all trades take place on the floor of the exchange. You must then contact the clearinghouse and tell them what happened. An exchange for physicals differs from a delivery in that the traders actually exchanged the goods, the contract is not closed on the floor of the exchange, and the two traders privately negotiated the terms of the transaction.

10. **B**   The put seller or writer is agreeing to buy, not sell, at a specific price.

11. **C**   Buying a call, buying a futures contract, or buying a forward gives the investor the chance to buy more stock. However, neither of these strategies provides a way to hedge the existing equity position. A put option provides the opportunity to sell the stock.

12. **B**   The futures price is an estimate of the future spot price.

13. **D**   European options are less flexible for traders than American options because of the limitation on when they can be exercised, which is only on the expiration date. Traders gain more flexibility with American options that can be exercised at any time on or before expiration.

14. **B**   American-style options are traded throughout the world. The "American" label simply identifies the option as having the right to be exercised before maturity. American-style options are worth at least as much as European-style options and are the predominant type of options contract traded.

15. **C**   A swap consists of a series of forward commitments on multiple "settlement" dates. A strap is an options strategy and a stack is a type of hedge.

16. **A**   This is the definition of derivative securities. Options, futures, and forwards are examples of types of derivative securities.

COST VOLUME PROFIT ANALYSIS

STUDY MANUAL – BUSINESS ENVIRONMENT & CONCEPTS
CHAPTER 9

Study Tip: People get tired of studying, especially when studying seems to get into a rut. As long as you are preparing efficiently, do not make any changes. However, if putting in the hours of study has become a real trial, try changing your location. For example, if you normally study in your den, begin working at the kitchen table for a few days. Creating any type of change can be refreshing, and it can keep the preparation process from becoming drudgery.

COST-VOLUME-PROFIT ANALYSIS

A. The purpose of cost-volume-profit analysis is to determine the volume of production and sales necessary to break even (i.e., zero profit) or to attain a specific profit goal.

B. In applying breakeven analysis, certain basic assumptions are made to simplify the analysis. These assumptions are essential to the analysis:

1. The company is operating within a relevant range.

2. At any level of production, fixed costs will remain the same within the relevant range.

3. Variable costs will be incurred at a constant rate per unit at any level within the company's relevant range of production.

4. Sales mix remains constant if the company sells more than one product. Sales mix is the percentage of sales from each product (i.e., 25 percent from Product A, 50 percent from Product B, and 25 percent from Product C).

5. Although it is not an essential assumption, it is also generally assumed that inventory levels remain constant. Either there are no beginning or ending inventories, or beginning inventories are equal to ending inventories.

C. The relationships of cost, volume, and profit can be visualized in Figure 1:

©2007 Kaplan CPA Review

STUDY MANUAL – BUSINESS ENVIRONMENT & CONCEPTS
CHAPTER 9

Figure 1: Cost/Volume/Profit Graph

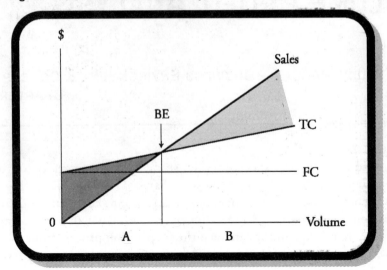

1. In this graph, total cost at any volume of production can be measured on line TC (total costs), while sales revenue can be measured at any volume on the sales line.

2. The breakeven point is noted as point BE.

3. At a volume indicated by A, there would be a loss equal to the difference between sales and total costs at that volume, indicated by the dark shading.

4. At a volume indicated by B, there would be a profit equal to the difference between sales and total costs indicated by the lighter shading.

D. A second type of graph that is used in cost-volume-profit analysis is a profit-volume graph as presented in Figure 2:

Figure 2: Profit/Volume Graph

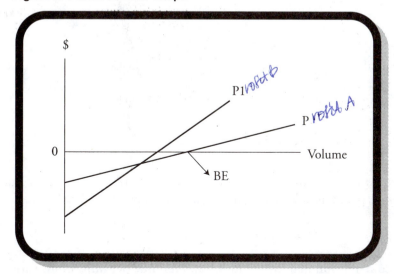

1. In this graph, P represents the profit at any given level of production for a particular product.

2. BE would be the breakeven point, and there would be a loss at volumes lower than BE and a profit at volumes higher than BE.

3. Line P1 represents the profit line for another product. Since the loss is greater for P1 than for P at 0 production, fixed costs are apparently higher for that product. Since line P1 is steeper than line P, however, the contribution margin per unit is higher. (The slope of the line is equal to the per-unit contribution margin.)

    a. Contribution margin equals sales minus variable costs.

    b. It is the amount left over, after covering variable costs, that contributes toward covering fixed costs and eventually profits.

CALCULATION OF CONTRIBUTION MARGIN AND BREAKEVEN SALES IN UNITS

A. The variable cost per unit is deducted from the sales price per unit, giving the contribution margin per unit.

   Sales price per unit − Variable cost per unit = Contribution margin per unit

B. The contribution margin per unit is divided into fixed costs to determine the number of units required to break even.

STUDY MANUAL – BUSINESS ENVIRONMENT & CONCEPTS
CHAPTER 9

$$\text{breakeven units} = \frac{\text{fixed costs}}{\text{contribution margin per unit}}$$

C. When the company sells more than one product, there will generally be an established sales mix.

In these cases, for analysis purposes, one sales unit should consist of a proportionate amount of the products sold. For example, if a company sells twice as much of product A as product B, one sales unit would consist of 2A + 1B.

TARGET PROFIT

A similar approach is used to determine the number of units required to achieve a certain profit. The profit may be stated as a certain dollar amount or a percentage of sales.

A. When profit is expressed as a dollar amount:

1. Compute the contribution margin per unit (sales revenue per unit minus variable costs per unit).

2. Add the amount of profit to the fixed costs.

3. Divide the fixed cost plus profit by the contribution margin per unit.

4. The result is the number of units required to earn the desired profit.

$$\text{desired sales level in units} = \frac{\text{fixed costs} + \text{profit before tax}}{\text{contribution margin per unit}}$$

B. When profit is expressed as a percentage of sales:

1. Compute the profit as a dollar amount per unit by multiplying the profit percentage by the sales price.

2. Compute contribution margin minus profit by subtracting variable costs per unit plus profit per unit from the sales price.

3. The result will be divided into fixed costs to give the units required to earn the desired profit.

C. When sales are expected to be higher than the amount needed for breakeven, the excess is considered the margin of safety, or sales minus breakeven sales.

1. In dollar terms, the margin of safety represents the amount by which sales can drop before incurring losses.

2. The margin of safety can also be expressed as a percentage of sales.

Page 258   ©2007 Kaplan CPA Review

STUDY MANUAL – BUSINESS ENVIRONMENT & CONCEPTS
CHAPTER 9

BREAKEVEN AND COST-VOLUME-PROFIT ANALYSIS

Breakeven and cost-volume-profit analysis can be summarized with the following formula:

	Sales in Units	Sales in Dollars
Breakeven sales	$\dfrac{\text{fixed costs}}{\text{contribution margin/unit}}$	$\dfrac{\text{fixed costs}}{\text{contribution margin ratio}}$
Sales for target level of profit	$\dfrac{\text{fixed costs + profit}}{\text{contribution margin/unit}}$	$\dfrac{\text{fixed costs + profit}}{\text{contribution margin ratio}}$

Sales for Target Level of Profit per Unit	Sales for Target Level of Profit Percentage
$\dfrac{\text{fixed costs + profit}}{\text{contribution margin/unit - profit/unit}}$	$\dfrac{\text{fixed costs + profit}}{\text{contribution margin ratio - profit percentage}}$

Example: Breakeven Calculation

The following data pertain to two types of products manufactured by Korn Corp.

	Amounts per Unit	
	Sales Price	Variable Costs
Product Y	$120	$70
Product Z	$500	$200

Fixed costs total $300,000 annually. The expected mix in units is 60 percent for Product Y and 40 percent for Product Z.

1. What is Korn's breakeven sales in units?
   A. 857.
   B. 1,111.
   C. 2,000.
   D. 2,459.

2. What is Korn's breakeven sales in dollars?
   A. $300,000.
   B. $420,000.
   C. $475,000.
   D. $544,000.

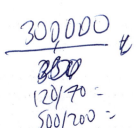

©2007 Kaplan CPA Review

STUDY MANUAL – BUSINESS ENVIRONMENT & CONCEPTS
CHAPTER 9

3. Adly Corp. wishes to earn a 30 percent return on its $100,000 investment in equipment used to produce Product X. Based on estimated sales of 10,000 units of Product X next year, the costs per unit would be as follows:

Variable manufacturing costs	$5
Fixed selling and administrative costs	$2
Fixed manufacturing costs	$1

At how much per unit should Product X be priced for sale?
A. $5.
B. $8.
C. $10.
D. $11.

Solutions:

1. **C** Product X and Product Z have contribution margins of $50 and $300, respectively. With a product mix of 60 percent Y and 40 percent Z, the weighted-average contribution margin is (60 percent × $50) + (40 percent × $300), or $150.00. Divided into fixed costs of $300,000, this gives a breakeven point of 2,000 units.

2. **D** The 2,000 units needed to break even would consist of 60 percent Y at $120 per unit ($144,000) and 40 percent Z at $500 per unit ($400,000), for a total of $544,000.

3. **D** Since Adly is looking for a 30 percent return on an investment of $100,000, it is seeking to earn a profit of $30,000 per year. Based on a volume of 10,000 units, this means that each unit must contribute $3 to profit in addition to covering the costs of $8 per unit to manufacture. This would require a sales price of $11 per unit.

STUDY MANUAL – BUSINESS ENVIRONMENT & CONCEPTS
CHAPTER 9

QUESTIONS: COST VOLUME PROFIT ANALYSIS

1. Consider the following regression equation:

   $$\text{Sales}_i = 10.0 + 1.25\ \text{R\&D}_i + 1.0\ \text{ADV}_i - 2.0\ \text{COMP}_i + 8.0\ \text{CAP}_i$$

   where sales is dollar sales in millions, R&D is research and development expenditures in millions, ADV is dollar amount spent on advertising in millions, COMP is the number of competitors in the industry, and CAP is the capital expenditures for the period in millions of dollars. Which of the following is NOT a correct interpretation of this regression information?
   A. If R&D and advertising expenditures are $1 million each, there are five competitors, and capital expenditures are $2 million, expected sales are $8.25 million.
   B. If a company spends $1 million more on capital expenditures (holding everything else constant), sales are expected to increase by $8.0 million.
   C. One more competitor will mean $2 million less in sales (holding everything else constant).
   D. Increasing advertising dollars by $1 million (holding everything else constant) will result in $1 million additional sales.

2. If the coefficient of correlation between two variables is zero, how might a scatter diagram of these variables appear?
   A. Under this condition, a scatter diagram could not be plotted on a graph.
   B. Random points.
   C. A least squares line that slopes up to the right.
   D. A least squares line that slopes down to the right.

3. The purpose of a flexible budget is to:
   A. eliminate cyclical fluctuations in production reports by ignoring variable costs.
   B. compare actual and budgeted results at virtually any level of production.
   C. reduce the total time in preparing the annual budget.
   D. allow management some latitude in meeting goals.

4. The following information pertains to Rica Company:

Sales (50,000 units)	$1,000,000
Direct materials and direct labor	300,000
Factory overhead:	
Variable	40,000
Fixed	70,000
Selling and general expenses:	
Variable	10,000
Fixed	60,000

©2007 Kaplan CPA Review
Page 261

STUDY MANUAL – BUSINESS ENVIRONMENT & CONCEPTS
CHAPTER 9

Assuming direct labor is a variable cost, how much was Rica's breakeven point in number of units?
A. 10,000.
B. 18,571.
C. 26,000.
D. 9,848.

5.   In an income statement prepared as an internal report using the absorption costing method, which of the following terms should appear?

	Contribution margin	Gross profit (margin)
A.	No	No
B.	Yes	Yes
C.	No	Yes
D.	Yes	No

6.   During Year 4, a department's three-variance overhead standard costing system reported unfavorable spending and volume variances. The activity level selected for allocating overhead to the product was based on 80 percent of practical capacity. If 100 percent of practical capacity had been selected instead, how would the reported unfavorable spending and volume variances be affected?

	Spending variance	Volume variance
A.	Increased	Increased
B.	Unchanged	Unchanged
C.	Increased	Unchanged
D.	Unchanged	Increased

7.   The budgeted total variable overhead cost for C machine hours is:
A. BC minus DO.
B. AB.
C. BC.
D. AC minus DO.

Use the following information to answer Questions 8 and 9.

Bates Co. incurred the following costs:

Direct materials and direct labor	$600,000
Variable factory overhead	80,000
Straight-line depreciation:	
Production machinerY	70,000
Factory building	50,000

8.   Under absorption costing, the inventoriable costs are:
A. $680,000.
B. $730,000.
C. $750,000.
D. $800,000.

Page 262   ©2007 Kaplan CPA Review

9. Under variable (direct) costing, the inventoriable costs are:
A. $600,000.
B. $680,000.
C. $720,000.
D. $750,000.

10. The fixed portion of the semivariable cost of electricity for a manufacturing plant is a:

	Period cost	Product cost
A.	Yes	No
B.	Yes	Yes
C.	No	Yes
D.	No	No

11. Brooks Company uses the following flexible budget formula for the annual maintenance cost in department T:

Total cost = $7,200 + $0.60 per machine hour

The July operating budget is based upon 20,000 hours of planned machine time. Maintenance cost included in this flexible budget is:
A. $11,400.
B. $12,000.
C. $12,600.
D. $19,200.

12. Ral Co.'s target gross margin is 60% of the selling price of a product that costs $5.00 per unit. The product's selling price per unit should be:
A. $17.50.
B. $12.50.
C. $8.33.
D. $7.50.

13. The fixed portion of the semivariable cost of electricity for a manufacturing plant is a:

	Conversion cost	Product cost
A.	No	No
B.	No	Yes
C.	Yes	Yes
D.	Yes	No

STUDY MANUAL – BUSINESS ENVIRONMENT & CONCEPTS
CHAPTER 9

14. The following relationships pertain to a year's budgeted activity for the Smythe Company:

Direct-labor hours	300,000	400,000
Total costs	$129,000	$154,000

What are the budgeted fixed costs for the year?
A. $25,000.
b. $54,000.
c. $75,000.
d. $100,000.

Use the following information to answer Questions 15 and 16.

Maintenance expenses of a company are to be analyzed for purposes of constructing a flexible budget. Examination of past records disclosed the following costs and volume measures:

	Highest	Lowest
Cost per month	$39,200	$32,000
Machine hours	24,000	15,000

15. Using the high-low-point method of analysis, the estimated variable cost per machine hour is:
A. $1.25.
B. $12.50.
C. $0.80.
D. $0.08.

16. Using the high-low technique, the estimated annual fixed cost for maintenance expenditures is:
A. $447,360.
B. $240,000.
C. $230,400.
D. $384,000.

Page 264

©2007 Kaplan CPA Review

STUDY MANUAL – BUSINESS ENVIRONMENT & CONCEPTS
CHAPTER 9

Use the following information to answer Questions 17 through 21.

The following data relate to a year's budgeted activity for Patsy Corporation, a single product company:

	Units
Beginning inventory	30,000
Production	120,000
Available	150,000
Sales	110,000
Ending inventory	40,000

	Per Unit
Selling price	$5.00
Variable manufacturing costs	1.00
Variable selling costs	2.00
Fixed manufacturing costs (based on 100,000 units)	0.25
Fixed selling costs (based on 100,000 units)	0.65

Total fixed costs remain unchanged within the relevant range of 25,000 units to total capacity of 160,000 units.

17.   The projected annual breakeven sales in units for Patsy Corporation is:
A. 30,000.
B. 37,143.
C. 45,000.
D. 50,000.

18.   The projected net income for Patsy Corporation for the year under direct (variable) costing is:
A. $110,000.
B. $127,500.
C. $130,000.
D. $150,000.

19.   If all the variances are charged to cost of goods sold, the projected net income for Patsy Corporation for the year under absorption costing is:
A. $122,500.
B. $127,500.
C. $130,000.
D. $132,500.

20.   A special order is received to purchase 10,000 units to be used in an unrelated market. Given the original data, what price per unit should be charged on this order to increase Patsy Corporation's net income by $5,000?
A. $3.50.
B. $4.40.
C. $5.00.
D. $6.50.

©2007 Kaplan CPA Review
Page 265

STUDY MANUAL – BUSINESS ENVIRONMENT & CONCEPTS
CHAPTER 9

21.   Concerning the data for Patsy Corporation, assume selling price increases by 20%; variable manufacturing costs increase by 10%; variable selling costs remain the same; and total fixed costs increase to $104,400. How many units must now be sold to generate a profit equal to 10% of the contribution margin?
A. 36,000.
B. 40,000.
C. 43,320.
D. 45,390.

22.   Kent Co.'s operating percentages were as follows:

Sales		100%
Cost of sales		
Variable	50%	
Fixed	10	60
Gross profit		40
Other operating expenses		
Variable	20	
Fixed	15	35
Operating income		5%

Kent's sales totaled $2,000,000. At what sales level would Kent break even?
A. $1,900,000.
B. $1,666,667.
C. $1,250,000.
D. $833,333.

23.   Jago Co. has 2 products that use the same manufacturing facilities and cannot be subcontracted. Each product has sufficient orders to utilize the entire manufacturing capacity. For short-run profit maximization, Jago should manufacture the product with the:
A. Lower total manufacturing costs for the manufacturing capacity.
B. Lower total variable manufacturing costs for the manufacturing capacity.
C. Greater gross profit per hour of manufacturing capacity.
D. Greater contribution margin per hour of manufacturing capacity.

24.   The following information pertains to Mete Co.:

Sales	$400,000
Variable costs	80,000
Fixed costs	20,000

Mete's breakeven point in sales dollars is:
A. $20,000.
B. $25,000.
C. $80,000.
D. $100,000.

Page 266
©2007 Kaplan CPA Review

25. In an income statement prepared as an internal report using the direct (variable) costing method, fixed selling and administrative expenses would:
A. Be used in the computation of the contribution margin.
B. Be used in the computation of operating income but not in the computation of the contribution margin.
C. Be treated the same as variable selling and administrative expenses.
D. Not be used.

26. At the end of Killo Co.'s first year of operations, 1,000 units of inventory remained on hand. Variable and fixed manufacturing costs per unit were $90 and $20, respectively. If Killo uses absorption costing rather than direct (variable) costing, the result would be a higher pretax income of:
A. $0.
B. $20,000.
C. $70,000.
D. $90,000.

27. Quo Co. rented a building to Hava Fast Food. Each month Quo receives a fixed rental amount plus a variable rental amount based on Hava's sales for that month. As sales increase so does the variable rental amount, but at a reduced rate. Which of the following curves reflects the monthly rentals under the agreement?

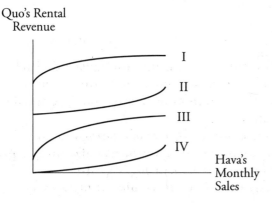

A. I.
B. II.
C. III.
D. IV.

Use the following information to answer Question 28.

The diagram below is a cost-volume-profit chart.

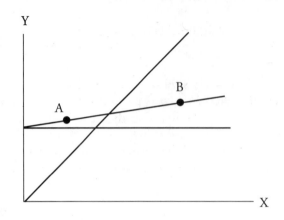

28. At point A compared to point B, as a percentage of sales revenues:

	Variable costs are:	Fixed costs are:
A.	Greater	Greater
B.	Greater	Same
C.	Same	Same
D.	Same	Greater

29. The most likely strategy to reduce the breakeven point would be to:
    A. increase both the fixed costs and the contribution margin.
    B. decrease both the fixed costs and the contribution margin.
    C. decrease the fixed costs and increase the contribution margin.
    D. increase the fixed costs and decrease the contribution margin.

30. Buff Co. is considering replacing an old machine with a new machine. Which of the following items is economically relevant to Buff's decision? (Ignore income tax considerations.)

	Carrying amount of old machine	Disposal value of new machine
A.	Yes	No
B.	No	Yes
C.	No	No
D.	Yes	Yes

31. The Lantern Corporation has 1,000 obsolete lanterns that are carried in inventory at a manufacturing cost of $20,000. If the lanterns are remachined for $5,000, they could be sold for $9,000. If the lanterns are scrapped, they could be sold for $1,000. What alternative is more desirable and what are the total relevant costs for that alternative?
    A. Remachine and $5,000.
    B. Remachine and $25,000.
    C. Scrap and $20,000.
    D. Neither, as there is an overall loss under either alternative.

32. Jarvis Co. has fixed costs of $200,000. It has two products that it can sell, Tetra and Min. Jarvis sells these products at a rate of 2 units of Tetra to 1 unit of Min. The contribution margin is $1 per unit for Tetra and $2 per unit for Min. How many units of Min would be sold at the breakeven point?
   A. 44,444.
   B. 50,000.
   C. 88,888.
   D. 100,000.

Use the following information to answer Questions 33 and 34.

Taylor, Inc., produces only two products, Acdom and Belnom. These account for 60% and 40% of the total sales dollars of Taylor, respectively. Variable costs (as a percentage of sales dollars) are 60% for Acdom and 85% for Belnom. Total fixed costs are $150,000. There are no other costs.

33. What is Taylor's breakeven point in sales dollars?
   A. $150,000.
   B. $214,286.
   C. $300,000.
   D. $500,000.

34. Assuming that the total fixed costs of Taylor increase by 30%, what amount of sales dollars would be necessary to generate a net income of $9,000?
   A. $204,000.
   B. $464,000.
   C. $659,000.
   D. $680,000.

35. Thomas Company sells products X, Y, and Z. Thomas sells three units of X for each unit of Z, and two units of Y for each unit of X. The contribution margins are $1.00 per unit of X, $1.50 per unit of Y, and $3.00 per unit of Z. Fixed costs are $600,000. How many units of X would Thomas sell at the breakeven point?
   A. 40,000.
   B. 120,000.
   C. 360,000.
   D. 400,000.

36. In an income statement prepared using the variable costing method, fixed factory overhead would:
   A. Not be used.
   B. Be used in the computation of the contribution margin.
   C. Be used in the computation of operating income but not in the computation of the contribution margin.
   D. Be treated the same as variable factory overhead.

©2007 Kaplan CPA Review

STUDY MANUAL – BUSINESS ENVIRONMENT & CONCEPTS
CHAPTER 9

37. Cuff Caterers quotes a price of $60 per person for a dinner party. This price includes the 6% sales tax and the 15% service charge. Sales tax is computed on the food plus the service charge. The service charge is computed on the food only. At what amount does Cuff price the food?
A. $56.40.
B. $51.00.
C. $49.22.
D. $47.40.

38. Cardinal Company needs 20,000 units of a certain part to use in its production cycle. The following information is available:

Cost to Cardinal to make the part:	
Direct materials	$4
Direct labor	16
Variable overhead	8
Fixed overhead applied	10
	$38
Cost to buy the part from the Oriole Company	$36

If Cardinal buys the part from Oriole instead of making it, Cardinal could not use the released facilities in another manufacturing activity. 60% of the fixed overhead applied will continue regardless of what decision is made.

In deciding whether to make or buy the part, the total relevant costs to make the part are:
A. $560,000.
B. $640,000.
C. $720,000.
D. $760,000.

39. Product Cott has sales of $200,000, a contribution margin of 20%, and a margin of safety of $80,000. What is Cott's fixed cost?
A. $16,000.
B. $24,000.
C. $80,000.
D. $96,000.

40. In an income statement prepared as an internal report using the variable costing method, which of the following terms should appear?

	Gross profit (margin)	Operating income
A.	Yes	Yes
B.	Yes	No
C.	No	No
D.	No	Yes

Page 270   ©2007 Kaplan CPA Review

STUDY MANUAL – BUSINESS ENVIRONMENT & CONCEPTS
CHAPTER 9

41. The following information pertains to Sisk Co.:

Sales (25,000 units)	$500,000
Direct materials and direct labor	150,000
Factory overhead:	
Variable	20,000
Fixed	35,000
Selling and general expenses:	
Variable	5,000
Fixed	30,000

Sisk's breakeven point in number of units is:
A. 4,924.
B. 5,000.
C. 6,250.
D. 9,286.

42. Using the variable costing method, which of the following costs are assigned to inventory.?

	Variable selling and administrative costs	Variable factory overhead costs
A.	Yes	Yes
B.	Yes	No
C.	No	No
D.	No	Yes

43. Motor Company manufactures 10,000 units of Part M-1 for use in its production annually. The following costs are reported:

Direct materials	$20,000
Direct labor	55,000
Variable overhead	45,000
Fixed overhead	70,000
	$190,000

Valve Company has offered to sell Motor 10,000 units of Part M-1 for $18 per unit. If Motor accepts the offer, some of the facilities presently used to manufacture Part M-1 could be rented to a third party at an annual rental of $15,000. Additionally, $4 per unit of the fixed overhead applied to Part M-1 would be totally eliminated. Should Motor accept Valve's offer, and why?
A. No, because it would be $5,000 cheaper to make the part.
B. Yes, because it would be $10,000 cheaper to buy the part.
C. No, because it would be $15,000 cheaper to make the part.
D. Yes, because it would be $25,000 cheaper to buy the part.

©2007 Kaplan CPA Review
Page 271

STUDY MANUAL – BUSINESS ENVIRONMENT & CONCEPTS
CHAPTER 9

44. The following information pertains to Clove Co. for the year ending December 31, 20XX:

Budgeted sales	$1,000,000
Breakeven sales	700,000
Budgeted contribution margin	600,000
Cashflow breakeven	200,000

Clove's margin of safety is:
A. $300,000.
B. $400,000.
C. $500,000.
D. $800,000.

Use the following information to answer Questions 45 and 46.

Selected information concerning the operations of Kern Company for the year ended December 31, 20XX, is available as follows:

Units produced	10,000
Units sold	9,000
Direct materials used	$40,000
Direct labor incurred	$20,000
Fixed factory overhead	$25,000
Variable factory overhead	$12,000
Fixed selling and administrative expenses	$30,000
Variable selling and administrative expenses	$4,500
Finished goods inventory, Jan. 1, 20XX	None

There were no work-in-process inventories at the beginning and end of 20XX.

45. What would be Kern's finished goods inventory cost at December 31, 20XX, under the variable (direct) cost method?
A. $7,200.
B. $7,650.
C. $8,000.
D. $9,700.

46. Which costing method, absorption or variable costing, would show a higher operating income for 20XX and by what amount?

	Costing method	Amount
A.	Absorption costing	$2,500
B.	Variable costing	$2,500
C.	Absorption costing	$5,500
D.	Variable costing	$5,500

Page 272   ©2007 Kaplan CPA Review

47. Del Co. has fixed costs of $100,000 and breakeven sales of $800,000. What is its projected profit at $1,200,000 sales?
A. $50,000.
B. $150,000.
C. $200,000.
D. $400,000.

48. Manor Company plans to discontinue a department with a contribution to overhead of $24,000 and allocated overhead of $48,000, of which $21,000 cannot be eliminated. The effect of this discontinuance on Manor's pretax profit would be a (an):
A. Decrease of $3,000.
B. Increase of $3,000.
C. Decrease of $24,000.
D. Increase of $24,000.

49. Gandy Company has 5,000 obsolete desk lamps that are carried in inventory at a manufacturing cost of $50,000. If the lamps are reworked for $20,000, they could be sold for $35,000. Alternatively, the lamps could be sold for $8,000 to a jobber located in a distant city. In a decision model analyzing these alternatives, the sunk cost would be:
A. $8,000.
B. $15,000.
C. $20,000.
D. $50,000.

50. On January 1, Lake Co. increased its direct labor wage rates. All other budgeted costs and revenues were unchanged. How did this increase affect Lake's budgeted break-even point and budgeted margin of safety?

	Budgeted break-even point	Budgeted margin of safety
A.	Increase	Increase
B.	Increase	Decrease
C.	Decrease	Decrease
D.	Decrease	Increase

51. When using a flexible budget, a decrease in production levels within a relevant range:
A. Decreases variable cost per unit.
B. Decreases total costs.
C. Increases total fixed costs.
D. Increases variable cost per unit.

©2007 Kaplan CPA Review

STUDY MANUAL – BUSINESS ENVIRONMENT & CONCEPTS
CHAPTER 9

52. When production levels are expected to decline within a relevant range, and a flexible budget is used, what effect would be anticipated with respect to each of the following?

	Variable costs per unit	Fixed costs per unit
A.	No change	No change
B.	Increase	No change
C.	No change	Increase
D.	Increase	Increase

53. In an income statement prepared as an internal report, total fixed costs normally would be shown separately under:

	Absorption costing	Variable costing
A.	No	No
B.	No	Yes
C.	Yes	Yes
D.	Yes	No

54. Based on potential sales of 500 units per year, a new product has estimated traceable costs of $990,000. What is the target price to obtain a 15% profit margin on sales?
   A. $2,329.
   B. $2,277.
   C. $1,980.
   D. $1,935.

55. The following information pertains to Syl Co.:

Sales	$800,000
Variable costs	160,000
Fixed costs	40,000

What is Syl's breakeven point in sales dollars?
   A. $200,000.
   B. $160,000.
   C. $50,000.
   D. $40,000.

STUDY MANUAL – BUSINESS ENVIRONMENT & CONCEPTS
CHAPTER 9

Use the following information to answer Questions 56 and 57.

Gordon Company began its operations on January 1, and produces a single product that sells for $10 per unit. Gordon uses an actual (historical) cost system. In 20XX, 100,000 units were produced and 80,000 units were sold. There was no work-in-process inventory at December 31. Manufacturing costs and selling and administrative expenses for the year were as follows:

	Fixed costs	Variable costs
Raw materials	—	$2.00 per unit produced
Direct labor	—	1.25 per unit produced
Factory overhead	$120,000	0.75 per unit produced
Selling and administrative	70,000	1.00 per unit sold

56.   What would be Gordon's operating income under the variable (direct) costing method?
        A. $114,000.
        B. $210,000.
        C. $234,000.
        D. $330,000.

57.   What would be Gordon's finished goods inventory at December 31 under the absorption costing method?
        A. $80,000.
        B. $104,000.
        C. $110,000.
        D. $124,000.

58.   Cook Co.'s total costs of operating five sales offices last year were $500,000, of which $70,000 represented fixed costs. Cook has determined that total costs are significantly influenced by the number of sales offices operated. Last year's costs and number of sales offices can be used as the bases for predicting annual costs. What would be the budgeted costs for the coming year if Cook were to operate seven sales offices?
        A. $700,000.
        B. $672,000.
        C. $614,000.
        D. $586,000.

59.   The following information pertains to Rica Company:

Sales (50,000 units)	$1,000,000
Direct materials and direct labor	300,000
Factory overhead:	
Variable	40,000
Fixed	70,000
Selling and general expenses:	
Variable	10,000
Fixed	60,000

©2007 Kaplan CPA Review
Page 275

What was Rica's contribution margin ratio?
A. 66%.
B. 65%.
C. 59%.
D. 35%.

60. Break-even analysis assumes that over the relevant range:
A. Unit revenues are nonlinear.
B. Unit variable costs are unchanged.
C. Total costs are unchanged.
D. Total fixed costs are nonlinear.

61. A scatter chart depicting the relationship between sales and salesmen's automobile expenses is set forth below:

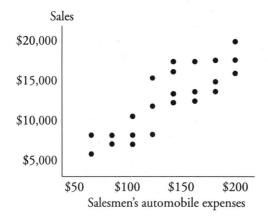

What can we deduce from the chart about the relationship between sales and salesmen's automobile expenses?
A. A high degree of linear correlation.
B. A high degree of nonlinear correlation.
C. No apparent correlation.
D. Both sales and salesmen's automobile expenses are independent variables.

62. Day Mail Order Co. applied the high-low method of cost estimation to customer order data for the first 4 months of the year. What is the estimated variable order filling cost component per order?

Month	Orders	Cost
January	1,200	$3,120
February	1,300	3,185
March	1,800	4,320
April	1,700	3,895
	6,000	$14,520

A. $2.00.
B. $2.42.
C. $2.48.
D. $2.50.

STUDY MANUAL – BUSINESS ENVIRONMENT & CONCEPTS
CHAPTER 9

63.   Waldo Company, which produces only one product, provides its most current month's data as follows:

Selling price per unit	$80
Variable costs per unit:	
Direct materials	21
Direct labor	10
Variable manufacturing overhead	3
Variable selling and administrative	6
Fixed costs:	
Manufacturing overhead	$76,000
Selling and administrative	58,000
Units:	
Beginning inventory	0
Month's production	5,000
Number sold	4,500
Ending inventory	500

Based upon the above information, what is the total contribution margin for the month under the variable costing approach?
A. $46,000.
B. $180,000.
C. $207,000.
D. $226,000.

©2007 Kaplan CPA Review
Page 277

STUDY MANUAL – BUSINESS ENVIRONMENT & CONCEPTS
CHAPTER 9

ANSWERS: COST VOLUME PROFIT ANALYSIS

1. **A** Predicted sales, under the conditions expressed in choice A, would be = $10 + 1.25 + 1 – 10 + 16 = $18.25 million. Simply populate the equation with the "givens" in A to arrive at the $18.25.

2. **B** When a correlation analysis produces a coefficient of zero, the implication is that there is absolutely no causal connection between the two variables. Plotting the points would show them as random points forming no pattern or cluster whatever.

3. **B** This is the definition of a flexible budget. Compared to a static budget, which shows only one level of production, the flexible budget shows budgeted costs and revenues for any level of production. As levels of production change, the costs and revenues will change as well. The flexible budget provides that information. Variance analysis is made more meaningful with flexible budgets.

4. **A** Fixed costs are $70,000 plus $60,000 = $130,000. Variable costs are $300,000 plus $40,000 plus $10,000 (direct materials and direct labor are variable costs) or $350,000. Sales of $1,000,000 minus variable costs of $350,000 equals contribution margin of $650,000. Per unit, contribution margin is $650,000/50,000 units, or $13.00. Breakeven in units is: Fixed costs\Contribution margin per unit. So, $130,000/$13 = 10,000 units.

   Remember the breakeven formulas: BE sales dollars = Fixed costs/Contribution margin ratio. BE sales units = Fixed costs/Contribution margin per unit in dollars. Why? Breakeven is where fixed costs equal contribution margin, therefore yielding zero profit.

5. **C** *Contribution margin* is a term associated with variable (direct) costing; however, it is not applicable to absorption costing. Contribution margin is sales less all variable costs, and it is from this amount that all fixed costs (manufacturing, selling, and administrative) are deducted to determine operating income.

   Under absorption costing, cost of goods sold includes both variable and fixed manufacturing costs, and sales less cost of goods sold is referred to as *gross profit or gross margin*. Remember: absorption costing is used for external reporting; variable or direct costing is not allowed for external reporting.

6. **D** The overhead spending (budget) variance is the difference between actual overhead costs and budgeted overhead costs at the actual level of activity achieved. The activity level used to determine the predetermined rate for overhead allocation has no effect on this variance.

   The overhead volume variance is the difference between budgeted overhead costs at the standard level of activity for the production achieved and applied overhead costs. It is attributable to the overapplication or underapplication of fixed costs, due to production at an activity level other than where the predetermined overhead rate was set. If the activity level used to determine the predetermined overhead rate was increased (80 percent of practical capacity to 100 percent), the fixed overhead application rate would decrease and less fixed overhead would be applied per unit of activity achieved. This would result in an increase in an unfavorable (underapplied) or a decrease in a favorable (overapplied) volume variance.

Page 278   ©2007 Kaplan CPA Review

STUDY MANUAL – BUSINESS ENVIRONMENT & CONCEPTS
CHAPTER 9

7. **A** The overhead spending (budget) variance is:

    line BC = total costs at C machine hours

    line DO = fixed costs total cost at zero machine hours

    variable cost = total cost – fixed costs

    $\qquad$ = BC – DO

8. **D** $600,000 + $80,000 + $70,000 + $50,000 = $800,000 (all manufacturing costs).

9. **B** $600,000 + $80,000 = $680,000 (only variable manufacturing costs).

10. **C** The cost of electricity for a manufacturing plant (fixed and variable) would be classified as overhead, which is an element of conversion costs (direct material and direct labor) and a product cost. A period cost is a noninventoriable cost which is deducted as an expense in the current period.

11. **C**

Fixed maintenance cost per month ($7,200/12)	$600
Variable cost (20,000 hrs. × $0.60)	12,000
Total maintenance cost budget for July	$12,600

12. **B** If the gross profit of the product is 60%, then its cost must be 40% (1.00 less 60%). Since the dollar cost of the product is $5.00 per unit, then that must equal 40% of the selling price. $5.00 divided by 40% = $12.50.

13. **B** The cost of electricity for a manufacturing plant (fixed and variable) would be classified as overhead which is an element of conversion costs (DL & OH) and is a product cost.

    Note: This cost would not be a period cost which is an expense.

14. **B** High-low points method:

	High	Low	Change
Direct-labor hours	400,000	300,000	100,000
Total costs	$154,000	$129,000	$25,000

    The change between the high and low points isolates the variable costs which are $.25 per hour ($25,000 / 100,000 hours). At the high point, total variable costs are $100,000 (400,000 hours × $.25). Therefore, total fixed costs budgeted are $54,000 ($154,000 – $100,000). Budgeted fixed costs can also be calculated using the low point.

    (300,000 hrs. $.25 = $75,000 total variable costs + $54,000 fixed costs = $129,000 total costs)

©2007 Kaplan CPA Review

STUDY MANUAL – BUSINESS ENVIRONMENT & CONCEPTS
CHAPTER 9

15. **C**   The high-low method is used to isolate the fixed and variable portions of costs by analysis of the high and low points of activity.

	Cost	Machine Hours
High	$39,200	24,000
Low	32,000	15,000
Change	$7,200	9,000
Change per machine hour		$\frac{\$7,200}{\$9,000} = \$0.80$

By definition of a variable cost (changes proportionately with changes in volume), the $.80 per machine hour change is the variable portion of the maintenance costs.

16. **B**   Computation of Fixed Costs:

	High	Low
Total costs	$39,200	$32,000
Less: Variable costs from above:		
24,000 × $0.80	19,200	
15,000 × $0.80		12,000
Fixed costs per month	$20,000	$20,000

Note: Only one computation is needed; however, both are shown to illustrate that the result is the same. 12 × $20,000 = $240,000 total annual fixed costs.

17. **C**

Selling price per unit	$5.00
Less: Variable cost per unit	3.00
Contribution margin	$2.00
Fixed Cost mfg. (0.25 × 100,000 units)	$25,000
Fixed cost selling (0.65 × 100,000 units)	65,000
Total fixed costs	$90,000

$$\text{B.E.P} = \frac{\text{Fixed costs}}{\text{Contribution margin}} = \frac{\$90,000}{\$2} = 45,000 \text{ units}$$

18. **C**

Total contribution margin ($2 × 110,000 units)	$220,000
Less: Total fixed costs	90,000
Net income	$130,000

19. **D**   If all variances are charged to cost of goods sold, the net income under absorption costing will differ from that under direct costing by the amount of fixed cost assigned to the increase or decrease in inventory. If inventory increases, fixed costs are transferred to the following period, thereby increasing net income under absorption costing. If inventory decreases, fixed costs from prior periods are expensed, thereby reducing net income.

Increase in inventory 10,000 units * $.25 fixed manufacturing costs per unit = $2,500 fixed cost transferred to the next period. Therefore, net income under absorption costing is $132,500 – ($130,000 + $2,500).

Page 280   ©2007 Kaplan CPA Review

STUDY MANUAL – BUSINESS ENVIRONMENT & CONCEPTS
CHAPTER 9

20. **A**   (Selling price – $3 variable cost) × 10,000 units = $5,000 net income

$$10,000 (X - 3) \quad = 5000$$
$$10,000X - 30,000 \quad = 5000$$
$$10,000X \quad = 35,000$$
$$X = 35,000 \times 10,000 = \underline{\$3.50} \text{ selling price}$$

21. **B**

Selling price ($5.00 × 1.20)	$6.00
Less: V.C. mfg. ($1.00 × 1.10	(1.10)
V.C. selling	(2.00)
Contribution margin	$2.90
Less: Profit per unit (0.1 × $2.90	0.29
Adjusted C.M. per unit	$2.61

units = $104,400 / 2.61 = <u>40,000</u> units

OR

$$\text{\# units} = \frac{FC + Profit}{CM}$$

$$X = \frac{\$140,400 + 0.29(X)}{2.90}$$

$$2.90X = \$104,400 + 0.29X$$
$$2.90X - 0.29 = \$104,400$$
$$2.61X = \$104,400$$
$$X = \$104,400/2.61 = \underline{40,000} \text{ units}$$

22. **B**   BEP = Fixed Costs % Contribution Margin %:

Fixed cost:		$200,000
Cost of goods sold (10% × $2,000,000 sales)		300,000
Other expenses (15% × $2,000,000 sales)		$500,000
Contribution margin %		
Selling price		100%
Less: Variable cost %		
Cost of goods sold	50%	
Other expenses	20%	70%
Contribution margin %		30%

BEC = FC / CM% = $500,000 / 30% = <u>$1,666,667</u>

23. **D**   As both products can utilize full capacity, the greatest profit will result from the greatest contribution margin (selling price – variable costs) for capacity. Fixed costs are irrelevant as they are not effected by the decision.

©2007 Kaplan CPA Review
Page 281

STUDY MANUAL – BUSINESS ENVIRONMENT & CONCEPTS
CHAPTER 9

24. **B**

$$BEP \text{ in dollar sales} = \text{Fixed costs / contribution margin \%}$$
$$= \$20,000 / 80\%*$$
$$= \underline{\$25,000}$$

$$*\text{Contribution margin \%} = 1 - (\text{variable cost / sales})$$
$$= 1 - (\$80,000 / \$400,000)$$
$$= 1 - 0.20$$
$$= 80\%$$

25. **B** Under the direct or variable costing method, variable costs are deducted from revenue to determine contribution margin, and all fixed costs (manufacturing, selling, general and administrative) are then deducted to obtain net income or income from operations.

The contribution margin is calculated in two steps:

1. Revenue less variable cost of goods sold = Contribution margin: manufacturing

2. Contribution margin: manufacturing less other variable costs (S, G & A) = Contribution margin: final

26. **B** $20,000.

Increase in inventory	1,000 units
Fixed manufacturing costs per unit	× $20
Fixed manufacturing costs included in ending inventory	$20,000

If inventory increases (production exceeds sales), absorption costing results in greater net income than direct (variable) costing, due to the fixed manufacturing costs included in inventory.

27. **A** Generally when you plot activity on a graph, your vertical axis (Y) is your cost, while your horizontal axis (X) is your activity. Since there is a fixed rental cost, this would be plotted by a straight horizontal line originating part way up on the Y axis at the zero level of activity (X), thus indicating I or II as possible answers. The variable portion of the rent is based upon sales, which is added to the straight fixed line at increasingly smaller increments as sales (plotted on the X axis) are increased. Therefore, A or line I is your answer. Answer (b) is incorrect because it shows larger increments being added to the fixed costs.

28. **D** Breakeven (cost-volume-profit) analysis assumes sales revenue per unit and variable cost per unit are constant within the relevant range. Therefore, variable cost as a percentage of sales revenue would be the same at all levels of activity within the relevant range.

Breakeven (CVP) analysis assumes that total fixed costs remain constant within the relevant range. Therefore, fixed costs as a percentage of sales revenue would be greater at lower levels of activity (a) than at higher levels of activity (b).

29. **C** Breakeven point represents your fixed costs divided by your contribution margin. Mathematically, by decreasing your numerator (fixed costs) or increasing your denominator (contribution margin), your breakeven point must decrease.

STUDY MANUAL – BUSINESS ENVIRONMENT & CONCEPTS

CHAPTER 9

30. **B** The original cost and carrying value (cost less accumulated depreciation) of an old asset is a "sunk cost" for replacement decisions as the replacement would not affect these amounts. A sunk cost is a cost which has been incurred and will not be changed by any future decisions. It is, therefore, irrelevant to a decision and excluded in its analysis.

The disposal value (fair market value) of the new asset (or the old asset) is a cash flow that will only result if the replacement is made and the old asset is disposed of. Because it is dependent upon the replacement decision it is relevant to the decision.

31. **A** Remachine and $5,000.

	Alternatives	
	Remachine	Scrap
Proceeds	$9,000	$1,000
Additional cost	5,000	0
Net proceeds	$4,000	$1,000

The inventory carrying value of $20,000 is not relevant to the decision since under either alternative the $20,000 is a cost (sunk cost).

32. **B** Fixed costs = $200,000.

Contribution margin–Tetra = $1
Contribution margin–Min = $2

For every unit of Min sold, two units of Tetra are sold. Therefore, the combined contribution margin for each unit of Min sold would be: (1 unit * $2) + (2 units * $1) = $4.

Breakeven = Fixed costs / Contribution margin
= $200,000 / 4
= 50,000 units (Min)

Proof: (50,000 Min * $2) + (100,000 Tetra * $1) = $200,000 (Fixed costs)

33. **D** $500,000.

Weighted average of variable costs to sales::

	Percent of Sales	*Percent of VC*	*Value*
A	60	60	36%
B	40	85	<u>34%</u>
			70%

Sales	1.00 (100%)
Variable cost	0.70 (70%)
Contribution	0.30 (30%)

©2007 Kaplan CPA Review

Page 283

STUDY MANUAL – BUSINESS ENVIRONMENT & CONCEPTS
CHAPTER 9

34. **D** $680,000.

Fixed cost = $150,000 + 30% ×150,000 =	$195,000
Add: Net income generated	9,000
	$204,000

Breakeven: $\dfrac{\$204,000}{0.30^1} = \$680,000$

Alternatively, the .30 composite contribution rate could be computed by subtracting the percent of variable cost from 100% and multiplying percent of sales by the result, for example:

A 60% × (100% – 60%) = 24%
B 40% × (100% – 85%) = 6%
                             30%

35. **B**

	Ratio	CM	Total CM
X	3	$1.00	$3.00
Y	6	1.50	9.00
Z	1	3.00	3.00
			$15.00

$BEP = \dfrac{FC}{CM} = \dfrac{600,000}{15} = 40,000 \text{ (of 3x, 6y, 1z)}$

$\text{\# of X at BEP} = 40,000 \times 3 = 120,000$

36. **C**   Under the direct or variable costing method, variable costs are deducted from sales revenue to determine contribution margin and all fixed costs (overhead, selling, general and administrative) are then deducted to obtain net income or income from operations. The contribution margin is calculated in two steps:

1. Sales revenue less (variable) cost of goods sold = Contribution margin: manufacturing.

2. Contribution margin: manufacturing less other variable costs (S, G & A) = Contribution margin: final.

37. **C** $49.22.

$60	=	Food cost	+	Service charge	+	Sales tax
	=	FC	+	15% FC	+	0.06 (FC + 15% FC)
	=	FC	+	0.15 FC	+	0.06 (1.15 FC)
	=		1.15FC			
	=		1.219 FC			
60	=		FC			
1.219						
$49.22	=		Food Cost			

Page 284
©2007 Kaplan CPA Review

STUDY MANUAL – BUSINESS ENVIRONMENT & CONCEPTS
CHAPTER 9

38. **B** $640,000.

Relevant costs per unit:

DM	$4
DL	16
VOH	8
FOH @ 40%	4
	$32 × $20,000 = $640,000

The fixed overhead of $6 per unit will continue regardless; therefore, only the cost that will not be incurred if part is bought outside is considered.

39. **B** $24,000 B.E.P.:

Sales	200,000
Less: margin of safety	(80,000)
Sales at break-even point	120,000
Contribution margin	× 0.20
Fixed cost	24,000

BEP in $Sales = Fixed Costs / Contribution Margin %.

Therefore, Fixed Cost = BEP $Sales × Contribution Margin %.

40. **D** Gross profit (margin) is a term associated with absorption costing; however, it is not applicable to variable (or direct) costing. Under variable (direct) costing, the cost of goods sold includes only the variable costs associated with the inventory sold and sales less (variable) cost of goods sold is referred to as contribution margin-manufacturing. Operating income applies to both variable and absorption costing.

41. **B**

	Total	Per unit (25,000 units)
Sales	$500,000	$20.00
Less: Variable costs:		
Direct materials and labor	(150,000)	(6.00)
Overhead	(20,000)	(0.80)
Selling and general	(5,000)	(0.20)
Contribution margin	$325,000	$13.00

42. **D** Under direct or variable costing, product costs or inventoriable costs include only variable manufacturing costs (direct material, direct labor and variable overhead). Variable selling costs are used in the calculation of contribution margin; however, they are not a product cost (inventoriable).

©2007 Kaplan CPA Review

Page 285

STUDY MANUAL – BUSINESS ENVIRONMENT & CONCEPTS
CHAPTER 9

43. **A**

Direct materials	$20,000
Direct labor	55,000
Variable overhead	45,000
Avoidable fixed overhead ($4 × 10,000)	40,000
Foregoe rent	15,000
Cost to make	$175,000
Cost to buy ($18 × 10,000)	180,000
Additional cost of buying	$5,000

44. **A** $300,000 margin of safety.

Margin of safety is the excess of actual or budgeted sales ($1,000,000) over sales at the breakeven point ($700,000). It is the amount by which sales could decrease before a loss occurs.

45. **A**

Direct material ($40,000 / 10,000)	$4.00
Direct labor ($20,000 / 10,000)	2.00
Variable overhead ($12,000 / 10,000)	1.20
Per unit cost	× 1,000
Ending inventory units	$7,200

46. **A**

Fixed cost per unit ($25,000 / 10,000)	$2.50
Increase in inventory units	× 1,000
Fixed costs assigned to inventory	$2,500

47. **A** $50,000.

$$BEP\ \$Sales = FC/CM\%$$
$$\$800,000 = \$100,000/CM\%$$
$$1/8 = CM\%$$

Sales	$1,200,000
– Sales @ BEP	800,000
Sales over BEP	$400,000
CM%	× 1/8
Profit @ $1,200,00 Sales	$50,000

48. **B**

Allocated overhead	$48,000
Less: Non avoidable overhead	(21,000)
Decrease in overhead cost	27,000
Less decrease in contribution margin	(24,000)
Increase in income	$3,000

49. **D** Sunk costs are costs that will not change or be affected by the selection of available alternatives. In this situation, the prior manufacturing costs of $50,000 will be unaffected by subsequent processing or sale.

STUDY MANUAL – BUSINESS ENVIRONMENT & CONCEPTS
CHAPTER 9

50. **B**   Increase budgeted breakeven; Decrease margin of safety.

An increase in direct labor costs (a variable cost) would decrease the contribution margin (selling price – variable costs) and result in an increase in the breakeven point (FC/CM).

Margin of safety is the excess of actual or budgeted sales over sales at the breakeven point. It is the amount by which sales could decrease before a loss occurs. An increase in the breakeven point, resulting from an increase in direct labor costs, would cause a decrease in margin of safety.

51. **B**   Within the relevant range, **total** fixed costs do not change and variable cost per unit does not change (total variable costs change proportionately with activity). Therefore, a decrease in the production level (within the relevant range) would result in an increase in fixed costs per unit as the total fixed costs are allocated to fewer units and a decrease in total variable costs as they change proportionally with activity or production.

52. **C**   Within the relevant range, variable costs per unit do not change and *total* fixed costs do not change. Therefore, a decline in the production level (within the relevant range) would result in no change in variable costs per unit while fixed costs per unit would increase.

53. **B**   Under the direct or variable costing method, variable costs are deducted from sales revenue to determine contribution margin and **all** fixed costs (overhead, selling, general and administrative) are then deducted to obtain net income or income from operations. The contribution margin is calculated in two steps:

1. Sales revenue less (variable) cost of goods sold = Contribution margin: manufacturing

2. Contribution margin: manufacturing less other variable costs (S, G & A) =
   Contribution margin: final

Under the absorption costing method, each cost classification (cost of goods sold, selling, general and administrative, etc.) includes both its fixed cost and variable cost components.

54. **A** $2,329 Target price.

$$\text{Sales revenue} = \text{Cost of goods/cost percentage}$$
$$= \$990,000 / 0.85$$
$$= \$1,164,706$$
$$\text{Target price} = \text{Sales revenue} / \text{\# units}$$
$$= \$1,164,706 / 500$$
$$= \underline{\$2,329}$$

Cost percentage: If profit margin on sales is 15%, then the cost of goods sold percentage is 85% (100% – 15%).

©2007 Kaplan CPA Review   Page 287

STUDY MANUAL – BUSINESS ENVIRONMENT & CONCEPTS
CHAPTER 9

55. **C** The breakeven point in sales dollars represents your fixed costs divided by your contribution margin percentage. Fixed costs are given, but the contribution margin must be determined.

Sales	$800,000	100%
Variable costs	160,000	20%
Contribution margin	$640,000	80%
Fixed costs	$40,000	
Dividend by contribution margin	80%	
Breakeven sales	$50,000	

56. **B**

Selling price	$10
Less: Variable costs	5
Contribution margin	5
# units sold	× 80,000
Total contribution	400,000
Less: Fixed costs	$190,000
Net income	$210,000

57. **B** A

Absorption Cost per unit:	
Raw materials	2.00
Direct labor	1.25
Overhead	0.75
Variable	
Fixed ($120,000 / 100,000 units)	1.20
	5.20
Ending inventory (100,000 – 80,000)	× 20,000
	$104,000

Note: Selling and administrative costs are not part of the product costs.

58. **B** This is a problem in the analysis of variable and fixed costs. Since costs are either variable or fixed, then of the $500,000 in total costs, $430,000 must be variable ($500,000 less $70,000 in fixed). It takes $430,000 in variable costs to run five sales offices, or $86,000 per office. If seven offices are being run, then:

7 offices @ $86,000 =	$602,000
Fixed costs	70,000
Total costs	$672,000

59. **B** $$\text{Contribution margin ratio} = \frac{\text{Contribution margin}}{\text{Selling price}} = \frac{\$13}{\$20} = 0.65$$

Note: Can also be calculated based on total contribution margin and sales ($650,000 ÷ $1,000,000 = .65).

60. **B** Within the relevant range, variable costs per unit do not change.

A basic assumption of break-even / C.V.P. analysis is linearity; therefore, answers (a) and (d) are incorrect. As variable cost per unit are unchanged, total variable cost changes proportionately with activity. Therefore, total cost change and answer (c) is incorrect.

Page 288   ©2007 Kaplan CPA Review

STUDY MANUAL – BUSINESS ENVIRONMENT & CONCEPTS
CHAPTER 9

61. **A**   The grouping of plotted dots clearly shows a thrust from lower left to upper right. Such a pattern clearly invites the reader to read the dots as a broad line thereby implying the linear correlation. The regularity and density of the dots implies a high degree of such correlation.

62. **A**

	Orders	Cost
High	1,800	$4,320
Low	1,200	3,120
Change	600	$1,200

$$\frac{\text{Change in cost}}{\text{Change in order}} \quad \frac{\$1,200}{600} = \$2 \text{ per order}$$

63. **B**   Contribution margin is sales – all variable cost. Therefore, sales minus direct materials, direct labor, variable manufacturing overhead and variable selling and administrative = contribution margin: $80 – (21 + 10 + 3 + 6) = $40 per unit x 4,500 units sold = $180,000 total contribution margin.

©2007 Kaplan CPA Review
Page 289

Cost Accounting

Study Manual – Business Environment & Concepts
Chapter 10

Study Tip: Do not dwell on whether you are going to pass or fail the CPA exam. That is pure speculation and can harm your chances. Your only goal is to add a point or two to your score every day. That is a reasonable goal and one that will bring you success faster than you might think possible.

Introduction

Cost measurement relates to the determination of and accounting for the various costs of products or services sold by a company. Manufacturing, merchandizing, and service companies all use cost measurement for determining cost of sales and income, for determining the carrying value of inventories, and for evaluating and measuring performance. As an efficiency measure, a snack food manufacturer will calculate the cost of the snack crackers sold and the snack crackers remaining on its balance sheet in various stages of inventory, as well as the cost per pound of materials used. A professional services firm will calculate the cost of consulting services provided to clients and may calculate cost per hour of a project as a means of evaluating a project manager.

Basic Terms and Concepts

A. Gross profit margin is net revenue (sales) minus cost of goods sold. Net revenue or net sales is total revenues (sales) reduced by any sales discounts or sales returns and allowances.

B. Fixed costs are costs that do not change in total, regardless of increases or decreases in production volume within the relevant range. The relevant range is a range of manufacturing volume within which each cost will either remain fixed or will vary in direct proportion to volume.

   1. Beyond the relevant range of volume output, even fixed costs are subject to change. For example, the relevant range of a snack food company might be between 1 million and 1.25 million pounds of product per week, operating with two 8-hour shifts per day. In order to produce more than 1.25 million pounds, fixed costs for supervisor salaries would increase because a third shift would need to be added.

   2. Fixed costs remain fixed in total, so the amount per unit varies as the volume of output varies. There are usually some fixed components of overhead, but direct

Page 290   ©2007 Kaplan CPA Review

materials and direct labor are not usually fixed. There will usually be fixed costs in the nonmanufacturing (operating) category as well.

C. Variable costs are costs that increase or decrease in total amount in direct proportion to increases or decreases in production, within the relevant range. Variable costs do not change on a per-unit basis but vary in total. Variable costs include:

VC = DM + DL + VOh

1. Direct materials.

2. Direct labor.

3. Variable overhead.

There will usually be variable costs in the nonmanufacturing (operating) category as well.

D. Controllable costs are costs that are controllable by a manager or supervisor, and they must be defined in the context of the business unit whose costs are being measured.

1. A manufacturing plant manager would have control over the amount of raw materials that are used in the production of the product.

2. The plant manager would not have control over the allocation of interest expense from the corporate office to each of the plants within the company. (The interest expense would be a controllable cost to the corporate office person responsible for financing the company, perhaps the vice president of finance.)

3. To facilitate decision making, a company will identify responsibility centers, in which specific individuals or groups can be held responsible for certain costs or revenues that they control. Responsibility centers may be cost centers, profit centers, or investment centers.

   a. A cost center has control over, and responsibility for, costs. The center has no control over sales or marketing activities. The manager of a cost center will try to minimize costs.

   b. A profit center has control over, and responsibility for, both revenues and costs. The manager of a profit center will try to maximize profits.

   c. An investment center has control over, and responsibility for, revenues, costs, and the acquisition of assets. The manager of an investment center has a higher degree of responsibility than the manager of a cost or profit center.

E. Sunk costs are past committed costs that are now irrevocable. They are not relevant to future decisions. Examples of sunk costs are advertising for a campaign that has already been aired or published, research costs for a new product that have already been incurred, and last year's repairs for a vehicle that now needs to be scrapped.

F. Accounting costs are costs that are recognized using accrual basis accounting and that are generally recorded in the company's financial statements using generally accepted

©2007 Kaplan CPA Review

accounting principles (GAAP). Opportunity costs are not accounting costs, but are very important to economists.

G. Opportunity costs are the benefits lost from rejecting the option that was not selected. Since opportunity costs are not actually incurred, they are not recorded in the accounting records. They are, however, relevant costs for decision making and should be considered in evaluating a proposed alternative course of action.

H. Relevant costs are expected future costs that will differ between alternatives.

   1. Irrelevant costs, on the other hand, are unaffected by the decision.

   2. Relevance is an attribute of the situation, not of a particular cost; the identical cost may be relevant in one circumstance and irrelevant in another.

   3. If the decision is whether to attend a seminar in New York or in Rome, Italy, the cost of airfare is definitely relevant. However, if the registration fee is the same regardless of location, then the fee would be irrelevant. Note that relevant costs are future costs.

I. Standard costs. A standard cost is nothing more than a per-unit "budget" for a cost element. In a standard cost system, management will determine the amount the business activity (usually in manufacturing) should cost, and compare this to the amount that it actually costs.

   1. Standard costs are determined using:

      a. Historical data.

      b. Inputs from employees and supervisory personnel.

      c. Data relevant to the industry.

      d. The technology pertinent to the business/manufacturing process.

   2. When products and services are costed using standard costs, variances are measured as the difference between the standard cost and the actual cost.

   3. Management will analyze these variances to determine the root cause of the difference:

      a. Whether the business process should be changed.

      b. Whether the standard itself should be revised.

J. Correlation analysis. In order to determine if there is a relationship between two or more factors within a company, such as a relationship between production volume and total manufacturing costs, it is often assumed that one of the factors is an independent variable, such as production volume. The other is the dependent variable, manufacturing costs, which will be a function of production volume. Before one can define what the relationship is between a dependent and an independent variable, it must be determined if there is a relationship at all.

1. The technique used to determine if there is a relationship between the dependent and the independent variable is referred to as *correlation analysis.*

2. In applying correlation analysis, certain formulae are applied to comparative data indicating the production volumes and corresponding manufacturing costs for selected periods.

3. The more data available, the more precise the result will be.

4. A coefficient of correlation is computed that must fall within the range from −1 to +1.

    a. A coefficient of correlation approximating −1 indicates that there is a strong inverse relationship between the dependent and independent variables.

    b. A coefficient approximating +1 indicates that there is a strong direct relationship between the dependent and independent variables.

    c. A coefficient approximating zero indicates that there is no relationship between the dependent and independent variables.

5. The coefficient of correlation is squared to give a coefficient of determination.

6. This coefficient of determination defines the relationship between the dependent and independent variable. (For exam purposes, it is not necessary to know the specific formula in this area, but you should understand what the results mean.)

K. Regression analysis. Once it has been established that a relationship exists between a dependent and an independent variable (using correlation analysis), the relationship itself must be defined. In the example of the relationship between production and costs, a formula may be computed to determine what total costs would be at various levels of production.

The general technique used to define the relationship between the dependent and independent variables is referred to as *regression analysis.* Within the category of regression analysis, there are several common techniques in use. These include the scatter diagram approach, the 2-point high-low method, and the sum of the least squares.

1. The scatter diagram approach is the least technical approach of the three. Under this method:

    a. A graph is set up on which the *y*-axis (vertical) is considered total cost, and the *x*-axis (horizontal) is considered production volume.

    b. Various data from previous periods are plotted on the graph as dots, with each dot indicating a production volume and total cost.

c. After numerous points are plotted on the graph, a line is drawn that most closely approximates the dots. This is assumed to be the cost function.

d. The point at which the line crosses the *y*-axis is the fixed cost per period.

e. The slope of the line is the variable cost per unit. The slope is the change in the total cost from one point to the next divided by the change in the production volume.

2. The 2-point high-low method can only be applied when there is a very strong correlation between the dependent and the independent variable. It involves selecting data for two periods:

a. A period in which production and costs were high.

b. A period in which production and costs were low.

c. The method would be similar to the scatter diagram approach using only the highest and lowest points on the diagram and drawing a straight-line intercepting them.

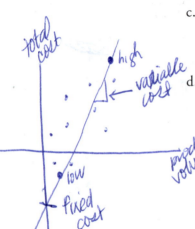

d. If a company were to measure overhead for several periods and select the highest and lowest amounts, they might determine:

	Overhead	Direct Labor
High point	$19,800	3,650 hours
Low point	$13,400	2,050 hours
Difference	$6,400	1,600 hours

They could conclude that by working 1,600 additional hours, they incurred an additional $6,400 in overhead. This indicates that variable overhead is $6,400/1,600, or $4 per hour. At 2,050 hours, total variable overhead would have been $8,200, indicating fixed overhead of $5,200.

$13,400 − (2,050 hours × $4/hour) = $5,200

3. The sum of the least squares is a method that is more precise than either of the others. It is a means of finding the line that most closely approximates the data, such as in the scatter diagram approach, but the line is determined algebraically, rather than by estimation.

a. The sum of the least squares method is used to find the line for which the sum of all the distances between each point and the line, squared, is minimized.

b. The distances are squared to eliminate negative numbers.

c. If the distances between the points and two individual lines are summed, both could appear equally good as negative distances will offset positive distances.

STUDY MANUAL – BUSINESS ENVIRONMENT & CONCEPTS
CHAPTER 10

   d. When the distances are squared, the sum for one line will be lower than for any other line.

   e. In applying the sum of the least squares method, various data are used from numerous periods. The more periods used, the greater the accuracy of the results, assuming there is a relationship between the variables. The data is organized such that for each period, x is the production quantity (independent variable) while y is the total cost for the period (dependent variable). While the CPA Exam does not usually test the actual calculations involved in this technique (they can be performed easily with a spreadsheet or statistical routine), the ultimate outcome is a formula for the linear representation representing the best fit through all the data points. (In other words, you end up with the formula for a line: $y = a + bx$, where y = total costs; a = fixed costs; b = variable cost per unit; and x = total units.)

L. In a manufacturing company, there are two common formats used for presentation of an income statement. One method is used for internal reporting purposes and is not acceptable for financial reporting purposes. This method is referred to as the *direct, variable,* or *prime costing method*.

   1. Under the direct or variable method, the following principles are applied:

      a. Cost of goods sold includes only variable manufacturing costs. These are direct materials, direct labor, and variable overhead.

      b. All variable expenses, including variable selling and general and administrative costs as well as variable manufacturing costs, are deducted from revenues to compute a contribution margin.

      c. Inventory costs include only variable manufacturing costs.

      d. All fixed costs, including fixed manufacturing overhead, are charged to expense in the period incurred. No fixed costs are included in inventory.

         Sales
         – Variable manufacturing costs (for those units sold)
         – Variable selling, general, and administrative costs
         = Contribution margin
         – Fixed manufacturing costs
         – Fixed selling, general, and administrative costs
         = Operating income

   2. The format acceptable for financial reporting purposes is the conventional income statement, referred to as the *absorption method*. Under the absorption method, the following principles are followed:

Kaplan CPA Review
Page 295

a. Cost of goods sold includes proportionate amounts of all manufacturing costs including variable and fixed manufacturing costs.

b. Cost of goods sold is deducted from revenues to compute gross profit.

c. Inventory costs include proportionate amounts of all manufacturing costs, variable and fixed.

d. All selling, general, and administrative expenses, variable and fixed, are deducted from the gross profit as expenses of the period.

3. The format for a statement under the absorption method is as follows:

Sales

− Cost of goods sold

= Gross profit

− Selling, general, and administrative expenses

= Operating income

4. In the direct method, all fixed costs are recognized as expenses in the period incurred. Under the absorption method, the fixed manufacturing costs are allocated between inventories and cost of sales. As a result, in periods when inventories increase, the fixed costs included in the increase in inventories would be expensed under the direct method.

5. In periods when inventories increase, the absorption method will result in greater profits than under the direct method. The amount of the difference will be the increase in the number of units in inventory multiplied by the amount of fixed manufacturing costs per unit. In periods when inventories decrease, the inverse is true.

M. JIT Inventory.

1. Many companies will try to save costs by using a just-in-time system, which has the following characteristics.

a. A just-in-time (JIT) inventory system attempts to schedule all purchases and production so that inventory components will arrive both at the start of manufacturing and at each point in the system at the very moment they are needed.

b. Materials are ordered in smaller quantities, which:

- Minimizes inventory carrying costs.
- Avoids both loss and breakage.
- Reduces funds tied up in inventory.

STUDY MANUAL – BUSINESS ENVIRONMENT & CONCEPTS
CHAPTER 10

    c.   In the perfect system, a JIT system is engineered to smooth out the process so that production takes less time.

- Employees never have to wait for goods.
- There is never a backlog at any point.

2. A challenge in JIT systems is to ensure that materials are available when needed.

    a.   It is important for the company to minimize the lead time necessary for obtaining materials.

    b.   The company must reduce the number of vendors they do business with and make certain that a very strong relationship is maintained with the remaining vendors.

    c.   Since smaller quantities are being ordered, more orders are placed, and the company will keep suppliers aware of expected production schedules.

3. Another challenge of a JIT system is the elimination of those operations that do not add value to the goods being produced. All nonvalue-adding operations cannot be eliminated, but through the maintenance of strong relationships with vendors, they can be significantly reduced.

CATEGORIES OF COSTS AND COST TERMS

Cost accounting is used to cost inventory and determine cost of sales for a manufacturing company.

A. In general, costs can be separated into nonmanufacturing and manufacturing.

1. Nonmanufacturing costs are operating expenses more specifically referred to as selling, general, and administrative expenses. They are also referred to as *period costs* because they are charged to expense in the period incurred.

2. Manufacturing costs, also referred to as *product costs,* are incurred in the factory and are separated into three basic areas. These costs become part of the carrying value of inventory and are charged against income when the inventory is sold.

    a.   Direct materials are those materials that become an integral part of the final product. Direct materials:

- Are used directly in the production of the product
- Are significant in terms of costs and quantities
- Can be traced to production

    b.   Direct labor is the labor required to convert raw materials into finished products. It is the labor used directly in the production of the product.

©2007 Kaplan CPA Review
Page 297

STUDY MANUAL – BUSINESS ENVIRONMENT & CONCEPTS
CHAPTER 10

    c.   Manufacturing overhead (factory overhead) consists of all other (production-related) factory costs except direct materials and direct labor. It includes items such as indirect labor, indirect materials, factory rent, factory utilities, factory insurance, and depreciation of the factory and factory equipment.

    3.   A cost is either a product cost or a period cost and cannot be both.

B.   Manufacturing costs are also categorized by nature.

    1.   They can be either of two kinds of costs:

        a.   Prime costs, which include direct materials and direct labor.

        b.   Conversion costs, which include direct labor and manufacturing overhead.

    2.   Direct labor is a prime cost because it is part of the actual product, and it is a conversion cost because it is an element of cost required to convert raw materials into finished product.

THREE APPROACHES USED TO ACCUMULATE MANUFACTURING COSTS

A.   There are three approaches that may be used to accumulate manufacturing costs to determine inventory amounts and cost of sales. These approaches include an actual cost system, a normal cost system, and a standard cost system.

    1.   Under an actual cost system, all costs (including direct materials, direct labor, and manufacturing overhead) are charged to production on the basis of the actual costs being incurred.

    2.   Under a normal cost system, actual direct materials and direct labor are charged to production, while manufacturing overhead is applied to production evenly with a standard application base. Differences between actual overhead and overhead applied are analyzed and charged to inventories and/or cost of sales.

    3.   Under a standard cost system, all costs are charged to production on the basis of predetermined standard amounts. Differences between actual costs and standard amounts are analyzed for all types of manufacturing costs.

B.   Actual and normal cost systems may be used for either external financial reporting purposes or for internal management reporting purposes. A standard cost system may be used only for internal reporting purposes.

BASIC CHARACTERISTICS OF ACTIVITY-BASED COSTING

A.   Some companies will apply a technique referred to as *activity-based costing (ABC)* for determining the cost of an output.

Page 298   ©2007 Kaplan CPA Review

1. Under activity-based costing, costs are accumulated by activity rather than by department or function for purposes of product costing.

2. ABC is often used where factory overhead is a major component of product cost.

3. ABC is relevant in organizations that manufacture products as well as in those that provide services.

B. In an activity-based costing system, every separate activity from the inception of a product to its completion is identified, and multiple cost drivers, or activities, are used as a basis for overhead cost allocation.

1. Cost drivers are the factors that contribute to increasing or decreasing costs.

2. Overhead costs are assigned to products based on these activities rather than on a departmental accumulation of cost. Twenty to thirty separate cost drivers might be used, which assign overhead in a more accurate fashion.

3. Activities utilizing the same cost driver can be grouped into cost pools to simplify the process.

4. Activities are classified as either value-adding (making the product better) or nonvalue-adding (an activity such as storage that does not improve the product).

5. In addition, under the activity-based costing approach, those activities that do not add value to the product are reduced to the extent possible (e.g., handling, setup time for machines, rework units).

OVERHEAD

A. Unlike direct materials and direct labor, actual overhead is not generally charged directly to the jobs or process as it is incurred, but is instead applied or allocated. The allocation is usually based on budgeted amounts for an entire year utilizing a predetermined overhead rate.

B. The overhead rate is determined by analyzing factory overhead and selecting a denominator base (activity) that appears to have a direct relationship to the amount of overhead cost incurred. The factor should be a cost driver for overhead.

1. The base may be direct labor hours when:

   a. Overhead consists largely of labor-related costs, and employees are paid varying wages based upon their individual skills and efficiency.

   b. Overhead costs are largely labor related, employees are paid similar wages, and costs fluctuate more with the amount of labor time spent than with the amount of money spent on labor.

©2007 Kaplan CPA Review

STUDY MANUAL – BUSINESS ENVIRONMENT & CONCEPTS
CHAPTER 10

2.   The base may be machine hours when overhead is largely made up of depreciation and equipment-related costs due to a highly automated manufacturing process.

3.   The base may be raw material quantities used when overhead consists largely of material-handling costs due to expensive or fragile material used.

C.   Example: Looking at selected budgeted items for the period, various predetermined denominator bases for applying factory overhead could be calculated. Assume the following budget amounts.

Capacity is 200,000 direct labor hours.

Direct labor wages are $1,200,000.

Production is 100,000 units.

Machine hours are 50,000 hours.

Factory overhead is $900,000.

Various overhead applications rates can be calculated as shown in Figure 1.

Figure 1: Various Overhead Application Rates Calculations

Overhead Rate Based on:	Calculation		Overhead Application Rate
Direct labor hours	$\dfrac{\text{factory overhead}}{\text{direct labor hour}}$	$\dfrac{\$900,000}{200,000 \text{ hour}}$	$4.50 per labor hour
Direct labor dollars	$\dfrac{\text{factory overhead}}{\text{direct labor wages}}$	$\dfrac{\$900,000}{\$1,200,000}$	75% of direct labor dollars
Machine hours	$\dfrac{\text{factory overhead}}{\text{machine hours}}$	$\dfrac{\$900,000}{50,000 \text{ hours}}$	$18.00 per machine hour
Units of production	$\dfrac{\text{factory overhead}}{\text{units produced}}$	$\dfrac{\$900,000}{100,000 \text{ hours}}$	$9.00 per unit

D.   As actual overhead costs are incurred, they are *not* recorded directly to the work-in-process inventory account, but rather are accumulated in a separate account, called factory overhead control.

1.   This control account includes all actual overhead costs, regardless of the source.

2.   At the end of the accounting period, it is compared to the amount applied (see below).

Page 300   ©2007 Kaplan CPA Review

3. The entry to record the actual (incurred) overhead is:

Factory overhead control	$250,000
Wages payable (indirect labor)	$120,000
Accumulated depreciation (factory equipment and building)	$55,000
Rent payable	$40,000
Inventory of supplies (indirect materials)	$10,000
Prepaid insurance (factory insurance)	$5,000
Utilities payable	$5,000
Cash, etc.	$15,000

E. Factory overhead is then charged or applied to production based on the volume of the activity base.

1. If, for example, the company were to use direct labor hours as the base for applying overhead, a unit requiring two direct labor hours would be charged with $9.00 ($4.50 × 2) of manufacturing overhead.

2. Amounts applied to production are added to work-in-process inventory and accumulated in an account established for that purpose, generally called factory (or manufacturing) overhead applied.

3. Assuming that $238,500 (53,000 direct labor hours × $4.50 per hour) of overhead is applied, the journal entry for application of overhead would be:

Work-in-process control	$238,500	
Factory overhead applied		$238,500

4. At the end of the accounting period, the balance in the overhead control account represents the total amount of overhead actually incurred during the period. The balance in the overhead applied account represents the amount charged to production (work-in-process).

5. An excess of overhead applied compared to actual overhead incurred is called *overapplied (overabsorbed) overhead.* An excess of actual overhead incurred compared to applied overhead is called *underapplied (underabsorbed) overhead.*

6. At the end of the accounting period, the overapplied or underapplied overhead is generally closed directly to the cost of goods sold account, which contains most of the overhead (recorded as goods are sold). The closing journal entry is a debit to

STUDY MANUAL – BUSINESS ENVIRONMENT & CONCEPTS
CHAPTER 10

factory overhead applied and a credit to factory overhead control with the difference being debited or credited to cost of goods sold to balance the entry:

Factory overhead applied	238,500	
←Cost of goods sold (underapplied)	11,500	
Factory overhead control		250,000

7. Most companies use a normal cost system, in which overhead is applied to production in proportion to the overhead base, rather than an actual cost system.

   a. This ensures that overhead is charged to production on a systematic basis.

   b. A normal cost system eliminates the possibility that disproportionate amounts of overhead will be charged to units produced during either peak or slack periods.

8. In an actual cost system, if overhead costs include a high percentage of fixed costs, lower amounts of overhead are charged to units produced during peak periods, and higher amounts are charged to units produced during slack periods. (In a normal cost system, similar amounts are charged to production during peak and slack periods.)

   a. During peak periods, overhead will tend to be overapplied, while during slack periods overhead will tend to be underapplied.

   b. Overapplied amounts will offset underapplied amounts, and if overhead and the overhead base have been reasonably estimated, the net amount will be relatively low.

COST SYSTEMS

There are two types of accounting systems used to accumulate the costs of manufacturing so that amounts can be computed for ending inventories, cost of goods manufactured, and cost of sales. (The CPA Exam often requires the valuation of ending work-in-process inventory.)

A. A process cost system is used for the manufacture of large volumes of output (mass production) where the individual units are relatively inexpensive and homogeneous.

   1. Costs are accumulated on a period-by-period basis.

   2. Total costs for the period are accumulated and divided by the number of units produced during the period to compute unit cost. More specifically, a procedure is used to determine unit cost.

      a. The first step is to evaluate the physical flow of units. The physical flow is converted into equivalent (whole) units of production (direct materials, direct labor, and factory overhead).

Page 302   ©2007 Kaplan CPA Review

b. The accumulated costs for direct materials, direct labor, and factory overhead are divided by their respective equivalent units to derive the cost per equivalent unit.

c. The ending work-in-process inventory can be valued by multiplying the equivalent units in the ending inventory by the respective cost per equivalent unit.

3. Calculation of equivalent units (EU) of production.

   a. When applying process costing, the units processed may be whole units (both started and completed during a period) or partial units (beginning work-in-process that is finished this period, or ending work-in-process that is started but not finished). Partial units are converted to equivalent full units.

   b. In the simplest example, if there are 100 units that are 50 percent complete, the EU is 50. In other words, the amount of work done to finish half of 100 is the same amount of work it would take to completely finish 50 units.

   c. Not all costs will necessarily be incurred uniformly. For example, a unit may be 50 percent complete as to labor and 100 percent complete as to materials. Therefore, EU is calculated for each type of cost.

   d. Under the weighted-average method of computing equivalent units:

      - Beginning inventory of partially complete units is considered to be 100 percent complete during the current period. (This is just an assumption of this method.) So, even if a unit is half complete in beginning work-in-process due to work done last period, it is still considered 100 percent complete in the current period.
      - Therefore, EU is equal to the sum of the following:
        ♦ 100 percent of units completed this period
        ♦ The units in ending work-in-process multiplied by the percentage complete for that cost category

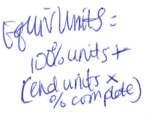

   e. Under the modified first in, first out (FIFO) approach, equivalent units includes:

      - Percentage required to complete the beginning work-in-process inventory (only the percentage completed in the current period) x units in beginning work-in-process inventory
      - Plus units started and completed in the current period
      - Plus percentage of work done in the current period on the ending work-in-process inventory.

   Example:

   Beginning work-in-process inventory = 10 units, 40% complete before the period begins.

Study Manual – Business Environment & Concepts
Chapter 10

Units started and complete this period = 60 units, 100% complete

Ending work-in-process inventory = 20 units, 65% complete this period

- Under the weighted-average approach, EU would be 10 + 60 + (20 × 65%).
- Under the FIFO approach, EU would be (10 × 60%) + 60 + (20 × 65%).
- Note the difference: under the weighted-average approach, all work on the beginning inventory is considered to be done in the current period. Under the FIFO approach, only the work actually done in the current period is considered.

    f.   Once the EU is calculated, the next step is to determine cost per unit.

- The basic calculation is to take manufacturing costs and divide by the EU.
- If you are using the weighted-average approach, the manufacturing costs will include the costs of the beginning inventory, since the EU calculation assumed all units were manufactured in the current period.
- If you are using the FIFO approach, the manufacturing costs will include only the costs actually incurred this period, and *not* the costs brought forward in the beginning inventory.

B. A job order cost system is used for the manufacture of a small volume of units where the individual units are relatively expensive and heterogeneous and are often produced to the customer's specification.

   1. Costs are attributed to specific units or batches of units on a job-by-job basis.

   2. The costs of those units sold are treated as cost of sales with other costs remaining in inventories.

   3. In a job order cost system, a job cost sheet is maintained for each job, and costs are entered onto the sheet as they are incurred.

      a. The job cost sheet serves as a subsidiary ledger.

      b. Simultaneously, all of the costs are charged to general ledger accounts that tie in to the total of the subsidiary ledger accounts.

C. Comparison of job order and process costing.

   1. Both job order and process costing attempt to accumulate the manufacturing costs (direct materials, direct labor, and factory overhead).

   2. A different emphasis is placed on these costs in job order and process costing.

      a. In job order costing, direct labor is proportionately larger relative to total product cost because it generally uses more highly skilled labor, which is paid more. It also takes more labor per unit to produce than would be the case with mass production.

b. For job order costing, the emphasis is on direct material and direct labor, which together are called *prime cost*.

c. For process costing, the emphasis is on direct material. Direct labor and factory overhead are generally combined and called *conversion cost*.

INVENTORY ACCOUNTS

A. Unlike nonmanufacturing companies where there is only one inventory for units purchased, in manufacturing there are three inventories: materials, work-in-process, and finished goods. Along with these inventory accounts there is also a cost of goods sold account.

B. The material account traditionally represents all direct and indirect materials to be used in the factory.

1. For the CPA Exam, the material account usually contains only direct materials.

2. There is usually a beginning inventory, purchases, and an ending inventory.

3. All materials used are assumed to be direct materials and are transferred to the work-in-process account.

C. The work-in-process account is an accumulation of all factory costs.

1. Direct materials are usually recorded into work-in-process from material requisitions. Direct labor is accumulated in work-in-process from payroll records.

. All other factory costs (factory overhead) are generally applied to work-in-process based on a predetermined rate, as discussed above.

3. The inputs into work-in-process (direct materials, direct labor, and factory overhead) are called *total manufacturing cost*s.

4. There is usually a beginning work-in-process inventory and an ending work-in-process inventory. The credit to the work-in-process account is called *cost of goods manufactured or cost of goods completed*.

D. The finished goods account represents all goods ready for sale.

1. It usually starts with a beginning inventory.

2. The cost of goods manufactured from work-in-process is put into finished goods and added to the beginning inventory to arrive at merchandise available for sale.

3. When the ending finished goods inventory is deducted from merchandise available for sale, the difference is transferred to the cost of goods sold account.

4. The cost of goods sold account includes the outputs from finished goods and, at the end of the period, an increase (debit) for underapplied overhead or a decrease (credit) for overapplied overhead.

COST FLOW FOR MANUFACTURING

The cost flow for manufacturing involves the following accounts:

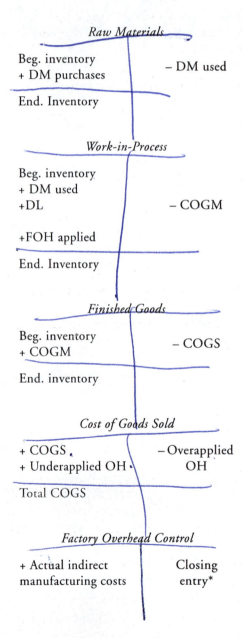

Factory Overhead Applied

– Closing entry*	+ FOH applied

* The amount required to balance the closing entry is the underapplied/overapplied overhead that is debited/credited to the cost of goods sold.

COST OF GOODS MANUFACTURED

An area frequently tested on the exam is cost of goods sold and cost of goods manufactured. The difference between net sales and the amount computed as cost of goods sold is referred to as the *gross profit* or *gross margin*.

A. For a nonmanufacturing company (retailer), cost of goods sold is computed using a basic formula:

    Beginning merchandise inventory

    + Net merchandise purchases

    = Cost of goods available for sale

    – Ending merchandise inventory

    = Cost of goods sold

B. For a manufacturing company, cost of goods sold is computed in several steps.

1. In the first step, the amount of raw (direct) materials put into the manufacturing process is computed:

    Beginning direct materials inventory

    + Net direct material purchases

    = Direct materials available for use

    – Ending direct materials inventory

    = Direct materials used

2. The cost of goods manufactured (Manufacturing Schedule) is then computed:

    Note: This is an analysis of the work-in-process T-account.

    Direct materials used (from previous)

    + Direct labor

    + Manufacturing overhead applied

STUDY MANUAL – BUSINESS ENVIRONMENT & CONCEPTS
CHAPTER 10

= Manufacturing costs added during the period

+ Beginning work-in-process inventory

– Ending work-in-process inventory

= Cost of goods manufactured

3. The cost of sales is then computed as follows:

Beginning finished goods inventory

+ Cost of goods manufactured (from previous)

= Cost of goods available for sale

– Ending finished goods inventory

+ Underapplied manufacturing overhead OR

– Overapplied manufacturing overhead

= Cost of goods sold

COST BEHAVIOR

Costs can be classified by many different attributes and in many different categories, including the broad classification of fixed, variable, and semivariable costs. These classifications are referred to as *cost behavior*. These cost definitions are valid within a relevant range, which is a range of activity within which it is assumed that each cost will either remain fixed or will vary in direct proportion to volume.

A. A fixed cost is a cost that does not change relative to production volume within the relevant range. Fixed costs remain fixed in total, while they vary on a per-unit basis. Fixed costs can be classified as:

1. Fixed factory overhead.

2. Fixed operating expenses.

B. A variable cost is a cost that increases or decreases in direct proportion to increases or decreases in production within the relevant range. Variable costs vary in total, while they are fixed on a per-unit basis. Variable costs can be classified as:

1. Direct materials.

2. Direct labor.

3. Variable overhead.

4. Variable operating expenses.

C. A mixed cost or semivariable cost is a cost that contains both a fixed and a variable component. It increases as the level of production increases but is not directly proportionate because of the fixed component.

   1. Factory overhead can be semivariable (e.g., factory utilities).

   2. Operating expenses can be semivariable, like sales salaries where there is a guaranteed fixed portion and an additional amount based on a percentage of sales.

RELATIONSHIP BETWEEN PRODUCTION VOLUME AND FIXED AND VARIABLE COSTS

A. When a company incurs a cost that has some portion variable and some portion fixed, it will often need to determine what relationship the cost has to production volume. In other words, it will have to separate the variable and fixed portions. This is particularly important for budgeting purposes and for the evaluation of performance.

B. The variable portion may be related to a variety of factors, such as the number of units produced, the number of direct labor hours worked, the number of hours that machines were in use, or some other measure of volume. As a result, in order to separate the fixed and variable portions, the relationship between the variable portion and some specific factor must be determined first.

C. When costs include a fixed and variable portion, the relationship between that cost and volume of production can be visually presented as in Figure 2:

Figure 2: Fixed, Variable, and Total Costs

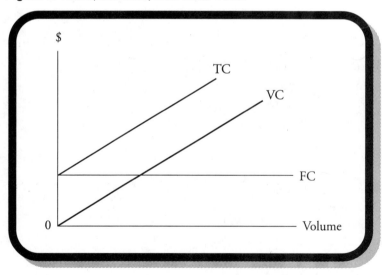

In the graph, fixed costs (FC) remain the same regardless of volume, and variable costs (VC) vary in direct proportion to volume. The resulting total cost (TC) will equal the total fixed and variable components at any volume.

STUDY MANUAL – BUSINESS ENVIRONMENT & CONCEPTS
CHAPTER 10

QUESTIONS: COST ACCOUNTING

1. A job order cost system uses a predetermined factory overhead rate based on expected volume and expected fixed costs. At the end of the year, underapplied overhead might be explained by which of the following situations?

	Actual volume	Actual fixed costs
A.	Less than expected	Greater than expected
B.	Less than expected	Less than expected
C.	Greater than expected	Greater than expected
D.	Greater than expected	Less than expected

2. Lawton Company produces canned tomato soup and is budgeting sales of 250,000 units for the month of January. Actual inventory units at January 1 and budgeted inventory units at January 31 are as follows:

	Units
Actual inventory at January 1:	
Work-in-process	None
Finished goods	75,000
Budgeted inventory at January 31:	
Work-in-process (75% processed)	16,000
Finished goods	60,000

How many equivalent units of production is Lawton budgeting for January?
A. 251,000.
B. 253,000.
C. 235,000.
D. 247,000.

3. In a job order cost system, the use of indirect materials previously purchased usually is recorded as a decrease in:
A. stores control.
B. work-in-process control.
C. factory overhead control.
D. factory overhead applied.

4. In a process cost system, the application of factory overhead usually would be recorded as an increase in:
A. work-in-process control.
B. factory overhead control.
C. finished goods control.
D. cost of goods sold.

STUDY MANUAL – BUSINESS ENVIRONMENT & CONCEPTS

CHAPTER 10

5. Tolbert Manufacturing Company uses a standard cost system in accounting for the cost of production of its only product, Product A. The standards for the production of one unit of Product A are as follows:
    - Direct materials: 10 feet of item 1 at $0.75 per foot and 3 feet of item 2 at $1 per foot.
    - Direct labor: 4 hours at $3.50 per hour.
    - Manufacturing overhead: applied at 150% of standard direct labor costs.

    There was no inventory on hand at July 1, year 2. Following is a summary of costs and related data for the production of Product A during the year ended June 30, year 3.
    - 100,000 feet of item 1 were purchased at $0.78 per foot.
    - 30,000 feet of item 2 were purchased at $0.90 per foot.
    - 8,000 units of Product A were produced that required 78,000 feet of item 1, 26,000 feet of item 2, and 31,000 hours of direct labor at $3.60 per hour.
    - 6,000 units of Product A were sold.

    At June 30, year 3, there are 22,000 feet of item 1, 4,000 feet of item 2, and 2,000 completed units of product A on hand. All purchases and transfers are "charged in" at standard.

    For the year ended June 30, year 3, the total debits to the raw materials account for the purchase of item 1 would be:
    A. $58,500.
    B. $78,000.
    C. $75,000.
    D. $60,000.

6. For the year ended June 30, year 3, the total debits to the work-in-process account for direct labor would be:
    A. $108,500.
    B. $115,100.
    C. $111,600.
    D. $112,000.

7. The Forming Department is the first of a two-stage production process. Spoilage is identified when the units have completed the Forming process. Costs of spoiled units are assigned to units completed and transferred to the second department in the period spoilage is identified. The following information concerns Forming's conversion costs in May:

	Units	Conversion Costs
Beginning work-in-process (50% complete)	2,000	$10,000
Units started during May	8,000	75,500
Spoilage – normal	500	
Units completed and transferred	7,000	
Ending work-in-process (80% complete)	2,500	

©2007 Kaplan CPA Review

Page 311

STUDY MANUAL – BUSINESS ENVIRONMENT & CONCEPTS
CHAPTER 10

Using the weighted average method, what was Forming's conversion cost transferred to the second production department?
A. $59,850.
B. $64,125.
C. $67,500.
D. $71,250.

8. When should process-costing techniques be used in assigning costs to products?
A. If the product is manufactured on the basis of each order received.
B. When production is only partially completed during the accounting period.
C. If the product is composed of mass-produced homogeneous units.
D. In situations where standard costing techniques should not be used.

9. A job order cost system uses a predetermined factor overhead rate based on expected volume and expected fixed cost. At the end of the year, underapplied overhead might be explained by which of the following situations?

	Actual volume	Actual fixed costs
A.	Greater than expected	Greater than expected
B.	Greater than expected	Less than expected
C.	Less than expected	Greater than expected
D.	Less than expected	Less than expected

10. In order to compute equivalent units of production using the FIFO method of process costing, work for the period must be broken down to units:
A. completed during the period and units in ending inventory.
B. completed from beginning inventory, started and completed during the month, and units in ending inventory.
C. started during the period and units transferred out during the period.
D. processed during the period and units completed during the period.

11. A process costing system was used for a department that began operations in January. Approximately the same number of physical units, at the same degree of completion, were in work in process at the end of both January and February. Monthly conversion costs are allocated between ending work in process and units completed. Compared to the FIFO method, would the weighted average method use the same or a greater number of equivalent units to calculate the monthly allocations?

	Equivalent units for weighted average compared to FIFO	
	January	February
A.	Same	Same
B.	Greater number	Greater number
C.	Greater number	Same
D.	Same	Greater number

Page 312   ©2007 Kaplan CPA Review

STUDY MANUAL – BUSINESS ENVIRONMENT & CONCEPTS

CHAPTER 10

12. Walton, Incorporated, had 8,000 units of work in process in Department A on October 1. These units were 60% complete as to conversion costs. Materials are added in the beginning of the process. During the month of October, 34,000 units were started and 36,000 units completed. Walton had 6,000 units of work in process on October 31. These units were 80% complete as to conversion costs. By how much did the equivalent units for the month of October using the weighted-average method exceed the equivalent units for the month of October using the first-in, first-out method?

	Materials	Conversion costs
A.	0	3,200
B.	0	4,800
C.	8,000	3,200
D.	8,000	4,800

13. Information for the month of May concerning Department A, the first stage of Wit Corporation's production cycle, is as follows:

	Materials	Conversion Costs
Work in process, beginning	$4,000	$3,000
Current costs	20,000	16,000
Total costs	$24,000	$19,000
Equivalent units based on weighted-average method	100,000	95,000
Average unit costs	$0.24	$0.20
Goods completed		90,000 units
Work in process, end		10,000 units

Material costs are added at the beginning of the process. The ending work in process is 50% complete as to conversion costs. How would the total costs accounted for be distributed, using the weighted-average method?

	Goods completed	Work in process, end
A.	$39,600	$3,400
B.	$39,600	$4,400
C.	$43,000	$0
D.	$44,000	$3,400

©2007 Kaplan CPA Review

Page 313

STUDY MANUAL – BUSINESS ENVIRONMENT & CONCEPTS
CHAPTER 10

14. The Wiring Department is the second stage of Flem Company's production cycle. On May 1, the beginning work in process contained 25,000 units which were 60% complete as to conversion costs. During May, 100,000 units were transferred in from the first stage of Flem's production cycle. On May 31, the ending work in process contained 20,000 units which were 80% complete as to conversion costs. Material costs are added at the end of the process. Using the weighted-average method, the equivalent units were:

	Transferred-in costs	Materials	Conversion costs
A.	100,000	125,000	100,000
B.	125,000	105,000	105,000
C.	125,000	105,000	121,000
D.	125,000	125,000	121,000

15. The Cutting Department is the first stage of Mark Company's production cycle. Conversion costs for this department were 80% complete as to the beginning work-in-process and 50% complete as to the ending work-in-process. Information as to conversion costs in the Cutting Department for January is as follows:

	Units	Conversion Costs
Work-in-process at January 1	25,000	$22,000
Units started and costs incurred during January	135,000	$143,000
Units completed and transferred to next department during January	100,000	$19,000

Using the FIFO method, what was the conversion cost of the work-in-process in the Cutting Department at January 31?
A. $33,000.
B. $38,100.
C. $39,000.
D. $45,000.

16. Under Heller Company's job order cost system, estimated costs of defective work (considered normal in the manufacturing process) are included in the predetermined factory overhead rate. During March, Job No. 210 for 2,000 hand saws was completed at the following costs per unit:

Direct materials	$5
Direct labor	4
Factory overhead (applied at 150% of direct-labor	6
	$15

Page 314   ©2007 Kaplan CPA Review

Final inspection of Job No. 210 disclosed 100 defective saws which were reworked at a cost of $2 per unit for direct labor, plus overhead at the predetermined rate. The defective units on Job No. 210 fall within the normal range. What is the total rework cost and to what account should it be charged?

	Rework cost	Account charged
A.	$200	Work-in-process
B.	$200	Factory overhead control
C.	$500	Work-in-process
D.	$500	Factory overhead control

17. In its April production, Hern Corp., which does not use a standard cost system, incurred total production costs of $900,000, of which Hern attributed $60,000 to normal spoilage and $30,000 to abnormal spoilage. Hern should account for this spoilage as:

A. Period cost of $90,000.

B. Inventoriable cost of $90,000.

C. Period cost of $60,000 and inventoriable cost of $30,000.

D. Inventoriable cost of $60,000 and period cost of $30,000.

18. Walden Company has a process cost system using the FIFO cost flow method. All materials are introduced at the beginning of the process in Department 1. The following information is available for the month of January:

	Units
Work-in-process, 1/1 (40% complete as to conversion costs)	500
Started in January	2,000
Transferred to Department 2 during January	2,100
Work-in-process, 1/31 (25% complete as to conversion costs)	400

What are the equivalent units of production for the month of January?

	Materials	Conversion
A.	2,500	2,200
B.	2,500	1,900
C.	2,000	2,200
D.	2,000	2,000

19. Axe Co. has a job order cost system. The following debits (credits) appeared in the work-in-process account for the month of March:

March	Description	Amount
1	Balance	$2,000
31	Direct materials	12,000
31	Direct labor	8,000
31	Factory overhead	6,400
31	To finished goods	(24,000)

©2007 Kaplan CPA Review

STUDY MANUAL – BUSINESS ENVIRONMENT & CONCEPTS
CHAPTER 10

Axe applies overhead to production at a predetermined rate of 80% based on direct labor cost. Job No. 9, the only job still in process at the end of March has been charged with direct labor of $1,000. The amount of direct materials charged to Job No. 9 was:

A. $12,000.
B. $4,400.
C. $2,600.
D. $1,500.

20.   Barkley Company adds materials at the beginning of the process in department M. Data concerning the materials used in March production are as follows:

	Units
Work-in-process at March 1	16,000
Started during March	34,000
Completed and transferred to next department during March	36,000
Normal spoilage incurred	4,000
Work-in-process at March 31	10,000

Using the weighted-average method, the equivalent units for the materials unit cost calculation are:

A. 30,000.
B. 34,000.
C. 40,000.
D. 46,000.

21.   In a traditional job order cost system, the issue of indirect materials to a production department increases:

A. Stores control.
B. Work in process control.
C. Factory overhead control.
D. Factory overhead applied.

22.   Barnett Company adds materials at the beginning of the process in department M. Conversion costs were 75% complete as to the 8,000 units in work-in-process at May 1, and 50% complete as to the 6,000 units in work-in-process at May 31. During May 12,000 units were completed and transferred to the next department. An analysis of the costs relating to work-in-process at May 1 and to production activity for May is as follows:

	Costs	
	Materials	Conversion
Work-in-process, 5/1	$9,600	$4,800
Cost added in May	15,600	14,400

Page 316   ©2007 Kaplan CPA Review

Using the weighted-average method, the total cost per equivalent unit for May was:

A. $2.47.
B. $2.50.
C. $2.68.
D. $3.16.

23. Assuming that there was no beginning work in process inventory, and the ending work in process inventory is 50% complete as to conversion costs, the number of equivalent units as to conversion costs would be:

A. The same as the units placed in process.
B. The same as the units completed.
C. Less than the units placed in process.
D. Less than the units completed.

24. Assuming that there was no beginning work in process inventory, and the ending work in process inventory is 100% complete as to material costs, the number of equivalent units as to material costs would be:

A. The same as the units placed in process.
B. The same as the units completed.
C. Less than the units placed in process.
D. Less than the units completed.

25. During March Bly Co.'s Department Y equivalent unit product costs, computed under the weighted-average method, were as follows:

Materials	$1
Conversion	3
Transferred-in	5

Materials are introduced at the end of the process in Department Y. There were 4,000 units (40% complete as to conversion cost) in work-in-process at March 31. The total costs assigned to the March 31 work-in-process inventory should be:

A. $36,000.
B. $28,800.
C. $27,200.
D. $24,800.

26. In a job order cost system, the use of indirect materials previously purchased usually is recorded as a decrease in:

A. Stores control.
B. Work-in-process control.
C. Factory overhead control.
D. Factory overhead applied.

©2007 Kaplan CPA Review

Page 317

STUDY MANUAL – BUSINESS ENVIRONMENT & CONCEPTS
CHAPTER 10

27. In a process cost system, the application of factory overhead usually would be recorded as an increase in:
    A. Cost of goods sold.
    B. Work in process control.
    C. Factory overhead control.
    D. Finished goods control.

28. Which of the following is a disadvantage of using a process costing system versus job order costing?
    A. It is difficult to determine cost of goods sold when partial shipments are made before completion.
    B. It is difficult to ensure that material and labor are accurately charged to each specific job.
    C. It involves the calculation of stage of completion of goods-in-process and the use of equivalent units.
    D. It is expensive to use as a good deal of clerical work is required.

STUDY MANUAL – BUSINESS ENVIRONMENT & CONCEPTS
CHAPTER 10

ANSWERS: COST ACCOUNTING

1. **A** Overhead is applied to production with a predetermined overhead rate. The amount of overhead applied is equal to the predetermined rate multiplied by the actual or standard activity base for the volume of production achieved. The predetermined overhead rate is calculated as the fraction expected overhead/expected activity base. The numerator is in dollars, and the denominator is in units of the chosen activity base (such as direct labor hours).

   Underapplied overhead means that actual overhead costs were greater than the overhead applied to production (work-in-process).

   Examine the overhead rate calculation (the fraction) to see why it was underapplied. Either an increase in overhead costs above the expected level (numerator) or a decrease in the level of production below the expected level (activity base) (denominator) would result in underapplied overhead.

2. **D**

Sales		250,000 units
+	Ending inventory – finished goods	60,000 units
–	Beginning inventory – finished goods	75,000) units
	Required production	235,000 units
+	Ending inventory – work-in-process (16,000 × 75%)	12,000 EFU
–	Beginning inventory – work-in-process	0
	Production required	247,000 EFU

3. **A** When indirect materials are *purchased* they are charged to (increase) store supplies (an inventory account). When indirect materials are used they are charged (debited) to factory overhead control and credited against (decrease) store supplies.

4. **A** Applied factory overhead is charged (debited) to work-in-process and credited to the factory overhead control account. This increases work-in-process inventory and decreases the control account. Factory overhead is NOT applied directly to finished goods or cost of goods sold, but is included in the cost of the units transferred to these accounts.

5. **C** All purchases are "charged in" at standard. Therefore, the debit to raw materials for the purchase of item 1 would be: 100,000 ft. × $0.75 = $75,000.

6. **D** Debits to work-in-process for direct labor: 8,000 units × 4 hrs. × $3.50 = $112,000 (standard amounts and standard cost).

©2007 Kaplan CPA Review
Page 319

STUDY MANUAL – BUSINESS ENVIRONMENT & CONCEPTS
CHAPTER 10

7. **B** $67,500.

Computation of equivalent finished units (conversion costs)	
Units finished and transferred out	7,000
+ Normal spoilage – finished	2,000
+ Ending inventory 2,500 × 80%	2,000
E.F.U. – at average	9,500

Conversion cost per E.F.U. (wt. aver.)	
Beginning inventory conversion cost	10,000
Current period conversion cost	75,500
Total conversion cost	$85,500
E.F.U. – conversion cost	/9,500
Conversion cost per E.F.U.	$9.00

Conversion costs transferred to Dept. 2	
Units finished and transferred out	7,000
Normal spoilage	500
	7,500
Conversion cost per unit	× $9
	$67,500

Note: Cost of spoiled units are assigned to units completed and transferred out; therefore, they are included in the E.F.U. computation.

8. **C** Process-costing techniques should be used when the product is composed of mass-produced, homogeneous units. This does not preclude the use of standard costing (d). Answer (a) refers to job order costing.

9. **C** Actual volume: Less than expected; Actual fixed cost: Greater than expected.

Overhead is applied to production with a predetermined overhead rate. The amount of overhead applied is equal to the predetermined rate times the actual or standard activity base for the volume of production achieved.

Underapplied overhead means that actual overhead costs were greater than the overhead applied to production (work-in-process). Therefore, either an increase in overhead costs or a decrease in the level of production (activity base) would result in underapplied overhead.

10. **B** This reflects the fact that the equivalent units include (1) those beginning inventory units that were completed, (2) the completed units all of whose costs were incurred in the current period, and (3) the partially completed units in ending inventory.

11. **D** The difference between FIFO and Weighted Average equivalent finished units (EFU) is the EFU of beginning inventory. Under the FIFO method, the EFU of beginning work-in-process inventory are excluded from the EFU computation for the period; however, under the Weighted Average method, these EFU are included in the EFU calculation.

For January, the EFU for Weighted Average and FIFO would be the same because there was no beginning inventory of work-in-process.

For February, the beginning inventory of work-in-process (January's ending inventory) would cause the Weighted Average EFU to be greater than the FIFO EFU for the month.

Page 320   ©2007 Kaplan CPA Review

STUDY MANUAL – BUSINESS ENVIRONMENT & CONCEPTS

CHAPTER 10

12. **D**   8,000 material; 4,800 conversion costs

Computation of equivalent units for material:

	FIFO	W/A
Finished	36,000	36,000
+ Ending WIP	(1) 6,000	6,000
	42,000	42,000
– Beginning WIP	(1) 8,000	–
	34,000	42,000 + 8,000

(1) Material added at the beginning of the process

Computation of equivalent units for conversion costs:

	FIFO	W/A
Finished	36,000	36,000
+ Ending WIP – 6,000 ×80%	4,800	4,800
	40,800	40,800
– Beginning WIP – 8,000 × 60%	4,800	–
	36,000	40,800 + 4,800

13. **A** $39,600 and $3,400:

Completed goods 90,000 × ($0.24 + $0.20) =	$39,600
Goods in process	3,400
Total costs ($24,000 + $19,000) =	$43,000

The above is all that is needed for the answer, because the total costs are $43,000, the goods in process are $3,400. Computation of goods in process:

Material 10,000 × 0.24 (100%) =	$2,400
Conversion cost 10,000 × 0.20 (50%) =	1,000
	$3,400

©2007 Kaplan CPA Review

STUDY MANUAL – BUSINESS ENVIRONMENT & CONCEPTS
CHAPTER 10

14. **C** 125,000; 105,000; 121,000.

B.I. WIP	25,000
+ Transferred in	100,000
Total units	125,000 (Also, E.U. – Transferred in)
– E.I. WIP	20,000
Finished units	105,000

Use finished units plus ending inventory of WIP to compute equivalent units.

	M	C.C.	Transferred-in
Finished	105,000	105,000	105,000
E.I. WIP 20,000 × 0%	–		
20,000 × 80%		16,000	
20,000 × 100%			20,000
	105,000	121,000	125,000

15. **C** EFU Computation:

Finished	100,000
EFU in ending inventory (60,000 × 50% complete)	30,000
Less: EFU in beginning inventory (25,000 × 80% complete)	(20,000)
	110,000

Unit cost computation:

Period Cost	/	EFU	=	Unit Cost
143,000		110,000		1.30

Cost of ending WIP = $1.30   30,000 EFU = $39,000

Note ending inventory of 60,000 units = 25,000 B.I. + 135,000 started – 100,000 completed.

16. **D** Rework cost:

Labor cost (100 units × $2)	$200
Overhead ($200 D.L. × 1.5)	300
	$500

The cost of rework should be charged to the factory overhead control account, as the predetermined rate used to apply overhead (cost jobs) during the period includes an estimate for such costs.

17. **D** The cost of normal spoilage ($60,000) is a product cost which should be absorbed by the good units produced and included in the recorded cost of both work-in-process and finished goods inventories.

The cost of abnormal spoilage ($30,000) is a period cost and should be expensed in the current period.

Page 322   ©2007 Kaplan CPA Review

STUDY MANUAL – BUSINESS ENVIRONMENT & CONCEPTS
CHAPTER 10

18. **D**

	Materials	Conversion
Finished unit	2,100	2,100
Ending inventory		
400 × 100%	400	
400 × 25%		100
Less: beginning inventory		
500 × 100%	(500)	
500 ×40%		(200)
E.F.U.(FIFO)	2,000	2,000

19. **C**

Work-in-process March 1	$2,000
Add: Direct materials	12,000
Direct labor	8,000
Factory overhead	6,400
Less: Transferred to finished goods	(24,000)
Work-in-process March 31	$4,400
Less: Direct labor	(1,000)
Factory overhead ($1,000 × 80%)	(800)
Direct materials, Job #9	$2,600

20. **D**

Finished units	36,000
Ending inventory (10,000 × 100%)	10,000
EFU – average	46,000

Note: Materials are added at the beginning of the process in dept. M; therefore, the units in the ending inventory are 100% complete as to materials.

Normal spoilage is a cost of good production (product cost); therefore, units of normal spoilage (or loss) are excluded from the E.F.U. computation.

21. **C** When indirect materials were initially purchased, they would be charged to the stores control. However, when they are issued to a production department, they would be charged (increased) to the factory overhead control account.

©2007 Kaplan CPA Review

STUDY MANUAL – BUSINESS ENVIRONMENT & CONCEPTS
CHAPTER 10

22. **C**

E.F.U. Computation	Materials	Conversion
Finished units	12,000	12,000
Ending inventory		
6,000 units × 100%	6,000	
6,000 units × 50%		3,000
Wt. Avg. EFU	18,000	15,000

Unit Cost Computation:

	Beg. Inv. Cost	+	Period Cost	= Total Cost/EFU	=	Unit Cost
Materials	$9,600		$15,600	$25,200/18,000	=	$1.40
Conversion	$4,800		$14,400	$19,200/15,000	=	1.28
Total cost per EFU						$2.68

23. **C** EFU Computations:

Finished units   #

+ $\dfrac{\text{Ending inventory EFU}}{\text{EFU average}}$ #   × 50% complete

− $\dfrac{\text{Beginning inventory}}{\text{EFU FIFO}}$ 0

As there is no beginning inventory, average EFU are equal to FIFO EFU and the answer to this question is the same for both methods.

As there is no beginning inventory, and ending inventory is 50% complete:

1. EFU is less than units placed in process (all units started have not been completed) – Answer C.

2. EFU are less than units started; therefore answer A is incorrect.

3. EFU are greater than units completed; therefore answers B and D are incorrect.

24. **A** EFU Computations:

Finished units   #

+ $\dfrac{\text{Ending inventory EFU}}{\text{EFU average}}$ #   × 100% complete

− $\dfrac{\text{Beginning inventory}}{\text{EFU FIFO}}$ 0

As there is no beginning inventory, average EFU are equal to FIFO EFU and the answer to this question is the same for both methods. As there is no beginning inventory and ending inventory is 100% complete:

1. EFU are equal to the units started (answer C) and therefore answer C is incorrect.

2. EFU are greater than units completed; therefore, answers B and D are incorrect.

STUDY MANUAL – BUSINESS ENVIRONMENT & CONCEPTS
CHAPTER 10

25. **D**

	Units		% Complete		Unit Cost		Total Cost
Materials	4,000	×	0%	×	$1	=	$0
Conversion	4,000	×	40%	×	$3	=	4,800
Transferred in	4,000	×	100%	×	$5	=	20,000
							$24,800

26. **A**   When indirect materials are purchased they are charged to (increase) store supplies (an inventory account). When indirect materials are used they are charged to factory overhead control and credited against (decrease) store supplies.

27. **B**   Applied factory overhead is charged (debited) to work-in-process and credited to the factory overhead control account. This increases work-in-process inventory and decreases the control account. Factory overhead is not applied directly to finished goods or cost of goods sold, but is included in the cost of the units transferred to these accounts.

28. **C**   Process costing involves the use of equivalent units, and equivalent units depend on estimates of the stage of completion, which is not an exact science. For example, it is difficult for an auditor or an accountant to walk on the floor of a manufacturing plant at twelve midnight on December 31 and view 100 machines in various stages of production and say that on the average the stage of completion is X. Whereas, in a job order system, to build houses for example, the cost of direct materials and direct labor can be traced directly to the job (house) without any estimation

©2007 Kaplan CPA Review

Page 325

COST ACCOUNTING: OTHER AREAS

STUDY MANUAL – BUSINESS ENVIRONMENT & CONCEPTS
CHAPTER 11

Study Tip: Don't make any sudden changes in your sleeping or eating habits right before you take the CPA exam. Keep life as normal as possible so that there is not any unnecessary stress on you. The CPA exam is a challenge; don't make your body and your mind have to adapt to new circumstances at this critical juncture.

JOINT PRODUCTS

A. In some circumstances, firms will create more than one product from one raw material input. The various products manufactured from the same group of raw materials are referred to as joint products. Consider the paper products industry: the raw material trees may be processed into paper napkins, paper plates, and copier paper.

B. In a typical situation, raw materials are processed until a certain point is reached at which the various products can be separated. This point is referred to as the *split-off point*. All costs incurred in processing the raw materials prior to the split-off point pertain to all of the products in production and are referred to as *joint product costs*.

C. Costs that are incurred after the split-off point that pertain to a particular product are referred to as *separable costs*.

D. The goal of joint product costing is to allocate joint costs fairly among the ultimate finished products.

E. There are two common methods of allocating joint product costs. They may be allocated according to the units of volume of output, or according to the relative sales values of the output.

   1. Under the units of output method, the same amount of joint product cost is allocated to each unit. The total of the costs is divided by the total number of units, resulting in a per-unit cost. The joint product costs are then allocated to all units.

   2. The relative sales value method is the more commonly used of the two. It is considered the fairer method since it allocates costs based on relative value, rather than according to volume.

Page 326   ©2007 Kaplan CPA Review

a. Under the relative sales value method, the sales value of each product is determined at the earliest point at which the product could be sold. Even if a product is generally processed further and sold at a later point, the sales price is determined at the earlier point.

b. If any separable costs pertain to a particular product, they are deducted from the sales value of that product. The result is considered the net realizable value and generally referred to as the *relative sales value*.

c. The relative sales values of all of the products are added together to compute a total. A ratio is computed for each product by taking the relative sales value of that product divided by the total of the values.

d. The amount of joint product costs allocated to each product will be the ratio for that product multiplied by the total of the joint product costs.

BY-PRODUCTS

A. When two or more products result from a single manufacturing process or a single group of materials, the products are not always joint products. If a product does not materially contribute to the revenues of the company, the product is considered a by-product.

B. There are several methods of accounting for by-products. Each of the following methods is acceptable.

1. Allocate no costs to by-products. Revenues will be treated as an "Other Income" item.

2. Allocate costs to the by-product equal to the net revenues generated by it or its net realizable value. The result will be a breakeven situation for the by-product.

3. Allocate no costs to the by-product and reduce the costs allocated to the main product by the net revenues generated by the by-product.

STUDY MANUAL – BUSINESS ENVIRONMENT & CONCEPTS
CHAPTER 11

Example: Joint costs

Axe Co. produces joint products J and K from a process that yields by-product B. The cost assigned to by-product B is its market value less additional costs incurred after split-off. Information concerning a batch produced in April at a joint cost of $60,000 is as follows:

Product	Units Produced	Additional Costs (after split-off)	Market Values
J	1,000	$15,000	$50,000
K	2,000	$10,000	$40,000
B	4,000	$2,000	$5,000

How much of the joint cost should be allocated to the joint products?
A. $53,000.
B. $55,000.
C. $57,000.
D. $58,000.

Solution:

The answer is C. The cost assigned to B is its market value ($5,000), less additional costs incurred after split-off ($2,000) = $3,000. Total joint costs are $60,000 less costs for B, $3,000 = $57,000.

BUDGETING

A. An operating budget is a quantitative expression of management's objectives and a means of monitoring progress toward achievement of those objectives.

1. The operating budget is a more comprehensive extension of the planning and control processes that were illustrated under standard costing. That is, standard costing may be perceived as a subset of the operating budget.

2. Operating budgets include not just planning and controlling product costs, but also marketing and administrative costs, revenues, cash inflows, and cash outflows.

3. The first step in developing the operating budget is the sales forecast. The process ends with the completion of the budgeted income statement, the cash budget, and the budgeted balance sheet.

4. The presentation in the budgeted financial statements is similar to that in the regular financial statements except that we are dealing with the future rather than the past.

B. The following budgets are commonly prepared for a manufacturing operation:

1. Sales budget. The foundation upon which the sales budget and all other parts of the operating budget rest is the sales forecast. If this forecast has been carefully and accurately prepared, the succeeding steps in the budget process will be that much more reliable.

   sales budget (dollars) = projected units to be sold × projected sales price per unit

2. Production budget. The quantities for the production budget must be closely tied in with the sales budget and the desired inventory levels. Essentially, the production budget is the sales budget adjusted for inventory changes.

   production budget (units) = projected units to be sold + desired ending inventory (units) − expected beginning inventory (units)

3. Raw materials purchase budget. This is one of the first cost budgets to be prepared, as the purchasing quantities and delivery schedules must be quickly established in order for raw materials to be available when required. Usually there is a specification sheet or formula for each product showing the type and quantity of each raw material per unit of production.

   raw materials purchase budget (units) = production budget (units) × std. qty. of direct materials per unit + desired ending inventory (units of raw material) − expected beginning inventory (units of raw material)

   raw materials purchase budget (dollars) = raw materials purchase budget (units) × projected purchase cost per unit

4. Direct labor budget. The direct labor requirements are usually developed by engineers based on time studies. The direct labor budget must be coordinated with the production budget, the purchasing budget, and all other parts of the operating budget. Indirect labor will be included in the factory overhead budget.

   direct labor budget (dollars) = production budget (units) × standard direct labor hours per unit × standard direct labor rate per hour

5. Factory (manufacturing) overhead budget. Department heads should be held accountable for expenses incurred in their departments. Budgets are commonly used in controlling factory overhead costs. Prior to the period in question, a budget that shows anticipated factory overhead costs is prepared. Actual factory overhead costs are later compared with those budgeted as a means of evaluating managerial performance. Two commonly used budgeting approaches are static budgets and flexible budgets.

STUDY MANUAL – BUSINESS ENVIRONMENT & CONCEPTS
CHAPTER 11

a. Static budgets show anticipated costs at one level of activity justified on the assumption that production will not materially deviate from the level selected.

factory overhead budget = total fixed factory overhead + total variable factory overhead

- When the majority of factory overhead costs are unaffected by activity, or when productive activity is stable, the static budget would be the appropriate tool.
- However, such a situation is rare because factory overhead contains many variable costs, such as indirect labor, indirect materials, and supplies. Also, production levels usually fluctuate in response to fluctuations in customer demand.

b. Flexible budgets show anticipated costs at different activity levels. (The formula below assumes overhead is allocated on the basis of direct labor hours. There are other possibilities, such as direct labor dollars, pounds of direct materials, etc.)

factory overhead budget = total fixed factory overhead + total budgeted direct labor hours × variable expense rate per direct labor hour

- This eliminates the problems associated with static budgets in terms of fluctuations in productive activity.
- Actual costs incurred must be compared with budgeted costs that would have been incurred at the same activity level. The comparison of actual cost to standard cost at the same activity level is the only meaningful comparison for performance evaluation purposes and makes flexible budgets a more realistic form of budgeting.
- For better control, the fixed and variable expenses are separated in a flexible budget. Fixed expenses have total dollar values assigned, while variable expenses have rates assigned, based on, for example, direct labor hours.

6. Budgeted ending inventories. Budgeted inventory amounts at month-end or year-end are needed for direct materials and finished goods inventory in order to prepare the cost of goods sold budget and the budgeted balance sheet.

budgeted ending inventory cost = desired ending inventory (units) × standard cost per unit

7. Cash budget. Cash disbursements are based on the individual budgets previously prepared, with needed adjustments to change from the accrual basis to the cash basis. In preparing the cash budget, the beginning cash balance is added to the estimated cash receipts to show the expected amount of cash available each month. From this amount the expected cash disbursements are deducted to determine the excess (or deficiency) of cash at the end of the month.

cash balance, ending = cash balance, beginning + cash receipts for the period – cash disbursements for the period

Page 330   ©2007 Kaplan CPA Review

CAPITAL BUDGETING

A. Capital budgeting refers to long-range decision making.

1. Capital budgeting involves the planning and controlling of long-term expenditures and obtaining of capital on a long-range basis.

2. Capital budgeting decisions are generally material in value and scope and are of greater risk than short-range decisions.

3. These decisions frequently involve applications of present value techniques.

B. Decisions involving capital budgeting techniques may include make-versus-buy decisions, deciding between alternative investments, deciding between different methods of obtaining capital, decisions whether to accept or reject certain projects, and similar decisions involving the use of or obtaining of capital.

C. Various techniques are used in making capital budgeting decisions. The most prevalent methods include the accounting rate of return, the time-adjusted rate of return, the payback method, and the net present value method.

COST OF CAPITAL

A. One factor common to all problems concerning capital budgeting is the company's cost of capital. The cost of capital is the amount that the company must pay in order to obtain capital, usually expressed in terms of an interest rate.

B. Capital can usually be obtained in one of two ways: issuance of debt or issuance of stock. Typically, both debt and equity are involved, in which case a weighted-average cost of capital is computed.

1. When stock is issued, the cost of capital is the dividend paid per period, plus stock price appreciation. When divided by the proceeds from the issuance of the stock, this gives the cost of capital rate.

2. When debt securities are issued, the cost of capital is the interest, net of tax, that is paid on the new debt. Dividing by the proceeds from the issuance of the debt will give a rate as well.

C. The cost of capital is expressed as an interest rate and is the rate to which the return on investment is compared in determining if the investment is favorable or unfavorable.

STUDY MANUAL – BUSINESS ENVIRONMENT & CONCEPTS
CHAPTER 11

APPLYING CAPITAL BUDGETING TECHNIQUES

A. Accounting rate of return. This is a method of evaluating investments in which the rate of return is compared to the company's cost of capital.

1. If the computed rate exceeds the cost of capital, the investment is acceptable. If the computed rate is lower, the investment is unacceptable, and if the computed rate equals the cost of capital, we are indifferent to the investment.

2. The accounting rate of return involves a simple computation in which the increase in accounting net income per year is divided by the amount of the investment. (The increase in accounting net income is that amount that is expected to be attributable to the new project that is being considered and evaluated.)

3. In some circumstances, the accounting rate of return may be computed based on average investment, rather than the total investment. In this case, the annual increase in accounting net income is divided by the average investment, which is the initial investment plus the salvage value divided by two.

4. The greatest advantage of using the accounting rate of return is that it is easy to compute.

5. There are two major weaknesses.

   a. The accounting rate of return is based on the increase in accounting net income, rather than cash flows. It does not indicate the increase in funds available to the company.

   b. The accounting rate of return does not take into account the time value of money.

Example: Accounting rate of return

Saratoga Company is planning to purchase a new machine for $600,000. The new machine will be depreciated on the straight-line basis over a 6-year period with no salvage, and a full year's depreciation will be taken in the year of acquisition. The new machine is expected to produce cash flow from operations, net of income taxes, of $150,000 a year in each of the next six years. The accounting (book value) rate of return on the initial investment is expected to be:

A. 8.3 percent.
B. 12.0 percent.
C. 16.7 percent.
D. 25.0 percent.

STUDY MANUAL – BUSINESS ENVIRONMENT & CONCEPTS
CHAPTER 11

Solution:

The answer is A.

Expected cash flow from operations	$150,000
Less: depreciation ($600,000/6 years)	100,000
Net income	$50,000

$$\frac{\text{net income}}{\text{investment}} = \frac{\$50,000}{\$600,000} = 8.3\%$$

B. Time-adjusted rate of return. The time-adjusted or internal rate of return computes the actual rate of return on an investment based on increases in cash flows rather than accounting income and takes into account the time value of money.

1. The biggest disadvantage of the time-adjusted rate of return is that it is relatively difficult to compute because trial-and-error methods must be applied. It is particularly difficult if payments are not equal from period to period. The calculation requires use of a financial calculator or computer spreadsheet.

2. The time-adjusted rate of return for an investment is the discount (interest) rate that will make the present (or discounted) value of annual cash flows from the project equal to the initial outlay for the investment.

3. A time-adjusted rate of return above the minimum rate of return specified by management (called the *hurdle rate*) is considered acceptable. When mutually exclusive projects are being compared, the project with the highest time-adjusted rate of return will be preferred.

4. The computation becomes much more difficult when the investment has a salvage value, as the present value of the salvage value must also be taken into account. This method is applied in computing the implicit interest rate in a lease. It may be done by trial and error, financial calculator, or by computer program.

5. The time-adjusted rate of return is computed using the following procedures:

    a. The annual increase in cash flow resulting from having made the investment is computed. This will include any increases in revenues or decreases in cash costs. Decreases or increases in noncash costs, such as depreciation, are also taken into account due to the effect on income taxes. (It is the income tax amount that is used in calculating cash flows; taxes are a cash outflow.) It is assumed that the cash flows are the same each year.

    b. The annual increase in cash flows is divided into the investment. This gives us a present value factor.

©2007 Kaplan CPA Review
Page 333

STUDY MANUAL – BUSINESS ENVIRONMENT & CONCEPTS
CHAPTER 11

c. Using a present value table for an annuity, looking at the appropriate row for the number of periods equal to the life of the investment, we find the factor that is closest to the one computed in the preceding step.

d. If the factor equals the one computed, the interest rate at the top of that column will be the time-adjusted rate of return. If the factor is different, we must interpolate between the two interest rates whose factors are just higher and just lower than the factor computed.

Example: Time-adjusted rate of return

Kipling Company invested in an eight-year project. It is expected that the annual cash flow from the project, net of income taxes, will be $20,000. Information on present value factors is as follows:

Present value of $1 at 12% for eight periods	0.404
Present value of an ordinary annuity of $1 at 12% for eight periods	4.968

Assuming that Kipling based its investment decision on a time-adjusted (internal) rate of return of 12 percent, how much did the project cost?
A. $160,000.
B. $99,360.
C. $80,800.
D. $64,640.

Solution:

The answer is B. Multiply the annual cash flow ($20,000) by the present value of an ordinary annuity of $1 at 12 percent for eight periods (4.968) to arrive at the project cost of $99,360.

C. Payback. The payback method involves computing the annual increase in cash flows from the investment and dividing the amount into the net investment. The result will be the number of periods it will take to recover the investment.

1. This number of periods is then compared to a predetermined payback period based on the company's cost of capital. If the computed period is shorter, the investment is acceptable. If the computed period is longer, the investment is unacceptable, and if the computed period equals the predetermined period, we are indifferent to the investment.

2. The major weakness with the payback method is that it does not take into account whether the investment is profitable, only how long it will take to recover the amount invested. It also ignores the time value of money.

3. The major advantage of the method is that it is relatively easy to compute.

Example: Payback period

The Womark Company purchased a new machine on January 1, 2006, for $90,000 with an estimated useful life of five years and a salvage value of $10,000. The machine will be depreciated using the straight-line method. The machine is expected to produce cash flow from operations (net of income taxes) of $36,000 a year in each of the next five years. The payback period would be:

A. 2.2 years.
B. 2.5 years.
C. 4.0 years.
D. 4.5 years.

Solution:

The answer is B.

$$\frac{\text{investment}}{\text{cash flow}} = \frac{\$90,000}{\$36,000} = 2.5 \text{ years}$$

D. Net present value. The net present value is considered another excellent method. It takes into account cash flows and the time value of money, and it is not too difficult to compute.

1. Under the net present value method, the present value of the increase in annual cash flows is computed using the company's cost of capital. In addition, the present value of the salvage value, if any, is computed and added to the amount. This total is then reduced by the amount of the net investment to be made.

2. If the net amount is positive, the return on the investment exceeds the company's cost of capital and is acceptable. If the net amount is negative, the return is less than the company's cost of capital and is unacceptable. If the net amount is zero, the return on investment is equal to the company's cost of capital and the company will be indifferent to the investment.

3. The major disadvantage associated with this method is that it is difficult to compare investment alternatives when the investment amounts are different.

STUDY MANUAL – BUSINESS ENVIRONMENT & CONCEPTS
CHAPTER 11

Example: Net present value

Hillsdale Company purchased a machine for $480,000. The machine has a useful life of six years and no salvage value. Straight-line depreciation is to be used. The machine is expected to generate cash flow from operations, net of income taxes, of $140,000 in each of the six years. Hillsdale's desired rate of return is 14 percent. Information on present value factors is as follows:

Period	Present Value of $1 at 14%	Present Value of an Ordinary Annuity of $1 at 14%
1	0.877	0.877
2	0.769	1.647
3	0.675	2.322
4	0.592	2.914
5	0.519	3.433
6	0.456	3.889

What is the net present value?
A. $63,840
B. $64,460
C. $218,880
D. $233,340

Solution:

The answer is B.

Present value of cash inflows: $140,000 × 3.889	$544,460
Less: initial investment	480,000
Net present value	$64,460

INVENTORY MANAGEMENT

A. There are several costs associated with inventories. Some costs result from carrying too much inventory and some result from not carrying enough inventory. The costs associated with maintaining quantities of inventory are referred to as carrying costs. Costs of maintaining low levels of inventory include the costs associated with running out of inventory, stockout costs, and the cost of placing and receiving orders.

1. Stockout costs are composed primarily of lost revenues. When a company can backorder inventory items, insufficient inventory will not necessarily result in lost sales. The company will simply fill the order when the inventory becomes available. As a result, the stockout cost will be low and a company will be willing to carry low levels of inventory. Other companies may not be able to backorder

and will lose sales as a result of insufficient quantities of inventory on hand. These companies will tend to carry greater quantities of inventories.

2. Carrying costs include costs such as insurance on inventories, interest that would be earned if the amounts invested in inventories could be redirected, costs of handling and storage, costs of spoilage and obsolescence, and any other costs that may be associated with large quantities of inventory.

    a. Carrying costs are usually expressed as a cost of carrying one unit in inventory for one year.

    b. When carrying costs for a company are relatively high, the company will tend to carry lower levels of inventory than when carrying costs are relatively low.

3. Order costs are those costs associated with placing an order for inventory. When order costs are high, the company will wish to place fewer orders and will carry higher levels of inventory. The inverse is true when order costs are low. They include the costs of:

    a. The purchasing department.

    b. Receiving inventory.

    c. Putting the inventory into stock.

B. When a company can determine the average costs of carrying one unit of inventory for one year (S), knows the cost of placing an order (P), and knows the annual demand for inventory expressed in units (A), it can determine the most economical amount of inventory that should be ordered each time inventory is ordered. This is referred to as the *economic order quantity* (EOQ) and is computed with the following formula:

$$EOQ = \sqrt{\frac{2AP}{S}}$$

This formula may be used to compute the optimum size of a purchase order or of a production run.

C. When a company orders inventory according to the economic order quantity, the total cost associated with inventory will be at its lowest. If actual demand should be lower than the demand used to compute the economic order quantity, total costs associated with inventories may be lower, but by recomputing the economic order quantity, they could be reduced even further.

D. The cost of placing orders is computed by taking the annual demand and dividing by the economic order quantity to determine the number of orders to be placed. This number is multiplied by the cost of placing one order.

STUDY MANUAL – BUSINESS ENVIRONMENT & CONCEPTS
CHAPTER 11

E. The cost of carrying units is computed by multiplying the average inventory, usually one-half of the economic order quantity plus safety stock, if any, by the cost of carrying one unit in inventory for one year.

F. A company must be able to determine when to place an order for inventory, called the *reorder point.* The reorder point is:

1. The point in time when there is enough inventory left to meet the demand for the period from the time an order is placed to the time it is received.

2. Computed by multiplying the average daily demand by the average lead time.

G. When a company has a high stockout cost, it may carry a safety stock. It will order goods when inventory is equal to the reorder point plus the safety stock.

1. Safety stock will be the excess inventory required in case the lead time exceeds the average lead time or the daily demand exceeds the average daily demand.

2. Safety stock is computed by multiplying the maximum lead time by the maximum daily demand and subtracting from the amount computed as the normal reorder point.

3. When a company maintains a safety stock, the reorder point will be increased by the amount of safety stock.

4. The reorder point may be calculated as the maximum lead time multiplied by the maximum daily demand.

Example: Safety stock and order point

The following information relates to Eagle Company's material A:

Annual usage in units	7,200
Working days per year	240
Normal lead time in working days	20
Maximum lead time in working days	45

Assuming that the units of material A will be required evenly throughout the year, the safety stock and reorder point would be:

	Safety stock	Reorder point
A.	600	750
B.	600	1,350
C.	750	600
D.	750	1,350

Solution:

The answer is D.

Maximum lead time = 45 days

Normal lead time = 20 days

Therefore, cushion time = 45 – 20, or 25 days

Average daily usage = 7,200/240 = 30

Safety stock = 25 × 30 = 750

Reorder point = 45 × 30 = 1,350

COSTS IN SHORT-TERM DECISION MAKING

The following costs are commonly found in decision-making questions on the CPA Exam.

A. Incremental or differential costs are the additional costs to purchase or manufacture one or more additional units. Incremental costs usually consist of variable costs, as, within the relevant range, fixed costs would be unchanged.

B. Opportunity costs are the benefits lost from rejecting the second-best option. Since opportunity costs are not actually incurred, they are not recorded in the accounting records. They are, however, relevant costs for decision making and should be considered in evaluating a proposed alternative course of action.

C. Sunk costs are past committed costs that are now irrevocable. They are not relevant to future decisions and should not be considered in an analysis, except for salvage value and possible tax effects relating to disposition of assets.

D. Relevant costs are expected future costs that will differ between alternatives. Irrelevant costs, on the other hand, are unaffected by the decision.

   1. Relevance is not an attribute of a particular cost.

   2. An identical cost may be relevant in one circumstance and irrelevant in another.

TYPES OF SHORT-TERM DECISIONS

A. Discontinuing a segment (product line). Quantitatively, a segment should be dropped if, by doing so, the reduction in costs exceeds the revenue lost. The qualitative factors include:

   1. The impact of discontinuing the segment on the rest of the business.

   2. Management's ability to use resources in an alternative manner.

       Often the elimination of a product line causes the sales of other lines to decrease. Both the qualitative and quantitative elements must be measured before arriving at a decision to drop a segment.

STUDY MANUAL – BUSINESS ENVIRONMENT & CONCEPTS
CHAPTER 11

The following example pertains to divisions. The same format could be followed for evaluating other types of segmenting, such as product lines or services provided.

Example: Discontinuing a segment

Large Corporation currently operates two divisions that had operating results for the year ended December 31, year 2, as follows:

	West Division	East Division
Sales	$600,000	$300,000
Variable costs	$310,000	$200,000
Contribution margin	$290,000	$100,000
Fixed costs for the division	$110,000	$70,000
Margin over direct costs	$180,000	$30,000
Allocated corporate costs	$90,000	$45,000
Operating income (loss)	$90,000	($15,000)

Since the East Division also sustained an operating loss during year 1, Large's president is considering the elimination of this division. Assume that the East Division's fixed costs could be avoided if the division was eliminated. If the East Division had been eliminated on January 1, year 2, Large Corporation's year 2 operating income would have been equal to what amount?

Solution

Decrease in revenue		$300,000
Cost savings:		
Variable costs	$200,000	
Fixed costs	$70,000	($270,000)
Decrease in Large Corporation's operating income		$30,000
Operating income before eliminating East Division (combined)		$75,000
Operating income if East Division is eliminated		$45,000

By eliminating the East Division, income would decrease from $75,000 ($90,000 - $15,000) to $45,000, a difference of $30,000. Another way to look at this is: The East Division has a margin over its direct costs of $30,000, which is available to cover corporate allocated costs. By eliminating the East Division, the West Division must cover all the allocated corporate costs. The company is better off by keeping the East Division as long as it contributes to the corporate allocated costs.

B. Sell or process further. Joint products are the result of a single production process that yields two or more products. Examples include the chemical, petroleum, and wood industries, as well as producers of cattle or dairy products.

Page 340   ©2007 Kaplan CPA Review

STUDY MANUAL – BUSINESS ENVIRONMENT & CONCEPTS
CHAPTER 11

1. If external markets exist for semifinished products, the manufacturer must decide which products are more profitable to sell at the split-off point and which ones should be processed further before sale.

2. The split-off point is that point where the separate products emerge from the joint process.

3. The costs incurred before split-off are irrelevant in determining whether or not the products should be processed further. They need to be considered only in determining whether or not the entire process should be undertaken.

4. Incremental analysis provides the basis for solving the "sell or process further" problem.

   a. If the additional revenue earned by processing further is greater than the additional cost, the product should be processed further.

   b. If the converse is true, the product should be sold at the split-off point.

Example: Sell or process further

The Prime Cut Meat Company produces three joint products—hamburger, steak, and roast beef—from a joint process. Total joint costs are equal to $43,000. Each of the three joint products can be (1) sold at the split-off point to a competing meat company (who will complete the necessary processing) or (2) finished by the Prime Cut Meat Company and sold to retailers. Relevant costs and revenues appear below:

Product	Total Sales Value at Split-Off	Total Additional Processing Costs	Total Final Sales Value
Hamburger	$10,000	$2,000	$14,000
Steak	$14,000	$3,000	$20,000
Roast Beef	$13,000	$6,000	$17,000

Which products should be sold at the split-off point and which products should be processed further?

STUDY MANUAL – BUSINESS ENVIRONMENT & CONCEPTS
CHAPTER 11

Solution:

	Hamburger	Steak	Roast Beef
Incremental revenue	$4,000 (1)	$6,000 (2)	$4,000 (3)
Incremental cost	$2,000	$3,000	$6,000
Incremental income	$2,000	$3,000	
Decremental income			($2,000)

Computations

Total final sales value	$14,000	$20,000	$17,000
Total sales value of split-off	–$10,000	–$14,000	–$13,000
Incremental revenue	$4,000(1)	$6,000(2)	$4,000(3)

Hamburger and steak should be processed further while roast beef should be sold at the split-off point.

C. Special orders: accept or reject. In addition to producing and selling on a regular basis, a firm may be in a position to accept a special one-time order for its products at below normal price.

1. Fixed costs generally are not considered because they are fully absorbed by the normal output.

2. The fixed costs that are considered relevant should be considered in the analysis only when expected to change presently or in the future because of the specific decision to accept the additional business.

3. If the special order increases the activity level to the point of requiring additional supervision, plant, equipment, insurance, or property taxes, those fixed costs are relevant. Generally, a special order should be accepted if the following three conditions occur:

   a. The incremental revenue exceeds the incremental cost of the order.

   b. The facilities used are idle and have no other, more profitable, use.

   c. The order does not disrupt the market for the firm's regular output.

Example: Special order

Speedie Company, which manufactures sneakers, has enough idle capacity available to accept a special order of 20,000 pairs of sneakers at $6 a pair. The normal selling price is $10 a pair. Variable manufacturing costs are $4.50 a pair, and fixed manufacturing costs are $1.50 a pair. Speedie will not incur any selling expenses as a result of the special order. What would the effect on operating income be if the special order could be accepted without affecting normal sales?

Page 342   ©2007 Kaplan CPA Review

STUDY MANUAL – BUSINESS ENVIRONMENT & CONCEPTS
CHAPTER 11

Solution

Incremental sales (20,000 @ $6.00)	$120,000
Incremental costs (20,000 @ $4.50)	$90,000
Incremental income	$30,000

D. Make or buy decisions. When idle equipment, space, and/or labor exist, management is presented with the choice of producing parts internally rather than purchasing them. This choice is known as the *make or buy decision.*

1. Frequently, the manufactured components can be produced at lower incremental costs than those charged by external suppliers.

2. If a firm can produce as economically as potential suppliers, it can save the profit a supplier would normally earn.

   a. The costs of the "make" alternative include the incremental manufacturing costs such as direct labor, direct materials, and variable overhead.

   b. Allocated fixed costs that remain unchanged in total when the parts are manufactured are irrelevant to make or buy decisions. They will be incurred regardless of whether the component is bought or made.

   c. If an additional capital investment is made, the costs and the timing of the cash flows must also be considered.

3. Another quantitative consideration to be examined is the possibility of alternative uses for the idle capacity.

   a. New products, instead of component parts, could be manufactured and the contribution margin from these products should be considered the opportunity costs of making the components.

   b. Alternatively, if unused equipment or space were leased or rented, the resulting profit would then be regarded as the opportunity cost of the "make" decision.

Example: Make or buy

Plainfield Company manufactures Part G for use in its production cycle. The cost per unit for 10,000 units of Part G are as follows:

Direct materials	$3
Direct labor	$15
Variable overhead	$6
Fixed overhead	$8
	$32

Verona Company has offered to sell Plainfield 10,000 units of Part G for $30 per unit. If Plainfield accepts Verona's offer, the released facilities could be used to save $45,000 in

---

©2007 Kaplan CPA Review

STUDY MANUAL – BUSINESS ENVIRONMENT & CONCEPTS

CHAPTER 11

relevant costs in the manufacture of Part H. In addition, $5 per unit of the fixed overhead applied to Part G would be totally eliminated. What alternative is more desirable and by what amount is it more desirable?

Cost to Manufacture Part G

Direct materials	$3	
Direct labor	$15	
Variable overhead	$6	
Fixed overhead	$5 (portion eliminated if bought)	
Per-unit	$29 × 10,000 =	$290,000
Opportunity cost		$45,000
Total cost to manufacture		$335,000

Cost to Buy Part G

Purchase price 10,000 × $30/unit	$300,000
Savings if Part G is bought	$35,000

RETURN ON INVESTMENT

After company divisions have been established and the related authorities and responsibilities assigned, it is vital that an adequate system be developed for measuring the performance of both the divisions and the division managers.

There are many approaches to an evaluation program. Their selection depends on the needs of the enterprise and the wishes of management. For example, should performance be gauged in terms of net income, net sales, or net income in relation to investment? No one answer will suit the needs of all companies. However, one of the most common methods of performance measurement in use is the return on investment (ROI).

A. The return on investment or return on capital method is used to measure the performance of borrowers. The rate of return on investment for the total company is usually computed by dividing net income by total assets. Alternatives to total assets may be plant investment, invested capital, or capital employed.

B. The ROI method has many important advantages over most other methods. It is simple to compute and can be used to measure and compare divisional or company performance, returns on competing companies, returns on competing capital projects, and many other factors, thereby permitting management to select the most favorable option from alternatives.

STUDY MANUAL – BUSINESS ENVIRONMENT & CONCEPTS
CHAPTER 11

C. A simple way to express ROI is with an equation. The ROI equation is generally shown in two parts, the investment turnover and the earnings ratio or profit margin. The investment turnover is stated as:

$$\text{investment turnover} = \frac{\text{sales}}{\text{total assets}}$$

The earnings ratio shows the sales-expense relationship and is stated as:

$$\text{earnings ratio} = \frac{\text{net income}}{\text{sales}}$$

1. Investment turnover indicates management's efficiency in using available assets to generate sales volume and earnings.

2. The earnings ratio indicates the percentage of profit in each dollar of sales.

3. The ROI equation is made up of both of the above components:

ROI = Investment turnover × Earnings ratio

4. Upon superficial examination, it appears that the equation could be simplified by canceling out sales in the two components. If this were done, however, the importance of the two separate variables, investment turnover and earnings ratio, would be lost.

Example: ROI

The Truhlar Company wishes to measure its operations for the year ended 20X4. Using the following data, compute the investment turnover and the earnings ratio:

Net income (25% of sales): $30,000
ROI: 15%

residual income = net income − (investment × imputed interest rate)
$60,000 − ($400,000 × 296) = $60,000 − $48,000 = $12,000

Solution

$$\text{Sales} = \frac{\$30,000 \text{ net income}}{25\%} = \$120,000$$

$$\text{Plant investment} = \frac{\text{net income}}{\text{ROI}} = \frac{\$30,000}{15\%} = \$200,000$$

$$\text{Investment turnover} = \frac{\text{sales}}{\text{plant investment}} = \frac{\$120,000}{\$200,000} = 60\%$$

$$\text{Earnings ratio} = \frac{\text{net income}}{\text{sales}} = \frac{\$30,000}{\$120,000} = 25\%$$

©2007 Kaplan CPA Review

Page 345

STUDY MANUAL – BUSINESS ENVIRONMENT & CONCEPTS
CHAPTER 11

D. Residual income. One of the stated shortcomings of ROI is its emphasis on rate of return rather than on absolute dollars. To overcome this, some companies use a target rate or imputed interest rate, and the excess of net income above this figure is considered the residual income. The formula for residual income is:

Residual income = Net income – (Investment × Imputed interest rate)

1. An important advantage of this method is that a particular division may expand as long as it earns a rate in excess of the charge for invested capital (imputed interest).

2. Under this method, managers generally concentrate on increasing dollars rather than improving only the ROI percentage rate.

STUDY MANUAL – BUSINESS ENVIRONMENT & CONCEPTS
CHAPTER 11

QUESTIONS: COST ACCOUNTING: OTHER AREAS

1. At December 31, year 4, Zar Co. had a machine with an original cost of $84,000, accumulated depreciation of $60,000, and an estimated salvage value of zero. On December 31, year 4, Zar was considering the purchase of a new machine having a five-year life, costing $120,000, and having an estimated salvage value of $20,000 at the end of five years. In its decision concerning the possible purchase of the new machine, how much should Zar consider as sunk cost at December 31, year 4?
   A. $4,000
   B. $120,000
   C. $100,000
   D. $24,000

2. What is the normal effect on the numbers of cost pools and allocation bases when an activity-based cost (ABC) system replaces a traditional cost system?

	Cost polls	Allocation bases
A.	No effect	No effect
B.	Increase	Increase
C.	Increase	No effect
D.	No effect	Increase

3. In an activity-based costing system, what should be used to assign a department's manufacturing overhead costs to products produced in varying lot sizes?
   A. A single cause-and-effect relationship
   B. A product's ability to bear cost allocations
   C. Multiple cause-and-effect relationships
   D. Relative net sales values of the products

4. Book Co. uses the activity-based costing approach for cost allocation and product costing purposes. Printing, cutting, and binding functions make up the manufacturing process. Machinery and equipment are arranged in operating cells that produce a complete product starting with raw materials. Which of the following are characteristics of Book's activity-based costing approach?

   I. Cost drivers are used as a basis for cost allocation.
   II. Costs are accumulated by department or function for purposes of product costing.
   III. Activities that do not add value to the product are identified and reduced to the extent possible.

   A. I and II.
   B. I and III.
   C. II and III.
   D. I only.

©2007 Kaplan CPA Review

Page 347

STUDY MANUAL – BUSINESS ENVIRONMENT & CONCEPTS
CHAPTER 11

5.   The benefits of a just-in-time system for raw materials usually include
   A. maximization of the standard delivery quantity, thereby lessening the paperwork for each delivery.
   B. decrease in the number of deliveries required to maintain production.
   C. elimination of nonvalue-adding operations.
   D. increase in the number of suppliers, thereby ensuring competitive bidding.

6.   When a manager is concerned with monitoring total cost, total revenue, and net profit conditioned upon the level of productivity, an accountant would normally recommend:

	Flexible budgeting	Standard costing
A.	Yes	No
B.	Yes	Yes
C.	No	Yes
D.	No	No

Use the following information to answer Questions 7 through 10.

	Fabrication	Assembly	General Factory Administration	Factory Maintenance	Factory Cafeteria
Direct-labor costs	$1,950,000	$2,050,000	$90,000	$82,100	$87,000
Direct-material costs	$3,130,000	$950,000	–	$65,000	$91,000
Manufacturing-overhead	$1,650,000	$1,850,000	$70,000	$56,100	$62,000
Direct-labor hours	562,500	437,500	31,000	27,000	42,000
Number of employees	280	200	12	8	20
Square-footage occupied	88,000	72,000	1,750	2,000	4,800

The Parker Manufacturing Company has two production departments (fabrication and assembly) and three service departments (general factory administration, factory maintenance, and factory cafeteria.) A summary of costs and other data for each department prior to allocation of service-department costs for the year ended June 30, 2006, appears above.

The costs of the general-factory-administration department, factory-maintenance department, and factory cafeteria are allocated on the basis of direct-labor hours, square-footage occupied, and number of employees, respectively. There are no manufacturing-overhead variances. Round all final calculations to the nearest dollar.

Page 348   ©2007 Kaplan CPA Review

7. Assuming that Parker elects to distribute service-department costs directly to production departments without interservice department cost allocation, the amount of factory-maintenance department costs which would be allocated to the fabrication department would be
    A. $0.
    B. $111,760.
    C. $106,091.
    D. $91,440.

8. Assuming the same method of allocation as in item 1, the amount of general-factory-administration department costs which would be allocated to the assembly department would be
    A. $0.
    B. $63,636.
    C. $70,000.
    D. $90,000.

9. Assuming that Parker elects to distribute service-department costs to other service departments (starting with the service department with the greatest total costs) as well as the production departments, the amount of factory-cafeteria department costs which would be allocated to the factory-maintenance department would be (Note: Once a service department's costs have been reallocated, no subsequent service-department costs are recirculated back to it.)
    A. $0.
    B. $96,000.
    C. $3,840.
    D. $6,124.

10. Assuming the same method of allocation as in item 3, the amount of factory-maintenance department costs which would be allocated to the factory cafeteria would be
    A. $0.
    B. $5,787.
    C. $5,856.
    D. $148,910.

11. Which measures would be useful in evaluating the performance of a manufacturing system?

    I.   Throughput time.
    II. Total setup time for machines/Total production time.
    III. Number of rework units/Total number of units completed.

    A. I and II only.
    B. II and III only.
    C. I and III only.
    D. I, II, and III.

STUDY MANUAL – BUSINESS ENVIRONMENT & CONCEPTS
CHAPTER 11

12. Gram Co. develops computer programs to meet customers' special requirements. How should Gram categorize payments to employees who develop these programs?

	Direct costs	Value-adding costs
A.	Yes	Yes
B.	Yes	No
C.	No	No
D.	No	Yes

13. Spoilage occurring during a manufacturing process can be considered normal or abnormal. The proper accounting for each of these costs is

	Normal	Abnormal
A.	Product	Period
B.	Product	Product
C.	Period	Product
D.	Period	Period

14. In developing a predetermined factory overhead application rate for use in a process costing system, which of the following could be used in the numerator and denominator?

	Numerator	Denominator
A.	Actual factory overhead	Actual machine hours
B.	Actual factory overhead	Estimated machine hours
C.	Estimated factory overhead	Actual machine hours
D.	Estimated factory overhead	Estimated machine hours

15. Following are Mill Co.'s production costs for October:

Direct materials	$100,000
Direct labor	90,000
Factory overhead	4,000

What amount of costs should be traced to specific products in the production process?
A. $194,000.
B. $190,000.
C. $100,000.
D. $90,000.

16. Direct labor cost is a

	Conversion cost	Prime cost
A.	No	No
B.	No	Yes
C.	Yes	Yes
D.	Yes	No

Page 350   ©2007 Kaplan CPA Review

STUDY MANUAL – BUSINESS ENVIRONMENT & CONCEPTS
CHAPTER 11

17. What is the normal effect on the numbers of cost pools and allocation bases when an activity-based cost (ABC) system replaces a traditional cost system?

	Cost pools	Allocation bases
A.	No effect	No effect
B.	Increase	No effect
C.	No effect	Increase
D.	Increase	Increase

18. In an activity-based costing system, what should be used to assign a department's manufacturing overhead costs to products produced in varying lot sizes?
    A. A single cause and effect relationship.
    B. Multiple cause and effect relationships.
    C. Relative net sales values of the products.
    D. A product's ability to bear cost allocations.

19. A direct labor overtime premium should be charged to a specific job when the overtime is caused by the:
    A. Increased overall level of activity.
    B. Customer's requirement for early completion of job.
    C. Management's failure to include the job in the production schedule.
    D. Management's requirement that the job be completed before the annual factory vacation closure.

20. Baker Co., a manufacturer, had inventories at the beginning and end of its current year as follows:

	Beginning	End
Raw materials	$22,000	$30,000
Work in process	40,000	48,000
Finished goods	25,000	18,000

During the year the following costs and expenses were incurred:

Raw materials purchased	$300,000
Direct-labor cost	120,000
Indirect factory labor	60,000
Taxes and depreciation on factory building	20,000
Salesmen's salaries	40,000
Office salaries	24,000
Utilities (60% applicable to factory, 20% to salesroom, 20% to office)	50,000

Baker's cost of goods sold for the year is:
    A. $514,000.
    B. $521,000.
    C. $522,000.
    D. $539,000.

©2007 Kaplan CPA Review   Page 351

STUDY MANUAL – BUSINESS ENVIRONMENT & CONCEPTS
CHAPTER 11

21. Nile Co.'s cost allocation and product costing procedures follow activity-based costing principles. Activities have been identified and classified as being either value-adding or nonvalue-adding as to each product. Which of the following activities, used in Nile production process, is nonvalue-adding?
    A. Design engineering activity.
    B. Heat treatment activity.
    C. Drill press activity.
    D. Raw materials storage activity.

22. Book Co. uses the activity-based costing approach for cost allocation and product costing purposes. Printing, cutting, and binding functions make up the manufacturing process. Machinery and equipment are arranged in operating cells that produce a complete product starting with raw materials. Which of the following are characteristics of Book's activity-based costing approach?

    I. Cost drivers are used as a basis for cost allocation.
    II. Costs are accumulated by department or function for purposes of product costing.
    III. Activities that do not add value to the product are identified and reduced to the extent possible.

    A. I only.
    B. I and II.
    C. I and III.
    D. II and III.

23. The benefits of a just-in-time system for raw materials usually include:
    A. Elimination of nonvalue adding operations.
    B. Increase in the number of suppliers, thereby ensuring competitive bidding.
    C. Maximization of the standard delivery quantity, thereby lessening the paperwork for each delivery.
    D. Decrease in the number of deliveries required to maintain production.

24. Fab Co. manufactures textiles. Among Fab's manufacturing costs were the following salaries and wages:

Loom operators	$120,000
Factory foremen	45,000
Machine mechanics	30,000

    What was the amount of Fab's direct labor?
    A. $195,000.
    B. $165,000.
    C. $150,000.
    D. $120,000.

Page 352   ©2007 Kaplan CPA Review

25. Wages paid to factory machine operators of a manufacturing plant are an element of:

	Prime cost	Conversion cost
A.	No	No
B.	No	Yes
C.	Yes	No
D.	Yes	Yes

26. Property taxes on a manufacturing plant are an element of:

	Conversion cost	Period cost
A.	Yes	No
B.	Yes	Yes
C.	No	Yes
D.	No	No

27. In process 2, material G is added when a batch is 60 percent complete. Ending work-in-process units, which are 50 percent complete, would be included in the computation of equivalent units for:

	Conversion cost	Material G
A.	Yes	No
B.	No	Yes
C.	No	No
D.	Yes	Yes

28. A flexible budget is appropriate for a (an):

	Administrative budget	Marketing budget
A.	Yes	Yes
B.	Yes	No
C.	No	No
D.	No	Yes

29. Nonfinancial performance measures are important to engineering and operations managers in assessing the quality levels of their products. Which of the following indicators can be used to measure product quality?

I.   Returns and allowances.
II. Number and types of customer complaints.
III. Production cycle time.

A. I and II only.
B. I and III only.
C. II and III only.
D. I, II, and III.

STUDY MANUAL – BUSINESS ENVIRONMENT & CONCEPTS
CHAPTER 11

30. Birk Co. uses a job order cost system. The following debits (credit) appeared in Birk's work-in-process account for the month of April:

April	Description	Amount
1	Balance	$4,000
30	Direct materials	24,000
30	Direct labor	16,000
30	Factory overhead	12,800
30	To finished goods	(48,000)

Birk applies overhead to production at a predetermined rate of 80% of direct labor cost. Job No. 5, the only job still in process on April 30 has been charged with direct labor of $2,000. What was the amount of direct materials charged to Job No. 5?
A. $3,000
B. $5,200
C. $8,800
D. $24,000

31. The flexible budget for a producing department may include:

	Direct labor	Factory overhead
a.	No	Yes
b.	No	No
c.	Yes	No
d.	Yes	Yes

32. Boa Corp. distributes service department overhead costs directly to producing departments without allocation to the other service department. Information for the month of June is as follows:

	Service Departments	
	Maintenance	Utilities
Overhead costs incurred	$20,000	$10,000
Service provided to departments:		
Maintenance		10%
Utilities	20%	
Producing-A	40%	30%
Producing-B	40%	60%
Totals	100%	100%

The amount of maintenance department costs distributed to Producing-A department for June was:
A. $8,000
B. $8,800
C. $10,000
D. $11,000

Page 354   ©2007 Kaplan CPA Review

33. In manufacturing its products for the month of March, Elk Co. incurred normal spoilage of $5,000 and abnormal spoilage of $9,000. How much spoilage cost should Elk charge as a period cost for the month of March?
   A. $0
   B. $5,000
   C. $9,000
   D. $14,000

34. In developing a factory overhead application rate for use in a process costing system, which of the following could be used in the numerator?
   A. Actual direct labor hours.
   B. Estimated direct labor hours.
   C. Actual factory overhead costs.
   D. Estimated factory overhead costs.

35. Parat College allocates support department costs to its individual schools using the step method. Information for May is as follows:

	Support departments	
	Maintenance	Power
Costs incurred	$99,000	$54,000
Service percentages provided to:		
Maintenance	-	10%
Power	20%	-
School of Education	30%	20%
School of Technology	50%	70%
	100%	100%

   What is the amount of May support department costs allocated to the School of Education?
   A. $40,500
   B. $42,120
   C. $46,100
   D. $49,125

36. Each of the following is a method by which to allocate joint costs except
   A. Relative sales value.
   B. Relative profitability.
   C. Relative weight, volume, or linear measure.
   D. Average unit cost.

STUDY MANUAL – BUSINESS ENVIRONMENT & CONCEPTS
CHAPTER 11

Use the following information to answer Questions 37 and 38.

Forward, Inc., manufactures products P, Q, and R from a joint process. Additional information is as follows:

		Product		
	P	Q	R	Total
Units produced	4,000	2,000	1,000	7,000
Joint cost	$36,000	?	?	$60,000
Sales value at split- off	?	?	$15,000	$100,000
Additional costs if processed further	$ 7,000	$ 5,000	$ 3,000	$ 15,000
Sales value if processed further	$70,000	$30,000	$20,000	$120,000

37. Assuming that joint costs are allocated using the relative-sales-value-at-split-off approach, what were the joint costs allocated to products Q and R?
    A. $12,000 for Q and $12,000 for R.
    B. $14,400 for Q and $9,600 for R.
    C. $15,000 for Q and $9,000 for R.
    D. $16,000 for Q and $8,000 for R.

38. Assuming that joint costs are allocated using the relative-sales-value-at-split-off approach, what was the sales value at split-off for product P?
    A. $58,333.
    B. $59,500.
    C. $60,000.
    D. $63,000.

39. A processing department produces joint products Ajac and Bjac, each of which incurs separable production costs after split-off. Information concerning a batch produced at a $60,000 joint cost before split-off follows:

Product	Separable costs	Sales value
Ajac	$8,000	$ 80,000
Bjac	22,000	40,000
Total	$30,000	$120,000

    What is the joint cost assigned to Ajac if costs are assigned using the relative net realizable value?
    A. $16,000
    B. $40,000
    C. $48,000
    D. $52,000

Page 356   ©2007 Kaplan CPA Review

STUDY MANUAL – BUSINESS ENVIRONMENT & CONCEPTS

CHAPTER 11

40. Kode Co. manufactures a major product that gives rise to a by-product called May. May's only separable cost is a $1 selling cost when a unit is sold for $4. Kode accounts for May's sales by deducting the $3 net amount from the cost of goods sold of the major product. There are no inventories. If Kode were to change its method of accounting for May from a by-product to a joint product, what would be the effect on Kode's overall gross margin?
    A. No effect.
    B. Gross margin increases by $1 for each unit of May sold.
    C. Gross margin increases by $3 for each unit of May sold.
    D. Gross margin increases by $4 for each unit of May sold.

41. The method of accounting for joint-product costs that will produce the same gross-profit rate for all products is the
    A. Relative sales-value method.
    B. Physical-measure method.
    C. Actual-costing method.
    D. Services-received method.

42. Ohio Corporation manufactures liquid chemicals A and B from a joint process. Joint costs are allocated on the basis of relative-sales-value at split-off. It costs $4,560 to process 500 gallons of product A and 1,000 gallons of product B to the split-off point. The sales value at split-off is $10 per gallon for product A and $14 for product B. Product B requires an additional process beyond split-off at a cost of $1 per gallon before it can be sold. What is Ohio's cost to produce 1,000 gallons of product B?
    A. $3,360.
    B. $3,660.
    C. $4,040.
    D. $4,360.

43. Which of the following statements best describes a by-product?
    A. A product that is produced from material that would otherwise be scrap.
    B. A product that has a lower unit selling price than the main product.
    C. A product created along with the main product whose sales value does not cover its cost of production.
    D. A product that usually produces a small amount of revenue when compared to the main product revenue.

44. At the split-off point, products may be salable or may require further processing in order to be salable. Which of the following have both of these characteristics?

	By-products	Joint products
A.	No	No
B.	No	Yes
C.	Yes	No
D.	Yes	Yes

©2007 Kaplan CPA Review

Page 357

STUDY MANUAL – BUSINESS ENVIRONMENT & CONCEPTS
CHAPTER 11

45. Which of the following is (are) acceptable regarding the allocation of joint product cost to a by-product?

	None allocated	Some portion allocated
A.	Acceptable	Not acceptable
B.	Acceptable	Acceptable
C.	Not acceptable	Acceptable
D.	Not acceptable	Not acceptable

46. For purposes of allocating joint costs to joint products, the sales price at point of sale, reduced by cost to complete after split-off, is assumed to be equal to the
   A. Joint costs.
   B. Total costs.
   C. Net sales value at split-off.
   D. Sales price less a normal profit margin at point of sale.

47. The diagram below represents the production and sales relationships of joint products P and Q. Joint costs are incurred until split-off, then separable costs are incurred in refining each product. Market values of P and Q at split-off are used to allocate joint costs.

   If the market value of P at split-off increases and all other costs and selling prices remain unchanged, then the gross margin of

	P	Q
A.	Increases	Decreases
B.	Increases	Increases
C.	Decreases	Decreases
D.	Decreases	Increases

48. Actual sales values at split-off point for joint products Y and Z are not known. For purposes of allocating joint costs to products Y and Z, the relative sales value at split-off method is used. An increase in the costs beyond split-off occurs for product Z, while those of product Y remain constant. If the selling prices of finished products Y and Z remain constant, the percentage of the total joint costs allocated to Product Y and Product Z would
   A. Decrease for Product Y and increase for Product Z.
   B. Decrease for Product Y and Product Z.
   C. Increase for Product Y and decrease for Product Z.
   D. Increase for Product Y and Product Z.

Page 358 ©2007 Kaplan CPA Review

STUDY MANUAL – BUSINESS ENVIRONMENT & CONCEPTS

CHAPTER 11

Use the following information to answer Questions 49 through 51.

As the accounting consultant for Leslie Company you have compiled data on the day-to-day demand rate from Leslie's customers for Product A and the lead time to receive Product A from its supplier. The data are summarized in the following probability tables:

Demand for Product A

Unit Demand per Day	Probability of Occurrence
0	0.45
1	0.15
2	0.30
3	0.10
	1.00

Lead Time for Product A

Lead Time in Days	Probability of Occurrence
1	0.40
2	0.35
3	0.25
	1.00

Leslie is able to deliver Product A to its customers the same day that Product A is received from its supplier. All units of Product A demanded but not available, due to a stock-out, are backordered and are filled immediately when a new shipment arrives.

49. The probability of the demand for Product A being nine units during a three-day lead time for delivery from the supplier is
   A. .00025.
   B. .10.
   C. .025.
   D. .25.

50. If Leslie reorders 10 units of Product A when its inventory level is 10 units, the number of days during a 360-day year that Leslie will experience a stock-out of Product A is:
   A. 0.75 days.
   B. 36 days.
   C. 10 days.
   D. 0 days.

©2007 Kaplan CPA Review

Page 359

STUDY MANUAL – BUSINESS ENVIRONMENT & CONCEPTS
CHAPTER 11

51.   Leslie has developed an inventory model based on the probability tables and desires a solution for minimizing total annual inventory costs. Included in inventory costs are the costs of holding Product A, ordering and receiving Product A, and incurring stockouts of Product A. The solution would state:
   A. At what inventory level to reorder and how many units to reorder.
   B. Either at what inventory level to reorder or how many units to reorder.
   C. How many units to reorder but not at what inventory level to reorder.
   D. At what inventory level to reorder but not how many units to reorder.

52.   A sales office of Helms, Inc., has developed the following probability distribution for daily sales of a perishable product.

X (Units Sold)	P (Sales = X)
100	.2
150	.5
200	.2
250	.1

   The product is restocked at the start of each day. If the Company desires a 90% service level in satisfying sales demand, the initial stock balance for each day should be
   A. 250.
   B. 160.
   C. 200.
   D. 150.

53.   Your client wants your advice on which of two alternatives he should choose. One alternative is to sell an investment now for $10,000. Another alternative is to hold the investment three days after which he can sell it for a certain selling price based on the following probabilities:

Selling Price	Probability
$5,000	.4
$8,000	.2
$12,000	.3
$30,000	.1

   Using probability theory, which of the following is the most reasonable statement?
   A. Hold the investment three days because the expected value of holding exceeds the current selling price.
   B. Hold the investment three days because of the chance of getting $30,000 for it.
   C. Sell the investment now because the current selling price exceeds the expected value of holding.
   D. Sell the investment now because there is a 60% chance that the selling price will fall in three days.

54. To assist in an investment decision, Gift Co. selected the most likely sales volume from several possible outcomes. Which of the following attributes would that selected sales volume reflect?
A. The mid-point of the range.
B. The median.
C. The greatest probability.
D. The expected value.

55. Dough Distributors has decided to increase its daily muffin purchases by 100 boxes. A box of muffins costs $2 and sells for $3 through regular stores. Any boxes not sold through regular stores are sold through Dough's thrift store for $1. Dough assigns the following probabilities to selling additional boxes:

Additional sales	Probability
60	0.6
100	0.4

What is the expected value of Dough's decision to buy 100 additional boxes of muffins?
A. $28.
B. $40.
C. $52.
D. $68.

56. Joe Neil, CPA, has among his clientele a charitable organization that has a legal permit to conduct games of chance for fund-raising purposes. Neil's client derives its profit from admission fees and the sale of refreshments, and therefore wants to "break even" on the games of chance. In one of these games, the player draws one card from a standard deck of 52 cards. A player drawing any one of four "queens" wins $5, and a player drawing any one of 13 "hearts" wins $2. Neil is asked to compute the price that should be charged per draw, so that the total amount paid out for winning draws can be expected to equal the total amount received from all draws. Which one of the following equations should Neil use to compute the price (P)?

A. $5 - 2 = \dfrac{35}{52}P$

B. $\dfrac{4}{52}(5) + \dfrac{13}{52}(2) = \dfrac{35}{52}P$

C. $\dfrac{4}{52}(5-P) + \dfrac{13}{52}(2-P) = P$

D. $\dfrac{4}{52}(5) + \dfrac{13}{52}(2) = P$

STUDY MANUAL – BUSINESS ENVIRONMENT & CONCEPTS
CHAPTER 11

57. The following information pertains to three shipping terminals operated by Krag Co.:

Terminal	Percentage of cargo handled	Percentage of error
Land	50	2
Air	40	4
Sea	10	14

Krag's internal auditor randomly selects one set of shipping documents, ascertaining that the set selected contains an error. The probability that the error occurred in the Land Terminal is
A. 2%
B. 10%
C. 25%
D. 50%

58. Which of the following may be used to estimate how inventory warehouse costs are affected by both the number of shipments and the weight of materials handled?
A. Economic order quantity analysis.
B. Probability analysis.
C. Correlation analysis.
D. Multiple regression analysis.

59. A quantitative technique used to make predictions or estimates of the value of a dependent variable from given values of an independent variable(s) is
A. Linear programming.
B. Regression analysis.
C. Trend analysis.
D. Queuing theory.

60. Your client, a retail store, is interested in the relationship between sales (independent variable) and theft losses (dependent variable). Using the proper formula, you compute the coefficient of correlation at 0.95. What can you definitely conclude about these factors (sales and theft losses)?
A. An increase in sales causes an increase in theft losses.
B. Movement of these factors is in opposite directions.
C. Movement of these factors is entirely unrelated.
D. Movement of these factors is in the same direction.

61. Multiple regression analysis involves the use of

	Dependent variables	Independent variables
a.	One	More than one
b.	More than one	More than one
c.	More than one	One
d.	One	One

Page 362   ©2007 Kaplan CPA Review

62. What is the appropriate range for the coefficient of correlation (r)?
    A. $0 \backslash r \backslash 1$.
    B. $-1 \backslash r \backslash 1$.
    C. $-100 \backslash r \backslash 100$.
    D. $-infinity \backslash r \backslash infinity$.

63. Multiple regression analysis
    A. Establishes a cause and effect relationship.
    B. Is not a sampling technique.
    C. Involves the use of independent variables only.
    D. Produces measures of probable error.

64. Multiple regression differs from simple regression in that it
    A. Provides an estimated constant term.
    B. Has more dependent variables.
    C. Allows the computation of the coefficient of determination.
    D. Has more independent variables.

65. Which of the following tables should be used to calculate the amount of the equal periodic payments which would be equivalent to an outlay of $3,000 at the time of the last payment?
    A. Amount of 1.
    B. Amount of an annuity of 1.
    C. Present value of an annuity of 1.
    D. Present value of 1.

66. Which of the following tables would show the largest value for an interest rate of 5% for six periods?
    A. Amount of 1 at Compound Interest.
    B. Present Value of 1 at Compound Interest.
    C. Amount of Annuity of 1 per Period.
    D. Present Value of Annuity of 1 per Period.

67. Jarvis wants to invest equal semi-annual payments in order to have $10,000 at the end of 20 years. Assuming that Jarvis will earn interest at an annual rate of 6% compounded semiannually, how would the periodic payment be calculated?
    A. $10,000 divided by the future amount of an ordinary annuity of 40 payments of $1 each at an interest rate of 3% per period.
    B. $10,000 divided by the present value of an ordinary annuity of 40 payments of $1 each at an interest rate of 3% per period.
    C. The future amount of an ordinary annuity of 20 payments of $1 each at an interest rate of 6% per period divided into $10,000.
    D. The present value of an ordinary annuity of 40 payments of $1 each at an interest rate of 3% per period divided by $10,000.

STUDY MANUAL – BUSINESS ENVIRONMENT & CONCEPTS
CHAPTER 11

68. For the next 2 years, a lease is estimated to have an operating net cash inflow of $7,500 per annum, before adjusting for $5,000 per annum tax basis lease amortization, and a 40% tax rate. The present value of an ordinary annuity of $1 per year at 10% for 2 years is $1.74. What is the lease's after-tax present value using a 10% discount factor?
    A. $2,610
    B. $4,350
    C. $9,570
    D. $11,310

69. Scott, Inc., is planning to invest $120,000 in a ten-year project. Scott estimates that the annual cash inflow, net of income taxes, from this project will be $20,000. Scott's desired rate of return on investments of this type is 10%. Information on present value factors is as follows:

	At 10%	At 12%
Present value of $1 for ten periods	0.386	0.322
Present value of an annuity of $1 for ten periods	6.145	5.650

Scott's expected rate of return on this investment is
    A. Less than 10%, but more than 0%.
    B. 10%.
    C. Less than 12%, but more than 10%.
    D. 12%.

70. Residual income is income
    A. To which an imputed interest charge for invested capital is added.
    B. From which an imputed interest charge for invested capital is deducted.
    C. From which dividends are deducted.
    D. To which dividends are added.

Use the following information to answer Questions 71 and 72.

Tam Co. is negotiating for the purchase of equipment that would cost $100,000, with the expectation that $20,000 per year could be saved in after-tax cash costs if the equipment were acquired. The equipment's estimated useful life is 10 years, with no residual value, and would be depreciated by the straight-line method. Tam's predetermined minimum desired rate of return is 12%. Present value of an annuity of 1 at 12% for 10 periods is 5.65. Present value of 1 due in 10 periods at 12% is 0.322.

71. Net present value is
    A. $5,760
    B. $6,440
    C. $12,200
    D. $13,000

Page 364   ©2007 Kaplan CPA Review

STUDY MANUAL – BUSINESS ENVIRONMENT & CONCEPTS
CHAPTER 11

72.   Payback period is
        A. 4.0 years.
        B. 4.4 years.
        C. 4.5 years.
        D. 5.0 years.

73.   Which of the following capital budgeting techniques implicitly assumes that the
        cash flows are reinvested at the company's minimum required rate of return?

	Net present value	Internal rate of return
a.	Yes	Yes
b.	Yes	No
c.	No	Yes
d.	No	No

74.   Pole Co. is investing in a machine with a 3 year life. The machine is expected to
        reduce annual cash operating costs by $30,000 in each of the first 2 years and by
        $20,000 in year 3. Present values of an annuity of $1 at 14% are:

Period 1	0.88
2	1.65
3	2.32

        Using a 14% cost of capital, what is the present value of these future savings?
        A. $59,600
        B. $60,800
        C. $62,900
        D. $69,500

75.   The Polar Company is planning to purchase a new machine for $30,000. The
        payback period is expected to be five years. The new machine is expected to
        produce cash flow from operations, net of income taxes, of $7,000 a year in each
        of the next three years and $5,500 in the fourth year. Depreciation of $5,000 a
        year will be charged to income for each of the five years of the payback period.
        What is the amount of cash flow from operations, net of taxes, that the new
        machine is expected to produce in the last (fifth) year of the payback period?
        A. $1,000.
        B. $3,500.
        C. $5,000.
        D. $8,500.

76.   Under the internal rate of return capital budgeting technique, it is assumed that
        cash flows are reinvested at the
        A. Cost of capital.
        B. Hurdle rate of return.
        C. Rate earned by the investment.
        D. Payback rate.

©2007 Kaplan CPA Review
Page 365

STUDY MANUAL – BUSINESS ENVIRONMENT & CONCEPTS
CHAPTER 11

77. Lin Co. is buying machinery it expects will increase average annual operating income by $40,000. The initial increase in the required investment is $60,000, and the average increase in required investment is $30,000. To compute the accrual accounting rate of return, what amount should be used as the numerator in the ratio?
A. $20,000
B. $30,000
C. $40,000
D. $60,000

78. Doro Co. is considering the purchase of a $100,000 machine that is expected to result in a decrease of $25,000 per year in cash expenses after taxes. This machine, which has no residual value, has an estimated useful life of 10 years and will be depreciated on a straight-line basis. For this machine, the accounting rate of return based on initial investment would be
A. 10%
B. 15%
C. 25%
D. 35%

79. The discount rate (hurdle rate of return) must be determined in advance for the
A. Payback period method.
B. Time adjusted rate of return method.
C. Net present value method.
D. Internal rate of return method.

80. Neu Co. is considering the purchase of an investment that has a positive net present value based on Neu's 12% hurdle rate. The internal rate of return would be
A. 0.
B. 12%.
C. >12%.
D. <12%.

81. The basic difference between a master budget and a flexible budget is that a master budget is
A. Only used before and during the budget period and a flexible budget is only used after the budget period.
B. For an entire production facility and a flexible budget is applicable to single departments only.
C. Based on one specific level of production and a flexible budget can be prepared for any production level within a relevant range.
D. Based on a fixed standard and a flexible budget allows management latitude in meeting goals.

Page 366 ©2007 Kaplan CPA Review

STUDY MANUAL – BUSINESS ENVIRONMENT & CONCEPTS
CHAPTER 11

82.   The Fresh Company is preparing its cash budget for the month of May. The following information is available concerning its accounts receivable:

Estimated credit sales for May	$200,000
Actual credit sales for April	$150,000
Estimated collections in May for credit sales in May	20%
Estimated collections in May for credit sales in April	70%
Estimated collections in May for credit sales prior to April	$ 12,000
Estimated write-offs in May for uncollectible credit sales	$8,000
Estimated provision for bad debts in May for credit sales in May	$7,000

What are the estimated cash receipts from accounts receivable collections in May?
A. $142,000.
B. $149,000.
C. $150,000.
D. $157,000.

83.   Glo Co., a manufacturer of combs, budgeted sales of 125,000 units for the month of April. The following additional information is provided:

	Number of units
Actual inventory at April 1	
Work-in-process	None
Finished goods	37,500
Budgeted inventory at April 30	
Work-in-process (75% processed)	8,000
Finished goods	30,000

How many equivalent units of production did Glo budget for April?
A. 126,500
B. 125,500
C. 123,500
D. 117,500

©2007 Kaplan CPA Review

STUDY MANUAL – BUSINESS ENVIRONMENT & CONCEPTS
CHAPTER 11

84. The economic order quantity formula assumes that
   A. Periodic demand for the good is known.
   B. Carrying costs per unit vary with quantity ordered.
   C. Costs of placing an order vary with quantity ordered.
   D. Purchase costs per unit differ due to quantity discounts.

85. For inventory management, ignoring safety stocks, which of the following is a valid computation of the reorder point?
   A. The economic order quantity.
   B. The economic order quantity multiplied by the anticipated demand during the lead time.
   C. The anticipated demand during the lead time.
   D. The square root of the anticipated demand during the lead time.

86. The economic order quantity formula assumes that
   A. Purchase costs per unit differ due to quantity discounts.
   B. Costs of placing an order vary with quantity ordered.
   C. Periodic demand for the good is known.
   D. Erratic usage rates are cushioned by safety stocks.

87. What effect, if any, will a last-in, first-out or first-in, first-out inventory method have on an Economic Order Quantity?
   A. No effect.
   B. LIFO will increase the order quantity in times of rising prices.
   C. LIFO will reduce the order quantity in times of rising prices.
   D. FIFO will increase the order quantity in times of rising prices.

Use the following information to answer Questions 88 and 89.

Brady Sporting Goods Incorporated buys baseballs at $20 per dozen from its wholesaler. Brady will sell 36,000 dozen baseballs evenly throughout the year. Brady desires a 10% return on its inventory investment. In addition, rent, insurance, taxes, etc., for each dozen baseballs in inventory is $0.40. The administrative cost involved in handling each purchase order is $10.

88. What is the economic order quantity?
   A. Approximately 448.
   B. Approximately 500.
   C. Approximately 548.
   D. Approximately 600.

89. Assuming that Brady ordered in order sizes of 800 dozen evenly throughout the year, what would be the total annual inventory expenses to sell 36,000 dozen baseballs?
   A. $1,315.
   B. $1,320.
   C. $1,338.
   D. $1,410.

Page 368   ©2007 Kaplan CPA Review

STUDY MANUAL – BUSINESS ENVIRONMENT & CONCEPTS
CHAPTER 11

90.   Which changes in costs are most conducive to switching from a traditional inventory ordering system to a just-in-time ordering system?

Cost per purchase order	Inventory unit carrying costs
A. Increasing	Increasing
B. Decreasing	Increasing
C. Decreasing	Decreasing
D. Increasing	Decreasing

91.   The Aron Company requires 40,000 units of Product Q for the year. The units will be required evenly throughout the year. It costs $60 to place an order. It costs $10 to carry a unit in inventory for the year. What is the economic order quantity?
A. 400.
B. 490.
C. 600.
D. 693.

92.   Politan Company manufactures bookcases. Set up costs are $2.00. Politan manufactures 4,000 bookcases evenly throughout the year. Using the economic-order-quantity approach, the optimal production run would be 200 when the cost of carrying one bookcase in inventory for one year is
A. $0.05.
B. $0.10.
C. $0.20.
D. $0.40.

93.   The following information relates to Eagle Company's material A:

Annual usage in units	7,200
Working days per year	240
Normal lead time in working days	20
Maximum lead time in working days	45

Assuming that the units of material A will be required evenly throughout the year, the safety stock and order point would be

	Safety Stock	Order Point
A.	600	750
B.	600	1,350
C.	750	600
D.	750	1,350

94.   The economic order quantity formula can be used to determine the optimum size of a

	Production run	Purchase order
A.	Yes	No
B.	Yes	Yes
C.	No	Yes
D.	No	No

©2007 Kaplan CPA Review

STUDY MANUAL – BUSINESS ENVIRONMENT & CONCEPTS
CHAPTER 11

95.   Key Co. changed from a traditional manufacturing operation with a job order costing system to a just-in-time operation with a back-flush costing system. What is (are) the expected effects(s) of these changes on Key's inspection costs and recording detail of costs tracked to jobs in process?

Inspection costs	Detail of costs tracked to jobs
A. Decrease	Decrease
B. Decrease	Increase
C. Increase	Decrease
D. Increase	Increase

96.   Under the balanced scorecard concept developed by Kaplan and Norton, employee satisfaction and retention are measures used under which of the following perspectives?
A. Customer.
B. Internal business.
C. Learning and growth.
D. Financial.

97.   Which of the following steps in the strategic planning process should be completed first?
A. Translate objectives into goals.
B. Determine actions to achieve goals.
C. Develop performance measures.
D. Create a mission statement.

Page 370   ©2007 Kaplan CPA Review

STUDY MANUAL – BUSINESS ENVIRONMENT & CONCEPTS
CHAPTER 11

ANSWERS: COST ACCOUNTING: OTHER AREAS

1. **D** A *sunk cost* is a cost that has been incurred and will not be changed by any future decision; it is therefore irrelevant to a decision and excluded in its analysis. The original cost of an asset less its accumulated depreciation (book value) is a sunk cost for replacement decisions, as the replacement would not affect these amounts.

2. **B** Activity-based costing identifies the activities or transactions that cause costs to be incurred (cost drivers). Costs are accumulated (homogeneous cost pools) by activities and then assigned to products based upon the product's use of these activities in its production. Multiple cost drivers are usually employed in costing a single product as multiple activities are used in its production. The result is more accurate cost assignments.

3. **C** Activity-based costing identifies the activities or transactions that cause costs to be incurred (cost drivers). Costs are then assigned to products based upon the product's use of these activities in its production. Multiple cost drivers are usually employed in costing a single product as multiple activities are used in its production.

4. **B** Activity-based costing assigns costs to products based upon the product's use of activities (cost drivers) that caused the costs to be incurred. Costs are accumulated (homogeneous cost pools) by activities (cost drivers) rather than by department or function as in more traditional costing systems. Nonvalue-added activities (cost drivers), such as movement of product, storage, setup, and inspection are minimized or eliminated without adversely affecting the product or service.

5. **C** Just-in-time strongly advocates the elimination of nonvalue-added operations. JIT recommends reducing the number of suppliers (for higher quality and consistency); minimizing the standard delivery quantity (less goods on hand to store and move); and increasing the number of deliveries (again decreasing inventory and other nonvalue-added steps).

6. **B** Flexible budgeting is a reporting system wherein the planned level of activity is adjusted to the actual level of activity before the budget to actual comparison report is prepared. It may be appropriately employed for any item that is affected by the level of activity.

    In standard costing, product costs are predetermined and set up as a goal to be attained. Actual performance is compared to the standard. A primary objective of a standard costing system is to control costs.

7. **B** Share of

	Square footage	% of Total	Factory maint. costs
Fabrication	88,000	55	$111,760
Assembly	72,000	45	91,440
Total	160,000	100	$203,200

    Total factory maintenance costs = $82,100 + $65,000 + $56,100 = $203,200.

©2007 Kaplan CPA Review
Page 371

STUDY MANUAL – BUSINESS ENVIRONMENT & CONCEPTS
CHAPTER 11

8. **C**   Share of General Factory

	Direct Labor Hrs.	% of Total	Administration Costs
Fabrication	562,500	56.25	$ 90,000
Assembly	437,500	43.75	70,000
Total	1,000,000	100.00	$160,000

Total general-factory-administration costs = $90,000 + $70,000 = $160,000.

9. **C**   Factory cafeteria will be allocated first because it has the greatest total costs.

Share of

	No. of Employees	% of Total	Cafeteria costs
Fabrication	280	56.0	$134,400
Assembly	200	40.0	96,000
Gen.-Factory-Admin.	12	2.4	5,760
Factory Mtce.	8	1.6	3,840
Total	500	100.0	$240,000

Total factory cafeteria costs = $87,000 + $91,000 + $62,000 = $240,000.

10. **A**   Factory cafeteria costs were allocated before factory maintenance costs. Once a service department's costs have been allocated, no subsequent service-department costs are recirculated back to it (per #3 above).

11. **D**   All of these nonfinancial measures would be useful in evaluating a manufacturing system.

Throughput time: Total production time required for a units production
    measure of capacity and efficiency.
Setup time to total production time: Nonvalue-added function as a % of total production time
    measure of efficiency.
Rework units as a % total units
    measure of quality of production.

12. **A**   Programmers for a computer programming company would be classified as direct labor which would be both a direct cost and a value-added cost of program development.

13. **A**   The cost of normal spoilage is "absorbed" by the surviving units while abnormal spoilage is recognized immediately; that is, in the current period.

14. **D**   Numerator: Estimated factory overhead; Denominator: Estimated machine hours.

Predetermined overhead = rate	Budget estimate of overhead cost
	Budget estimate of activity base

Only answer (d) has estimates for both overhead costs (the numerator) and an activity base (the denominator).

15. **B**   Only direct manufacturing costs (direct materials and direct labor) should be traced to specific products. The other manufacturing costs, called indirect costs, should be allocated based upon activity cost drivers which only approximates the amount of cost incurred by the specific product.

Page 372

©2007 Kaplan CPA Review

STUDY MANUAL – BUSINESS ENVIRONMENT & CONCEPTS
CHAPTER 11

16. **C** Direct labor is an element of both prime costs and conversion costs. Prime costs are direct material and direct labor. Conversion costs include direct labor and overhead costs.

17. **D** Activity based costing identifies the activities or transactions that cause costs to be incurred (cost drivers). Costs are accumulated (homogeneous cost pools) by activities and then assigned to products based upon the product's use of these activities in its production. Multiple cost drivers are usually employed in costing a single product as multiple activities are used in its production.

18. **B** Activity based costing identifies the activities or transactions that cause costs to be incurred (cost drivers). Costs are then assigned to products based upon the product's use of these activities in its production. Multiple cost drivers are usually employed in costing a single product as multiple activities are used in its production.

19. **B** Generally, an overtime premium is charged to overhead, and allocated to all jobs, as the arbitrary scheduling of jobs should not affect the cost of jobs worked on during overtime. However, if an overtime premium is due to a specific job or customer's requirements, it is appropriately charged to that job, increasing its costs.

20. **B** Computation of CGS Using Manufacturing Costs

Raw Material Beginning Inventory		$ 22,000
Purchases		300,000
		322,000
Less: Ending Inventory		30,000
Cost of Materials Used	$292,000	
Work in Process Beginning Inventory		40,000
Direct Material		292,000
Direct Labor		120,000
Overhead:		
Indirect Labor	60,000	
Taxes & Depr. on Factory	20,000	
Utilities chgd. to Factory		
60%× 50,000	30,000	110,000
		562,000
Less: Ending Inv. of WIP		48,000
Cost of Goods Manufactured		$514,000
Finished Goods Beg. Inv.		25,000
Add: Cost of Goods Mfg.		514,000
		539,000
Less: Fin. Goods End. Inv.		18,000
Cost of Goods Sold		$521,000

21. **D** In the production process, storing raw materials until they are needed represents a non-value added step, whereas engineering, heat treatment or drilling represents improving the product. In addition, storage requires handling costs, cost of holding inventory, possible breakage or misappropriation, while inventory simply waits for use at a later time.

22. **C** Activity based costing assigns costs to products based upon the product's use of activities (cost drivers) which caused the costs to be incurred. Costs are accumulated (homogeneous cost pools) by activities (cost drivers) rather than by department or function as in more traditional costing systems. Nonvalue-added activities (cost drivers), such as movement of product, storage, set up, and inspection are minimized or eliminated without adversely affecting the product or service.

©2007 Kaplan CPA Review

Page 373

STUDY MANUAL – BUSINESS ENVIRONMENT & CONCEPTS
CHAPTER 11

23. **A**   Just-in-time strongly advocates the elimination of non-value added operations. In contrast with answers (b), (c) and (d), JIT recommends reducing the number of suppliers (for higher quality and consistency); minimizing the standard delivery quantity (less goods on hand to store and move); and increasing the number of deliveries (again decreasing inventory, and other non-value added steps).

24. **D**   A loom operator's salary or wages would be classified as direct labor, as the loom operator works directly on the manufacture of the product. The salary or wages of factory foremen and machine mechanics are indirect labor costs and appropriately classified as overhead.

25. **D**   Wages paid to factory machine operators are classified as direct labor. Direct labor is an element of prime costs (DM & DL) and an element of conversion costs (DL & OH).

26. **A**   Property taxes on a manufacturing plant are classified as overhead which is an element of conversion costs (DL & OH). They would not be a period cost (which is an expense) as they are included as a product cost in overhead.

27. **A**   Because Material G is added when a batch is 60% complete, the units in ending inventory, which are only 50% complete, would not have any Material G and would not be included in the computation of EFU for Material G. The ending inventory would be included in the computation of conversion costs (DL + overhead) EFU as they are 50% complete in process 2.

EFU computation:		
Finished units	# units	
+ Ending inventory EFU	# units	% complete
EFU average		
– Beginning inventory EFU	# units	% complete
EFU FIFO		

28. **A**   Flexible budgeting is a reporting system wherein the planned level of activity is adjusted to the actual level of activity before the budget to actual comparison report is prepared. It may be appropriately employed for any item which is affected by the level of activity (such as production, administration, and marketing).

29. **A**   Product quality is best indicated by the returns and allowances made to customers, as well as their complaints about the product. The production cycle time refers only to the efficiency, not the quality.

30. **B** $5,200-Direct materials, Job #5.

Work in process, April 1		$ 4,000
Add:	Direct materials	24,000
	Direct labor	16,000
	Factory overhead	12,800
Less:	Transferred to finished goods	(48,000)
Work-in-process, April 30		$ 8,800
Less:	Direct labor	(2,000)
	Overhead ($2,000 80%)	(1,600)
Direct materials, Job #5		$ 5,200

STUDY MANUAL – BUSINESS ENVIRONMENT & CONCEPTS

CHAPTER 11

31. **D**   Flexible budgeting is a reporting system wherein the planned level of activity is adjusted to the actual level of activity before the budget comparison report is prepared. It may appropriately be employed for any item which is affected by the level of activity (such as direct labor and overhead).

32. **C**

Producing Dept.	% Services Provided	Allocation %	Allocated Maintenance Cost
A	40	50%	$10,000
B	40	50%	10,000
	80		$20,000

As service department costs are allocated directly to producing departments, without allocation to other service departments, only the percentage of services provided to the producing departments A and B are relevant for the allocation.

33. **C**   The cost of normal spoilage is a product cost which should be absorbed by the good units produced and included in the recorded cost of both work-in-process and finished goods inventories.

The cost of abnormal spoilage ($9,000) is a period cost and should be expensed in the current period.

34. **D**   Predetermined = Budget estimate overhead cost

Rate   Budget estimate activity base

35. **C** $46,100

Maintenance	Power	Education	Technology
Costs incurred (to allocate)	99,000	54,000	
Allocation of Maintenance Costs:			
Power 20% x 99,000	(19,800)	19,800	
Education 30% x 99,000	(29,700)		29,700
Technology 50% x 99,000	(49,500)		49,500
	--0--	73,800	
Allocation of Power Costs:			
* Maintenance	--0--		
** Education 2/9 x 73,800		(16,400)	16,400
Technology 7/9 x 73,800 (		57,400)	57,400
		--0--	46,100	106,900

* Once a service department's cost is allocated, no reallocation to that department is made under the step method.
** Maintenance department service percentage (10%) is not used as its cost has already been allocated.

Service percentage:	Education	20
	Technology	70
	Total	90

Education percentage = 2/9.
Under the step method, generally the service department with the greatest inter-service department percentage or cost is allocated first.

36. **B**   Relative profitability is inappropriate because profitability itself is affected by the allocation method; that is, there is circularity of reasoning.

©2007 Kaplan CPA Review

Page 375

STUDY MANUAL – BUSINESS ENVIRONMENT & CONCEPTS
CHAPTER 11

37. **C** $15,000 for Q and $9,000 for R

Joint cost allocated to R:

Sales value R at split-off	$ 15,000

Joint Cost × $60,000 = $9,000

Sales value of P, Q and R at split-off $100,000

Joint cost allocated to Q:

To P	$36,000
To R	9,000
$45,000	
Balance to Q	15,000
Total Joint Cost	$60,000

38. **C** $60,000

P's Joint Cost $\dfrac{\$36,000}{\text{Total Joint Cost } \$60,000} = 60\%$

60% × Total Sales Value at split-off – $100,000 = $60,000

39. **C**   48,000

	Sales – Value	Separable = Cost	N.R.V.	Relative NRV
Ajac	80,000	8,000	72,000	72/90 = 80%
Bjac	40,000	22,000	18,000	18/90 = 20%
			90,000	

Joint cost allocated to Ajac:

80% x $60,000 = $48,000

40. **B** $1 increase per unit sold

Increase in sales revenue	$4 per unit
Increase in cost of goods sold*	3 per unit
Increase in gross profit	1 per unit

* As unit would no longer be considered a by-product, cost of goods sold would **not** be reduced by the net realizable value of the units sold.

41, **A**   The relative sales-value method under which joint-product costs are prorated to **each** product according to total sales value will result in a uniform gross-profit rate for **all** products.

e.g.:	Product A	Product B	Total
Sales Value	$100 (1/3)	$200 (2/3)	$300
Less: Joint Costs	50 (1/3)	100 (2/3)	150
Gross Profit	$ 50 (50%)	$100 (50%)	$150 (50%)

STUDY MANUAL – BUSINESS ENVIRONMENT & CONCEPTS

CHAPTER 11

42. **D** Sales value at split-off:

A	500 gal. × $10	$ 5,000
B	1,000 gal. × $14	14,000
	Total	$19,000

Joint cost allocated to B:

$4,560 × 14,000/19,000	$ 3,360

Cost of subsequent processing

1,000 gal. × $1	1,000
Total cost of 1,000 gal. of B	$ 4,360

43. **D** A by-product is a product of relatively small value which is obtained during production of the main product. Answer (d) would be the best description of this.

44. **D** The "split-off point" occurs when two or more products which are produced simultaneously can be specifically identified and separated as individual products. These products may or may not require subsequent processing in order to be salable. Classification of simultaneously produced products as "joint products" or "by-products" is determined by their relative sales values. Simultaneously produced products of more than nominal value are classified as joint products, while those of relatively small or insignificant sale value are classified as by-products.

45. **B** The cost of by-products may include an allocation of joint costs; however, this allocation is normally not made.

46. **C** The relative sales value of joint products may be unknown at the point of split-off or because of extensive subsequent processing required to make the product salable, may be difficult to determine. In such cases, it is recommended that the subsequent costs be applied as a reduction in revenue on a dollar-for-dollar basis and the remaining revenue used as the sales value at split-off for assignment of joint cost.

47. **D** Under the relative sales value at split-off method of allocating joint costs, an increase in the market value of P at split-off would increase the proportion and amount of joint costs allocated to P and decrease the joint costs allocated to Q. As all other costs and selling prices remain unchanged, the increase in joint costs allocated to P would result in a decrease in P's gross margin while the decrease in joint costs allocated to Q would result in an increase in Q's gross margin.

48. **C** When the actual sales value at the split-off point is not known, the final sales value is reduced by costs subsequent to the split-off point to determine the relative value at split-off. Therefore, if subsequent costs for product Z increase while those of Y remain constant, Z's relative value would decrease resulting in less joint costs being allocated to Z and more being allocated to Y.

49. **A** The probability of the lead time being 3 days is 25%, and the probability of demand being 3 units in a day is 10%. The probability of 3 days of demand being 3 units ($3 × 3 = 9$) coupled with a 3-day lead time is as follows:

   $$25 × 0.1 × 0.1 × 0.1 = 0.00025$$

50. **D** Maximum possible lead time is 3 days, and the maximum possible demand on any day is 3 units. Therefore, the maximum possible demand during lead time is 9 units (3 days × 3 units per day). If 10 units are ordered when inventory is 10 units, there will be at least one unit in inventory when the shipment arrives.

©2007 Kaplan CPA Review

Page 377

STUDY MANUAL – BUSINESS ENVIRONMENT & CONCEPTS
CHAPTER 11

51. **A**   In order to control the cost of stock-outs as well as ordering and carrying costs, the model would have to state when to order (reorder point) as well as how many units to order (EOQ).

52. **C**   The probability of demand being greater than 200 units is 10%; therefore, the probability that sales will be 200 units or less is 90% (100% – 10%). The 90% probability for sales of 200 or less units could also be determined by adding the individual probabilities for sale of 200 units or less (0.2 + 0.5 + 0.2).

53. **A**   Computation of expected selling price

Selling price	×	Probability of selling price	=	Expected value
$ 5,000		0.4		$ 2,000
8,000		0.2		1,600
12,000		0.3		3,600
30,000		0.1		3,000
Expected Selling Price				$10,200

    This solution does not provide for an analysis or evaluation of the individual's aversion to risk.

54. **C**   Most probability problems have you compute the expected value from a series of possible outcomes, each weighted with its own likelihood of occurrence. However, in this problem, the company only wants to select the *most likely* sales volume figure. That would be the one with the greatest probability of occurrence.

55. **C** $52.

Additional sales 60 boxes		
#60 boxes × ($3 selling price – $2 cost)	$60	
#40 boxes × ($1 selling price – $2 cost)	(40)	
Profit	$20	
Probability	× 0.6	
Expected value		$12
Additional sales 100 boxes		
#100 boxes × ($3 selling price – $2 cost)	$100	
-0- boxes × ($1 selling price)	-0-	
Profit	$100	
Probability	× 0.4	
Expected Profit		40
Expected profit (value) of decision		$52

56. **D**   Because the games of chance are to break even, the price charged (P) is to equal the expected payoff of the games.

    The expected value of the payoffs are as follows:

    Queens $\dfrac{4}{52}$ ($5) The probability of drawing a queen from the deck of cards is 4/52.

    Hearts $\dfrac{13}{52}$ ($2) The probability of drawing a heart from the deck of cards is 13/52.

    Therefore, P = $\dfrac{4}{52}$ ($5) $+\dfrac{13}{52}$ ($2)

STUDY MANUAL – BUSINESS ENVIRONMENT & CONCEPTS
CHAPTER 11

57. C

Terminal	% of Cargo	Expected Error % of Error	Occurrence Rate	Probability Error is from Terminal
Land	50%	2%	1.0%	1.0/4.0 = 25%
Air	40%	4%	1.6%	1.6/4.0 = 40%
Sea	10%	14%	<u>1.4%</u>	1.4/4.0 = <u>35%</u>
		4.0%		100%

58. D Regression analysis is a mathematical technique used to predict the value of one variable and its changes (the dependent variable) based upon the value of some other variable (the independent variable). Simple regression analysis involves the use of only one independent (explanatory) variable, while multiple regression analysis allows for more than one independent variable.

59. B Regression analysis develops a mathematical function or formula. A function yields dependent variable values from independent variable values.

60. D 0.95 as a coefficient of correlation is very high (the maximum is at 1.0), thus showing a definite cause-effect relationship. (b) and (c) are obviously incorrect. (a) is incorrect because it does not provide for the fact that a decrease in sales would be associated with a decrease in theft. (d) is correct because it covers both possibilities, or, in other words, it is more correct than (a).

61. A Regression analysis (simple or multiple) is a sampling technique which measures the relationship (does not establish) of a dependent variable to one or more independent variables. If one independent variable is used the method is referred to as simple regression. If more than one independent variable is used the method is referred to as multiple regression.

62. B Maximum correlation exists between +1 and –1.

63. D The coefficient of correlation and coefficient of determination are measures of probable error. Answers (a), (b) and (c) are incorrect as regression analysis (simple or multiple) is a sampling technique which measures the relationship (does not establish) of a dependent variable to one or more independent variables.

64. D Regression analysis is a sampling technique which measures the relationship of a dependent variable to one or more independent variables. If one independent variable is used, the method is referred to as simple regression. If *more than one independent variable* is used, the method is referred to as *multiple regression*.

65. B The equal periodic payments are an annuity and the $3,000 is the future value of the annuity; therefore, the appropriate table of interest factors is the compound value (future value) of an annuity of $1.

66. C Compound value factors are larger than present value factors as they include principal plus interest for a given period. Annuity factors are larger than single sum factors as they represent a series of payments for a period.

©2007 Kaplan CPA Review

Page 379

STUDY MANUAL – BUSINESS ENVIRONMENT & CONCEPTS
CHAPTER 11

67. **A**   1) Payments are to be semi-annual for 20 years. Therefore, there will be 40 payments.

2) Because the annual interest rate is 6%, the semi-annual rate equals 3%.

3) Because we are dealing with compounding, we are interested in future values.

Answer (a) is the only choice which reflects 1-3 listed above. If (a) is reduced to a formula, it can be more readily seen that it results in the appropriate answer:

Period payment needed = $\dfrac{\$10,000 \text{ at the end of 20 years}}{40 \text{ payments at 3\%}}$

68. **D** $11,310

Net cash inflow before tax	$ 7500
– Lease amortization	(5000)
	$ 2500
– Tax (2500 x 40%)	(1000)
	$ 1500
+ Lease amortization	5000
Net cash inflow after taxes	$ 6500
Present value factor	× 1.74
	$11,310

69. **C**   The true rate of return is that rate which equates the present value of the future returns with the cost of the investment.

PV   = FV × PVIF
120,000 = 20,000 × PVIF
$\dfrac{120,000}{20,000}$ = PVIF

6.000   = PVIF

As the factor is between the factors for 10% and 12% the rate of return is less than 12% and more than 10%.

70. **B**   An investment's residual income is the accounting income from the investment less an allowance for a return **on** investment (invested capital).

71. **D** $13,000 net present value.

Present value of benefit*	
$20,000 × 5.65	$113,000
–Investment (present value)	100,000
Net present value	$ 13,000

* The accounting rate of return may also be based on average investment (Investment/2).

STUDY MANUAL – BUSINESS ENVIRONMENT & CONCEPTS
CHAPTER 11

72. **D**   5.0 year payback period.

Payback period	=	Investment cost
		Annual cash flows
	=	$\dfrac{\$100,000}{\$\ 20,000} = \underline{5.0}$ years

73. **B**   Both the internal rate of return method and the net present value method of capital budgeting employ compound interest computations and tables, and these tables explicitly assume reinvestment at the interest rate used (refer to construction of compound interest tables in text). The net present value method uses the cost of capital as the discount rate and therefore assumes reinvestment at this rate which is the minimum rate of return allowable from investments. The internal rate of return provides for a discount rate equal to the rate of return earned by the project, which may be equal to, greater than, or less than the minimum rate of return allowable from investment. Therefore, the internal rate of return allows for reinvestment at a rate which may be greater or less than the minimum rate assured on investments.

74. **C** $62,900.

Period	Annuity		P.V. Factor		Present Value
1-3	$20,000	x	2.32	=	$46,400
1-2	10,000	x	1.65	=	16,500
					$62,900
			or		
1-2	$30,000	x	1.65	=	$49,500
3	20,000	x	.67*	=	13,400
					$62,900

* 3rd period factor   =   2.32 (3 period annuity factor)
  − 1.65 (2 period annuity factor)
  .67 (3 period single sum factor)

75. **B**

Cost of machine		$30,000
Less: Cash flow		
First 3 years $7,000 × 3	$21,000	
4th year	5,500	26,500
Required cash flow Year 5		$ 3,500

76. **C**   The internal rate of return method provides for a discount rate equal to the rate of return earned by the investment or project. Compound interest computations and tables employed by the internal rate of return method explicitly assume reinvestment at the interest rate used (refer to construction of compound interest tables in text).

77. **C**   The ratio to determine the accounting rate of return is the annual operating income from the investment divided by either the initial increase or average investment. The numerator in this problem is $40,000.

78. **B**

Net cash flow after taxes		$25,000
Less depreciation expense ($100,000 ÷ 10)		10,000
Net income after taxes		$15,000
Accounting Rate of Return (based on initial investment)	=	Net income ÷ initial investment
	=	$15,000 ÷ $100,000
	=	15%

©2007 Kaplan CPA Review

STUDY MANUAL – BUSINESS ENVIRONMENT & CONCEPTS
CHAPTER 11

79. **C** The Net Present Value method discounts future cash flow benefits using the cost of capital as the discount rate. Answer (a) is incorrect as the payback method does not employ a discount rate. Answers (b) and (d) are incorrect as they are the same method and it solves for the discount rate which equates the investment cost and the future cash benefits.

80. **C** The net present value method discounts future cash inflows by a predetermined percentage (12%) and compares that amount to the cash outlay to acquire the investment. If there is a positive NPV, it means the rate of return is greater than the stated hurdle rate.

81. **C** The master budget is the budget plan for a planned level of operation.

   Flexible budgeting is a reporting system wherein the planned level of activity is adjusted to the actual level of activity before the budget to actual comparison report is prepared.

82. **D** Collection on credit sales of

May 20% × $200,000	$ 40,000
April 70% × $150,000	105,000
Prior to April	12,000
	$157,000

83. **C**

Sales	125,000 units
Less: Decrease in finished goods inventory	(7,500) units
Required production	117,500 units
Add: Increase in work-in-process	
(8,000 × 75%)	6,000 E.F.U.
Production required	123,500 E.F.U.

   (E.F.U. = Equivalent Finished Units)

84. **A** The E.O.Q. formula is: $EOQ = \sqrt{\dfrac{2SO}{C}}$, where:

S	=	Total units sold / Demand during the period
O	=	Ordering costs per order
C	=	Carrying cost per unit

   Periodic demand (S) for the goods is assumed to be known. Carrying costs and ordering costs are assumed to be constant. Therefore, answers (b) and (c) are incorrect. Purchase cost per unit is not part of the EOQ model; therefore, answer (d) is incorrect.

85. **C** Perfection, ignoring safety stocks, is to replenish supplies as they reach zero level.

86. **C** The economic order quantity is based upon demand (usage or sales), ordering cost per order (assumed constant) and carrying cost per unit of inventory (assumed constant).

   $$EOQ = \sqrt{\dfrac{2SO}{C}}$$, where:

   S = units sold or manufactured
   O = cost per order (set-up cost)
   C = cost of carrying one unit in inventory

STUDY MANUAL – BUSINESS ENVIRONMENT & CONCEPTS
CHAPTER 11

87. **A** A LIFO or FIFO inventory method will have no effect on the EOQ, because EOQ does not deal with pricing of inventory. It merely indicates the amount of inventory which should be purchased at one time in order to minimize carrying and ordering costs.

88. **C** Q = Annual quantity in units
P = Cost of placing an order
S = Annual cost of storage for one unit

$$
\begin{aligned}
EOQ &= \sqrt{\frac{2QP}{S}} \\
&= \sqrt{\frac{2 \times 36,000 \times \$10}{\$0.40 + (10\% \times \$20)}} \\
&= \sqrt{300,000} \\
&= \text{approximately } 548
\end{aligned}
$$

Note that the annual cost of storage includes rent, taxes, insurance, etc., plus the cost of borrowing or the return that could be earned by an alternate investment of funds.

89. **D** Total annual inventory expenses:

1) Order costs:
   Number of orders (36,000 / 800) =   45
   Cost per order   × $10 $ 450
2) Inventory costs:
   Average inventory (800 × 2) =   400 units
   Cost of storage for one unit   × $2.40   960
                                                        $1,410

90. **B** JIT inventory system results in more frequent, small orders and ideally eliminates inventory. A decrease in purchase order costs and/or an increase in inventory carry costs would make JIT more attractive.

91. **D** 693.

$$
\begin{aligned}
EOQ &= \sqrt{\frac{2SO}{C}} = \sqrt{\frac{2(40,000)(\$60)}{\$10}} \\
EOQ &= \sqrt{\frac{4,800,000}{10}} = \sqrt{480,000} = 693
\end{aligned}
$$

The above may also be accomplished by trial and error as follows:

Cost of ordering:	Cost of carrying:
(a) 40,000 ÷ 400 = 100 orders × $60 = $6,000	400 ÷ 2 = 200 × $10 = $2,000
(b) 40,000 ÷ 490 = 86 orders × $60 = $4,898	490 ÷ 2 = 245 × $10 = $2,450
(c) 40,000 ÷ 600 = 67 orders × $60 = $4,000	600 ÷ 2 = 300 × $10 = $3,000
(d) 40,000 ÷ 693 = 57 orders × $60 = $3,420	693 ÷ 2 = 347 × $10 = $3,470

©2007 Kaplan CPA Review

STUDY MANUAL – BUSINESS ENVIRONMENT & CONCEPTS
CHAPTER 11

92. **D**

$$EOQ = \sqrt{\frac{2 \cdot S \cdot O}{C}}$$

$$200 = \sqrt{\frac{2 \cdot 4000 \cdot 2}{C}}$$

$$40,000 = \frac{16,000}{C}$$

$$C = \underline{\underline{\$0.40}}$$

93. **D**   7,200 annual usage ÷ 240 days = 30 units per day
Reorder point equals maximum usage during lead time

30 units per day × 45 days =	1350

Safety stock equals the difference between maximum and normal usage during lead time.

Maximum usage	1350
Normal usage 30 × 20 days	600
	750

94. **B**   The economic order quantity formula can be used to determine the optimum size of either a production run or purchase order. For production runs, the costs associated with setting up a production run are used in the numerator as "O". For purchase orders, the costs associated with placing an order are used in the numerator as "O".

95. **A**   A just-in-time operation generally improves quality as defective inventory must be corrected immediately; there are no inventory pools to hold defective units. Therefore, inspection costs should decrease with a J.I.T. operation.

J.I.T. operations simplify accounting by charging costs directly to cost of goods sold (no inventory). If inventory exists, the inventory is "backed out" of the cost of goods sold account. Backing the inventory amount out of cost of goods sold is referred to as backflush accounting. This process decreases the detail of costs tracked to jobs.

96. **C**   The balance scorecard approach is an outgrowth of the old goal congruence concept. In both ideas, the effort was to look at the tradeoffs associated with each decision. For example, a company may invest $100,000 in a machine that is more efficient and increases profits versus investing in R&D. The decision may be the right one but at some point the scorecard has to be balanced and the company has to invest in R&D. A typical scorecard includes profitability; customer satisfaction; innovation; learning and growth; and efficiency, quality and time. Employee satisfaction and retention are a part of learning and growth.

97. **D**   The creation of a mission statement is always the first step in the strategic planning process. The mission statement outlines the essential reasons for its existence. Choices (a), (b) and (c) are steps that follow the mission statement.

VARIANCE ANALYSIS

STUDY MANUAL – BUSINESS ENVIRONMENT & CONCEPTS
CHAPTER 12

Study Tip: Always focus on learning the essentials of each topic. The CPA exam rarely gets into much depth on any topic, but instead prefers to focus on testing a very broad range of questions. It is better to know the essentials about every topic than to know any topic in serious depth and detail.

STANDARD COSTS

A. A company can employ a cost accounting system that records manufacturing-related activity using actual costs (actual or normal cost system) or standard costs (standard cost system).

   1. In a standard cost system, management will determine the amount that the manufacturing activity should have cost and compare this to the amount that it actually cost.

   2. This determination is based on historical data, inputs from factory employees and supervisory personnel, data relevant to the industry, and the technology that relates to the manufacturing process.

B. Although external financial statements under a standard cost system are not generally acceptable, the use of standard costing is a means of allowing management to evaluate performance of the manufacturing and related departments on a management-by-exception basis.

   1. Under the concept of management-by-exception, material differences between expected performance and actual performance are investigated.

   2. Both favorable or unfavorable differences, referred to as *variances,* are examined.

C. There are several factors that must be considered in setting standards, including economic conditions, the efficiency or inefficiency of the production process, availability of qualified laborers, and quality of materials. There are also several different methods for selecting standards:

   1. Standards based on past performance are not widely used. The major reason is that inefficiencies of previous periods are perpetuated. This method also neglects changes in economic conditions and other factors from one period to the next.

©2007 Kaplan CPA Review

Page 385

2. Basic standards are developed when the standard cost system is initiated but they do not change at any time in the future. These standards are not realistic, and over long periods of time become somewhat meaningless.

3. Perfection or ideal standards are based upon perfect conditions and perfect efficiency. These are unrealistic and often counterproductive. Employees will not attempt to attain standards that cannot be accomplished reasonably.

4. Currently attainable standards are the ones most commonly in use. They are usually strict enough so that substantial effort is required to attain them, but lax enough so that they can be achieved by a reasonably efficient manufacturing system.

D. An item that should be considered when establishing standards is the level of quality control that the company desires to maintain.

1. Standards might be met as a result of sacrificing quality, but the overall cost to the company could be higher than if the standards had not been met.

2. Many companies will establish quality-control procedures to make certain that products meet qualitative standards at a cost that does not exceed the benefits of adhering to those standards.

3. The costs associated with such a quality-control program include prevention costs, appraisal costs, internal failure costs, and external failure costs.

   a. Prevention costs relate to the procedures a company can establish to prevent errors from occurring. They include:

   - Overall quality planning and standard setting.
   - Designing and operating a quality-assurance program.
   - Quality training for employees.
   - Preventative maintenance on tools and equipment.
   - Supplier training and evaluation.
   - Engineering studies to improve quality performance.

   b. Appraisal costs relate to the procedures that a company can establish to determine if the quality-control procedures are working as planned. They include:

   - Statistical process control procedures.
   - Inspection.
   - Testing.
   - Quality audits.

   c. Internal failure costs relate to the procedures that will be followed when errors are not prevented but are detected before the product is actually shipped to customers. They include:

   - Rework.
   - Scrap.

- Downtime.

d. External failure costs relate to the procedures that will be followed when errors are not prevented and are not detected until the product is in the hands of customers. They include:

- Warranty repairs.
- Handling of customer complaints.
- Repacking and freight.
- Product liability claims.

E. Each of the three component costs of manufacturing (direct materials, direct labor, and factory overhead) can be analyzed to determine if actual productivity materially differed from standard or planned productivity. To determine the standard productivity, each component of manufacturing is studied, and standards are created. Specifically, standards are created for the direct material price, direct material usage, direct labor rate, direct labor usage, and factory overhead, all segregated into fixed and variable components. Variances between actual and standard productivity can be evaluated, and appropriate action, if any, can be taken.

VARIANCE ANALYSIS

Formulae are presented below for the computation of variances. Based on the approach presented, a positive number will indicate an unfavorable variance and a negative number will indicate a favorable variance. This section will present the computation and analysis of the variances of direct materials, direct labor, and factory overhead. A favorable variance indicates that the actual amount is less than the standard amount; an unfavorable variance indicates that the actual amount is greater than the standard amount.

A. Direct Materials Variances.

1. The direct materials price variance is computed as follows:

   direct materials price variance = (actual unit price − standard unit price) × actual quantity purchased

   a. If prices varied during the year, the actual unit price would be a weighted-average purchase price.

   b. The actual quantity is the quantity purchased (not quantity used), because price variances for materials are isolated and recorded in total at the time of the purchase.

2. Analysis of variance:

   a. If the variance is favorable, it indicates the company spent less money than expected, which may or may not benefit the company. If less money was spent but a lower quality material was purchased, the quality of the finished product may not be good, and sales may decline. If the quality was the same, however, then this favorable variance benefited the company.

    b.   If the variance is unfavorable, management must determine whether the purchasing department is not functioning properly, or if the standard price is unreasonable.

3.   Responsibility: The purchasing department is usually responsible for direct materials price variances.

4.   Direct materials efficiency (quantity or usage) variance is computed as follows:

direct materials efficiency variance = (actual quantity used – standard quantity allowed*) × standard unit price

*standard quantity allowed = standard quantity per unit × equivalent production

    a.   Equivalent production represents all direct materials used for completed units as well as units still in process. Equivalent production is defined as the sum of the units still in process restated in terms of completed units, plus total units actually completed.

    b.   Use of the standard unit price eliminates the effect of price changes so that the variance will reflect only changes in quantity.

5.   Analysis of variance:

    a.   If the variance is favorable, it indicates less material was used than anticipated.

       •   This benefits the company if the direct materials were used efficiently.
       •   It could have a negative effect if an incorrect quantity of direct materials was used, reducing the quality of the product.

    b.   If the variance is unfavorable, management must determine whether the direct materials are being used inefficiently (perhaps the workers need more/better training), or if the direct materials were of inferior quality, causing more usage (related to direct materials price variance—perhaps cheaper, lesser quality materials were purchased), or if the standard quantity was incorrect.

6.   Responsibility: Usually the production department or cost center that controls the input of direct materials into the production process is responsible for the direct materials efficiency (quantity or usage) variance.

B. Direct Labor Variances.

1.   The direct labor price (rate) variance is computed as follows:

direct labor price variance = (actual hourly wage rate – standard hourly wage rate) × actual number of direct labor hours worked

a. The actual hourly wage rate represents the weighted-average wage rate for all employees.

b. Actual hours worked are used in order to compare the actual payroll to what the payroll should have been for the hours actually worked.

2. Analysis of variance:

a. If the variance is favorable, it means lower wages per hour were paid than anticipated.

b. If the variance is unfavorable, management must determine whether workers are properly assigned to their jobs, or if external factors affect the variance (new minimum wage, new union contracts). If external factors affect the variance, or if the standard is incorrect, management must compute a new standard.

3. Responsibility: Usually the supervisor of the department or cost center where the work is performed is responsible for the direct labor price (rate) variance.

4. The direct labor efficiency variance is computed as follows:

direct labor efficiency variance = (actual direct labor hours worked – standard direct labor hours allowed*) × standard direct hourly wage rate

*standard direct labor hours allowed = standard number of direct labor hours per unit × equivalent production

a. Equivalent production is used because it represents all direct labor used for completed units as well as units still in process.

b. The standard direct labor hourly rate is used so that the variance will reflect changes in quantity only and eliminate the effect of rate differentials.

5. Analysis of variance:

a. If this variance is favorable, it indicates that fewer direct labor hours were used than anticipated. This benefits the company if the labor was efficient; however, if inferior production resulted, this could reduce the quality of the product and cause a negative impact on the entity.

b. If this variance is unfavorable, management must determine whether the workers are inefficient, if inferior direct materials (related to direct materials price variance) caused the workers to spend more time on the product, or if the standard was incorrect.

6. Responsibility: Usually the supervisor of the department or cost center in which the work is performed is responsible for the direct labor efficiency variance.

©2007 Kaplan CPA Review

STUDY MANUAL – BUSINESS ENVIRONMENT & CONCEPTS
CHAPTER 12

7. Comparison of the calculation of direct materials and direct labor variances: The techniques for calculating direct materials and direct labor variances are similar.

C. Factory overhead variances are similar to direct materials and direct labor variances in that predetermined costs are compared with actual costs. However, because factory overhead includes many types of costs, which are both variable and fixed, the procedures for determining the variances are different. Analysis of factory overhead variances includes a volume variance in addition to price and efficiency variances.

1. Budgets are frequently used to control factory overhead costs. Two common budgets are:

a. Static budgets, which show anticipated costs at one level of activity. When factory overhead is unaffected by activity, or when productive activity is stable, the static budget is useful. However, these circumstances are rare, so the static budget is not frequently used.

b. Flexible budgets, which show anticipated costs at different activity levels. To be useful, actual costs must be compared with the standard costs at the actual level of activity, not the expected level of activity that is used in the static budget.

2. Three common methods for computing factory overhead variances follow: 1-factor, 2-factor, and 3-factor methods. Note that in each of the three methods, the total variance is the same. However, each method provides a different level of detail for analyzing the variances. For example, all detailed components of the 3-factor variance, when added together, will equal the 2-factor components added together.

a. 1-factor analysis of factory overhead variances (the simplest and least useful):

overall factory overhead = actual factory overhead – applied factory overhead*

*applied factory overhead = standard direct labor hours allowed** × standard factory overhead application rate

**standard direct labor hours allowed = standard number of direct labor hours per unit × equivalent production

Note that factory overhead applied is calculated using the standard rate multiplied by the standard hours. This is different from normal costing, which multiplies the standard rate by the actual hours.

This method will provide a total factory overhead variance. However, without more details than this method provides, it will be difficult to identify the causes of the variance.

b. 2-factor analysis of factory overhead variances: Under this method, the factory overhead variance comprises two components: budget (controllable) variance and production volume (denominator or idle capacity) variance. The

Page 390   ©2007 Kaplan CPA Review

sum of these two components equals the 1-factor variance described previously.

- Budget (controllable) variance:

  budget (controllable) variance = actual factory overhead − budgeted factory overhead at std. direct labor hours allowed*

  *budgeted factory overhead at standard direct labor hours allowed = variable factory overhead (standard direct labor hours allowed × standard variable factory overhead application rate) + fixed** (budgeted) factory overhead

  **fixed costs as a lump sum

  - A variance will occur if a company actually spends more or less on factory overhead than expected and/or uses more or less than the number of direct labor hours allowed. It assumes a manager or supervisor can control these factors (hence, this is a controllable variance).
  - The shortcoming of this variance is that it does not distinguish between spending and efficiency. This variance looks at fixed overhead as a budgeted lump sum, and not as a budgeted per-unit amount. The next variance, production volume, uses fixed costs on a per-unit basis.

- Production volume (denominator or idle capacity) variance.

  production volume (denominator or idle capacity) variance = (denominator direct labor hours − standard direct labor hours allowed) × standard fixed* factory overhead application rate.\

  *fixed costs on a per-unit basis

- The denominator direct labor hours are the original budgeted, or normal capacity, hours used to determine the factory overhead application rate.
  - Fixed costs do not change with different levels of productive activity and remain constant throughout the relevant range.
  - When the unit cost for fixed factory overhead is calculated, a denominator such as direct labor hours is chosen, which has the effect of applying fixed costs as if they were variable costs.
  - When the actual direct labor hours are different from the expected (denominator), a variance occurs because the fixed costs are a specific amount, but have been either underapplied or overapplied based on the actual direct labor hours.
  - This variance is sometimes referred to as the *idle capacity variance* because there may be a correlation to the utilization of the plant.

c. 3-factor analysis of factory overhead variances: With this method, the factory overhead variance comprises three components: price (spending) variance, efficiency variance, and production volume variance.

STUDY MANUAL – BUSINESS ENVIRONMENT & CONCEPTS
CHAPTER 12

The sum of the price (spending) variance and the efficiency variance equals the budget variance in the 2-factor analysis. The production volume variance is the same as was computed in the 2-factor analysis.

The sum of the three components equals the same total variance as the 1- and 2-factor analyses.

- Price (spending) variance:

  price (spending) variance = actual factory overhead – budgeted factory overhead at actual direct labor hours worked*

  *budgeted factory overhead at actual direct labor hours worked = variable factory overhead (actual worked × standard variable factory rate) + fixed (budgeted) factory overhead

  ◆ This variance is similar to the budget variance (2-factor analysis) except that the budget variance uses standard direct labor hours allowed, whereas the price (spending) variance uses actual direct labor hours worked.
  ◆ This variance is referred to as a *spending variance* because it is caused by price changes or changes in operating conditions. If this variance is a result of external forces (e.g., utility company increasing its rates), then these costs are not controllable by management.

- Efficiency variance.

  efficiency variance = (actual direct labor hours worked – standard direct labor hours allowed) × standard variable factory overhead application rate

  This variance will indicate the savings or additional costs of variable overhead due to efficiency or inefficiency of direct laborers.

- Production volume variance is the same as for the 2-factor analysis method.

Note: All the factory overhead variance calculations outlined assume the factory overhead application rate is based on direct labor hours. If another base is used (such as direct labor cost, direct materials cost, and machine hours), the method remains the same, and only the equations change to reflect the proper denominator base.

SUMMARY OF VARIANCES

One Factor: Total factory overhead variance = Actual factory overhead – Applied factory overhead

Two Factor: Total factory overhead variance = Budget variance + Production volume variance

Page 392   ©2007 Kaplan CPA Review

STUDY MANUAL – BUSINESS ENVIRONMENT & CONCEPTS
CHAPTER 12

Three Factor: Total factory overhead variance = Price (spending) variance + Efficiency variance + Production volume variance

Example: Variance analysis

Strontium, Inc., maintains a standard cost system and has budgeted 100,000 direct labor hours of capacity for year 7 based on an expected production of 50,000 units. Manufacturing overhead is applied to production based on direct labor hours. At 100,000 direct labor hours, manufacturing overhead has been budgeted as follows:

	Total	Capacity in Direct Labor Hours	Manufacturing Overhead Rates
Variable	$100,000	/100,000	= $1.00
Fixed	$150,000	/100,000	= $1.50
Total	$250,000		$2.50

Standards per unit were set as follows:

Direct Materials	5 yards @ $2.00	$10.00
Direct Labor	2 hours @ $4.00	$8.00
Manufacturing Overhead	2 hours @ $2.50	$5.00
		$23.00

During year 7, the following transactions occurred:

a. Direct materials purchased: 300,000 yards at $1.90 (no beginning inventory existed).

b. Direct materials used: 256,000 yards.

c. Direct labor cost: 97,000 hours at $4.20 per hour.

d. Manufacturing overhead incurred:

Fixed	$145,000
Variable	$103,000

Manufacturing overhead was applied based on direct labor hours.

e. 48,000 units were started and completed, of which 40,000 units were sold (no beginning finished goods inventory existed).

©2007 Kaplan CPA Review
Page 393

STUDY MANUAL – BUSINESS ENVIRONMENT & CONCEPTS
CHAPTER 12

Calculate all variances as follows:

1. Material variances:

   a. Direct materials price variance.

   b. Direct materials quantity variance.

2. Labor variances:

   a. Direct labor rate variance.

   b. Direct labor efficiency variance.

3. Total overhead variance.

4. Manufacturing overhead variances (3-variance method):

   a. Overhead spending variance.

   b. Overhead efficiency variance.

   c. Overhead volume variance.

5. Overhead budget variance (2-variance method).

Solutions:

1.

   a. MPV = (AP - SP) × AQ ($1.90 – $2.00) × 300,000 = $30,000 favorable

   b. MQV = (AQ - SQ) × SP (256,000 – 240,000) × $2.00 = $32,000 unfavorable

   SQ = 48,000 units × 5 yards/unit

2.

   a. LRV = (AR - SR) × ADLH

   ($4.20 – $4.00) × 97,000 = $19,400 unfavorable

   b. LEV = (ADLH – SDLH) × SR

   (97,000 – 96,000) × $4.00 = $4,000 unfavorable

   SDLH = 48,000 units × 2 DLH/unit

3. Total OH variance = Act OH – Applied OH – $248,000 – $240,000 = $8,000 unfavorable

Page 394   ©2007 Kaplan CPA Review

Applied OH = SDLH × Standard OH rate 96,000 × $2.50 = $240,000

4.

    a.   OH spending variance = Act OH − Bud at ADLH ($248,000 − $247,000) = $1,000 unfavorable

        Bud at ADLH = 97,000 DLH × $1/DLH + $150,000 = $97,000 + $150,000 = $247,000

    b.   OH eff. variance = (ADLH - SDLH) × Std. VOH rate (97,000 − 96,000) × $1 = $1,000 unfavorable

    c.   OH vol. var. = (bud DLH − SDLH) × Std. FOH rate (100,000 − 96,000) × $1.50 = $6,000 unfavorable

        Bud DLH = Normal capacity of 50,000 units × 2DLH/unit

5.   OH budget variance = Act OH − Bud at SDLH ($248,000 − $246,000) = $2,000 unfavorable

    Bud at SDLH = 96,000 DLH × $1/DLH + $150,000 = $96,000 + $150,000 = $246,000

Example: Variance analysis (FAV or UNFAV)

Use the following information for Questions 1 through 5.

Bilco, Inc., produces bricks and uses a standard costing system. On the diagram in Figure 1, the line OP represents Bilco's standard material cost at any output volume expressed in direct material pounds to be used. Bilco had identical outputs in each of the first three months of 20X5, with a standard cost of V in each month. Points Ja, Fe, and Ma represent the actual pounds used and actual costs incurred in January, February, and March, respectively.

Figure 1

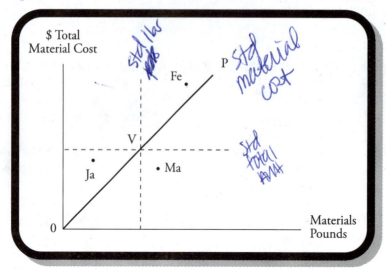

For Questions 1 through 5, determine whether each variance is favorable (F) or unfavorable (U).

1. January material price variance.

2. January material usage variance.

3. February material price variance.

4. February material usage variance.

5. March material net variance.

Solutions:

Questions 1 through 5 require the interpretation of the graph showing the standard cost of materials at a certain level of production.

If the company were to use the standard number of pounds of materials, the point would appear on the vertical hyphenated line. A point to the left indicates that a lower number of pounds were used, and a point to the right indicates that a greater number of pounds were used.

If the company were to pay the standard price per pound, the point would appear on the diagonal solid line. A point below the line, which would be to the right of it, indicates a lower price per pound. A point above the line, which would be to the left of it, indicates a higher price per pound.

If the company were to pay the standard total amount for materials, the point would appear on the horizontal hyphenated line. A point below the line indicates the total amount paid was less, while a point above the line indicates the total amount paid was greater.

1. U   Because the point indicating the cost of materials used in January appears above the solid diagonal line, the price per pound of materials was greater than the standard price indicating an unfavorable price variance.

2. F   Because the point indicating the cost of materials used in January appears to the left of the vertical hyphenated line, the number of pounds used for January production was lower than the standard amount indicating a favorable usage variance.

3. U   Because the point indicating the cost of materials used in February appears above the solid diagonal line, the price per pound of materials was greater than the standard price indicating an unfavorable price variance.

4. U   Because the point indicating the cost of materials used in February appears to the right of the vertical hyphenated line, the number of pounds used for February production was higher than the standard amount indicating an unfavorable usage variance.

5. F. Because the point indicating the cost of materials used in March appears below the horizontal hyphenated line, the total cost of materials was lower than the standard cost indicating a favorable total material variance.

RECORDING VARIANCES IN THE ACCOUNTING RECORDS

A. The pricing of all inventories (raw materials, work-in-process, and finished goods) is a major concern of cost accountants because of its influence on the reporting of income. When standard costing is used, a decision must be made whether to price inventories at standard cost or at actual cost. Disposition of variances will differ according to which inventory costing basis is used.

B. If inventory is to be shown at standard costs, the variances will simply be charged off as a period cost. If inventory is to be shown at actual costs, the variances will be prorated among work-in-process inventory, finished goods inventory, and cost of goods sold so as to approximate actual costs. In such cases, variances are treated as product costs. The proration should be based on a ratio (or fraction) of quantities (pounds, yards, equivalent units) or dollars in each account to total quantities or dollars of all accounts to be restated.

C. Immaterial or insignificant variances may be treated as period costs (with a direct adjustment to cost of goods sold). If end-of-period inventories are immaterial or insignificant, variances may also be treated as period costs (by a direct adjustment to cost of goods sold). On the other hand, if variances and end-of-period inventories are material, the variances are treated as product costs and prorated as explained above.

STUDY MANUAL – BUSINESS ENVIRONMENT & CONCEPTS
CHAPTER 12

QUESTIONS: VARIANCE ANALYSIS

1. Under the two-variance method for analyzing overhead, which of the following variances consists of both variable and fixed overhead elements:

Controllable budget variance	Volume variance
A. No	Yes
B. Yes	Yes
C. Yes	No
D. No	No

2. Which of the following is one of the purposes of standard costs?
    A. To use them as a basis for product costing for external reporting purposes.
    B. To replace budgets and budgeting.
    C. To simplify costing procedures and expedite cost reports.
    D. To eliminate having to account for underapplied or overapplied factory overhead at the end of the period.

3. If a company follows a practice of isolating variances at the earliest point in time, what would be the appropriate time to isolate and recognize a direct material price variance? When:
    A. material is purchased.
    B. material is used in production.
    C. purchase order is originated.
    D. material is issued.

4. How should a usage variance that is significant in amount be treated at the end of an accounting period?
    A. Charged or credited to cost of goods manufactured.
    B. Allocated among work-in-process inventory, finished goods inventory, and costs of goods sold.
    C. Allocated among cost of goods manufactured, finished goods inventory, and cost of goods sold.
    D. Reported as a deferred charge or credit.

5. Palo Corp. manufactures one product with a direct labor standard of two hours at $6 per hour. During March, 500 units were produced using 1,050 hours at $6.10 per hour. The unfavorable direct labor efficiency variance is:
    A. $105.
    B. $100.
    C. $305.
    D. $300.

6. Before allocation of standard variances, the balance in the material usage variance account for item 2 was a:
    A. $1,000 credit.
    B. $2,000 debit.
    C. $2,600 debit.
    D. $600 debit.

Page 398   ©2007 Kaplan CPA Review

7. If all standard variances are prorated to inventories and cost of goods sold, the amount of material-usage variance for item 2 to be prorated to raw materials inventory would be:
    A. $0.
    B. $333 credit.
    C. $333 debit.
    D. $500 debit.

8. If all standard variances are prorated to inventories and cost of goods sold, the amount of material-price variance for item 1 to be prorated to raw materials inventory would be:
    A. $660 debit.
    B. $0.
    C. $647 debit.
    D. $600 debit.

9. Which of the following is the most probable reason a company would experience an unfavorable labor rate variance and a favorable labor efficiency variance?
    A. Because of the production schedule, workers from other production areas were assigned to assist this particular process.
    B. The mix of workers assigned to the particular job was heavily weighted towards the use of new relatively lower-paid, unskilled workers.
    C. The mix of workers assigned to the particular job was heavily weighted towards the use of higher-paid, experienced individuals.
    D. Defective materials caused more labor to be used in order to produce a standard unit.

10. What type of direct material variances for price and usage will arise if the actual number of pounds of materials used exceeds standard pounds allowed but actual cost is less than standard cost?

	Usage	Price
A.	Favorable	Favorable
B.	Unfavorable	Favorable
C.	Favorable	Unfavorable
D.	Unfavorable	Unfavorable

11. During year 4, a department's three-variance overhead standard costing system reported unfavorable spending and volume variances. The activity level selected for allocating overhead to the product was based on 80 percent of practical capacity. If 100 percent of practical capacity had been selected instead, how would the reported unfavorable spending and volume variances be affected?

	Spending variance	Volume variance
A.	Increased	Increased
B.	Unchanged	Unchanged
C.	Increased	Unchanged
D.	Unchanged	Increased

©2007 Kaplan CPA Review

STUDY MANUAL – BUSINESS ENVIRONMENT & CONCEPTS
CHAPTER 12

12. Under the two-variance method for analyzing overhead, which of the following variances consists of both variable and fixed overhead elements?

Controllable (budget) variance	Volume variance
A. Yes	Yes
B. Yes	No
C. No	No
D. No	Yes

13. Which of the following standard costing variances would be least controllable by a production supervisor?
   A. Overhead volume.
   B. Overhead efficiency.
   C. Labor efficiency.
   D. Material usage.

14. What is the normal year-end treatment of immaterial variances recognized in a cost accounting system utilizing standards?
   A. Reclassified to deferred charges until all related production is sold.
   B. Allocated among cost of goods manufactured and ending work-in-process inventory.
   C. Closed to cost of goods sold in the period in which they arose.
   D. Capitalized as a cost of ending finished goods inventory.

15. Palo Corp. manufactures one product with a standard direct labor cost of 2 hours at $6.00 per hour. During March, 500 units were produced using 1,050 hours at $6.10 per hour. The unfavorable direct labor efficiency variance is:
   A. $100.
   B. $105.
   C. $300.
   D. $305.

16. A standard cost system may be used in:
   A. Neither process costing nor job order costing.
   B. Process costing but not job order costing.
   C. Either job order costing or process costing.
   D. Job order costing but not process costing.

Question 17 is based on the following information:

Tolbert Manufacturing Company uses a standard-cost system in accounting for the cost of production of its only product, product A. The standards for the production of one unit of product A are as follows:

- Direct materials: 10 feet of item 1 at $.75 per foot and 3 feet of item 2 at $1.00 per foot.
- Direct labor: 4 hours at $3.50 per hour.
- Manufacturing overhead: applied at 150% of standard-direct-labor costs.

Page 400   ©2007 Kaplan CPA Review

There was no inventory on hand at July 1, year 2. Following is a summary of costs and related data for the production of product A during the year ended June 30, 2006.

- 100,000 feet of item 1 were purchased at $.78 per foot.
- 30,000 feet of item 2 were purchased at $.90 per foot.
- 8,000 units of product A were produced which required 78,000 feet of item 26,000 feet of item 2, and 31,000 hours of direct labor at $3.60 per hour.
- 6,000 units of product A were sold.

At June 30, year 3, there are 22,000 feet of item 1, 4,000 feet of item 2, and 2,000 completed units of product A on hand. All purchases and transfers are "charged in" at standard.

17. For the year ended June 30, year 3, the total debits to the raw-materials account for the purchase of item 1 would be:
    A. $75,000.
    B. $78,000.
    C. $58,500.
    D. $60,000.

18. In connection with a standard cost system being developed by Flint Co., the following information is being considered with regard to standard hours allowed for output of one unit of product:

	Hours
Average historical performance for the past three years	1.85
Production level to satisfy average consumer demand over a seasonal time span	1.60
Engineering estimates basked on attainable performance	1.50
Engineering estimates based on ideal performance	1.25

To measure controllable production inefficiencies, what is the best basis for Flint to use in establishing standard hours allowed?
    A. 1.25.
    B. 1.50.
    C. 1.60.
    D. 1.85.

19. The following were among Gage Co.'s year 1 costs:

Normal spoilage	$5,000
Freight out	10,000
Excess of actual manufacturing costs over standard costs	20,000
Standard manufacturing costs	100,000
Actual prime manufacturing costs	80,000

©2007 Kaplan CPA Review

STUDY MANUAL – BUSINESS ENVIRONMENT & CONCEPTS
CHAPTER 12

Gage's year 1 actual manufacturing overhead was:
A. $40,000.
B. $45,000.
C. $55,000.
D. $120,000.

20.   What does a credit balance in a direct-labor efficiency variance account indicate?
A.   The average wage rate paid to direct labor employees was less than the standard rate.
B.   The standard hours allowed for the units produced were greater than actual direct-labor hours used.
C.   Actual total direct-labor costs incurred were less than standard direct-labor costs allowed for the units produced.
D.   The number of units produced was less than the number of units budgeted for the period.

21.   Information on Material Company's direct-material costs is as follows:

Actual units of direct materials used	20,000
Actual direct-material costs	$40,000
Standard price per unit of direct materials	$2.10
Direct-material efficiency variance-favorable	$3,000

What was Material's direct-material price variance?
A. $1,000 favorable.
B. $1,000 unfavorable.
C. $2,000 favorable.
D. $2,000 unfavorable.

22.   Information on Kennedy Company's direct-material costs is as follows:

Standard unit price	$3.60
Actual quantity purchased	1,600
Standard quantity allowed for actual production	1,450
Materials purchase price variance-favorable	$240

What was the actual purchase price per unit, rounded to the nearest penny?
A. $3.06.
B. $3.11.
C. $3.45.
D. $3.75.

23.   Lab Corp. uses a standard cost system. Direct labor information for Product CER for the month of October is as follows:

Standard rate	$6.00 per hour
Actual rate paid	$6.10 per hour
Standard hours allowed for actual production	1,500 hours
Labor efficiency variance	$600 unfavorable

Page 402   ©2007 Kaplan CPA Review

What are the actual hours worked?
A. 1,400.
B. 1,402.
C. 1,598.
D. 1,600.

24. Air, Inc., uses a standard cost system. Overhead cost information for Product CO for the month of October is as follows:

Total actual overhead incurred	$12,600
Fixed overhead budgeted	$3,300
Total standard overhead rate per direct labor hour	$4.00
Variable overhead rate per direct labor hour	$3.00
Standard hours allowed for actual production	3,500

What is the overall (or net) overhead variance?
A. $1,200 favorable.
B. $1,200 unfavorable.
C. $1,400 favorable.
D. $1,400 unfavorable.

Questions 25 and 26 are based on the following information:

Data on Goodman Company's direct-labor costs is given below:

Standard direct-labor hours	30,000
Actual direct-labor hours	29,000
Direct-labor usage (efficiency) variance–favorable	$4,000
Direct-labor rate variance–favorable	$5,800
Total payroll	$110,200

25. What was Goodman's actual direct-labor rate?
A. $3.60.
B. $3.80.
C. $4.00.
D. $5.80.

26. What was Goodman's standard direct-labor rate?
A. $3.54.
B. $3.80.
C. $4.00.
D. $5.80.

STUDY MANUAL – BUSINESS ENVIRONMENT & CONCEPTS
CHAPTER 12

27.   During 20X0, a department's three-variance overhead standard costing system reported unfavorable spending and volume variances. The activity level selected for allocating overhead to the product was based on 80% of practical capacity. If 100% of practical capacity had been selected instead, how would the reported unfavorable spending and volume variances be affected?

	Spending variance	Volume variance
A.	Increased	Unchanged
B.	Increased	Increased
C.	Unchanged	Increased
D.	Unchanged	Unchanged

28.   If over- or underapplied overhead is interpreted as an error in allocating actual costs against the production of the year, this suggests that the over- or underapplied overhead of this year should be:
   A. Carried forward in the overhead control account from year to year.
   B. Eliminated by changing the predetermined overhead rate in subsequent years.
   C. Apportioned among the work-in-process inventory, the finished goods inventory, and the cost of goods sold.
   D. Treated as a special gain or loss occurring during the year.

29.   Yola Co. manufactures one product with a standard direct labor cost of four hours at $12.00 per hour. During June, 1,000 units were produced using 4,100 hours at $12.20 per hour. The unfavorable direct labor efficiency variance was:
   A. $1,220.
   B. $1,200.
   C. $820.
   D. $400.

30.   Under the two-variance method for analyzing factory overhead, the factory overhead applied to production is used in the computation of the:

	Controllable (budget) variance	Volume variance
A.	Yes	No
B.	Yes	Yes
C.	No	Yes
D.	No	No

31.   Carr Co. had an unfavorable materials usage variance of $900. What amounts of this variance should be charged to each department?

	Purchasing	Warehousing	Manufacturing
A.	$0	$0	$900
B.	$0	$900	$0
C.	$300	$300	$300
D.	$900	$0	$0

Page 404   ©2007 Kaplan CPA Review

STUDY MANUAL – BUSINESS ENVIRONMENT & CONCEPTS
CHAPTER 12

32. The variable factory overhead rate under the normal-volume, practical-capacity, and expected activity levels would be the:
A. Same except for normal volume.
B. Same except for practical capacity.
C. Same except for expected activity.
D. Same for all three activity levels.

33. Lanta Restaurant compares monthly operating results with a static budget. When actual sales are less than budget, would Lanta usually report favorable variances on variable food costs and fixed supervisory salaries?

	Variable food costs	Fixed supervisory salaries
A.	Yes	Yes
B.	Yes	No
C.	No	Yes
D.	No	No

Items 34 and 35 are based on the following information:

The following information relates to a given department of Herman Company for the fourth quarter year 4:

Actual total overhead (fixed plus variable)	$178,500
Budget formula	$110,000 plus $0.50 per hour
Total overhead application rate	$1.50 per hour
Spending variance	$8,000 unfavorable
Volume variance	$5,000 favorable

The total overhead variance is divided into three variances-spending, efficiency, and volume.

34. What were the actual hours worked in this department during the quarter?
A. 110,000.
B. 121,000.
C. 137,000.
D. 153,000.

35. What were the standard hours allowed for good output in this department during the quarter?
A. 105,000.
B. 106,667.
C. 110,000.
D. 115,000.

©2007 Kaplan CPA Review
Page 405

STUDY MANUAL – BUSINESS ENVIRONMENT & CONCEPTS
CHAPTER 12

Questions 36 and 37 are based on the following information:

Beth Company's budgeted fixed factory overhead costs are $50,000 per month plus a variable factory overhead rate of $4 per direct labor hour. The standard direct labor hours allowed for October production were 18,000. An analysis of the factory overhead indicates that, in October, Beth had an unfavorable budget (controllable) variance of $1,000 and a favorable volume variance of $500. Beth uses a two-way analysis of overhead variances.

36.   The actual factory overhead incurred in October is:
   A. $121,000.
   B. $122,000.
   C. $122,500.
   D. $123,000.

37.   The applied factory overhead in October is:
   A. $121,000.
   B. $122,000.
   C. $122,500.
   D. $123,000.

38.   The following information is available from the Tyro Company:

Actual factor overhead	$15,000
Fixed overhead expenses, actual	$7,200
Fixed overhead expenses, budgeted	$7,000
Actual hours	3,500
Standard hours	3,800
Variable overhead rate per direct labor hour	$2.50

Assuming that Tyro uses a three-way analysis of overhead variances, what is the spending variance?
   A. $750 favorable.
   B. $750 unfavorable.
   C. $950 favorable.
   D. $1,500 unfavorable.

39.   Information on Fire Company's overhead costs is as follows:

Actual variable overhead	$73,000
Actual fixed overhead	$17,000
Standard hours allowed for actual production	32,000
Standard variable overhead rate per direct-labor hour	$2.50
Standard fixed overhead rate per direct-labor hour	$0.50

What is the total overhead variance?
   A. $1,000 unfavorable.
   B. $6,000 favorable.
   C. $6,000 unfavorable.
   D. $7,000 favorable.

Page 406

©2007 Kaplan CPA Review

Questions 40 and 41 are based on the following:

The figure below depicts a factory overhead flexible budget line DB and standard overhead application line OA. Activity is expressed in machine hours with Point V indicating the standard hours required for the actual output in September. Point S indicates the actual machine hours (inputs) and actual costs in September.

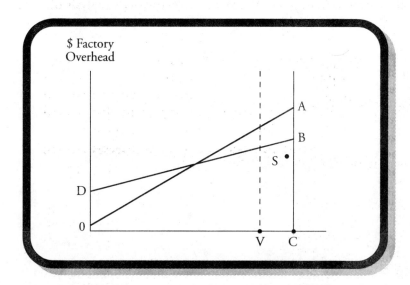

40. Are the following overhead variances favorable or unfavorable?

	Volume (capacity) variance	Efficiency variance
A.	Favorable	Favorable
B.	Favorable	Unfavorable
C.	Unfavorable	Favorable
D.	Unfavorable	Unfavorable

41. The standard direct material cost to produce a unit of Lem is 4 meters of material at $2.50 per meter. During May, 4,200 meters of material costing $10,080 were purchased and used to produce 1,000 units of Lem. What was the material price variance for May?
    A. $400 favorable.
    B. $420 favorable.
    C. $80 unfavorable.
    D. $480 unfavorable.

STUDY MANUAL – BUSINESS ENVIRONMENT & CONCEPTS
CHAPTER 12

42. Sender, Inc. estimates parcel mailing costs using data shown on the chart below.

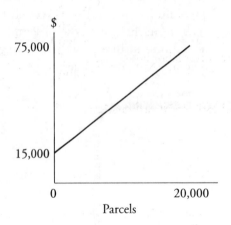

What is Sender's estimated cost for mailing 12,000 parcels?
A. $36,000.
B. $45,000.
C. $51,000.
D. $60,000.

43. The following direct labor information pertains to the manufacture of product Glu:

What is the standard direct labor cost per unit of product Glu?
A. $30.
B. $24.
C. $15.
D. $12.

44. Under the two-variance method for analyzing factory overhead, the actual factory overhead is used in the computation of the:

	Controllable (budget) variance	Volume variance
A.	Yes	Yes
B.	Yes	No
C.	No	No
D.	No	Yes

45. Which of the following variances would be useful in calling attention to a possible short-term problem in the control of overhead costs?

	Spending variance	Volume variance
A.	No	No
B.	No	Yes
C.	Yes	No
D.	Yes	Yes

46. The following information pertains to Roe Co.'s manufacturing operations:

Standard direct labor hours per unit	2
Actual direct labor hour	10,500
Number of units produced	5,000
Standard variable overhead per standard direct labor hour	$3
Actual variable overhead	$28,000

Roe's unfavorable variance overhead efficiency variance was:
A. $0.
B. $1,500.
C. $2,000.
D. $3,500.

47. Information on Cox Company's direct-material costs for the month of January was as follows:

Actual quantity purchased	18,000
Actual unit purchase price	$3.60
Materials purchase price variance–unfavorable (based on purchases)	$3,600
Standard quantity allowed for actual production	16,000
Actual quantity used	15,000

For January there was a favorable direct-material usage variance of:
A. $3,360.
B. $3,375.
C. $3,400.
D. $3,800.

48. Companies in what type of industry may use a standard cost system for cost control?

	Mass production industry	Service industry
A.	Yes	Yes
B.	Yes	No
C.	No	No
D.	No	Yes

49. On the diagram below, the line OW represents the standard labor cost at any output volume expressed in direct labor hours. Point S indicates the actual output at standard cost, and Point A indicates the actual hours and actual cost required to produce S.

Which of the following variances are favorable or unfavorable?

	Rate variance	Efficiency variance
A.	Favorable	Unfavorable
B.	Favorable	Favorable
C.	Unfavorable	Unfavorable
D.	Unfavorable	Favorable

STUDY MANUAL – BUSINESS ENVIRONMENT & CONCEPTS
CHAPTER 12

50. Under the three-variance method for analyzing factory overhead, which of the following is used in the computation of the spending variance?

	Budget allowance based on actual hours	Budget allowance based on standard hours
A.	Yes	No
B.	Yes	Yes
C.	No	Yes
D.	No	No

51. Under the two-variance method for analyzing factory overhead, the budget allowance based on standard hours allowed is used in the computation of the

	Controllable (budget) variance	Volume variance
A.	Yes	Yes
B.	Yes	No
C.	No	No
D.	No	Yes

52. Dahl Co. uses a standard costing system in connection with the manufacture of a "one size fits all" article of clothing. Each unit of finished product contains 2 yards of direct material. However, a 20% direct material spoilage calculated on input quantities occurs during the manufacturing process. The cost of the direct material is $3 per yard. The standard direct material cost per unit of finished product is:

A. $4.80.
B. $6.00.
C. $7.20.
D. $7.50.

Questions 53 and 54 are based on the following data:

The following information pertains to Nell Company's production of one unit of its manufactured product during the month of June:

Standard quantity of materials	5 lbs.
Standard cost per lb.	$0.20
Standard direct labor hours	0.4
Standard wage per hour	$7.00
Materials purchased	100,000 lbs.
Cost of materials purchased	$0.17 per lb.
Materials consumed for manufacture of 10,000 units	60,000 lbs.
Actual direct labor hours required for 10,000 units	3,900
Actual direct labor cost per hour	$7.20

The materials price variance is recognized when materials are purchased.

Page 410   ©2007 Kaplan CPA Review

STUDY MANUAL – BUSINESS ENVIRONMENT & CONCEPTS
CHAPTER 12

53. Nell's materials price variance for June was:
     A. $3,000 favorable.
     B. $3,000 unfavorable.
     C. $2,000 favorable.
     D. $2,000 unfavorable.

54. Nell's labor efficiency variance for June was:
     A. $780 favorable.
     B. $780 unfavorable.
     C. $700 favorable.
     D. $700 unfavorable.

STUDY MANUAL – BUSINESS ENVIRONMENT & CONCEPTS
CHAPTER 12

ANSWERS: VARIANCE ANALYSIS

1. **C** Under the two-variance method, the controllable (budget) variance is the difference between the actual overhead and the budgeted overhead. Both of these contain variable and fixed costs and either fixed or variable costs can vary from the budget.

    The volume variance is due solely to fixed costs. It is the difference between the budgeted overhead and applied overhead, based upon the same level of activity as the budget. Because the budget and applied activity bases are the same, budgeted variable overhead will equal applied variable overhead, and any volume variance is due solely to fixed costs.

    Note: The answer is the same for both actual and standard costing. The difference between actual and standard, under the two-variance method, is the activity base used for the budgeted overhead. Under actual costing, the activity base used would be the actual activity base achieved, while under standard costing, it would be the standard activity base for the production achieved.

2. **C** Standard costing simplifies costing procedures by using one predetermined standard cost rather than recalculating costs each time actual costs change. Then, variances from standard are analyzed.

    Standard costs do not replace budgets and budgeting; standards are a per-unit measure (e.g., standard cost per pound of corn or standard labor rate per hour), whereas budgets are for totals, not just units. Standard costing is not allowed for inventory costing for external reporting purposes. Using standard costing does not eliminate the need to account for overapplied or underapplied overhead.

3. **A** Since the material price variance relates to the difference between standard price and actual price and might be viewed as measuring the performance of the company's purchasing department, the variance should be determined on the basis of the units purchased and should therefore be computed when the purchase occurs.

4. **B** This method provides for allocation among all units that were handled during the period. If the usage variance is immaterial, it is acceptable accounting practice to charge it off to cost of goods sold.

5. **D**

Actual direct labor hours used	1,050
Standard direct labor hours allowed	1,000
500 units × 2 hours per unit	
Excess hours	50
Standard direct labor rate	× $6
Direct labor efficiency variance	$300 (UF)

Page 412 　　　　　©2007 Kaplan CPA Review

STUDY MANUAL – BUSINESS ENVIRONMENT & CONCEPTS
CHAPTER 12

6. **B**   Material-usage variance for item 2:

Units		Price	
Actual	×	Standard	
26,000 ft.		$1.00	$26,000
Standard	×	Standard	
24,000 ft.*		$1.00	24,000
Unfavorable variance (debit)			$2,000

*8,000 units × 3 ft. per unit

7. **A**   The material-usage variance does not arise until the materials are placed into production. Therefore, no part of the variance will be prorated to raw materials inventory.

8. **A**

Actual price paid per foot	$0.78
Less: Standard price per foot	$0.75
Material price (unfavorable variance per foot)	$0.03
Ending raw-materials inventory	22,000 ft.
Price variance per foot	× $0.03
Material price variance to be prorated to raw materials	$ 660 dr.

9. **C**   An unfavorable labor rate variance suggests that the labor cost was higher than anticipated, and a favorable labor efficiency variance implies that more productive work occurred than had been expected.

10. **B**   Actual number of pounds in excess of standard is unfavorable; actual cost being less than standard cost is favorable.

11. **D**   The overhead spending (budget) variance is the difference between actual overhead costs and budgeted overhead costs at the actual level of activity achieved. The activity level used to determine the predetermined rate for overhead allocation has no effect on this variance.

12. **B**   Under the two variance method: The controllable (budget) variance is the difference between the actual overhead and the budgeted overhead. Both of these contain variable and fixed costs and either fixed or variable costs can vary from the budget.

13. **A**   The amount being produced within a period (volume) is driven by the sales forecast, which is generally more controllable by the sales department rather than the production department. Production then, in turn, controls material, labor and overhead efficiency or usage.

14. **C**   Because the amounts are immaterial, allocation is not warranted; hence, they are treated as a determinant of the current period's earnings only.

15. **C**   :

Actual direct labor hours used	1,050
Standard direct labor hours allowed 500 units × 2 hours per unit	1,000
Excess hours	50
Standard direct labor rate	× $6
Direct labor efficiency variance	$300 (UF)

©2007 Kaplan CPA Review   Page 413

STUDY MANUAL – BUSINESS ENVIRONMENT & CONCEPTS
CHAPTER 12

16. **C** Standard costs may be used in either job order costing or process costing. Standard costing is a cost estimation technique used for control purposes and to simplify costing procedures and expedite cost reports. The system of recording costs (job order or process) is independent of the costs to be recorded (standard or actual).

17. **A** All purchases are "charged in" at standard. Therefore, the debit to raw materials for the purchase of item 1 would be: 100,000 ft. × $.75 = $75,000.

18. **B** The best basis upon which standards should be established is always the normal, or currently attainable performance. Setting them at the ideal or theoretical maximum capacity creates standards which may never be met, resulting in frustration amongst the workers and rendering the cost reports meaningless. By establishing performance standards too low, they may cause workers to reduce their output in order to hit the low standards, unknown to management.

19. **A** $40,000 actual overhead.:

Standard manufacturing costs	$100,000
Add: Excess of actual manufacturing costs over standard costs	20,000
Total actual manufacturing costs	$120,000
Less: Actual prime costs (direct materials and direct labor)	(80,000)
Actual manufacturing overhead costs	<u>$40,000</u>

20. **B** A credit balance indicates a favorable variance, with standard hours allowed being greater than actual hours used.

21. **C** 2,000 favorable.

Set-up information given:
20,000   ?   = $40,000
20,000   2.10 =   ?

Fill in the blanks:
20,000 $2.00 = $40,000
20,000 $2.10 = $42,000   Fav. 2,000 CR

or simply 20,000   (2.10 - 2.00) = $2,000 FAVORABLE

22. **C**

Actual quantity 1,600 @ std. price $3.60	= 5,760
Less: Favorable price variance	(240)
Actual quantity 1,600 @ actual price	5,520
/actual quantity	<u>/1,600</u>
=actual price per unit	<u>$3.45</u>

STUDY MANUAL – BUSINESS ENVIRONMENT & CONCEPTS

CHAPTER 12

23. **D**   1,600. Set up a variance computation schedule and work backwards.

Standard Hours	×	Standard rate	
1,500	×	$6.00	= $9,000
Actual hours	×	Standard rate	
(1)	×	$6.00	= (2)

$600 (bracketing the $9,000 and (2) values)

(2) = $9,000 + $600 unfavorable variance or $9,600

(1) = $9,600 $6.00 or $1,600

Also, since the efficiency variance is the difference between actual hours and standard hours times the standard rate, the variance can be divided by $6.00 ($600   6.00 = 100 hours + 1,500 hours = 1,600)

24. **C** $1,400 favorable

The net overhead variance is the difference between actual overhead, $12,600, and overhead applied to product cost or standard.:

Actual overhead	$12,600
Standard 3,500 hours allowed × total overhead rate per hour $4.00	14,000
Favorable total variance	$1,400

25. **B**

$$\text{Actual hours} \times \text{actual rate} = \text{Total payroll}$$

$$\text{Actual rate} = \frac{\text{Total payroll}}{\text{Actual hours}}$$

$$= \frac{\$110,200}{29,000}$$

$$= \$3.80$$

26. **C**

Rate variance = Actual hours × the difference between the standard and actual rates (D)

$$\$5,800 = 29,000 \, D$$
$$D = \$0.20 \text{ per hour}$$

Because the rate variance is favorable, the standard rate must be $.20 more than the actual rate of $3.80, or $4.00.

©2007 Kaplan CPA Review

STUDY MANUAL – BUSINESS ENVIRONMENT & CONCEPTS
CHAPTER 12

27. **C**   Spending variance-unchanged; Volume variance-increased.

The overhead spending (budget) variance is the difference between actual overhead costs and budgeted overhead costs at the actual level of activity achieved. The activity level used to determine the predetermined rate for overhead allocation has no effect on this variance.

The overhead volume variance is the difference between budgeted overhead costs at the standard level of activity for the production achieved and applied overhead costs. It is attributable to the over- or under-application of fixed costs, due to production at an activity level other than where the predetermined overhead rate was determined. If the activity level used to determine the predetermined overhead rate was increased (80% of practical capacity to 100%), the fixed overhead application rate would decrease and less fixed overhead would be applied per unit of activity achieved. This would result in an increase in an unfavorable (underapplied) or a decrease in a favorable (overapplied) volume variance.

28. **C**   If over- or underapplied overhead is interpreted as an error in allocating actual costs, then this error should be corrected by prorating the variance to the components affected: cost of goods sold and ending inventories.

(Note: Over- or underapplied overhead is the difference between actual overhead and overhead applied at a predetermined rate.)

29. **B**   An unfavorable direct labor efficiency variance represents the number of actual hours required over the number of standard labor hours allowed for that level of output, multiplied by the standard labor rate. For making 1,000 we were allowed:

1,000 units @ 4 hours per unit =	4,000 hours allowed
Actual hours	4,100
Excess hours over standard	100
Standard rate	$12
Variance	$1,200

30. **C**   Under the two variance method of overhead analysis:

Controllable Variance = actual overhead vs. budgeted overhead at standard activity base allowed for the production achieved (if using standard costs) or budgeted overhead at actual activity base used (if using actual costing techniques-not standard costing).

Volume Variance = budgeted overhead at standard activity base (or actual activity base if not using standard costing) vs. applied overhead.

31. **A**   Material usage variances cannot occur until materials are placed into production. Production does not occur in purchasing and warehousing. Purchasing and warehousing may be charged the material purchase price variance.

32. **D**   The variable overhead rate would be the same for all three activity levels. By definition, variable overhead would be the same per unit, machine hour, etc., within a relevant range of capacity.

Page 416   ©2007 Kaplan CPA Review

STUDY MANUAL – BUSINESS ENVIRONMENT & CONCEPTS

CHAPTER 12

33. **B** A static budget is not adjusted to the actual level of activity before the budget to actual comparison report is prepared. Therefore, a level of activity below the budget level would usually result in favorable variance for variable cost items (total cost changes with change in the level of activity). However, fixed cost items (total cost does not change with changes in the level of activity) would not usually show favorable (or unfavorable) variances as the cost would not differ from budget as a result of the decrease in activity.

34. **B** :

Actual overhead	$178,500
Less: Spending variance	8,000 Unf
Budget	170,500
Less: Fixed costs	110,000
Variance	$60,500 /$0.50 = 121,000 hours

35. **D** :

Overhead rate	$1.50
Variable portion	0.50
Fixed portion	$1.00
Fixed cost	$110,000
Normal volume	110,000 hours
Volume variance	$5,000 /$1 = 5,000 hours
Standard hours	110,000 + 5,000 = 115,000

Total variance computation:

Actual	178,500	
Budget	170,500	8,000 UNF
110,000 + 121,000 × 0.50		
Efficiency	167,500	3,000 UNF
110,00 + 115,000 × 0.50		
Volume	172,500	5,000 FAV
115,000 × 1.50		

This answer is based on the use of standard hours in computing the efficiency variance. This is not the only way this variance can be computed, but the question does not allow for alternative answers.

36. **D**

$123,000		$122,000
Budget $50,000 + 18,000 ×$4 =		$122,000
Add: Budget variances (unfavorable)		1,000
Actual overhead		$123,000

©2007 Kaplan CPA Review

STUDY MANUAL – BUSINESS ENVIRONMENT & CONCEPTS
CHAPTER 12

37. **B**

$122,500

Actual overhead		
(see previous solution)	$123,000	
Budget $50,000 + 18,000 × $4	122,000	Unf. $1,000 Budget Var.
Applied overhead	[1]122,500	Fav. $500 Volume Var.

[1]Add the volume variance to Budget $122,000 + $500 = $122,500

Note: For further practice compute the total overhead rate and normal activity:

Total overhead rate = $122,500/18,000 = $6.80 (rounded)

Normal = $6.80 – $4.00 = $2.80 (fixed portion of rate)

FC $50,000/2.80 = 17,857 labor hours

38. **A**

$750 favorable

Actual overhead	$15,000	
Budget (actual hours)		
$7,000 + 3,500 × $2.50	$15,750	$750 spending var. (favorable)
* Budget (standard hours)		
$7,000 + 3,800 × $2.50	$16,500	$750 efficiency var. (favorable)

* Not required. The volume variance cannot be determined with the facts given.

39. **B**

Actual overhead: variable	73,000	
Actual overhead: fixed	17,000	90,000
Applied overhead		
Variable 2.50 × 32,000 std. hrs.	80,000	
Fixed 0.50 × 32,000 std. hrs.	16,000	96,000
Favorable variance (overapplied)		6,000

40. **B** Volume variance-favorable; Efficiency variance-unfavorable.

The overhead volume variance is the difference between budgeted overhead costs at the standard level of activity for the production achieved (line DB, overhead flexible budget line) and applied overhead costs (line OA, standard overhead application line). As line OA (applied overhead) is above line OB (budgeted overhead) at point V, the standard hours required for actual output, the volume variance is favorable (applied over head exceeds budget at standard).

The overhead efficiency variance is the difference between budgeted overhead at the actual level of activity and budgeted overhead at the standard level of activity for the production achieved. As point S, the actual level of activity (machine hours) is greater than (is to the right of) point V, the standard hours required for actual output, the budget at actual activity exceeds the budget at standard activity and the overhead efficiency variance is unfavorable.

STUDY MANUAL – BUSINESS ENVIRONMENT & CONCEPTS
CHAPTER 12

41. **B** Material price variance= Actual quantity (actual price vs. standard price)
$$= \$4,200 \ (\$2.40 - \$2.50)$$
$$= \underline{\underline{\$420}}$$
Actual price $=\ \$10,080\ /\ 4200$ meters $=\ \$2.40$
The variance is favorable as the actual price is less than the standard price.

42. **C** $51,000.

$$\frac{\text{Change in cost}}{\text{Change in units}} = \frac{75,000-15,000}{20,000} = \frac{\$60,000}{20,000} = \begin{matrix} \$3 \ \text{Variable cost} \\ \text{per unit} \end{matrix}$$

Total cost of 12,000 units:	
Variable cost ($3 × 12,000)	$36,000
Fixed cost	15,000
Total cost	$51,000

43. **A** $30 standard direct labor costs per unit.

Weekly wages per worker	$500
Add: Benefits treated as direct labor	100
	$600
# of productive hours per week, per worker	/40
Standard direct labor costs per hour	$15
# hours required per unit	× 2
Standard direct labor costs per unit	$30

44. **B** Under the two variance method of overhead analysis:

Controllable variance = actual overhead vs. budgeted overhead at standard activity base allowed for the production achieved.

Volume variance = budgeted overhead at standard activity base allowed for the production achieved vs. applied overhead based upon standard activity base allowed for production achieved.

45. **C** The spending (budget) variance is considered a measure of the control of spending in that actual overhead costs are compared with budgeted overhead costs at the actual activity achieved.

The volume (capacity) variance does not relate to the control of overhead costs as it is attributable to the over- or under-application of fixed costs, due to production at an activity level other than where the predetermined overhead rate was originally determined.

©2007 Kaplan CPA Review

Page 419

STUDY MANUAL – BUSINESS ENVIRONMENT & CONCEPTS
CHAPTER 12

46. **B**   Overhead is generally applied based upon direct labor hours. The unfavorable overhead efficiency variance represents the number of actual hours required over the number of standard labor hours allowed for that level of output, multiplied by the standard variable overhead rate. For making 5,000 units we were allowed:

5,000 units @ 2 hours per unit =	10,000	hours allowed
Actual hours	10,500	
Excess hours over standard	500	
Standard rate	$3	
Variance	$1,500	

47. **C**   .

Actual unit price	$3.60
Less unfavorable price variance per unit	
$3,600 / 18,000	(0.20)
Standard price per unit	3.40
Standard quantity allowed	16,000
Actual quantity used	15,000
Quantity difference (favorable)	1,000
Standard price per unit	× $3.40
Favorable quantity variance	$3,400

48. **A**   A Standard cost system can be used for cost control by/for any company, product, process or service for which standard costs can be established.

49. **D**   As point A is above line OW (standard), the actual rate exceeds the standard rate for the direct labor hours used, therefore, the rate variance is unfavorable.

    As point A is to the left of point S, the actual direct labor hours used were less than the standard hours allowed for the actual output, therefore, the efficiency variance is favorable.

50. **A**   Under the three (3) variance method, the spending variance is the difference between actual overhead and the budget for overhead at actual activity base.

51. **A**   Under the two variance method of overhead analysis:

    Controllable variance= actual overhead vs. budgeted overhead at standard activity base allowed for the production achieved.

    Volume variance =Budgeted overhead at standard activity base allowed for the production achieved vs. applied overhead based upon standard activity base allowed.

52. **D**

Direct materials requirement per unit	
(2 yards per finished unit / 80%*)	2.5 yards
Cost per yard	× $3
Standard direct materials cost per unit	$7.50

    * If direct material spoilage is 20% of input quantities, output quantities are 80% of input (100% - 20%).

Page 420   ©2007 Kaplan CPA Review

STUDY MANUAL – BUSINESS ENVIRONMENT & CONCEPTS
CHAPTER 12

53. **A**   Actual quantity purchased @ actual cost = 100,000 lbs @ $.17 = $17,000
         Actual quantity purchased @ standard cost = 100,000 lbs. @ $.20 = 20,000
         Favorable material price variance (on purchases) $ 3,000

54. **C**   Actual hours @ standard rate = 3,900 hrs. @ $7 = $27,300
         Standard hours @ standard rate = 4,000 hrs. @ $7 =   28,000
         Favorable labor efficiency variance $ 700
         Standard hours = .4 hrs./unit × 10,000 units produced = 4,000 standard hrs.

©2007 Kaplan CPA Review

IT: IT FUNDAMENTALS

STUDY MANUAL – BUSINESS ENVIRONMENT & CONCEPTS
CHAPTER 13

Study Tip: Many CPA exam candidates complain that they do not have a sufficient amount of time to study. It is important to learn to study at times that would otherwise be wasted. Study at lunch, while exercising, or while waiting for the bus. If candidates can make use of these wasted moments, they usually discover that they do have enough time to adequately prepare.

A. Systems, Data, and Information.

- A *system* is a set of interrelated components that interact to achieve a goal. Most systems are composed of smaller subsystems and vice versa.
- Every organization has goals, and the sub-systems should be designed to maximize achievement of the organization's goals–even to the detriment of the subsystem itself. For example, the production department (a subsystem) of a company might have to forego its goal of staying within its budget in order to meet the organization's goal of delivering product on time.
- *Goal conflict* occurs when the activity of a subsystem is not consistent with another subsystem or with the larger system.
- *Goal congruence* occurs when the subsystem's goals are in line with the organization's goals.
- The larger and more complicated a system, the more difficult it is to achieve goal congruence.
- The *systems concept* encourages integration (i.e., minimizing the duplication of recording, storing, reporting, and processing).
- *Data* are facts that are collected, recorded, stored, and processed by an information system.
- Organizations collect data about *events* that occur, *resources* that are affected by those events, and *agents* who participate in the events
- *Information* is different from data. Information is data that have been organized and processed to provide meaning to a user. Usually, more information and better information translates into better decisions. However, when you get more information than you can effectively assimilate, you suffer from *information overload*. When you've reached the overload point, the quality of decisions declines while the costs of producing the information increases.
- The value of information can be measured as its benefits minus its costs. Costs are more difficult to quantify.
- Characteristics that make information useful:
    - Relevance—reduces uncertainty by helping predict or confirm.
    - Reliability—dependable and free from error or bias.
    - Completeness—doesn't leave out anything important.

Page 422   ©2007 Kaplan CPA Review

STUDY MANUAL – BUSINESS ENVIRONMENT & CONCEPTS
CHAPTER 13

- ◆ Timeliness—received in time to affect the decision.
- ◆ Understandability—presented so it's comprehensible and useful.
- ◆ Verifiability—independent people would produce the same result.
- ◆ Accessibility—available when needed in a usable format.
- Information is provided to both external and internal users.
  - ◆ External users primarily use information that is either mandatory (e.g., required by government) or essential (needed to conduct business).
  - ◆ In providing mandatory or essential information, the focus should be on minimizing costs, meeting regulatory requirements, and meeting minimum standards of reliability and usefulness.
- Internal users primarily use discretionary information.
  - ◆ The primary focus in producing this information is ensuring that benefits exceed costs, i.e., the information has positive value.

B. Hardware.

1 **Input devices**—keyboard, mouse, trackball, track pads, light pens, audio/voice input devices, barcode scanners, optical character readers, point of sale devices, scanners.

2 **Processors.**

- The central processing unit (CPU) is the primary handler of the processing of information in a computer, and is also known as the "brains of the computer."
- The CPU control unit interprets and executes program instructions and logic, and the arithmetic logic unit performs arithmetic and logical calculations.
- Most processors require random access memory (RAM).
- Faster processor ratings (in megahertz or gigahertz - cycles per second) and higher amounts of RAM will make the overall system more efficient.
- Cache memory and read-only memory (ROM) are two other forms of physical memory.
- Cache memory is a special high-speed storage device, either a reserved section of main memory or an independent device. Two types of caching are commonly used in personal computers: memory caching and disk caching.
  - ◆ A memory cache is a portion of memory made of high-speed static RAM (SRAM) instead of the slower and cheaper dynamic RAM (DRAM) used for main memory.
  - ◆ Memory caching is effective because most programs access the same data or instructions over and over.
  - ◆ By keeping as much of this information as possible in SRAM, the computer avoids accessing the slower DRAM.

Disk cache is a portion of RAM used to speed up access to data on a disk. The RAM can be part of the disk drive itself (hard disk cache) or it can be RAM in the computer (soft disk cache).

Read only memory (ROM)—memory that is pre-programmed and not erasable, used for things you never want to erase such as boot programs.

©2007 Kaplan CPA Review
Page 423

3. **Storage.**

- There are two methods of accessing information within a storage device:
- Random access—information directly accessed on storage device (e.g. Hard drives, Optical drives).
- Sequential access—specific data must be processed in the order in which it is stored on the storage device (e.g. Tape drives).

Primary storage—Main memory (physical memory or RAM) is internal to the computer. A computer can manipulate only data that is loaded into main memory. RAM is volatile, meaning that you will lose data if power is interrupted. The amount of main memory determines how many programs can be running at one time and how much data can be readily available.

Secondary storage is non-volatile—Examples include storage devices such as tapes, diskettes, zip drives, hard drives, floppy diskettes, CDs, DVDs, and USB drives which are used for permanent storage.

4. **Output devices.**

- Printers (all types), monitors, sound cards, speakers.
- Input and output devices together are referred to as peripherals since you typically plug them into the CPU "box."

5. **Server.**

- A Server is a computer or a software application that provides network services to all of the client computers attached to the network.

C. Systems software.

Systems software includes *operating systems* and *utility programs* (such as compilers, translators, debuggers, etc.) that manage and control the activities of the computer.

1. Operating systems automate the management of computer resources and enable applications to be loaded and run. Examples of operating systems are:

- Linux
- Windows XP
- Windows CE
- Mac OSX
- UNIX
- VMS
- AIX

For example, it is the operating system that enables the data input from the keyboard to get to the processor, and the documents created by the user to get to the printer. The operating system is the heart of the machine. Operating systems can be:

- Multi-user: Allows two or more users to run programs at the same time.
- Multi-processing: Supports running a program on more than one CPU.
- Multi-tasking: Allows more than one program to run concurrently.

An operating system (OS) is the program that, after being initially loaded into the computer by a boot program, manages all the other programs in a computer.

- The other programs are called applications.
- The application programs make use of the operating system by making requests for services through a defined application program interface (API).
- In addition, users can interact directly with the operating system through a user interface such as a command language or a graphical user interface (GUI).

An operating system performs these services for applications:

- In a multitasking operating system where multiple programs can be running at the same time, the operating system determines which applications should run in what order and how much time should be allowed for each application before giving another application a turn.
- It manages the sharing of internal memory among multiple applications.
- It handles input and output to and from attached hardware devices, such as hard disks, printers, and communications ports.
- It sends messages to each application or interactive user (or to a system operator) about the status of operation and any errors that may have occurred.
- It can offload the management of what are called batch jobs (for example, printing) so that the initiating application is freed from this work.
- On computers that can provide parallel processing, an operating system can manage how to divide the program so that it runs on more than one processor at a time.

2. Utilities are special purpose programs that usually manage some component of the system architecture, such as a printer driver.

D. Application software—application specific software, controlled by systems software, such as spreadsheet, word processing applications and database management systems.

E. Networks—communication networks come in several levels, varying from linking (networking) a couple of computers together all the way to the Internet. They rely on client server technology—the physical and logical division between user applications and the shared data that must be available to all users (such as databases and print queues). Types of networks include:

LANs (local area networks) - link several different user machines, printers, and/or databases to other shared devices within a limited geographic area, often within the same building. A LAN will be connected using one of three common designs: Bus, Ring, or Star. There are three major component categories:

STUDY MANUAL – BUSINESS ENVIRONMENT & CONCEPTS
CHAPTER 13

- Computers and peripheral devices (printers, modems, etc.) with network adapters (NICs, or network interface cards).
- At least one server, which provides services to the network, such as file servers, printer servers, database servers, and web servers.
- A communications channel to connect them—wired or wireless—but always dedicated communication media.

WANs (wide area networks) link distributed users and local area networks. They are used to provide broad geographical coverage, perhaps even global coverage. WANs use currently existing phone lines to communicate, which they do not own.

VAN (value added networks) are a secure long distance communications system designed and maintained by an independent provider. These provide communications services beyond the mere transmission of data. For example, they might batch transactions together and send them at a certain time during the day. They are used in Electronic Data Interchange.

Internet provides a network that connects various secured WANs.

- It allows communication between dissimilar technology platforms.
- Web browsers are software programs that allow users to browse various data sources on the internet.
- Internet service providers (ISPs) provide access to the internet.
- Nobody "owns" the Internet.
- The Internet is available to everyone.

An **Intranet** uses Internet protocols to establish a network internal to the company. It links internal documents and databases using web-based technology.

Extranets allow companies such as suppliers and distributors to link to a corporate intranet.

- Access is limited to those areas necessary for conducting business.

Virtual Private Networks (VPNs) allow you to send information over the Internet, but encrypts it in such a way that it is private and secure. In concept, this is similar to a private network, but runs on the internet, so that the costs are lower than an actual private network.

F. Generations of computer software languages.

Programming Languages:

- 1st generation—machine language.
- 2nd generation—assembly language.
- 3rd generation—high level programming languages (C--, Java).
- 4th generation—programming languages, often used to access databases, which are closer in their commands to actual human language ("find all records where date is July 31). SQL and Focus are examples of 4GL (or, 4th generation programming languages).

Page 426   ©2007 Kaplan CPA Review

- 5th generation – languages used for artificial intelligence (AI). AI is the computing capability that allows computer programs to process information in the same way, or in a similar way, to the way a human processes information. In other words, it allows computers to think like people, rather than in rigid logical routines. Neural networks and robotics are applications of AI.

G. Distinguish between online and batch processing.

Application Processing Modes:

- Online real time represents direct access processing where transactions are processed in order of occurrence.
- Batch processed transactions are processed in groups (batches) of similar transactions.

H. Know the definition of CITP.

Certified Information Technology Professional (CITP)—Recently developed by the AICPA to recognize CPAs who can provide skilled professional services within IT. This professional should be able to provide services on:

- Project Management.
- Relationships between IT and the business processes.
- Competence in IT.

I. Data validation.

Data validation techniques are used to ensure that valid data are input into the system. Examples include the following:

- A **field check** determines if the characters in a field are of the proper type. For example, a check on a field such as US Zip code that is supposed to contain only numeric values, would indicate an error if it contained any alphanumeric characters.
- A **sign check** determines if the data in a field have the appropriate arithmetic sign. For example, the quantity-ordered field should never be negative.
- A **limit check** tests a numeric amount to ensure that it does not exceed a predetermined value. For example, the regular hours-worked field in weekly payroll input must be less than or equal to 40 hours. Similarly, the hourly wage field should be greater than or equal to the minimum wage.
- A **range check** is similar to a limit check except that it has both upper and lower limits.
- A **size check** ensures that the input data will fit into the assigned field. For example, the value 456,789,876 will not fit into a six digit field.
- A **completeness check** on each input record determines if all required data items have been entered. For example, sales transaction records should not be accepted for processing unless they include the customer's complete address.
- A **validity check** compares the ID code or account number in transaction data with similar data in the master file to verify that the account exists. For example, if a sale to customer 4567 is entered, the computer must verify the existence of

©2007 Kaplan CPA Review

STUDY MANUAL – BUSINESS ENVIRONMENT & CONCEPTS
CHAPTER 13

customer 4567 in the customer database to confirm that the sale was made to a valid customer.

- A **reasonableness test** determines the correctness of the logical relationship between two data items. For example, a $1,000 monthly salary increase may be appropriate for an executive, but it is an unlikely raise for a file clerk.

COMPUTER-BASED STORAGE CONCEPTS

Record, field, character, array.

- Following are some computer-based storage concepts that should be understood:
  - *Entity*—something about which information is stored. Example: Students are an entity in the university.
  - *Attribute*—characteristics of interest with respect to the entity. A student's GPA is an attribute of a student.
  - *Field*—the physical space where an attribute is stored, e.g. a GPA field.
  - *Record*—the set of attributes stored for a particular instance of an entity, e.g., all the information stored about student John Doe is John Doe's record. John's record might contain his address, his GPA, his telephone number, his student ID, etc.
  - *Data Value*—the intersection of the row and column, i.e., a particular field for a particular record. John's address (where name identifies the row and address identifies the column) would be a data value.
  - *File*—a group of related records, e.g., all the students enrolled in the School of Management might constitute a file.
  - *Master File*—a file that stores cumulative information about an organization's entities. Conceptually similar to a ledger in that (1) the file is permanent; (2) it exists across fiscal periods; and (3) changes are made to the file to reflect effects of new transactions. A master file might include all the courses completed by students, along with their course final grade.
  - *Transaction File*—a file that contains records of individual transactions (events) during a fiscal period. Similar to a journal in that the files are temporary and maintained for one period. A transaction file might be all the tuition payments made by all the students for a given semester.
  - *Database*—a set of inter-related, centrally coordinated files. A database might include all students, and all information about the students, such as address, grades, tuition payments, major, high school attended, etc.

DATABASE SYSTEMS

- In file-oriented systems, programmers must know the physical location and layout of records used by a program. They must reference the location, length, and format of every field they utilize. When data is used from several files, this process becomes more complex.
- Database systems overcome this problem by separating the storage and use of data elements. Two separate views of the data are provided: (1) a logical (conceptual) view, and (2) a physical view. Separating these views facilitates application development,

Page 428 — ©2007 Kaplan CPA Review

because programmers can focus on coding the logic and not be concerned with storage details.

- The DBMS (database management system) translates users' logical views into instructions as to which data should be retrieved from the database. The operating system translates DBMS requests into instructions to physically retrieve data from various disks. The DBMS handles the link between the physical and logical views of the data. This interface allows the user to access, query, and update data without reference to how or where it is physically stored. The user only needs to define the logical data requirements.

- Separating logical and physical views also means that users can change their conceptualizations of the data relationships without making changes in the physical storage. Furthermore, the database administrator can change the physical storage of the data without affecting users or application programs.

- A *schema* describes the logical structure of a database. There are three levels of schema:
  - *Conceptual level*—The organization-wide view of the *entire* database (i.e., the big picture). Lists all data elements and the relationships between them.
  - *External level*—A set of individual user views of portions of the database, i.e., how each user sees the portion of the system with which he interacts. These individual views are referred to as *subschema*.
  - *Internal level*—A low-level view of the database. It describes how the data are actually stored and accessed, including record layouts, definitions, addresses, and indexes.

- The DBMS uses the mappings to translate a request by a user or program for data (expressed in logical names and relationships) into the indexes and addresses needed to physically access the data.

- Accountants are frequently involved in developing conceptual- and external-level schema.

- An employee's access to data should be limited to the subschema of data that is relevant to the performance of his job.

- A key component of a DBMS is the *data dictionary*. The data dictionary contains information about the structure of the database. For each data element, there is a corresponding record in the data dictionary describing that element. Information provided for each element includes a description or explanation of the element; the records in which it is contained; its source, the length and type of the field in which it is stored, the programs in which it is used, the outputs in which it is contained, the authorized users of the element, and other names for the element.

- Accountants should participate in the development of the data dictionary because they have a good understanding of the data elements in a business organization, as well as where those elements originate and how they are used.

- The DBMS usually maintains the data dictionary. It is often one of the first applications of a newly implemented database system. Inputs to the dictionary include records of new or deleted data elements and changes in names, descriptions, or uses of existing elements. Outputs include reports that are useful to programmers, database designers, and IS (information system) users in designing and implementing the system, documenting the system, and creating an audit trail.

- *DBMS Languages*—Every DBMS must provide a means of performing the three basic functions of creating a database, changing a database, and querying a database.

- The set of commands used to create the database is known as *data definition language (DDL)*. DDL is used to build the data dictionary, initialize or create the database, describe the logical views for each individual user or programmer, and specify any limitations or constraints on security imposed on database records or fields.
  - The set of commands used to change the database is known as *data manipulation language (DML)*. DML is used for maintaining the data, including updating data, inserting data, and deleting portions of the database
  - The set of commands used to query the database is known as *data query language (DQL)*. DQL is used to interrogate the database, including retrieving records, sorting records, ordering records, and presenting subsets of the database. The DQL usually contains easy-to-use, powerful commands that enable users to satisfy their own information needs.
- Many DBMS packages also include a *report writer*, a language that simplifies the creation of reports. Users typically specify what elements they want printed and how the report should be formatted. The report writer then searches the database, extracts specified data, and prints them out according to specified format.
- Users typically have access to both DQL and report writer. Access to DDL and DML are typically restricted to employees with administrative and programming responsibilities.

Batch processing

Updating can be done through several approaches:

- *Batch Processing*—Source documents are grouped into batches, and control totals are calculated. Periodically, the batches are entered into the computer system, edited, sorted, and stored in a temporary file. The temporary transaction file is run against the master file to update the master file. Output is printed or displayed, along with error reports, transaction reports, and control totals.
- *Online Batch Processing*—Transactions are entered into a computer system as they occur and stored in a temporary file. Periodically, the temporary transaction file is run against the master file to update the master file. The output is printed or displayed.

Point of Sale Processing (POS):

- An integrated transaction system that delivers information in real time.
- Immediately updates inventory, sales, and financial statement each time a POS transaction is completed.
- Usually the POS system is centralized so that secure data can be shared throughout the organization.
- POS systems integrate an entity's web site, catalogues, and stores with the rest of the organization.

Real-time processing

- *Online, Real-time Processing*—Transactions are entered into a computer system as they occur. The master file is immediately updated with the data from the transaction. Output is printed or displayed.

Distributed processing

- Distributed Processing – The distribution of computer processing work among multiple computers linked by a communications network.

STUDY MANUAL – BUSINESS ENVIRONMENT & CONCEPTS
CHAPTER 13

QUESTIONS: IT: IT FUNDAMENTALS

1. Which one of the following situations would most likely provide the best way to secure data integrity for a personal computer environment?
    A. Provision of personal computers to all users.
    B. Trained, proficient user group.
    C. All computers linked to a local area network (LAN).
    D. Adequate program documentation.

2. In a computer system environment, the procedures that include the equipment configuration, program, and data files to be used as well as description of conditions that may require interruption of a program execution are known as:
    A. operating documentation.
    B. application controls.
    C. administrative documentation.
    D. systems documentation.

3. Computers located throughout an organization's different remote facilities that are networked to fulfill information processing needs are referred to as:
    A. a local area network (LAN).
    B. interactive processing.
    C. centralized processing.
    D. distributed data processing.

4. A software tool used for ad hoc, online access to items in a database would *most likely* be a(n):
    A. query utility program.
    B. application generator.
    C. report generator.
    D. terminal emulation software.

5. A system where several minicomputers are connected for communication and data transmission purposes, but where each computer can also process its own data, is known as a:
    A. distributed data processing network.
    B. centralized network.
    C. decentralized network.
    D. multidrop network.

6. The input device used in a department store where the sales clerk passes a light pen over the price tag to record the purchase is a(n):
    A. mark-sense reader.
    B. optical scanner.
    C. touch-tone device.
    D. laser bar code scanner.

Page 432   ©2007 Kaplan CPA Review

STUDY MANUAL – BUSINESS ENVIRONMENT & CONCEPTS
CHAPTER 13

7. All of the following are computer input devices **EXCEPT** a(n):
   A. plotter.
   B. mouse.
   C. magnetic ink character recognition device.
   D. light pen.

8. In distributed data processing, a ring network:
   A. has all computers linked to a host computer and each linked computer routes all data through the host computer.
   B. links all communication channels to form a loop.
   C. attaches all channel messages along one common line with communication to the appropriate location via direct access.
   D. organizes itself along hierarchical lines of communication usually to a central host computer.

9. The main components of the central processing unit of a computer are:
   A. semiconductors, on-line devices, and memory.
   B. arithmetic-logic unit, control unit, and primary memory.
   C. random access memory, read only memory, and auxiliary storage.
   D. primary storage, input-output devices, and arithmetic-logic unit.

10. Access time in relation to computer processing is the amount of time it takes to:
    A. transmit data from a remote terminal to a central computer.
    B. complete a transaction from initial input to output.
    C. perform a computer instruction.
    D. retrieve data from memory.

11. Banks are required to process many transactions from paper documents (e.g. checks, deposit slips) during the course of an average business day. This requires a reliable, yet economical form of input. The *most* common source of automation device used by banks is:
    A. a disk pack.
    B. magnetic tape.
    C. bar coding.
    D. magnetic ink character recognition.

12. A local area network (LAN) is *best* described as a:
    A. computer system that connects computers of all sizes, workstations, terminals, and other devices within a limited proximity.
    B. system to allow computer users to meet and share ideas and information.
    C. electronic library containing millions of items of data that can be reviewed, retrieved, and analyzed.
    D. method to offer specialized software, hardware and data handling techniques that improve effectiveness and reduce costs.

©2007 Kaplan CPA Review
Page 433

STUDY MANUAL – BUSINESS ENVIRONMENT & CONCEPTS
CHAPTER 13

13. One advantage of a database management system is:
A. that each organizational unit takes responsibility and control for its own data.
B. the cost of the data processing department decreases as users are not responsible for establishing their own data handling techniques.
C. a decreased vulnerability as the database management system has numerous security controls to prevent disasters.
D. the independence of the data from the application programs which allows the programs to be developed for the user's specific need without having to be concerned with data capture problems.

14. A flat file structure is used in database management systems when:
A. a complex network structure is employed.
B. a network based structure is used and a complex database schema is developed.
C. a simple network structure is employed.
D. a relational database model is selected for use.

15. The possibility of erasing a large amount of information stored on magnetic tape most likely would be reduced by the use of:
A. File protection rings.
B. Check digits.
C. Completeness tests.
D. Conversion verification.

16. On magnetic discs, more than one file may be stored on a single physical file, while in multiprogramming computer operations, several programs may be in core storage at one time. In both cases, it is important to prevent the intermixing or overlapping of data. This is accomplished by a technique known as:
A. boundary protection.
B. file integrity.
C. paging.
D. interleaving.

17. A technique for controlling identification numbers (part number, man number, etc.) is:
A. self-checking digits.
B. echo checks.
C. parity control.
D. file protection.

18. Errors in data processed in a batch computer system may **NOT** be detected immediately because:
A. transaction trails in a batch system are available only for a limited period of time.
B. there are time delays in processing transactions in a batch system.
C. errors in some transactions cause rejection of other transactions in the batch.
D. random errors are more likely in a batch system that in an on-line system.

Page 434   ©2007 Kaplan CPA Review

STUDY MANUAL – BUSINESS ENVIRONMENT & CONCEPTS
CHAPTER 13

19. Misstatements in a batch computer system caused by incorrect programs or data may not be detected immediately because:
   A. errors in some transactions may cause rejection of other transactions in the batch.
   B. the identification of errors in input data typically is not part of the program.
   C. there are time delays in processing transactions in a batch system.
   D. the processing of transactions in a batch system is not uniform.

STUDY MANUAL – BUSINESS ENVIRONMENT & CONCEPTS
CHAPTER 13

ANSWERS: IT: IT FUNDAMENTALS

1. **C** Answer C is correct as the best way to secure data integrity among the five methods listed. Linking all computers to a LAN would improve security, allowing the control over who has access to which programs and files, and allowing for the automatic back-up of all data daily. Answer A is not correct because the provision of personal computers to all users would reduce data integrity by increasing the number of opportunities to introduce error or fraud into the system. Answer B is not correct because while a trained, proficient user group may reduce the accidental destruction of data, it would not guarantee that the users would always do the right thing. They might be overly confident and take short cuts or they might use their knowledge to commit fraud. Answer D is not correct because the use of adequate documentation does not guarantee that everyone will read it nor that they will avoid the commission of fraud.

2. **A** Answer A is correct. Operating documentation is prepared for the computer operator so that he or she can run the program. It includes the equipment configuration, instructions for entering data on the console, and descriptions of conditions which cause the program to halt. Answer B is incorrect because they are controls built into a specific computer application. Answer C is not correct because administrative documentation includes overall standards, policies, and procedures for the computer facility. Answer D is not correct because systems documentation is a complete description of all aspects of each application, including flowcharts and program listings.

3. **D** Answer D is correct because distributed data processing does distribute computers to a company's remote locations and link them together. Answer A is not correct because a LAN links equipment within a limited geographical area such as one building. Answer B is not correct because interactive processing simply refers to an operating system which permits the user and the computer to interact, with the system responding within a reasonable time to the user. Answer C is not correct because centralized processing refers to the consolidation of all equipment and personnel within the same geographical area.

4. **A** A utility program is a pre-written program to perform, primarily, housekeeping functions. One such function could be to query a database, or to request specific information from it. Answer B is not correct because an application generator is software which facilitates the writing of programs. Answer C is not correct because a report generator is software which lets the user specify the data elements to be printed. Answer D is not correct because terminal emulation software makes a computer behave like a terminal so that it can access another (usually much larger) computer.

5. **A** Distributed data processing distributes computers at remote locations and links them. Each computer can do its own processing, but data can be shared because of common standards. Answer B is not correct because a centralized network performs all processing centrally, with only dumb terminals at the remote locations. Answer C is not correct because a decentralized network uses independent processors at each location, with little concern about communication and transmission among them. Answer D is not correct because a multidrop network is normally a centralized system using dumb terminals rather than minicomputers, and having most terminals linked together with only one (or a few) linked directly to the main computer.

6. **B** An optical scanner is used by a clerk with a light pen to read actual characters or numbers which have been typewritten, computer-printed, or hand-written. Choice A is incorrect. A mark-sense reader reads optical marks and is used for grading multiple choice tests.

Page 436   ©2007 Kaplan CPA Review

STUDY MANUAL – BUSINESS ENVIRONMENT & CONCEPTS
CHAPTER 13

Choice C is incorrect. A touch-tone device is used for inputting data by using a touch-tone telephone. Choice D is incorrect. A laser bar code scanner reads bar codes, such as the universal produce code (UPC) which is found on grocery products and which is read with scanners that emit an intense light and are built into the counter or hand-held.

7. **A**   A plotter is an output device. It is a special type of printer used for producing graphical output. Generally, a plotter has a moving writing arm which draws across the paper. An architect would be interested in such a device. Choice B is incorrect. A mouse is a small input device which sends signals to the computer as it moves across a surface (a desk) and can be used to point to objects on the computer screen and activate them by clicking a button on the mouse. Choice C is incorrect. Magnetic ink character recognition (MICR) devices send input to the computer as they read characters and numbers printed with magnetic ink, most frequently from the bottom of bank checks. Choice D is incorrect. A light pen sends data to the computer using photoelectric circuitry through the computer screen.

8. **B**   A ring network is indeed wired like a ring, or a loop, such that each link passes communication through its neighbor. And a distributed data processing distributes the hardware in a manner where it may be tailored to the needs of that location's processing. All data does not need to go through the host (choice A)in a ring, although it would in a star network. There is not direct access (choice C)in a ring, but rather communication must pass through other links; it is a bus network which uses one common line with direct access. A ring is not a hierarchical (choice D) configuration, but rather a loop; it is a tree network which is hierarchical.

9. **B**   The ALU, the control unit, and primary storage are the three main components of the CPU. Other components are peripheral units. On-line devices [choice A] are not in the CPU. Auxiliary storage (choice C) is not in the CPU. Input-output devices (choice D) are not in the CPU.

10. **D**   The amount of time required to retrieve or access data from memory is access time. The time to transmit data from a remote terminal [choice A] applies only in networks and refers to transmittal rather than access. The time to complete a transaction (choice B) may involve multiple accesses and waiting; this is actually throughput time. The performance of a computer instruction (choice C) is very fast and may involve no accessing at all.

11. **D**   MICR is indeed the method used by banks, with necessary data (such as the bank identifier and the customer's account number) preprinted on the check with magnetic ink. A disk pack [choice A] is a storage unit, not a source automation device. Magnetic tape (choice B) is a storage unit, not a source automation device. Bar coding (choice C) is used on grocery products and many other items, but not on bank checks.

12. **A**   A LAN is within a limited proximity (local) and connects computers of all sizes. A LAN does not allow users to meet (choice B). A LAN may or may not provide access to an electronic library (choice C). A LAN may or may not improve effectiveness and reduce costs (choice D) and may not involve specialized hardware.

13. **D**   Data independence is a feature of a DBMS. Applications do not "own" data. Rather, data records are common, maintained by the DBMS which allows access to authorized users. New applications may be developed without concern about the data's physical structure. In a DBMS, units do not "own" their own data [choice A]. In a DBMS, users are not responsible for their own data [choice B] because applications do not typically "own"

©2007 Kaplan CPA Review
Page 437

STUDY MANUAL – BUSINESS ENVIRONMENT & CONCEPTS
CHAPTER 13

proprietary data and the DP department is concerned with data storage. A DBMS should have controls built in [choice C] because it is in fact more vulnerable than a file-oriented system as different users are all accessing common data.

14. **D** A relational database model does use flat files, or tables, which may be related to one another by means of common fields, columns or attributes. A complex network structure [choice A] links records together in an intricate variety of ways; they are not neatly stored in flat files. A network with a complex schema [choice B] links records together in an intricate variety of ways; they are not neatly stored in flat files. A simple network [choice C] links records together in an intricate variety of ways; they are not neatly stored in flat files.

15. **A** A file protection ring is a removable plastic or metal ring, the presence or absence of which prevents an employee from writing on a magnetic tape and thereby prevents the accidental destruction of a magnetic tape file. Answers B, C and D are other examples of input and processing controls.

16. **A** Boundary protection is a method of protecting access to unauthorized areas of a device such as a magnetic disc or drum. Sections of core storage are also partitioned so that more than one program can be operated at the same time. This method prevents overlapping of operations of one partition to another.

17. **A** One method for controlling identification numbers is to include an appended check digit as part of the number which is a result of some mathematical process that is applied to each digit in the number. The additional digit created is the result of this mathematical process.

18 **B** Batch processing is a technique in which items to be processed are collected into groups to permit convenient and efficient processing. The records of all transactions affecting a particular master file are accumulated over a period of time, then arranged in a sequence and processed against the master file. Because transactions are accumulated over a period of time, there will be time delays in processing transactions and errors may not be detected immediately.

19. **C** Misstatements may not be detected immediately because a batch computer system processes transactions in a batch or group, instead of individually. Therefore, there is a delay between the transaction and the processing while the transactions are accumulated. Choice (a) is incorrect because an error in one transaction will not cause the rejection of other transactions but rather the rejection of the entire batch until the errors are corrected. Choice (b) is incorrect because input controls typically are designed into the system to reduce the chance of errors being introduced when the transactions are entered. Choice (d) is incorrect because processing of transactions in a batch is intended to be uniform since all are processed at the same time by the same program.

Page 438   ©2007 Kaplan CPA Review

IT: BUSINESS INFORMATION SYSTEMS

STUDY MANUAL – BUSINESS ENVIRONMENT & CONCEPTS
CHAPTER 14

Study Tip: The biggest enemy that any CPA exam candidate faces is procrastination. Adequate preparation requires a significant number of hours. It is easy to put off doing the studying that is necessary. There is always something that absolutely has to be done prior to studying: paying the bills, washing the dishes, taking out the garbage, mowing the grass, etc. Eventually, the dishes get washed but the candidate never manages to get around to studying. Study first so you can avoid procrastination.

WHAT IS AN ACCOUNTING INFORMATION SYSTEM (AIS)?

- An AIS is a system that collects, records, stores, and processes data to produce information for decision makers.
- An AIS can use advanced technology, be a simple paper-and-pencil system, or be something in between. Technology is simply a tool to create, maintain, or improve a system.
- The functions of an AIS are to:
  - Collect and store data about events, resources, and agents.
  - Transform that data into information that management can use to make decisions about events, resources, and agents.
  - Provide adequate controls to ensure that the entity's resources (including data) are available when needed, as well as accurate and reliable.

WHY STUDY ACCOUNTING INFORMATION SYSTEMS?

- It's fundamental to accounting.
  - It helps accountants understand how information systems are designed, implemented and used, how financial information is reported, and how that information is used to make decisions.
  - While other accounting courses focus on how data is provided and used, an AIS course focuses on how data is collected and transformed and how its reliability is ensured.
- The skills are critical to career success.
  - Auditors need to evaluate accuracy and reliability of information.
  - Tax accountants need to have confidence in the accuracy of client data.
  - Systems work is considered the most important activity performed by accountants in private industry and not-for-profits.
  - Systems design is often an important aspect of management consulting.
- The AIS course complements other systems courses by emphasizing accountability and control rather than design and implementation.

©2007 Kaplan CPA Review

Page 439

STUDY MANUAL – BUSINESS ENVIRONMENT & CONCEPTS
CHAPTER 14

- AIS topics make up about 25% of the Business Environment and Concepts section of the CPA exam.
- AIS topics impact corporate strategy and culture.
  - AIS design is affected by IT, organization strategy, and organization culture.
  - IT affects the organization's business strategy.
  - The AIS affects organization culture by altering the dispersion and availability of information.

ROLE OF THE AIS IN THE VALUE CHAIN

- The objective of most organizations is to provide value to their customers. While "adding value" is a commonly used buzzword, in its genuine sense, it means making the value of the finished component greater than the sum of its parts. It may mean making it faster, making it more reliable, providing better service or advice, providing something in limited supply (like O-negative blood or rare gems), providing enhanced features, or customizing it.
- Value is provided by performing a series of activities referred to as the value chain. These include primary and support activities (sometimes referred to as "line" and "staff" activities respectively).
- Primary activities include:
  - Inbound logistics—receiving, storing, and distributing inputs.
  - Operations—transforming inputs into outputs.
  - Outbound logistics—distributing goods or services to customers.
  - Marketing and sales—helping customers buy the product.
  - Service—post-sale support, such as repair and maintenance.
- Support activities include:
  - Firm infrastructure—accountants, lawyers, administration, AIS.
  - Human resources—recruiting, hiring, training, and compensating.
  - Technology—R&D, website development, and other activities to improve products or services.
  - Purchasing—buying inputs and other resources.
- Information technology can significantly impact the efficiency and effectiveness with which the preceding activities are carried out. An organization's value chain can be connected with the value chains of its customers, suppliers, and distributors. The linking of these separate value chains creates a larger system known as a supply chain. IT can facilitate synergistic linkages that improve the performance of each company's value chain.
- There is variation in the degree of structure used to make decisions:
  - Structured decisions—repetitive and routine, can be delegated to lower-level employees; relate to day-to-day performance of specific tasks.
  - Semi-structured decisions—have incomplete rules and require some subjectivity; relate to utilizing resources to accomplish organizational objectives (e.g., budgeting).
  - Unstructured decisions—Nonrecurring and non-routine; require much subjectivity; involves setting those objectives and the policies to achieve them.

INFORMATION AND COMMUNICATION

The primary purpose of the AIS is to gather, record, process, store, summarize, and communicate information about an organization. So accountants must understand how transactions are initiated, data are captured in or converted to machine-readable form, computer files are accessed and updated, data are processed, and information is reported to internal and external parties. Accountants must also understand the accounting records and procedures, supporting documents, and specific financial statement accounts involved in processing and reporting transactions. The preceding items facilitate an audit trail which allows for transactions to be traced from origin to financial statements and vice versa.

MONITORING

Monitoring can be accomplished with a series of ongoing events or by separate evaluations. Key methods of monitoring performance include: performing ERM (enterprise risk management) evaluation, implementing effective supervision, using responsibility accounting, monitoring system activities, tracking purchased software, conducting periodic audits, employing a computer security officer and security consultants, engaging forensic specialists, installing fraud detection software, and implementing a fraud hotline.

BUSINESS CYCLES

- A *transaction* is an agreement between two entities to exchange goods or services OR any other event that can be measured in economic terms by an organization (e.g., sell goods to customers; depreciate equipment).
- The **transaction cycle** is a process that begins with capturing data about a transaction and ends with an information output, such as a set of financial statements.
- Many business activities are paired in give-get exchanges.
- The basic exchanges can be grouped into five major transaction cycles.
  - **Revenue cycle**—Interactions with customers. Give goods; get cash.
  - **Expenditure cycle**—Interactions with suppliers. Give cash; get goods.
  - **Production cycle**—Give labor and raw materials; get finished product.
  - **Human resources/payroll cycle**—Give cash; get labor.
  - **Financing cycle**—Give cash; get cash.
- Thousands of transactions can occur within any of these cycles, but there are relatively few types of transactions in a cycle.
- Every transaction cycle relates to other cycles and interfaces with the general ledger and reporting system, which generates information for management and external parties.
- The revenue cycle gets finished goods from the production cycle, provides funds to the financing cycle, and provides data to the general ledger and reporting system.
- The expenditure cycle gets funds from the financing cycle, provides raw materials to the production cycle, and provides data to the general ledger and reporting system.
- The production cycle gets raw materials from the expenditure cycle, gets labor from the HR/payroll cycle, provides finished goods to the revenue cycle, and provides data to the general ledger and reporting system.

STUDY MANUAL – BUSINESS ENVIRONMENT & CONCEPTS
CHAPTER 14

- The HR/payroll cycle gets funds from the financing cycle, provides labor to the production cycle, and provides data to the general ledger and reporting system.
- The financing cycle gets funds from the revenue cycle, provides funds to the expenditure and HR/payroll cycles, and provides data to the general ledger and reporting system.
- The general ledger and reporting system gets data from all of the cycles and provides information for internal and external users.
- Many accounting software packages implement the different transaction cycles as separate modules. Not every module is needed in every organization (e.g., retail companies don't have a production cycle). Some companies may need extra modules. So the implementation of each transaction cycle can differ significantly across companies.
- However the cycles are implemented, it is critical that the AIS be able to accommodate the information needs of managers and integrate financial and non-financial data.

IMPORTANT TYPES OF APPLICATIONS

1. Enterprise Resource Planning systems (ERP Systems) are integrated software packages designed to provide complete integration of an organization's business information processing systems.

   - Larger ERP systems are integrated with Computer Aided Design (CAD) systems and other engineering systems to improve productivity, reduce lead-time and costs, and enhance product quality.
   - Basic business information systems activities include:
     - Data entry (manually and electronically).
     - Billing.
     - Collections.
     - Inventory Management.
     - Purchasing.
     - Payments.
     - Human Resources and Payroll.
     - Financial Reporting.
     - Logistics.
     - Planning and Budgeting.
   - A key feature of an ERP system is that there is one database of information which is linked to all the applications within the company.
     - One database receives, stores, and feeds data back to all affected systems.
     - For example, when a sales person enters an order, the following systems can be updated from this one data element: sales orders, inventory, production schedules, and purchase orders (P.O.s for the necessary materials to create a product for sale in a manufacturing company or for additional products for sale in a merchandising company.)
   - Additionally, ERP systems can collect and store non-financial data. Information such as employee or customer addresses, employee numbers, customer profiles, etc. can be stored as well.

2. Decision Support Systems (DSS):

- Management will make decisions based on the outputs or results of the DSS.
- Examples are spreadsheets, project planning software, databases, ad-hoc querying, etc.

3. Executive Information Systems (EIS) or Executive Support Systems (ESS):

- Preprogrammed executions or business intelligence based on a desired set of outputs or results.
- Such systems provide just the needed data in a format that is easily accessed and understood, whether graphical or tabular.
- These are implemented to support executive-level decision making.
- Examples are "Red/Yellow/Green" or "Traffic Light" reports, sales/marketing systems providing real time price quotes/trends of commodities to senior management.

4. Group Support Systems (GSS):

- These systems collaborate many users' information and generate analyses, recommendations, or solutions.
- Examples are company calendar or meeting scheduling system and document sharing.

5. Expert Systems (ES:)

- These systems perform an extremely complex synthesis of data from many environments to emulate problem-solving techniques.
- For example, one complex company system monitors the systems of Human Resources, Accounting, sales/marketing, and corporate property to recommend optimal product mixes (modeling).

6. Intelligent Agents:

- These are decision support systems with automated assistance and advice based on lessons learned from patterns in data input.
- Examples are spelling and grammar checking, help wizards, and auto-formatting.

7. Customer Relationship Management Systems (CRM):

- A customer service system designed to manage all data related to customers, such as marketing, field service, and contract management.
- CRM has become the primary focus of managers and CIOs for prioritizing new systems acquisitions.
- An example would be large customer service center phone banks.
- The objective of a CRM is to retain customers.

8. Management Reporting Systems (MRS):

©2007 Kaplan CPA Review

Page 443

STUDY MANUAL – BUSINESS ENVIRONMENT & CONCEPTS
CHAPTER 14

- An accounting information subsystem that produces "Special Purpose" reports for internal purposes.

These MRS generate financial statements and other financial reports based on the needs of the company.

STUDY MANUAL – BUSINESS ENVIRONMENT & CONCEPTS
CHAPTER 14

QUESTIONS: IT: BUSINESS INFORMATION SYSTEMS

1. All of the following are examples of a decision support system (DSS) **EXCEPT**:
   A. financial modeling application.
   B. transaction processing system.
   C. database query application.
   D. sensitivity analysis application.

2. Which one of the following terms *best* describes a decision support system (DSS)?
   A. Management reporting system.
   B. Formalized system.
   C. Structured system.
   D. Interactive system.

3. In order to prevent, detect, and correct errors and unauthorized tampering, a payroll system should have adequate controls. The *best* set of controls for a payroll system includes:
   A. batch and hash totals, record counts of each run, proper separation of duties, passwords and user codes, and backup copies of activity and master files.
   B. employee supervision, batch totals, record counts of each run, and payments by check.
   C. passwords and user codes, batch totals, employee supervision, and record counts of each run.
   D. sign test, limit tests, passwords and user codes, online edit checks and payments by check.

4. An accounting information system must include certain source documents in order to control purchasing and accounts payable. For a manufacturing organization, the *best* set of documents should include:
   A. purchase requisitions, purchase orders, inventory reports of goods needed, and vendor invoices.
   B. purchase orders, receiving reports, and inventory reports of goods needed.
   C. purchase orders, receiving reports, and vendor invoices.
   D. purchase requisitions, purchase orders, receiving reports, and vendor invoices.

5. Which one of the following statements about an accounting information system (AIS) is **INCORRECT**?
   A. AIS supports day-to-day operations by collecting and sorting data about an organization's transactions.
   B. The information produced by AIS is made available to all levels of management for use in planning and controlling an organization's activities.
   C. AIS is best suited to solve problems where there is great uncertainty and ill-defined reporting requirements.
   D. AIS is often referred to as a transaction processing system.

©2007 Kaplan CPA Review
Page 445

STUDY MANUAL – BUSINESS ENVIRONMENT & CONCEPTS
CHAPTER 14

6. Which one of the following features is *least likely* to apply to the transaction processing cycle of an accounting information system?
   A. Data records are chiefly historical in nature.
   B. Most of the sources of data are an organization's recurring transactions.
   C. Data are usually financial in nature.
   D. Data records are the basis of predictive systems.

7. Which one of the following statements about an executive information system (EIS) is **INCORRECT**? The EIS:
   A. is likely to be one of the most widely used and the largest of the information subsystems in a business organization.
   B. helps executives monitor business conditions in general and assists in strategic planning to control and operate the company.
   C. is designed to accept data from many different sources; combine, integrate, and summarize the data; and to display this data in a format that is easy to understand and use.
   D. provides information that is highly aggregated; however, the details supporting the aggregated data are accessible.

8. Which of the following statements *most likely* represents a disadvantage for an entity that keeps microcomputer-prepared data files rather than manually prepared files?
   A. Attention is focused on the accuracy of the programming process rather than errors in individual transactions.
   B. It is usually easier for unauthorized persons to access and alter the files.
   C. Random error associated with processing similar transactions in different ways is usually greater.
   D. It is usually more difficult to compare recorded accountability with physical count of assets.

STUDY MANUAL – BUSINESS ENVIRONMENT & CONCEPTS
CHAPTER 14

ANSWERS: IT: BUSINESS INFORMATION SYSTEMS

1. **B**   A transaction processing system is not a DSS. A transaction processing system processes (usually accounting) transactions at the basic level of an organization, providing outputs usually on scheduled reports. A DSS, on the other hand, provides support for unstructured or semistructured decisions and suggests possible choices, accessing a database or a decision-making model. Answer (a) is not correct because a financial modeling application is an example of a DSS. These systems provide support for unstructured or semi-structured decisions and suggest possible choices, accessing a database or a decision making model. Answer (c) is not correct because a database query application is an example of a DSS. These systems provide support for unstructured or semistructured decisions and suggest possible choices, accessing a database or a decision-making model. Answer (d) is not correct because a sensitivity analysis application is an example of a DSS. Sensitivity analysis involves making changes to some parameters or inputs and observing the impact of such changes on the result. DSSs, likewise, provide support for unstructured or semistructured decisions and suggest possible choices, accessing a database or a decision-making model.

2. **D**   A DSS is interactive. The user's active involvement is essential, providing inputs and reacting to outputs as the DSS suggests decision choices. Answer (a) is not correct because a management reporting system may only provide reports to management, rather than accepting inputs from the manager and providing decision choices. Answer (b) is not correct because a formalized system refers to the documented, official, methods of sending, receiving, and processing information in an organization. Answer (c) is not correct because a structured system is one in which solutions may be automated because of readily defined rules. DSSs are used in unstructured or semistructured environments.

3. **A**   This is a good combination of controls. Batch and hash totals and record counts will detect input errors or skipped records. Proper separation of duties will prevent unauthorized tampering and could help detect errors. Passwords and user codes can prevent unauthorized tampering. And backup copies can help correct errors when files are damaged.

4. **D**   This is a good combination. The purchase requisition is evidence that some user needs the goods. The purchase order specifies the price and quantity authorized by the purchasing department. The receiving report is evidence of the quantity actually received. The vendor invoice is evidence of the vendor's request to be paid for the specified quantity (which should be matched with the receiving report and purchase order) and price (which should be matched with the purchase order).

5. **C**   An AIS is generally designed to process routine transactions on a regular basis. Its decisions are very structured. Thus, unlike a decision support system, an AIS is not well-suited to solve problems where there is great uncertainty or ill-defined reporting requirements. Choice (a) is incorrect. An AIS is designed for day-to-day processing of accounting transactions, at the operational level of a company. Transactions are often collected and sorted for batch processing. Choice (b) is incorrect. Unlike other information systems, which might be available only for top management, accounting information is generally used by all levels of management for their functions of planning, controlling, and evaluating performance. Choice (d) is incorrect. Although there are other types of information systems, such as operational support systems, decision support systems, and executive information systems, AISs are considered transaction processing systems because they process accounting transactions at the basic level of the organization.

©2007 Kaplan CPA Review
Page 447

STUDY MANUAL – BUSINESS ENVIRONMENT & CONCEPTS
CHAPTER 14

6. **D** Processing transactions is the basic level of an accounting information system. The transactions could be for accounts receivable, accounts payable, payroll, etc. These records are designed for controlling the basic cycles of the company, and they are not designed for their predictive ability. Choice (a) is incorrect. The data records for transaction processing cycles, such as accounts receivable, accounts payable, or payroll, are designed for storage and processing of historical information. Choice (b) is incorrect. While there are some nonrecurring transactions, most of the transactions in these cycles are recurring ones, such as sales, purchases, and payroll. Choice (c) is incorrect. Accounting transactions do turn economic data about the company and its external relationships into financial information.

7. **A** An EIS is not designed to be widely used. It is tailored to the needs of a specific executive. For example, an EIS for the treasurer, will include measuring tools needed to control that specific function, such as interest rates and cash balances. Choice (b) is incorrect. The executive information systems of the various executives will have some elements in common for all the executives about the business conditions and some specific elements to help each executive in controlling functional areas. Choice (c) is incorrect. An EIS includes traditional internal company data and also nontraditional data from external sources (such as stock quotes and breaking news) integrated in a way that is not so complex that it would be difficult to use. Choice (d) is incorrect. Executives, with their broad scope of responsibility, must see information in aggregated form; however, if they are interested in probing, they should have access to the supporting detail.

8. **B** In manual accounting systems, records are kept and files are prepared by individuals who are responsible and accountable for security of and access to those files and records. In order to alter the records, an unauthorized individual would have to manually access the files and manually make changes. Accessing and altering files in a microcomputer-based accounting system is usually easier. If an unauthorized individual successfully enters the computer system, he or she may be able to access and alter many records. The microcomputer-prepared data files could then be changed electronically, leaving no indication that an unauthorized individual entered the system and changed data. Answer (a) is incorrect because, although it may be true that attention is focused on programming rather than individual transactions, this is not necessarily a disadvantage of a microcomputer-based system. Answer (c) is incorrect because random error is usually less in a microcomputer-based system since transactions are processed uniformly. Answer (d) is incorrect because it is not more difficult to compare records with physical counts if an entity has microcomputer-prepared records.

IT: System Operation

Study Manual – Business Environment & Concepts
Chapter 15

Study Tip: When you are studying a complicated subject such as the equity method of accounting, it is good to remind yourself that you do not need to be perfect. There is no need to shoot for a grade of 100. You only have to make a grade of 75 in order to pass the CPA exam and that means that you can miss a lot of questions and still pass. That is quite different from school where teachers write most tests looking for students who can answer all of the questions. On the CPA exam, any grade above 75 indicates that the candidate studied too hard.

TRANSACTION PROCESSING: THE DATA PROCESSING CYCLE

- Accountants play an important role in data processing. They answer questions such as: What data should be entered and stored? Who should be able to access the data? How should the data be organized, updated, stored, accessed, and retrieved? How can scheduled and unanticipated information needs be met? To answer these questions, they must understand data processing concepts.
- An important function of the AIS is to efficiently and effectively process the data about a company's transactions. In **manual** systems, data is entered into paper journals and ledgers. In **computer-based** systems, the series of operations performed on data is referred to as the data processing cycle.
- The data processing cycle consists of four steps: (1) data input, (2) data storage, (3) data processing, and (4) information output.

DATA INPUT

- The first step in data processing is to capture the data. This capture is usually triggered by a business activity. Data is captured about the **event** that occurred, the **resources** affected by the event, and the **agents** who participated.
- A number of actions can be taken to improve the accuracy and efficiency of data input:
  - Turnaround documents.
  - Source data automation.
  - Well-designed source documents and data entry screens.
  - Using prenumbered documents or having the system automatically assign sequential numbers to transactions.
  - Verifying transactions.

©2007 Kaplan CPA Review

Page 449

STUDY MANUAL – BUSINESS ENVIRONMENT & CONCEPTS
CHAPTER 15

DATA STORAGE

- Data needs to be organized for easy and efficient access. Let's start with some vocabulary terms with respect to data storage.
- A **ledger** is a file used to store cumulative information about resources and agents. We typically use the word ledger to describe the set of t-accounts. The t-account is where we keep track of the beginning balance, increases, decreases, and ending balance for each asset, liability, owners' equity, revenue, expense, gain, loss, and dividend account.
- The **general ledger** is the summary level information for all accounts. Detail information is not kept in general ledger accounts.
- The **subsidiary ledgers** contain the detail accounts associated with the related general ledger account. The related general ledger account is often called a **control** account. The sum of the subsidiary account balances should equal the balance in the control account.
- **Coding** is a method of systematically assigning numbers or letters to data items to help classify and organize them. There are many types of codes, including sequence codes, block codes, and group codes.
- With **sequence codes**, items such as checks or invoices are numbered consecutively to ensure no gaps in the sequence. The numbering helps ensure that all items are accounted for and that there are no duplicate numbers (which would suggest errors or fraud).
- When **block codes** are used, blocks of numbers within a numerical sequence are reserved for a particular category.
- When **group codes** are used, two or more subgroups of digits are used to code an item. Group coding schemes are often used in assigning general ledger account numbers. The following guidelines should be observed:
  - The code should be consistent with its intended use, so make sure you know what users need.
  - Provide enough digits to allow room for growth.
  - Keep it simple in order to minimize costs, facilitate memorization, and ensure employee acceptance.
  - Make sure it's consistent with the company's organization structure and other divisions of the organization.
- The **chart of accounts** is a list of all general ledger accounts an organization uses. Group coding is often used for these numbers, for example:
  - The first section identifies the major account categories, such as asset, liability, revenue, etc.
  - The second section identifies the primary sub-account, such as current asset or long-term investment.
  - The third section identifies the specific account, such as accounts receivable or inventory.
  - The fourth section identifies the subsidiary account (e.g., the specific customer code for an account receivable).
- The structure of the chart of accounts is an important AIS issue, as it must contain sufficient detail to meet the organization's needs.
- In manual systems and some accounting packages, the first place that transactions are entered is the **journal**.

Page 450   ©2007 Kaplan CPA Review

- A **general journal** is used to record nonroutine transactions, such as loan payments, summaries of routine transactions, adjusting entries, and closing entries.
- A **special journal** is used to record routine transactions. The most common special journals are cash receipts, cash disbursements, credit sales, and credit purchases.
- An **audit trail** exists when there is sufficient documentation to allow the tracing of a transaction from beginning to end or from the end back to the beginning. The inclusion of posting references and document numbers enable the tracing of transactions through the journals and ledgers and, therefore, facilitate the audit trail.
- When transaction data is captured on a source document, the next step is to record the data in a journal. A journal entry is made for each transaction showing the accounts and amounts to be debited and credited.
- When **routine transactions** occur, they are initially recorded in **special journals** (e.g., cash receipts, cash disbursements, credit sales, credit purchases). When **nonroutine transactions** occur, they are recorded in the *general journal.*
- Periodically, the transactions in the special journal are totaled, and a summary entry is made in the general journal. The individual line items in the special journal are posted to the subsidiary ledger accounts, and the items in the general journal are posted to the general ledger.
- Periodically, the balances in the general ledger control accounts are compared to the sums of the balances in the related subsidiary accounts.

DATA PROCESSING

- Once data about a business activity has been collected and entered into a system, it must be processed.
- There are four different types of file processing:
  - **Updating data** to record the occurrence of an event, the resources affected by the event, and the agents who participated (e.g., recording a sale to a customer).
  - **Changing data** (e.g., a customer address).
  - **Adding data** (e.g., a new customer).
  - **Deleting data** (e.g., removing an old customer that has not purchased anything in five years).
- Updating can be done through several approaches:
- **Batch Processing**—Source documents are grouped into batches, and control totals are calculated. Periodically, the batches are entered into the computer system, edited, sorted, and stored in a temporary file. The temporary transaction file is run against the master file to update the master file. Output is printed or displayed, along with error reports, transaction reports, and control totals.
- **Online Batch Processing**—Transactions are entered into a computer system as they occur and stored in a temporary file. Periodically, the temporary transaction file is run against the master file to update the master file. The output is printed or displayed.
- **Online, Real-time Processing**—Transactions are entered into a computer system as they occur. The master file is immediately updated with the data from the transaction. Output is printed or displayed.

INFORMATION OUTPUT

- The final step in the information process is information output.
- This output can be in the form of:

©2007 Kaplan CPA Review

- **Documents**—Records of transactions or other company data, such as paychecks or purchase orders. Documents generated at the end of the transaction processing activities are known as **operational documents** (as opposed to source documents). They can be printed or stored as electronic images.
- **Reports**—Used by employees to control operational activities and by managers to make decisions and design strategies. They may be produced on a regular basis, on an exception basis, or on demand. Organizations should periodically reassess whether each report is needed.
- **Queries**—User requests for specific pieces of information. They may be requested periodically or one time and can be displayed on the monitor (soft copy) or on paper (hard copy).
- Output can serve a variety of purposes:
  - Financial statements can be provided to both external and internal parties.
  - Some outputs are specifically for internal use:
- For planning purposes, such as budgets and sales forecasts.
- For management of day-to-day operations (e.g., delivery schedules).
- For control purposes, such as performance reports.
- For evaluation purposes, such as employee error rates.
- With managerial reports, you get what you measure. If you're not very careful about what you measure, there can be dysfunctional results, such as managers foregoing needed equipment maintenance to stay within a budget.

ROLE OF THE AIS

- The traditional AIS captured financial data. Nonfinancial data was captured in other, sometimes redundant, systems.
- Enterprise resource planning (ERP) systems are designed to integrate all aspects of a company's operations (including both financial and nonfinancial information) with the traditional functions of an AIS.

THE AIS AND CORPORATE STRATEGY

- Corporations have unlimited opportunities to invest in technology but limited resources with which to do so. Consequently, they must identify the improvements likely to yield the highest return. This decision requires an understanding of the entity's overall business strategy.
- Michael Porter suggests that there are two basic business strategies companies can follow—either a product-differentiation strategy or a low-cost strategy.
- A **product differentiation strategy** involves setting your product apart from those of your competitors (i.e., building a "better" mousetrap by offering one that's faster, has enhanced features, etc).
- A **low-cost strategy** involves offering a cheaper mousetrap than your competitors. The low cost is made possible by operating more efficiently.
- Sometimes a company can do both, but they normally have to choose.
- Porter also argues that companies must choose a strategic position among three choices:
  - **Variety-based** strategic position—Offers a subset of the industry's products or services (e.g., an insurance company that only offers life insurance).

- **Needs-based** strategic position—Serves most or all of the needs of a particular group of customers in a target market (e.g., farm bureau insurance companies that tailors products to the needs of farmers).
- **Access-based** strategic position—Serves a subset of customers who differ from others in terms of factors such as geographic location or size (e.g., providing satellite internet to rural users who do not have access to cable or DSL).

- These strategic positions are not mutually exclusive and can overlap
- Choosing a strategic position is important because it helps a company focus its efforts as opposed to trying to be everything to everybody (e.g, a radio station that tries to play all types of music will probably fail).
- It's critical to design the organization's activities so that they reinforce one another in achieving the selected strategic position. The result is synergy, which is difficult for competitors to imitate.
- The growth of the Internet has profoundly affected the way value chain activities are performed:
  - Inbound and outbound logistics can be streamlined for products that can be digitized, like books and music.
  - The Internet allows companies to cut costs, which impacts strategy and strategic position.
  - Because the Internet is available to everyone, intense price competition can result. The outcome may be that many companies shift from low-cost to product-differentiation strategies.
  - The Internet may impede access-based strategic positions.
- The AIS should help a company adopt and maintain its strategic position. Requires that data be collected about each activity and requires the collection and integration of both financial and nonfinancial data.
- The authors believe that accounting and information systems should be closely integrated and that the AIS should be the primary information system to provide users with information they need to perform their jobs.

STUDY MANUAL – BUSINESS ENVIRONMENT & CONCEPTS
CHAPTER 15

QUESTIONS: IT: SYSTEM OPERATION

1. The indexed-sequential-access method (ISAM) is an approach to file
    organization:
    A. in which each data record has a pointer filed containing the address of the
        next record in the list.
    B. where an index of record pointers of some of the file attributes are maintained
        in a list.
    C. utilizes an algorithm to convert a record key into a storage address to assist
        with later retrieval.
    D. where records are stored sequentially in a direct access file and organized by a
        primary key stored in an index record.

2. Block codes:
    A. are generally used to identify missing items from a set of documents or
        records.
    B. allow a user to number items sequentially.
    C. allow a user to assign meaning to particular segments of a coding scheme.
    D. are randomly calculated groups of numbers used as a control check.

3. The real-time feature normally would be *least* useful when applied to accounting
    for a firm's:
    A. bank account balances.
    B. property and depreciation.
    C. customer accounts receivable.
    D. merchandise inventory.

4. A fundamental programming technique which allows computers to be utilized
    effectively in solving repetitive problems is:
    A. dynamic reallocation.
    B. indexed sequential access.
    C. graceful degradation.
    D. looping.

5. Which of the following is a characteristic of an integrated system for data
    processing?
    A. An integrated system is a real-time system where files for different functions
        with similar information are separated.
    B. A single input record describing a transaction initiates the updating of all files
        associated with the transaction.
    C. Parallel operations strengthen internal control over the computer processing
        function.
    D. Files are maintained according to organizational functions such as
        purchasing, accounts payable, sales, etc.

Page 454   ©2007 Kaplan CPA Review

6. An electronic data processing technique, which collects data into groups to permit convenient and efficient processing, is known as:
   A. document-count processing.
   B. multprogramming.
   C. batch processing.
   D. generalized-audit processing.

7. Which of the following controls is a processing control designed to ensure the reliability and accuracy of data processing?

	Limit test	Validity check test
a.	Yes	Yes
b.	No	No
c.	No	Yes
d.	Yes	No

8. In an accounting information system, which of the following types of computer files *most likely* would be a master file?
   A. Inventory subsidiary.
   B. Cash disbursements.
   C. Cash receipts.
   D. Payroll transactions.

STUDY MANUAL – BUSINESS ENVIRONMENT & CONCEPTS
CHAPTER 15

ANSWERS: IT: SYSTEM OPERATION

1. **D** ISAM files are stored sequentially by primary key on a direct access device, such as a disk. In addition, there is a separate index or directory in which the system may look up a key and find that record's disk address. Thus, records may be processed sequentially, but may also be accessed directly for queries. ISAM records do not have pointer fields embedded in them [choice (a)] like a linked list; rather, there is a separate index for such pointers. It is not some of the attributes [choice (b)] for which the index is maintained. ISAM does not utilize an algorithm [choice (c)] the way that randomization does.

2. **C** Lock coding does reserve a block of numbers or letters for a particular segment. To identify missing items [choice (a)], sequential coding would be used. To number items sequentially [choice (b)], sequential coding would be used. Block codes are not randomly calculated and not used as a control check [choice (d)].

3. **B** The real time feature of a computer is best used on accounting data that requires frequent inquiries. Property depreciation would have the least reason for the real time feature.

4. **D** A loop is a sequence of instructions that can be executed repetitively. Each repetition is called a cycle, and cycling continues until a specified criteria is satisfied.

5. **B** An integrated data processing system is a system designed to minimize duplicate operations and duplicate records. The most important characteristic would be a single input record describing a given transaction which initiates the updating of all files associated with the transaction.

6. **C** Batch processing is a technique in which items to be processed are collected into groups (batches) to permit convenient and efficient processing.

7. **B** Edit checks are computer-programmed routines that are designed to detect data entry errors. Accordingly, a direct output of the edit checks of sales data being entered into a system would be a file or list of all sales transactions rejected by the edit checks. Answers (a) and (d) are incorrect because missing sales invoices and voided shipping documents would not be reflected on output generated from edit checks on data entry because sales invoices and shipping documents are generated after sales data are entered into the system. Answer (c) is incorrect because a printout of user codes and passwords would relate to general controls over access rather than application controls over data entry.

8. **A** Master files contain permanent data such as general ledge accounts. Answers (b), (c) and (d) are all examples of transaction files, which are subsequently used to update the master file.

Page 456   ©2007 Kaplan CPA Review

IT: IT ROLES AND RESPONSIBILITIES

STUDY MANUAL – BUSINESS ENVIRONMENT & CONCEPTS
CHAPTER 16

Study Tip: A key to passing the CPA exam is to break each topic into learnable segments. Normally, each topic is composed of several different specific steps. Break the topic into those steps and then learn each one individually. Passing the CPA exam becomes quite difficult when a candidate attempts to learn a major topic as a single whole. That is similar to trying to eat a watermelon without cutting it into pieces. People come to understand the topic better when they are faced with a segment of information that is small enough to be learnable.

Systems Administrators are responsible for ensuring that the different parts of an information system operate smoothly and efficiently. A system administrator must be knowledgeable about website architecture and infrastructure, network security, firewall products, and basic hardware functionality. A system administrator will generally bear responsibility for the following:

1. Setting up servers.

2. Configuring system capacity (space).

3. Establishing and maintaining e-mail accounts and e-mail mailing lists.

4. Security procedures for intranets.

5. Installing firewall software.

6. System and data backups.

7. Implementing updates to software and hardware.

Network Managers ensure that all applicable devices are linked to the organization's internal and external networks and that the networks operate continuously and properly.

Security Management ensures that all components of the system are secure and protected from all internal and external threats. Responsibilities include security of software and systems and granting appropriate access to systems via user authentication, password set-up, and maintenance.

Change Management. These individuals manage all changes to an organization's information system to ensure they are made smoothly and efficiently and to prevent errors and fraud.

©2007 Kaplan CPA Review   Page 457

Users. Users of the system record transactions, authorize data to be processed, and use output.

Systems Analysts help users determine their information needs and then design an information system to meet those needs.

1. Systems analysts are the "designers" of the system.

2. Systems analysts determine user requirements (through interviews and observations) and write new system specifications.

3. They understand and prepare data flow diagrams (and other documentation) of systems.

4. These analysts study information-related problems and propose solutions.

Programmers take the design provided by systems analysts and create an information system by writing the computer programs.

Systems programmers convert a designer's specifications into the system, bringing multiple systems together to achieve a common purpose.

1. They modify and adapt system software [including operating systems] and other utility software.

2. A systems programmer would develop an operating system for a microcomputer, for example, but would not be involved in developing the applications that run on that microcomputer.

Applications programmers convert a designer's specifications into applications programs.

1. They code, test, and debug applications programs, and configure and customize existing applications.

2. An example of an applications program might be a general ledger system, a payroll system, or a word processing system.

Computer operators run the software in the company's computers. They ensure that data are input properly and correctly processed and needed output is produced.

Information System Librarian. The librarian maintains custody of corporate databases, files, and programs in a separate storage area called the information system library.

1. In the world of Information Technology, librarians manage, protect, and store software, data files, backup files, etc., to protect it from damage, misappropriation or unauthorized use.

2. They maintain records of data, programs, and document usage.

Data Control. The data control group ensures that source data have been properly approved, monitors the flow of work through the computer, reconciles input and output, maintains a record of input errors to ensure their correction and resubmission, and distributes systems output.

Database Administrators (DBAs) In general, a DBA is responsible for the planning, development and maintenance of databases. A DBA should ensure the following:

1. Data consistency throughout the database.

2. Clear definitions of the types of data stored.

3. Customer satisfaction with the data.

4. Security and recoverability of data.

Network Administrators

1. Install and support the computer and telecommunication hardware and software.

2. Help users acquire, setup, and properly utilize various computer networks.

Web Administrators

1. Web administrators are responsible for the operation and support of a web server and for content hosted on that server (including updates and maintenance).

2. A web server is a software application that uses the hypertext transfer protocol (recognized as http://).

3. A web server is usually run on a computer that is connected to the Internet.

4. There are many web server software applications, including public domain software from Apache and commercial applications from Microsoft and Oracle.

Help Desk Personnel answer help line calls and e-mails, resolves user problems, and obtain technical support and vendor support when necessary.

STUDY MANUAL – BUSINESS ENVIRONMENT & CONCEPTS
CHAPTER 16

CIO

1. A Chief Information Officer, also referred to as the vice president of information technology, generally reports to the Chief Executive Officer (CEO).

2. The CIO is responsible for efficient and effective functions of existing systems and for planning for the development and technical resources for future systems.

3. The CIO is ultimately in control of hardware and software operations for the entire company.

SEGREGATION OF DUTIES IN INFORMATION TECHNOLOGY FUNCTIONS

A. In general, segregation of duties refers to the assignment of job duties, tasks and responsibilities in such a manner that no individual employee can both carry on and cover up errors or irregularities.

B. Without proper segregation of duties, an organization may fail to achieve input accuracy or update accuracy; ultimately leading to misleading record keeping and management decisions.

C. The general model for segregation of duties follows:

1 Authorization (approval).

2 Execution (physical activity such as pick, move, ship).

3 Recordation (record or post).

4 Safeguarding resources (physically protect and maintain accountability of physical resources).

D. The IT function will primarily carry out control plans related to just recordation between the following specific areas:

1. Users.

2. Information system library.

3. Data control.

4. Computer operations.

5. Programming.

6. System analysis.

Page 460   ©2007 Kaplan CPA Review

E. It is the responsibility of management in other areas to primarily ensure proper safeguard, authorization, and execution.

Figure 1

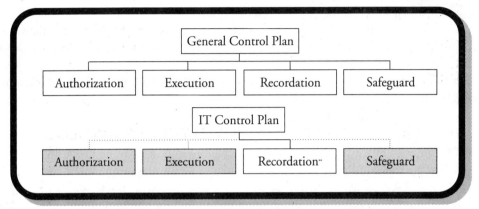

F. Because of the trend toward systems integration, procedures that were once performed by separate individuals are now combined. This increases the opportunity for an individual to commit fraudulent acts, which makes segregation of duties extremely important in the overall security of systems and data.

G. The division of authority and responsibility must be clearly demonstrated among the various components of the information technology function, including:

1 Systems administration.

2 Network management.

3 Security management.

4 Change management.

5 Users.

6 Systems analysis.

7 Programming.

8 Computer operations.

9 Library.

10 Data control.

H. Consider some examples:

1. If a computer programmer was also a user of the Payroll system, she would be able to implement changes to the program to increase her own pay amount.

STUDY MANUAL – BUSINESS ENVIRONMENT & CONCEPTS
CHAPTER 16

    2.   If a programmer in a bank had access to actual, live data to test new programs, he might be able to delete his car loan balance from the bank's systems.

  I.   Compare this discussion of segregation of duties in IT to the traditional concept as it is applied in the accounting control environment.

        1.   In accounting, we think of segregation of duties related to the different stages of a business transaction.

        2.   We separate authorizing transactions from recording transactions from maintaining custody of physical assets.

In the IT function, we are segregating duties related to access—access to hardware, software, files, systems and procedures.

STUDY MANUAL – BUSINESS ENVIRONMENT & CONCEPTS
CHAPTER 16

QUESTIONS: IT: IT ROLES & RESPONSIBILITIES

1. Which one of the following tasks is *least likely* to be undertaken in the implementation phase of an accounting software application?
   A. Obtain and install hardware.
   B. Enter and verify test data.
   C. Identify inputs and outputs.
   D. Document user procedures.

2. A systems analyst who is responsible for the development of an organization's information system is *least likely* to perform which one of the following functions?
   A. Analyze the present system.
   B. Prepare computer program specifications.
   C. Design computer applications.
   D. Develop and code computer programs.

3. An information system (IS) project manager is currently in the process of adding a systems analyst to the IS staff. The new systems analyst will be involved with the testing of the new computerized system. At which stage of the systems development life cycle will the analyst be primarily used?
   A. Conceptual design.
   B. Cost-benefit analysis.
   C. Requirements definition.
   D. Implementation.

4. The process of learning how the current system functions, determining the needs of users, and developing the logical requirements of proposed system is referred to as:
   A. systems maintenance.
   B. systems analysis.
   C. systems feasibility study.
   D. systems design.

5. Which one of the following *best* reflects the basic elements of a data flow diagram?
   A. Data sources, data flows, computer configurations, flowchart, and data storage.
   B. Data source, data destination, data flows, transformation processes, and data storage.
   C. Data flows, data storage, and program flowchart.
   D. Data flows, program flowchart, and data destination.

6. Which one of the following *best* depicts the path of data as it moves through an information system?
   A. Program flowcharts.
   B. Computer system flowcharts.
   C. Decision table.
   D. HIPO chart.

©2007 Kaplan CPA Review

Page 463

STUDY MANUAL – BUSINESS ENVIRONMENT & CONCEPTS
CHAPTER 16

7. All of the following are included in the systems implementation process
    EXCEPT:
    A. training.
    B. documentation.
    C. systems design.
    D. testing.

8. The analysis tool for the systems analyst and steering committee to use in
    selecting the *best* systems alternative is:
    A. cost benefit analysis.
    B. systems design.
    C. decision tree analysis.
    D. user selection.

9. In the organization of the information systems function, the *most* important
    separation of duties is:
    A. not allowing the data librarian to assist in data processing operations.
    B. assuring that those responsible for programming the system do not have
        access to data processing operations.
    C. having a separate information officer at the top level of the organization
        outside of the accounting function.
    D. using different programming personnel to maintain utility programs from
        those who maintain the application programs.

10. Information systems steering committees:
    a. should consist of systems specialist and end users that plan and direct projects
        throughout the systems life cycle.
    b. should consist of systems management, the controller, and other management
        personnel and should establish policies with regard to an organization's
        information system.
    c. are found in organizations that have had a history of information system
        problems with the focus of the committee being the overseeing of
        information systems development.
    d. utilize a top down approach to the solution of the information system
        problems.

11. In the computer program development process, a problem will *most likely* result
    when:
    A. programmers take a longer amount of time to perform programming tasks
        than expected.
    B. written specifications from the user are used to develop detail program code.
    C. programmers use specialized application tools to simulate the system being
        programmed.
    D. user specifications are inadvertently misunderstood.

Page 464 ©2007 Kaplan CPA Review

12. Which of the following *most likely* represents a weakness in the internal control structure of an EDP system?
    A. The systems analyst reviews output and controls the distribution of output from the EDP department.
    B. The accounts payable clerk prepares data for computer processing and enters the data into the computer.
    C. The systems programmer designs the operating and control functions of programs and participates in testing operating systems.
    D. The control clerk establishes control over data received by the EDP department and reconciles control totals after processing.

13. Daylight Corporation's organization chart provides for a controller and an EDP manager, both of whom report to the financial vice-president. Internal control would **NOT** be strengthened by:
    A. Assigning the programming and operating of the computer to an independent control group which reports to the controller.
    B. Providing for maintenance of input data controls by an independent control group which reports to the controller.
    C. Rotating periodically among machine operators the assignments of individual application runs.
    D. Providing for review and distribution of computer output by an independent control group which reports to the controller.

14. Which of the following employees in a company's electronic data processing department should be responsible for designing new or improved data processing procedures?
    A. Flowchart editor.
    B. Programmer.
    C. Systems analyst.
    D. Control-group supervisor.

15. Which of the following control procedures most likely could prevent EDP personnel from modifying programs to bypass programmed controls?
    A. Periodic management review of computer utilization reports and systems documentation.
    B. Segregation of duties within EDP for computer programming and computer operations.
    C. Participation of user department personnel in designing and approving new systems.
    D. Physical security of EDP facilities in limiting access to EDP equipment.

STUDY MANUAL – BUSINESS ENVIRONMENT & CONCEPTS
CHAPTER 16

ANSWERS: IT: IT ROLES & RESPONSIBILITIES

1. **C** Answer (c) is correct because the identification of inputs and outputs must occur well before implementation. Inputs and outputs of the current system are identified during systems analysis, while inputs and outputs of the new system are developed during the design phase. Answer (a) is not correct because hardware installation often takes place during the implementation phase of an application. Answer (b) is not correct because testing the system is usually part of the implementation phase. Answer (d) is not correct because completing the documentation usually takes place during the implementation phase.

2. **D** Answer (d) is correct because developing and coding computer programs is the responsibility of a programmer. Answer (a) is not correct. Analyzing the present system is, by definition, what a systems analyst does. Answer (b) is not correct because preparing computer program specifications would be done by the systems analyst during the design phase. Answer (c) is not correct because designing computer applications would be done by the systems analyst when he or she does systems design.

3. **D** The implementation stage of the systems development life cycle includes training users in the new system and testing the system. Answer (a) is not correct because conceptual design includes activities such as evaluating design characteristics and developing design specifications. Answer (b) is not correct because cost-benefit analysis is an activity that should be done at the end of each major stage of the systems development life cycle, before advancing to the next stage. Answer (c) is not correct because the requirements definition is done early in the systems development life cycle, during systems analysis.

4. **B** Systems analysis is that stage of the systems development life cycle which includes the initial investigation of the current system, the systems survey, the feasibility study, and the determination of information needs and system requirements. Answer (a) is not correct because systems maintenance is that ongoing stage of the systems development life cycle which involves doing necessary modifications and improving the system. Answer (c) is not correct because the systems feasibility study is a task that occurs during the systems analysis stage of the systems development life cycle. Answer (d) is not correct because systems design is that stage of the systems development life cycle which includes developing design specifications, and designing output, inputs, and databases.

5. **B** Data flow diagrams contain rectangles representing entities, circles (or "bubbles") representing processes, parallel lines representing data storage, and arrows representing the data flows among the previous three shapes. Entities, processes, and storage may at different times be sources or destinations of data. Choice (a) is incorrect. Computer configurations are not shown on a data flow diagram, which shows the flow of data independent of specific media used. And a flowchart is a different representation which shows files and processes. Choice (c) is incorrect. A program flowchart is a different representation which shows the internal logic of a program. Choice (d) is incorrect. A program flowchart is a different representation which shows the internal logic of a program.

6. **B** Computer system flowcharts use specific shapes to represent specific physical media used for files and processes. It shows input documents, output reports, tape files, disk files, terminal input, computer processes, and manual processes. Arrows connecting those shapes depict the path of data through the information system. Choice (a) is incorrect. Program flowcharts show only the internal logic of a particular program. They do not

Page 466   ©2007 Kaplan CPA Review

broadly show data moving through the information system. Choice (c) is incorrect. Decision tables show in tabular form the internal logic of a particular program or the actions to be taken given specific conditions. They do not broadly show data moving through the information system. Choice (d) is incorrect. HIPO is an acronym for hierarchy + input process output. These charts show functions as blocks in a hierarchical chart, with lower-level blocks as subfunctions of higher level ones. They do not show the path of data moving through an information system.

7. **C** Systems design must occur much earlier in the systems development process than during implementation. One would hope that the system is designed well before it is implemented. Choice (a) is incorrect. Training and educating system users does occur during systems implementation. Choice (b) is incorrect. Although some of it might occur earlier, documentation is completed during systems implementation. Choice (d) is incorrect. Testing of the new system would occur during systems implementation.

8. **A** Cost benefit analysis should be used for selecting the best systems alternative. The costs of each alternative should be evaluated against the benefits. Choice (b) is incorrect. Systems design is a phase in which the new system is broadly designed by matching user needs to the application. Selection of alternatives is not involved in this phase. Choice (c) is incorrect. Decision tree analysis involves laying out the various paths of possibilities and attaching probabilities to each branch. Expected values are computed. It is not well suited for selecting the best systems alternative. Choice (d) is incorrect. Users' preferences are to be considered, but the users may not be in the best position to weigh all of the costs of each alternative against benefits.

9. **B** Separating the programming function from the operating function is considered the most critical. Programmers have too much knowledge of the controls, or lack of controls, built into the program. Thus, in operating, the programmers could circumvent controls. The data librarian [choice (a)] may assist in operations if necessary but should not have access to equipment. It is permissible to have the top information officer [choice (c)] reporting to an accounting officer. It is permissible and common to have the same programmers maintaining both utility programs [choice (d)] and application programs.

10. **B** Steering committees set priorities for the information systems function, choosing which projects are most important for the company. Thus they should include upper management from the information systems department, as well as management from most other functional areas. It is usually management rather than end users [choice (a)] who serve on the steering committee, and the committee, with its broad representation, does not get involved to the level of directing particular projects through their life cycles. Steering committees [choice (c)] help assure that the information systems function performs according to the company's priorities; thus, they would more likely be found in organizations without system problems, but should exist in all computerized companies. Top-down [choice (d)], which focuses first on the information needs of top management, and bottom-up, which focuses first on the users and operators, are approaches to developing applications and are independent of the existence of a steering committee.

11. **D** It is almost certain that misunderstanding user specifications will result in serious problems in program development. Programmers taking a longer time than expected (a) might cause budget problems but would not damage the quality of the programs. Written user specifications (b) would in fact be quite helpful in developing code. Specialized tools (c) are becoming a popular method for expediting quality programming.

©2007 Kaplan CPA Review

STUDY MANUAL – BUSINESS ENVIRONMENT & CONCEPTS
CHAPTER 16

12. **A**   A data control group should review output and control the distribution of output from the EDP department. The systems analyst designs and evaluates systems and prepares program specifications for programmers. These two functions should be separated. Answer (b) may be acceptable, especially in an on-line system. Answers (c) and (d) describe appropriate functions of a programmer and a control clerk.

13. **A**   The assignment of programmers and the operation of a computer are the prime responsibilities of an EDP manager. An independent control group should function between the user department and the EDP department. Items (b), (c) and (d) are good examples of internal control within an EDP system.

14. **C**   A systems analyst has the primary responsibility for the design of new and improved data processing procedures.

15. **B**   In order to prevent unauthorized program modification, the duties of analysts, programmers and operators should be segregated. Specifically, systems analysts and computer operators should not do the technical programming and should not have access to the programmer's work. Answer (a) is incorrect because review of utilization reports and system documentation may detect control problems but will not prevent control problems, such as EDP personnel modifying programs. Answer (c) is incorrect because designing new systems is unrelated to preventing program changes. Answer (d) is incorrect because limiting physical access to equipment may not prevent modification of programs if programs can be accessed from off-site.

Page 468   ©2007 Kaplan CPA Review

IT: DISASTER RECOVERY AND BUSINESS CONTINUITY

STUDY MANUAL – BUSINESS ENVIRONMENT & CONCEPTS
CHAPTER 17

Study Tip: Forget the past. People often approach the CPA exam talking about previous failures, either on the exam itself or in school. "I was never a very good student" is a common refrain. The past is not important. If you use good, quality preparation materials and are willing to invest a sufficient amount of time studying, you can pass. Do not let something that occurred in the past hold you back from success today.

DISASTER RECOVERY PLANNING

This should include alternate processing sites in case of emergency. For most companies, duplicate equipment is too costly. Therefore, arrangements must be made with vendors and other external service agencies for alternate processing facilities.

    a.   **Hot site**—A fully equipped data center in a bunker-like environment that requires a subscriber's fee.

    b.   **Cold site**—An air-conditioned space with necessary communications in which equipment can be moved (such as a mobile facility). Less expensive than a hot site.

Disaster recovery planning devises plans for the restoration of computing and communications services after they have been disrupted by an event such as an earthquake, flood, or terrorist attack. Disaster recovery plans focus primarily on the technical issues involved in keeping systems up and running, such as which files to back up and the maintenance of backup computer systems or disaster recovery services.

For example, MasterCard maintains a duplicate computer center in Kansas City, Missouri, to serve as an emergency backup to its primary computer center in St. Louis. Rather than build their own backup facilities, many firms contract with disaster recovery firms, such as Comdisco Disaster Recovery Services in Rosemont, Illinois, and SunGard Recovery Services, headquartered in Wayne, Pennsylvania. These disaster recovery firms provide hot sites housing spare computers at locations around the country where subscribing firms can run their critical applications in an emergency.

Business continuity planning focuses on how the company can restore business operations after a disaster strikes. The **business continuity plan** identifies critical business processes and determines action plans for handling mission-critical functions if systems go down.

©2007 Kaplan CPA Review

Page 469

STUDY MANUAL – BUSINESS ENVIRONMENT & CONCEPTS
CHAPTER 17

Business managers and information technology specialists need to work together on both types of plans to determine which systems and business processes are most critical to the company. They must conduct a business impact analysis to identify the firm's most critical systems and the impact a systems outage would have on the business. Management must determine the maximum amount of time the business can survive with its systems down and which parts of the business must be restored first.

ENSURING BUSINESS CONTINUITY

Management should establish a disaster recovery process, coordinated with the overall business continuity strategy, for all IT processes for internal and external functions. Contingency planning goes beyond just the backup of computer data and programs. Contingency planning includes backup and restoration of the physical computer facilities, supplies, key resources, and personnel.

There are many different data backup and recovery procedures available, any number of which can be a part of the overall contingency plan:

As companies increasingly rely on digital networks for their revenue and operations, they need to take additional steps to ensure that their systems and applications are always available. Many factors can disrupt the performance of a website, including denial of service attacks, network failure, heavy internet traffic, and exhausted server resources. Computer failures, interruptions, and downtime translate into disgruntled customers, millions of dollars in lost sales, and the inability to perform critical internal transactions. Downtime refers to periods of time in which a system is not operational.

Firms such as those in the airline and financial services industries with critical applications requiring online transaction processing have traditionally used fault-tolerant computer systems for many years to ensure 100% availability. In online transaction processing, transactions entered online are immediately processed by the computer. Multitudinous changes to databases, reporting, and requests for information occur each instant.

Fault-tolerant computer systems contain redundant hardware, software, and power supply components that create an environment that provides continuous, uninterrupted service. Fault-tolerant computers contain extra memory chips, processors, and disk storage devices to back up a system and keep it running to prevent failure. They use special software routines or self-checking logic built into their circuitry to detect hardware failures and automatically switch to a backup device. Parts from these computers can be removed and repaired without disruption to the computer system.

Fault tolerance should be distinguished from **high-availability computing**. Both fault tolerance and high-availability computing are designed to maximize application and system availability. Both use backup hardware resources. However, high-availability computing helps firms recover quickly from a crash, whereas fault tolerance promises continuous availability and the elimination of recovery time altogether. High-availability computing environments are a minimum requirement for firms with heavy electronic commerce processing or for firms that depend on digital networks for their internal operations.

Page 470   ©2007 Kaplan CPA Review

High-availability computing requires an assortment of tools and technologies to ensure maximum performance of computer systems and networks, including redundant servers, mirroring, load balancing, clustering, high-capacity storage, and good disaster recovery and business continuity plans. The firm's computing platform must be extremely robust with scalable processing power, storage, and bandwidth.

Load balancing distributes large numbers of access requests across multiple servers. The requests are directed to the most available server so that no single device is overwhelmed. If one server starts to get swamped, requests are forwarded to another server with more capacity.

Mirroring uses a backup server that duplicates all the processes and transactions of the primary server. If the primary server fails, the backup server can immediately take its place without any interruption in service. However, server mirroring is very expensive because each server must be mirrored by an identical server whose only purpose is to be available in the event of a failure.

   a.   Maintains copies of the primary site's programs and data.

   b.   Physically separate sites are updated simultaneously.

   c.   Mirror site can take over in a few seconds.

   d.   Popular with e-business for seamless online commerce.

High-availability clustering links two computers together so that the second computer can act as a backup to the primary computer. If the primary computer fails, the second computer picks up its processing without any pause in the system. (Computers can also be clustered together as a single computing resource to speed up processing.)

   a.   Used to disperse processing load among several servers

   b.   If one server fails, another server can take over.

   c.   Cluster servers are essentially mirror sites of each other.

Researchers are exploring ways to make computing systems recover even more rapidly when mishaps occur, an approach called **recovery-oriented computing**. This work includes designing systems that can recover quickly and implementing capabilities and tools to help operators pinpoint the sources of faults in multicomponent systems and easily correct their mistakes.

STUDY MANUAL – BUSINESS ENVIRONMENT & CONCEPTS
CHAPTER 17

QUESTIONS: IT: DISASTER RECOVERY & BUSINESS CONTINUITY

1.   A critical aspect of a disaster recovery plan is to be able to regain operational capability as soon as possible. In order to accomplish this, an organization can have an arrangement with its computer hardware vendor to have a fully operational facility available that is configured to the user's specific needs. This is *best* known as a(n):
     A. uninterruptible power system.
     B. parallel system.
     C. cold site.
     D. hot site.

STUDY MANUAL – BUSINESS ENVIRONMENT & CONCEPTS
CHAPTER 17

ANSWERS: IT: DISASTER RECOVERY & BUSINESS CONTINUITY

1. **D** A hot site is a fully operational facility that is available on short notice and configured to the specific needs of the disaster-stricken user. Choice (a) is incorrect. An uninterruptible power system involves a power supply operating as a buffer between the power from the electric utility and the user, smoothing fluctuations in power (surges or dips) and providing some back-up power in the event of a total power loss. Choice (b) is incorrect. A parallel system would be another company which uses the same computer system. Choice (c) is incorrect. A cold site is a location which has everything necessary to function as a fully operational facility in the event of a disaster except for the computer equipment and software, which would have to be delivered in the event of an emergency.

IT: BUSINESS IMPLICATIONS

STUDY MANUAL – BUSINESS ENVIRONMENT & CONCEPTS
CHAPTER 18

Study Tip: Believe in yourself. Thousands of people just like you pass the CPA exam each year. They are no smarter and no better educated. They just use good quality materials and they put in the time and the energy. You can do it also. The CPA exam is challenging, but it is certainly not impossible. People will constantly tell you that you cannot pass. Tell them to go away. There is nothing more important that you can bring to the CPA exam than a belief that you can do the work and make it happen.

ELECTRONIC COMMERCE

There are many ways to classify electronic commerce transactions. One is by looking at the nature of the participants in the electronic commerce transaction. The three major electronic commerce categories are business-to-consumer (B2C) e-commerce, business-to-business (B2B) e-commerce, and consumer-to-consumer (C2C) e-commerce.

- Business-to-consumer (B2C) electronic commerce involves retailing products and services to individual shoppers. BarnesandNoble.com, which sells books, software, and music to individual consumers, is an example of B2C e-commerce.
- Business-to-business (B2B) electronic commerce involves sales of goods and services among businesses. Milacron's website for selling machinery, mold bases, and related tooling, supplies, and services to companies engaged in plastics processing is an example of B2B e-commerce.
- Consumer-to-consumer (C2C) electronic commerce involves consumers selling directly to consumers. For example, eBay, the giant Web auction site, enables people to sell their goods to other consumers by auctioning the merchandise off to the highest bidder.

Another way of classifying electronic commerce transactions is in terms of the participants' physical connection to the Web. Until recently, almost all e-commerce transactions took place over wired networks. Now mobile phones and other wireless handheld digital appliances are Internet enabled to send text messages, access websites, and make purchases. Companies are offering new types of web-based products and services that can be accessed by these wireless devices. The use of handheld wireless devices for purchasing goods and services from any location has been termed mobile commerce or m-commerce. Both business-to-business and business-to-consumer e-commerce transactions can take place using m-commerce technology.

Today, about 80% of B2B e-commerce is based on proprietary systems for electronic data interchange (EDI). Electronic data interchange (EDI) enables the computer-to-computer exchange between two organizations of standard transactions, such as invoices, bills of lading, shipment schedules, or purchase orders. Transactions are automatically transmitted from one information system to another through a network, eliminating the printing and handling of paper at one end and the inputting of data at the other. Each major industry in the United States and much of the rest of the world has EDI standards that define the structure and information fields of electronic documents for that industry.

EDI originally automated the exchange of documents such as purchase orders, invoices, and shipping notices. Although some companies still use EDI for document automation, firms engaged in just-in-time inventory replenishment and continuous production use EDI as a system for continuous replenishment. Suppliers have online access to selected parts of the purchasing firm's production and delivery schedules and automatically ship materials and goods to meet prespecified targets without intervention by firm purchasing agents.

Although many organizations still use private networks for EDI, companies are increasingly turning to the Internet for this purpose because it provides a much more flexible and low-cost platform for linking to other firms. Using the Internet, businesses can extend digital technology to a wider range of activities and broaden their circle of trading partners.

Take procurement, for example. Procurement involves not only purchasing goods and materials but also sourcing, negotiating with suppliers, paying for goods, and making delivery arrangements. Businesses can now use the Internet to locate the most low-cost supplier, search online catalogs of supplier products, negotiate with suppliers, place orders, make payments, and arrange transportation. They are not limited to partners linked by traditional EDI networks but use the Web to work with any other business linked to the Internet. E-procurement over the Internet provides new opportunities for lowering costs and improving service because Internet technology enables businesses to cast their nets more widely.

The Internet and Web technology enable businesses to create new electronic storefronts for selling to other businesses with multimedia graphic displays and interactive features similar to those for B2C commerce. Alternatively, businesses can use Internet technology to create extranets or electronic marketplaces for linking to other businesses for purchase and sale transactions. Extranets are private intranets extended to authorized users outside the company.

Internet Based Transactions

Attributes:

- Elimination of staff positions is often a by-product.
- Acceleration of business processes.
- Direct links to suppliers' systems and to other separate physical locations (ERP system).
- Price efficiency for buyers.
- Directly reach consumers via internet commerce.

STUDY MANUAL – BUSINESS ENVIRONMENT & CONCEPTS
CHAPTER 18

Automated Data Entry includes:

- Bar Coding.
- Optical Character Readers.
- Scanners.

Digital Image Processing Systems:

- Systems for capture, storage retrieval and presentations of images.
- Usually for business documents, historically used for large mainframe computers, now seen on personal computers (scanners).
- Digital imaging takes a tremendous amount of storage space—therefore 'write once, read many' (WORM) storage systems are less expensive.

Electronic Mail (e-mail):

- Electronic transmission of nonstandard messages between two parties.
- E-mail is a weak form of e-business because of the nonstandard formats between parties (freeform).
- Usually attachments within e-mail.
- E-mail lists with certain attributes are sold to vendors.
- Business recording activities still need to occur.

Electronic Document Management (EDM):

- The capturing, storage, management and control of electronic data images for supporting management decisions.
- Relies on digital image processing.
- Inexpensive alternative to a paper system.
- Two categories:
  - Document storage and retrieval—such as for mortgages, certificates, public documents.
  - Business event data processing—passing e-documents along at different stages of a process, such for approvals and feedback.
- Benefits of an EDM environment:
  - Reduction of paper costs and handling costs.
  - Improved staff productivity.
  - Better customer service.
  - Faster processing.

Electronic Data Interchange (EDI):

- Computer to computer exchange of business data in a structured format that allows direct processing.
- Standardized EDI format: ANSI (American National Standards Institute).

Page 476   ©2007 Kaplan CPA Review

STUDY MANUAL – BUSINESS ENVIRONMENT & CONCEPTS
CHAPTER 18

Internet Commerce:

- Computer-to-computer exchange of business data in structured or semistructured formats.
- In effect, an implementation of EDI on the Internet.

Network Providers:

- Companies that provide a link to the Internet through their networks for a fee.
- Benefits include e-mail services, mailboxes, space allocation for web development, and remote connection to other computer sites.

Security:

- Over 90% of internet users want more security for e-commerce related transactions.
- Internet assurance services provide limited assurance for vendors' website
- Example is WebTrust, a commercially provided internet security product.
- Anti-fraud software and a secure environment needed for credit card transactions.

Electronic Store Fronts are internet-created resources for displaying goods and services.

- Benefits: improved competition, responsiveness, global visibility, reduced costs, improvement of existing processes and requirement to rethink controls.
- Risks include hackers, fraud.

Issues and concerns in e-business:

- Mode of the payment.
- Security of the payment transaction.
- Privacy of individuals.
- Trust, authentication and non-repudiation.
- Jurisdictional and legal issues.

Definitions:

1. **Electronic funds transfer** (EFT) Also referred to as the automated clearing house (ACH)

   - Used for direct deposit and automated deposit of funds between financial institutions.
   - Reduces the problem of 'float'.
   - Other technology advances to reduce float include electronic checks and electronic lockboxes.

2. **Point of sale transactions** (POS)

   - An integrated transaction system that delivers information in real time.
   - Immediate inventory, sales, and financial statement updates each time a POS transaction is completed.

©2007 Kaplan CPA Review

Page 477

STUDY MANUAL – BUSINESS ENVIRONMENT & CONCEPTS
CHAPTER 18

- Usually the POS system is centralized so that secure data can be shared throughout the organization.
- POS systems integrate an entity's website, catalogues, and stores with the rest of the organization.

3. **Domain**—a group of computers and devices on a network that are administered as a unit with common rules and procedures. Within the Internet, domains are defined by an IP address. All devices sharing a common part of the IP address are said to be in the same domain.

4. **Domain name server** (DNS)—an internet service that translates domain names into IP addresses. The domain name Server is used to maintain records of the web server aliases associated with the computer.

5. **Home page**—a document in HTML format displayed as the initial document or page when a web browser establishes a connection with a Web Server.

6. **HTML**—Hypertext Markup Language (HTML) is the authoring language used to create documents accessed via the world wide web. HTML defines the structure and layout of all documents accessible via the world wide web by using a variety of tags and attributes. A document may contain textual content, images, links to other documents (and possibly other applications) as well as formatting instructions for display on a screen.

7. **Uniform resource locator** (URL)—A uniform resource locator, or URL, is the Internet address of a web document or other Internet resource accessible via the World Wide Web. The first part of the address indicates what protocol is being used (for example FTP, HTTP) and the second part specifies the IP address or the domain name where the resource is located and may also include a directory name and a filename.

8. **World wide web**—The World Wide Web (also known as WWW, or the Web) is a hypermedia-based distributed information system based on the client/server communications model.

9. **XBRL** stands for extensible business reporting language, which is language for electronic communication of business and financial data.

Page 478   ©2007 Kaplan CPA Review

IT: IT CONTROL ISSUES

STUDY MANUAL – BUSINESS ENVIRONMENT & CONCEPTS
CHAPTER 19

Study Tip: Learn to study when other candidates are not studying. Get up early and study for an hour in the morning or study on Friday evening rather than going out. Study at lunch or on holidays. On each part of the exam, roughly 40% to 45% of the candidates are going to pass. If you can find time to study when others are not, it will help you get into that top 40% to 45%.

CONTROL OBJECTIVES, THREATS, AND PROCEDURES

A well-designed AIS should provide adequate controls to ensure that the following objectives are met: (1) all transactions are properly authorized; (2) all recorded transactions are valid; (3) all valid and authorized transactions are recorded; (4) all transactions are recorded accurately; (5) assets are safeguarded from loss or theft; (6) business activities are performed efficiently and effectively; (7) the company is in compliance with all applicable laws and regulations; and (8) all disclosures are full and fair.

There are several actions a company can take with respect to any cycle to reduce threats of errors or irregularities. These include: (1) using simple, easy-to-complete documents with clear instructions (enhances accuracy and reliability); (2) using appropriate application controls, such as validity checks and field checks (enhances accuracy and reliability); (3) providing space on forms to record who completed and who reviewed the form (encourages proper authorizations and accountability); (4) prenumbering documents (encourages recording of valid and only valid transactions); and (5) restricting access to blank documents (reduces risk of unauthorized transaction).

CONTROL AND AIS

Why AIS Threats Are Increasing—Control risks have increased in the last few years because there is a proliferation of computers, servers, and users, and because distributed and wide-area networks make data widely available.

- Vocabulary terms:
  - A **threat** is any potential adverse occurrence or unwanted event that could injure the AIS or the organization.
  - The **exposure** or **impact** of the threat is the potential dollar loss that would occur if the threat became a reality.
  - The **likelihood** is the probability that the threat will occur.
- Companies are now recognizing control risks and taking positive steps to achieve better control, including security staffs, education, enforcement, secure

©2007 Kaplan CPA Review

Page 479

STUDY MANUAL – BUSINESS ENVIRONMENT & CONCEPTS
CHAPTER 19

environments, and building control into the development process. Accountants must understand how to protect systems from threats, and have a good understanding of IT and its capabilities and risks. Management must make security and control a top priority.

- Control objectives are the same regardless of the data processing method, but a computer-based AIS requires different policies and procedures to achieve that control.
- In today's dynamic business environment, companies must balance the need for innovation and creativity with the need for control systems to avoid excessive risks or harmful behaviors.
- **Internal control** is the process implemented by the board of directors, management, and those under their direction to provide reasonable assurance that the following control objectives are achieved: (1) assets (including data) are safeguarded; (2) records are maintained in sufficient detail to accurately and fairly reflect company assets; (3) accurate and reliable information is provided; (4) there is reasonable assurance that financial reports are prepared in accordance with GAAP; (5) operational efficiency is promoted and improved (6) adherence to prescribed managerial policies is encouraged; and (7) the organization complies with applicable laws and regulations.
- Internal control is a **process** that permeates an organization's activities and provides **reasonable**, rather than absolute, assurance. Internal control systems are susceptible to errors, poor decisions, and override; and internal control objectives are often at odds with each other (e.g., controls to safeguard assets may also reduce operational efficiency).
- Internal controls perform three important functions:
  - **Preventive controls** deter problems before they arise.
  - **Detective controls** discover problems quickly when they do arise.
  - **Corrective controls** remedy problems by identifying the cause, correcting errors, and modifying the system to prevent recurrences.
- Internal controls are often classified as:
  - **General controls** to ensure the environment is stable and well-managed.
  - **Application controls** to prevent, detect, and correct transaction errors and fraud.

THREATS

Information systems are becoming increasingly more complex and society is becoming increasingly more dependent on these systems. Companies face four types of threats to their information systems: (1) natural and political disasters, (2) software errors and equipment malfunction, (3) unintentional acts, and (4) intentional acts (computer crime).

THREATS IN SALES ORDER ENTRY

The primary objectives of this process:

- Accurately and efficiently process customer orders.
- Ensure that all sales are legitimate and that the company gets paid for all sales.
- Minimize revenue loss arising from poor inventory management.

Threat No. 1—Incomplete or inaccurate customer orders:

- Causes inefficiencies and customer dissatisfaction.
- Controls include: data entry controls, such as completeness checks; automatic lookup of reference data like customer address; and reasonableness tests comparing quantity ordered to past history.

Threat No. 2—Sales to customers with poor credit:

- Causes uncollectible sales and loss of revenues and assets.
- Control: follow proper authorization procedures for credit sales.

Threat No. 3—Orders that are not legitimate:

- Can cause poor credit decisions.
- Controls include: appropriate authorization evidenced by receipt of a signed purchase order and/or digital signatures and maximum caution in online credit card transactions with retail customers.

Threat No. 4—Carrying too much or too little merchandise:

- Causes lost sales or excess carrying costs and product markdowns.
- Controls include: accurate inventory control and sales forecasting systems; online, real-time inventory systems; periodic physical counts of inventory; and regular review of sales forecasts to make adjustments.

THREATS IN SHIPPING

The primary objectives of the shipping process are:

- Fill customer orders efficiently and accurately.
- Safeguard inventory.

Threat No. 5—Shipping errors:

- May cause customer dissatisfaction, lost sales, and loss of assets.
- Controls include: online shipping systems that check quantities shipped, bar code scanners and RFID tags to record picking and shipping, application controls such as field checks and completeness tests can reduce errors, and postponing printing of packing slip and bill of lading until accuracy of the shipment has been verified.

Threat No. 6—Theft of inventory:

- Causes loss of assets and inaccurate inventory records.
- Controls include: securing inventory and restricting access, documentation of inventory transfers, releasing inventory for shipping only with approved sales orders, employees who handle inventory should sign the documents or enter their codes online to ensure accountability, wireless communication and RFID tags to provide real-time tracking, and periodic physical counts of inventory.

THREATS IN BILLING

The primary objectives of the billing process are to ensure:

- Customers are billed for all sales.
- Invoices are accurate.
- Customer accounts are accurately maintained.

Threat No. 7—Failure to bill customers:

- Causes loss of assets and revenues and inaccurate sales, inventory and accounts receivable data.
- Controls include: segregate shipping and billing functions; sequentially prenumber sales orders, picking tickets, packing slips, and sales invoices; and in invoiceless systems, ensure every shipment is recorded, since the shipment triggers recording of the account receivable.

Threat No. 8—Billing errors:

- May cause loss of assets or customer dissatisfaction
- Controls include: use a computer to retrieve prices, check quantities on packing slip against quantities on sales order, and use bar code scanners to reduce data entry errors.

Threat No. 9—Errors in maintaining customer accounts:

- Causes customer dissatisfaction and loss of sales and may indicate theft of cash.
- Controls include: conduct edit checks, reconcile batch totals to detect posting errors, compare number of accounts updated with number of checks received, reconciliations performed by an independent party, and monthly customer statements.

THREATS IN CASH COLLECTION

The primary objective of the cash collection process:

- Safeguard customer remittances.

Threat No. 10—Theft of cash:

- Causes loss of cash.
- Controls include: segregation of duties; minimizing money handling; prompt documentation and restrictive endorsements of remittances; two people opening e-mail together; remittance data sent to accounts receivable while cash and checks are sent to cashier; checking that total credits to accounts receivable equal total debits to cash; sending copy of remittance list to internal auditing to be compared with validated deposit slips and bank statements; monthly statements to customers; cash registers that automatically produce a written record of all cash received; inducements to customers to scrutinize receipts; daily deposit of all remittances in the bank; and bank reconciliations done by an independent party.

GENERAL CONTROL ISSUES

Two general objectives pertain to activities in every cycle:

- Accurate data should be available when needed.
- Activities should be performed efficiently and effectively.

Threat No. 11—Loss, alteration, or unauthorized disclosure of data:

- Could threaten a company's continued existence and could cause errors in reporting and/or in responding to customers. Could cause customer dissatisfaction, loss of sales, and legal sanctions or fines.
- Controls include: file backups, file labels, strong access controls, modification of default settings on ERP systems, encryption, and secure transmissions.

Threat No. 12—Poor performance:

- Can damage customer relations and reduce profitability.
- Controls: prepare and review performance reports.

Access Control

Access control consists of all the policies and procedures a company uses to prevent improper access to systems by unauthorized insiders and outsiders. To gain access, a user must be authorized and authenticated. Authentication refers to the ability to know that a person is who she claims to be. Access control software is designed to allow only authorized persons to use systems or to access data using some method for authentication.

Authentication is often established by using passwords known only to authorized users. An end user uses a password to log onto a computer system and may also use passwords for accessing specific systems and files. However, users often forget passwords, share them, or choose poor passwords that are easy to guess, which compromises security. Passwords can also be "sniffed" if transmitted over a network or stolen through social engineering.

E-commerce has led to the proliferation of password-protected websites. If users employ passwords to access multiple systems and they reuse a password for more than one system, a hacker gaining access to one user account may be able to gain access to others.

Sometimes systems use **tokens** such as smart cards for access control. A token is a physical device similar to an identification card that is designed to prove the identity of a single user.

Biometric authentication represents a promising new technology that can overcome some of the limitations of passwords for authenticating system users. Biometric authentication is based on the measurement of a physical or behavioral trait that makes each individual unique. It compares a person's unique characteristics, such as fingerprints, face, or retinal image, against a stored set profile of these characteristics to determine whether there are any differences between these characteristics and the stored profile. If the two profiles

STUDY MANUAL – BUSINESS ENVIRONMENT & CONCEPTS
CHAPTER 19

match, access is granted. The technology is expensive, and fingerprint and facial recognition technologies are just beginning to be used for security applications.

SECURITY CONTOLS IN AIS

- An AIS should provide information useful for decision making. To be useful, information must be reliable, which means accurate, complete, and timely; available when needed; and protected from loss, compromise, and theft.
- The Trust Services framework developed by the AICPA and the Canadian Institute of Chartered Accountants (CICA) identified five basic principles that contribute to systems reliability: security, confidentiality, privacy, processing integrity, and availability.
- Security is the foundation of systems reliability. Security procedures restrict access to only authorized users and protect confidentiality and privacy of sensitive information; provide for processing integrity; and protect against attacks.

SECURITY AS A MANAGEMENT ISSUE

- Security is a top management issue—not an IT issue. Management is responsible for the accuracy of various internal reports and financial statements produced by the organization's IS. Management must certify the accuracy of the financial statements and maintain effective internal controls.
- The Trust Services framework identifies four essential requirements for successfully implementing the five principles of systems reliability:
  - Develop and document policies.
  - Effectively communicate those policies to all authorized users.
  - Design and employ appropriate control procedures to implement those policies.
  - Monitor the system, and take corrective action to maintain compliance with the policies.
- Top management involvement and support is necessary to satisfy each of the preceding requirements.
- **Policy Development**—A comprehensive set of security policies should be developed before designing and implementing specific control procedures. This process begins with taking an inventory of information systems hardware, software, and databases. Once the resources have been identified, they need to be valued in order to select the most cost-effective control procedures.
- **Effective Communication of Policies**—Security policies must be communicated to and understood by employees, customers, suppliers, and other authorized users. Regular reminders and compliance training should be employed. Management must actively support these policies, and sanctions should apply to violators.
- **Design and Employ Appropriate Control Procedures**—Control frameworks such as COBIT and Trust Services identify a variety of specific control procedures and tools that can be used to mitigate various security threats. Determining the optimal level of investment in security involves evaluating cost-benefit tradeoffs.
- **Monitor and Take Remedial Action**—Technology advances create new threats and alter the risks associated with existing threats. Effective control involves a continuous cycle of:
  - Developing policies to address identified threats.
  - Communicating those policies to employees.

Page 484
©2007 Kaplan CPA Review

- Implementing specific control procedures to mitigate risk.
- Monitoring performance.
- Taking corrective action in response to problems.

THE TIME-BASED MODEL OF SECURITY

- Given enough time and resources, any preventive control can be circumvented. Detection and correction must be timely, especially for information security, because once preventive controls have been breached, it takes little time to compromise the organization's economic and information resources.
- The time-based model evaluates the effectiveness of an organization's security by measuring and comparing the relationships among three variables:
  - P = Time it takes an attacker to break through the organization's preventive controls.
  - D = Time it takes to detect that an attack is in progress.
  - C = Time to respond to the attack.
- If $P > (D + C)$, then security procedures are deemed effective. Otherwise, security is ineffective.

DEFENSE-IN-DEPTH

- Defense-in-depth involves using multiple layers of controls to avoid having a single point of failure. Computer security involves using a combination of firewalls, passwords, and other preventive procedures to restrict access. Redundancy also applies to detective and corrective controls.
- Major types of **preventive controls** used for defense-in-depth include:
  - **Authentication controls** to identify the person or device attempting access.
  - **Authorization controls** to restrict access to authorized users. These controls are implemented with an access control matrix and compatibility tests.
  - **Training** to teach employees why security measures are important and teach them to use safe computing practices.
  - **Physical access controls** to protect entry points to the building, to rooms housing computer equipment, to wiring, and to devices such as laptops, cell phones, and PDAs.
  - **Remote access controls** include routers, firewalls, and intrusion prevention systems to prevent unauthorized access from remote locations.
- A **border router** connects the IS to the Internet.
- Behind the router is the main **firewall**. It works with the border router to filter information trying to enter or leave the organization.
- Data is transmitted over the Internet in packets through a protocol called TCP/IP. A set of rules called an **access control list** (ACL) determines which packets are allowed in and which are dropped. **Stateful packet filtering** examines the header of each packet in isolation. **Deep packet filtering** examines the data in the body of a packet to provide more effective access control. Deep packet filtering is the heart of a new type of filter called **intrusion prevention systems**.
- **Internal firewalls** can be used to segment different departments within an organization.

STUDY MANUAL – BUSINESS ENVIRONMENT & CONCEPTS
CHAPTER 19

- Web servers and e-mail servers are placed in a separate network outside the corporate network referred to as the **demilitarized zone**.
- Special attention must be paid to use of rogue modems by employees. Wireless access and dial-up modems require special security procedures.
  - **Host and application hardening** procedures involve the use of supplemental preventive controls on workstations, servers, printers, and other devices. Special attention should be paid to host configuration, user accounts, and software design.
  - **Encryption** provides the final barrier. It involves transforming normal text, called **plaintext**, into unreadable gibberish, called **ciphertext**. Decryption reverses the process.
- The factors that determine the strength of an encryption system are the length of the key, key management policies, and the nature of the encryption algorithm.
- There are both symmetric and asymmetric encryption systems. Symmetric systems use the same key to encrypt and decrypt. Asymmetric systems use both a public and a private key. E-business uses symmetric encryption to encode most data, since it is faster, and uses asymmetric encryption to safely send the symmetric key to the recipient.
- **Hashing** transforms plaintext into a short code called a **hash**.
- A **digital signature** is a hashed document that has been encrypted with the sender's private key.
- A **digital certificate** certifies the owner of a particular public key.
- An organization that issues public and private keys and records the public key in a digital certificate is a **certificate authority**.
- Preventive controls are never 100% effective, so organizations implement controls to enhance security by monitoring the effectiveness of preventive controls and detecting incidents in which they have been circumvented. **Detective controls** include:
  - **Log analysis**—the process of examining logs which record who accesses the system and the actions they take.
  - **Intrusion detection systems** (IDS) automate the monitoring of logs of network traffic permitted to pass the firewall. The most common analysis is to compare the logs to a database containing patterns of known attacks.
  - **Managerial reports** can be created to disclose the organization's performance with respect to the COBIT objectives. Key performance indicators include downtime caused by security incidents, number of systems with IDS installed, and the time needed to react to security incidents once they are reported.
  - **Security testing** includes:
    - **Vulnerability scans**, which use automated tools designed to identify whether a system contains any well-known vulnerabilities.
    - **Penetration testing** which involves an authorized attempt by either an internal audit team or external security consulting firm to break into the organization's IS.
- **Corrective controls** include the following:

Page 486   ©2007 Kaplan CPA Review

- A **computer emergency response team** (CERT), consisting of technical specialists and senior operations management, to deal with major incidents. The CERT leads the organization's incident response process through four steps, which must be practiced regularly:
  - Recognizing that a problem exists.
  - Containing the problem.
  - Recovery.
  - Follow up.
- A **chief security officer** is a designated individual with organizationwide responsibility for security. This individual should report to the COO or CEO and be independent of the IS function. The CSO must understand the technology; disseminate information about fraud, security breaches, and consequences; work with the person in charge of building security; and impartially assess the IT environment.
- **Patch management** involves fixing known vulnerabilities and installing the latest updates to anti-virus software, firewalls, operating systems, and application programs.

According to the Trust Services framework, reliable systems satisfy five principles:

- Security (discussed above).
- Confidentiality.
- Privacy.
- Processing integrity.
- Availability.

CONFIDENTIALITY

- Reliable systems protect confidential information from unauthorized disclosure. Confidential information includes sensitive data produced internally as well as that shared by business partners. Each organization will develop its own definitions, which usually include: business plans, pricing strategies, client and customer lists, and legal documents.
- Encryption is a fundamental control procedure for protecting the confidentiality of sensitive information. Confidential information should be encrypted while stored and during transmission to trusted parties.
- The internet provides inexpensive transmission, but data is easily intercepted. Encryption solves the interception issue. If data is encrypted before sending it, a **virtual private network (VPN)** is created.
- It is critical to encrypt any sensitive information stored in devices that are easily lost or stolen, such as laptops, PDAs, cell phones, and other portable devices. Many organizations have policies against storing sensitive information on these devices, but 81% of users do so anyway.
- Encryption alone is not sufficient to protect confidentiality. Access controls and strong authentication techniques are also needed. Strong controls should be used to limit the actions (read, write, change, delete, copy, etc.) that authorized users can perform when accessing confidential information. Access to system outputs should also be controlled.

©2007 Kaplan CPA Review

STUDY MANUAL – BUSINESS ENVIRONMENT & CONCEPTS
CHAPTER 19

- It is especially important to control disposal of information resources. Special procedures are needed for information stored on magnetic and optical media.
- Controls to protect confidentiality must be continuously reviewed and modified to respond to new threats created by technological advances. Many organizations now prohibit visitors from using cell phones while touring their facilities because of the threat caused by cell-cams. Phone conversations routed over the Internet are also vulnerable.
- Employee use of e-mail and instant messaging (IM) probably represents two of the greatest threats to the confidentiality of sensitive information.

PRIVACY

- In the Trust Services framework, the privacy principle is closely related to the confidentiality principle. The primary difference is that privacy focuses on protecting personal information about customers rather than organizational data. Key controls for privacy are the same that were previously listed for confidentiality.
- Federal and some state regulations require organizations to protect the privacy of customer information.
- The Trust Services privacy framework of the AICPA and CICA lists ten internationally recognized best practices for protecting the privacy of customers' personal information:
  - **Management**—Establish policies and procedures to protect privacy of personal information collected. Assign responsibility to a particular person or group.
  - **Notice**—Notify individuals when their information is collected.
  - **Choice and consent**—Give customers a choice to opt out (U.S.) or opt in (Europe) to the collection of their personal information.
  - **Collection**—Means collect only what is needed.
  - **Use and retention**—Means retain only as long as needed.
  - **Access**—Allow customers to access, review, and delete their information.
  - **Disclosure to Third Parties**—Provide to third parties only per policy and require the same protection.
  - **Security**—Take reasonable steps to protect the information from loss or unauthorized disclosure.
  - **Quality**—Maintain the integrity of the information.
  - **Monitoring and enforcement**—Assign a third party to assure and verify compliance.
- A related concern involves the overwhelming volume of spam—unsolicited e-mail that contains either advertising or offensive content. A 2003 Congressional Act, **CAN-SPAM**, provides criminal and civil penalties for violation of the law, applies to commercial e-mail, and covers most legitimate e-mail sent by organizations to customers, suppliers, or donors to non-profits. CAN-SPAM guidelines include:
  - The sender's identity must be clearly displayed in the message header.
  - The subject field in the header must clearly identify the message as an advertisement or solicitation.
  - The body must provide recipients with a working link that can be used to "opt out" of future e-mail.
  - The body must include the sender's valid postal address.

- Organizations should not send e-mail to randomly generated addresses or set up websites designed to harvest e-mail addresses of potential customers.
- Organizations need to train employees on how to manage personal information collected from customers. One privacy-related issue is identity theft. Organizations have an ethical and moral obligation to implement controls to protect databases that contain their customers' personal information.

PROCESSING INTEGRITY

- A reliable system produces information that is accurate, timely, reflects results of only authorized transactions, and includes outcomes of all activities engaged in by the organization during a given period of time. Reliability requires controls over both data input quality and the processing of the data.
- Five categories of integrity controls are designed to meet the preceding objectives:
  - **Source data controls**—Companies must establish control procedures to ensure that all source documents are authorized, accurate, complete, properly accounted for, and entered into the system or sent to their intended destination in a timely manner. Source data controls include forms design; prenumbered forms sequence tests; turnaround documents; cancellation and storage of documents; authorization and segregation of duties; visual scanning; check digit verification; and RFID security.
  - **Data entry controls**—Once data is collected, data entry control procedures are needed to ensure that it is entered correctly. The following tests were described previously under data validation:
    - A **field check.**
    - A **sign check.**
    - A **limit check.**
    - A **range check.**
    - A **completeness check.**
    - A **validity check.**
    - A **reasonableness test.**
  - In addition to the preceding controls, when using batch processing, the following data entry controls should be incorporated: sequence checks, error logs, and batch totals. Online data entry controls include: automatic entry of data, prompting, preformatting, closed-loop verification, transaction logs, and error messages.
  - **Processing Controls**—Controls to ensure that data is processed correctly include:
    - **Data Matching**—Involves matching two or more items before processing can proceed.
    - **File Labels**—External and internal labels to ensure that the correct and most current files are being updated.
    - Recalculation of batch totals.
    - Cross-footing balance test.
    - Write-protection mechanisms.
    - **Database processing integrity measures**—include database administrators, data dictionaries, and concurrent update controls.
    - Data conversion controls.
  - **Data transmission controls**—Organizations need controls to minimize the risk of data transmission errors. When the receiving unit detects a data transmission

STUDY MANUAL – BUSINESS ENVIRONMENT & CONCEPTS
CHAPTER 19

error, it asks the sending unit to re-send. This action is usually done automatically. Sometimes, the system may not be able to accomplish automatic resubmission and will ask the sender to retransmit the data. There are two basic types of data transmission controls:

- **Parity checking**—adds an additional bit to the digit being transmitted. The receiving device performs parity checking to verify that the proper number of bits is received (odd or even) for each character.
- **Message acknowledgment techniques** include:
  - **Echo checks**—The sending unit calculates a summary statistic, and the receiving unit recalculates it to see that they match.
  - **Trailer records**—The sending unit stores control totals in a trailer record, and the receiving unit uses that information to verify the entire message was received.
  - **Numbered batches**—Batches being transmitted are numbered sequentially. The receiving unit uses those numbers to properly assemble the batches.
- **Output controls**—Careful checking of system output provides additional control over processing integrity. Output controls include:
  - **User review of output** for reasonableness, completeness, and to be sure they are the intended recipient.
  - **Reconciliation procedures** involve reconciling all transactions and system updates to control reports, etc., and reconciling control account balances to totals of subsidiary accounts.
  - **External data reconciliation** involves reconciling stored data with data from outside the system.

AVAILABILITY

Reliable systems are available for use whenever needed. Threats to system availability originate from many sources, including hardware and software failures, natural and man-made disasters, human error, worms and viruses, and denial-of-service attacks, and other sabotage. Organizations must develop disaster recovery and business continuity plans to enable them to quickly resume normal operations after such an event.

Steps to minimize the risk of system downtime include: physical and logical access controls, good computer security to minimize risk of theft or sabotage, preventive maintenance, use of redundant components to provide fault tolerance, surge protection devices, and an uninterruptible power supply.

Risks associated with natural and man-made disasters can be reduced with proper location and design of rooms housing mission-critical servers and databases.

Training is especially important. Well-trained operators are less likely to make mistakes and more able to recover if they do. Security awareness training, particularly concerning safe e-mail and web-browsing practices, can reduce risk of virus and worm infection.

Anti-virus software should be installed, run, and kept current. E-mail should be scanned for viruses at both the server and desktop levels. Newly acquired software and disks, CDs,

Page 490   ©2007 Kaplan CPA Review

or DVDs should be scanned and tested first on a machine that is isolated from the main network.

Disaster recovery and business continuity plans are essential if an organization hopes to survive a major catastrophe. The objectives of a disaster recovery and business continuity plan are to: minimize the extent of the disruption, damage, and loss; temporarily establish an alternative means of processing information; resume normal operations as soon as possible; and train and familiarize personnel with emergency operations. Key components of effective disaster recovery and business continuity plans include: data backup procedures, provisions for access to replacement infrastructure (equipment, facilities, phone lines, etc.), thorough documentation, periodic testing, and adequate insurance.

CHANGE MANAGEMENT CONTROLS

Organizations constantly modify their information systems to reflect new business practices and to take advantage of advances in IT. Controls are needed to ensure that such changes don't negatively impact reliability. Existing controls related to security, confidentiality, privacy, processing integrity, and availability should be modified to maintain their effectiveness after the change. Change management controls need to ensure adequate segregation of duties is maintained in light of the modifications to the organizational structure and adoption of new software.

Important change management controls include: documentation of change requests in a standard format; approval of change requests at various levels of management; thorough testing; updated program, system, and procedure documentation; procedures for emergency changes; back-out plans; and monitoring of user rights and privileges.

COMPUTER FRAUD

The U.S. Department of Justice defines **computer fraud** as any illegal act for which knowledge of computer technology is essential for its perpetration, investigation, or prosecution.

- In using a computer, fraud perpetrators can steal more of something in less time and with less effort. They may also leave very little evidence, which can make these crimes more difficult to detect.
- Computer systems are particularly vulnerable to computer crimes for several reasons:
  - Individuals can steal, destroy, or alter massive amounts of data in very little time.
  - Access provided to customers and vendors creates added vulnerability.
  - Computer programs only need to be altered once, and they will operate that way until the system is no longer in use or someone notices.
  - Modern systems are accessed by PCs, which are inherently more vulnerable to security risks and difficult to control.
  - Computer systems face a number of unique challenges.
- Computer frauds cost billions of dollars each year, and their frequency is increasing because:
  - Not everyone agrees on what constitutes computer fraud.
  - Many computer frauds go undetected.

STUDY MANUAL – BUSINESS ENVIRONMENT & CONCEPTS
CHAPTER 19

- Many that are detected are not reported.
- There are a growing number of competent computer users aided by easier access.
- Some folks believe "it can't happen to us."
- Many networks have a low level of security.
- Instructions on how to perpetrate computer crimes and abuses are readily available on the Internet.
- Law enforcement is unable to keep up.

- **Economic espionage**—the theft of information and intellectual property, is growing especially fast. This growth has led to the need for investigative specialists or cybersleuths.

- **Computer Fraud Classification**—frauds can be categorized according to the data processing model: input frauds; processor frauds, computer instruction frauds, stored data frauds, and output frauds.

- **Input fraud** is the simplest and most common way to commit a fraud. Altering computer input requires little computer skills. It can take a number of forms, including disbursement frauds, inventory frauds, payroll frauds, cash receipt frauds, and fictitious refund frauds.

- **Processor fraud** involves computer fraud committed through unauthorized system use. It includes theft of computer time and services. Incidents could involve employees surfing the Internet, using the company computer to conduct personal business, or using the company computer to conduct a competing business.

- **Computer instruction fraud** involves tampering with the software that processes company data. It may include modifying the software, making illegal copies, using it in an unauthorized manner, or developing a software program or module to carry out an unauthorized activity. Computer instruction fraud used to be one of the least common types of frauds because it required specialized knowledge. Today, these frauds are more frequent.

- **Data fraud** involves altering or damaging a company's data files; or copying, using, or searching the data files without authorization. In many cases, disgruntled employees have scrambled, altered, or destroyed data files. Theft of data often occurs so that perpetrators can sell the data.

- **Output fraud** involves stealing or misusing system output. Output is usually displayed on a screen or printed on paper. Unless properly safeguarded, screen output can easily be read from a remote location using inexpensive electronic gear. This output is also subject to prying eyes and unauthorized copying. Fraud perpetrators can use computers and peripheral devices to create counterfeit outputs, such as checks.

STUDY MANUAL – BUSINESS ENVIRONMENT & CONCEPTS
CHAPTER 19

COMPUTER FRAUD AND ABUSE TECHNIQUES

Perpetrators have devised many methods to commit computer fraud and abuse. These include:

- Adware	- Packet sniffers
- Data diddling	- Password cracking
- Data leakage	- Phishing
- Denial of service attacks	- Piggybacking
- Eavesdropping	- Round-down technique
- Email threats	- Salami technique
- Email forgery (aka, **spoofing**)	- Social engineering
- Hacking	- Software piracy
- Phreaking	- Spamming
- Hijacking	- Spyware
- Identity theft	- Keystroke loggers
- Internet misinformation	- Superzapping
- Internet terrorism	- Trap doors
- Logic time bombs	- Trojan horse
- Masquerading or impersonation	- War dialing
	- War driving
	- Viruses
	- Worms

PREVENTING AND DETECTING COMPUTER FRAUD

Organizations must take every precaution to protect their information systems. Certain measures can significantly decrease the potential for fraud and any resulting losses:

- **Make fraud less likely to occur**—By creating an ethical culture, adopting an appropriate organizational structure, requiring active oversight, assigning authority and responsibility, assessing risk, developing security policies, implementing human resource policies, supervising employees effectively, training employees, requiring vacations, implementing development and acquisition controls, and prosecuting fraud perpetrators vigorously.
- **Increase the difficulty of committing fraud**—By designing strong internal controls, segregating duties, restricting access, requiring appropriate authorizations, utilizing documentation, safeguarding assets, requiring independent checks on performance, implementing computer-based controls, encrypting data, and fixing software vulnerabilities.
- **Improve detection methods**—By creating an audit trail, conducting periodic audits, installing fraud detection software, implementing a fraud hotline, employing a computer security officer, monitoring system activities, and using intrusion detection systems.

©2007 Kaplan CPA Review

Page 493

STUDY MANUAL – BUSINESS ENVIRONMENT & CONCEPTS
CHAPTER 19

- **Reduce Fraud Losses**—By maintaining adequate insurance, developing disaster recovery plans, backing up data and programs, and using software to monitor system activity and recover from fraud.

SOX AND THE FOREIGN CORRUPT PRACTICES ACT

- In 1977, Congress passed the **Foreign Corrupt Practices Act**. Its primary purpose was to prevent the bribery of foreign officials to obtain business. A significant effect was to require that corporations maintain good systems of internal accounting control.
- In the late 1990s and early 2000s, a series of multimillion-dollar accounting frauds made headlines. Congress responded with passage of the **Sarbanes-Oxley Act of 2002** (SOX). SOX applies to publicly held companies and their auditors.
- Important aspects of SOX include: (1) creation of the Public Company Accounting Oversight Board (PCAOB) to oversee the auditing profession; (2) new rules for auditors, audit committees, and management; and (3) new internal control requirements, requiring that management attest to the adequacy of internal controls. The auditor must attest to and report on management's assessment on internal controls.
- The SEC further mandated that management must base its evaluation of internal control on a recognized control framework. The most likely framework is the COSO model discussed later.
- **Levers of Control**—Many people feel there is a basic conflict between creativity and controls. Robert Simons has espoused four levers of controls to help companies reconcile this conflict:
  - A concise **belief system** to communicate core values to employees.
  - A **boundary system** to set limits.
  - A **diagnostic control system** to ensure efficient and effective achievement of important controls.
  - An **interactive control system** to help top-management with high-level activities that demand regular attention, such as strategic development.

RISK ASSESSMENT AND RISK RESPONSE

There are two types of risk: Inherent risk is the risk that exists before management takes any control steps. Residual risk is the risk that still remains after control steps. Companies should assess inherent risk, develop a response, and then assess residual risk. The steps in risk assessment and response are:

- Identify the events or threats that confront the company.
- Estimate the likelihood of each event occurring.
- Estimate the potential loss from each threat.
- Identify controls to guard against the threat.
- Estimate costs and benefits of implementing such controls.
- If it's cost beneficial, then reduce the risk by implementing controls; otherwise, avoid, share, or accept the risk.

Page 494

©2007 Kaplan CPA Review

STUDY MANUAL – BUSINESS ENVIRONMENT & CONCEPTS
CHAPTER 19

CONTROL ACTIVITIES

Control activities are policies, procedures, and rules that provide reasonable assurance that management's control objectives are met and their risk responses are carried out. They generally fall into one of the following categories: (1) proper authorization of transactions and activities; (2) segregation of duties; (3) project development and acquisition controls; (4) change management controls; (5) design and use of documents and records; (6) safeguard assets, records, and data; and (7) independent checks on performance.

- **Proper Authorization of Transactions and Activities**—Management must establish policies and empower employees to perform activities within policy. This empowerment is called **authorization**. There are typically at least two levels of authorization. With **general authorization**, management authorizes employees to handle routine transactions without special approval. **Special authorization** is required for transactions that are of significant consequences; management review and approval is required.
- **Segregation of Duties**—Segregation of duties in the accounting function means that no employee should have responsibility for more than one of the following with respect to related assets:
  - **Authorization**—approving transactions and decisions.
  - **Recording**—Preparing source documents; maintaining journals, ledgers, or other files; preparing reconciliations; and preparing performance reports.
  - **Custody**—Handling cash, maintaining an inventory storeroom, receiving incoming customer checks, writing checks on the organization's bank account.
- If two or more employees work together to override these controls, there is **collusion**.
- Within the systems function, procedures once performed by separate individuals are combined. Therefore, anyone who has unrestricted access to the computer, its programs, and live data could have the opportunity to perpetrate and conceal fraud. To combat this threat, organizations must implement effective segregation of duties within the IS function. Authority and responsibility must be divided clearly among the following functions: systems administration, network management, security management, change management, users, systems analysts, programming, computer operations, information systems library, and data control.
- **Project Development and Acquisition Controls**—Involves a formal, appropriate, and proven methodology to govern the development, acquisition, implementation, and maintenance of information systems and related technologies. This approach should contain appropriate controls for management review and approval, user involvement, analysis, design, testing, implementation, and conversion. The following basic control principles should be applied to systems development: develop a strategic master plan, incorporate project controls, create a data processing schedule, utilize a steering committee, and use system performance measurements and post-implementation review.
- **Change Management Controls**—Change management is the process of making sure that system changes do not negatively affect systems reliability, security, confidentiality, integrity, or availability.
- **Design and Use of Adequate Documents and Records**—Proper design and use of documents and records helps ensure accurate and complete recording of all relevant transaction data. Form and content should be kept as simple as possible. Documents

©2007 Kaplan CPA Review

Page 495

STUDY MANUAL – BUSINESS ENVIRONMENT & CONCEPTS
CHAPTER 19

that initiate a transaction should contain a space for authorization. Those used to transfer assets should have a space for the receiving party's signature. Documents should be sequentially prenumbered and should provide an audit trail.

- **Safeguard Assets, Records, and Data**—Cash, inventory, information, and other assets all need to be protected. Insiders pose the greatest risk to information. It is important to maintain accurate records of all assets, periodically reconcile recorded amounts to physical counts, restrict access to assets, and protect records and documents.

- **Independent Checks on Performance**—Internal checks to ensure that transactions are processed accurately are an important control element. These checks should be performed by someone independent of the party responsible for the activities. They typically include: top-level reviews, analytical reviews, reconciliation of independently maintained sets of records, comparison of actual quantities with recorded amounts, double-entry accounting, and independent review.

STUDY MANUAL – BUSINESS ENVIRONMENT & CONCEPTS

CHAPTER 19

QUESTIONS: IT: IT CONTROL ISSUES

1. Ryan Company has an accounting information system that operates in a client/server environment. Which one of the following situations is *least likely* to provide Ryan with an appropriate security environment?
    A. Use of application passwords.
    B. Power-on passwords for personal computers.
    C. Installation of anti-virus programs.
    D. Placing complete systems application controls under one individual.

2. Which one of the following controls is *least likely* to be closely associated with assuring the accuracy and completeness of data in computer-processed master files?
    A. Source data controls.
    B. File maintenance controls.
    C. Online data entry controls.
    D. Logical access controls.

3. Feedback, feedforward, and preventive controls are important types of control systems and procedures for an accounting information system. Which one of the following is in the **CORRECT** order of feedback, feedforward, and preventive control systems?
    A. Cash budgeting, capital budgeting, and hiring qualified employees.
    B. Inventory control, capital budgeting, and cash budgeting.
    C. Cash budgeting, cost accounting variances, and separation of duties.
    D. Cost accounting variances, cash budgeting, and organizational independence.

4. Which one of the following is **NOT** considered a typical risk associated with outsourcing (the practice of hiring an outside company to handle all or part of the data processing)?
    A. Inflexibility.
    B. Loss of control.
    C. Less availability of expertise.
    D. Locked-in relationship with a vendor.

5. Data input validation routines include:
    A. terminal logs.
    B. passwords.
    C. hash totals.
    D. backup controls.

6. In designing systems of internal control, which of the following types of controls are the *best* to include in the design in order to be fully effective?
    A. Preventive, detective, and corrective controls.
    B. Feedforward, batch, and on-line controls.
    C. Management, personnel, and administrative controls.
    D. Edit, input verification, and output controls.

©2007 Kaplan CPA Review

Page 497

STUDY MANUAL – BUSINESS ENVIRONMENT & CONCEPTS
CHAPTER 19

7. Which of the following *best* describe the interrelated components of a system of internal control?
    A. Organizational structure, management philosophy, and planning.
    B. Control environment, risk assessment, control activities, information and communication systems, and monitoring.
    C. Risk assessment, backup facilities, responsibility accounting, and natural laws.
    D. Legal environment of the firm, management philosophy, and organizational structure.

8. Which of the following computer documentation would an auditor *most likely* utilize in obtaining an understanding of the internal control structure?
    A. Systems flowcharts.
    B. Record counts.
    C. Program listings.
    D. Record layouts.

9. Which of the following is a computer test made to ascertain whether a given characteristic belongs to the group?
    A. Parity check.
    B. Validity check.
    C. Echo check.
    D. Limit check.

10. When EDP programs or files can be accessed from terminals, users should be required to enter a(an):
    A. parity check.
    B. personal identification code.
    C. self-diagnosis test.
    D. echo check.

11. If a control total were computed on each of the following data items, which would *best* be identified as a hash total for a payroll EDP application?
    A. Total debits and total credits.
    B. Net pay.
    C. Department numbers.
    D. Hours worked.

12. Which of the following controls is a processing control designed to ensure the reliability and accuracy of data processing?

	Limit test	Validity check test
A.	Yes	Yes
B.	No	No
C.	No	Yes
D.	Yes	No

Page 498

©2007 Kaplan CPA Review

STUDY MANUAL – BUSINESS ENVIRONMENT & CONCEPTS

CHAPTER 19

13. Which of the following is an example of a validity check?
    A. The computer ensures that a numerical amount in a record does not exceed some predetermined amount.
    B. As the computer corrects errors and data are successfully resubmitted to the system, the causes of the errors are printed out.
    C. The computer flags any transmission for which the control field value did not match that of an existing file record.
    D. After data for a transaction are entered, the computer sends certain data back to the terminal for comparison with data originally sent.

14. An entity has the following invoices in a batch:

Invoice #	Product	Quantity	Unit price
201	F10	150	$ 5.00
202	G15	200	$10.00
203	H20	250	$25.00
204	K35	300	$30.00

    Which of the following numbers represents the record count?
    A. 1.
    B. 4.
    C. 810.
    D. 900.

15. An entity has the following invoices in a batch:

Invoice #	Product	Quantity	Unit price
201	F10	150	$ 5.00
202	G15	200	$10.00
203	H20	250	$25.00
204	K35	300	$30.00

    Which of the following *most likely* represents a hash total?
    A. FGHK80.
    B. 4.
    C. 204.
    D. 810.

16. Jones, an auditor for Farmington Co., noted that Acme employees were using computers connected to Acme's network by wireless technology. On Jones' next visit to Acme, Jones brought one of Farmington's laptop computers with a wireless network card. When Jones started the laptop to begin work, Jones noticed that the laptop could view several computers on Acme's network and Jones had access to Acme's network files. Which of the following statements is the *most likely* explanation?
    A. Acme's router was improperly configured.
    B. Farmington's computer had the same administrator password as the server.
    C. Jones had been given root account access on Acme's computer.
    D. Acme was not using security on the network.

©2007 Kaplan CPA Review

Page 499

STUDY MANUAL – BUSINESS ENVIRONMENT & CONCEPTS
CHAPTER 19

17.   Which of the following risks can be minimized by requiring all employees accessing the information systems to use passwords?
   A.   Collusion.
   B.   Data entry errors.
   C.   Failure of server duplicating function.
   D.   Firewall vulnerability.

18.   What is the primary advantage of using an application firewall rather than a network firewall?
   A.   It is less expensive.
   B.   It offers easier access to applications.
   C.   It provides additional user authentication.
   D.   It is easier to install.

STUDY MANUAL – BUSINESS ENVIRONMENT & CONCEPTS
CHAPTER 19

ANSWERS: IT: IT CONTROL ISSUES

1. **D** Answer (d) is correct because if one individual has complete authority over systems applications controls, he or she could too easily bypass those controls. Answer (a) is not correct because application passwords are helpful in prohibiting access to software to only those authorized to use it. Answer (b) is not correct because power-on passwords are helpful in prohibiting access to the system to only those authorized to have access. Answer (c) is not correct because anti-virus programs are helpful in scanning disks and files introduced into the system for destructive virus software.

2. **D** Answer (d) is correct because logical access relates to the ability to use computer equipment to access data. Accordingly, while helpful, these controls would not be as closely associated with assuring accuracy and completeness of data as the other choices. Answer (a) is not correct because source data controls would be helpful in assuring that data entered from source information are correct and complete. Answer (b) is not correct because these controls over the addition, deletion, and changing of records in files would be useful in assuring their accuracy and completeness. Answer (c) is not correct because controls over the entry of data during on-line processing would help assure the accuracy and completeness of files.

3. **D** Cost accounting variances are feedback controls since they provide feedback, after the fact, of the degree of manufacturing efficiency. Cash budgeting is a feedforward control, since it can warn in advance of any looming problems. Organizational independence, properly enforced, is a preventive control, since it prevents unauthorized people from performing an incompatible function.

4. **C** With outsourcing, the hope is that by using a company that specializes in data processing, there would be more expertise available than by doing the data processing in-house where it is auxiliary to our main business. Choice (a) is incorrect. The outside company may be inflexible in that it may want us to use its payroll systems, for example, rather than one designed specifically for us. Also, for another example, it may be closed for certain holidays when we need service. Choice (b) is incorrect. There is a potential loss of control when the data processing employees do not work for us, but work instead for the outside company. Choice (d) is incorrect. A locked-in relationship is a concern because the outside company may be processing our customer records and we cannot take the chance of losing any processing days by switching to another vendor.

5. **C** Hash totals are totals in a batch of input transactions that, by themselves, are meaningless, such as the total of the employee numbers, or the total of the vendor numbers. But such a total may be checked later in the processing to verify that no errors were made in their entry, thus providing input validation. Terminal logs [choice (a)] may show which programs were accessed, but provide no input validation. Passwords [choice (b)] assure that only authorized users gain access, but do not validate input. Backup controls [choice (d)] assure that copies of files are maintained, but do not validate input.

6. **A** Preventive controls (designed to prevent errors or fraud), detective controls (designed to detect errors or fraud), and corrective controls (designed to correct errors or fraud) comprise a collectively exhaustive way to classify controls. Feedforward controls (b) may be used with batch or online computer systems; this answer does not comprise all controls. Management, personnel, and administrative controls (c) fails to include many computer and operational controls. Edit, input verification, and output controls (d) relate only to computer input and output.

©2007 Kaplan CPA Review
Page 501

STUDY MANUAL – BUSINESS ENVIRONMENT & CONCEPTS
CHAPTER 19

7. **B** These five components have been described as key. The control environment sets the overall tone, risk assessment identifies and analyzes risk, control activities ensure the following of management policies, information and communication systems provide information necessary for responsibilities to be met, and monitoring assesses the control structure. Planning (a) is not a component, while the other two are part of the control environment. Backup facilities, responsibility accounting, and natural laws (c) are not components. The factors in choice (d) are part of the control environment.

8. **A** A system's flowchart is a pictorial representation of the processing steps in moving an item through processing. The question deals with understanding the internal control structure. Therefore, a flowchart would aid the auditor in understanding the flow of the system.

9. **B** A validity check is a hardware check that determines whether or not a particular character is a legitimate member of the permissible character set (alphanumeric, numeric, etc.).

10. **B** Access controls deal with ensuring that only authorized people can use EDP programs or files. An example is an online access password system, such as a personal identification code. Answer (a) is applied by the computer to assure that bits are not lost during the process. Answer (d) is a check upon the accuracy of a data transfer operation.

11. **C** A hash total is a sum of numbers in a specified field of a record, or of a batch of records, used for checking and control purposes. A hash total is distinguishable from other control totals in that it is not meaningful for the accounting records and is not usually added. Answer (c) best meets the definition for a hash total.

12. **A** A limit test is designed to limit, for example, the number of hours an employee can be paid in any week and, therefore, ensure the reliability and accuracy of data processing. A validity check test is designed to check that an employee is a current employee (valid) before processing a payroll transaction for that person and, therefore, ensures the reliability and accuracy of data processing.

13. **C** Validity checks are computer-programmed routines that determine whether or not a particular character is legitimate. An example of a validity check would be a comparison of input data fields to existing file records to determine if the characters being entered are valid. If the validity check is operating properly, the computer will flag any transmissions for which the control field value (input data) did not match that of an existing file record. Answer (a) is incorrect because it is an example of a limit test, which is a computerized check to determine that data values do not exceed or fall below some determined limit. Answer (b) is incorrect because it is an example of an error log, which is a record or listing of each rejected item. Answer (d) is incorrect because it is an example of a data entry or data conversion control, which determines that the data being entered agrees with the data originally sent.

14. **B** In a batch processing system, a record count is the number of items included in the batch to be processed.

15. **D** In a batch processing system, a hash total is the sum of items in the batch that are not usually totaled. In this question, if you add the invoice numbers, they total 810. The totaling of invoice numbers is an example of a hash total.

Page 502   ©2007 Kaplan CPA Review

STUDY MANUAL – BUSINESS ENVIRONMENT & CONCEPTS

CHAPTER 19

16. **D** Acme did not have security protecting access to the network. Answer (a) is incorrect because a router is a switching device linking incoming messages over the Internet. Answer (b) is incorrect because it appears there were no passwords used. Answer (c) is incorrect because there is nothing in the data suggesting this happened. Jones would not necessarily be given root account access by Acme.

17. **D** Passwords limit unauthorized access to the system and data. Answers (a), (b) and (c) can occur with or without the use of passwords.

18. **C** A firewall is software used to prevent unauthorized access to information. It separates one segment from another. By placing a firewall on the application software rather than the entire network, it provides an additional layer of authentication to the data by the user at the specific application level.

IT: FLOWCHARTS

STUDY MANUAL – BUSINESS ENVIRONMENT & CONCEPTS
CHAPTER 20

Study Tip: The AICPA provides a free six-month subscription to their research database for candidates who have received their NTS (notice to sit). Have you subscribed to this excellent free resource? If not, go to www.cpa-exam.org and do so now. It's a tremendous benefit for practicing your research skills for the simulations.

Popular forms of flowcharting include:

- **Document flowchart**—showing the flow of documents and information between departments or participants in the system. There is usually a column for each participant.
- **Program flowchart**—showing the sequence of operations that a computer performs in executing a program.
- **System flowchart**—showing the relationship among inputs, processing, and outputs in a system.

DOCUMENT FLOWCHART

The standard flow chart symbols are illustrated in Figures 1–3.

STUDY MANUAL – BUSINESS ENVIRONMENT & CONCEPTS
CHAPTER 20

Figure 1: Flow Chart Symbols

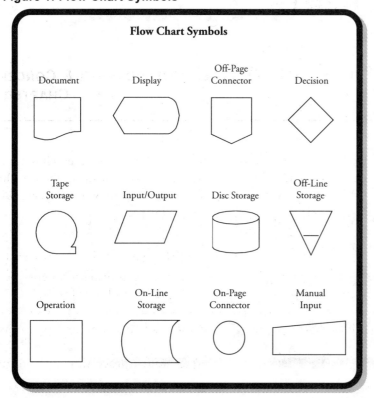

Figure 2: Sales Order Processing

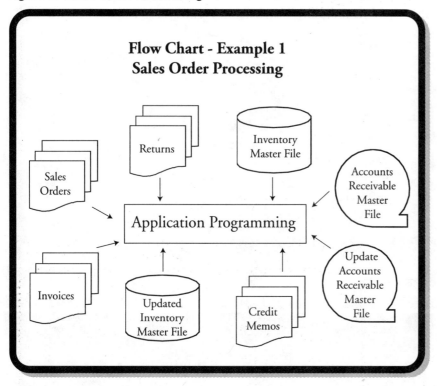

STUDY MANUAL – BUSINESS ENVIRONMENT & CONCEPTS
CHAPTER 20

Figure 3: Purchase Order Processing

Flow Chart - Example 2
Purchase Order Processing

Purchase Requisition · Shipment Receipt · Returns · Invoices

Accounts Payable Master File → **Application Programming** ← Inventory Master File

Updated Accounts Payable Master File · Updated Inventory Master File · Purchase Orders · Debit Memos

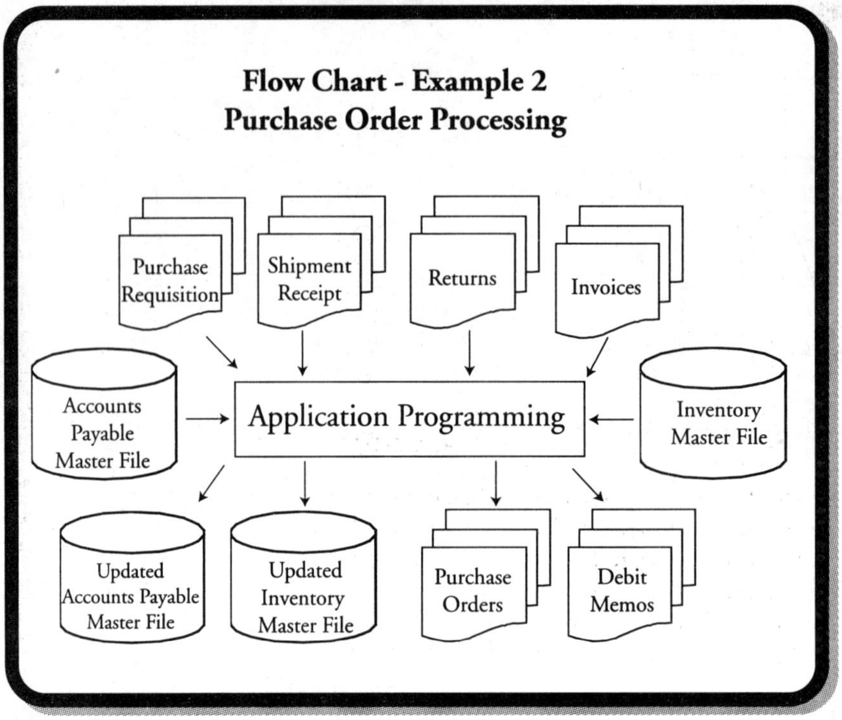

PROGRAM FLOWCHARTING

The major symbols used in **program** flowcharting are shown in Figure 4.

Page 506   ©2007 Kaplan CPA Review

Figure 4: Major Program Symbols

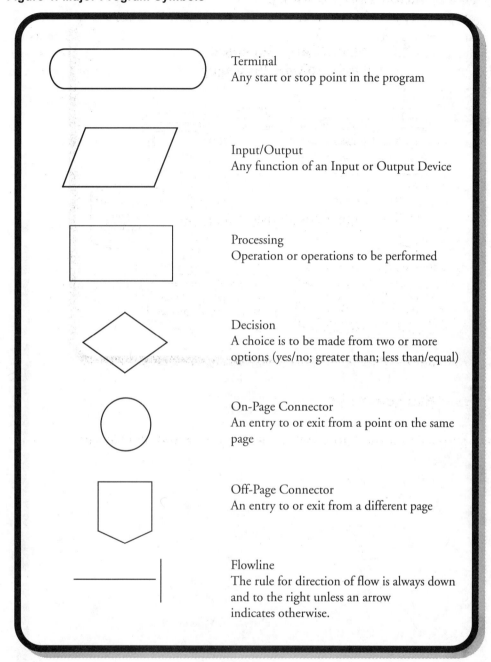

Study Manual – Business Environment & Concepts
Chapter 20

System Flowcharting

The major symbols used in **system** flowcharting refer to tapes, hardcopy printouts, paper handling, and the like. The system flowchart represents an entire accounting system, while a program flowchart will be the specific computer activity in just one part of the system. Major system symbols are shown in Figure 5.

Figure 5: Major System Symbols

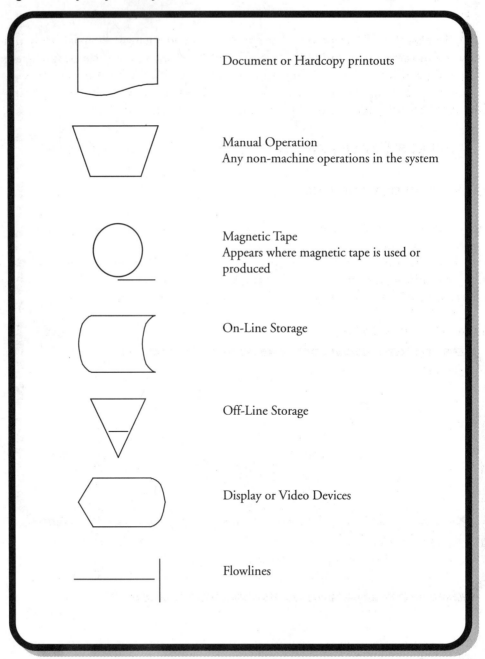

ECONOMICS OF THE FIRM

STUDY MANUAL – BUSINESS ENVIRONMENT & CONCEPTS
CHAPTER 21

Study Tip: To pass the CPA exam, you need to invest an adequate amount of study time. The amount will vary significantly based on a number of factors, but most people need to plan on spending at least 60 to 120 hours in preparing for Business Environment & Concepts. Before getting started, make sure you know when you will have enough time available. It is very difficult to pass this exam without enough study hours.

BUSINESS CYCLES AND REASONS FOR BUSINESS CYCLES

BASIC TERMINOLOGY FOR BUSINESS CYCLES

A. The business cycle is characterized by fluctuations in economic activity around a long-term growth trend line. It is the short-term ups and downs in the economy. Real gross domestic product (GDP) and the rate of unemployment are key variables used when determining the current phase of the cycle. The phases of the business cycle are illustrated in Figure 1. (GDP will be explained in more detail later.)

Figure 1: Business Cycles

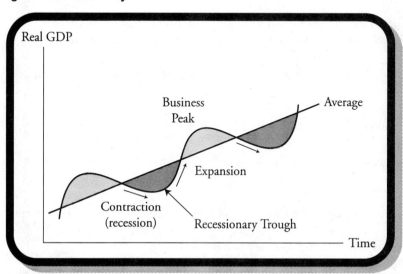

B. As to the length of each phase, recent experience has shown that the contractionary periods are becoming shorter, and the expansionary periods are becoming longer.

C. A recession is defined as a period during which real GDP declines for two or more consecutive quarters. Both the contractionary and recessionary trough phases constitute a recession. A depression is a prolonged and very severe recession.

D. A peak is defined as the highest point in profits and growth resulting from an expansion, just before the economy slides into a contraction. At the peak, economic forces begin to cause shortages in the supplies of inputs and constraints on productive capacity, which causes higher costs and higher prices.

E. A trough is defined as the low point in profits and growth and is characterized by excess capacity, low corporate profits, and a corporate focus on cutting costs in payroll and other areas.

THE GENERAL STAGES OF THE BUSINESS CYCLE

A. Recovery: The economy begins to show signs that a recession is ending.

   1. Consumers, governments, and businesses begin to increase their demand for goods and services.

   2. Providers of goods and services begin to increase aggregate supply.

   3. Corporate profits begin to stabilize and economic growth begins to increase, heading toward its long-term growth trend line.

   4. Companies begin to notice a decrease in any excess capacity and may begin to increase their workforce.

B. Early expansion: The recovery takes hold and the momentum of the recovery increases. Attractive investments include stocks in general and real estate.

C. Late expansion: The recovery has continued, and confidence and momentum are high.

   1. Attractive investments include bonds and interest-sensitive stocks.

   2. Lumping together early and late expansion into "expansion" is sometimes referred to as a *boom.*

D. Slowing (contraction), entering recession: Growth rates turn flat and then negative.

   1. This is the opposite of the recovery stage.

   2. Attractive investments include bonds and interest-sensitive stocks.

E. Recession (or slump): Typically the money supply will be expanded, but recovery may take time. Attractive investments include commodities and stocks.

Factors Affecting Business Cycle

A. Aggregate output or aggregate supply are terms used to describe the total goods and services produced by the economy over a certain period of time.

B. Aggregate demand, conversely, is the total goods and services that all segments of the economy are willing and able to purchase at a given "overall price level."

C. The overall price level refers to an average of all prices of all goods and services. The overall price level is not a price that a purchaser of goods and services would pay for a specific item. Think of overall price level as a price index. Consider a simple example to illustrate overall price level:

   1. If prices of airline tickets increase, a consumer who travels by air might decide to switch to travel by train.

   2. However, if overall price levels increase, then both air travel and train travel would increase, and there would be no advantage to switching to train travel.

D. The shifts in aggregate supply and aggregate demand largely drive the economy through the ups and downs of business cycles.

E. As shown in Figure 2, the aggregate demand (AD) curve depicts all equilibrium combinations of goods and services demanded at a given price level.

Figure 2: Aggregate Demand

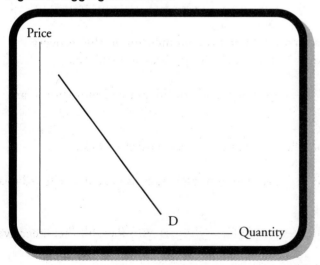

   1. The aggregate demand curve represents the effects of decisions made by all market participants and is downward sloping.

   2. The downward slope is indicative of the inverse (opposite direction) relationship between price and quantity demanded (in the aggregate) by consumers.

STUDY MANUAL – BUSINESS ENVIRONMENT & CONCEPTS
CHAPTER 21

3. The aggregate demand curve represents the quantity demanded of a good at all price levels, given the current level of wealth (income) in the economy.

    a. For example, the number of $25 steak dinners you are willing to purchase will depend to some degree on how much money you have.

    b. In other words, a general increase in wealth will cause an increased demand for goods and services at every price level, and the AD curve will shift to the right.

    c. By "shift to the right," we simply mean that the entire curve will move to the right, maintaining the same downward slope, indicating that at every price consumers will demand (consume) more.

F. The aggregate supply curve depicts the amount of goods and services that firms, in the aggregate, are willing to produce (supply) at any given price level. As with demand, we must always make a clear distinction between long-run aggregate supply (LRAS), which represents the long-run productive capacity of the economy, and short-run aggregate supply (SRAS), which represents short-run deviations from the long-run potential.

    1. There is dispute among economists about the shape of the aggregate supply curve.

    2. In general, though, think of the long-term aggregate supply curve as a vertical line.

CAUSES OF SHIFTS IN AGGREGATE DEMAND AND AGGREGATE SUPPLY

A. Changes in the following shift aggregate demand and supply:

    1. Real wealth.

    2. Real interest rate.

    3. Expectations about direction of economy.

    4. Expected rate of inflation.

    5. Income abroad.

    6. Exchange rate.

    7. Resource base.

    8. Technology.

    9. Institutional changes.

10. Resource prices.

11. Supply shocks.

EFFECTS OF THE BUSINESS CYCLE ON AN ENTITY'S FINANCIAL POSITION AND BUSINESS OPERATIONS

A. Effects on the Firm:

1. If consumers decide to consume less today, they necessarily have to save more (given some level of income).

2. Inventories will accumulate on store shelves, production will be cut, and workers will be laid off.

3. The economy will move from point E (full employment, GDP_f) to point A (under-employment, GDP_u).

4. The reduction in demand places downward pressure on wage rates and prices. As workers and suppliers begin to accept the lower wage rate, employment and output will rise due to the favorable shift in resource prices. While the long-run result is solely a reduction in prices, the short-run results are:

    a. Decline in output.

    b. Reduction in prices (a decline in prices).

5. If consumers decide to consume more, it will cause a shift to the right in AD resulting in GDP moving above full employment, GDP_f.

6. In the short run, both output and prices rise (reducing unemployment).

7. In the long run, the increased resource costs (higher wages and other inputs) will reduce SRAS, leading solely to higher prices.

Figure 3 illustrates the long-run and short-run impacts of an unanticipated change in AD.

©2007 Kaplan CPA Review

Page 513

STUDY MANUAL – BUSINESS ENVIRONMENT & CONCEPTS
CHAPTER 21

Figure 3: Long-Run and Short-Run Impacts of an Unanticipated Change in AD

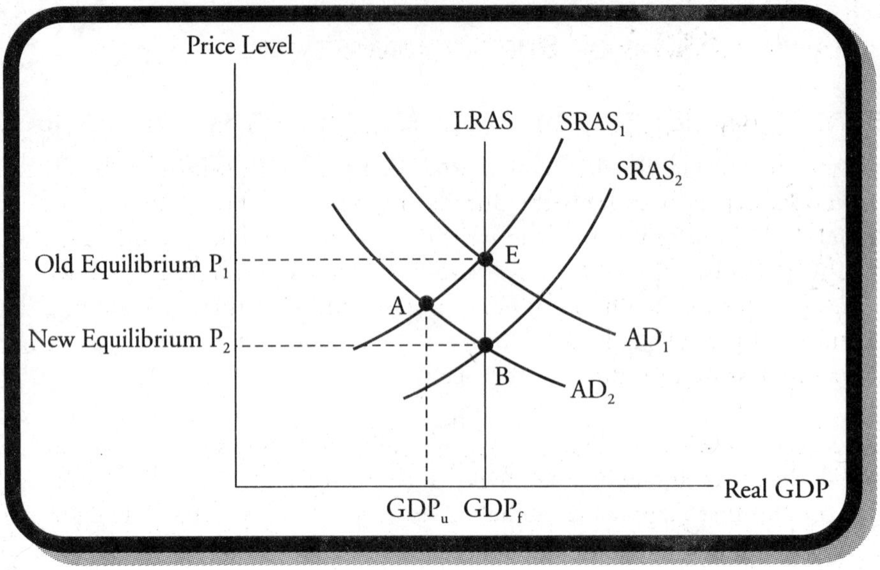

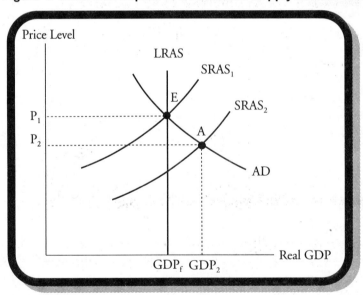

Figure 4 illustrates the short-run impact of an unanticipated change in AS.

Figure 4: Short-Run Impact of a Favorable Supply Shock

B. Three self-correcting mechanisms tend to stabilize the economy after a shock or in response to changes in the business cycle:

1. Consumption demand: Demand is relatively stable over the business cycle leading to increased (decreased) saving when the economy is in an expansion (recession).

2. Real interest rates: Changes in real interest rates will help to stabilize aggregate demand and redirect economic fluctuations.

3. Resource prices: Changes in real resource prices will dampen economic cycles.

LAWS OF SUPPLY AND DEMAND

A. According to the law of demand, there exists an inverse relationship between the price of a good in the market and the quantity that consumers are willing to buy. People's desire for goods typically exceeds the purchasing power of their incomes, forcing them to make choices. People will choose those alternatives that enhance their welfare most for the price they pay, and an increase in the cost of an item relative to alternatives reduces its likelihood of being purchased. Substitutes are goods that perform similar functions. The availability of substitutes is the main reason that consumers buy less of a product as its price increases.

B. It can be seen in panel (a) of Figure 5 that the demand curve slopes downward to the right, indicating that the quantity demanded increases as the price decreases. Some goods are much more responsive to changes in price than are others. The greater the number of viable substitutes for a good, the more responsive its demand is to price changes. When interpreting the demand curve, remember that we have assumed that factors other than price, such as consumer income, have not changed significantly.

Figure 5: Supply and demand curves

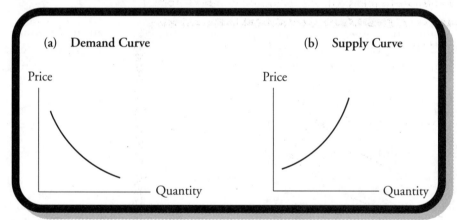

C. Elastic and inelastic demand curves. When substitutes are readily available, a product is likely to have a relatively flat (more horizontal) demand curve. For example, if the price of tacos increases, consumers can and will readily substitute hamburgers. This means the demand for tacos is highly elastic (i.e., a price increase is likely to significantly decrease demand).

D. When substitutes are not readily available, a product will have a relatively steep (more vertical) demand curve (i.e., its demand is relatively inelastic). For example, if the price of gasoline increases, demand will not decline much because there are few substitutes.

E. The law of supply states that there is a direct relationship between the price of a good and the amount of that good that will be supplied in the marketplace. All else held constant, a higher price will increase the supply of goods produced and offered for

STUDY MANUAL – BUSINESS ENVIRONMENT & CONCEPTS
CHAPTER 21

sale. Existing producers will produce more, and new suppliers will enter the market. This relationship is described by the supply curve presented in panel (b) of Figure 5.

F. An economic profit results when sales revenue exceeds the cost of production, including opportunity costs. An economic loss results when sales revenue is less than the cost of production, including all opportunity costs. A product's opportunity cost of production is the return that the firm's resources would have earned elsewhere had they not been devoted to the production of the product. This includes the firm's cost of capital. In a market economy, profits and losses are important in that they determine whether firms remain solvent and prosperous, and which firms are driven out of the market. In market economies, profit potential encourages entrepreneurs to identify the need for new or additional products, gather investment funds, and risk those funds by accumulating assets to produce and sell a service or product.

G. Elastic and inelastic supply curves. Given a price change, the responsiveness of supply differs between goods. When a price change leads to a large change in quantity supplied, the supply curve is elastic. This would be the case when producers can add resources inexpensively. When a price change leads to a small change in supply, the supply curve is inelastic.

SHIFTS IN AND MOVEMENTS ALONG SUPPLY AND DEMAND CURVES

A. The demand curve isolates the impact that price has on the amount of a product purchased. As indicated in panel (a) of Figure 6, a movement along a specific demand curve represents the change in quantity demanded resulting from a change in price.

B. Some factors, however, cause the entire demand curve to shift. This is illustrated in panel (b) of Figure 6.

C. Demand curve shifts are called *changes in demand* and are caused by the following factors.

   1. Changes in consumer income. When consumers have more money, they can buy more of everything at a given price, so the aggregate demand curve shifts to the right.

   2. Changes in the prices of related goods (substitutes and complements). The price of butter goes up, so consumers buy less butter and more margarine. The demand curve for margarine shifts to the right.

Page 516 ©2007 Kaplan CPA Review

Figure 6: Movements Along vs. Shifts in Demand Curves

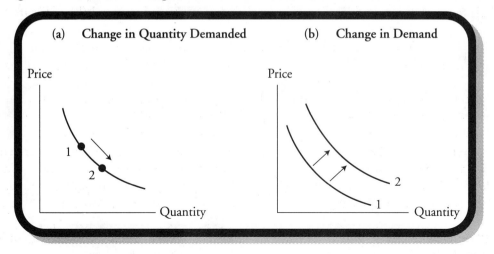

3. Changes in consumer expectations. Consumers expect the price of cars to rise next month, so they buy a new car now before the price increases later. The demand curve for new autos temporarily shifts to the right.

4. Changes in the number of consumers in the market. As cities grow and shrink and as international markets open to domestic markets, the change in the number of customers shifts the demand curves of many products.

5. Demographic changes. In recent years, the number of people ages 15 to 24 in the United States declined by more than 5 million. This change will shift demand curves to the left for such things as jeans and pizza.

6. Changes in consumer tastes and preferences. As consumer tastes and preferences change, the demand curves for various products will shift.

D. Other things held constant, the supply curve summarizes the willingness of producers to offer a product at a given price. The change in the quantity supplied as price changes represents movements along the supply curve. This is illustrated in panel (a) of Figure 7.

E. Some factors may cause producers to change the quantity they are willing to supply at all price levels simultaneously. These changes will shift the supply curve as shown in panel (b) of Figure 7:

Figure 7: Movements Along vs. Shifts in Supply Curves

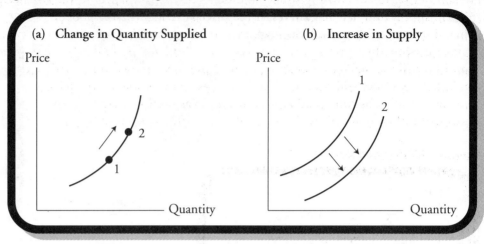

F. The following are some of the reasons for a shift in the supply curve:

1. Changes in resource prices. Higher costs in the resource markets will reduce supply (shift the supply curve left) and increase price in the product markets based on these resources.

2. Changes in technology. The discovery of new, lower-cost production techniques will reduce the opportunity cost of production and increase supply in the product markets (i.e., increase the amount supplied at all prices, see Figure 7).

MARKETS

A. Short-run equilibrium. In the short run, there is not enough time for sellers to fully adjust to changing market conditions. Producers are only able to increase the supply of a good offered for sale by using more labor and raw materials. New plant and equipment cannot be brought on line in the short run. In the short run, the *market price* of goods will change in the direction that brings the price consumers are willing to pay into balance with the price at which producers are willing to sell. The balance between the amount supplied and the amount demanded that brings about market equilibrium is created by price alone.

B. Long-run equilibrium. In the long run, adequate time exists for producers to adjust fully to changes in market conditions. Producers have the time to alter their productive factors and increase or decrease the physical size of their plants. Production will increase supply as long as the return exceeds the opportunity cost of producing the item. When returns exceed opportunity costs, capital will flow into the industry and output will expand. This increased production will cause prices to fall, eliminating the excess profits. If opportunity costs exceed returns from production, firms will remove capital from the production process, thus reducing supply and causing prices to rise.

C. A market is an economic system, incorporating the trading arrangements of buyers and sellers that underlie the forces of supply and demand. Equilibrium occurs when the conflicting forces creating supply and demand are in balance. In the absence of shifts in supply and demand curves, if the price is so high that supply exceeds demand, some businesses will decrease their prices to sell their excess inventory while others elect to reduce production. The result is a reduction in both price and quantity supplied until the market is in equilibrium. Conversely, if demand exceeds supply, the price of the product will rise, resulting in a reduction in quantity demanded as consumers find substitutes and increased supply as producers add capacity. As illustrated in Figure 8, this will occur until the market is in equilibrium:

Figure 8: Market Equilibrium

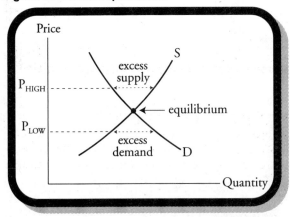

Figure 9 summarizes the equilibrium adjustment process to shifts in supply and demand. Keep in mind that the market adjustment process described here is not completed instantaneously. Economic information is sent out and reacted to gradually.

Figure 9: Summary of Effects of Shifts in Demand and Supply

		Change in Equilibrium	
Change	Shift in Demand/Supply Curve	Price	Quantity
Increase in demand	Shift in demand curve to the right	Increase	Increase
Decrease in demand	Shift in demand curve to the left	Decrease	Decrease
Increase in supply	Shift in supply curve to the right	Decrease	Increase
Decrease in supply	Shift in supply curve to the left	Increase	Decrease

Figure 10 illustrates that when supply is reduced, the supply curve shifts from S1 to S2, and the initial impact will be a steep rise in prices from P1 to P2. This is because the slope of the demand curve is fixed in the short run. As consumers adjust their habits and seek alternatives, the long-run demand curve will flatten and prices will fall to P3.

Figure 10: Equilibrium Adjustment Process

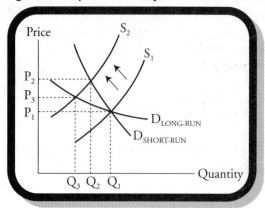

D. A shortage exists when the amount of a good offered by sellers is less than the amount demanded by buyers at the existing price. An increase in price will eliminate the shortage. A surplus exists when more of a good is willingly offered for sale than the quantity demanded at that price. The price is then above the equilibrium price. Shortages will lead to higher equilibrium prices; surpluses will lead to lower equilibrium prices.

E. The invisible hand principle refers to the tendency of market prices to direct individuals pursuing their own interests into productive activities that also promote the economic well-being of society. The market does this by:

1. Communicating information to decision makers. Without the information provided by market prices, it would be impossible for decision makers to determine how intensely a good is desired relative to its opportunity costs.

2. Coordinating actions of market participants. Prices direct producers to undertake those projects that are demanded most intensely by consumers.

3. Motivating economic players. Market prices establish a reward-penalty structure that induces the participants to work, cooperate with others, use efficient production methods, supply goods that are desired, and invest for the future.

4. Pricing products and providing order to the market. The market process works automatically without the need for any government decision or central planners. The market system sets prices and determines production and distribution channels without any outside control.

MARKET INFLUENCES ON BUSINESS STRATEGIES

A. The demand for a resource indicates how much of the resource firms will employ at each possible price. Other things equal, there is a negative relationship between price and quantity demanded.

B. As the price of the resource rises, firms substitute for the resource and use other resources whose prices have not increased.

STUDY MANUAL – BUSINESS ENVIRONMENT & CONCEPTS
CHAPTER 21

C. Along with substituting for higher-priced resources, firms will tend to cut back overall output and reduce the quantity demanded of higher-priced resources. This latter effect occurs because the increase in the cost of only one resource will make the total cost of production higher at each level of production.

D. As the price of a resource rises, firms pass along the increased cost to consumers in the form of higher final good prices. This lowers the quantity demanded for the final good or service, and the firm uses less of all resources.

THE INFLUENCE OF THREE FACTORS THAT CAUSE SHIFTS IN THE DEMAND CURVE FOR A RESOURCE

A. Three factors can shift resource demand.

1. An increase in a resource's productivity will lead to firms substituting for other inputs and toward the resource that is now more productive. Furthermore, the firm will tend to increase output and use even more of the resource.

2. An increase in the prices of other resources will lead to an increase in the demand for a given resource as firms substitute for the now higher-priced resources.

3. An increase in the demand for the final good will lead to an increase in the price of the final good and the revenue each unit of resource input will yield.

   Hence, there will be an increase in the demand for all resources in the production of the final good that experienced the increased demand.

THE MARGINAL REVENUE PRODUCT OF A RESOURCE AND ITS INFLUENCE ON THE DEMAND FOR THAT RESOURCE

A. Marginal revenue product. If a firm uses an additional unit of an input while holding other inputs constant, the output of the final good or service should increase by some amount. That increase in output is the marginal product of that last unit of resource employed. The increase in revenue from producing and selling the marginal product is called the **marginal revenue product** (MRP).

1. If the firm is a price-taker in the market for the final good, the marginal revenue product is the result of multiplying the marginal product by the price of the final product. A price-taker is a buyer or seller small enough to have no effect on the market price of a good; a price-taker "takes" the price in the market but does not control it. This is also called the value of marginal product.

2. If the firm is not a price-taker, producing and selling the last unit lowers its market price. This will complicate the computation of marginal revenue product, but it does not change the basic definition. The profit-maximizing firm will increase the use of each resource until the marginal revenue product equals the cost (price) of the last unit of resource input.

©2007 Kaplan CPA Review
Page 521

B. MRP and demand. If other resource inputs are held constant, the law of diminishing marginal returns will lead to the marginal product of a given resource falling as more of it is used. This necessarily means that the marginal revenue product will fall as the firm employs more of the resource.

1. The profit-maximizing firm will increase the use of a resource until the marginal revenue product equals the resource's price.

2. If all other resource inputs are fixed, a firm's demand for the variable resource is the marginal revenue product schedule for the various amounts of the resource employed.

As illustrated in Figure 11, for a given resource used (holding all other resources constant in production), a graph of the marginal revenue product curve is identical to the demand curve, except the axes are labeled differently:

Figure 11: Marginal Revenue Product (Demand)

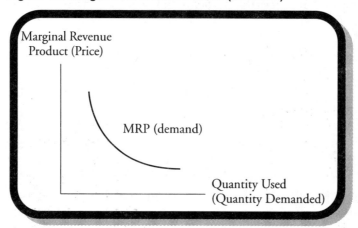

C. Factors that shift the marginal revenue product schedule will shift demand. These factors include:

1. Price of the final product.

2. Productivity of the resource.

3. Price of substituted resources used.

An increase in each of these will increase the marginal revenue product at each level of resource use. Therefore, an increase in each of these will increase the demand for the resource and vice versa.

THE FACTORS THAT INFLUENCE THE SUPPLY OF AND DEMAND FOR RESOURCES IN THE SHORT RUN AND LONG RUN

A. Influence on elasticity of demand.

STUDY MANUAL – BUSINESS ENVIRONMENT & CONCEPTS
CHAPTER 21

1. In the short run, the elasticity of demand for the final good and the degree to which a resource has substitutes in production determine the demand for a resource. If there are no good substitutes for the resource in production and/or the demand for the final good is inelastic, the demand for the resource will tend to be inelastic.

2. In the long run, firms will have time to find more substitutes in production, and the elasticity of demand for final goods will be more elastic as well. Therefore, the demand for a resource is more elastic in the long run than it is in the short run. This is the standard argument that everything is variable in the long run.

3. Other things held constant, the quantity supplied of a resource increases with an increase in its price. The supply curve for a specific resource will slope upward to the right. For example, if the working conditions in firms stay the same and firms raise wages, employees will supply more labor. This is because workers will shift away from other activities (e.g., leisure) to offer more labor. If wages increase but working conditions decrease, the quantity supplied may not increase. A change in working conditions amounts to a shift of the supply curve. The same analysis applies to other resources.

B. Influence on elasticity of supply.

1. In the short run, the elasticity of supply is determined by resource mobility, which is defined as how easily the resource can be transferred from one use to another.

    a. If a resource has few other uses (e.g., a machine for a specific task), it has low resource mobility and a low elasticity of supply.

    b. If the resource has many alternative uses (e.g., unskilled labor), its supply will be more elastic.

        Caution: The term *resource mobility* does not necessarily apply to how easily the resource can move physically. Land is not mobile, but it can have high resource mobility if it can easily be converted from, for example, corn to wheat production or even to a parking lot. A plot of land with an existing 40-story building is not resource-mobile because it would be difficult and costly to relocate the building and apply the land to an alternative use.

2. In the long run, resource mobility increases, and so does the elasticity of supply for a given resource. In the market for skilled labor, workers can invest in human capital to increase the supply of specific types of laborers such as doctors, accountants, or mechanics. Machines and land can be modified for new uses. Therefore, over longer periods of time, the quantity supplied of a resource is much more responsive to changes in price.

CONSUMER CHOICE IN AN ECONOMIC FRAMEWORK

A. Consumer choice is an economic concept that relies on the following assumptions:

©2007 Kaplan CPA Review
Page 523

1. Individuals have limited incomes so they must make choices.

2. Consumers make decisions purposefully to maximize their welfare or satisfaction.

3. Substitute goods are available.

4. Perfect information is never available, but consumers make the most informed decisions possible.

5. As consumption increases, the marginal utility (i.e., the benefit derived from consuming the next unit) decreases. For example, your 12th consecutive soda does not taste nearly as good as your first soda. This is known as the *law of diminishing marginal utility of consumption.*

B. Consumer demand curve. Figure 12 represents a general demand curve for a good or service.

1. A consumer's demand curve slopes downward from left to right, indicating that the lower the price, the higher the quantity demanded.

2. The quantity demanded changes as the current price of the good changes.

3. The quantity demanded is inversely related to price (i.e., the lower the price, the more the demand and vice versa).

Note that this is movement up and down the same demand curve.

C. Market demand curve. The market demand schedule is the relationship between the amount demanded by all consumers in the market and the market price for a particular good or service. It is simply the aggregation of the individual consumer's demand curves. As with an individual's demand curve, the market demand curve in Figure 12 exhibits an inverse relationship between price and quantity:

Figure 12: Demand Curve for a Good or Service

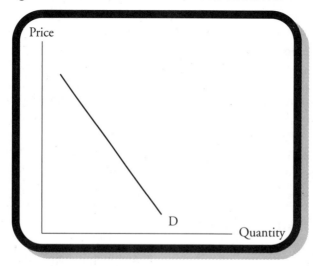

D. The law of diminishing marginal utility. The shape of an individual's demand curve may be explained with the law of diminishing marginal utility.

1. The price at any point along a demand curve represents the marginal benefit to a consumer (the maximum price the consumer would pay for an additional unit). For a real movie buff, the marginal benefit of seeing a third movie during a week may be significantly greater than the marginal benefit of a third movie to a casual moviegoer. Therefore, the demand curve for the movie buff will be higher than the demand curve for the casual moviegoer.

2. Consumers will maximize their satisfaction (total utility) by ensuring that the last dollar spent on each item yields an equal degree of marginal utility. The marginal utility of item X divided by its price equals the marginal utility of Y divided by its price. If MU_X/P_X is greater than MU_Y/P_Y, the consumer should consume more of good X. For example, assume you go to a sports bar with $10 in your pocket. You buy nine bags of potato chips and one soda pop. After eating two bags of chips and finishing the soda pop, you realize that you did not follow the above instructions. Your marginal utility for soda pop exceeds your marginal utility for chips due to your thirst.

E. Price change and consumer choice. Consumer choice may be explained by two microeconomic concepts, both of which result from a change in price:

1. The substitution effect. If a good becomes cheaper relative to other goods, you will consume more of that good.

2. The income effect. As the price of a good drops, your real income rises and you will consume more of that good (and other goods).

F. The cost of time. Time is money, or so the saying goes. In any case, like money, time is scarce to the consumer. The less time or money that must be spent on a particular good or service, the more attractive it becomes. For example, if you can spend all afternoon fixing your car using parts that cost $50, or pay someone to fix it for a total cost of $60, you may be inclined to have someone else do the job.

G. Marginal vs. total value. If everyone needs water, and sports cars are clearly luxury goods, then why is water so cheap? The answer is that the total value of an item is its market price plus the consumer surplus, the difference between the maximum amount that you would be willing to pay for a product and the amount that you actually pay. Your willingness to pay for additional units depends on your valuation of the marginal unit (that is the next unit to be consumed), not the value of all the units you want taken together. In other words, in a land where water is plentiful, the marginal cost/value of another gallon of water is quite low. Given the choice between a glass of water and a diamond, you would no doubt opt for the diamond. If you were dying of thirst in the middle of a desert, however, the marginal value you place on water would be much higher than the marginal value of diamonds. A whole pocketful of diamonds won't be worth much, unless you value dying wealthy!

H. Why demand curves shift. As illustrated in Figure 13, a change in demand is a change in the amount of a good or service consumed at a given price and is represented by a shift in the demand curve:

Figure 13: Shift in Demand

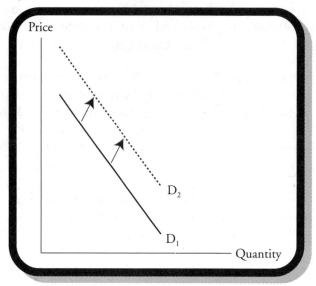

A shift in demand may be explained by several factors:

1. Changes in consumer income. The more you can afford, the more you will buy. So, as your income increases, your demand curve will shift to the right.

2. Changes in the number of consumers in the market. As cities grow and shrink and as international markets open to domestic markets, changes in the number of consumers change (shift) the demand curves of many products.

3. Changes in prices of closely related goods—substitutes and complements. If two goods are similar to one another (perform the same function), they are substitutes. If the price of one rises relative to the other, demand for the other (the substitute) will rise (shift upward to the right). If the price falls relative to the substitute, demand for the substitute falls (shifts left). If two goods are consumed together—like syrup and pancakes—they are complements. An increase in the price of one of the goods will cause the demand for the other to drop. (The demand curve for the complement will shift downward to the left.)

4. Changes in market demographics. Changes in the population can have a large influence in markets. Population increases make demand curves shift to the right.

5. Changes in consumer preferences. If a product becomes fashionable, its demand curve shifts out to the right. Once the product goes out of favor with consumers, its demand curve shifts back to the left.

6. Changes in consumer price expectations. If consumers expect the price of cars to rise next month, they may elect to buy a car now. It is important that you

recognize that the preceding factors may cause a change in demand (i.e., a shift in the demand curve to the right or left). This means that the quantity demanded at the same price changes. A shift in demand is distinctly different from a change in the quantity demanded, which is represented by movement along an existing demand curve and results from a change in price.

I. The following are some of the reasons consumers have different preferences and make different choices.

1. Individual personalities. The preferences behind any one choice are frequently complex. Take a car for instance. Some consumers may want nothing more than a means of transportation and will be satisfied with a standard automobile. Others may like the feel of a powerful engine and opt for a high-performance vehicle. Furthermore, the individual consumer's choice is not always independent of other consumers.

2. Time and risk. Attitudes about time and risk help shape consumer preferences. Consumers generally prefer to receive a good now rather than later. Consumers have different attitudes toward risk, and some are willing to spend money to reduce risk and others are not. For example, some people buy flood insurance while others do not, some people pay more for brand names, while others pay less for generic products, and so forth.

3. Advertising. A strong factor influencing consumer choice is advertising. Advertising conveys information about price, quality, and availability. Supporters of advertising say it helps consumers make informed decisions, while advertising's critics claim it is wasteful, misleading, and manipulative. Economics is neutral on this argument.

PRICE AND INCOME ELASTICITY OF DEMAND

A. The price elasticity of demand measures the change in the quantity demanded in response to a change in market price (i.e., a movement along a demand curve).

Figure 14 illustrates the general categories of price elasticity of demand. A discussion of each is presented below:

1. If a small percentage price change results in a large percentage change in quantity demanded, the demand for that good is said to be highly elastic. Apples are an example of an elastic good. The absolute value of price elasticity is > 1, meaning that the percentage change in Q is greater than the percentage change in P.

2. If a large percentage price change results in a small percentage change in quantity demanded, demand is relatively inelastic. Gasoline is an example of a relatively inelastic good. The absolute value of price elasticity is < 1, meaning that the percentage change in Q is less than the percentage change in P.

3. A perfectly elastic demand curve is horizontal, and elasticity = 1. If the price increases, none will be consumed.

4. A perfectly inelastic demand curve is vertical, and elasticity = 0. If the price changes, there will be no effect on the quantity demanded.

Figure 14: Price Elasticity of Demand

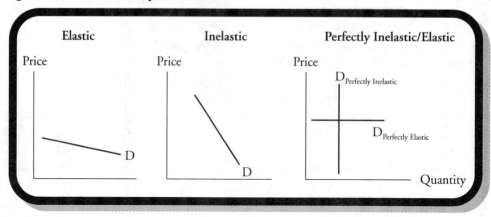

Example: Price elasticity

If the price of product A is increased from $1 per unit to $1.10 per unit, the demand will decrease from 5.0 million units to 4.8 million units. What is the price elasticity of demand for product A, and is product A an elastic good?

Answer

Percentage change in quantity = (4.8 − 5.0)]/[(5.0 + 4.8)/2] = −0.2/4.9 = −0.041 = −4.1%.

Percentage change in price = (1.10 − 1.00)]/[(1.10 + 1.00)/2] = 0.10/1.05 = 0.095 = 9.5%.

Price elasticity of demand for product A = −4.1%/9.5% = −0.43.

Because the price elasticity of demand is below 1.0 (ignoring the sign), demand for product A is inelastic.

Consider the demand curve presented in Figure 15.

Figure 15: Price Elasticity of Demand

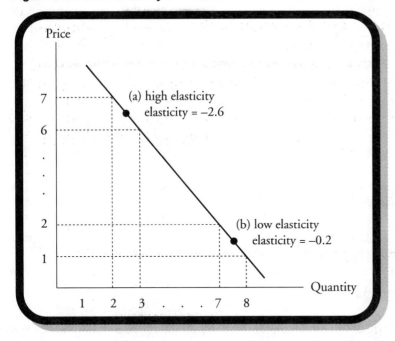

At point *a*, (higher price range), the price elasticity of the good is greater than at point *b* (lower price range).

Point *a* has more price elasticity than point *b*.

Price elasticity in the $6 to $7 range is:

$$[(2-3)/2.5]/[(7-6)/6.5] = -2.6$$

Point *b* has less price elasticity than point *a*.

Price elasticity in the $1 to $2 range is:

$$[(7-8)/7.5]/[(2-1)/1.5] = -0.2$$

B. Income elasticity of demand is the sensitivity of demand to changes in consumer income. The income elasticity of demand measures the sensitivity of the quantity demanded to an increase or decrease in a consumer's income. The demand curve shifts when income changes.

THE TENDENCY OF THE PRICE ELASTICITY OF DEMAND TO INCREASE IN THE LONG RUN

A. Generally speaking, as the price of a product rises, consumers will reduce their consumption of that product by a larger amount in the long run than in the short run. So, the price elasticity of demand for most products is greater in the long run than in the short run. This economic reality is often called the second law of demand.

STUDY MANUAL – BUSINESS ENVIRONMENT & CONCEPTS
CHAPTER 21

B. The price elasticity of demand is greater in the long run as consumers are able to make greater adjustments to the change in prices. Consider the situation in the 1970s when oil and gas prices rose significantly from historic levels. Early adjustment to the increased price may have involved simply driving less (picking a closer vacation spot, taking the bus to work, or carpooling) or keeping the house at a slightly lower temperature in the winter.

$$\text{income elasticity} = \frac{\text{percentage change in quantity demanded}}{\text{percentage change in income}}$$

C. Over time other substitutions were made. People bought smaller cars, chose to live closer to work, installed more home insulation, and equipped their homes with efficient wood-burning stoves as an alternative source of heat. These longer-run adjustments to price increases are the reason that demand is more elastic in the long run than in the short run. Over time, consumers were able to reduce their petroleum fuel consumption by a much greater amount in response to the price increase than they did in the short run.

TOTAL REVENUE, TOTAL EXPENDITURES, AND PRICE ELASTICITY OF DEMAND

A. An important application of price elasticity is to estimate how total consumer expenditures on a product change when the price changes. There are three ways to do this:

1. Consider an individual's elasticity of demand.

2. Consider the combined elasticity of demand for all consumers of the product.

3. Consider the elasticity of demand for an individual business that produces the product.

   In the two following points, we consider how total consumer expenditures change to affect total revenue.

B. Total expenditures and price elasticity of demand.

1. When demand is inelastic, the percentage change in unit sales is less than the percentage change in price. Therefore, an increase in price leads to an increase in total expenditure on the good. Certain medicines (e.g., insulin) or alcohol are examples of this.

2. When demand is elastic, quantity demanded is more responsive to a change in price. Therefore, an increase in price leads to a decrease in total expenditure on the good. A particular brand of cornflakes or toothpaste would be an example of this.

Page 530   ©2007 Kaplan CPA Review

3. With *unitary* price elasticity (i.e., the change in price equals the change in quantity demanded at all price levels), total expenditures remain unchanged when unit price changes.

C. Total revenue and price elasticity of demand. Instead of looking at total market demand, we can consider how price affects the total revenue for an individual firm. First, demand for an individual firm is more elastic than the demand for the entire market.

   1. When a firm's demand curve is inelastic, total revenue rises when the firm increases the price. Conversely, total revenue declines when the firm decreases the price.

   2. When price is elastic, total revenue falls when the firm increases the price, and total revenue rises when the firm decreases the price. With unitary elasticity, total revenue is unaffected by a price change. Recall that price elasticity changes as we move up and down the firm's demand curve.

   3. A firm can maximize its revenue where demand is of unitary elasticity. Because firms are more interested in enhancing profits than revenue, it is important to understand that for many firms (particularly those with substantial fixed costs), profits will be maximized at or near the same point where revenue is maximized.

THE FACTORS THAT INFLUENCE PRICE AND INCOME ELASTICITY OF DEMAND

Note that the slope is constant but elasticity is changing.

A. Price elasticity of demand is determined by two factors:

   1. The availability of substitutes is the most important determinant of the price elasticity of demand. If good substitutes are available, a price increase in one product will induce consumers to switch to a substitute good. As such, elasticity of demand is a result of the availability of good substitutes.

   2. The relative amount of budget spent on a product is a second important determinant of the price elasticity of demand. When a relatively small portion of your budget is spent on a particular good, that good will tend to be price inelastic.

B. An inferior good has negative income elasticity. As income increases (decreases), quantity demanded decreases (increases). Inferior goods include such things as bus travel and margarine. The opposite type of good, a normal good, has positive income elasticity meaning that, as income increases (decreases), demand for the good increases (decreases). Normal goods include things like bread and tobacco.

C. Generally, normal goods that have low-income elasticities (absolute values between 0 and 1) are considered necessities. Normal goods with high-income elasticities (absolute values greater than 1) are generally considered luxury goods.

©2007 Kaplan CPA Review

STUDY MANUAL – BUSINESS ENVIRONMENT & CONCEPTS
CHAPTER 21

Example: Income elasticity

Suppose that your income has risen by $10,000 from a base rate of $50,000. During this period, your demand for bread has increased from 100 loaves per year to 110 loaves per year. Given this information, determine whether or not bread is a necessity or a luxury good.

Answer

The percentage change in income is 18.2% = ($60,000 − $50,000)/$55,000, while the percentage change in the quantity of bread demanded is 9.5% = (110 − 100)/105. Hence, the income elasticity of bread is 0.52 = 9.5/18.2. Since its income elasticity of demand is less than 1.0, bread is a necessity.

CONSUMER INDIFFERENCE CURVES

A. Indifference curves map out the consumer's preferences between two choices. For example, panel (a) of Figure 16 shows the combinations of apples and oranges that have equal preference (equal utility) for an individual. Since these combinations show equal preference levels, the consumer is said to be *indifferent* between any of the points along the curve. This means that the consumer will be indifferent between (would derive the same utility from) a basket containing six apples and two oranges or a basket having four apples and three oranges.

B. To formalize the concept of indifference curves, let us state that an indifference curve is a convex-shaped curve, where all points on the curve represent combinations of goods that are equally preferred by (produce the same utility for) the individual. This general concept is illustrated in panel (b) of Figure 16, where each set of points represents equal preferences between goods A and B:

Figure 16: Consumer Indifference Curves

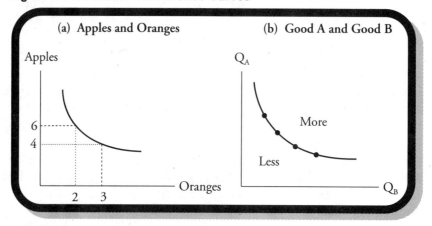

C. The following are the general characteristics of indifference curves:

1. More is preferred to less. Figure 17 illustrates, using indifference curves, that more is preferred to less. As indicated, higher indifference curves represent greater utility than lower curves. That is, investors receive more utility from a

combination of good A and good B on indifference curve I3 than a combination on I1.

Figure 17: Set of Consumer Indifference Curves

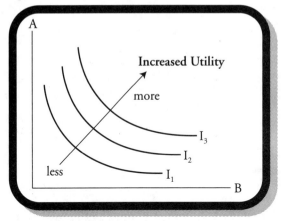

2. Substitutable goods. Since goods may be substituted, indifference curves slope downward to the right.

3. Diminishing utility. The utility of a good declines the more it is consumed. Therefore, indifference curves are convex.

4. Infinite and nonintersecting. There are an infinite number of indifference curves and they do not intersect.

CONSUMPTION-OPPORTUNITY CONSTRAINT AND THE BUDGET CONSTRAINT AS THEY RELATE TO INDIFFERENCE CURVE ANALYSIS

A. Budget constraints represent all combinations of goods that consumers can purchase within a given budget. These constraints separate the consumption opportunities that can be obtained from those that cannot be obtained. As shown in Figure 18, the optimal level of consumer satisfaction will be the tangency point between the budget constraint line and the highest obtainable indifference curve.

STUDY MANUAL – BUSINESS ENVIRONMENT & CONCEPTS
CHAPTER 21

Figure 18: Utility Maximizing With a Budget Constraint

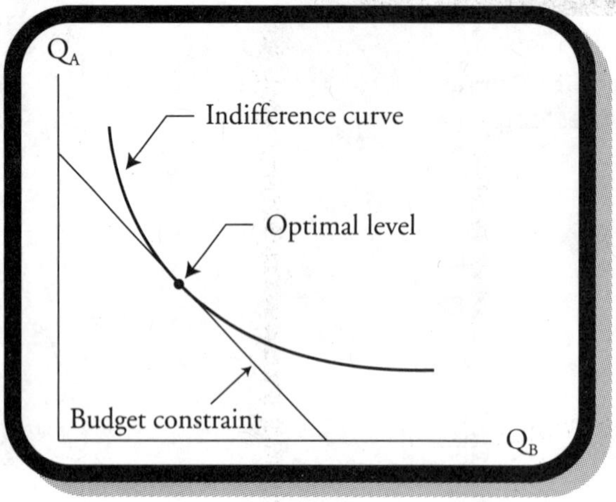

B. Consumption-opportunity constraint. This analysis applies both in the cases of barter and an economy with money. In the money economy, the budget-constraint line applies. In a barter economy, the *consumption-opportunity constraint* line applies. This line indicates different bundles of goods that can be acquired (three fish and four loaves of bread or six fish and two loaves of bread, etc.). In either case, it is the relative price of each good that determines the slope of the line and, thus, the optimal level of consumption of each good or bundle of goods.

THE DIFFERENCE BETWEEN THE INCOME EFFECT AND THE SUBSTITUTION EFFECT

A. If the price of one good changes, the budget constraint changes and a consumer's optimal combination of X and Y will change as well. We illustrate this for an increase in the price of X in Figure 19. Since fewer units of X can now be purchased at the higher price, the budget constraint becomes steeper (shifts from B_1 to B_2). The new optimal consumption bundle is at point c. In this example, the consumer chooses a fairly large decrease in consumption of X (X_1 to X_2) and a small increase in the consumption of Y (Y_1 to Y_2).

B. The total decrease in the consumption of good X in response to the price increase can be separated (theoretically) into two separate effects:

1. A substitution effect, because the relative price (slope of the budget constraint) has changed

2. An income effect, because less consumption is possible with the same income when the price of X rises.

Page 534   ©2007 Kaplan CPA Review

STUDY MANUAL – BUSINESS ENVIRONMENT & CONCEPTS

CHAPTER 21

Figure 19: Effect on Optimal Consumption of an Increase in the Price of X

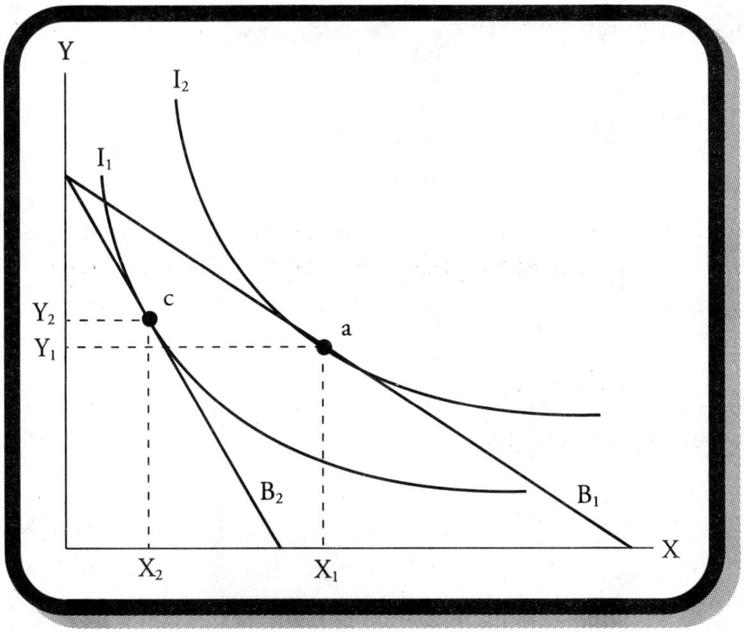

C. The *substitution effect* is always negative for a price increase; a consumer will choose less X and more Y in order to maximize utility. You can think of the substitution effect as the change in consumption that would result if the consumer faced the new prices but received just enough additional income so that his or her optimal consumption bundle was still on the same indifference curve. This is illustrated in Figure 20 by the budget constraint labeled B_1'. B_1' is drawn to be tangent to indifference curve I_2 but to have a slope that reflects the new relative prices (it is parallel to B_2). The substitution effect of an increase in the price of X is shown as a reduction in the consumption of X from X_1 to X_2, since the optimal consumption bundle along B_1' is point *b*.

STUDY MANUAL – BUSINESS ENVIRONMENT & CONCEPTS
CHAPTER 21

Figure 20: Income and Substitution Effect of an Increase in the price of X

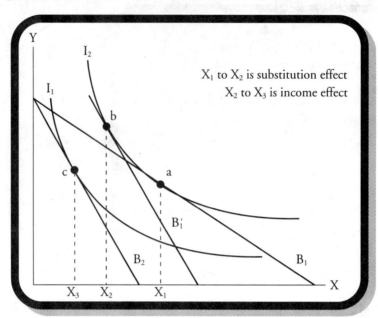

D. The *income effect* can be positive or negative. Recall that the consumption of a normal good decreases when income is reduced, but for an inferior good, consumption increases when income falls. In Figure 20, the good is a normal good; the effect of a reduction in income is a reduction in the amount of X consumed. The effect on the consumption of X of a decrease in income is the further decrease in consumption of X from X_2 to X_3.

E. To summarize, when the price of X rises, the budget constraint shifts and optimal consumption (Figure 20) changes from bundle *a* to bundle *c*. The substitution effect of the increase in the price of X is shown by the tangent point to a hypothetical budget line that has the new slope but is tangent to "old" indifference curve, I_2. The change in the quantity of X between bundle *b* and bundle *c* is the income effect and is illustrated by a parallel shift of the budget constraint to the left from B_1' to B_2.

THE LAW OF DIMINISHING RETURNS AND ITS IMPACT ON A COMPANY'S COSTS

A. The law of diminishing returns states that as more and more resources (e.g., labor) are devoted to a production process holding the quantity of other inputs constant, the output increases, but at a decreasing rate. For example, if an acre of corn needs to be picked, the addition of a second and third worker is highly productive. But if you already have 300 workers in the field, the productive capacity of the 301st worker is not near that of the second worker.

B. Concepts related to the law of diminishing returns are as follows:

1. Total product is the total output of goods associated with a specific rate of resource input. As resource input increases, total product increases.

2. Marginal product is the increase in total output associated with an additional unit of input.

3. Average product equals the total output (product) divided by the units of the variable input required to produce that level output.

   Note: The marginal product of an input decreases at higher input levels because all other inputs are held constant.

STUDY MANUAL – BUSINESS ENVIRONMENT & CONCEPTS
CHAPTER 21

QUESTIONS: ECONOMICS OF THE FIRM

1.　The law of demand states that, given a decrease in:
　A.　real output, demand will increase.
　B.　real output, demand will decrease.
　C.　price, demand will increase.
　D.　price, demand will decrease.

2.　The law of supply states that, given a decrease in:
　A.　real output, supply will decrease.
　B.　price, supply will decrease.
　C.　real output, supply will increase.
　D.　price, supply will increase.

3.　Which of the following indicates the typical slope of the supply-and-demand curves?

	Supply curve	Demand curve
A.	Flat	Vertical
B.	Upward to the left	Upward to the left
C.	Upward to the right	Downward to the right
D.	Vertical	Flat

4.　If the admission price for a rock concert is raised from $25 to $30 causing attendance to drop from 60,000 to 40,000, the price elasticity of the demand for attending the concert is:
　A.　–2.20.
　B.　–1.67.
　C.　0.60.
　D.　2.20.

5.　Which of the following will **NOT** cause the demand curve to shift? A change in:
　A.　the relative price of a complementary good.
　B.　the price of a product.
　C.　consumer preferences.
　D.　the price of a substitute good.

6.　Movements along and shifts in a demand curve result from changes in:

	Movements	Shifts
A.	quantity demanded	consumer income
B.	quantity demanded	price of a good
C.	consumer tastes	price of a good
D.	consumer tastes	consumer income

Page 538　　　　　　　　　　　©2007 Kaplan CPA Review

STUDY MANUAL – BUSINESS ENVIRONMENT & CONCEPTS
CHAPTER 21

7. Income elasticity is defined as the:
    A. change in income divided by the percentage change in the quantity demanded.
    B. percentage change in income divided by the percentage change in the quantity demanded.
    C. change in quantity demanded divided by the change in income.
    D. percentage change in the quantity demanded divided by the percentage change in income.

8. When household incomes go down and the quantity of a product demanded goes up, the product is:
    A. a necessity.
    B. an inferior good.
    C. a luxury good.
    D. a normal good.

9. Which of the following measures would indicate that a good is a luxury good?
    A. Low income elasticities.
    B. High income elasticities.
    C. Income elasticity of one.
    D. Not enough information given to determine answer.

10. If marginal cost is above the average cost, when you produce your next unit:
    A. average cost will be flat.
    B. average cost will decline.
    C. marginal cost will remain unchanged.
    D. average cost will increase.

11. Indifference curves slope downward to the right because:
    A. of diminishing marginal utility.
    B. demand for goods declines when prices increase.
    C. goods are substitutable.
    D. demand for luxury goods is more sensitive to income changes.

12. Under the substitution effect, if the price of one good relative to another increases, individuals will consume along the:
    A. lower indifference curve.
    B. higher indifference curve.
    C. same indifference curve.
    D. lower budget constraint line.

©2007 Kaplan CPA Review

13. Assume that Richard Rojas, journalist, can purchase some combination of good A and good B. The income elasticity for both goods is 0.6, and Rojas has been consuming 10 of each good. Which of the following statements about the income effect and the substitution effect with regard to Rojas is FALSE?
    A. If Rojas's boss decreases his salary, Rojas's budget constraint line will shift inward, and he will consume less of each good.
    B. If Rojas's boss gives him a salary increase, Rojas will likely purchase more of good A than of good B.
    C. If the price of good A increases relative to good B, Rojas will purchase more of good B due to the substitution effect.
    D. If the price of good A decreases relative to good B, Rojas's budget constraint line will rotate.

14. In the graph below, the axes X and Y represent the amount of good X or good Y consumed, respectively. The consumer moved along the path in the order points a, b, and then c. Based on the information in the graph, which of the following statements about the income and substitution effects is FALSE?

    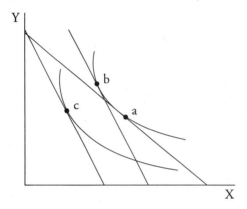

    A. The movement from b to c likely resulted from an increase in the price of good X.
    B. The consumer's income decreased during the time it took to move from point a to point c.
    C. Good X and good Y are both normal goods.
    D. The movement from a to b represents the substitution effect.

15. Marginal cost is defined as the:
    A. sum of total fixed and variable cost.
    B. cost of making an additional sale.
    C. average manufacturing cost.
    D. total cost of producing an additional unit of output.

16. Given a shift to the left in the demand curve, which of the following identifies the short-run response and long-run response of supply relative to beginning supply?

	Short-run response	Long-run response
A.	Decrease modestly	Increase modestly
B.	Decrease modestly	Decrease substantially
C.	Increase modestly	Decrease substantially
D.	Increase modestly	Increase substantially

STUDY MANUAL – BUSINESS ENVIRONMENT & CONCEPTS
CHAPTER 21

17. All of the following factors will cause a demand curve to shift EXCEPT changes in:
A. consumer tastes and preferences.
B. the prices of related goods.
C. the number of consumers in the market.
D. the cost of production for the product.

18. If buyers are expecting higher prices for rice in the future, what is *mostly likely* to happen now in the rice market?
A. The demand for rice will increase.
B. Prices for rice will fall.
C. The demand for rice will decrease.
D. The supply of rice will decrease.

19. Mitsubishi has recently discovered a new way to produce flat-screen televisions. This new process is expected to reduce the company's costs by 23%. Which of the following choices *best* describes the effect on the supply curve?
A. Shift the supply curve left.
B. Shift the supply curve right.
C. Movement along the supply curve upward.
D. Movement along the supply curve downward.

20. Fiscal policy refers to the:
A. manipulation of government spending and taxes to stabilize domestic output, employment, and the price level.
B. manipulation of government spending and taxes to achieve greater equality in the distribution of income.
C. altering of the interest rate to change aggregate demand.
D. fact that equal increases in government spending and taxation will be contractionary.

21. Expansionary fiscal policy is so named because it:
A. involves an expansion of the nation's money supply.
B. necessarily expands the size of government.
C. is aimed at achieving greater price stability.
D. is designed to expand real GDP.

22. Suppose that the economy is in the midst of a recession. Which of the following policies would be consistent with active fiscal policy? A:
A. congressional proposal to incur a Federal surplus to be used for the retirement of public debt
B. reduction in agricultural subsidies and veterans' benefits
C. postponement of a highway construction program
D. reduction in Federal tax rates on personal and corporate income

23. An appropriate fiscal policy for a severe recession is:
A. a decrease in government spending.
B. a decrease in tax rates.
C. appreciation of the dollar.
D. an increase in interest rates.

©2007 Kaplan CPA Review
Page 541

STUDY MANUAL – BUSINESS ENVIRONMENT & CONCEPTS
CHAPTER 21

24. An appropriate fiscal policy for severe demand-pull inflation is:
    A. an increase in government spending.
    B. depreciation of the dollar.
    C. a reduction in interest rates.
    D. a tax rate increase.

25. If both the supply and the demand for a good increase, the market price will:
    A. rise only in the case of an inelastic supply function.
    B. fall only in the case of an inelastic supply function.
    C. not be predictable with only these facts.
    D. rise only in the case of an elastic demand function.

26. The sum of the average fixed costs and the average variable costs for a given output is known as:
    A. long-run average cost.
    B. average product.
    C. total cost.
    D. average total cost.

27. In any competitive market, an equal increase in both demand and supply can be expected to always:
    A. increase both price and market-clearing quantity.
    B. decrease both price and market-clearing quantity.
    C. increase market-clearing quantity.
    D. increase price.

28. A perfectly inelastic supply curve in a competitive market:
    A. means the equilibrium price must be zero.
    B. says the market supply curve is horizontal.
    C. exists when firms cannot vary input usage.
    D. can only exist in the long run.

29. In the theory of demand, the marginal utility per dollar of a product:
    A. increases when consumption expands.
    B. decreases when consumption expands.
    C. is used to explain why demand curves are vertical.
    D. explains why short-run supply curves are upward sloping.

30. Because of the existence of economies of scale, business firms may find that:
    A. each additional unit of labor is less efficient than the previous unit.
    B. as more labor is added to a factory, increases in output will diminish in the short run.
    C. increasing the size of a factory will result in lower average costs.
    D. increasing the size of a factory will result in lower total costs.

Page 542   ©2007 Kaplan CPA Review

31. In microeconomics, the distinguishing characteristic of the long run on the supply side is that:
    A. only supply factors determine price and output.
    B. only demand factors determine price and output.
    C. firms are not allowed to enter or exit the industry.
    D. all inputs are variable.

32. Any business firm that has the ability to control price of the product it sells:
    A. faces a downward-sloping demand curve.
    B. does not have any entry or exit barriers in its industry.
    C. has a supply curve that is horizontal.
    D. has a demand curve that is horizontal.

33. If a group of consumers decide to boycott a particular product, the expected result would be:
    A. an increase in the product price to make up lost revenue.
    B. a decrease in the demand for the product.
    C. an increase in product supply because of increased availability.
    D. that companies in the industry would experience higher economic profits.

34. Product demand becomes more elastic the:
    A. greater the number of substitute products available.
    B. greater the consumer income.
    C. greater the elasticity of supply.
    D. higher the input costs.

35. If a product's demand is elastic and there is a decrease in price, the effect will be:
    A. a decrease in total revenue.
    B. no change in total revenue.
    C. a decrease in total revenue and the demand curve shifts to the left.
    D. an increase in total revenue.

36. The movement along the demand curve from one price-quantity combination to another is called a(n):
    A. change in demand.
    B. shift in the demand curve.
    C. change in the quantity demanded.
    D. increase in demand.

37. In the pharmaceutical industry where a diabetic must have insulin no matter what the cost and where there is no other substitute, the diabetic's demand curve is *best* described as:
    A. perfectly elastic.
    B. perfectly inelastic.
    C. elastic.
    D. inelastic.

STUDY MANUAL – BUSINESS ENVIRONMENT & CONCEPTS
CHAPTER 21

38. If a product has a price elasticity of demand of 2.0, the demand is said to be:
    A. perfectly elastic.
    B. perfectly inelastic.
    C. elastic.
    D. inelastic.

39. Demand for a product tends to be price inelastic if:
    A. the product is considered a luxury item.
    B. few good complements for the product are available.
    C. few good substitutes are available for the product.
    D. people spend a large share of their income on the product.

STUDY MANUAL – BUSINESS ENVIRONMENT & CONCEPTS
CHAPTER 21

ANSWERS: ECONOMICS OF THE FIRM

1. **C** The law of demand states that, given an increase in price, demand will decrease. This relationship exists because higher prices induce some consumers to purchase substitute goods and/or simply forgo the use of the product.

2. **B** The law of supply states that, given an increase in price, supply will increase and vice versa. This relationship exists because higher prices induce current producers to produce more units and new producers to enter the market.

3. **C** Given that price is on the vertical axis and quantity on the horizontal axis, the supply curve slopes upwards to the right indicating that supply increases as price increases. The demand curve slopes downward to the right indicating that demand increases as price decreases.

4. **A** Price elasticity of demand is calculated by dividing the percent change in quantity demanded by the percent change in price, using the average value of the variable in the computations. The percent change in quantity demanded is $(40,000 - 60,000)/((60,000 + 40,000)/2) = -0.4$. The percent change in price is $(30 - 25)/((30 + 25)/2) = 0.1818$. The price elasticity of demand is $-0.40/0.1818 = -2.2$.

5. **B** A change in the price of a product is movement along the demand curve. Other factors that cause a shift in the demand curve are: changes in prices of complementary or substitute goods, changes in consumer preferences or consumer income, changes in consumer expectations regarding future prices of products, changes in the number of consumers in the market, demographic changes.

6. **A** Movements along a demand curve result from changes in the quantity demanded from a change in the price of the good. Shifts in the demand curve are caused by the following factors: changes in consumer income, changes in the prices of related goods, changes in consumer expectations, changes in the number of consumers in the market, demographic changes, and changes in consumer tastes and preferences.

7. **D** Income elasticity is defined as the percentage change in quantity demanded divided by the percentage change in income. Normal goods have positive values for income elasticity and inferior goods have negative income elasticity.

8. **B** When household incomes go down and the quantity demanded of a product goes up, the product is an inferior good. Inferior goods include things like bus travel and margarine.

9. **B** Generally, normal goods that have low income elasticities (absolute values between 0 and 1) are considered necessities. Normal goods with high income elasticities (absolute value greater than 1) are considered luxury goods.

10. **D** If marginal cost is above the average cost, when you produce your next unit, average cost will increase. Because marginal cost is the cost of producing the next unit, and because this cost is above the firm's average cost per unit, the average cost per unit must increase, if only slightly. Based on the information provided in the question, there is no way to know what will happen to the marginal cost of future units produced.

11. **C** Indifference curves slope downward to the right because goods are substitutable. The curve shows all possible combinations of two goods that give equal utility to the individual.

©2007 Kaplan CPA Review
Page 545

STUDY MANUAL – BUSINESS ENVIRONMENT & CONCEPTS
CHAPTER 21

12. **C**   Under the substitution effect, individuals will consume along the *same* indifference curve simply buying more of one product over another product. Under the income effect, individuals will consume along a *different* indifference curve by purchasing more or less of all products.

13. **B**   For normal goods (income elasticity between 0 and 1), an increase in salary will shift the budget constraint line outward and Rojas will consume more of *both* good A and good B.

    The other statements are true. The substitution effect occurs when the price of one good relative to the price of another increases or decreases. If the price of one good changes relative to the price of another good, the slope of the budget line rotates and a new tangency point is created with respect to a particular indifference curve. The result is that Rojas will give up some of one good for the other. *Remember:* Under the substitution effect, goods will be consumed along the same indifference curve, whereas under the income effect, they will be consumed along a *different* indifference curve.

14. **A**   The movement from b to c represents the *income* effect and likely resulted from a *decrease in the consumer's income*. An inward shift of the budget constraint line (such as that in the graph) indicates that the consumer's income has decreased.

    The other statements are true. Since the consumption of both goods fell from the income effect (parallel shift in the budget constraint line), both goods are normal goods. The substitution effect results in a slope change in the budget constraint line and occurs when the price of one good relative to another increases. (The consumer consumes less of one good and more of the other.)

15. **D**   Marginal cost is defined as the cost of producing an additional unit of output.

16. **B**   Given a shift to the left in the demand curve, the lower price that results forces producers to produce fewer units. A producer can usually produce fewer units by working employees less, but to reduce production even more requires shutdown of plant and equipment, which takes time. In the long run, given the shutdown of plant and equipment, production can be reduced even more.

17. **D**   Changes in the cost of production for the product will not cause a shift in the demand curve. Changes in production costs will cause the supply curve to shift. Therefore, this will result in a movement along a specific demand curve, resulting from a change in price. Factors that cause a demand curve to shift are changes in: consumer income, the prices of related goods, consumer expectations, the number of consumers in the market, consumer tastes and preferences, and demographics.

18. **A**   A change in consumer expectations is one factor that can shift the demand curve. If consumers expect prices to rise in the future, the demand curve will shift to the right as consumers attempt to lock in purchases prior to a price increase.

19. **B**   The discovery of new, lower cost production techniques will reduce the opportunity cost of production and increase supply in the product markets.

20. **A**   The cost to produce an item is a determinant of the supply curve for the item. Answer B is not correct because the price of the item is a determinant of the demand for an item. Answer C is not correct because the tastes of the consumer is a determinant of demand. Answer D is not correct because the prices of substitute and complementary goods is a determinant of demand.

Page 546   ©2007 Kaplan CPA Review

STUDY MANUAL – BUSINESS ENVIRONMENT & CONCEPTS
CHAPTER 21

21. **D** The quantity supplied varies directly with price and the quantity demanded varies indirectly with price. Answer A is not correct because the quantity supplied varies directly with price. Answer B is not correct because the quantity demanded varies indirectly with price. Answer C is not correct because the quantity supplied varies directly with price and the quantity demanded varies indirectly with price.

22. **C** An equilibrium price can be disrupted by any change in the supply and or the demand curve. Answer A is not correct because such a price would lead to a surplus. Answer B is not correct because such a price would lead to a deficiency in demand. Answer D is not correct because an equilibrium price leads to an equality of the quantities demanded and supplied, not necessarily (or even likely) a complete satisfaction of consumer demand for the good or service.

23. **D** A downward and to the right shift in the supply curve with no change in the demand curve will result in a lower price and a larger equilibrium quantity. Answer A is not correct because a downward and to the right shift in the supply curve with no change in the demand curve will decrease the equilibrium price. Answer B is not correct because a downward and to the right shift in the supply curve with no change in the demand curve will result in an increase in the equilibrium quantity. Answer C is not correct because a downward and to the right shift in the supply curve with no change in the demand curve will result in a lower price and a larger equilibrium quantity.

24. **B** The supply curve will shift to the left, the demand curve will remain unchanged, prices will increase and the quantity demanded will decline. Answer A is not correct because the supply curve will shift to the left and speculative homes are no longer built. Answer C is not correct because a downward shift in the supply curve would suggest an increased supply at all price points (contrary to the removal of speculative homes) and an increased supply would imply a reduction in price. Answer D is not correct because the supply curve will shift to the left as speculative homes are no longer constructed. That shift in the supply curve with no change in the demand curve will result in an increase in price.

25. **C** The effect on the market price will only be predictable when the extent of the change in demand or supply is known. That information is not given among the choices. Answer A is not correct because the increase in supply is inconsistent with an inelastic supply function. Answer B is not correct because the increase in supply is inconsistent with an inelastic supply function. Answer D is not correct because the increase in demand is inconsistent with an inelastic demand function.

26. **D** Explicit costs are of two types—fixed costs and variable costs. The sum of the average fixed costs and average variable costs is equal to the average total costs. Answer A is not correct because the long-run average cost includes opportunity costs. Answer B is not correct because average product is the total physical product divided by the number of units of the factor employed. Answer C is not correct because the total cost is the sum of the total variable costs and the total fixed costs.

27. **C** The market clearing quantity is the quantity purchased which leaves no frustrated consumers. If the increase in both demand and supply were equal, that increase in supply would be purchased and there would be no frustrated consumers. Thus, the quantity purchased would increase. Answer A is not correct because it is not likely that the price would increase because the supply increased. Answer B is not correct because it is not likely that the price would decrease because the demand increased. Answer D is not correct because both demand and supply increase equally.

©2007 Kaplan CPA Review
Page 547

STUDY MANUAL – BUSINESS ENVIRONMENT & CONCEPTS
CHAPTER 21

28. **C**   A perfectly inelastic supply curve is a vertical line, and it implies that a change in price will not impact the quantity offered in the market. That would be the case where firms cannot vary input usage. Answer A is not correct because an equilibrium price of zero would mean that it is a free good. Answer B is not correct because a horizontal supply curve is used to represent a perfectly elastic supply curve, not an inelastic one. Answer D is not correct because a perfectly inelastic supply curve is more likely to occur in the short run, than in the long run. In the long run, producers may be able to adjust to lower or higher demand for the product.

29. **B**   The principle of diminishing marginal utility states that additional utility declines as quantity consumed increases. Answer A is not correct because the principle of diminishing marginal utility states just the opposite is true. One tires of something the more he or she has of it. Answer C is not correct because a vertical demand curve implies that the demand remains unchanged as price changes. That is contrary to the principle of diminishing marginal utility. Answer D is not correct because it implies that marginal utility increases as supply increases. Utility is independent of supply.

30. **C**   Economies of scale are declines in long-run average costs that are caused by increased plant size. Answers A and B are not correct because they describe the law of diminishing returns. Answer D is not correct because increasing the size of the factory might lower average costs, but it will not lower total costs.

31. **D**   In the long run, the firm has the opportunity to change the factors of production. The firm can expand or contract in response to changes in consumer demand. Thus, in the long run all inputs are variable. Answer A is not correct because in the long run the demand factors play a role in determining price and output. Answer B is not correct because supply factors play a role in determining price and output. Answer C is not correct because in the long run firms are assumed to enter and exit the industry.

32. **A**   A business that has the ability to control the price of the product it sells is a monopolistic firm. In such a situation the firm faces the market demand curve because the firm is the single seller in the market. Market demand curves have a negative slope (downward sloping). Answer B is not correct because such a firm is monopolistic, and industries in which monopolism exists have barriers to entry and exit. Answer C is not correct because in the case of a monopolist, one cannot predict the supply curve without knowing the demand curve. In a sense a monopolist has no supply curve. Answer D is not correct because in a monopolistic industry, the firm faces the market demand curve and market demand curves have negative slopes (downward sloping).

33. **B**   A boycott would decrease the demand at all price levels and result in a shift in the demand curve to the left. Answer A is not correct because a lower quantity would be sold at the same price. Answer C is not correct because there would be no increase in availability. The supply curve would be dictated by the cost of production, not by the demand curve. Answer D is not correct because the quantity demanded would be lower at every price level with no change in the cost of production. Thus, profits would decline.

34. **A**   Product demand elasticity refers to the extent to which demand will change in response to changes in price. If there are substitute products, the demand will be more elastic than if there were no substitute products. With substitute products, if the price goes up, the consumer will merely shift demand to the substitute products. Answer B is not correct because when the consumer has greater income, there is decreasing marginal utility. The decreasing marginal utility causes the consumer to be less likely to reduce demand as the price increases. Thus, increased income would result in less elasticity of demand. Answer

Page 548 ©2007 Kaplan CPA Review

STUDY MANUAL – BUSINESS ENVIRONMENT & CONCEPTS

CHAPTER 21

C is not correct because the elasticity of supply is independent of the elasticity of demand. Answer D is not the correct answer because higher input costs might influence the price, but it will not influence the elasticity of demand.

35. **D** Because the product's demand is elastic, the revenue effect of the increase in quantity is greater than the revenue effect of the decrease in price. The result is a net increase in total revenue. Answer A is not correct because when the product's demand is elastic, the revenue effect of the increase in quantity is greater than the revenue effect of the decrease in price. Thus, the total revenue would not decrease. Answer B is not correct because when the product's demand is elastic, the revenue effect of the increase in quantity is greater than the revenue effect of the decrease in price. Thus, the total revenue would not stay the same. Answer C is not correct because elasticity of demand refers to changes in the quantity demanded as price changes. It does not refer to shifts in the demand curve.

36. **C** This highlights an important distinction between a change in the quantity demanded and a shift in the demand curve. When the change is along a specific demand curve, as it is in this question, it is referred to as a change in the quantity demanded. In contrast, if the demand curve itself changes, that is referred to as a shift in the demand curve. Answer A is not correct because a change in demand would imply a shift in the demand curve, not movement along the existing demand curve. Answer B is not correct because a shift in the demand curve means a movement of the demand curve in response to a change in the demand. Answer D is not correct because an increase in demand would imply a shift in the demand curve, not movement along the existing demand curve.

37. **B** A product that is a necessity is often characterized by inelastic demand. Thus, the quantity demanded does not change much in response to a change in the price of the product. Answer A is not correct because the term "perfectly elastic" implies that there would be a major change in the quantity demanded for any small change in the price. Answer C is not correct because the term "elastic" implies that there would be a significant change in the quantity demanded for any small change in the price. Answer D is not correct because of the phrase in the question which states "no matter what cost." That phrase suggests that this answer, although a good answer, may not be the best answer.

38. **C** A price elasticity of 2.0 suggests that the percentage change in quantity will be twice the percentage change in price. Such a change is not perfectly elastic, but it is elastic. Answer A is not correct because perfectly elastic demand would have a price elasticity of demand of infinity. Answer B is not correct because perfectly inelastic demand would have a price elasticity of demand of zero. Answer D is not correct because a price elasticity of less than 1 is characteristic of inelastic demand.

39. **C** If there are few substitutes and the product is considered a necessity, then any increase in price will not have much of an impact on demand. Answer A is not correct because luxury items are items for which there are a significant number of substitutes. Thus, if the price goes up, the demand for the item might be significantly reduced. Answer B is not correct because complements are products that are sold in conjunction with the main product. The fact that there is a complement for the product has no real impact on the elasticity of demand for the primary product. Answer D is not correct because such a generalization is not warranted. This is true because some people spend a large portion of their income on necessities and some people spend a large portion of their income on luxuries. The statement may be more true for those who spend a large portion of their income on necessities.

©2007 Kaplan CPA Review

Page 549

Economics: Competitive Environment of the Firm

Study Manual – Business Environment & Concepts
Chapter 22

Study Tip: Never think about failing. When studying for the CPA exam, it is easy to become obsessed with failure. That attitude can sap your energy and prevent you from putting out your best effort. You should focus entirely on one goal: adding points to your score. That is the one and only obsession that will eventually get you to a passing score.Markets

A. Short-run equilibrium. In the short run, there is not enough time for sellers to fully adjust to changing market conditions. Producers are only able to increase the supply of a good offered for sale by using more labor and raw materials. New plant and equipment cannot be brought on line in the short run. In the short run, the *market price* of goods will change in the direction that brings the price consumers are willing to pay into balance with the price at which producers are willing to sell. The balance between the amount supplied and the amount demanded that brings about market equilibrium is created by price alone.

B. Long-run equilibrium. In the long run, adequate time exists for producers to adjust fully to changes in market conditions. Producers have the time to alter their productive factors and increase or decrease the physical size of their plants. Production will increase supply as long as the return exceeds the opportunity cost of producing the item. When returns exceed opportunity costs, capital will flow into the industry and output will expand. This increased production will cause prices to fall, eliminating the excess profits. If opportunity costs exceed returns from production, firms will remove capital from the production process, thus reducing supply and causing prices to rise.

C. A market is an economic system, incorporating the trading arrangements of buyers and sellers that underlie the forces of supply and demand. Equilibrium occurs when the conflicting forces creating supply and demand are in balance. In the absence of shifts in supply and demand curves, if the price is so high that supply exceeds demand, some businesses will decrease their prices to sell their excess inventory while others elect to reduce production. The result is a reduction in both price and quantity supplied until the market is in equilibrium. Conversely, if demand exceeds supply, the price of the product will rise, resulting in a reduction in quantity demanded as consumers find substitutes and increased supply as producers add capacity. As illustrated in Figure 4.8, this will occur until the market is in equilibrium.

Page 550   ©2007 Kaplan CPA Review

Figure 1: Market Equilibrium

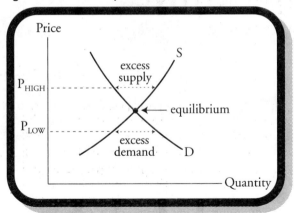

Figure 2 summarizes the equilibrium adjustment process to shifts in supply and demand. Keep in mind that the market adjustment process described here is not completed instantaneously. Economic information is sent out and reacted to gradually

Figure 2: Summary of Effects of Shifts in Demand and Supply

		Change in Equilibrium	
Change	*Shift in Demand/Supply Curve*	*Price*	*Quantity*
Increase in demand	Shift in demand curve to the right	Increase	Increase
Decrease in demand	Shift in demand curve to the left	Decrease	Decrease
Increase in supply	Shift in supply curve to the right	Decrease	Increase
Decrease in supply	Shift in supply curve to the left	Increase	Decrease

Figure 3 illustrates that when supply is reduced, the supply curve shifts from S_1 to S_2, and the initial impact will be a steep rise in prices from P_1 to P_2. This is because the slope of the demand curve is fixed in the short run. As consumers adjust their habits and seek alternatives, the long-run demand curve will flatten and prices will fall to P_3.

Figure 3: Equilibrium Adjustment Process

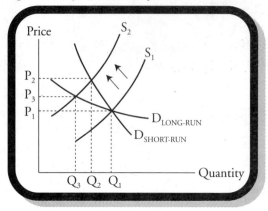

D. A shortage exists when the amount of a good offered by sellers is less than the amount demanded by buyers at the existing price. An increase in price will eliminate the shortage. A surplus exists when more of a good is willingly offered for sale than the quantity demanded at that price. The price is then above the equilibrium price. Shortages will lead to higher equilibrium prices; surpluses will lead to lower equilibrium prices.

E. The invisible hand principle refers to the tendency of market prices to direct individuals pursuing their own interests into productive activities that also promote the economic well-being of society. The market does this by:

1. Communicating information to decision makers. Without the information provided by market prices, it would be impossible for decision makers to determine how intensely a good is desired relative to its opportunity costs.

2. Coordinating actions of market participants. Prices direct producers to undertake those projects that are demanded most intensely by consumers.

3. Motivating economic players. Market prices establish a reward-penalty structure that induces the participants to work, cooperate with others, use efficient production methods, supply goods that are desired, and invest for the future.

4. Pricing products and providing order to the market. The market process works automatically without the need for any government decision or central planners. The market system sets prices and determines production and distribution channels without any outside control.

LABOR MARKET INDICATORS

A. Key indicators for the labor market are:

1. The civilian labor force is made up of those individuals who are at least 16 years old and are either currently employed or actively seeking employment. Note that not all people over 16 years of age are included in the labor force.

2. The labor-force participation rate is the number of persons 16 or older who are either employed or actively seeking employment as a percentage of the civilian population 16 or older.

3. The rate of unemployment is the percentage of people in the civilian labor force who are unemployed.

   Unemployment rate = Number of unemployed/Number in the labor force.

4. Unemployed workers include those classified as:

   a. Laid off.

   b. Reentrants into labor force.

   c. New entrants.

   d. Left last job willingly.

   e. Fired or terminated.

B. Problems encountered when measuring the unemployment rate include:

1. Workers waiting recall. Workers who have been laid off but are waiting to be recalled to their old jobs are counted as unemployed.

2. Discouraged workers. Workers who have become discouraged and have given up looking for employment are not counted as unemployed. This problem accounts for the anomaly that occurs when the economy turns up and the unemployment rate jumps. When once-discouraged workers start looking for jobs, they are then counted as unemployed.

3. Part-time workers. Workers looking for full-time employment but settling for part-time work are considered employed.

C. Frictional unemployment results from constant changes in the economy that prevent qualified workers from being matched with existing job openings in a timely manner. There are two causes of frictional unemployment.

1. The primary cause is imperfect information. Information regarding prospective employees and employers is costly and sometimes hard to find.

STUDY MANUAL – BUSINESS ENVIRONMENT & CONCEPTS
CHAPTER 22

2. A secondary cause is the job search conducted by both employees and employers. Both parties seek the best possible match and will spend time looking for information regarding that match. Both parties will conduct their searches until the costs and benefits of the search are equal.

D. Structural unemployment is caused by structural changes in the economy that eliminate some jobs while generating job openings for which unemployed workers are not qualified. Structural unemployment differs from frictional unemployment in that workers do not currently have the skills needed to perform the newly created jobs.

E. Cyclical unemployment is caused by a change in the general level of economic productivity. When the economy is operating at less than full capacity, positive levels of cyclical unemployment will be present. At levels *above* full capacity, negative cyclical unemployment will exist.

F. Full employment is the economic condition that exists when cyclical unemployment is zero. Note, however, that both structural and frictional unemployment continue to exist even when the economy is at full employment. In other words, there is some level of unemployment that is expected when the economy is at full employment.

G. The natural rate of unemployment is that rate of unemployment present when the economy is at its full employment rate of production or output. In the recent past, the natural rate of unemployment has risen due to changes in the composition of the labor force, namely, an increase in young workers entering the labor force. The natural rate of unemployment can persist for an indefinite period of time and is typically associated with the economy's maximum long-run rate of output.

H. Generally, movements in the unemployment rate and real GDP occur in opposite directions. If real GDP or real output in the economy is rising, it seems logical that unemployment would be lower because entities need more workers to produce the higher volumes of output. In contrast, when real output is decreasing, the unemployment rate would most likely be rising.

I. The Phillips curve is a graph of the inverse relationship between the rate of inflation and the rate of unemployment (see Figure 4). The major flaw with the Phillips curve is that the model ignores the effects of expectations.

Page 554   ©2007 Kaplan CPA Review

J. There are two conclusions arising from modern analysis of the Phillips curve:

Figure 4: The Phillips Curve (pre-1970)

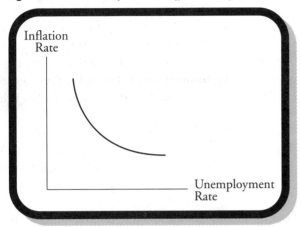

1. Expansionary macroeconomic policies will cause inflation, without permanently reducing unemployment.

2. When inflation exceeds expectations, unemployment falls below its natural level. It is the difference between expected and actual inflation that influences unemployment, not the absolute magnitude of inflation.

THE STAGES OF THE PRODUCT LIFE CYCLE AND COMPETITIVE ADVANTAGE

A. The product life cycle model shown in Figure 5 is often used to predict industry sales. A typical consumer product goes through four stages in its life cycle.

Figure 5: Product Life Cycle Stages

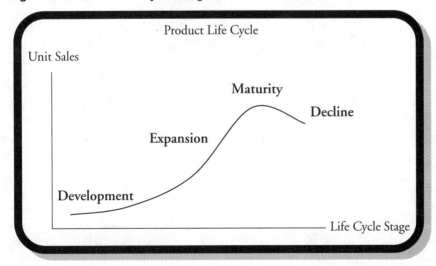

STUDY MANUAL – BUSINESS ENVIRONMENT & CONCEPTS
CHAPTER 22

1. Development stage. In this first stage, firms are designing and developing new and innovative products. Sales are low because consumers are unfamiliar with the product. However, there is also little competition. Global positioning satellite (GPS) applications to consumer products are examples of products currently in the development stage.

2. Expansion stage. Demand increases as consumer recognition of the product increases. Because of the accelerating sales and lack of competition, profits are high. MP3 players are currently in the expansion stage of the product life cycle.

3. Maturity stage. The high profit potential attracts additional competitors, which reduces profit margins. Industry sales are still increasing, but at a decreasing rate. At the beginning of the 21st century, personal computers have moved into the maturity stage of the product life cycle.

4. Decline stage. As consumers lose interest in the product and move on to better and cheaper substitutes, industry sales fall and margins erode. The industry experiences large losses, and firms exit the industry. The classic example of a product in the decline stage is the typewriter.

ANALYSIS IN TERMS OF SUPPLY AND DEMAND, THE MARKETS FOR LABOR, LOANABLE FUNDS, AND FOREIGN EXCHANGE

A. The labor market. Resource markets coordinate the supply and demand for resources like raw materials and labor services. We focus on the labor market, where people offer their labor for a price per time period, the wage rate. Just as it is in the markets for final goods and services, the quantity demanded for labor is inversely related to the wage rate. When the wage rate rises, firms will lower the quantity demanded as they substitute more nonhuman resources for labor and cut back production. The supply curve of labor is upward-sloping, which reflects the fact that workers will reduce leisure time and work more if the wage increases. Just as there are many markets for goods and services, there are many labor markets: one for each skill, experience, and occupational category.

B. The loanable funds market. As is the case for all resources, the market for labor is affected by the market for the final good or service that uses it in production.

1. An increase in the demand for the final good or service will increase the price for it and, thus, increase the demand for the labor used to produce the good or service. Likewise, a change in the labor market can increase or decrease the supply of a final good or service.

2. Demands for higher wages will eventually be passed along as higher prices in the final good or service. If businesses anticipate a recession, for example, they may reduce their demand for loanable funds. This will lead to a fall in the interest rate and the number of loans. As another example, if a given population's average age is increasing, and they begin to save more for retirement, the supply of funds will increase. This will have a negative effect on interest rates, and the number of loans will increase.

Page 556   ©2007 Kaplan CPA Review

C. The foreign exchange market. A foreign exchange market is where the currency of country X is traded for the currency of country Y. The higher the exchange rate for a foreign currency, say currency X, the lower the quantity demanded of currency X. When there is a high exchange rate, foreigners will not want to purchase as many of the goods priced in currency X, because they will be relatively more expensive.

1. At higher exchange rates, holders of currency X will increase the quantity they supply. If the exchange rate is high, holders of currency X find that the goods, services, and investments priced in currency Y are relatively cheaper. The holders of currency X will exchange it to obtain the currency of country Y to purchase the relatively cheaper goods and services.

2. An increase in the preference for goods from country Y will increase the exchange rate for that country's currency. If investment opportunities are more attractive in country Y, that will increase the exchange rate for that country's currency, too.

INDUSTRY LIFE CYCLE AND HOW TO IDENTIFY AN INDUSTRY'S STAGE IN ITS LIFE CYCLE

A. Figure 6 depicts a general illustration of the industry life cycle. This figure shows sales on the vertical axis and the phases of a firm's life cycle on the horizontal axis.

Figure 6: Industry Life Cycle

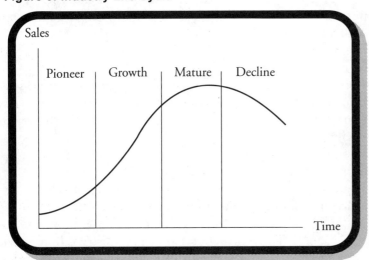

B. The following descriptions can be used to identify an industry's stage in its life cycle.

1. Pioneering phase. This is the start-up phase, where the industry experiences limited growth in sales and low, or even negative, profit margins. Demand is low, and firms in the industry are faced with substantial developmental costs.

2. Rapid accelerating growth phase. During this stage, markets develop for the industry's products, and demand grows rapidly. There is limited competition among the few firms in the industry, and sales growth and profit margins are high and accelerating.

3. Mature growth phase. Sales growth is still above normal but ceases to accelerate. Competitors enter the market, and profit margins start to decline.

4. Stabilization and market maturity phase. This is the longest phase. Industry sales growth rates approach the average growth rate of the economy. Fierce competition produces slim profit margins, and ROE becomes normal.

5. Deceleration of growth and decline. Demand shifts away from the industry. Growth of substitute products causes declining profit margins.

THE BASIC FORCES THAT DETERMINE INDUSTRY COMPETITION

A. In addition to life cycle analysis, industry sales (and earnings) forecasts should be preceded with an evaluation of the competitive structure of the industry. This is necessary because the profitability of a specific firm in an industry is heavily influenced by the competitive environment in which it does business and the profitability of the industry as a whole.

B. A widely cited author, Michael Porter, believes that the competitive environment of an industry determines the ability of firms within that industry to sustain above-average rates of return on invested capital. In his widely cited book, *Competitive Strategy: Techniques for Analyzing Industries and Competitors* (New York: Free Press, 1980), Porter published "Porter's five factors" for determining the intensity of competition within an industry.

C. Porter's five competitive forces that determine industry competition are:

1. Rivalry among the existing competitors. Rivalry is high when many equal-sized firms compete within an industry. Slow growth leads to competition when firms fight for market share, and high fixed costs lead to price cutting as firms try to operate at full capacity.

2. Threat of new entrants. The easier it is to enter the market, the greater the potential for competition. Barriers to entry (e.g., very high start-up costs, regulation, economies of scale) help limit competition.

3. Threat of substitute products. The profit potential in an industry is limited when many substitute products exist. This availability of substitute products restricts the price that firms may charge. There are higher levels of competition and lower profit margins for more commodity-like products.

4. Bargaining power of buyers. A limited number of buyers or a high concentration of buyers relative to sellers places the buying firms in an advantageous position over sellers. This means the buying firms have significant control over prices.

5. Bargaining power of suppliers. A limited number of selling firms or a high concentration of sellers relative to buyers places the selling firms in an advantageous position over buyers. This means the selling firms have significant control over prices. Suppliers are more powerful if there are just a few of them or

if they are more concentrated than the buying firms. This enables sellers to control prices.

THE EFFECTS OF BUSINESS CYCLES ON INDUSTRY CLASSIFICATION (I.E., GROWTH, DEFENSIVE, CYCLICAL)

A. The *business cycle* is characterized by fluctuations in economic activity. Real gross domestic product (GDP) and the rate of unemployment are key variables used when determining the current phase of the cycle.

B. Recent experience has shown that contractionary periods are becoming shorter and expansionary periods are becoming longer. A recession is defined as a period during which real GDP declines for two or more consecutive quarters. A recession includes both the contractionary and recessionary trough phases. A depression is a prolonged and very severe recession.

C. The business cycle reaction approach classifies industries by their behavior during the various phases of the business cycle. The general classifications are as follows:

1. Growth industry stocks experience accelerating sales and high profit margins during all phases of the business cycle. The biotechnology industry is an example of a growth industry.

2. Defensive industry stocks are much less cyclical than the overall market because demand for their products tends to be relatively independent of the business cycle. Food, beverage, and utility companies are examples of defensive industries.

3. Cyclical industry stocks vary directly with the business cycle because product demand tends to increase during the expansion and peak phases and drop off significantly during the recessionary phase. Automobile, heavy equipment, and machine tool companies are examples of cyclical industries.

D. Classifying industries in terms of life cycle phase and business cycle reaction provides a convenient point of reference from which follow-up analysis can proceed. When following such a classification, however, one must remember that not all firms in the industry are the same and that classifications can change over time.

THE IMPACT OF EXTERNAL FACTORS ON INDUSTRIES

A. Every industry is subject to a variety of outside forces that can have a fundamental impact on the industry's fortunes (or even survival). Five such outside forces are:

1. Technology. For industries in the pioneer phase attempting to introduce new technologies, the concern is whether or not the innovation will be successful. For mature industries, the concern is whether or not competition from new technologies will supplant the old technology. In the latter case, a company is typically faced with a choice of copying or acquiring the competition to survive.

©2007 Kaplan CPA Review

STUDY MANUAL – BUSINESS ENVIRONMENT & CONCEPTS
CHAPTER 22

2. Government. Government, through regulations, taxes, and subsidies, has its hands in almost every phase of industry. Examples of governmental involvement include litigation against the tobacco companies, environmental mandates, and export subsidies.

3. Social changes. Most social changes are either lifestyle or fashion changes. Fashion changes tend to be more short-term in nature and, as a result, are relatively unpredictable. Lifestyle changes generally occur over a longer-term horizon, which makes them easier to incorporate into the analysis. One example of lifestyle change is the trend toward two-income families. The result of this change has been an increase in demand for child day care.

4. Demography. Demography is concerned with the population's vital statistics. One relevant trend in these statistics is the aging of the population in the United States and other developed economies. Industries that provide services to older individuals (e.g., health care and financial services) will tend to prosper as the population ages.

5. Foreign influences. Virtually all industries are exposed to foreign influences. For example, most U.S. firms use oil even though they do not import or export it. Since more than 50 percent of oil consumed in the United States is imported, these firms are exposed to changes in oil prices. Moreover, a foreign competitor with a comparative advantage can decimate an entire industry, while increasing prosperity in foreign countries creates new demand for output from U.S. industries.

FACTORS THAT AFFECT INDUSTRY PRICING PRACTICES

A. In addition to supply and demand, at least four factors contribute to a firm's profitability and pricing decisions:

1. Product segmentation. This refers to a firm's ability to differentiate its product over various market segments (e.g., branded versus generic products) and charge premium prices.

2. Industry concentration. The fewer the competitors, the greater the concentration. The greater the concentration, the greater the likelihood that pricing actions will be broadly coordinated, thus reducing the probability of serious price competition.

3. Ease of industry entry. Greater ease of entry will have the effect of reducing prices toward the marginal cost of production. Industries that have large barriers to entry (e.g., large capital outlays for facilities) will find it easier to maintain premium pricing.

4. Supply input price. For example, chemical companies rely on oil as a major input to their production processes. A change in the price of oil will have major implications for the profitability of the chemical industry.

Page 560   ©2007 Kaplan CPA Review

THE TWO FUNDAMENTAL QUESTIONS DETERMINING THE CHOICE OF COMPETITIVE STRATEGY

A. If the firm's goal is to make money, the competitive strategy is its battle plan for achieving that goal. Two central questions provide the basis for the firm's choice of a competitive strategy:

1. Industry attractiveness. Is the industry attractive in terms of long-term profitability potential?

2. Competitive advantage. What determines the firm's relative competitive position within its industry?

B. The firm typically has little control over the industry's long-term attractiveness, but it has a great deal of control over its choice of competitive position.

HOW COMPETITIVE FORCES DETERMINE INDUSTRY PROFITABILITY

A. The attractiveness or profitability of any industry is determined by the interaction of the following five competitive forces (Porter's Five Forces):

1. Entry barriers (or threat of new entrants). Entry barriers for new competitors are a function of economies of scale, product differentials, brand identity, capital requirements, access to distribution channels, government policy, and cost advantages.

2. Threat of substitutes. The threat of substitutes is a function of the relative price performance of substitutes, buyer propensity to substitute, and switching costs.

3. Bargaining power of buyers. The bargaining power of buyers is a function of bargaining leverage and price sensitivity.

    a. The degree of bargaining leverage is determined by buyer concentration, buyer volume, buyer information, available substitutes, and switching costs.

    b. The degree of price sensitivity is determined by price relative to total purchases, brand identity, product differences, quality and performance, and buyer profits.

4. Bargaining power of suppliers. Suppliers' bargaining power is determined by differentiation of inputs, presence of substitute inputs, supplier concentration, importance of volume to the supplier, and threat of forward integration.

5. Rivalry among existing competitors. The degree of competitive rivalry in an industry is a function of industry growth, fixed costs, value added, product differences, brand identity, diversity of competitors, exit barriers, and informational complexity.

STUDY MANUAL – BUSINESS ENVIRONMENT & CONCEPTS
CHAPTER 22

B. These five factors determine the level of long-term average industry profitability through their collective effect on return on investment and its components: prices, costs, and required investment. Firms in industries that face intense competition and are threatened by substitute products or the entry of new competitors, for example, will typically earn unattractive returns.

C. Satisfying buyer needs is a prerequisite to a firm's viability within its industry. However, satisfying buyers alone does not determine firm profitability. It is the ability of the firm to charge customers for the *value-added component* of their products that determines profitability. If there is intense industry competition, this value-added component of price may be driven to zero through competition, or it may be extracted by suppliers. It is the industry structure that determines who gets to keep the value added component of price.

D. Short-term profitability is determined by supply-and-demand factors, whereas long-term profitability is determined by industry structure. Industry structure underlies long-term supply-and-demand imbalances because:

1. Entry barriers determine the number of new entrants.

2. Intensity of rivalries determines how capacity and output are expended.

3. Exit barriers preclude firms from leaving the market when demand falls off.

THE BASIC TYPES OF COMPETITIVE ADVANTAGE AND THE GENERIC STRATEGIES FOR ACHIEVING COMPETITIVE ADVANTAGE

A. The firm's relative position in an industry determines its overall profitability. It is the firm's competitive strategy that determines its relative position. A firm with a sustainable competitive advantage in an industry is likely to realize above-average returns for an extended period of time, even in an industry with an overall unfavorable structure.

B. Competitive strategy is determined by two choices. First, the firm must choose a competitive approach to competitive advantage based on either:

1. Product differentiation.

2. Cost leadership.

C. The firm must choose a broad or narrow scope. Combining these two generic approaches to competitive advantage with the scope of the firm's strategy yields four generic competitive strategies.

1. Cost leadership/broad scope.

2. Differentiation/broad scope.

3. Cost focus/narrow scope.

Page 562   ©2007 Kaplan CPA Review

4.   Differentiation focus/narrow scope.

D.   Generic competitive strategies:

1.   Cost leadership. The goal of the cost leader is to be the industry's low-cost producer. The cost leader tries to achieve low operating costs in all market segments in which it operates. Cost advantages can arise from economies of scale, technological innovation, or special access to raw materials.

   a.   Cost leaders will be above-average industry performers if their products are priced at or just below the average industry price. However, to achieve cost leadership, the cost leader must maintain differentiation parity: consumers must perceive the firm's product as being similar to the competitors' products.

   b.   A successful cost leader earns a higher profit margin than the rest of the industry because its prices are comparable and its costs are lower.

   c.   Cost leadership requires that a firm achieve the lowest production costs and not be one of several firms trying to be the cost leader. If there is more than one, competition will be fierce.

2.   Differentiation. A firm that is seeking to differentiate itself selects one or more product attributes that buyers perceive to be important and then strives to meet the buyers' needs. The differentiator charges a higher price for its differentiated product. Differentiation can be based on the product itself, the method of delivery, or the approach used to market the product or service.

   a.   A differentiator attempts to achieve cost parity with other industry participants (i.e., it attempts to keep its cost in line with other firms).

   b.   The differentiator generates higher than average profit margins by charging higher prices and maintaining approximately the same cost structure as do its competitors.

3.   Cost focus. A firm that employs a cost focus strategy seeks a competitive cost advantage in a narrow subsector of the industry's overall market.

   a.   The firm optimizes its strategy to achieve a competitive advantage in specific subsectors and forsakes any competitive advantage in the others.

   b.   A cost focuser will earn above-average returns if it can achieve differentiation parity in its chosen subsector.

   c.   The target segment of the market must have some unique aspect to it from which the focuser can achieve significant cost reductions, and the interaction of the five forces should have a positive influence on segment structure (i.e., the segment structure should be attractive).

©2007 Kaplan CPA Review

STUDY MANUAL – BUSINESS ENVIRONMENT & CONCEPTS
CHAPTER 22

4. Differentiation focus. A differentiation focus strategy is similar to cost focus, except the firm tries to achieve differentiation in a narrow segment of the industry. For this strategy to succeed:

    a. The firm must maintain cost parity in the sectors in which it competes and be able to differentiate its product.

    b. The segment must remain structurally attractive.

THE DIFFICULTIES AND RISKS OF SIMULTANEOUSLY USING MORE THAN ONE OF THE GENERIC STRATEGIES

A. A stuck-in-the-middle firm is one that tries to achieve both cost leadership and product differentiation at the same time, but fails at both. Stuck-in-the-middle firms compete at a disadvantage to those that achieve cost leadership or differentiation. Differentiators will be able to charge a higher price, and cost leaders will face a lower cost structure. The stuck-in-the-middle firm's profit margin will be squeezed from both sides.

B. A firm can, however, operate under different competitive strategies if it can separate its operations into distinctly separate operating units. Each of these operating units then pursues a different competitive strategy. If a firm is lucky enough to be able to be a cost leader and a product differentiator, the potential rewards are great.

C. A firm can also achieve both cost leadership and product differentiation if all competitors are stuck in the middle, its costs are affected by its market share, or it is the first to develop a new, innovative technology.

DIFFICULTIES IN SUSTAINING A COMPETITIVE ADVANTAGE WITH ANY GENERIC STRATEGY

A. The key to a firm's success is to create and sustain a competitive advantage relative to its competitors. In practice, sustaining a competitive advantage with any of the generic strategies is probably more difficult than creating it in the first place.

B. Changes in the structure of the industry can alter a firm's competitive position by changing the sustainability of a generic strategy or the size of the potential profits to be achieved by pursuing that strategy.

C. The premise of the generic strategies is that the firm creates barriers that make it difficult for its competitors to imitate its strategy. However, fierce competition in most industries makes these barriers temporary at best.

D. Each of the generic strategies has risks, and those risks represent opportunities for competitors to erode the firm's competitive advantage.

E. For example, a differentiator is vulnerable to competition from smaller differentiation focusers, each working to achieve even greater differentiation in its own selected industry segments.

Page 564   ©2007 Kaplan CPA Review

1. This is what happened to the large, traditional retailers when the category killers like Home Depot, Barnes and Noble, and Best Buy were able to capture some of the industry profits by differentiating in narrow segments of the retail industry.

2. The result is that the firm must continually work to improve its position by introducing new methods of differentiation (if it is a differentiator), developing new, cheaper production methods (if it is a cost leader), or exploiting new industry segments (if it is a focuser).

THE ROLE OF A GENERIC STRATEGY IN THE STRATEGIC PLANNING PROCESS

A. The firm's generic competitive strategy should be at the center of the firm's strategic plan. If the ultimate corporate goal is to create value by achieving a competitive advantage, then the generic strategy is the firm's road map for achieving that goal. Therefore, the strategic planning process should be guided and informed by the firm's generic strategy.

B. Firms that fail to do this make one or more of the following mistakes:

1. Their strategic plan is merely a list of unrelated action items that does not lead to a sustainable competitive advantage.

2. Price and cost forecasts are based on current market conditions and competitive positions and fail to take into account how industry structure will influence future, long-term industry profitability and each competitor's position in the industry.

3. They categorize business units as build, hold, or harvest, failing to realize that these are not business strategies, but rather means of achieving them.

4. They focus on market share as a measure of competitive position, failing to recognize that market share is the result, and not the cause, of a sustainable competitive advantage.

DIFFERENTIATE BETWEEN A PRODUCT LIFE CYCLE AND BROADER INDUSTRY TRENDS IN PRODUCT DEVELOPMENT

A. The life cycle model suffers from a severe shortcoming: most industries are not single-product industries.

B. Hence, even though products move through the stages of the life cycle (sometimes very quickly), an industry may simultaneously have one product in decline and another in expansion.

C. Multiproduct industries can be more stable, and the industry life cycle can be much longer than the individual product cycle. For example, even though software products move through the life cycle from development to decline in a matter of months, the

---

©2007 Kaplan CPA Review

STUDY MANUAL – BUSINESS ENVIRONMENT & CONCEPTS
CHAPTER 22

software industry is continually developing new software, and industry software sales are growing.

THE SIGNIFICANCE OF REGRESSION TOWARD THE MEAN AS A TENDENCY IN INDUSTRY PROFITS

A. An important conclusion to draw from the product life cycle model is that profits attract competition from other firms, which forces down prices and eventually reduces profits to a long-run normal level.

B. Conversely, continuing industry losses eventually thin out the competition and increase profit margins until the long-run normal profit level is reached. In other words, industry profits tend to regress toward the mean in the long run.

C. Any long-term forecast of industry profits should account for this fact: margins in high-profit industries will fall, and margins in low-profit industries will rise.

FACTORS THAT MAY CONTRIBUTE TO CHANGES IN A COMPANY'S MARKET SHARE OF INDUSTRY SALES

A. Given that market shares of firms within an industry are slow to change, if we know projected industry sales, we can estimate firm sales as:

Forecasted firm sales = Forecasted industry sales × Forecasted market share

B. Changes in market share may be driven by:

1. Changing consumer preferences.

2. Firms entering and leaving the industry.

3. The competitive advantage of the firms in the industry.

4. Change in demand due to changes in economic conditions.

5. Competitors' marketing strategies.

ENTRY BARRIERS THAT MAY PROTECT COMPANIES AGAINST COMPETITION FROM POTENTIAL MARKET ENTRANTS

A. Barriers to entry take the form of:

1. Economies of scale, which exist because some firms in certain industries are faced with declining average total costs (ATC) over the entire output range from which consumers will buy. In this case, the relatively larger firms in the market benefit from lower unit costs. This makes entry very expensive, since new entrants must be large from the beginning.

Page 566 ©2007 Kaplan CPA Review

2. Government licensing and legal barriers, which create barriers to entry in certain industries such as electric utilities, where the exclusive right to supply electricity in certain areas is legally granted.

3. Patents or exclusive rights of production, which are granted to producers of new and innovative products. This encourages research and development.

4. Resource control, which relates to the single firm that has sole control over a resource essential for entry into an industry; it can eliminate potential competitors.

HOW A PROFIT-MAXIMIZING MONOPOLIST SETS PRICES AND DETERMINES OUTPUT

A. The demand curve for a monopolist slopes downward to the right, reflecting the fact that higher prices result in lower demand. Monopolists will expand output until marginal revenue (MR) equals marginal cost (MC). This will maximize profit. Due to high entry barriers, monopolist profits do not attract new market entrants. Therefore, positive economic profits can exist in the long run.

B. Do monopolists charge the highest possible price? The answer is no, because monopolists want to maximize profits, not price. Monopolists will not make profits if the ATC line is always above the demand curve. For example, if someone held a patent on a machine that could be used just one time to convert a $5 bill into a $10 bill, but the ATC of producing the machine was $6, the monopolist would not make a profit.

Figure 7 shows the revenue-cost structure facing the monopolist. Note that production will expand until MR = MC at optimal output Q^*. To find the price at which it will sell Q^* units you must go to the demand curve. Note that the demand curve itself does not determine the optimal behavior of the monopolist. Just as with the pure competition model, optimal quantity is where MR = MC. For a profit to be ensured, the demand curve must lie above the ATC curve at the optimal quantity point (i.e., P – C > 0).

Figure 7: Monopolistic Short-Run Costs and Revenue

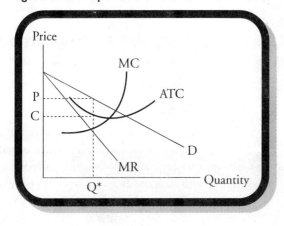

C. Once again, profit maximization (optimal output) for a monopolistic firm occurs when MR = MC. As shown in Figure 8, profit per unit at this point is P – C. On the other hand, a monopolist will lose money when the ATC curve lies above the demand curve (i.e., P – C < 0). This is illustrated in Figure 8.

Figure 8: Losses for a Monopolistic Firm

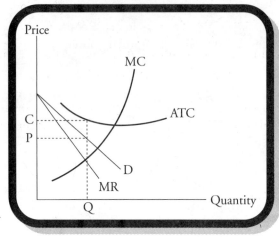

D. Monopolists are price-searchers and have imperfect information regarding demand. Therefore, they must experiment with different prices.

THE DIFFERENCE BETWEEN A MONOPOLY AND AN OLIGOPOLY

A. A monopoly market structure has the following characteristics:

1. One seller of a specific, well-defined product that has no good substitutes.

2. Barriers to entry are high.

B. Oligopoly is a market structure characterized by:

1. A small number of sellers.

2. Interdependence among competitors (decisions made by one firm affect the demand, price, and profit of others in the industry).

3. Significant barriers to entry that often include large economies of scale.

4. Products may be similar or differentiated.

C. In contrast to a monopolist, oligopolists are highly dependent upon the actions of their rivals when making business decisions. Price determination in the auto industry is a good example. Automakers tend to play follow the leader and announce price increases in close synchronization. They are not working explicitly together, but the actions of one producer have a large impact on the others. The barriers to entry are large. It would take an enormous capital investment to start a new auto company because the large economies of scale that are achieved by the oligopolist pose a significant barrier.

PRICE AND OUTPUT UNDER OLIGOPOLY, WITH AND WITHOUT COLLUSION

A. Collusion is the agreement among firms to avoid various competitive practices, particularly price competitions. Figure 4.27 shows the price/output decision when collusion is present and when it is not. Since collusion is the avoidance of competition, the oligopolist will produce Q_1 units and sell at a price of P_1. So, with collusion, price increases and output decreases like with a monopoly.

B. Also shown in Figure 9 is that if competition is fierce, price reduction will occur until the point where long-run average total cost (LRATC) is equal to price. At output level Q_2, zero economic profits are achieved and price is reduced to P_2.

Figure 9: The Effects of Collusion

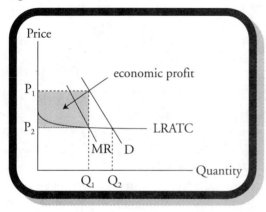

WHY OLIGOPOLISTS HAVE A STRONG INCENTIVE TO COLLUDE AND TO CHEAT ON COLLUSIVE AGREEMENTS

A. Oligopolists will recognize that they cannot maximize profits when they are in fierce competition, so they will have a strong incentive to collude. Hence, they will form associations, or cartels, to set prices and output so as to maximize profits. They will stay at Q_1 and P_1 in Figure 9.

B. The demand curve facing an individual oligopolist is very elastic so that a small decrease in price will provide a large change in quantity demanded. Therefore, if a firm increases its price, it will lose customers. If the firm decreases its price, the firm will steal customers from its rivals. This elasticity of demand creates an incentive for firms to cheat on collusion agreements. It also makes price increases very difficult to sustain unless the entire industry follows suit. This tends to explain the "follow-the-leader" behavior.

OBSTACLES TO COLLUSION AMONG OLIGOPOLISTIC COMPANIES

A. Obstacles to collusive behavior among oligopolistic companies include:

1. Number of oligopolists. When the number of oligopolists is large, effective collusion is less likely.

2. Monitoring partners. Collusion is less attractive when it is difficult to detect and eliminate price cuts. In other words, if cheating is difficult to detect, fewer firms will be willing to enter into collusive agreements.

3. Low entry barriers. New entrants will see the "premium" pricing that is available and enter the market (outside the oligopoly) with more attractive pricing in an attempt to steal market share.

4. Unstable demand conditions. Unstable demand can lead to differing opinions between oligopolists as to how to best serve the industry's clientele.

5. Vigorous antitrust action. Antitrust actions may increase the cost of collusion.

6. Limits of the oligopoly model. Firms gain when they collude. However, collusion also has its costs. Game theory is frequently used to analyze the behavior of oligopolists. Game theory analyzes the strategic choices made by competitors in a conflict situation, such as decisions made by members of an oligopoly.

GOVERNMENT POLICY ALTERNATIVES THAT ARE INTENDED TO REDUCE THE PROBLEMS STEMMING FROM HIGH BARRIERS TO ENTRY

A. A natural monopoly is one in which economies of scale are so pronounced that total industry production should be produced by only one firm. Here, average total cost (ATC) is a declining function of output. Most utilities fit into the definition of natural monopoly. Thus, restructuring an industry to allow natural monopolies is one policy alternative.

B. Regulators often attempt to reduce artificial barriers to trade such as licensing requirements, quotas, and tariffs. This will increase competition and efficiency.

C. Regulators often attempt to place price controls on the protected producer. Since monopolists are allocatively inefficient, government regulation may be aimed at improving resource allocation by placing price ceilings on monopoly pricing. Regulators may accomplish this through average cost pricing or marginal cost pricing.

1. Average cost pricing is the most common form of regulation. Average cost pricing forces monopolists to reduce price to where the firm's ATC intersects the market demand curve. This will:

   a. Increase output and decrease price.

   b. Increase social welfare.

   c. Ensure the monopolist a normal profit (zero economic profit, i.e., $P - C = 0$).

2. Marginal cost pricing forces the monopolist to lower price to the point where the firm's MC curve intersects market demand, which increases output and reduces price but causes the monopolist to incur a loss, requiring a government subsidy. Regulators often go astray when dealing with the problems associated with markets with high barriers to entry. The reasons for this include:

   a. Lack of information. Regulators may not know the firm's ATC, MC, and demand schedule.

   b. Cost shifting. The firm has no incentive to reduce costs, since this will cause the regulator to reduce the price. If the firm allows costs to rise, the regulator will allow a price increase.

   c. Quality regulations. It is easier to regulate price than it is to regulate quality. If the firm faces falling profits due to a cost squeeze, it may let quality deteriorate.

   d. Special interest effect. The firm may try to influence regulation by political manipulation designed to influence who gets placed on the regulatory board.

D. In the real world, a monopoly firm does not operate in a static environment. If a monopoly is profitable, rivals will seek to develop substitute products. Dynamic competition in the form of technological change and the development of new substitutes will threaten the position of the monopolist. Dynamic competition may cause the monopolist to act in ways inconsistent with the behavior dictated by the monopoly model. Instead of maximizing profits, the monopolist may:

   1. Charge less and produce more to discourage potential rivals.

   2. Work harder on new product development. This will enable the monopolist to maintain control of the market through the patent system.

THE CONDITIONS THAT CHARACTERIZE COMPETITIVE PRICE-SEARCHER MARKETS

A. Monopolistic competition is another name for competitive price-searcher markets.

B. The following market and product features define monopolistic competition:

   1. A large number of independent sellers.

   2. Each seller produces a differentiated product.

   3. Low barriers to entry.

   4. Downward sloping demand curve and highly elastic demand.

STUDY MANUAL – BUSINESS ENVIRONMENT & CONCEPTS
CHAPTER 22

HOW PRICE-SEARCHERS CHOOSE PRICE AND OUTPUT COMBINATIONS

A. Monopolistic competitors face downward sloping demand curves due to differentiated products. This demand curve is highly elastic (flat) because of the availability of close substitutes. Think about the market for toothpaste. All toothpaste is basically the same, but differentiation occurs as a result of taste preferences, influential advertising, and the reputation of the seller. However, if the price of Crest skyrocketed, you could easily switch to Colgate.

B. The price/output decision. Panel (a) of Figure 4.28 describes the short-run price/output characteristics of monopolistic competition for a single firm. As Figure 4.28 indicates, price-searchers maximize profits by producing where marginal revenue (MR) equals marginal cost (MC) and by charging the price from the demand curve. Here the firm earns positive economic profits because price, P^*, exceeds average total cost (ATC), C^*. Due to low barriers to entry, rivals will enter the market in pursuit of economic profits.

Panel (b) of Figure 10 shows the long-run condition for a representative firm after new firms have entered the market. As indicated, the entry of new firms shifts the demand curve down to the point where price equals average total cost ($P^* = C^*$) such that economic profit is zero. The monopolistic competitor continues to produce at the quantity where MR = MC.

Figure 10: Short-Run and Long-Run Price-Searcher Markets with Low Barriers to Entry

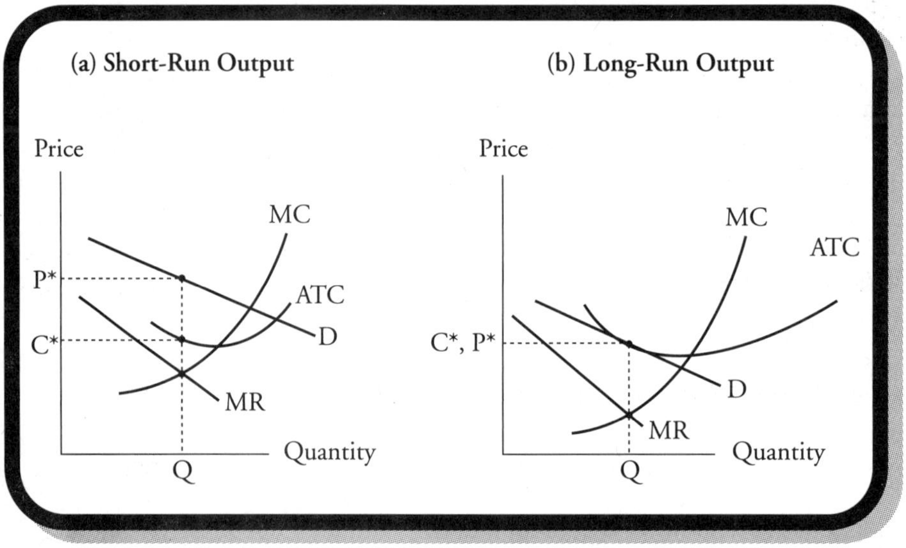

HOW PRICE DISCRIMINATION INCREASES OUTPUT AND REDUCES ALLOCATIVE INEFFICIENCY

A. Price discrimination is the practice of charging different consumers different prices for the same product or service. Examples are different prices for airline tickets based on whether a Saturday night stay is involved (separates business travelers and leisure travelers) and different prices for movie tickets based on age.

Page 572   ©2007 Kaplan CPA Review

Figure 11: Monopolistic vs. Pure Competition

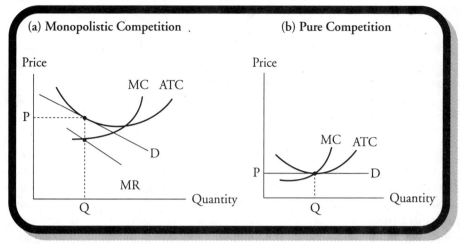

B. For price discrimination to work, the seller must:

1. Face a downward sloping demand curve.

2. Have at least two identifiable groups of customers with different price elasticities of demand for the product.

3. Be able to prevent the customers paying the lower price from reselling the product to the customers paying the higher price.

C. Company gains from price discrimination. As long as the previous conditions are met, profits can be increased through price discrimination.

D. Winners and losers. Price discrimination reduces the allocative inefficiencies that result from pricing above marginal cost. The major benefit is more output. The firm gains from those customers with inelastic demand curves while still providing goods to customers with more elastic demand curves. This may even cause production to take place when it would not otherwise.

THE DIFFERENCE BETWEEN PRICE-TAKERS AND PRICE-SEARCHERS

A. Price-takers produce a small amount of output relative to the market and face a horizontal (perfectly elastic) demand curve. They can sell all of their output at the prevailing market price, but if they set their output price higher than the market price, they would sell nothing. The term *price-taker market* means the same thing as *purely competitive market*.

B. Price-searchers have significant control on total supply and face a downward sloping demand curve. They can set their own prices, but the higher the price, the less they sell.

STUDY MANUAL – BUSINESS ENVIRONMENT & CONCEPTS
CHAPTER 22

CONDITIONS THAT CHARACTERIZE A PURELY COMPETITIVE (PRICE-TAKER) MARKET

A. Pure competition assumes the following characteristics:

1. All the firms in the market produce a homogeneous product.

2. There are a large number of independent firms.

3. Each seller is small relative to the total market.

4. There are no barriers to entry or exit.

B. Producers in a purely competitive market must sell their product at the going market price or be shut out of the market. The market's (not the individual firm's) supply and demand determines the price.

C. Under pure competition, individual firms have no control over price. As illustrated in Figure 12, the individual firm's demand schedule is perfectly elastic (horizontal).

Figure 12: Price-Taker Demand

THE EFFECTS OF PRICE CEILINGS AND PRICE FLOORS

A. A price ceiling is an upper limit on the price a supplier can charge. If the ceiling is above the equilibrium price, it will have no effect. As illustrated in Figure 13, if the ceiling is below the equilibrium price, the result will be a shortage characterized by quantity demanded, Q_d, exceeding quantity supplied, Q_s.

1. In such a case, price is no longer an effective means of rationing the good or service. Price ceilings lead to the following:

   a. Consumers may have to wait in long lines to make a purchase. They pay a price in terms of the time they spend in line.

   b. Suppliers may engage in discrimination, such as selling to friends and relatives first.

c. Suppliers sell at the ceiling price, but take bribes to do so.

d. Suppliers may also reduce the quality of the goods produced to a level commensurate with the ceiling price.

2. Rent controls provide a good example of how a price ceiling can distort a market. Renters must wait for units to become available. Renters may have to bribe landlords to rent at the ceiling price. The quality of the apartments will fall. Other inefficiencies can develop. For example, a renter might be reluctant to take a new job across town because it means giving up a rent-controlled apartment and risking not finding another apartment near the new place of work.

Figure 13: Price Ceiling

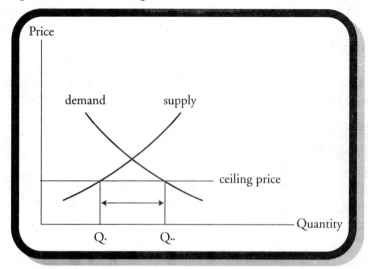

B. A price floor is a minimum price that a buyer can offer for a good, service, or resource. If the floor is below the equilibrium price, it will not have an effect. Figure 14 shows that if the floor is above the equilibrium price, the result will be a surplus characterized by quantity supplied exceeding quantity demanded, Q_d.

Figure 14: Price Floor

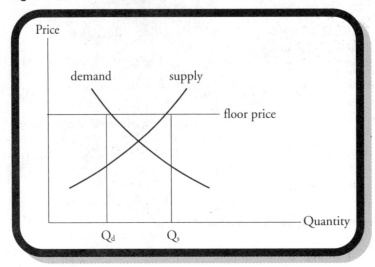

1. Price floors often lead to the following:

    a. Suppliers will divert resources to the production of the good with the anticipation of selling the good at the floor price, but then will not be able to sell all they produce.

    b. Consumers will buy less of a product if the floor is above the equilibrium price and substitute other consumption goods for the good with the controlled price. Both situations lead to inefficiencies.

2. The minimum wage in the United States is an excellent example of a price floor. Firms cannot employ all the workers who want to work at the minimum wage. Since firms must pay at least the minimum wage for the workers hired, firms then substitute away from labor and use more capital than might be optimal. Furthermore, firms might lower the nonpecuniary (nonmonetary) benefits offered to workers (e.g., good working conditions and training). Most dramatic is the large number of unemployed, low-skilled workers who may be willing to work at a wage lower than the minimum wage, but firms cannot legally hire them.

SUPPLY CHAIN MANAGEMENT

CHARACTERISTICS OF SUPPLY CHAIN MANAGEMENT

Supply chain management requires a sharing of information among the suppliers, manufacturers, distributors, and retailers. For example, if retailers gather good information on consumer demand and share this information with the distributors and manufacturers, there will be a better flow of production and sales. In turn, if the manufacturers share information with the suppliers there will be even better information all along the supply chain. This improved flow of information or forecasts will reduce inventories and make the entire process more efficient. Supply chain management is now more important as the markets have become more global and the relationships between initial suppliers, manufacturers, distributors, retailers, and customers have become more complex. The emphasis on supply chain management also increased as a result of total quality management (TQM) applications and the increased use of outsourcing for inputs.

A. Supply chain management is the organization of activities between a company and its suppliers in an effort to provide for profitable development, production, and delivery of goods to customers. The goal is to focus on the entire supply chain to improve the levels of efficiencies at every level.

B. Supply chains are sometimes called value chains to reflect value added as goods and services progress all the way to final delivery to the customer. An example of a typical supply chain is given:

Supplier A

Supplier B Storage…Manufacturing…Storage…Distributor…Retailer…Consumer

Supplier C

C. A number of areas for analysis and information sharing in supply chain management include the following:

1. Customers: What products/services are to be sold?

2. Forecasting: Predict quantity and timing of consumer wants.

3. Design: Consider the customers' wants, manufacturing capabilities, and timing to get to the market.

4. Purchasing: Compare potential suppliers while meeting the needs of manufacturing operations. This is a link between an organization and its suppliers.

5. Inventory: Balance the need to meet demands while managing the cost of holding inventory.

6. Suppliers: How will the quality of supplier goods be monitored while maintaining on-time delivery, flexibility, and good relations with suppliers?

7. Processing: How will quality be controlled and how will work be scheduled?

8. Location: What is the best location of facilities along the supply chain?

9. Logistics: What is the best way to move and store materials?

STUDY MANUAL – BUSINESS ENVIRONMENT & CONCEPTS
CHAPTER 22

TRANSFER PRICES AND THE IMPLICATIONS OF DIFFERENT METHODS OF ESTABLISHING TRANSFER PRICES

Transfer prices are internal prices set by the parent company for transfers of goods and services within the company. If one subsidiary supplies an intermediate product for another subsidiary, or for the parent company, the transaction is not a market sale. The firm must choose an appropriate transfer price to use to account for the sale of one subsidiary and purchase of the other subsidiary. The transfer price may be set to approximate a market price if that information is available. In many cases it is impossible to apply the principles of market pricing to transfer prices.

A. Transfer prices may be set too low. This hurts the accounting profits of the subsidiary supplying the product and helps the accounting profits of the subsidiary using the product as an input. If the transfer price is set too high it helps the subsidiary supplying the product and hurts the subsidiary using the product as an input. If a subsidiary is judged as a profit center, the level of the transfer price is crucial to performance.

B. The transfer price should be set to optimize the value of the firm. If market prices are not easily obtained, the firm may choose to lower taxes by setting a higher price for the subsidiary supplying the product if it is in a lower tax bracket than the subsidiary using the product.

STUDY MANUAL – BUSINESS ENVIRONMENT & CONCEPTS
CHAPTER 22

QUESTIONS: COMPETITIVE ENVIRONMENT OF THE FIRM

1. Supply Chain Management systems rely upon which of the following?
   A. Many suppliers.
   B. Frequent competitive bidding.
   C. Cooperation between purchasing and suppliers.
   D. Short-term contracts.

2. Government price regulations in competitive markets that set maximum or ceiling prices below the equilibrium price will in the short run:
   A. cause demand to decrease.
   B. cause supply to increase.
   C. create shortages of that product.
   D. have no effect on the market.

3. In competitive product markets, equilibrium price in the long run is:
   A. a fair price all consumers can afford.
   B. set equal to the total costs of production.
   C. set equal to the total fixed costs of production.
   D. set equal to the marginal costs of production.

4. In the short run, the supply curve in a competitive market shows a positive relationship between price and quantity supplied because:
   A. a higher price causes an increase in demand so the market stays in equilibrium.
   B. of the law of diminishing returns.
   C. as the size of a business firm increases, price must rise.
   d. increases in output imply a shift in consumer preferences allowing a higher price.

5. Economic markets that are characterized by monopolistic competition have all of the following characteristics **EXCEPT**:
   A. one seller of the product.
   B. economies or diseconomies of scale.
   C. heterogeneous products.
   D. downward-sloping demand curves for individual firms.

6. When markets are perfectly competitive, consumers:
   A. must search for the lowest price for the products they buy.
   B. have goods and services produced at the lowest cost in the long run.
   C. must choose the brands they buy solely on the basis of informational advertising.
   d. do not receive any consumer surplus unless producers choose to overproduce.

©2007 Kaplan CPA Review

Page 579

STUDY MANUAL – BUSINESS ENVIRONMENT & CONCEPTS
CHAPTER 22

7. The manner in which cartels set and maintain price above the competitive market price is to:
   A. avoid product differentiation in order to decrease demand for the product.
   B. advertise more so market demand increases.
   C. encourage the introduction of higher-priced substitute products.
   D. require cartel members to restrict output.

8. In a competitive market for the labor where demand is stable, if workers try to increase their wage:
   A. employment must fall.
   B. labor supply must increase.
   C. government must set a maximum wage below the equilibrium wage.
   D. firms in the industry must become smaller.

9. The competitive model of supply and demand predicts that a surplus can only arise if there is a:
   A. maximum price above the equilibrium price.
   B. minimum price below the equilibrium price.
   C. technological improvement in the means of production.
   D. minimum price above the equilibrium price.

10. In markets that are imperfectly competitive, such as monopoly and monopolistic competition, firms produce at an output where:
    A. price equals marginal cost.
    B. marginal cost equals marginal revenue.
    C. total revenue is maximized.
    D. price equals average cost.

11. Price tends to fall in competitive markets when there is a(n):
    A. increase in demand for the product.
    B. decrease in quantity demanded of the product.
    C. decline in available labor.
    D. increase in interest rates.

12. Monopolistic competition is characterized by:
    A. a relatively large number of sellers who produce differentiated products.
    B. a relatively small number of sellers who produce differentiated products.
    C. one or two companies producing similar products.
    D. a relatively large number of sellers who produce a standardized product.

13. Which one of the following is **NOT** a key assumption of perfect competition?
    A. Firms sell a homogeneous product.
    B. Customers are indifferent about which firm they buy from.
    C. The level of a firm's output is small relative to the industry's total output.
    D. Each firm can price its product above the industry price.

14. A market with many independent firms, low barriers to entry, and product differentiation is **BEST** classified as:
    A. a monopoly.
    B. a natural monopoly.
    C. monopolistic competition.
    D. an oligopoly.

15. Which one of the following would cause the demand curve for a commodity to shift to the left?
    A. A rise in the price of a substitute product.
    B. A rise in average household income.
    C. A rise in the price of a complementary commodity.
    D. A rise in the population.

STUDY MANUAL – BUSINESS ENVIRONMENT & CONCEPTS
CHAPTER 22

ANSWERS: COMPETITIVE ENVIRONMENT OF THE FIRM

1. **C** Supply Chain Management systems are based on purchasers and suppliers working together under long-term contracts to reduce the cost of the product or service and also to reduce the cost of the delivery and documentation. Answer A is not correct because under Supply Chain Management systems purchasing managers establish partnerships with one or few suppliers. Answer B is not correct because under Supply Chain Management systems the purchasing manager and the supplier enter into a long-term contract to induce the supplier to participate as a partner with the purchaser. Answer D is not correct because in order to establish a partnership between the purchaser and the supplier, there is a need for long-term contracts.

2. **C** If the maximum price is set below the equilibrium price, the supply will not be sufficient to meet the demand. Thus, there will be a shortage of the product. Answer A is not correct because demand is independent of supply. Answer B is not correct because supply will not increase if the market-clearing price cannot be realized. Answer D is not correct because regulations that set minimum prices are likely to have an impact on the market in most situations.

3. **D** In a competitive market, the forces of demand and supply will, in the long run, cause price to equal marginal cost. If price is higher than marginal cost, additional production will be forthcoming. If price is lower than marginal cost, producers will quit producing. Answer A is not correct because a competitive market cannot assure a fair price that all consumers can afford. The disposable income of the consumers dictates whether or not they can afford the product at the equilibrium price. Some will be able to afford it and some will not. Answer B is not correct because a price set equal to the total cost of production fails to recognize that the total cost should be divided by the number of units produced. Answer C is not correct because a price set equal to the total fixed cost of production fails to recognize that the total fixed cost should be divided by the total number of units produced. Even then, the variable costs per unit would be ignored.

4. **B** In the short run the addition of variable inputs to fixed resources yields additional output; but the amount of additional output diminishes as more variable inputs are used. Thus, as price increases, the amount of product supplied will increase until the marginal cost is equal to the marginal revenue. Answer A is not correct because a higher price does not usually cause an increase in demand. The increase in demand is what would likely cause a higher price. Answer C is not correct because as the size of the business firm increases, the price must fall if the demand remains unchanged. Answer D is not correct because increases in supply do not always imply a shift in consumer preference; it could be caused by the entry of a new producer in pursuit of excess profits.

5. **A** Monopolistic competition is characterized by a market in which a large number of firms sell differentiated products. Answer B is not correct because firms in a market characterized by monopolistic competition are faced with economies and dis-economies of scale. Answer C is not correct because the monopolistic competition market is characterized by a set of goods that are differentiated but have a large number of close substitutes. Answer D is not correct because the monopolistic competition market is faced with a downward sloping demand curve. As the price of the product declines, more will be demanded.

STUDY MANUAL – BUSINESS ENVIRONMENT & CONCEPTS
CHAPTER 22

6. **B**   In a purely competitive market, in the long run, an increase in market demand will cause the price to rise. Economic profit will result, and new firms will enter the industry in response to this profit. As new firms enter, the market supply increases causing price to fall to the point at which all firms are earning zero economic profit. Answer A is not correct because consumers will be able to buy the product at the same price from several sources. Answer C is not correct because informational advertising plays a limited role in perfectly competitive markets because there is little opportunity for product differentiation. Answer D is not correct because there is no such thing as overproduction because all of the production will be cleared at the market price.

7. **D**   Cartels control price by restricting output. The oil cartel is an example. The OPEC countries restrict output to increase price. Answer A is not correct because cartels do not seek to decrease demand. Answer B is not correct because advertising is not likely to influence demand for the homogeneous product that the cartel produces. Answer C is not correct because there is no evidence that cartels encourage the introduction of higher-priced substitute products. The effect of a cartel might be the introduction of lower-priced substitute products, e.g., natural gas substituted for oil.

8. **A**   If supply remains unchanged and there is a concerted effort to increase price, demand will fall and unemployment will increase. This is one of the arguments against the minimum wage. Answer B is not correct because it is possible that there is no additional labor supply available to respond to the increased wage. Answer C is not correct because there is no economic law that says that the government must interfere. Answer D is not correct because the firms may choose to substitute capital for labor in order to maintain production.

9. **D**   A minimum price above the equilibrium price will cause more to be produced than can be cleared by the price. This excess uncleared production is a surplus. Answer A is not correct because a maximum price above the equilibrium price means that the price will be set by the market at the equilibrium price. At the equilibrium price there will be no surplus. Answer B is not correct because the minimum price below the equilibrium price means that the price will be set by the market at the equilibrium price. At the equilibrium price there will be no surplus. Answer C is not correct because if there is technological improvement in the means of production the average cost would decrease and a new supply curve would result. Given no change in the demand curve, the equilibrium price would be adjusted downward; but there would be no surplus.

10. **B**   The monopolist produces a small output and charges a higher price than a perfectly competitive firm. The monopolist is encouraged to stop production when the marginal cost equals marginal revenue. Answer A is not correct because the firm in a perfectly competitive market will produce an output where price equals marginal cost and marginal cost and average cost will be equal. Answer C is not correct because the maximization of total revenue does not pay proper attention to the role that cost plays in influencing supply. Answer D is not correct because the firm in a perfectly competitive market will produce an output where price equals average cost and average cost and marginal cost will be equal at the output level.

11. **B**   Given an unchanging supply, the price of a product in a competitive market will decline as there is a decline in the demand for the product. Answer A is not correct because an increase in the demand for the product will cause a higher price. Answer C is not correct because when there is a decline in the available labor, the costs go up and the price is likely to rise. Answer D is not correct because as the interest rates increase, the costs will increase and the price is likely to rise.

©2007 Kaplan CPA Review   Page 583

STUDY MANUAL – BUSINESS ENVIRONMENT & CONCEPTS
CHAPTER 22

12. **A**   Monopolistic competition is the situation in which there are a large number of sellers who can, for a short period of time, create a monopoly by differentiating their product. Answer B is not correct because monopolistic competition is not characterized by a relatively small number of sellers. An oligopoly has a small number of sellers. Answer C is not correct because that choice describes a monopoly or an oligopoly. Answer D is not correct because that choice describes perfect competition.

13. **D**   If a firm in a perfectly competitive industry were to price its product above the industry price, the firm would sell nothing. This is true because the consumer could buy an identical product at a lower price just down the street. Answer A is not correct because it is a choice that describes a characteristic of perfect competition. Answer B is not correct because it is a choice that describes a characteristic of perfect competition. Answer C is not correct because it is a choice that describes a characteristic of perfect competition.

14. **C**   Monopolistic competition is characterized by many firms in a situation in which there can be product differentiation for a short period of time. An example is the fast food industry. One fast food chain will develop a new concept; and the others will soon be copying that concept. Answer A is not correct because a monopoly usually has only one firm. Answer B is not correct because a natural monopoly is a monopoly which is created because the economies of scale restrict competitors. An example would be power generation. Answer D is not correct because an oligopoly usually has only a few firms.

15. **C**   Complementary products are products that are sold in conjunction with the primary product. If the primary product is a razor, then the complementary product would be razor blades. Answer A is not correct because a rise in the price of a substitute product would cause the demand curve for this product to shift to the right. This would indicate a larger quantity demanded at all price levels. Answer B is not correct because a rise in the average household income would tend to shift the demand curve to the right indicating a larger quantity demanded at all price levels. Answer D is not correct because a rise in population would tend to shift the demand curve to the right indicating a larger quantity demanded at all price levels.

ECONOMICS: SENSITIVITY OF THE FIRM TO THE MACROECONOMY

STUDY MANUAL – BUSINESS ENVIRONMENT & CONCEPTS
CHAPTER 23

Study Tip: Make sure that occasionally, probably once a week or so, you take a break and get completely away from preparing for the CPA exam. Everyone needs to recharge their batteries now and then. If you spend too much time studying, you will gradually wear down and become inefficient. On your calendar, program in time for rest and relaxation on a regular basis.

ECONOMIC MEASURES AND REASONS FOR CHANGES IN THE ECONOMY

GROSS DOMESTIC PRODUCT (GDP)

Gross domestic product (GDP) is by far the most commonly used measure of economic performance. It is computed as the total market value of all domestically produced final goods and services during a given year. GDP is designed to measure the market value of production that flows through the economy.

A. GDP includes only goods and services purchased by their final or ultimate users, so GDP measures final production. Intermediate stages of production are not explicitly included. For example, the price of flour sold to a baker is not included in GDP. Value added during the intermediate steps (i.e., harvesting, milling, and baking) is included in the final selling price of the products sold by the baker.

B. GDP counts only the goods and services produced within the country's borders during the year, whether by citizens or foreigners. Sales of used or secondhand goods are excluded, but sales commissions charged on the sale of used products are included.

C. GDP excludes financial transactions and transfer payments since they do not represent current production. For example, stock and bond sales along with welfare and Social Security payments are excluded. These payments represent exchanges of goods, not production of goods.

D. GDP measures both output and income, which are equal. If the value of output per person increases, per capita income also increases. Thus, achieving a higher standard of living involves producing more output per worker (increasing productivity).

©2007 Kaplan CPA Review

GROSS NATIONAL PRODUCT (GNP)

A. The gross national product (GNP) is the total market value of all final goods and services produced by the *citizens* of a country, no matter where they are residing.

B. Prior to 1991 GNP was used to measure U.S. production.

C. GNP and GDP are closely related concepts. GDP is a measure of domestic output, regardless of who produces it (i.e., citizens or foreigners). GNP is a measure of the output produced by the citizens of a country, regardless of where they live.

D. GNP = GDP + Income earned by citizens from their work and investments abroad – Income earned by foreigners from their work and investments within the country.

MEASURING GROSS DOMESTIC PRODUCT (GDP)

GDP may be measured using either the expenditure approach or the resource cost/income approach. Both approaches yield the same results because aggregate expenditures must equal aggregate income.

A. Expenditure approach. The total expenditure approach considers total spending on all final goods and services produced during the year. The expenditure approach is a demand-based concept measured by summing the following expenditure items:

1. Personal consumption represents household purchases for consumption purposes, and represents the single largest component of GDP. Over two-thirds of GDP is accounted for by personal consumption. This category of expenditures includes durable goods, nondurable goods, and services.

2. Gross private investment (expenditures of business). This is an important component of GDP because it provides an indicator of the future productive capacity of the economy. Fixed investment (investment in capital goods) is a key component of future economic growth. GDP includes replacement purchases plus net additions to the stock of capital assets plus investments in inventories (+/–). Inventory investments are the changes in the stock of unsold goods held by a business during the period.

3. Government consumption and gross investment. Purchases of goods and services by federal, state, and local governments are included in GDP. Transfer payments (Social Security, welfare) are excluded.

4. Net exports of goods and services (+/–). Since we only want to measure domestic production, net exports are calculated as total exports (domestically produced goods and services purchased by consumers outside the country) minus total imports (foreign-produced goods and services purchased by domestic consumers).

B. Resource cost/income approach. The resource cost-income approach is a supply-oriented (i.e., production) approach and measures GDP by summing the following components:

1. Employee compensation.

2. Proprietors' income.

3. Rents.

4. Corporate profits.

5. Interest income.

6. Indirect business taxes.

7. Depreciation.

8. Net income of foreigners (the income foreigners earn domestically minus the income that domestic citizens earn abroad).

C. The difference between real and nominal GDP.

1. An important use of GDP is comparing levels of production over time. However, when nominal GDP (GDP measured in terms of current prices) changes from one period to the next, it reflects both changes in production and price changes. Therefore, economists attempt to filter out the impact of price changes by calculating GDP measured in terms of prices from some base year. This measure is called *real GDP*. Changes in real GDP correspond to real or actual changes in production.

2. Since nominal GDP is measured with current prices and real GDP is measured relative to the price level in some base year, we need a price index to indicate the relative price change between periods.

D. The difference between the GDP deflator and the consumer price index.

1. The GDP deflator is a general price index that corresponds to the price change exhibited by a very large market basket—all final goods and services produced. An important point to note is that the contents of the market basket of goods change every year depending on current production. The GDP deflator is useful for measuring economy-wide inflation. The current base year in the United States is 2000 (GDP deflator = 100).

2. The consumer price index (CPI) differs from the GDP deflator in several ways.

    a. A relatively small market basket is used.

    b. The market basket is fixed from year to year.

STUDY MANUAL – BUSINESS ENVIRONMENT & CONCEPTS
CHAPTER 23

    c.   The CPI measures consumer price changes and does not directly measure the price changes of items purchased by businesses and government.

        The net result of all these differences is very small.

- The CPI tends to overstate the inflation rate, because its market basket is fixed and does not consider that consumers will substitute away from goods that have risen dramatically in price.
- However, the CPI is useful for measuring inflation in the consumer goods sector.

E. Calculate real GDP, given nominal GDP and the GDP deflator.

    1. To calculate real GDP from nominal GDP, you need three pieces of information: These values are related as follows:

Example: Calculating Real GDP

Assume an economy's nominal GDP was $2.5 billion in 20X0 and $3.5 billion in 20X4. If the GDP deflator was 100.0 in 20X0 and 112.7 in 20X4, what is the change in real GDP over the period both in dollars and in percentage terms?

Answer

- Nominal GDP 20X0 = $2.5 billion.
- Real GDP 20X4 = $3.5 billion (100.0/112.7) = $3.1 billion. This is the 20X4 GDP in 20X0 dollars.
- Real increase in dollars: $3.1 – 2.5 = $0.6 billion.
- Real increase in percent: [(3.1 – 2.5)/2.5] = 0.24 or 24%.

Although nominal GDP rose by over 40 percent during the period (i.e., [(3.5 – 2.5)/ 2.5 = 0.40]), real GDP rose by only 24.0 percent.

F. The major limitations of GDP.

    1. GDP does not:

        a.   Count nonmarket production—specifically, homemaker services.

        b.   Count the underground economy—illegal activities and tax evasion.

        c.   Measure the value of leisure activities, the standard of living accounted for by a shorter workweek, or changing working conditions.

        d.   Measure the changing quality of goods and services.

        e.   Measure the cost of pollution and damage to the ecology.

Note: GDP is not a measure of the welfare of a society or its people, as it values a dollar spent on education the same as a dollar spent on alcohol. Instead it provides the

Page 588   ©2007 Kaplan CPA Review

information needed to track the performance of the economy. Without this information, policy makers would not be able to adopt corrective economic activities.

ALTERNATIVES TO GDP AND GNP

A. Alternative measures of domestic output and income, including GDP, GNP, national income, personal income, and disposable income

1. GDP is the total market value of all final goods produced within a country, regardless of the nationality of the producer.

2. GNP is the total market value of all final goods produced by the citizens of a country, regardless of where they reside.

3. National income (NI) is the total earnings, both domestic and foreign, of a nation's citizens.

4. Personal income (PI) is the total income received by individuals, including transfer payments such as social security and welfare.

5. Disposable income (DI) is personal income net of personal taxes.

LABOR MARKET INDICATORS

A. Key indicators for the labor market are:

1. The civilian labor force is made up of those individuals who are at least 16 years old and are either currently employed or actively seeking employment. Note that not all people over 16 years of age are included in the labor force.

2. The labor-force participation rate is the number of persons 16 or older who are either employed or actively seeking employment as a percentage of the civilian population 16 or older.

3. The rate of unemployment is the percentage of people in the civilian labor force who are unemployed.

    Unemployment rate = Number of unemployed/Number in the labor force.

4. Unemployed workers include those classified as:

    a. Laid off.

    b. Reentrants into labor force.

    c. New entrants.

    d. Left last job willingly.

STUDY MANUAL – BUSINESS ENVIRONMENT & CONCEPTS
CHAPTER 23

e.   Fired or terminated.

B.   Problems encountered when measuring the unemployment rate include:

1.   Workers waiting recall. Workers who have been laid off but are waiting to be recalled to their old jobs are counted as unemployed.

2.   Discouraged workers. Workers who have become discouraged and have given up looking for employment are not counted as unemployed. This problem accounts for the anomaly that occurs when the economy turns up and the unemployment rate jumps. When once-discouraged workers start looking for jobs, they are then counted as unemployed.

3.   Part-time workers. Workers looking for full-time employment but settling for part-time work are considered employed.

C.   Frictional unemployment results from constant changes in the economy that prevent qualified workers from being matched with existing job openings in a timely manner. There are two causes of frictional unemployment.

1.   The primary cause is imperfect information. Information regarding prospective employees and employers is costly and sometimes hard to find.

2.   A secondary cause is the job search conducted by both employees and employers. Both parties seek the best possible match and will spend time looking for information regarding that match. Both parties will conduct their searches until the costs and benefits of the search are equal.

D.   Structural unemployment is caused by structural changes in the economy that eliminate some jobs while generating job openings for which unemployed workers are not qualified. Structural unemployment differs from frictional unemployment in that workers do not currently have the skills needed to perform the newly created jobs.

E.   Cyclical unemployment is caused by a change in the general level of economic productivity. When the economy is operating at less than full capacity, positive levels of cyclical unemployment will be present. At levels *above* full capacity, negative cyclical unemployment will exist.

F.   Full employment is the economic condition that exists when cyclical unemployment is zero. Note, however, that both structural and frictional unemployment continue to exist even when the economy is at full employment. In other words, there is some level of unemployment that is expected when the economy is at full employment.

G.   The natural rate of unemployment is that rate of unemployment present when the economy is at its full employment rate of production or output. In the recent past, the natural rate of unemployment has risen due to changes in the composition of the labor force, namely, an increase in young workers entering the labor force. The natural rate of unemployment can persist for an indefinite period of time and is typically associated with the economy's maximum long-run rate of output.

Page 590   ©2007 Kaplan CPA Review

H. Generally, movements in the unemployment rate and real GDP occur in opposite directions. If real GDP or real output in the economy is rising, it seems logical that unemployment would be lower because entities need more workers to produce the higher volumes of output. In contrast, when real output is decreasing, the unemployment rate would most likely be rising.

I. The Phillips curve is a graph of the inverse relationship between the rate of inflation and the rate of unemployment (see Figure 1). The major flaw with the Phillips curve is that the model ignores the effects of expectations.

J. There are two conclusions arising from modern analysis of the Phillips curve:

Figure 1: The Phillips Curve (pre-1970s)

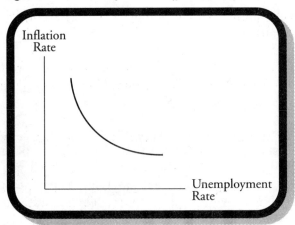

1. Expansionary macroeconomic policies will cause inflation, without permanently reducing unemployment.

2. When inflation exceeds expectations, unemployment falls below its natural level. It is the difference between expected and actual inflation that influences unemployment, not the absolute magnitude of inflation.

INFLATION

A. Inflation is a protracted period of rising prices. As inflation rises, the purchasing power of each dollar held declines. The inflation rate (i) is the rate of change in a given price index over a specified period of time. The annual inflation rate, i, may be calculated as shown in the following example:

Example: Calculating the Inflation Rate

Assume that a price index is 113.5 at the end of 20X3 and 119.9 at the end of 20X4. Calculate the inflation rate during 20X4.

STUDY MANUAL – BUSINESS ENVIRONMENT & CONCEPTS
CHAPTER 23

Answer

$$i = \frac{119.9 - 113.5}{113.5} = 5.6\%$$

B. Throughout the study of economics, you can see the differential effects of a change in a variable that was expected and a change that was not expected. You will find that, in most cases, unanticipated or unexpected shocks to an economy have a much greater impact on real economic outcomes than anticipated changes.

C. Unanticipated inflation is a change in prices that was not expected by rational decision makers. When inflation is unanticipated, the purchasing power of every dollar is unexpectedly eroded. Therefore, any income to be received in the future is now worth less in a present-value sense (i.e., the value today of the expected future income is reduced).

D. Now, think for a moment about potential winners and losers from a dose of unanticipated inflation. The definite losers are people who are currently holding long-term contracts in which they are to receive fixed payments. Fixed-rate mortgages, fixed-payment annuities, and other fixed-rate loans are examples of such contracts. The winners are the individuals or institutions that have made the promise to pay under those same fixed-rate contracts. If you own a home with a fixed-rate mortgage and unexpected inflation hits, you win and the bank loses. This is because you are able to repay the loan in the future with cheaper dollars. The opposite argument is true when prices are falling (deflation).

E. Anticipated inflation is reflected in all financial contracts (loans, mortgages, annuities, etc.). With anticipated changes in inflation, lenders will prefer to write variable-rate contracts, and anyone wishing to obtain a fixed-rate contract will have to pay a higher price (i.e., higher interest rate).

F. Increased risk. Unanticipated inflation may alter the outcome of certain long-term projects (e.g., the purchase of equipment or buying a business). This increases the risk associated with investing and discourages investment.

G. Price distortion. Inflation distorts the information delivered by prices that can lead to inefficient allocations in production and consumption.

H. Reduced output. In response to high or variable inflation, people tend to spend less time being productive and more time protecting themselves from inflation.

I. Demand-pull inflation results from high demand and is attributable to strong employment and increasing incomes. Demand-pull inflation results in the bidding up of prices.

J. Cost-push inflation results when businesses increase prices due to an increase in costs, other than labor costs.

K. Wage-push inflation results when businesses must bid up wages to keep employees (period of low unemployment), and therefore must raise their prices to cover increased wage costs.

L. Stagflation (stagnation and inflation at the same time) results when prices are rising while there is high unemployment. How does this seemingly impossible state of affairs occur? How can people have the income to drive up prices when there is high unemployment? The answer is that they do not.

M. Stagflation results from cost-push inflation, where there is an increase in the price of significant inputs other than labor. Consider the recent increase in the price of oil as a good example. In fact, the term *stagflation* originated during the oil crisis of the 1970s, when the price of petroleum products rose and firms had to absorb the increase and, even though prices rose, incomes of consumers did not rise and demand was sluggish (stagnating).

N. In the short run, there is not much that can be done about stagflation. In the long run, substitutes can be found for the higher-priced goods (hybrid cars, compared to SUVs).

DEFLATION

A. Deflation is the opposite of inflation: a sustained period of falling prices for most goods and services. This may sound like the proverbial "good thing," but read on. Initially, with falling prices, and assuming stable wages, consumers are happy. However, this may lead to consumers delaying purchases, wondering when the next price will fall. Also, businesses may face lower profits due to decreasing prices and may need to reduce payrolls. Now the consumer is not so happy. Further, declining prices may lead to lower interest rates, which leads to lower returns on investments.

B. The principal cause of deflation is too much capacity relative to demand. In general, this causes businesses to reduce capacity, including people. Generally, economists and businesspeople are not in favor of deflation.

MARKET INFLUENCES ON BUSINESS STRATEGIES

A. The demand for a resource indicates how much of the resource firms will employ at each possible price. Other things equal, there is a negative relationship between price and quantity demanded.

B. As the price of the resource rises, firms substitute for the resource and use other resources whose prices have not increased.

C. Along with substituting for higher-priced resources, firms will tend to cut back overall output and reduce the quantity demanded of higher-priced resources. This latter effect occurs because the increase in the cost of only one resource will make the total cost of production higher at each level of production.

STUDY MANUAL – BUSINESS ENVIRONMENT & CONCEPTS
CHAPTER 23

D. As the price of a resource rises, firms pass along the increased cost to consumers in the form of higher final good prices. This lowers the quantity demanded for the final good or service, and the firm uses less of all resources.

THE FACTORS THAT INFLUENCE THE SUPPLY OF AND DEMAND FOR RESOURCES IN THE SHORT RUN AND LONG RUN

A. Influence on elasticity of demand.

1. In the short run, the elasticity of demand for the final good and the degree to which a resource has substitutes in production determine the demand for a resource. If there are no good substitutes for the resource in production and/or the demand for the final good is inelastic, the demand for the resource will tend to be inelastic.

2. In the long run, firms will have time to find more substitutes in production, and the elasticity of demand for final goods will be more elastic as well. Therefore, the demand for a resource is more elastic in the long run than it is in the short run. This is the standard argument that everything is variable in the long run.

3. Other things held constant, the quantity supplied of a resource increases with an increase in its price. The supply curve for a specific resource will slope upward to the right. For example, if the working conditions in firms stay the same and firms raise wages, employees will supply more labor. This is because workers will shift away from other activities (e.g., leisure) to offer more labor. If wages increase but working conditions decrease, the quantity supplied may not increase. A change in working conditions amounts to a shift of the supply curve. The same analysis applies to other resources.

B. Influence on elasticity of supply.

1. In the short run, the elasticity of supply is determined by resource mobility, which is defined as how easily the resource can be transferred from one use to another.

   a. If a resource has few other uses (e.g., a machine for a specific task), it has low resource mobility and a low elasticity of supply.

   b. If the resource has many alternative uses (e.g., unskilled labor), its supply will be more elastic.

   Caution: The term *resource mobility* does not necessarily apply to how easily the resource can move physically. Land is not mobile, but it can have high resource mobility if it can easily be converted from, for example, corn to wheat production or even to a parking lot. A plot of land with an existing 40-story building is not resource-mobile because it would be difficult and costly to relocate the building and apply the land to an alternative use.

Page 594 ©2007 Kaplan CPA Review

2. In the long run, resource mobility increases, and so does the elasticity of supply for a given resource. In the market for skilled labor, workers can invest in human capital to increase the supply of specific types of laborers such as doctors, accountants, or mechanics. Machines and land can be modified for new uses. Therefore, over longer periods of time, the quantity supplied of a resource is much more responsive to changes in price.

DETERMINATION OF PRICES FOR RESOURCES IN A MARKET ECONOMY

A. Changing resource prices affect the decisions of producers about which input mix to use in production to minimize costs and the decisions of those providing the resources. Thus, resource prices are important in determining what will be produced and how it will be produced. The prices provide important signals about the values of various resources so that the choice of production methods and the choice of what to produce both reflect the relative scarcity of an economy's resources.

B. An increase in the price of labor will do both of the following:

1. Cause producers to use less labor and substitute more machinery (capital).

2. Cause suppliers/workers to provide more labor (consume less leisure).

   a. Both of these changes will increase the efficiency of the economy. If consumer tastes change so that a good becomes more valuable, the demand for the resources necessary to produce the good will increase, putting upward pressure on the price of those resources. In response to this price increase, other users of these resources will reduce their use of them and substitute other resources in their production processes.

   b. The prices of goods that are produced with these resources will rise, and consumers will adjust their consumption to reflect these price changes. Again, the response to changing resource prices will improve economic efficiency through its effect on both production and consumption decisions.

HOW CHANGING RESOURCE PRICES INFLUENCE RESOURCE UTILIZATION AND THE PERFORMANCE OF THE ECONOMIC SYSTEM

A. Clearly, prices play a coordinating function in the markets for resources. Resource prices signal how much of each resource should be employed in a given end product. Prices of resources ultimately measure the value that consumers of final goods and services place on the outputs produced by resources.

1. If consumers begin to value a final product more, the price of that product will rise, the marginal revenue of each resource used to produce that product will rise, and firms will employ more of those resources. To employ those resources, firms must lure them away from alternative uses. This raises the market price of resources used in producing the product. The prices of other resources will probably go up as well unless the tastes of consumers fall for some other final products.

2. Changes in consumer tastes and preferences occur frequently. When market prices change for final goods and services, this changes the price of resources.

3. Changing market prices divert resources from less-profitable uses to more profitable uses. This process will also allow resources to flow to their highest-valued social uses. Firms will tend to produce the goods most desired by consumers in the most efficient manner, and this enhances the performance of the economic system.

B. The two most popular aggregate measures of macroeconomic activity are gross national product (GNP) and gross domestic product (GDP).

1. GNP is the value of goods and services (or total income) produced by resources belonging to a nation and its citizens (irrespective of where the citizens reside).

2. GDP is the value of products produced domestically, irrespective of who owns the resources.

3. GDP and GNP are highly correlated. Since GNP measures *total income* and GDP measures *production*, GNP is more useful in predicting sales of consumption goods, and GDP is more useful in predicting sales of intermediate production goods.

C. The Bureau of Economic Analysis of the U.S. Department of Commerce publishes the index of 11 leading indicators every month. Leading indicators change before the level of economic activity changes, so they are very useful for prediction.

1. This index leads the level of economic activity by only six months on average, which makes it useful for forecasting economic activity only in the very short run.

2. A single change in the index is not as important as three or four consecutive changes in the same direction, which requires a substantial time lapse before you can detect or conclude a change in the direction of the economy. This behavior reduces the usefulness of the index in predicting intermediate or longer-term economic activity.

D. The extent to which macroeconomic conditions affect industry sales varies from one industry to another.

1. Some industry sales are very highly correlated with macroeconomic conditions. Examples include autos, airlines, and other luxury consumption goods that exhibit a high elasticity of demand. Estimating sales for such industries is relatively straightforward because you can use published projections of GDP growth rates as the inputs to a regression equation to obtain estimated industry sales.

2. Further, note that macroeconomic conditions affect not only the level of industry sales but also the composition of sales.

E. Macroeconomic conditions do not affect all industries in the same manner.

STUDY MANUAL – BUSINESS ENVIRONMENT & CONCEPTS
CHAPTER 23

1. Consumer staples have inelastic demand, so they are not affected as much by the peaks and troughs of the business cycle.

2. Interest-sensitive stocks typically lead the business cycle and are quite sensitive to the stages of the business cycle. These stocks are traditionally banks, utilities, and other dividend-producing instruments.

3. Capital goods companies perform well during the recovery phase, and luxury goods companies perform best during boom times in the economic cycle.

F. Macroconditions also affect the composition of industry sales and the market share of a firm within an industry. For example, during economic downturns, producers of low-cost products increase their market share at the expense of high-cost producers. This happens because consumers switch from high-cost, high-quality brands to low-cost, low-quality brands. The reverse is true during economic upturns.

G. Macroeconomic conditions can be predicted well only in the short run (six months to two years at best), thus reducing their usefulness for predicting long-run industry sales. For long-run projections, assume that in the long term, macroeconomic variables will approach their long-term averages. Predicting industry sales in the long run, therefore, is more a function of industry fundamentals than of macroeconomic conditions.

ANALYSIS IN TERMS OF SUPPLY AND DEMAND, THE MARKETS FOR LABOR, LOANABLE FUNDS, AND FOREIGN EXCHANGE

A. The labor market. Resource markets coordinate the supply and demand for resources like raw materials and labor services. We focus on the labor market, where people offer their labor for a price per time period, the wage rate. Just as it is in the markets for final goods and services, the quantity demanded for labor is inversely related to the wage rate. When the wage rate rises, firms will lower the quantity demanded as they substitute more nonhuman resources for labor and cut back production. The supply curve of labor is upward-sloping, which reflects the fact that workers will reduce leisure time and work more if the wage increases. Just as there are many markets for goods and services, there are many labor markets: one for each skill, experience, and occupational category.

B. The loanable funds market. As is the case for all resources, the market for labor is affected by the market for the final good or service that uses it in production.

1. An increase in the demand for the final good or service will increase the price for it and, thus, increase the demand for the labor used to produce the good or service. Likewise, a change in the labor market can increase or decrease the supply of a final good or service.

2. Demands for higher wages will eventually be passed along as higher prices in the final good or service. If businesses anticipate a recession, for example, they may reduce their demand for loanable funds. This will lead to a fall in the interest rate and the number of loans. As another example, if a given population's average age

©2007 Kaplan CPA Review

Page 597

STUDY MANUAL – BUSINESS ENVIRONMENT & CONCEPTS
CHAPTER 23

is increasing, and they begin to save more for retirement, the supply of funds will increase. This will have a negative effect on interest rates, and the number of loans will increase.

C. The foreign exchange market. A foreign exchange market is where the currency of country X is traded for the currency of country Y. The higher the exchange rate for a foreign currency, say currency X, the lower the quantity demanded of currency X. When there is a high exchange rate, foreigners will not want to purchase as many of the goods priced in currency X, because they will be relatively more expensive.

1. At higher exchange rates, holders of currency X will increase the quantity they supply. If the exchange rate is high, holders of currency X find that the goods, services, and investments priced in currency Y are relatively cheaper. The holders of currency X will exchange it to obtain the currency of country Y to purchase the relatively cheaper goods and services.

2. An increase in the preference for goods from country Y will increase the exchange rate for that country's currency. If investment opportunities are more attractive in country Y, that will increase the exchange rate for that country's currency, too.

THE IMPACT OF EXTERNAL FACTORS ON INDUSTRIES

A. Every industry is subject to a variety of outside forces that can have a fundamental impact on the industry's fortunes (or even survival). Five such outside forces are:

1. Technology. For industries in the pioneer phase attempting to introduce new technologies, the concern is whether or not the innovation will be successful. For mature industries, the concern is whether or not competition from new technologies will supplant the old technology. In the latter case, a company is typically faced with a choice of copying or acquiring the competition to survive.

2. Government. Government, through regulations, taxes, and subsidies, has its hands in almost every phase of industry. Examples of governmental involvement include litigation against the tobacco companies, environmental mandates, and export subsidies.

3. Social changes. Most social changes are either lifestyle or fashion changes. Fashion changes tend to be more short-term in nature and, as a result, are relatively unpredictable. Lifestyle changes generally occur over a longer-term horizon, which makes them easier to incorporate into the analysis. One example of lifestyle change is the trend toward two-income families. The result of this change has been an increase in demand for child day care.

4. Demography. Demography is concerned with the population's vital statistics. One relevant trend in these statistics is the aging of the population in the United States and other developed economies. Industries that provide services to older individuals (e.g., health care and financial services) will tend to prosper as the population ages.

Page 598   ©2007 Kaplan CPA Review

STUDY MANUAL – BUSINESS ENVIRONMENT & CONCEPTS
CHAPTER 23

5. Foreign influences. Virtually all industries are exposed to foreign influences. For example, most U.S. firms use oil even though they do not import or export it. Since more than 50 percent of oil consumed in the United States is imported, these firms are exposed to changes in oil prices. Moreover, a foreign competitor with a comparative advantage can decimate an entire industry, while increasing prosperity in foreign countries creates new demand for output from U.S. industries.

TOTAL REVENUE, TOTAL EXPENDITURES, AND PRICE ELASTICITY OF DEMAND

A. An important application of price elasticity is to estimate how total consumer expenditures on a product change when the price changes. There are three ways to do this:

1. Consider an individual's elasticity of demand.

2. Consider the combined elasticity of demand for all consumers of the product.

3. Consider the elasticity of demand for an individual business that produces the product.

   In the two following points, we consider how total consumer expenditures change to affect total revenue.

B. Total expenditures and price elasticity of demand.

1. When demand is inelastic, the percentage change in unit sales is less than the percentage change in price. Therefore, an increase in price leads to an increase in total expenditure on the good. Certain medicines (e.g., insulin) or alcohol are examples of this.

2. When demand is elastic, quantity demanded is more responsive to a change in price. Therefore, an increase in price leads to a decrease in total expenditure on the good. A particular brand of cornflakes or toothpaste would be an example of this.

3. With unitary price elasticity (i.e., the change in price equals the change in quantity demanded at all price levels), total expenditures remain unchanged when unit price changes.

C. Total revenue and price elasticity of demand. Instead of looking at total market demand, we can consider how price affects the total revenue for an individual firm. First, demand for an individual firm is more elastic than the demand for the entire market.

1. When a firm's demand curve is inelastic, total revenue rises when the firm increases the price. Conversely, total revenue declines when the firm decreases the price.

©2007 Kaplan CPA Review

Page 599

STUDY MANUAL – BUSINESS ENVIRONMENT & CONCEPTS
CHAPTER 23

2. When price is elastic, total revenue falls when the firm increases the price, and total revenue rises when the firm decreases the price. With unitary elasticity, total revenue is unaffected by a price change. Recall that price elasticity changes as we move up and down the firm's demand curve.

3. A firm can maximize its revenue where demand is of unitary elasticity. Because firms are more interested in enhancing profits than revenue, it is important to understand that for many firms (particularly those with substantial fixed costs), profits will be maximized at or near the same point where revenue is maximized.

THE FACTORS THAT INFLUENCE PRICE AND INCOME ELASTICITY OF DEMAND

Note that the slope is constant but elasticity is changing.

A. Price elasticity of demand is determined by two factors:

1. The availability of substitutes is the most important determinant of the price elasticity of demand. If good substitutes are available, a price increase in one product will induce consumers to switch to a substitute good. As such, elasticity of demand is a result of the availability of good substitutes.

2. The relative amount of budget spent on a product is a second important determinant of the price elasticity of demand. When a relatively small portion of your budget is spent on a particular good, that good will tend to be price inelastic.

B. An inferior good has negative income elasticity. As income increases (decreases), quantity demanded decreases (increases). Inferior goods include such things as bus travel and margarine. The opposite type of good, a normal good, has positive income elasticity meaning that, as income increases (decreases), demand for the good increases (decreases). Normal goods include things like bread and tobacco.

C. Generally, normal goods that have low-income elasticities (absolute values between 0 and 1) are considered necessities. Normal goods with high-income elasticities (absolute values greater than 1) are generally considered luxury goods.

Example: Income elasticity

Suppose that your income has risen by $10,000 from a base rate of $50,000. During this period, your demand for bread has increased from 100 loaves per year to 110 loaves per year. Given this information, determine whether or not bread is a necessity or a luxury good.

Answer

The percentage change in income is 18.2% = ($60,000 – $50,000)/$55,000, while the percentage change in the quantity of bread demanded is 9.5% = (110 – 100)/105. Hence, the income elasticity of bread is 0.52 = 9.5/18.2. Since its income elasticity of demand is less than 1.0, bread is a necessity.

CONSUMER INDIFFERENCE CURVES

A. Indifference curves map out the consumer's preferences between two choices. For example, panel (a) of Figure 2 shows the combinations of apples and oranges that have equal preference (equal utility) for an individual. Since these combinations show equal preference levels, the consumer is said to be *indifferent* between any of the points along the curve. This means that the consumer will be indifferent between (would derive the same utility from) a basket containing six apples and two oranges or a basket having four apples and three oranges.

B. To formalize the concept of indifference curves, let us state that an indifference curve is a convex-shaped curve, where all points on the curve represent combinations of goods that are equally preferred by (produce the same utility for) the individual. This general concept is illustrated in panel (b) of Figure 2, where each set of points represents equal preferences between goods A and B.

Figure 2: Consumer Indifference Curves

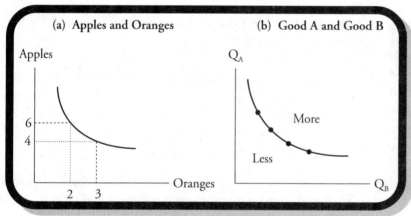

C. The following are the general characteristics of indifference curves:

1. More is preferred to less. Figure 3 illustrates, using indifference curves, that more is preferred to less. As indicated, higher indifference curves represent greater utility than lower curves. That is, investors receive more utility from a combination of good A and good B on indifference curve I_3 than a combination on I_1.

Figure 3: Set of Consumer Indifference Curves

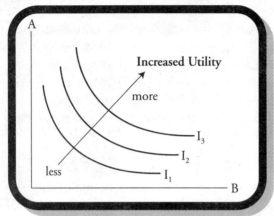

2. Substitutable goods. Since goods may be substituted, indifference curves slope downward to the right.

3. Diminishing utility. The utility of a good declines the more it is consumed. Therefore, indifference curves are convex.

4. Infinite and nonintersecting. There are an infinite number of indifference curves and they do not intersect.

CONSUMPTION-OPPORTUNITY CONSTRAINT AND THE BUDGET CONSTRAINT AS THEY RELATE TO INDIFFERENCE CURVE ANALYSIS

A. Budget constraints represent all combinations of goods that consumers can purchase within a given budget. These constraints separate the consumption opportunities that can be obtained from those that cannot be obtained. As shown in Figure 4, the optimal level of consumer satisfaction will be the tangency point between the budget constraint line and the highest obtainable indifference curve.

Figure 4: Utility Maximizing with a Budget Constraint

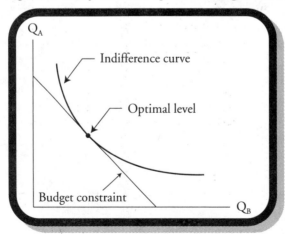

B. Consumption-opportunity constraint. This analysis applies both in the cases of barter and an economy with money. In the money economy, the budget-constraint line applies. In a barter economy, the *consumption-opportunity constraint* line applies. This line indicates different bundles of goods that can be acquired (three fish and four loaves of bread or six fish and two loaves of bread, etc.). In either case, it is the relative price of each good that determines the slope of the line and, thus, the optimal level of consumption of each good or bundle of goods.

THE DIFFERENCE BETWEEN THE INCOME EFFECT AND THE SUBSTITUTION EFFECT

A. If the price of one good changes, the budget constraint changes and a consumer's optimal combination of X and Y will change as well. We illustrate this for an increase in the price of X in Figure 5. Since fewer units of X can now be purchased at the higher price, the budget constraint becomes steeper (shifts from B_1 to B_2). The new optimal consumption bundle is at point c. In this example, the consumer chooses a fairly large decrease in consumption of X (X_1 to X_2) and a small increase in the consumption of Y (Y_1 to Y_2).

B. The total decrease in the consumption of good X in response to the price increase can be separated (theoretically) into two separate effects:

   1. A substitution effect, because the relative price (slope of the budget constraint) has changed

   2. An income effect, because less consumption is possible with the same income when the price of X rises.

Figure 5: Effect on Optimal Consumption of an Increase in the Price of X

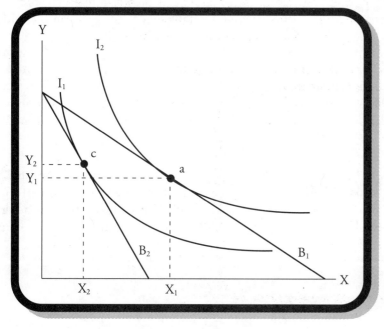

STUDY MANUAL – BUSINESS ENVIRONMENT & CONCEPTS
CHAPTER 23

C. The *substitution effect* is always negative for a price increase; a consumer will choose less X and more Y in order to maximize utility. You can think of the substitution effect as the change in consumption that would result if the consumer faced the new prices but received just enough additional income so that his or her optimal consumption bundle was still on the same indifference curve. This is illustrated in Figure 6 by the budget constraint labeled B¢. B¢ is drawn to be tangent to indifference curve I_2 but to have a slope that reflects the new relative prices (it is parallel to B_2). The substitution effect of an increase in the price of X is shown as a reduction in the consumption of X from X_1 to X_2, since the optimal consumption bundle along B¢ is point *b*.

Figure 6: Income and Substitution Effect of an Increase in the Price of X

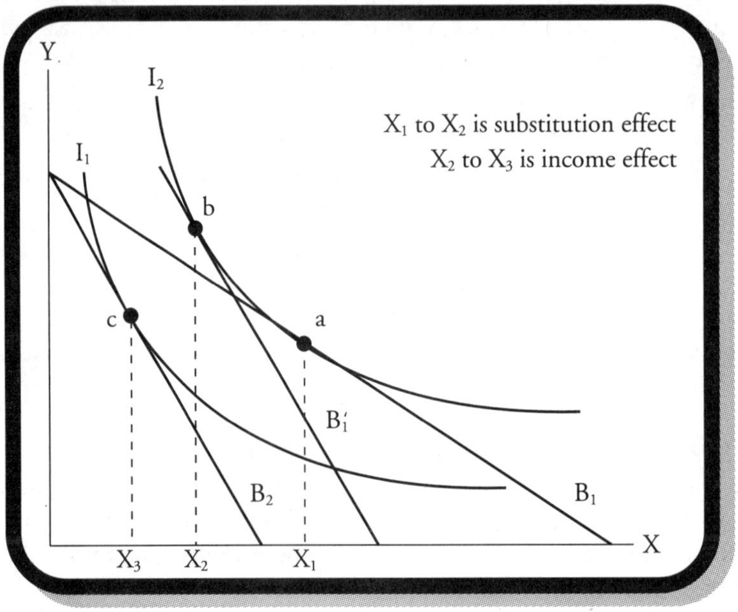

D. The *income effect* can be positive or negative. Recall that the consumption of a normal good decreases when income is reduced, but for an inferior good, consumption increases when income falls. In Figure 6, the good is a normal good; the effect of a reduction in income is a reduction in the amount of X consumed. The effect on the consumption of X of a decrease in income is the further decrease in consumption of X from X_2 to X_3.

E. To summarize, when the price of X rises, the budget constraint shifts and optimal consumption (Figure 6 changes from bundle a to bundle c. The substitution effect of the increase in the price of X is shown by the tangent point to a hypothetical budget line that has the new slope but is tangent to "old" indifference curve, I2. The change in the quantity of X between bundle b and bundle c is the income effect and is illustrated by a parallel shift of the budget constraint to the left from B¢ to B_2.

Page 604　　　　©2007 Kaplan CPA Review

STUDY MANUAL – BUSINESS ENVIRONMENT & CONCEPTS
CHAPTER 23

COSTS

The Difference between (A) Explicit Costs and Implicit Costs, (B) Economic Profit and Accounting Profit, and (C) the Short Run and the Long Run in Production

A. Demand reflects the preferences of consumers and how those preferences influence the allocation of final goods. Similarly, the costs of production influence the use of resources to produce those goods and reflect the many possible uses of those resources. Three types of cost are relevant to the allocation of resources to the production of final goods.

  1. Explicit costs are measurable operating expenses.

  2. Implicit costs are the returns the employed resource would have earned in its next best use. They include the opportunity cost of a firm's equity and owner-provided services.

  3. Total costs are the sum of both the explicit and implicit costs for all the resources used by the firm.

B. Economic profit considers both explicit and implicit costs. Accounting profit ignores implicit costs, such as the opportunity cost of equity capital. For this reason, accounting profits are generally higher than economic profits. When the firm's revenues are just equal to its total costs (explicit and implicit, including the normal rate of return), economic profits are zero.

C. In the short run, it is difficult to alter production methods. The short run is defined as that time period over which the size of plant and equipment cannot be changed. The length of the short run varies from industry to industry. The long run is the period of time necessary for the firm to change its production methods and resource uses. In the long run, all resources (inputs) are variable.

OPPORTUNITY COSTS, SUNK COSTS, FIXED COSTS, VARIABLE COSTS, MARGINAL COSTS, AND AVERAGE COSTS

A. Opportunity cost is the cost of forgoing the next best alternative investment with the resources being used. The opportunity cost of equity capital is the implied rate of return that investors require in order to encourage them to continue to supply the firm with capital. It is the rate of return that could be earned if the capital were put to the next best use.

B. Sunk costs are those costs already incurred and are not considered in current decisions.

C. Fixed costs remain unchanged in the short run. They are related to the passage of time, not the level of production. The expense on a current building lease is a fixed cost.

©2007 Kaplan CPA Review
Page 605

STUDY MANUAL – BUSINESS ENVIRONMENT & CONCEPTS
CHAPTER 23

D. Average fixed costs are fixed costs divided by output. Average fixed costs decline as output increases.

E. Variable costs (e.g., wages and raw materials) are incurred when the firm produces output. They are related to the level of production, not the passage of time.

F. Average variable cost equals the total variable cost divided by output.

G. Marginal cost is the cost of producing one additional unit of output.

H. Average total cost equals the total costs (fixed and variable) divided by the number of units produced.

THE DIFFERENCE BETWEEN ECONOMIC COSTS AND ACCOUNTING COSTS

A. Economic costs include both explicit and implicit costs.

B. Accounting costs usually include only explicit costs. They often do not include implicit costs, such as the labor of the owners of a firm or the cost of equity capital. Therefore, accounting costs are usually less than economic costs.

THE LAW OF DIMINISHING RETURNS AND ITS IMPACT ON A COMPANY'S COSTS

A. The law of diminishing returns states that as more and more resources (e.g., labor) are devoted to a production process holding the quantity of other inputs constant, the output increases, but at a decreasing rate. For example, if an acre of corn needs to be picked, the addition of a second and third worker is highly productive. But if you already have 300 workers in the field, the productive capacity of the 301st worker is not near that of the second worker.

B. Concepts related to the law of diminishing returns are as follows:

1. Total product is the total output of goods associated with a specific rate of resource input. As resource input increases, total product increases.

2. Marginal product is the increase in total output associated with an additional unit of input.

3. Average product equals the total output (product) divided by the units of the variable input required to produce that level output.

   Note: The marginal product of an input decreases at higher input levels because all other inputs are held constant.

Page **606** ©2007 Kaplan CPA Review

THE SHAPES OF THE SHORT-RUN MARGINAL COST, AVERAGE VARIABLE COST, AVERAGE FIXED COST, AND AVERAGE TOTAL COST CURVES

A. The concept of diminishing marginal returns and the short-run average/marginal cost structures are illustrated in Figure 7.

Figure 7: Cost Curves

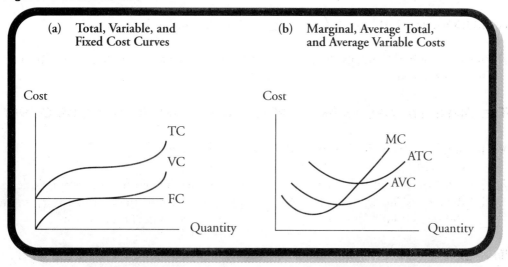

Panel (a) in Figure 7 shows that total cost (TC) is equal to variable cost (VC) plus fixed costs (FC). Here it is illustrated that as production increases, VC and TC increase at a decreasing rate, then flatten out, then increase at an increasing rate (TC and VC curves arch upward). This is where diminishing returns take effect.

Panel (b) of Figure 7 illustrates the unit cost structure. Here it can be seen that when marginal costs (MC) are below both average variable costs (AVC) and average total costs (ATC), the average falls. When the MC, the cost of producing the next unit, moves above the average cost line (AVC or ATC), the average will start to rise. Thus, MC = AVC when AVC is at its minimum. The same holds for ATC.

You should remember that diminishing marginal returns are only met after a point. Increasing marginal returns will exist at low levels of output corresponding to the downward sloping portion of the MC curve. Remember, the short run for the firm's cost curve is that period over which the quantities of inputs are fixed.

THE FACTORS THAT CAUSE COST CURVES TO SHIFT

A. Cost curves shift for the following reasons:

1. Changes in resource prices.

2. Changes in taxes paid.

3. Changes in regulations that increase costs (e.g., environmental regulations, safety regulations, etc.).

STUDY MANUAL – BUSINESS ENVIRONMENT & CONCEPTS
CHAPTER 23

    4.   Improvements in technology that lower production costs.

B.   Each of these factors can change the marginal cost of a unit of output. Lower input prices, lower taxes, reduced regulatory costs, and better technology will all lower the marginal cost for the firm. This will, in turn, lower the AVC and ATC.

STUDY MANUAL – BUSINESS ENVIRONMENT & CONCEPTS
CHAPTER 23

QUESTIONS: SENSITIVITY OF THE FIRM TO THE MACROECONOMY

1. When the expenditure approach is used to measure GDP, the major components are:
   A. consumption, investment, indirect business taxes, and depreciation.
   B. consumption, investment, government purchases, and net exports.
   C. employee compensation, rents, interest, corporate profits, and net exports.
   D. employee compensation, corporate profits, depreciation, and indirect business taxes.

2. Which one of the following most accurately describes the normal sequence of a business cycle?
   A. Expansion, contraction, recession, boom.
   B. Contraction, recession, expansion, boom.
   C. Boom, contraction, expansion, recession.
   D. Recession, contraction, expansion, boom.

3. A recession is defined as a decline in real gross domestic product (GDP) over:
   A. one year.
   B. two years.
   C. six months.
   D. two quarters.

4. If the consumer price index (CPI) was 135 this year and it was 122 the year before, the rate of inflation was:
   A. 9.6 percent.
   B. 10.7 percent.
   C. 13.0 percent.
   D. 9.04 percent.

5. In order to measure the contribution of many different types of goods and services to economic output, gross domestic product (GDP) uses:
   A. market prices.
   B. a combination of weights and measures.
   C. only the cost of production of goods and services.
   D. a combination of price indexes and costs of production of goods and services.

6. During the recession phase of a business cycle:
   A. the purchasing power of money is likely to decline rapidly.
   B. the natural rate of unemployment will increase dramatically.
   C. potential national income will exceed actual national income.
   D. actual national income will exceed potential national income.

7. The trough of a business cycle is generally characterized by:
   A. shortages of essential raw materials and rising costs.
   B. increasing purchasing power and increasing capital investments.
   C. rising costs and an unwillingness to risk new investments.
   D. unused productive capacity and an unwillingness to risk new investments.

©2007 Kaplan CPA Review

Page 609

STUDY MANUAL – BUSINESS ENVIRONMENT & CONCEPTS
CHAPTER 23

8. Recurring upswings and downswings in an economy's real Gross Domestic Product over time are called:
   A. recessions.
   B. business cycles.
   C. output yo-yos.
   D. total product oscillations.

9. In the United States, business cycles have occurred against a backdrop of a long-run trend of:
   A. declining unemployment.
   B. stagnant productivity growth.
   C. rising real Gross Domestic Product.
   D. rising inflation.

10. The immediate determinant of the volume of output and employment is the:
    A. composition of consumer spending.
    B. ratio of public goods to private goods production.
    C. level of total spending.
    D. size of the labor force.

11. In which of the following industries or sectors of the economy is output likely to be most strongly impacted by the business cycle?
    A. military goods.
    B. producer's durables (machinery or equipment).
    C. textile products (clothing).
    D. agricultural commodities (wheat or corn).

12. During a prolonged recession, we would expect output to fall the most in:
    A. the health care industry.
    B. the clothing industry.
    C. agriculture.
    D. the construction industry.

13. The phase of the business cycle in which real Gross Domestic Product declines is called:
    A. the peak.
    B. a recovery.
    C. a recession.
    D. the trough.

14. The phase of the business cycle in which real Gross Domestic Product is at a minimum is called:
    A. the peak.
    B. a recession.
    C. the trough.
    D. a recovery.

Page 610   ©2007 Kaplan CPA Review

15. Market economies have been characterized by:
    A. occasional instability of employment and price levels.
    B. uninterrupted economic growth.
    C. persistent full employment
    D. declining populations.

16. The production of durable goods varies more than the production of nondurable goods because:
    A. durable purchases are non-postponable.
    B. durable purchases are postponable.
    C. the producers of nondurables have monopoly power.
    D. Producers of durables are highly competitive.

17. A recession is a period in which:
    A. cost-push inflation is present.
    B. potential domestic output falls.
    C. demand-pull inflation is present.
    D. real domestic output falls.

18. The natural rate of unemployment is:
    A. higher than the full-employment rate of unemployment.
    B. lower than the full-employment rate of unemployment.
    C. that rate of unemployment occurring when the economy is operating at its full potential.
    D. found by dividing total unemployment by the size of the labor force.

19. If the unemployment rate is 9 percent and the natural rate of unemployment is 5 percent, then the:
    A. frictional unemployment rate is 5 percent.
    B. cyclical unemployment rate and the frictional unemployment rate together are 5 percent.
    C. cyclical unemployment rate is 4 percent.
    D. natural rate of unemployment will eventually increase.

20. The natural rate of unemployment:
    A. is fixed over time.
    B. is found by adding the cyclical and structural unemployment rates.
    C. may change from one decade to another.
    D. cannot be changed through public policy.

21. The natural rate of unemployment is the:
    A. unemployment rate experienced at the depth of a depression.
    B. full-employment unemployment rate.
    C. unemployment rate experienced by the least-skilled workers in the economy.
    D. unemployment rate experienced by the most-skilled workers in the economy.

STUDY MANUAL – BUSINESS ENVIRONMENT & CONCEPTS
CHAPTER 23

22. Cyclical unemployment results from:
    A. deficiency of aggregate spending.
    B. the decreasing relative importance of goods and the increasing relative importance of services in the economy.
    C. the everyday dynamics of a free labor market.
    D. technological change.

23. Structural unemployment:
    A. is also know as frictional unemployment.
    B. is the main component of cyclical unemployment.
    C. is said to occur when people are waiting to be called back to previous jobs.
    D. may involve a locational mismatch between unemployed workers and job openings.

24. The type of unemployment associated with a recession is called:
    A. frictional unemployment.
    B. structural unemployment.
    C. cyclical unemployment.
    D. seasonal unemployment.

25. Which of the following constitute the unemployment occurring at the natural rate of unemployment?
    A. frictional and cyclical unemployment.
    B. structural and frictional unemployment.
    C. cyclical and structural unemployment.
    D. frictional, structural, and cyclical unemployment.

26. All the following are characteristic of the recessionary stage of the business cycle **EXCEPT:**
    A. It eventually leads to a trough.
    B. Unemployment levels rise.
    C. Prices fall more rapidly than economic activity falls.
    D. Output levels decline.

27. If John's expectations of sustained economic growth are correct, which of the following correctly pairs an investment vehicle with an economic scenario, likely to exist under the growth assumption, that would make the investment attractive?
    A. Short-term debt instruments: sustained economic growth will cause a substantial increase in interest rates.
    B. Real estate: sustained economic growth will induce high inflation.
    C. Common stock: sustained economic growth will entail a neutral fiscal and monetary policy, but firms with prospects for consistent earnings growth will prosper.
    D. Cyclical common stocks: sustained economic growth will cause interest rates to fall, thus spurring demand.

28. Which of the following combinations of investments would be best for the investor in an environment of high inflation?

 I. Common stock in companies with large holdings of oil, precious metals, or land.
 II. Collectibles.
 III. Short-term liquid assets like U.S. Treasury bills and money market funds.
 IV. Common stock of public utility companies.

 A. I and II only.
 B. III and IV only.
 C. I, II, and III only.
 D. II, III, and IV only.

29. Which of the following combinations of investments would be best when the economy is undergoing deflation?

 I. Long-term bonds rated AA or higher.
 II. Long-term bonds raced CC or lower.
 III. Common stocks of firms with sizeable financial leverage.
 IV. Short-term U.S. Treasury bills.

 A. II and III only.
 B. I and IV only.
 C. I, II, and IV only.
 D. I, III, and IV only.

30. David believes that we are moving into a period of deflation. If David's expectations concerning deflation are correct, which of the following correctly pairs an investment vehicle with an appropriate logic?
 A. Savings and loan common stocks: deflation will cause savings and loans to lend at higher rates.
 B. Precious metals: deflation will cause these assets to increase in value.
 C. Long-term, high-quality bonds: deflation will cause interest rates to decrease.
 D. Short-term bonds: deflation will cause short-term interest rates to increase.

31. Tracy is concerned that inflation will increase soon. Given an inflationary economic environment, which one of the following investment vehicles would be most appropriate for Tracy to purchase?
 A. Automotive stocks: inflation will cause cyclical stocks to increase in value.
 B. Precious metals: inflation will cause these assets to increase in value.
 C. Long-term bonds: inflation will cause interest rates to increase.
 D. Short-term bonds: inflation will cause interest rates to decrease.

32. If an investor held long-term U.S. Treasury bonds currently, the investor would most likely sell them and hold money if he or she believed that interest rates will:
 A. Rise far above present levels.
 B. Not change from present levels.
 C. Fluctuate up and down within a narrow range.
 D. Fall below present levels.

STUDY MANUAL – BUSINESS ENVIRONMENT & CONCEPTS
CHAPTER 23

ANSWERS: SENSITIVITY OF THE FIRM TO THE MACROECONOMY

1. **B** Consumption, the largest part of GDP, includes purchases made by households, such as durable goods, nondurable goods, and services.

   Investments are important because they are an indicator of the economy's future productive capacity.

   Government purchases include federal, state, and local expenditures, not including payments to Social Security and welfare.

   Net exports of goods and services must be domestically produced goods and services purchased by consumers outside the country.

2. **B** The business cycle has four phases that normally occur in sequence: (1) contraction, (2) recession, (3) expansion, and (4) peak or boom.

3. **D** A recession is defined as a period during which real GDP declines for two or more successive quarters.

4. **B** $(135 – 122)/122 = 10.7\%$. The increase in the price index was 13 $(135 – 122)$. $13/122 = 10.7\%$.

   Another way to calculate this is $135/122 = 1.107$. Subtract one, to get 10.7%.

   Remember 122 means the price level has increased 22 percent since the base year of the price index, and, likewise, prices have risen 35 percent since the base year. The base year selected for comparison is always set to 100.

5. **A** The expenditure approach to measuring GDP uses market prices to calculate total expenditures on all final goods and services produced during the year.

6. **C** Productive capacity would support a higher national income than the actual income during a recession phase. Answer A is not correct because in a recession phase there is not likely to be inflation and it is inflation that causes the purchasing power of money to decline. Answer B is not correct because the natural rate of unemployment tends not to change. It represents the sum of the frictionally and the structurally unemployed. Answer D is not correct because potential national income is related to productive capacity. During a recession the actual production (GDP) is less than the productive capacity.

7. **D** At the trough, there is considerable unused capacity. However, because a trough is not recognized until the expansion is clearly under way, investments are postponed until it is clear the expansion is under way. Answer A is not correct because there are unlikely to be shortages of essential raw materials when production is at a reduced level. Likewise, in a trough, inflationary pressures are unlikely. Answer B is not correct because increased investment is not likely until it is clear that an expansion phase is under way. When the economy is in a trough, it is not clear how long it will remain that way. Answer C is not correct because rising costs are not usually present until the economy is well into the expansion phase as actual production approaches capacity and incomes increase as a result of reduced unemployment.

8. **B**   Business cycles are measured by changes in GDP. Answer A is not correct because recessions are caused only by the downswings in GDP. Answer C is not correct because "output yo-yos" is a nonsensical answer. Answer D is not correct because the answer is a nonsensical answer.

9. **C**   The trend line of GDP has been a growth trend line. Answer A is not a correct answer because the natural rate of unemployment tends to remain unchanged or even increase as the population grows. Answer B is not correct because the trend has been an increase in GDP and GDP reflects increases in production. Answer D is not correct because the trend in inflation has been declining as GDP increases.

10. **C**   Total spending has the greatest influence on production and higher production causes higher employment which will also increase spending. Thus, fiscal policy often increases government spending or decreases taxes in order to jump-start the economy. Answer A is not the correct answer because the volume of output is influenced by government, business, and consumer spending, not just consumer spending. Answer B is not correct because private goods and public goods production is part of the volume of output rather than a determinant of the volume of output. Answer D is not the correct answer because the size of the labor force is of no consequences to the volume of output. The size of the labor force is not the same as the unemployment rate; and it is the unemployment rate that is a determinant of the volume of output.

11. **B**   Durable goods are the types of goods that require considerable thought and analysis prior to the decision to invest. If the economy is in a recessionary phase, decision makers are faced with increasing unused capacity. They are not likely to invest in durable goods under those conditions. Answer A is not correct because the purchase of military goods is not likely to be influenced by the business cycle. Decisions about military acquisitions are more likely to be influenced by geopolitical considerations. Answer C is not correct because clothing is considered a necessity and its purchase is not the result of considerable thought and analysis. Answer D is not correct because agricultural commodities are considered necessities and their purchase is not preceded by considerable thought and analysis.

12. **D**   The construction industry is based on business decisions that require considerable thought and analysis. During a prolonged depression, there would be excess capacity and businesses are not likely to expand capacity through construction until such time as the expansionary phase is well under way. Answer A is not correct because the health care industry is based on purchases that are considered a necessity. Answer B is not correct because the clothing industry is based on purchases that are considered a necessity. Answer C is not correct because the agriculture industry is based on purchases that are considered a necessity.

13. **C**   A recession is characterized as a period during which production is measured by GDP declines for two or more quarters in a row. Answer A is not correct because the peak is the high point in the business cycle when there is neither increase or decrease. Answer B is not the correct answer because the recovery phase is the phase in which GDP increases. Answer D is not correct because the trough is the low point in the business cycle when there is neither increase or decrease.

14. **C**   The trough is the lowest point in the business cycle. Answer A is not correct because the peak is the highest point in the business cycle. Answer B is not correct because a recession is defined as an economy which has been in decline for two or more quarters. Answer D is not correct because a recovery is defined as an economy that has been through the trough and GDP is increasing.

©2007 Kaplan CPA Review   Page 615

STUDY MANUAL – BUSINESS ENVIRONMENT & CONCEPTS
CHAPTER 23

15. **A** Market economies are always subject to economic cycles. Economic cycles are characterized by instability of employment levels and price levels. Planned economies are not nearly as inclined toward instability. Answer B is not correct because, even though market economies tend to have long-term growth, the growth is frequently interrupted by business cycles. Answer C is not correct because market economies will always have frictional and structural unemployment (natural level of unemployment) plus cyclical unemployment because of business cycles. Answer D is not correct because market economies attract workers from other economies and thus, the population of countries with market economies tends to increase.

16. **B** Durable goods, as contrasted to consumer goods, are postponable. Durable goods include machinery, transportation equipment, and building construction. Answer A is not correct because it is nondurable goods (consumer goods such as toiletries, food, and clothing) that are regarded as non-postponable. Answer C is not correct because the producers of nondurable goods (toiletries, food, and clothing) operate in nearly perfectly competitive markets where there are many buyers and many sellers. Answer D is not correct because the producers of durable goods tend to operate in a market where there are many buyers but few sellers.

17. **D** Real domestic output, as measured by real GDP, falls during a recession. In fact, a recession is defined as a period in when GDP declines for two or more consecutive quarters. Answer A is not correct because no form of inflation is likely to be present when spending, employment, and GDP are declining as in a recession. Answer B is not correct because potential domestic output remains unchanged during a recession. Potential domestic output is measured by the productive capacity of the economy. Answer C is not correct because no form of inflation is likely to be present when spending, employment, and GDP are declining as in a recession.

18. **C** The natural rate of unemployment is what is left after the cyclical unemployment has been eliminated. That elimination of the cyclical unemployment is likely to occur when the economy is at the peak of a business cycle. Answer A is not correct because the natural rate of unemployment is essentially the same as the full-employment rate of unemployment. Answer B is not correct because the natural rate of unemployment is essentially the same as the full-employment rate of unemployment. Answer D is not correct because the answer is a nonsensical answer.

19. **C** The unemployment rate is the sum of the natural rate of unemployment plus the cyclical unemployment rate. Answer A is not correct because the natural rate of unemployment is the sum of the frictional unemployment rate and the structural unemployment rate. Answer B is not correct because the unemployment rate is the sum of the cyclical unemployment rate and the natural rate of unemployment. Answer D is not correct because one cannot draw conclusions about the increase or decrease of the natural rate of unemployment by knowing only the unemployment rate and the natural rate of unemployment. Changes in the natural rate of unemployment are gradual and they are related to changes in society.

20. **C** The natural rate of unemployment is likely to change from one decade to the next as a result of societal changes such as demographic changes and other societal changes. Answer A is not correct because the natural rate of unemployment is likely to change to reflect societal changes. Answer B is not correct because the natural rate of unemployment is the sum of the frictional unemployment and the structural unemployment. Answer D is not correct because the natural rate of unemployment is influenced by societal changes.

STUDY MANUAL – BUSINESS ENVIRONMENT & CONCEPTS
CHAPTER 23

21. **B** The natural rate of unemployment is the rate of unemployment that is experienced when there is no cyclical unemployment. Answer A is not correct because at the depth of a depression there would be considerable cyclical unemployment in addition to the always present natural rate of unemployment. Answer C is not correct because the unemployment rate of the least-skilled workers in the economy is not ordinarily measured. Answer D is not correct because the unemployment rate of the most-skilled workers in the economy is not ordinarily measured.

22. **A** Aggregate spending impacts GDP and a deficiency in aggregate spending will tend to reduce GDP. A reduction in GDP will result in cyclical unemployment. Answer B is not correct because if the decreasing GDP related to goods is offset by the increasing GDP related to services, there is not likely to be any increase in cyclical unemployment. Answer C is not correct because it is the natural rate of unemployment that results from the everyday dynamics of a free labor market. Answer D is not the correct answer because structural unemployment is caused by technological change.

23. **D** Structural unemployment is related to geographical separation between the location of the worker and the location of the job opening. Answer A is not correct because structural unemployment and frictional unemployment are components of the natural rate of unemployment. Answer B is not correct because structural unemployment is a component of the natural rate of unemployment. Answer C is not correct because people waiting to be called back to their previous jobs are classified as the frictionally unemployed.

24. **C** Cyclical unemployment is caused by declining GDP and declining GDP is associated with a recession. Answer A is not correct because frictional unemployment is a component of the natural rate of unemployment and the natural rate of unemployment is not likely to change in response to a recession. Answer B is not correct because structural unemployment is a component of the natural rate of unemployment and the natural rate of unemployment is not likely to change in response to a recession. Answer C is not correct because seasonal unemployment is unemployment caused by seasonal changes rather than changes in GDP.

25. **B** The natural rate of unemployment is the sum of structural unemployment and frictional unemployment. Answer A is not correct because cyclical unemployment is added to the natural rate of unemployment to obtain total unemployment. Answer C is not correct because structural unemployment is an element of the natural rate of unemployment but cyclical unemployment is not. Answer D is not correct because frictional, structural and cyclical unemployment, taken together, constitute total unemployment.

26. **C** Economic activity, when measured by GDP, falls but prices are not likely to fall quite as rapidly. Prices tend to be rather "sticky" in a recession. Answer A is not correct because a recession will eventually lead to a trough. Answer B is not correct because unemployment rises in a recession. Answer D is not correct because output levels, when measured by GDP, decline during a recession.

27. **C** During a period of sustained economic growth, the economy is growing within a desirable range of possible growth rates, enabling government policy to adopt a neutral posture. Firms capable of generating consistent earnings growth will be good investments during a period when moderate inflation is the norm. Answer A is not correct because as long as growth is sustained, as opposed to breaking away on the upside, there is little reason for the Federal Reserve to tighten money and cause higher interest rates. Therefore there is little advantage in remaining very liquid with short-term instruments. Answer B is incorrect because sustained economic growth means economic growth without an

©2007 Kaplan CPA Review

Page 617

STUDY MANUAL – BUSINESS ENVIRONMENT & CONCEPTS
CHAPTER 23

unacceptably high inflation rate. Answer D is incorrect because interest rates would not be expected to fall, since Federal Reserve policy would be neutral, and loan demand would not be weak under an environment of sustained economic growth.

28. **C** Investments 1, 2, and 3 are all well suited for an environment of high inflation. Tangible assets such as land, oil, precious metals, and collectibles have traditionally done well during such periods. High inflation is usually accompanied by high interest rates, since the inflation premium in the interest rate expands. During periods of rising interest rates, short-term liquid assets can be reinvested at higher and higher interest rates. Answer A is not correct because there is one more type of investment that would also be advantageous. Answer B is not correct because public utilities are highly leveraged with debt and the higher interest rates associated with high inflation would cause increasing costs. Answer D is not correct because public utilities are highly leveraged with debt and the higher interest rates associated with high inflation would cause increasing costs.

29. **B** Long-term AAA rated bonds will lock in the higher interest rates of the past, plus insure confidence that the debt will be serviced during the period when bankruptcies are increasing. Short-term U. S. Treasury bills have zero credit risk, and the purchasing power of this investment is increasing as prices for goods and services are falling as a result of deflation. Answer A is not correct because long-term bonds rated CC or lower and common stocks of firms with sizeable leverage are dangerous investments in deflation. The bonds risk default and the companies that are highly leveraged could experience a decline in earnings during a deflationary period. Those decreased earnings could make payment of interest on the debt difficult or impossible. Answer C is not correct because long-term bonds rated CC or lower are dangerous investments in deflation. The bonds risk default. Answer D is not correct because companies that are highly leveraged could experience a decline in earnings during a deflationary period. Those decreased earnings could make payment of interest difficult or impossible.

30. **C** Deflation is a period of tepid demand, declining prices of goods and services, declining interest rates, and rising bankruptcies among the weaker firms. Long-term bonds rated AA or higher are good investments in deflationary times. Answer A is incorrect because interest rates will be falling. A lender will be unable to lend at higher interest rates. Answer B is incorrect because tangible assets such as precious metals will decline in price during a deflationary economy. Answer D is incorrect because the economic logic is faulty. Short-term interest rates will decline in a deflationary economy.

31. **A** If interest rates rise far above the present levels, there will be a sharp drop in the price for bonds now held. By selling and holding cash, the investor could again buy the bonds when the price dropped, avoiding a possible capital loss and pocketing a substantial gain on the transactions. Answer B is not correct because holding the bonds will result in declining market price as interest rates increase. Answer C is not correct because it is an increase in interest rates that causes the market price of existing bonds to decline. Answer D is incorrect because if interest rates fall from present levels, the market value of the bonds would increase; thus, the investor should continue to hold them.

32. **B** Precious metals are good investments in inflationary periods. Answer A is incorrect because inflation causes interest rates to rise, which decreases demand for postponable, durable goods such as automobiles and houses. Answer C is incorrect because higher interest rates will cause long-term bond prices to decline. Answer D in incorrect because inflation will cause interest rates to increase, not decrease.

ECONOMICS: GOVERNMENT POLICIES

STUDY MANUAL – BUSINESS ENVIRONMENT & CONCEPTS
CHAPTER 24

Study Tip: Search on the Internet for stress management. The more you can relieve your stress, the better you will do on the CPA exam. And don't forget that when you sleep on what you have studied, it stays with you longer. Be sure to get a good night's sleep before you walk into the Prometric Center.

GOVERNMENTAL POLICIES DESIGNED TO PROMOTE ECONOMIC GROWTH

A. What kinds of governmental policies promote economic growth? Policies that:

1. Encourage high savings and high capital investment rates.

2. Emphasize the development of human capital.

3. Stabilize the macroeconomic environment through balanced budgets and tight monetary policy.

4. Encourage free trade.

5. Provide an adequate legal system (especially contract law).

6. Encourage low population growth.

7. Foster technological advancement, particularly in wealthy countries.

8. Provide technology to poorer countries.

B. Countries that succeed in implementing these policies usually reap large economic rewards in the form of higher economic growth.

MEASURING GROSS DOMESTIC PRODUCT (GDP)

GDP may be measured using either the expenditure approach or the resource cost/income approach. Both approaches yield the same results because aggregate expenditures must equal aggregate income.

STUDY MANUAL – BUSINESS ENVIRONMENT & CONCEPTS
CHAPTER 24

A. Expenditure approach. The total expenditure approach considers total spending on all final goods and services produced during the year. The expenditure approach is a demand-based concept measured by summing the following expenditure items:

1. Personal consumption represents household purchases for consumption purposes, and represents the single largest component of GDP. Over two-thirds of GDP is accounted for by personal consumption. This category of expenditures includes durable goods, nondurable goods, and services.

2. Gross private investment (expenditures of business). This is an important component of GDP because it provides an indicator of the future productive capacity of the economy. Fixed investment (investment in capital goods) is a key component of future economic growth. GDP includes replacement purchases plus net additions to the stock of capital assets plus investments in inventories (+/–). Inventory investments are the changes in the stock of unsold goods held by a business during the period.

3. Government consumption and gross investment. Purchases of goods and services by federal, state, and local governments are included in GDP. Transfer payments (Social Security, welfare) are excluded.

4. Net exports of goods and services (+/–). Since we only want to measure domestic production, net exports are calculated as total exports (domestically produced goods and services purchased by consumers outside the country) minus total imports (foreign-produced goods and services purchased by domestic consumers).

B. Resource cost/income approach. The resource cost-income approach is a supply-oriented (i.e., production) approach and measures GDP by summing the following components:

1. Employee compensation.

2. Proprietors' income.

3. Rents.

4. Corporate profits.

5. Interest income.

6. Indirect business taxes.

7. Depreciation.

8. Net income of foreigners (the income foreigners earn domestically minus the income that domestic citizens earn abroad).

C. The difference between real and nominal GDP.

1. An important use of GDP is comparing levels of production over time. However, when nominal GDP (GDP measured in terms of current prices) changes from one period to the next, it reflects both changes in production and price changes. Therefore, economists attempt to filter out the impact of price changes by calculating GDP measured in terms of prices from some base year. This measure is called *real GDP*. Changes in real GDP correspond to real or actual changes in production.

2. Since nominal GDP is measured with current prices and real GDP is measured relative to the price level in some base year, we need a price index to indicate the relative price change between periods.

D. The difference between the GDP deflator and the consumer price index.

1. The GDP deflator is a general price index that corresponds to the price change exhibited by a very large market basket—all final goods and services produced. An important point to note is that the contents of the market basket of goods change every year depending on current production. The GDP deflator is useful for measuring economy-wide inflation. The current base year in the United States is 2000 (GDP deflator = 100).

2. The consumer price index (CPI) differs from the GDP deflator in several ways.

    a. A relatively small market basket is used.

    b. The market basket is fixed from year to year.

    c. The CPI measures consumer price changes and does not directly measure the price changes of items purchased by businesses and government.

    The net result of all these differences is very small.

    - The CPI tends to overstate the inflation rate, because its market basket is fixed and does not consider that consumers will substitute away from goods that have risen dramatically in price.
    - However, the CPI is useful for measuring inflation in the consumer goods sector.

E. Calculate real GDP, given nominal GDP and the GDP deflator.

1. To calculate real GDP from nominal GDP, you need three pieces of information:

    a. The GDP deflator in the base year.

    b. The GDP deflator in the current period.

    c. The nominal GDP in the current year.

These values are related as follows:

©2007 Kaplan CPA Review

Page 621

STUDY MANUAL – BUSINESS ENVIRONMENT & CONCEPTS
CHAPTER 24

Example: Calculating Real GDP

Assume an economy's nominal GDP was $2.5 billion in 20X0 and $3.5 billion in 20X4. If the GDP deflator was 100.0 in 20X0 and 112.7 in 20X4, what is the change in real GDP over the period both in dollars and in percentage terms?

Answer

- Nominal GDP 20X0 = $2.5 billion.
- Real GDP 20X4 = $3.5 billion (100.0/112.7) = $3.1 billion. This is the 20X4 GDP in 20X0 dollars.
- Real increase in dollars: $3.1 – 2.5 = $0.6 billion.
- Real increase in percent: [(3.1 – 2.5)/2.5] = 0.24 or 24%.

Although nominal GDP rose by over 40 percent during the period (i.e., [(3.5 – 2.5)/ 2.5 = 0.40]), real GDP rose by only 24.0 percent.

F. The major limitations of GDP.

1. GDP does not:

   a. Count nonmarket production—specifically, homemaker services.

   b. Count the underground economy—illegal activities and tax evasion.

   c. Measure the value of leisure activities, the standard of living accounted for by a shorter workweek, or changing working conditions.

   d. Measure the changing quality of goods and services.

   e. Measure the cost of pollution and damage to the ecology.

Note: GDP is not a measure of the welfare of a society or its people, as it values a dollar spent on education the same as a dollar spent on alcohol. Instead it provides the information needed to track the performance of the economy. Without this information, policy makers would not be able to adopt corrective economic activities.

INTEREST RATES

A. The real interest rate is the difference between the nominal rate and the inflation rate. The real interest rate is what you are earning or paying when the effects of price increases (inflation) are removed.

B. Nominal interest rates are expressed in current dollars. This is the rate as stated by a savings account or loan agreement.

C. The effective interest rate is the true rate of interest after considering the number of compounding periods. Ten percent interest per year compounded annually is 10

Page 622   ©2007 Kaplan CPA Review

percent effective interest. However, a contract (stated or nominal) rate of 10 percent compounded quarterly results in an effective interest rate of more than 10 percent.

D. Financial institutions usually quote rates as stated annual interest rates, or nominal rates, along with a compounding frequency, as opposed to quoting rates as periodic rates—the rate of interest earned over a single compounding period. For example, a bank will quote a savings rate as 8 percent, compounded quarterly, rather than 2 percent per quarter.

E. The rate of interest that investors actually realize as a result of compounding is known as the *effective annual rate (EAR)*.

1. EAR represents the annual rate of return actually being earned after adjustments have been made for different compounding periods.

2. EAR may be determined as follows:

$$EAR = (1 + \text{Periodic rate})^m - 1$$

where:
Periodic rate = Nominal rate/m and m = Number of compounding periods per year

F. Obviously, the EAR for a stated rate of 8 percent compounded annually is not the same as the EAR for 8 percent compounded semiannually, or quarterly. Indeed, whenever compound interest is being used, the stated (nominal) rate and the actual (effective) rate of interest are equal only when interest is compounded annually. Otherwise, the EAR is greater than the stated rate.

G. The computation of EARs is necessary when comparing investments that have different compounding periods. It allows for an apples-to-apples rate comparison.

Example: Computing EAR

Compute EAR if the nominal (stated) rate is 12 percent, compounded quarterly.

Answer

Here, $m = 4$, so the periodic rate is $12\%/4 = 3\%$.

Thus, $EAR = (1 + 0.03)^4 - 1 = 1.1255 - 1 = 0.1255 = 12.55\%$.

Example: Computing EARs for a Range of Compounding Frequencies

Using a stated rate of 6 percent, compute EARs for semiannual, quarterly, monthly, and daily.

Answer

Semiannual effective rate = $(1 + 0.03)^2 - 1 = 1.06090 - 1 = 0.06090 = 6.090\%$.

©2007 Kaplan CPA Review

Quarterly effective rate = $(1 + 0.015)^4 - 1 = 1.06136 - 1 = 0.06136 = 6.136\%$.

Monthly effective rate = $(1 + 0.005)^{12} - 1 = 1.06168 - 1 = 0.06168 = 6.168\%$.

Daily effective rate = $(1 + 0.000164)^{365} - 1 = 1.06183 - 1 = 0.06183 = 6.183\%$.

Notice here that the EAR increases as the compounding frequency increases.

MONETARY POLICY

A. Monetarists believe that changes in the money supply exert a large influence on both prices and output. Monetarists blame both inflation and the business cycle on a mismanaged money supply. Since the money supply is such a powerful tool, monetarists feel that the best monetary policy is one of steady, predictable money growth. They believe that discretionary monetary policy should not be used to moderate fluctuations in prices and output.

B. Like fiscal policy, monetary policy also has a time lag. It can take anywhere from 5 months to 36 months after instituting a policy change until the policy exerts a significant impact on the economy. Furthermore, a restrictive policy aimed at controlling prices that misses the mark and is implemented when the economy is actually in recession will have disastrous effects. Both prices and output will fall further, exacerbating the recession. This aspect of timing supports the hands-off view of the monetarists.

C. The demand for money is largely determined by interest rates. This is illustrated in Figure 1, where the money demand schedule is shown to exhibit a downward slope. At higher interest rates, the opportunity cost of holding money increases, and people will desire to hold less money and more assets that are sensitive to changes in the price level.

D. Factors other than interest rates also affect the demand for money.

   1. As inflation increases, households and businesses need more money to buy costlier goods and services. Similarly, if the gross domestic product (GDP) rises, more goods and services are bought and sold, and more money is needed to conduct these transactions.

   2. In summary, as nominal GDP increases as the result of inflation and/or increased output, the demand for money also increases. This causes the entire demand curve to shift to the right.

   3. Over time, changes of an institutional nature, such as widespread credit card use and the greater availability of short-term credit in general, have decreased consumers' need to hold cash balances. These changes have decreased the demand for money (shifting the demand for the money curve to the left).

E. The supply of money is determined by the central bank, the Federal Reserve System (the Fed) in the United States, and is independent of the interest rate. This explains the vertical supply curve in Figure 1.

Figure 1: Supply and Demand for Money

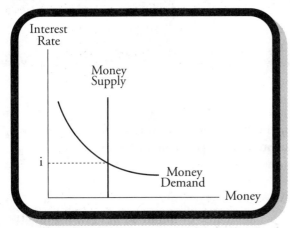

It is important that you note as the central bank increases the money supply, the real interest rate falls, which reduces the opportunity cost of holding money, and increases the demand for money.

F. When a monetary policy change is fully anticipated, contracts will reflect expected higher prices. Hence, both prices and interest rates will rise rapidly to their long-run equilibrium levels, leaving output unchanged.

G. Many labor contracts write escalator clauses (cost-of-living agreements) into the wage agreement in anticipation of inflation. These clauses adjust money wage rates upward as the price level rises.

Remember that policy changes always have more of an impact when they are unanticipated rather than anticipated.

H. If we break GDP into the price level and its real output component (Price × Real output), we obtain an identity known as the equation of exchange that in words, is stated as:

Money supply × Velocity = GDP = Price × Real output.

I. Velocity is the average number of times per year each dollar is used to buy goods and services: (Velocity = GDP/Money). Therefore, the money supply multiplied by velocity must equal nominal GDP. The equation of exchange must hold with velocity defined in this way. Letting money supply = M, velocity = V, price = P, and real output = Y, the equation of exchange may be symbolically expressed as:

$$MV = PY$$

J. The quantity theory of money states that an increase in the money supply will cause a proportional increase in prices.

K. The original proponents of the quantity theory felt that velocity and output were determined by institutional factors other than the money supply and were thus nearly constant. Therefore, if the money supply increases while velocity and quantities are fixed, prices must rise.

L. Rearranging the equation of exchange, we get: price = MV/Y. Since velocity (V) and real output (Y) change very slowly, an increase in the money supply (M) must result in a proportional increase in prices (inflation).

M. In the long run, an increase in the growth rate of money (expansionary policy) will be fully reflected in the price level. At the same time, individuals will begin to build expectations regarding future inflation.

N. When inflationary expectations are revised upward, the nominal interest rate also rises. (Remember that the nominal rate equals the real rate plus expected inflation.) Don't be confused. Just remember that, given expansionary monetary policy, the real interest rate falls in the short run and the nominal rate rises in the long run.

O. Modern analysis indicates that the long-run effect of rapid monetary growth differs from the short-run effects of an unanticipated shift.

    1. In the long run, the major consequences of rapid monetary growth are inflation and higher nominal interest rates.

    2. Rapid monetary growth will neither reduce unemployment nor stimulate real output in the long run.

P. Monetary policy actions affect short-term rates while long-term rates are influenced more by real factors and inflation expectations. The result is that the linkage between monetary policy and changes in output and prices is a weak one that exhibits significant time lags.

Q. If the Fed attempts to stimulate the economy by increasing the money supply, short-term interest rates are likely to decline. As interest rates decline, people are willing to hold more money because of the reduced opportunity cost of holding money.

R. As a result, the velocity of money declines. This tends to dampen the initial effects of the monetary policy and adds to the time lag.

S. Interest rates are not always a good indication of monetary policy. For example, an expansionary monetary policy is likely to lead to lower short-term interest rates. However, if the expansionary policy lasts long, the public will anticipate higher inflation causing interest rates to rise. Thus, interest rates are often a misleading indicator of monetary policy.

STUDY MANUAL – BUSINESS ENVIRONMENT & CONCEPTS

CHAPTER 24

EFFECTS OF MONETARY POLICY—A SUMMARY

A. An unanticipated shift to a more restrictive (expansionary) monetary policy will temporarily contract (expand) output and employment.

B. The effectiveness of a monetary policy change in stabilizing the economy is dependent upon the state of the economy when the effect of the policy change is observed.

1. Expansionary monetary policy when there is slack in the economy tends to increase output and employment.

2. Expansionary monetary policy when the economy is operating at the full-employment level tends to cause inflation.

3. Conversely, restrictive policy when the economy is operating beyond full capacity tends to reduce inflation, while a restrictive policy when the economy is at or below the full-employment level will cause a recession.

C. Persistent rapid money growth will cause inflation.

D. Nominal interest rates and the inflation rate are directly related.

E. There is only a loose year-to-year relationship between shifts in monetary policy and changes in output and price. This is because it takes time for the markets to adjust to changing demand conditions.

MONEY

A. Money provides an economic system with the following functions.

1. Medium of exchange. Money simplifies and reduces the cost of transactions.

2. Unit of account. Money serves as a unit of measure by which the values of goods can be compared.

3. Store of value. Money enables value to be stored and transported. It is also a liquid asset, meaning that it can be easily converted into other goods.

B. In the past, money's value was related to the value of some underlying asset, such as gold. Today's money is just paper (it is fiat money in that it has no intrinsic value nor is it backed by a commodity).

1. The paper has value because the government says that it has value. Regardless, money's main source of value is the same as any other commodity; value is determined by demand and supply.

©2007 Kaplan CPA Review

Page 627

STUDY MANUAL – BUSINESS ENVIRONMENT & CONCEPTS
CHAPTER 24

2. The unit value of money is quantified with reference to what it will purchase. Thus, there is an inverse relationship between the unit value of money and the level of prices. That is, an increase in price is equivalent to a decrease in the purchasing power of a money unit. So, in order for the purchasing power of money to be stable over time, the supply of money needs to be controlled.

C. The money supply is defined and measured according to the following two classifications.

    1. M1 is the narrowest definition of money and is defined as currency in circulation (coins and paper), checkable deposits maintained in depository institutions, and travelers' checks.

    2. M2 equals M1 plus savings deposits and time deposits less than $100,000 held in depository institutions plus money market mutual fund shares.

D. Money is a financial asset that provides the holder with future purchasing power. This must be distinguished from credit, which is a liability acquired when you borrow funds. Credit is not purchasing power but rather a facilitator of purchasing power. This is why the limit on your credit card does not count as part of the money supply.

E. In the United States, the Federal Reserve System (the Fed) is the central bank. It is charged with enforcing banking regulations and the implementation of monetary policy.

F. Under the Fed system, a bank's reserves are measured as vault cash plus deposits of the bank held at the Fed.

    1. Excess reserves are actual reserves held in excess of required reserves set by the Fed.

    2. Required reserves do not earn interest and may not be loaned to customers.

G. In a fractional reserve banking system, such as the Fed system, a bank is only required to hold a fraction of its deposits in reserve. The *required reserve ratio* is the term used to measure the reserve requirement. Deposits in excess of the required reserve may be loaned.

H. When a bank makes a loan, the borrower spends the money. The sellers who received the cash may deposit it in their banks. This action creates additional loanable funds, because only a fractional amount of the deposit is required by law to be held in reserve. This process of lending, spending, and depositing continues until the amount of excess reserves available for lending is zero. This is referred to as the multiplier effect.

I. The potential deposit expansion multiplier is the maximum potential increase in the money supply due to the multiplier effect.

Page 628   ©2007 Kaplan CPA Review

1. The actual deposit expansion multiplier will be less than the potential if some people decide to hold currency rather than deposit it into the bank, and if banks fail to loan out excess reserves.

2. It is important to note that money is created only when banks make loans, and a single bank can only lend out its excess reserves. It is the banking system as a whole that expands the money supply.

3. There is also a multiplier effect when the Fed decreases the monetary base through open market sales of Treasury securities.

4. To calculate the potential deposit expansion multiplier and the potential increase in the money supply, we use the following formulas:

   Potential deposit expansion multiplier = 1/Required reserve ratio.

   Potential increase in money supply = Potential deposit expansion multiplier × Increase in excess reserves.

J. For example, assume that the required reserve rate is 25 percent, and a bank finds itself with $1,000 in excess reserves. The bank can only lend out its own excess reserves of $1,000. If the borrower of the $1,000 deposits the cash in a second bank, the second bank will be able to lend its excess reserves of $750 (0.25 × $1,000). Those funds may be deposited in a third bank, which can then lend its excess reserve of $563. If this lending and depositing continues, the money supply may eventually expand to $4,000 [(1/0.25) × $1,000]. If no other banks took deposits or made loans, there would be no increase in the money supply.

K. A country's central bank (e.g., the Fed in the United States) controls the money supply with three policy tools: the required reserve ratio, open market operations, and the discount rate.

   1. As the required reserve ratio drops, each dollar of excess reserves can be multiplied more times. In other words, if the required reserve ratio falls, the money stock rises.

      a. It must be noted that lowering the required reserve ratio only increases the money supply if banks are willing to lend and their customers are willing to borrow.

      b. The results of a required reserve ratio change are hard to predict, so it is a seldom-used tool.

   2. Central bank's most powerful tool is open market operations.

      a. In the United States, the Fed buys and sells Treasury bonds, notes, and bills as a way to control the monetary base. The base is equal to the currency and coins in circulation plus bank reserves.

STUDY MANUAL – BUSINESS ENVIRONMENT & CONCEPTS
CHAPTER 24

   b.   If the Fed sells government securities, it sells a bond and receives cash in return. The individual who bought the bond must withdraw cash from his or her bank to pay the Fed.

   c.   When the Fed sells securities, the monetary base shrinks, excess reserves shrink, and the money supply is reduced. Similarly, if the Fed buys securities, it injects reserves into the banking system and the money supply increases.

   d.   This is the most commonly used tool of the Fed.

3.   In the United States, banks can borrow funds from the Fed if they have temporary shortfalls in reserves. The interest rate charged by the Fed is called the **discount rate**.

   a.   Since the Fed regulates banks and frowns upon borrowing too often to meet reserve requirements, banks try not to run short of reserves by loaning too much.

   b.   The idea behind this tool is that as the discount rate rises, this form of short-term borrowing is more expensive and banks will avoid reserve shortfalls even more aggressively. As the discount rate falls, however, borrowing from the Fed is less costly, and banks will tend to lend more aggressively.

L.   There is widespread use of the U.S. dollar outside the United States. As much as two-thirds of U.S. currency is held abroad, substantially reducing the reliability of M1.

M.   The increasing availability of low-fee stock and bond mutual funds has caused a shift of funds out of M2 components of the money supply.

N.   Debit cards and electronic money make it easier to transfer funds without the use of money. As the public holds less currency, reserves will accumulate in the banks, causing the money supply to grow rapidly if the Fed does not take offsetting action.

REGULATION

THE PURPOSE OF ECONOMIC REGULATION

A.   Economic regulation usually involves either of the following:

1.   Restrictions on prices.

2.   Restrictions on the structure of an industry.

B.   Traditionally, one goal of economic regulation is to protect consumers from the power of monopoly producers (e.g., electric utilities). Utility rate regulation seeks lower prices and expanded output by setting lower prices than a monopolist would charge, resulting in a higher equilibrium level of output.

Page 630   ©2007 Kaplan CPA Review

C. Economic regulation of industry structure is often based on a view that industries with high fixed costs and low marginal costs (e.g., airlines, railroads) are inherently unstable. Historically, rates were regulated to stabilize prices, and restrictions on the entry of new firms into such industries were promoted as a way to reduce harmful competition or stabilize competition within the industry.

How Economic Incentives and Political Activities Can Influence Regulatory Decisions and the Performance of the Regulatory Process.

A. Regulation. Consumers, regulators, and businesses affected by regulation have economic incentives to influence the nature and scope of regulation.

   1. Because regulation is a product of the political process, all of these groups may engage in political activities to influence regulatory decisions.

   2. Examples of such activities include hiring lobbyists, making political contributions, and organizing letter-writing campaigns by affected workers or groups.

B. Redistribution of wealth. Often, influence on the regulatory process is directed toward the redistribution of wealth rather than the maximization of overall wealth by economically efficient regulation.

   1. One important point about the nature of political activity affecting regulation is that often a small group will have a great economic stake in regulatory decisions, while the larger population will be affected in small ways.

   2. One example of such a special interest group is the taxicab industry. Existing companies have a strong economic incentive to limit new entry into the taxi business so that they can charge higher fares. To the average citizen, the small increase in fares is not enough to make this an important political issue. To the owner of a taxi company, however, the additional profits from limiting competition may be quite significant and make political contributions and lobbying activity very attractive.

C. Conflicts of interest. In regulated industries, affected firms have the greatest incentive to communicate with regulators, provide them with research that supports the firms' point of view, and influence regulators through political activities. Over time, the outcome is often that the regulators tend to share the views of the regulated firms on crucial issues.

D. Slow changes. The nature of the regulatory bureaucracy itself can lead to results that run counter to economic efficiency. Since regulations are most often the result of a cumbersome process, they are slow to change, even in the face of changing technology or industry structure. New building materials that are cheaper and/or better may be prohibited by existing building codes. Those wishing to produce or utilize such materials may face significant additional costs to get their use approved.

STUDY MANUAL – BUSINESS ENVIRONMENT & CONCEPTS
CHAPTER 24

    1. Advances in technology that provide new substitutes may make regulation of an industry unnecessary. Regulators have little incentive to recognize this, abolish their jobs, and increase societal wealth.

    2. In general, the regulatory bureaucracy has an incentive to undertake political activity to expand regulatory budgets and power by influencing legislative decisions.

E. Bias against approval. When regulators must specifically approve new products, there is a built-in bias against approval. If the FDA approves a new drug that turns out to cause significant side effects or deaths, the regulators are likely to face increased scrutiny and oversight, decreased influence and funding, and the real possibility of losing their jobs. On the other hand, delaying or failing to introduce even a potentially life-saving new drug will be unlikely to have such serious consequences. Regulation that is "too careful" is a more defensible error in the political arena. People whose health is impaired (or who die) are a less visible group and are less likely to sue and win large damage awards. There is built-in bias toward regulation that is too restrictive and leads to a less-than-optimal number of new drug introductions.

THE POTENTIAL EFFECT OF HEALTH AND SAFETY REGULATION ON DECISIONS MADE BY REGULATED FIRMS

A. The primary effect of health and safety regulation on an affected firm's decisions comes from the fact that such regulation increases the costs of production. The price will be increased and the output decreased compared to a situation without regulation.

B. When regulation increases the costs of bringing new products to market, as with the FDA approval process, some products will not be introduced as a result. Products that are only marginally profitable before increases in the cost of gaining regulatory approval can be money-losing propositions when these additional costs are considered.

C. The regulatory process is political and bureaucratic, making it much less flexible and responsive to changing conditions than competitive markets are. This can cause firms to be slow to innovate and adopt new methods, materials, and products.

THE UNINTENDED COSTS OF REGULATION

A. Costs. The costs of regulation include the direct cost of administration, monitoring, and enforcement, as well as the increased costs of production when safety rules are imposed. Some costs of regulation may be unintended.

B. Slow to innovate. If a company is protected from competition, it may be slow to innovate and adopt new technology or production methods. This represents an additional cost of regulation since production costs are higher than without the regulatory protection.

Page 632   ©2007 Kaplan CPA Review

C. Forgone cost savings. Safety regulation that once produced a desirable result can become outmoded and more costly if newer materials or construction methods that would reduce costs are prohibited. The forgone cost savings can be seen as one of the unintended costs of regulation.

D. Changes in incentives. Consumers will have less incentive to educate themselves about product safety characteristics, because they assume the regulations give them the level of safety they desire. This assumption may or may not be correct. The imposition of minimum gas mileage standards for passenger cars led to a greater use of plastic in cars to reduce weight. An unintended consequence of this standard is an increase in traffic fatalities compared to those that would have occurred with heavier (lower mileage) cars. Here, the unintended costs include the additional loss of life compared to the unregulated (market) result.

E. Forgone benefits. A good example of this is the FDA approval process. It is intended to save lives by preventing the sale of drugs that are dangerous. As the approval process lengthens to improve drug safety, lives will be lost due to the delays in the availability of new, potentially life-saving drugs. Any deaths that could have been prevented by more rapid approval are an additional cost of the regulatory process. Any forgone benefits of drugs not brought to market as a result of the cost of the approval process are considered part of the cost of regulation.

THE COSTS AND BENEFITS OF REGULATION AND HOW THESE COSTS AND BENEFITS ARE SHARED IN THE ECONOMY

A. So far in this review we've focused on the costs of regulation, but there are benefits as well, such as a decrease in pollution, and a reduction in injuries/deaths due to safety practices on the factory floor.

B. The question, from an economic perspective, is whether the benefits outweigh the costs. Both are difficult to quantify much of the time. Many of the costs of regulation are not immediately clear, and political activism and economic incentives can influence the regulatory process so that the stated benefits are not as certain or as large as they may first appear.

C. Empirical research, while not conclusive, suggests that the benefits of health and safety regulations do not significantly exceed the costs and that for the majority of U.S. federal regulations, the costs exceed the benefits. What the research does NOT indicate, however, is that the benefits of regulation substantially outweigh the costs, which calls into question the necessity of such regulation.

D. In addition, the costs and benefits of regulation are not shared equally among all the participants in the economy. Political influence in the regulatory process is often aimed at redistributing wealth rather than maximizing overall wealth through economically efficient regulation. A large, poorly organized and politically inactive group may share the costs of regulations that benefit only a few. The economically efficient solution would be to devote more resources to regulations that generate large benefits relative to their costs, and to modify or eliminate regulations that have large costs relative to their benefits.

STUDY MANUAL – BUSINESS ENVIRONMENT & CONCEPTS
CHAPTER 24

QUESTIONS: GOVERNMENT POLICIES

1.   If the Federal Reserve wanted to reduce the supply of money as part of an anti-inflation policy, it might:
     A. increase the reserve requirements.
     B. buy U.S. securities on the open market.
     C. lower the discount rate.
     D. buy U.S. securities directly from the Treasury.

2.   The Fed funds rate is the rate that:
     A. banks charge their best customers.
     B. the Fed charges banks to borrow from the Federal Reserve.
     C. banks charge each other for short-term borrowing and lending of excess reserves.
     D. the Treasury has to pay to borrow in the debt markets.

3.   An increase in spending by the government will cause which of the following to occur?
     A. A decrease in taxes.
     B. A downward shift in the aggregate demand curve.
     C. A decrease in real interest rates.
     D. An increase in prices.

4.   Proper timing of fiscal policy is important if the government is to achieve its goal of:
     A. injecting stimulus during a recession and restraint during an inflationary boom.
     B. generating revenues from taxes and sales equal to its expenditures.
     C. increasing the supply of loanable funds needed to place downward pressure on the real rate of interest.
     D. creating the supply of money needed to promote full employment, price stability, and rapid economic growth.

5.   Policy makers who want to offset the effects on output of an economic contraction caused by a shift in aggregate supply could use fiscal policy to shift aggregate:
     A. demand to the right.
     B. demand to the left.
     C. supply to the left.
     D. supply to the right.

Page 634   ©2007 Kaplan CPA Review

6. Fiscal policy refers to the:
   A. manipulation of government spending and taxes to stabilize domestic output, employment, and the price level.
   B. manipulation of government spending and taxes to achieve greater equality in the distribution of income.
   C. altering of the interest rate to change aggregate demand.
   D. fact that equal increases in government spending and taxation will be contractionary.

7. Expansionary fiscal policy is so named because it:
   A. involves an expansion of the nation's money supply.
   B. necessarily expands the size of government.
   C. is aimed at achieving greater price stability.
   D. is designed to expand real GDP.

8. Suppose that the economy is in the midst of a recession. Which of the following policies would be consistent with active fiscal policy?
   A. A Congressional proposal to incur a Federal surplus to be used for the retirement of public debt.
   B. A reduction in agricultural subsidies and veterans' benefits.
   C. A postponement of a highway construction program.
   D. A reduction in Federal tax rates on personal and corporate income.

9. An appropriate fiscal policy for a severe recession is:
   A. a decrease in government spending.
   B. a decrease in tax rates.
   C. appreciation of the dollar.
   D. an increase in interest rates.

10. An appropriate fiscal policy for severe demand-pull inflation is:
    A. an increase in government spending.
    B. depreciation of the dollar.
    C. a reduction in interest rates.
    D. a tax rate increase.

11. In an aggregate demand-aggregate supply diagram, equal decreases in government spending and taxes will:
    A. shift the AD curve to the right.
    B. increase the equilibrium GDP.
    C. not affect the AD curve.
    D. shift the AD curve to the left.

12. An expansionary fiscal policy is shown as a:
    A. rightward shift in the economy's aggregate demand curve.
    B. movement along an existing aggregate demand curve.
    C. leftward shift in the economy's aggregate supply curve.
    D. leftward shift in the economy's aggregate demand curve.

STUDY MANUAL – BUSINESS ENVIRONMENT & CONCEPTS
CHAPTER 24

13. Which of the following is not an item in the list of leading economic indicators?
    A. Changes in mutual fund balances.
    B. The length of the average work week.
    C. The money supply.
    D. The value of the index of consumer expectations.

14. In the United States, the money supply (M1) is comprised of:
    A. coins, paper currency, and checkable deposits.
    B. currency, checkable deposits, and Series E bonds.
    C. coins, paper currency, checkable deposits, and credit balances with brokers.
    D. paper currency, coins, gold certificates, and time deposits.

15. The value of money varies:
    A. inversely with the price level.
    B. directly with the volume of employment.
    C. directly with the price level.
    D. directly with the interest rate.

16. The difference between M1 and M2 is that:
    A. the former includes time deposits.
    B. the latter includes small time deposits, non-checkable savings accounts, money market deposit accounts, and money market mutual fund balances.
    C. the latter includes negotiable government bonds.
    D. the latter includes cash held by commercial banks and the U. S. Treasury.

17. The purchase of government securities from the public by the Fed will cause:
    A. commercial bank reserves to decrease.
    B. the money supply to increase.
    C. demand deposits to decrease
    D. the interest rate to increase.

18. Which of the following will increase commercial bank reserves?
    A. The purchase of government bonds in the open market by the Federal Reserve Banks.
    B. A decrease in the reserve ratio.
    C. An increase in the discount rate.
    D. The sale of government bonds in the open market by the Federal Reserve Banks.

19. If the Federal Reserve System buys government securities from commercial banks and the public:
    A. commercial bank reserves will decline.
    B. commercial bank reserves will be unaffected.
    C. it will be easier to obtain loans at commercial banks.
    D. the money supply will contract.

Page 636 ©2007 Kaplan CPA Review

20. Which of the following best describes the cause-effect chain of an easy money policy?
    A. A decrease in the money supply will lower the interest rate, increase investment spending, and increase aggregate demand and GDP.
    B. A decrease in the money supply will raise the interest rate, decrease investment spending, and decrease aggregate demand and GDP.
    C. An increase in the money supply will raise the interest rate, decrease investment spending, and decrease aggregate demand and GDP.
    D. An increase in the money supply will lower the interest rate, increase investment spending, and increase aggregate demand.

21. If the economy were encountering a severe recession, proper monetary and fiscal policies would call for:
    A. selling government securities, raising the reserve ratio, lowering the discount rate, and a budgetary surplus.
    B. buying government securities, reducing the reserve ratio, reducing the discount rate, and a budgetary deficit.
    C. buying government securities, raising the reserve ratio, raising the discount rate, and a budgetary surplus.
    D. buying government securities, reducing the reserve ratio, raising the discount rate, and a budgetary deficit.

22. Suppose the total market value of all final goods and services produced in a particular country in 20X1 is $500 billion and the total market value of final goods and services sold is $450 billion. We can conclude that:
    A. GDP in 20X1 is $450 billion.
    B. NDP in 20X1 is $450 billion.
    C. GDP in 20X1 is $500 billion.
    D. inventories in 20X1 fell by $50 billion.

23. In national income accounting, consumption expenditures include:
    A. purchases of both new and used consumer goods.
    B. consumer durable goods and consumer nondurable goods, but not services.
    C. consumer durable goods, consumer nondurable goods, and services.
    D. changes in business inventories.

24. Suppose that GDP was $200 billion in year 1 and that all other components of expenditures remained the same in year 2 except that business inventories increased by $10 billion. GDP in year 2 is:
    A. $180 billion.
    B. $190 billion.
    C. $200 billion.
    D. $210 billion.

STUDY MANUAL – BUSINESS ENVIRONMENT & CONCEPTS
CHAPTER 24

25. GDP differs from NDP in that:
   A. GDP is based on gross exports, while NDP is based on net exports.
   B. GDP includes, but NDP excludes, indirect business taxes.
   C. net investment is used in calculating GDP and gross investment is used in calculating NDP.
   D. gross investment is used in calculating GDP and net investment is used in calculating NDP.

26. NDP is:
   A. NI plus net foreign factor income earned in the U.S. plus indirect business taxes.
   B. NI plus corporate income taxes.
   C. GDP deflated for increases in the price level.
   D. GDP minus indirect business taxes.

27. If personal income exceeds national income in a particular year, we can conclude that:
   A. transfer payments exceeded the sum of social security contributions, corporate income taxes, and indirect business taxes.
   B. the sum of social security contributions, corporate income taxes, and undistributed corporate profits exceeded transfer payments.
   C. consumption of fixed capital and indirect business taxes exceeded personal taxes.
   D. transfer payments exceeded the sum of social security contributions, corporate income taxes, and undistributed corporate profits.

28. The amount of after-tax income received by households is measured by:
   A. discretionary income.
   B. national income.
   C. disposable income.
   D. personal income.

29. Real GDP measures:
   A. current output at current prices.
   B. current output at base year prices.
   C. base year output at current prices.
   D. base year output at current exchange rates.

30. The fact that nominal GDP has risen faster than real GDP:
   A. suggests that the base year of the GDP price index has been shifted.
   B. tells us nothing about what has happened to the price level.
   C. suggests that the general price level has fallen.
   D. suggests that the general price level has risen.

Page 638   ©2007 Kaplan CPA Review

31. The aggregate demand curve:
    A. is up-sloping because a higher price level is necessary to make production profitable as production costs rise.
    B. is down-sloping because production costs decline as real output increases.
    C. shows the amount of expenditures required to induce the production of each possible level of real output.
    D. shows the amount of real output that will be purchased at each possible price level.

32. Which one of the following would not shift the aggregate demand curve?
    A. A change in the price level
    B. Depreciation of the international value of the dollar
    C. A decline in the interest rate at each possible price level
    D. An increase in personal income tax rates

33. An increase in investment spending caused by higher expected rates of return will:
    A. shift the aggregate supply curve to the left.
    B. move the economy up along an existing aggregate demand curve.
    C. shift the aggregate demand curve to the left.
    D. shift the aggregate demand curve to the right.

34. The U.S. Gross Domestic Product (GDP) is defined as which of the following?
    A. The value of all goods and services produced.
    B. The value of all goods and services produced by Americans.
    C. The value of all goods and services produced in America.
    D. The value of all final goods and services produced in America.

35. All the following are "leading" indicators of the level of economic activity in the U.S. **EXCEPT**:
    A. New private housing construction starts.
    B. Common stock prices.
    C. Average weekly new claims for unemployment compensation.
    D. Size of the money supply.

36. Assume the following data for the U.S. economy in a recent year:

Personal consumption expenditures	$5,015 billion
Exports	$106 billion
Government purchases of goods/services	$1,040 billion
M1	$247 billion
Imports	$183 billion
Gross private domestic investment	$975 billion
Open market purchases by Federal Reserve	$4 billion

    Which of the following is the U.S. GDP based on the above information?
    A. $4,087 billion.
    B. $5,123 billion.
    C. $6,953 billion.
    D. $7,208 billion.

STUDY MANUAL – BUSINESS ENVIRONMENT & CONCEPTS
CHAPTER 24

37. A tightening of monetary policy would normally be expected to result in:
A. Higher bond and common stock prices.
B. Lower interest rates and stock prices.
C. Higher interest rates and lower stock prices.
D. Higher interest rates and higher stock prices.

38. If the Consumer Price Index rises during the year from 176.0 to 179.5, the rate of inflation during the year is:
A. 1.1%.
B. 1.9%.
C. 2.0%.
D. Answer cannot be determined from the information provided.

39. Which of the following is (are) among the elements of fiscal policy?

I. Government actions to raise or lower taxes.
II. Government actions to raise or lower the size of the money supply.
III. Government actions to raise or lower the amount it spends.

A. I only.
B. I and III only.
C. II and III only.
D. I, II, and III.

40. When the Federal Reserve engages in open market operations by buying government securities, which of the following is (are) likely to result?

I. Lower interest rates.
II. Lower size of the money supply.

A. I only.
B. II only.
C. Both I and II.
D. Neither I nor II.

41. When the Federal Reserve wants to tighten the availability of credit, it should so which of the following?

I. Sell government securities.
II. Raise the discount rate.

A. I only.
B. II only.
C. Both I and II.
D. Neither I nor II.

Page 640   ©2007 Kaplan CPA Review

42. The discount rate is the rate at which:
    A. the Federal Reserve will sell government securities.
    B. banks will lend to their best customers.
    C. the Treasury auctions off Treasury bills.
    D. the Federal Reserve will lend to member banks.

43. A raising of the reserve requirement by the Federal Reserve is likely to have all the following effects **EXCEPT:**
    A. Tighten the money supply.
    B. Lead to higher stock prices.
    C. Raise interest rates.
    D. Slow down the growth of GDP.

44. The federal government measures inflation with which of the following indicators?
    A. Dow Jones Index.
    B. Consumer Price Index.
    C. Consumer Confidence Index.
    D. Corporate profits.

45. Which of the following concepts compares the price of goods in a given year to a base year?
    A. Consumer Price Index.
    B. Consumer Confidence Index.
    C. Gross National Product.
    D. Net National Product.

STUDY MANUAL – BUSINESS ENVIRONMENT & CONCEPTS
CHAPTER 24

ANSWERS: GOVERNMENT POLICIES

1. **A** If the Fed increases reserve requirements, banks will have less money to supply, and the multiplier effect will work to cause the overall supply of money to contract.

2. **C** The Fed funds rate is the rate that banks charge each other for short-term borrowing and lending of excess reserves. Note that the Fed funds rate differs from the discount rate, which is the interest rate charged to banks when they borrow directly from the Fed.

3. **D** Expansionary fiscal policy, which is synonymous with running a deficit, will cause an upward shift in the aggregate demand curve resulting in higher prices. Paying off the deficit will result in higher taxes. The government will have to borrow funds to finance the deficit. Government borrowing increases the demand for loanable funds causing real interest rates to increase.

4. **A** If fiscal policy is going to reduce economic instability, changes in policy must inject stimulus during a recession and restraint during an inflationary boom.

5. **A** Fiscal policy affects the aggregate demand curve through changes in government spending or taxes. Increased government spending, or reduced taxes, could offset the output effects of a negative supply shock by increasing aggregate demand. Supply-side economics contends that fiscal policy also shifts the aggregate supply curve, but these effects are secondary to the impact on the aggregate demand curve.

6. **A** Fiscal policy makes use of government spending and taxation to regulate the economy for stability. Answer (b) is not correct because government spending and taxation do not have the purpose of achieving greater equality in the distribution of income. Answer (c) is not correct because it is monetary policy, not fiscal policy, that is used to alter the interest rate to change aggregate demand. Answer (d) is not correct because fiscal policy deals with government spending and taxation; but not with the fact that government spending and taxation will be contradictory. In fact the increase in government spending along with a reduction in taxation would be expansionary.

7. **D** The word expansionary explains it all. Answer (a) is not correct because fiscal supply is not designed to change the money supply. Answer (b) is not the correct answer because fiscal policy may or may not expand the size of government. Answer (c) is not the correct answer because monetary policy, not fiscal policy, is focused on price stability.

8. **D** A reduction in federal tax rates is an appropriate fiscal policy to bring the economy out of a recession. Answer (a) is not correct because such an action would use higher taxes to buy back federal debt instruments. Answer (b) is not correct because such actions would negatively impact aggregate demand. Answer (c) is not correct because such an action would involve a reduction in government spending.

9. **B** A decrease in taxes will increase aggregate demand. Answer (a) is not correct because a decrease in government spending will tend to decrease aggregate demand. Answer (c) is not correct because an appreciation of the dollar will tend to make exports more expensive in the world market, thus negatively impacting aggregate demand. Answer (d) is not correct because an increase in interest rates will tend to shift the aggregate demand curve to the left.

STUDY MANUAL – BUSINESS ENVIRONMENT & CONCEPTS
CHAPTER 24

10. **D** A tax rate increase is a fiscal policy and it is appropriate in that it will reduce customer spending and shift the aggregate demand curve inward. Answer (a) is not correct because an increase in government spending will move the aggregate demand curve outward. Answer (b) is not correct because depreciation of the dollar will cause exports to increase. Answer (c) is not correct because a reduction in interest rates will cause an outward shift in the aggregate demand curve and that will tend to increase the price level even more.

11. **D** Each of those two actions will tend to shift the aggregate demand curve inward and to the left because the decrease in government spending will have a greater impact than the impact of lower taxes. This is true because some of the lower taxes will be saved by consumers. Answer (a) is not correct because the government spending impact will be greater than the tax impact. Answer (b) is not correct because the aggregate supply will not change and the aggregate demand will shift to cause a lower price level. Answer (c) is not correct because the government spending impact on aggregate demand will be greater than the tax impact on aggregate demand.

12. **A** An expansionary fiscal policy will result in a rightward, or outward shift in the aggregate demand curve. Answer (b) is not correct because fiscal policy involves government spending and taxation and both are intended to shift the aggregate demand curve. Answer (c) is not correct because fiscal policy does not impact the aggregate supply curve. Answer (d) is not correct because the impact on the aggregate demand curve will be just the opposite.

13. **A** Changes in mutual fund balances are not part of the list of leading economic indicators. Answer (b) is not correct because the length of the average work week is in the list of leading economic indicators. Answer (c) is not correct because the money supply is in the list of leading economic indicators. Answer (d) is not correct because the value of the index of consumer expectations is in the list of leading economic indicators.

14. **A** M1 is the most liquid of the money supply classifications. Answer (b) is not correct because Series E bonds are not a part of the money supply. Answer (c) is not correct because credit balances with brokers is not a part of the money supply. Answer (d) is not correct because gold certificates are not a part of the money supply.

15. **A** As the price level increases, the value of money declines. Answer (b) is not correct because as the volume of employment increases, the price level is likely to increase and a price level increase will cause a decrease in the value of money. Answer (c) is not correct because the value of money declines as the price level increases. Answer (d) is not correct because inflation will tend to cause interest rates to increase and inflation causes the value of money to decline.

16. **B** The list provided in the question includes items that are included in M2, but not in M1. Answer (a) is not correct because M1 does not include time deposits. Answer (c) is not correct because the money supply does not include negotiable government bonds. Answer (d) is not correct because cash held in the U. S. Treasury is not included in the money supply.

17. **B** The purchase of government securities by the government puts money in the hands of consumers. Answer (a) is not correct because the purchase of government securities by the government will tend to cause commercial bank reserves to increase because it will put money in the hands of the people. Answer (c) is not correct because the purchase of government securities by the government will cause demand deposits to increase as people

©2007 Kaplan CPA Review
Page 643

STUDY MANUAL – BUSINESS ENVIRONMENT & CONCEPTS
CHAPTER 24

put the money in their bank accounts. Answer (d) is not correct because such an action will increase the money supply and the increase in the money supply will tend to cause interest rates to decrease.

18. **A**   The purchase of government bonds by the Fed will put money in the hands of people and those people will put the money in commercial banks. Answer (b) is not correct because only a specific policy decision by the Fed can change the reserve ratio. Answer (c) is not correct because only a specific policy decision by the Fed can change the discount rate. Answer (d) is not correct because the sale of government bonds will take money out of the hands of the people and the people will pay for the bonds by withdrawing money from the commercial banks.

19. **C**   The Fed's buying of government securities puts money in the hands of people and the people will deposit the money in commercial banks causing the bank to have more loanable reserves. Answer (a) is not correct because money will flow into the banks, not out of the banks. Answer (b) is not correct because money will flow into the banks and cause reserves to increase. Answer (d) is not correct because money will flow into the hand of the people.

20. **D**   An increase in the money supply will lower the interest rate, increase investment spending, and increase aggregate demand. Answer (a) is not correct because a decrease in the money supply will not cause a lower interest rate. Answer (b) is not correct because a decrease in the money supply may not result in a decline in GDP if the aggregate demand curve crosses the aggregate supply curve in the vertical range of the aggregate supply curve. Answer (c) is not correct because an increase in the money supply will reduce the interest rate.

21. **B**   The specified combination of Fed monetary policies and Federal Fiscal policies would be appropriate for a severe recession. Answer (a) is not correct because raising the reserve ratio and a budgetary surplus would be contrary actions in the face of a severe recession. Answer (c) is not correct because raising the reserve ratio, raising the discount rate, and a budgetary surplus are inconsistent with an attempt to overcome a severe recession. Answer (d) is not correct because raising the discount rate has the effect of reducing the money supply at a time when the money supply needs to increase to address the severe recession.

22. **C**   GDP measures the value of all final goods and services produced, not sold. Answer (a) is not correct because GDP measures the value of all final goods and services produced, not sold. Answer (b) is not correct because NDP is the value of all final goods and services produced within a nation's borders less depreciation. Answer (d) is not correct because the logic of changes in inventory would suggest that inventories increased rather than decreased.

23. **C**   Consumption expenditures include consumer durable goods, non-durable goods, and services. Answer (a) is not correct because consumption expenditures do not include second-hand goods because there is no production of those goods in the current year. Answer (b) is not correct because consumption expenditures do include the expenditures for services. Answer (d) is not correct because business inventories represent goods that have been produced but not yet purchased.

24. **D**   GDP measures the value of all final goods and services produced and the $10 billion increase in business inventories represents the only change from the prior year. Answer (a) is not correct because there is not information that would lead to that answer. Answer (b)

Page 644   ©2007 Kaplan CPA Review

is not correct because the change in business inventories was an increase, not a decrease. Answer (c) is not the correct answer because the change in business inventories suggests that more goods were produced in year 2 than in year 1.

25. **D** NDP is GDP less depreciation. Answer (a) is not correct because exports do not explain the difference between NDP and GDP. Answer (b) is not correct because indirect business taxes do not explain the difference between NDP and GDP. Answer (c) is not correct because gross investment is used in calculating GDP.

26. **A** Net foreign factor income and indirect business taxes explain the difference between NI and NDP. Answer (b) is not correct because corporate taxes are part of the difference between national income (NI) and personal income (PI). Answer (c) is not correct because GDP deflated for price level changes is called "Real GDP." Answer (d) is not correct because indirect business taxes is only one of the elements that explains the difference between NDP and NI.

27. **D** Personal income is equal to national income less social security contributions, less undistributed corporate profits, less corporate income taxes, plus transfer payments. Answer (a) is not correct because indirect business taxes are not an element in the difference between personal income and national income. Answer (b) is not correct because in such a situation, personal income would be less than national income. Answer (c) is not correct because indirect business taxes, consumption of fixed capital (depreciation), and personal taxes are not elements that explain the difference between national income and personal income.

28. **C** Disposable income is personal income less personal taxes. Answer (a) is not correct because discretionary income is the income available after making all payments on contractual obligations. Answer (b) is not correct because national income has not yet had taxes deducted. Answer (d) is not correct because personal income has not yet had personal taxes deducted.

29. **B** Real GDP measures current output at base year prices. Answer (a) is not correct because the word "Real" suggests that the measure is based on other than current prices. Answer (c) is not correct because Real GDP refers to the current year production. Answer (d) is not correct because exchange rates are not used to convert nominal GDP to real GDP.

30. **D** If nominal GDP rises faster than real GDP, it means that the general price level has risen. Answer (a) is not correct because the shifting of the base year is never done. Answer (b) is not correct because the relationship between nominal GDP and real GDP does reveal meaningful information about the price level. Answer (c) is not correct because if the price level had fallen, the real GDP would be lower than the previous year.

31. **D** The aggregate demand curve shows the relationship between the price level and real GDP. Answer (a) is not correct because the answer better describes the aggregate supply curve. Answer (b) is not correct because production costs are used to describe the slopes of the aggregate supply curve. Answer (c) is not correct because the aggregate demand curve shows the relationship between real GDP and some other variable other than "expenditures required."

32. **A** A change in the price level would result in an increase in real GDP without shifting the aggregate demand curve. Answer (b) is not correct because depreciation of the international value of the dollar will impact demand for exports and that will cause a shift in the aggregate demand curve. Answer (c) is not correct because the aggregate demand

©2007 Kaplan CPA Review

STUDY MANUAL – BUSINESS ENVIRONMENT & CONCEPTS
CHAPTER 24

curve shows the relationship between the price level and real GDP. Answer (d) is not correct because an increase in personal income tax rates will cause a shift in the aggregate demand curve.

33. **D** An increase in investment spending will cause the aggregate demand curve to shift to the right. Answer (a) is not correct because an increase in investment impacts the aggregate supply curve. Answer (b) is not correct because an increase in investment spending will not have an impact on the price level, one of the axis of the aggregate demand curve. Answer (c) is not correct because an increase in investment spending will have a positive impact on real GDP.

34. **D** Answer (a) is incorrect because it includes all intermediate goods, such as automobile transmissions along with the auto itself. Answer (b) is not correct because it includes intermediate goods and also because production in America by non-Americans is also included in GDP. Answer (c) is not correct because it includes all intermediate goods, such as automobile transmissions along with the auto itself.

35. **A** Building permits, not construction starts, is an item among the leading indicators of economic activity. Answer (b) is not correct because common stock prices is an item among the leading economic indicators. Answer (c) is not correct because average weekly new claims for unemployment compensation is an item among the leading economic indicators. Answer (d) is not correct because the size of the money supply is an item among the leading economic indicators.

36. **C** Consumption ($5,015) + Investment ($975) + Government ($1,040) – Net Imports ($183 - $106) = $6,953. Answer (a) is not correct because Consumption + Investment + Government – Net Imports = GDP. Answer (b) is not correct because Consumption + Investment + Government – Net Imports = GDP. Answer (d) is not correct because Consumption + Investment + Government – Net Imports = GDP.

37. **C** Tighter monetary policy means that actions are being taken by the Federal Reserve that will cause interest rates to rise, and rising interest rates will cause stock prices to be lower. Answer (a) is incorrect because tighter monetary policy suggests higher interest rates and higher interest rates will result in lower bond values and likely lower common stock prices. Answer (b) is incorrect because a tighter monetary policy will likely result in higher interest rates. Answer (d) is incorrect because a tighter monetary policy will likely result in higher interest rates which will cause lower stock prices.

38. **C** Answer (c) is the correct answer because (179.5 – 176.0) /176.0 = 2.0%. Answer (a) is not correct because (X –Y) / Y is the formula. Answer (b) is not correct because (X –Y) / Y is the formula. Answer (d) is not correct because (X –Y) / Y is the formula.

39. **B** Fiscal policy is implemented through the raising and lowering of taxes and through the raising and lowering of government spending. Answer (a) is not correct because there is another aspect to fiscal policy other than just taxation. Answer (c) is not correct because government actions to raise or lower the size of the money supply is an aspect of monetary policy, not fiscal policy. Answer (d) is not correct because government actions to raise or lower the size of the money supply is an aspect of monetary policy, not fiscal policy.

40. **A** The Fed's buying of government securities will increase the money supply and lower interest rates. Answer (b) is not correct because the Fed's buying of government securities will increase the money supply. Answer (c) is not correct because the Fed's buying of government securities will increase the money supply. Answer (d) is not correct because the Fed's buying of government securities will lower interest rates.

STUDY MANUAL – BUSINESS ENVIRONMENT & CONCEPTS
CHAPTER 24

41. **C** Both the selling of government securities and the raising of the discount rate will tend to tighten the availability of credit. Answer (a) is not correct because raising the discount rate will also tighten the availability of credit. Answer (b) is not correct because selling government securities will also tighten the availability of credit. Answer (d) is not correct because both the selling of government securities and the raising of the discount rate will tend to tighten the availability of credit.

42. **D** The discount rate is the rate at which the Fed will lend to member banks. Answer (a) is not correct because the rate at which the Fed will sell government securities is determined by the market. Answer (b) is not correct because the rate at which the banks will lend to their customers is determined by competition among banks. Answer (c) is not correct because the rate at which the Treasury auctions off Treasury bills is determined by the market.

43. **B** The raising of the reserve requirements will tend to raise interest rates and that will tend to cause lower stock prices. Answer (a) is not correct because a raising of the reserve requirements will tend to tighten the money supply. Answer (c) is not correct because the raising of the reserve requirement will tend to raise interest rates. Answer (d) is not correct because the raising of the reserve requirement will tend to raise interest rates and that will tend to slow down the growth of GDP.

44. **B** The Consumer Price Index measures inflation in the U.S. by comparing the price of a market basket in the current year to the price of the same market basket in the base year. Answer (a) is wrong because the Dow Jones Index is an average of a basket of blue-chip stocks. Answer (b) is incorrect because the Consumer Confidence Index is considered a variable in causing changes in business cycles.

45. **A** The Consumer Price Index measures inflation in the U.S. by comparing the price of a market basket in the current year to the price of the same market basket in the base year.

©2007 Kaplan CPA Review

Page 647

ECONOMICS: GLOBAL CURRENCY RISK AND HEDGING

STUDY MANUAL – BUSINESS ENVIRONMENT & CONCEPTS
CHAPTER 25

Study Tip: Believe in yourself. Thousands of people just like you pass the CPA exam each year. They are no smarter and no better educated. They just use good quality materials and they put in the time and the energy. You can do it also. The CPA exam is challenging, but it is certainly not impossible. People will constantly tell you that you cannot pass. Tell them to go away. There is nothing more important that you can bring to the CPA exam than a belief that you can do the work and make it happen.

IMPLICATIONS TO BUSINESS OF DEALINGS IN FOREIGN CURRENCIES

THE SIX POTENTIAL IMPEDIMENTS TO THE INTERNATIONAL FLOW OF CAPITAL

A. Psychological barriers. Unfamiliarity with international markets (e.g., language and information sources) may cause investors to limit foreign investment.

B. Legal restrictions. Institutional investors may be prohibited by domestic regulation from investing internationally. Additionally, local governments may impose restrictions on foreign investment flowing into or out of the country.

C. Transaction costs. Transaction costs are higher in international investing.

D. Discriminatory taxation. Foreign investments may be taxed at a higher rate than locally generated investments.

E. Political risks. Local government actions can cause changes in the value of invested funds.

F. Foreign currency risk. Foreign investors bear the risk of changes in the local-market value of invested funds, as well as the risk of changes in the exchange rate between the local foreign currency and investors' home currency.

FACTORS THAT FAVOR INTERNATIONAL MARKET INTEGRATION

A. While all of these impediments potentially limit capital flows and reduce the efficiency of world markets, international market integration only requires that a *sufficient number* of investors be able to move capital between markets. Three factors

Page 648

©2007 Kaplan CPA Review

have caused international capital mobility to increase dramatically over the past 20 years:

1. There are many private and institutional investors who are internationally active.

2. Essentially all major corporations have multinational operations.

3. Corporations and governments borrow and lend on an international scale.

   Given these developments, it is doubtful that markets are fully segmented today.

B. Real exchange rate movements are defined as changes in the nominal exchange rate that are not explained by inflation differentials. Suppose that the one-year inflation rate is 2 percent in the United States and 3 percent in Europe. The inflation differential is 1 percent. We would expect to see the euro depreciate by 1 percent against the dollar (remember, high inflation rate countries should expect to see their currencies depreciate). However, if the euro depreciates by 7 percent, there has been a real exchange rate depreciation of 6 percent (7 percent depreciation minus 1 percent inflation differential). In reality, most exchange rates uncertainty is due to these real changes, since inflation is highly predictable in the short run.

C. The firm's exchange rate exposure is the way the value of an individual company changes in response to a change in the *real* value of the local currency. We can estimate the currency exposure of a particular firm by regressing the firm's stock return on local currency changes. We can further refine this process with detailed analysis of the geographic distribution of the firm's sales and the currency origin of the firm's revenues and costs.

   For example, a German firm that imports products from the United States for resale in Germany has very different local currency exposure to the euro than a German firm that produces products in Germany and exports them for sale in the United States. Suppose the euro depreciates by 5 percent in real terms. The German importer is less competitive, and his or her euro profits fall because the goods purchased in the United States are more expensive (i.e., it takes more euros to buy the same goods). On the other hand, the exporter is helped by the depreciation of the euro. The exporter can effectively cut the U.S. dollar price of his or her goods without reducing his or her euro profits.

Example: Identifying a firm's currency exposure

Consider two different French firms:

Firm 1 produces electrical components in France for sale in Great Britain. Prices are set and paid in pounds, and costs are incurred in euros.

Firm 2 imports cars from Great Britain for sale in France.

Suppose the euro (the local currency) experiences real appreciation of 5 percent against the pound. Discuss how the value of each firm will be affected by appreciation of the euro against

STUDY MANUAL – BUSINESS ENVIRONMENT & CONCEPTS
CHAPTER 25

the pound. Explain how your answer changes if the change in value is completely explained by the inflation differential.

Answer

Firm 1 will be hurt by the appreciation of the euro. The currency appreciation effectively makes Firm 1's products more expensive in the British market, so sales will fall. Cost won't change, however, so profits and stock price will also likely fall.

Firm 2 will be helped by the euro appreciation because the currency change will make the British cars less expensive in the French market. The sales, profits, and value of Firm 2 should increase.

If the currency movements are purely nominal (i.e., completely explained by the inflation differential), nominal sales and profits for both firms will change, but real sales and profits (and value) will remain the same.

Note: Remember that importers are hurt by local currency depreciation, and exporters are helped by local currency depreciation.

D. Empirically, domestic economic activity (think GDP growth) is related to exchange rate movements. Two theories have been proposed to explain this relationship: the traditional model and the money demand model.

1. The traditional model has both a long-run and short-run component. In the long run, a decline in the value of a country's currency increases national competitiveness. That is, exports increase and economic activity is stimulated. However, the short-run impact is more negative. In the short run, if a country's currency depreciates in real terms, the cost of imports increases, causing a widening in the trade balance (exports minus imports) and an increase in domestic inflation. In the short run, currency depreciation tends to reduce economic activity. In the long run, the increased competitiveness of domestic industry will restore economic activity and reduce the trade gap. That is, the traditional model predicts that depreciation in the value of the local currency will cause an increase in the competitiveness of domestic industry and, thus, an increase in the stock value of domestic firms.

2. In the money demand model, an increase in real economic activity leads to an increase in the demand for the local currency. The increased local currency demand causes the value of the local currency to appreciate. Because stock prices are highly correlated with GDP growth, the money demand model explains the positive correlation between changes in local currency and stock returns.

   Bond prices are largely determined by long-term interest rates. Therefore, understanding the currency exposure of bonds requires understanding the relationship between exchange rates and interest rates. There are two conflicting theories that explain this relationship:

   a. Free markets theory. An increase in the domestic real rate of interest causes capital to flow into the domestic markets from abroad. The inflow of capital

Page 650 ©2007 Kaplan CPA Review

increases the demand for the local currency, causing an increase in its value. This creates negative local currency exposure for bond investors. That is, increases in interest rates decrease local currency bond values while the appreciating local currency increases the value of the bond in the foreign investor's domestic currency. (See Figure 1.

Figure 1: Free Market Theory of Bond Exposure

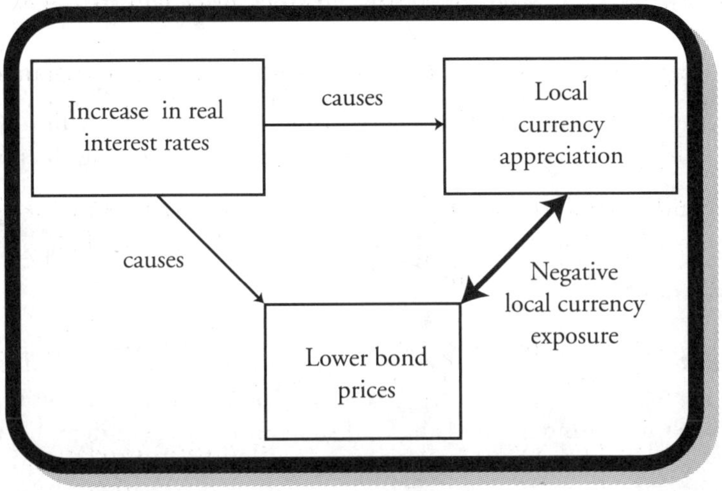

Note: It is important to distinguish between an increase in real interest rates and an increase in nominal interest rates caused by an increase in inflation. If rates increase because of higher anticipated inflation, the rate increase results in a decrease in the value of the currency.

    b.   Government intervention theory. Governments frequently attempt to maintain a target range for the value of their currency. If the value of the currency falls to the low end of the range, the local government will increase interest rates to support the currency. Likewise, a strong domestic currency will lead local governments to ease interest rates. This system (sometimes called the *leaning-against-the-wind policy*) induces positive local currency exposure. That is, increasing currency values (which helps foreign bond investors) leads to decreasing interest rates, increasing bond prices (which also helps foreign bond investors), and a positive local currency exposure for domestic bonds.

IMPACT OF CURRENCY EXCHANGE RATE MOVEMENTS ON A COMPANY THAT EXPORTS A HIGH PERCENTAGE OF ITS PRODUCTION

A. Currency exchange rates have considerable impact on companies with high levels of product exports.

B. The strengthening of an exporter's domestic currency has a negative effect on the exporter, since those goods become relatively more expensive to customers in the importing country with the weakening currency.

C. On the other hand, depreciation of the home currency will make the exporter's goods more attractive overseas and increase demand and net income.

GLOBAL CURRENCY RISKS AND HEDGING

A. Currency risk occurs because exchange rates are not fixed, causing the future value of assets, liabilities, cash flows, and contracts to change as the exchange rate changes.

1. Exchange rates are simply prices of a currency (euros/dollar = price of a dollar in terms of euros). $1.20/euro = 0.8333 euros/$. If exchange rates are allowed to float, the exchange rate is determined by supply-and-demand conditions in a currency market. For example, the price of euros in terms of dollars is the equilibrium exchange rate, as illustrated in Figure 2.

2. Shifts in the demand and supply for a currency will cause the exchange rate to move up or down.

   a. Increases in the demand for euros occur due to an increase in demand for euro exports, euro securities, or expectations about the euro going stronger. The economic fundamentals behind such an increase in demand for the euro would be relatively lower inflation in the euro zone, relatively higher real interest rates in the euro zone, and/or relatively lower income in the euro zone. This shift in demand is shown in Figure 2.

Figure 2: Shifts in the Demand for Euros

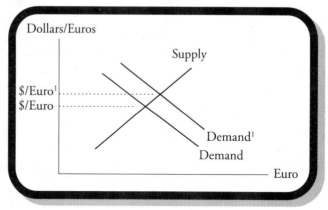

   b. Increases in the supply of euros occur due to increases in the demand for U.S. imports, relatively more attractive U.S. real interest rates, and/or relatively higher income in the euro zone. The shift in supply is shown in Figure 3.

Figure 3: Shifts in the Supply for Euros

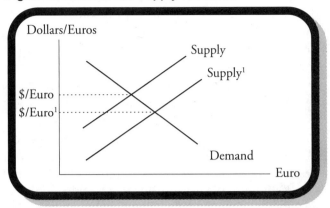

c. Fundamental factors that cause the dollar to be stronger are outlined below.

Fundamental Factor	$ Stronger (euro/$ rate up or $/euro rate down)
Inflation	Relatively higher in the euro zone
Real interest rates	Relatively higher in the United States
Income	Relatively higher in the euro zone
Expectations	Favor holding dollars
Central bank	Buy dollars and sell euros in the currency market

B. A fixed exchange rate is not allowed to move in response to normal market shifts in supply or demand. The disequilibrium must be managed by either forcing an equilibrium with trade restrictions or through intervention in the currency market by central banks to buy or sell a currency until the fixed rate is achieved. For example, using Figure 3, if the exchange rate is fixed above the equilibrium, the euro zone countries could restrict purchases of U.S. goods and securities (quotas and trade restrictions). This would force the supply of euros to be reduced back to the point where the fixed rate is established. Another alternative is for the central bank to buy euros, shifting demand out to the point where the fixed rate is achieved.

C. When a country's currency falls in value, the country should see an improvement in its trade account. It will export relatively more and import relatively less. The example below illustrates why this is true, everything else being equal.

Example: Exchange rates

Assume the exchange rate is $1.2 per euro. Also, assume a U.S. product costs $48 in the United States and 40 euros in the euro zone. The euro product costs 20 euros in the euro zone and $24 in the United States. Now, assume the value of the dollar rises and the euro falls to 1 euro per dollar.

STUDY MANUAL – BUSINESS ENVIRONMENT & CONCEPTS
CHAPTER 25

Answer

The U.S. product would sell for 48 euros in the euro zone and U.S. exports will fall. The euro product would sell for $20 in the United States and U.S. imports would rise. The change in the exchange rate effectively changes the prices of goods for export and import. The country with the lower valued currency will export more and import less.

D. An exposure to a currency represents a potential gain or loss due to movement of the currency's exchange rate. For example, an account receivable invoiced in pounds will gain in dollar value if the $/pound exchange rate goes up. The account receivable will lose in dollar value if the $/pound rate goes down. The exposure is illustrated below.

   AR exposure today = 1,000,000 pounds = $????
   Depends on the $/pound exchange rate

1. Exposures to changes in an exchange rate can be managed by hedging. For example, an account receivable for pounds will gain in dollar value if the $/pound exchange rate goes up and will lose dollar value if the $/pound rate goes down. This can be hedged by an account payable of the same amount and same maturity, since the gain or loss on the payable is just the opposite of the gain or loss on a receivable. A hedge is created by having offsetting exposures to the same currency or to currencies that are very highly correlated with each other.

2. Most currencies (at least major currencies) are allowed to float in response to changes in supply and demand for the currency in the global currency market. Major drivers of the shifts in supply and demand for a currency are inflation, real interest rates, and income (frequently called the country's fundamentals). If two countries follow similar domestic policies and have similar fundamentals, their currencies will remain stable with each other. But, most countries follow independent monetary and fiscal policies leading to different inflation rates, different real interest rates, and different rates of income growth. For this reason exchange rates tend to be volatile and currency risk must be managed.

   a. Countries with higher (lower) inflation will see the value of their currency fall (rise), everything else being equal. If the United States has higher inflation than countries in the euro zone, the euro/$ rate will fall. Higher inflation makes U.S. goods less attractive at the old exchange rate so a reduction in demand for dollars results in a falling value of the dollar (depreciation).

   b. Countries with higher (lower) real interest rates will see the value of their currency rise (fall). Demand for the currency with higher real rates shifts outward as investors seek the higher real rate of return. This makes the currency with the higher real rate go up (appreciate).

   c. Countries with higher (lower) income growth will see the value of their currency fall (rise). This relationship is a little harder to see. If the U.S. economy has higher income growth than the euro zone, the United States buys more from countries in the euro zone than they buy from the United

Page 654   ©2007 Kaplan CPA Review

STUDY MANUAL – BUSINESS ENVIRONMENT & CONCEPTS
CHAPTER 25

States. This is especially true for income-elastic exports and imports. The United States will have an increased demand for euros, but the demand for dollars will shift inward as less U.S. goods are bought, resulting in a lower euro/$ rate.

E. There are three types of currency risk exposure faced by the firm. Transaction exposure and operating exposure are real gains or losses. Translation exposure is an accounting exposure that is not realized unless the firm is liquidated.

1. Transaction exposure occurs when a monetary amount of another currency is to be either paid or received at a future date. The risk is that the value of the monetary amount of the foreign currency in terms of the domestic currency depends on what happens to the exchange rate between now and maturity. For example: Assume you have an account payable due in 60 days for 1 million euros. How many dollars will this payable cost? If the spot exchange rate in 60 days is $1.18 per euro, you will owe $1.18 million. But, if the value of the euro drops to $1.10, you will only owe $1.1 million. This is the currency risk/uncertainty of not knowing what the exchange rate will be.

2. Operating exposure occurs due to the effects unexpected changes in exchange rates have on nonmonetary assets and future cash flows from operations. Operating exposure is normally an ongoing exposure without a specific maturity. For example, you own a ski resort in Aspen. When the value of the dollar appreciates relative to European currencies, more of your potential customers will choose to ski in the Swiss Alps or other European spots. The dollar will buy more Swiss francs, making the trip to ski in Switzerland cheaper for U.S. skiers. This will hurt your operating cash flows, even though you do not have foreign currency assets, liabilities, or costs. Another example is a U.S. company producing in Canada but selling its products back in the United States. If the $/C$ goes up, sales back in the United States will go down (it takes more dollars to buy goods denominated in C$).

3. Translation exposure occurs because foreign currency accounts must be translated back into the home country's currency for consolidation. Depending on the translation method, some assets and liabilities are translated at the current exchange rate and some are translated at the old historic exchange rate. The imbalance that is created results in a translation gain or loss and is recorded in a cumulative translation adjustment account on the balance sheet (assuming FASB 52). There is no real loss, but there is an equity accounting entry to balance accounts.

Example: Translation

A subsidiary uses the euro as its functional currency and we must translate its balance sheet back into dollars. The firm has 20 million euros of exposed assets (exposed means it must be translated using the current spot rate) and 15 million euros of exposed liabilities.

©2007 Kaplan CPA Review
Page 655

STUDY MANUAL – BUSINESS ENVIRONMENT & CONCEPTS
CHAPTER 25

Answer

The net exposure is 5 million euros, since any movement of the euro that causes a gain or loss on assets will have the opposite effect on liabilities. If the spot rate ($/euro) used in translation falls by $0.07 then the translation gain or loss is equal to ($/euro 0.07)(5,000,000 euros) = $350,000. We had a translation gain of $350,000 due to the $0.07 appreciation per euro on our net exposure. We add this translation gain to the equity in a special cumulative account in the consolidated balance sheet.

F. Currency risk can be managed by using forward contracts, futures contracts, options, swaps, and internal balance sheet hedging to create offsetting exposures to whatever currency causes the currency risk. (Note that the financial contracts used for hedging are reviewed in the finance section.)

1. Balance sheet hedging should be used first before contractual hedging with financial contracts is used. Balance sheet hedging simply requires netting out assets and liabilities with exposures to the same currency. For example, if we have 10 million euros in assets and 10 million euros in liabilities, there is a perfect balance sheet hedge. On the other hand, if we have 15 million euros in assets and 10 million euros in liabilities, we have a 5 million euro net exposure to the $/euro rate. We would only use financial contracts to hedge the net exposure. We could also create a liability in euros for 5 million to achieve a hedge without using currency derivative contracts.

2. Forward currency contracts are provided by dealers on a bid-ask spread basis. The dealer quotes forward prices that can be locked in today for delivery at a future date. For example, if a firm has a 1-million euro account receivable in 90 days, the firm loses if the $/euro rate falls. The exposure is hedged by selling the 1 million euros to a dealer in the forward contract. The dealer will give a dollar quote for the euros today but with delivery in 90 days. Forwards are flexible and can be set for different amounts and different maturity dates. But, forward contracts are not liquid and are difficult to change.

3. Future currency contracts are much like forward contracts, but they are exchange traded. This makes futures much more liquid but they are not very flexible. Contracts are in standard amounts with only four delivery dates a year. Also, margins are required. However, futures do not have the counterparty risk of forward contracts. For example if a firm has a 70,000-pound account payable (owe pounds = short position) due in 90 days it could get an offsetting future on pounds (long position = buy pounds). These two positions have opposite and offsetting exposures. But, there may be a mismatch of maturities and amounts. The pound future is for 62,500 pounds per contract so a future for 70,000 pounds is not available. Also, the 90-day exposure of the account payable may not have the maturity date of the closest future contract.

4. Currency options are also available for hedging purposes. Options are traded on exchanges and in dealer markets. The option hedge has a unique characteristic. Options can be allowed to expire if the exchange rate movement does not cause a loss in the underlying exposure. This allows option hedges that are aimed at

Page 656   ©2007 Kaplan CPA Review

hedging only the direction of an exchange rate movement that causes a loss. For example, if there is an account receivable exposure to pounds, the exposure loses if the value of a pound falls (fewer dollars for the pounds received). But, if the value of the pound goes up, there is no need for a hedge. The option that gains when the value of a pound falls is a put on pounds. The pound put option matched with the pound account receivable hedges only falling pound values. If the pound goes up the put will expire without being exercised and the pounds received on the account receivable are sold at the market value. The premiums paid on the put are deducted from the pounds received, but upside potential for the exposure remains.

5. Swap contracts are also used to hedge currency exposure and are especially good for operating exposures. A currency swap is just an exchange of cash flows in one currency in exchange for cash flows in another currency. For example, assume a firm operates in the United Kingdom and earns pound cash flows over time. But, the firm uses dollar financing and has to make dollar interest payments. The firm has risk because it doesn't know if the dollar value of the pounds in the future will be sufficient to pay the dollar interest payments. For example, this firm could enter into a swap of pounds for dollars over a relatively long time period, such as five years. The current interest rate on pounds and the current interest rate on dollars will be used to set up the pound for dollar swap. A present value principal of pounds and dollars will be used based on the current spot rate and cash flows will be set by taking the interest rates multiplied by the present value. For example, if the spot rate is $1.60 per pound and the annual interest rate on the dollar is 5 percent and the rate on the pound is 6 percent, multiplied by the annual cash flows for the next five years would be as follows if the principal amount is 1 million pounds.

    Note: the swap is set up as two parallel loans. For example, one side gets $1,600,000 today and pays interest payments of $80,000 every year and a final payment of the $1,600,000 principal at the end of five years. The amounts not in boxes represent a similar parallel loan in pounds.

The following table provides a summary of hedging alternatives for different types of exposures.

Transactions Exposure	Hedging Alternatives
Account payable in euros	Buy euros forward
	Buy euros in futures market (long position)
	Buy a call option on euros (long call)
	Match AP with AR in euros
Account receivable in euros	Sell euros forward
	Sell euros in futures market (short position)
	Buy a put option on euros (long put)
	Match AR with AP in euros
Operating Exposure	Hedging Alternatives
Assets in euros	Liabilities in euros
Cash flows in euros or $ cash flows fall if $/euro fall	Swap euros for dollars

©2007 Kaplan CPA Review

Page 657

STUDY MANUAL – BUSINESS ENVIRONMENT & CONCEPTS
CHAPTER 25

Transactions Exposure	Hedging Alternatives
	Sell euro futures (short position)
	Buy puts on euros
	Sell euros forward
	Shift costs from dollars to euros
Costs in euros or $ cash flows fall if $/euro rises	Swap dollars for euros
	Buy euro futures (long position)
	Buy calls on euros
	Buy euros forward
	Shift revenues from dollars to euros
Translation Exposure	**Hedging Alternatives**
Exposed assets > exposed liabilities	Increase euro liabilities
	Don't worry, it will cancel out eventually
	Only in extreme cases would we use:
	Sell (short) euro futures
	Buy euro puts
Exposed assets < exposed liabilities	Increase euro assets
	Don't worry, it will cancel out eventually
	Only in extreme cases would we use:
	Buy (long) euro futures
	Buy (long) euro calls

MECHANICS OF A FORWARD CONTRACT

The party to the forward contract that agrees to buy the financial or physical asset has a long forward position and is called the long. The party to the forward contract that agrees to sell/deliver the asset has a short forward position and is called the short.

We will illustrate the basic forward contract mechanics through an example based on the purchase and sale of a Treasury bill (T-bill). Note that while forward contracts on T-bills are usually quoted in terms of a discount percentage from face value, we use dollar prices here to make the example easy to follow.

Consider a contract under which Party A agrees to buy a $1,000 face value 90-day T-bill from Party B 30 days from now at a price of $990. Party A is the long and Party B is the short. Both parties have removed uncertainty about the price they will pay or receive for the T-bill at the future date. If 30 days from now T-bills are trading at $992, the short must deliver the T-bill to the long in exchange for a $990 payment. If T-bills are trading at $988 on the future date, the long must purchase the T-bill from the short for $990, the contract price.

Each party to a forward contract is exposed to default risk, the probability that the other party (the counterparty) will not perform as promised. Typically, no money changes hands at the inception of the contract, unlike futures contracts in which each party posts an initial deposit called the *margin* as a guarantee of performance. At any point in time, including the settlement date, the party to the forward contract with the negative value will owe money to the other side. The other side of the contract will have a positive value of equal amount. Following this example, if the T-bill price is $992 at the (future)

Page 658   ©2007 Kaplan CPA Review

settlement date and the short does not deliver the T-bill for $990 as promised, the short has defaulted.

DETERMINING THE PRICE OF A FORWARD CONTRACT

The No-Arbitrage Principle

A. The price of a forward contract is not the price to purchase the contract, because the parties to a forward contract typically pay nothing to enter into the contract at its inception. Here, price refers to the contract price of the underlying asset under the terms of the forward contract. This price may be a U.S. dollar or euro price but it is often expressed as an interest rate or currency exchange rate.

   1. For T-bills, the price will be expressed as an annualized percentage discount from face value.

   2. For coupon bonds, it will usually be expressed as a yield to maturity.

   3. For the implicit loan in a forward rate agreement (FRA), it will be expressed as annualized London Interbank Offered Rate (LIBOR).

   4. For a currency forward, it is expressed as an exchange rate between the two currencies involved.

      However it is expressed, this rate, yield, discount, or dollar amount is the forward price in the contract.

B. The price that we wish to determine is the forward price that makes the values of both the long and the short positions zero at contract initiation. We will use the no arbitrage principle: there should not be a riskless profit to be gained by a combination of a forward contract position with positions in other assets. This principle assumes that:

   1. Transactions costs are zero.

   2. There are no restrictions on short sales or on the use of short sale proceeds.

   3. Both borrowing and lending can be done in unlimited amounts at the risk-free rate of interest.

HOW CREDIT RISK ARISES IN A FORWARD CONTRACT AND HOW MARKET VALUE IS A MEASURE OF THE CREDIT RISK TO A PARTY IN A FORWARD CONTRACT

A. At any date after initiation of a forward contract, it is likely to have positive value to either the long or the short. Recall that this value is the amount that would be paid to settle the contract in cash at that point in time.

STUDY MANUAL – BUSINESS ENVIRONMENT & CONCEPTS
CHAPTER 25

B. The party with the position that has positive value has credit risk in this amount because the other party would owe them that amount if the contract were terminated. The contract value and, therefore, the credit risk, may increase, decrease, or even change sign over the remaining term of the contract.

C. At any point in time, the market values of forward contracts, as we have calculated them, are a measure of the credit risk currently borne by the party to which a cash payment would be made to settle the contract at that time.

COMPARISON OF FUTURES AND FORWARD CONTRACTS

A. Futures contracts are very much like forward contracts. They are similar in that:

1. Deliverable contracts obligate the long to buy and the short to sell a certain quantity of an asset for a certain price on a specified future date.

2. Cash settlement contracts are settled by paying the contract value in cash on the expiration date.

3. Both forwards and futures are priced to have zero value at the time the investor enters into the contract.

B. There are important differences between futures and forward contracts, including:

1. Futures are marked to market at the end of every trading day. Forward contracts are not marked to market.

2. Forwards are private contracts and do not trade on organized exchanges. Futures contracts trade on organized exchanges.

3. Forwards are customized contracts satisfying the needs of the parties involved. Futures contracts are highly standardized.

4. Forwards are contracts with the originating counterparty; a single clearinghouse is the counterparty to all futures contracts.

5. Forward contracts are usually not regulated. The government regulates futures markets.

WHY THE FUTURES PRICE MUST CONVERGE TO THE SPOT PRICE AT EXPIRATION

A. The spot (cash) price of a commodity or financial asset is the price for immediate delivery. The futures price is the price today for delivery at some future point in time (the maturity date). The basis is the difference between the spot price and the futures price.

Basis = Spot price – Futures price

Page 660   ©2007 Kaplan CPA Review

B. As the maturity date nears, the basis converges toward zero. At expiration, the spot price must equal the futures price because the futures price has become the price today for delivery today, which is the same as the spot. Arbitrage will force the prices to be the same at contract expiration.

Example: Why the futures price must equal the spot price at expiration

Suppose the current spot price of silver is $4.65. Demonstrate by arbitrage that the futures price of a futures silver contract that expires in one minute must equal the spot price.

Answer

Suppose the futures price was $4.70. We could buy the silver at the spot price of $4.65, sell the futures contract, and deliver the silver under the contract at $4.70. Our profit would be $4.70 – $4.65 = $0.05. Because the contract matures in one minute, there is virtually no risk to this arbitrage trade.

Suppose instead the futures price was $4.61. Now we would buy the silver contract, take delivery of the silver by paying $4.61, and then sell the silver at the spot price of $4.65. Our profit is $4.65 – $4.61 = $0.04. Once again, this is a riskless arbitrage trade. Therefore, in order to prevent arbitrage, the futures price at the maturity of the contract must be $4.65.

FUTURES MARGINS AND MARKING TO MARKET

A. Margin in the futures markets is a performance guarantee: money deposited by both the long and the short. There is no loan involved and, consequently, no interest charges. Each exchange has a clearinghouse. The clearinghouse guarantees that traders in the futures market will honor their obligations. The clearinghouse does this by splitting each trade once it is made and acting as the opposite side of each position. To safeguard the clearinghouse, the exchange requires traders to post margin and settle their accounts on a daily basis. Before trading, the trader must deposit funds (called margin) with his or her broker (who, in return, will post margin with the clearinghouse).

B. Marking to market is the process of adjusting the margin balance in a futures account each day for the change in the value of the contract from the previous trading day, based on the settlement price. The futures exchanges can require a mark to market more frequently (than daily) under extraordinary circumstances.

DETERMINING THE VALUE OF A FUTURES CONTRACT

A. Like forward contracts, futures contracts have no value at contract initiation. Unlike forward contracts, futures contracts do not accumulate value changes over the term of the contract. Since futures accounts are marked to market daily, the value after the margin deposit has been adjusted for the day's gains and losses in contract value is always zero. The futures price at any point in time is the price that makes the value of a new contract equal to zero. The value of a futures contract strays from zero only

STUDY MANUAL – BUSINESS ENVIRONMENT & CONCEPTS
CHAPTER 25

during the trading periods between the times at which the account is marked to market:

Value of futures contract = Current futures price – futures price at last mark to market

B. If the futures price increases, the value of the long position increases. The value is set back to zero by the mark to market at the end of the mark-to-market period.

HOW FUTURES AND FORWARD PRICES DIFFER

A. There are a number of real-world complications that will cause futures and forward prices to be different. If investors prefer the mark-to-market feature of futures, futures prices will be higher than forward prices. If investors would rather hold a forward contract in order to avoid the marking to market of a futures contract, the forward price would be higher than the futures price. From a technical standpoint, the differences between the theoretical (no-arbitrage) prices of futures and forwards center on the correlation between interest rates and the mark-to-market cash flows of futures:

   1. Higher reinvestment rates for gains and lower borrowing costs to fund losses lead to a preference for the mark-to-market feature of futures, and higher prices for futures than forwards, when interest rates and asset values are positively correlated.

   2. A preference to avoid the mark-to-market cash flows will lead to a higher price for the forward relative to the future if interest rates and asset values are negatively correlated.

B. A preference for the mark-to-market feature will arise from a positive correlation between interest rates and the price of the contract asset. When the value of the underlying asset increases and the mark to market generates cash, reinvestment opportunities tend to be better due to the positive correlation of asset values with higher interest rates. When the value of the underlying asset decreases and the mark to market requires cash, borrowing costs tend to be lower due to the positive correlation.

C. The opposite result will occur when the correlation between the price of the underlying asset and interest rates is negative. Consider forwards and futures contracts on fixed-income prices. Fixed-income values fall when interest rates rise, so rates and values are negatively correlated. Borrowing costs are higher when funds are needed and reinvestment rates are lower when funds are generated by the mark to market of the futures contracts.

ABSOLUTE PURCHASING POWER PARITY AND RELATIVE PURCHASING POWER PARITY

A. On the most basic level, purchasing power parity (PPP) states that identical goods should have the same price regardless of the location. The law of one price focuses on a single, clearly comparable good and states that the same good should have the same

Page 662   ©2007 Kaplan CPA Review

real prices in all countries. For instance, a Starbucks latte should cost the same in San Francisco and Milan after adjusting for the U.S dollar/euro exchange rate. The relationship requires that competitive markets exist without transportation costs or tariffs.

B. Absolute purchasing power parity is an average version of the law of one price. Rather than focusing on a single good, absolute PPP focuses on a weighted average price level of a representative basket of goods and services. The absolute version of PPP states that the same basket of goods should have the same price in all countries after adjusting for the exchange rate. The equilibrium exchange rate occurs when the ratio of average price levels equalizes the prices of the baskets from each country. This version of PPP requires the unrealistic assumptions that there are no impediments to trade and that all consumers across the world have identical baskets of goods and services.

C. Relative purchasing power parity holds that exchange rate movements reflect differences in inflation rates between countries. It is the rate of inflation (i.e., the relative rate of change in prices) that is critical here. Hence, relative PPP requires only that the exchange rate be proportional to the ratio of the two price indexes. Movements in currencies provide a means of equilibrating purchasing power of currencies in an inflationary environment. In other words, the change in the real exchange rate is equal to the change in the nominal exchange rate minus the actual inflation differential between the two countries. In practical terms, currencies with high levels of inflation should depreciate relative to currencies with lower levels of inflation.

ELEMENTS OF BALANCE OF PAYMENTS AND THEIR ROLE IN EXCHANGE RATE DETERMINATION

A. The balance of payments is a summary of a country's international transactions. It ties together all financial flows for a country where all financial cash inflows are considered credits to the balance of payments and cash outflows are considered debits. The balance of payments consists of four accounts: the current account, the capital account, the financial account, and the official reserve account. The following balance of payments relationship must hold:

1. The current account encompasses the balance of trade merchandise and services, and income received or paid on existing investments. The current account consists of four components: merchandise trade balance, balance of services, net income (dividends and interest) received from existing investments, and current transfers of wealth, such as gifts to relatives and educational grants to foreign students.

2. The capital account represents unilateral transfers, such as financial assistance to foreign nations, debt forgiveness, expropriation losses, and investment capital given without future repayment. This account is generally very small in its impact on the balance of payments.

3. The financial account includes short-term and long-term capital flows resulting from direct investments and portfolio investments. Short-term capital flows

STUDY MANUAL – BUSINESS ENVIRONMENT & CONCEPTS
CHAPTER 25

represent deposits made by foreigners at domestic banks. Long-term capital flows include direct investments in the purchases of companies or real estate. The financial account excludes transactions made by the country's central bank.

4. The official reserve account is basically the net change in a government's international reserves. The reserves include foreign currency holdings and loans to foreign governments. The traditional approach to foreign exchange rate determination suggests that exchange rate adjustments are required to restore balance of payments equilibrium. This is a difficult model to implement, however. An analysis of these potential adjustments requires an estimate of trade flow elasticity in response to movements in exchange rates. Further, the model must be dynamic and complex enough to handle the impact of capital flows and the effect on the balance of payment components.

B. Ultimately, however, small changes in current account flows cannot substantiate the dramatic volatility in the exchange rate markets. That means an analysis of the elements of the balance of payments is not useful in explaining how exchange rates are determined. Therefore, additional models, such as the asset market approach, may provide more insight and be more useful.

FOREIGN EXCHANGE QUOTATIONS

A. Local nonbank public customer quotes (here the home country currency is quoted against the foreign currency) can be stated as:

1. Direct quotes, which are domestic currency per foreign currency: DC/FC. Usually quoted per 100 FC units, except for the U.S. dollar ($) and the British pound (£) where it is one unit. This is the usual method of quoting currencies.

2. Indirect quotes, which are foreign currency per domestic currency: FC/DC.

   a. To convert a direct quote to an indirect quote, or vice versa, you simply take the reciprocal of the one that you are given.

   b. For example, in Japan, a direct quote of 125 ¥/$ is equivalent to an indirect quote of 0.008 $/¥. Just use the $1/x$ key on your calculator to turn the indirect quote 125 ¥/$ into the direct quote of 0.008 $/¥.

PROTECTING A PORTFOLIO AGAINST CURRENCY RISKS

A. Currency risk is one of the most important factors in managing the risk of foreign investments. The underlying goal of a currency hedge is to minimize the portfolio's exposure to changes in exchange rates. Portfolio managers will typically use either futures or forward currency contracts to hedge their foreign investments. A basic hedging strategy would be to "hedge the principal," where a domestic investor offsets his or her currency exposure by entering into a foreign exchange contract in the same principal amount as his or her foreign investment. For example, a U.S. investor with Sf 5,000,000 invested in a Swiss company would sell futures contracts totaling Sf 5,000,000 worth of dollars. If the Swiss franc depreciates versus the dollar, the gain in

Page 664   ©2007 Kaplan CPA Review

the value on the futures position should offset the decline in value of the investment in the Swiss company. Alternatively, appreciation in the Swiss franc versus the dollar would result in a gain in the investment in the Swiss company and an equivalent loss on the futures contracts.

THE DIFFERENCE BETWEEN TRANSLATION RISK AND ECONOMIC RISK

A. Translation risk is the uncertainty in the actual amount that will be received, when the foreign investment is translated back into the domestic currency. The principal value of the foreign asset is translated at the prevailing exchange rate, so any change in the exchange rate affects the value of the asset when stated in terms of the domestic currency. The ideal currency hedge would smooth out any changes in the currencies of the two countries and achieve a foreign rate of return that is equal to a domestic rate of return. The optimal hedge ratio for translation risk is one.

B. Economic risk is separate from and in addition to translation risk. It occurs when the value of a foreign investment moves in reaction to a change in exchange rates. For example, assume an increase in a foreign currency causes a decrease in the value of a company based in the foreign country because the company's products will be more expensive to export, resulting in a drop in sales.

THE FACTORS TO CONSIDER IN HEDGING THE FUTURE VALUE OF A FOREIGN INVESTMENT

A. A typical "hedging the principal" strategy involves a portfolio manager selling forward/futures contracts equaling the amount of the portfolio. A French investor with a $100,000,000 portfolio would sell forward contracts on the U.S. dollar with a principal amount of $100,000,000. If, however, the portfolio changes in value, which it most likely will, the hedge is imperfect. If the portfolio increases in value to $105,000,000, the investor will have $5,000,000 that is unhedged. If the portfolio declines to $90,000,000, then it will be "overhedged" by $10,000,000.

B. Theoretically, portfolio managers should hedge the expected future value of their foreign portfolio. The expected future value is based on any expected changes in the price of the portfolio, plus any expected changes in exchange rates. The problem with this approach is that there may be a significant difference between expectations and actual performance, resulting in an improper hedge ratio. This method can be used more effectively with fixed-income securities than equities, because the future principal value and future income can be reasonably estimated. The hedge will still need to be adjusted as necessary for any changes in the price of the fixed-income securities due to changes in interest rates.

STUDY MANUAL – BUSINESS ENVIRONMENT & CONCEPTS
CHAPTER 25

QUESTIONS: GLOBAL CURRENCY RISK AND HEDGING

1. If the exchange rate value of the euro goes from $0.95 to $1.10, then the euro has:
    A. appreciated and the Dutch will find U.S. goods more expensive.
    B. depreciated and the Dutch will find U.S. goods cheaper.
    C. appreciated and the Dutch will find U.S. goods cheaper.
    D. depreciated and the Dutch will find U.S. goods more expensive.

2. A depreciation in the value of the U.S. dollar on the foreign exchange market will:
    A. make U.S. exports cheaper to foreigners.
    B. make imports less expensive for U.S. consumers.
    C. make U.S. exports more expensive for foreign consumers.
    D. cause the United States to run a balance of payments surplus in the long run.

3. If the exchange rate value of the English pound goes from $1.75 to $1.50, determine if the pound depreciates or appreciates relative to the dollar and if the English will find U.S. goods cheaper or more expensive.

	Pound	U.S. goods
A.	depreciated	cheaper
B.	appreciated	more expensive
C.	appreciated	cheaper
D.	depreciated	more expensive

4. In a floating exchange rate system, if there is an excess demand for:
    A. German goods by Americans, Americans will have to sell more goods to Germans so as to be able to buy more German goods.
    B. U.S. dollars by the British, then the British will sell pounds and buy dollars. This will cause the pound to depreciate relative to the dollar.
    C. British pounds by the Belgians, Belgians will lower their interest rates so as to enable their citizens to borrow more easily in order to buy British goods.
    D. Russian rubles by Spaniards, Russians will lower their interest rates so as to enable Spaniards to buy Russian goods on credit and satisfy their demand for Russian products.

5. In a flexible exchange rate system, exchange rates are determined by:
    A. governmental fiat.
    B. the total value of the country's gold reserves.
    C. trade restrictions.
    D. supply and demand in the market for the currency.

6. If the dollar appreciates it becomes:
    A. more expensive for foreigners to buy U.S. goods.
    B. cheaper for foreigners to buy U.S. goods.
    C. cheaper for foreigners to buy foreign goods.
    D. more expensive for foreigners to buy foreign goods.

Page 666   ©2007 Kaplan CPA Review

STUDY MANUAL – BUSINESS ENVIRONMENT & CONCEPTS

CHAPTER 25

7. U.S. export transactions create:
    A. a U.S. demand for foreign monies and the satisfaction of this demand decreases the supplies of dollars held by foreign banks.
    B. a U.S. demand for foreign monies and the satisfaction of this demand increases the supplies of dollars held by foreign banks.
    C. a foreign demand for dollars and the satisfaction of this demand decreases the supplies of foreign monies held by U.S. banks.
    D. a foreign demand for dollars and the satisfaction of this demand increases the supplies of foreign monies held by U.S. banks.

8. Other things equal, the financing of a U.S. import transaction:
    A. increases the supplies of foreign currency held by United States banks.
    B. increases U.S. interest rates.
    C. decreases the supplies of foreign currency held by U.S. banks.
    D. increases GDP in the United States.

9. Which of the following would contribute to a United States balance of payments deficit?
    A. Kawasaki builds a motorcycle manufacturing plant in Kansas City.
    B. United States tourists travel in large numbers to Europe.
    C. a wealthy Mexican citizen builds a mansion in Beverly Hills.
    D. Zaire pays interest on its debt to the United States.

10. Evidence of a chronic balance of payments deficit is:
    A. a decline in amount of the nation's currency held by other nations.
    B. an excess of exports over imports.
    C. diminishing reserves of foreign currencies.
    D. an increase in the international value of the nation's currency.

11. If a nation's goods exports are $55 billion, while its goods imports are $50 billion, we can conclude with certainty that this nation has a:
    A. balance of goods surplus.
    B. balance of payments surplus.
    C. positive balance on current account.
    D. positive balance on goods and services.

12. If the dollar price of yen rises, then:
    a. the yen price of dollars also rises.
    b. the dollar depreciates relative to the yen.
    c. the yen depreciates relative to the dollar.
    d. the dollar will buy fewer U.S. goods.

13. In considering euros and dollars, the rates of exchange for the euro and the dollar:
    A. are directly related.
    B. are inversely related.
    C. are unrelated.
    D. move in the same direction.

©2007 Kaplan CPA Review

Page 667

STUDY MANUAL – BUSINESS ENVIRONMENT & CONCEPTS
CHAPTER 25

14. If the exchange rate changes so that more Mexican pesos are required to buy a dollar, then:
    A. the peso has appreciated in value.
    B. Americans will buy more Mexican goods and services.
    C. more U.S. goods and services will be demanded by the Mexicans.
    D. the dollar has depreciated in value.

15. Appreciation of the Canadian dollar will:
    A. intensify an existing disequilibrium in Canada's balance of payments.
    B. make Canada's exports less expensive and its imports more expensive.
    C. make Canada's exports more expensive and its imports less expensive.
    D. make Canada's exports and imports both more expensive.

16. The U.S. demand for euros is:
    A. downsloping because, at lower dollar prices for euros, Americans will want to buy more European goods and services.
    B. downsloping because, at higher dollar prices for euros, Americans will want to buy more European goods and services.
    C. downsloping because the dollar price of euros and the euro price of dollars are directly related.
    D. upsloping because a higher dollar price of euros makes European goods and services more attractive to Americans.

17. Which of the following will generate a demand for country X's currency in the foreign exchange market?
    A. travel by citizens of country X in other countries.
    B. the desire of foreigners to buy stocks and bonds of firms in country X.
    C. the imports of country X.
    D. charitable contributions by country X's citizens to citizens of developing nations.

18. Under a system of freely flexible (floating) exchange rates, a U.S. trade deficit with Mexico will tend to cause:
    A. the United States government to ration pesos to U.S. importers.
    B. a flow of gold from the United States to Mexico.
    C. an increase in the peso price of dollars.
    D. an increase in the dollar price of pesos.

19. Under a system of freely floating exchange rates, an increase in the international value of a nation's currency will:
    A. cause an international surplus of its currency.
    B. contribute to disequilibrium in its balance of payments.
    C. cause gold to flow into that country.
    D. cause its imports to rise.

Page 668   ©2007 Kaplan CPA Review

STUDY MANUAL – BUSINESS ENVIRONMENT & CONCEPTS
CHAPTER 25

20. If the United States has full employment and the dollar dramatically depreciates in value, we can expect (other things equal):
   A. both U.S. imports and U.S. exports to rise.
   B. both U.S. imports and U.S. exports to fall.
   C. U.S. exports to fall and U.S. imports to increase.
   D. inflation to occur.

21. Suppose interest rates fall sharply in the United States but are unchanged in Great Britain. Other things equal, under a system of freely floating exchange rates we can expect the demand for pounds in the United States to:
   A. decrease, the supply of pounds to increase, and the dollar to appreciate relative to the pound.
   B. increase, the supply of pounds to increase, and the dollar may either appreciate or depreciate relative to the pound.
   C. increase, the supply of pounds to decrease, and the dollar to depreciate relative to the pound.
   D. decrease, the supply of pounds to increase, and the dollar to depreciate relative to the pound.

22. Countries engaged in international trade specialize in production based on:
   A. relative levels of GDP.
   B. comparative advantage.
   C. relative exchange rates.
   D. relative inflation rates.

23. Free trade based on comparative advantage is economically beneficial because:
   A. it promotes an efficient allocation of world resources.
   B. it increases competition.
   C. it provides consumers with a wider range of products.
   D. of all of the above reasons.

24. Country A limits other nation's exports to Country A to 1,000 tons of coal annually. This is an example of a(n):
   A. protective tariff.
   B. export subsidy.
   C. import quota.
   D. voluntary export restriction.

25. The current account in a nation's balance of payments includes:
   A. its goods exports and imports, and its services exports and imports.
   B. changes in its official reserves.
   C. purchases of foreign assets, and foreign purchases of assets.
   D. all of the above.

26. If a nation has a current account deficit and its official reserves account balance is zero, it must have a:
   A. surplus in its capital account.
   B. balance of payments deficit.
   C. balance of payments surplus.
   D. deficit in its capital account.

©2007 Kaplan CPA Review
Page 669

STUDY MANUAL – BUSINESS ENVIRONMENT & CONCEPTS
CHAPTER 25

27. In a nation's balance of payments, which one of the following items is always recorded as a positive entry?
    A. Goods imports.
    B. Changes in foreign currency reserves.
    C. U.S. purchases of assets abroad.
    D. Exports of services.

28. Assume that by devoting all of its resources to the production of X, nation Alpha can produce 40 units of X. By devoting all of its resources to Y, Alpha can produce 60Y. Comparable figures for nation Beta are 60X and 40Y. We can conclude that:
    A. the terms of trade will be 3X equals 1Y.
    B. Alpha should specialize in Y and Beta in X.
    C. Alpha should specialize in X and Beta in Y.
    D. there is no basis for mutually beneficial specialization and trade.

29. All the following are included in the U.S. current account in its balance of payments EXCEPT:
    A. U.S. imports of foreign goods.
    B. U.S. government spending in foreign countries.
    C. Direct investment by U.S. companies in foreign plants.
    D. U.S. purchases of services from foreigners.

30. If the U.S. balance in its current account is –$300 billion, and its balance in its capital account is –$100 billion, which of the following will happen to the U.S. holding of official reserve assets?
    A. It will go down by $200 billion.
    B. It will go down by $400 billion.
    C. It will go up by $200 billion.
    D. It will go up by $400 billion.

31. When management chooses to charge another subunit the price that the subunit charges to outside customers, the transfer pricing policy is:
    A. Market-based transfer pricing.
    B. Cost-based transfer pricing.
    C. Negotiated transfer pricing.
    D. Variable cost transfer pricing.

32. What is the effect on prices of U.S. imports and exports when the dollar depreciates?
    A. Import prices and export prices will decrease.
    B. Import prices will decrease and export prices will increase.
    C. Import prices will increase and export prices will decrease.
    D. Import prices and export prices will increase.

STUDY MANUAL – BUSINESS ENVIRONMENT & CONCEPTS

CHAPTER 25

ANSWERS: GLOBAL CURRENCY RISK AND HEDGING

1. **C**   An exchange rate is a ratio that describes how many units of one currency you can buy per unit of another currency. The numerator will be in the currency in which the quote is made and the denominator is the other unit of the currency you are comparing. A currency appreciates when it rises in value relative to another foreign currency. Likewise, a currency depreciates when it falls in value relative to another foreign currency. An appreciation in value of a currency makes that country's goods more expensive to residents of other countries. The depreciation of the value of a currency makes a country's goods more attractive to foreign buyers.

2. **A.** A depreciation of a currency makes a country's goods more attractive to foreign buyers.

    The choices, "Make imports less expensive for U.S. consumers," and "Make U.S. exports more expensive for foreign consumers," would be *true if the dollar was appreciating*. The balance of payments equation should always equal 0. Balance of payments (balance of international payments) is an overall accounting of a nation's international economic activity, summarizing a period's transactions between a nation and the rest of the world. Its component parts (current, capital, and financial accounts) will balance each other out.

3. **D**   An exchange rate is a ratio that describes how many units of one currency you can buy per unit of another currency. The numerator will be in the currency in which the quote is made and the denominator is the other unit of the currency you are comparing. A currency appreciates when it rises in value relative to another foreign currency and likewise, a currency depreciates when it falls in value relative to another foreign currency. An appreciation in value of a currency makes that country's goods more expensive to residents of other countries. The depreciation of the value of a currency makes a country's goods more attractive to foreign buyers.

4. **B**   In a floating exchange rate system, exchange rates between countries are based on the demand and supply of currencies relative to each other. If British demand dollars, they will sell pounds and buy dollars in exchange, thus depressing their own currency. The dollar will appreciate relative to the pound. Other choices are incorrect because they are not based on the supply-and-demand argument underlying floating exchange rates.

5. **D**   Exchange rates are determined by supply and demand. British importers needing dollars to purchase U.S. goods will buy U.S. dollars and sell British pounds. British exporters needing to convert dollars to pounds will sell dollars and buy pounds.

6. **A**   Appreciation is an increase in the value of a domestic currency relative to foreign currencies, leading to increased purchasing power of the domestic currency for foreign goods. As a result of appreciation of a domestic currency, domestic goods become more expensive to foreigners.

7. **D**   Foreign demand for U. S. dollars causes U. S. banks to obtain foreign currency. Answer (a) is not correct because a U. S. export transaction would not create demand for foreign monies. Answer (b) is not correct because a U. S. export transaction would not create demand for foreign monies. Answer (c) is not correct because foreign demand for dollars would not result in a decrease in the supplies of foreign monies held by U. S. banks.

©2007 Kaplan CPA Review

Page 671

STUDY MANUAL – BUSINESS ENVIRONMENT & CONCEPTS
CHAPTER 25

8. **C**   An import transaction will cause a reduction in foreign currency held by U. S. banks as dollars are given and foreign currency is received from the bank to effect the import transaction. Answer (a) is not correct because the domestic company that needs the foreign currency to effect the importation of goods will take foreign currency out of the U. S. banks. Answer (b) is not correct because there is relation between U. S. interest rates and the financing of a U. S. import transaction. Answer (d) is not correct because an import implies that there has been no increase in domestic production as a result of the transaction.

9. **B**   Tourists traveling to Europe is the same as an import of services from Europe. Answer (a) is not correct because Kawasaki would be paying domestic contractors with U. S. currency and thus there would be no impact on the U. S. balance of payments. Answer (c) is not correct because the Mexican citizen would be paying the domestic contractors with U. S. currency. Answer (d) is not correct because the payment by Zaire would not result in the decrease of Zaire's currency held by the U. S.

10. **C**   If a country has diminished reserves of foreign currencies, it is an indication of persistent balance of payments deficits. Answer (a) is not correct because the balance of payments does not refer to the amount of a nation's currency held by other nations. Answer (b) is not correct because exports and imports are only one element of a country's balance of payments. Answer (d) is not correct because a deficit would suggest that there is a large quantity of the country's currency in the banks of other countries. That large supply would put downward pressure on the country's currency.

11. **A**   When exports exceed imports, the country has a balance of goods, but it may or may not have a balance of payments surplus. Answer (b) is not correct because the balance of payments also includes service transactions, investment income, net transfers, and capital account transactions. Answer (c) is not correct because the balance in the current account also includes the transactions related to services, investments, and transfers in addition to the transactions related to goods. Answer (d) is not correct because the balance on goods and services includes services transactions in addition to goods transactions.

12. **B**   When one currency increases in value, the other declines in value. Answer (a) is not correct because both currencies cannot simultaneously rise. Answer (c) is not correct because the question implies that the yen has appreciated. Answer (d) is not correct because the relationship between the U. S. dollar and the yen has no influence on the extent to which the dollar will buy U. S. goods.

13. **B**   The rates of exchange for two are inversely related. Answer (a) is not correct because the relation of currency x to currency y is x/y but the relation of currency y to currency x is y/x. Answer (c) is not correct because the relation of currency x to currency y is x/y but the relation of currency y to currency x is y/x. Answer (d) is not correct because the relation of currency x to currency y is x/y but the relation of currency y to currency x is y/x.

14. **B**   More pesos to buy a dollar implies fewer dollars to buy a peso, therefore Americans will buy more Mexican goods and services. Answer (a) is not correct because more pesos required to buy a dollar implies that the peso has depreciated in value. Answer (c) is not correct because U. S. goods and services will be more expensive to Mexicans because more pesos will be required to obtain a dollar. Answer (d) is not correct because if the peso has declined in value relative to the dollar, then the dollar has appreciated in value in relation to the peso.

STUDY MANUAL – BUSINESS ENVIRONMENT & CONCEPTS
CHAPTER 25

15. **C** The higher value of the Canadian dollar will require more foreign currency for each Canadian dollar. The result will be that exports will be more expensive and imports will be less expensive. Answer (a) is not correct because appreciation of the Canadian dollar provides no basis for rendering a judgment concerning Canada's balance of payments. Answer (b) is not correct because the higher value of the Canadian dollar will require more foreign currency for each Canadian dollar. Answer (d) is not correct because a change in the value of a currency will impact exports in one direction and imports in the opposite direction.

16. **A** A downward sloping demand curve implies that a larger quantity will be demanded at a lower price. Answer (b) is not correct because at higher prices for euros, Americans will want to buy fewer European goods and services. Answer (c) is not correct because the relationship between dollars and euros is the inverse of the relationship between euros and the dollar. Answer (d) is not correct because the higher dollar price of euros will make European goods and services more expensive and less attractive to Americans.

17. **B** As foreigners seek to buy stocks and bonds of firms in country X, those foreigners will have to acquire the currency of country X. Answer (a) is not correct because such travel would cause the demand for the currencies of other countries to increase. Answer (c) is not correct because as country X imports from other countries, it will increase the demand for the currencies of other countries. Answer (d) is not correct because such contributions would be in the currencies of the developing nations.

18. **D** The U. S. will have to acquire pesos and that will cause an increase in the dollar price of pesos. Answer (a) is not correct because such a rationing system would restrict free trade with Mexico. Answer (b) is not correct because gold would only be used to deal with a persistent deficit balance of payments. Answer (c) is not correct because a trade surplus would be the cause of an increase in the peso price of dollars.

19. **D** As a nation's currency increases in value, goods and services purchased in other countries will become less expensive. Answer (a) is not correct because the fact that the exchange rates are free to float suggests that there will be neither a surplus nor a shortage. Answer (b) is not correct because a system of exchange rates that are free to float suggests that equilibrium will prevail at all times. Answer (c) is not correct because with exchange rates that can float freely, there would be no lack of balance in the balance of payments and thus no need for the use of gold to deal with the problem of deficits in the balance of payments.

20. **D** The depreciation of the dollar will tend to increase exports and when there is full employment, there will be a tendency toward inflation. Answer (a) is not correct because a change in the value of the dollar is not likely to simultaneously increase both imports and exports. Answer (b) is not correct because if the dollar depreciates in value, U. S. exports will rise. Answer (c) is not correct because U. S. imports will decline and U. S. exports will increase.

21. **C** Investors will increase their demand for pounds as they invest in Great Britain. Further, the increase in dollars offered for pounds will cause dollars to depreciate. Answer (a) is not correct because the demand for pounds increases as investors invest in Great Britain. Answer (b) is not correct because the dollar will depreciate as dollars are offered for the pounds which are in great demand in order to invest in Great Britain. Answer (d) is not correct because the demand for pounds increases as investors invest in Great Britain.

©2007 Kaplan CPA Review
Page 673

STUDY MANUAL – BUSINESS ENVIRONMENT & CONCEPTS
CHAPTER 25

22. **B** Comparative advantage causes countries to specialize in trade on goods and services for which they have a unique advantage. Answer (a) is not correct because the relative levels of GDP are not relevant in predicting the production in which a country will specialize. Answer (c) is not correct because specialization is related to an advantage one country has over another. Answer (d) is not correct because specialization is related to an advantage one country has over another.

23. **D** Answer (a) is not correct because this answer is only one of the reasons. Answer (b) is not correct because this answer is only one of the reasons. Answer (c) is not correct because this answer is only one of the reasons.

24. **C** The limitation is on imports into Country A. Answer (a) is not correct because there is no mention of a tariff to limit imports. Answer (b) is not correct because the question describes an import, not an export, situation. Answer (d) is not correct because the question describes an import, not an export, situation.

25. **A** The current account includes exports and imports of goods and services. Answer (b) is not correct because the official reserves are used to bring the balance of payments to zero. Answer (c) is not correct because the purchase of assets is included in the capital account portion of the balance of payments. Answer (d) is not correct because at least one of the other answers is incorrect.

26. **A** With zero official reserves account, the balance of payments balance relies on a surplus in the capital account to exactly offset the current account deficit. Answer (b) is not correct because there is never a balance of payments deficit. The official reserves account is sufficient to cause the balance of payments to be zero. Answer (c) is not correct because there is never a balance of payments surplus. The official reserves account is sufficient to cause the balance of payments to be zero. Answer (d) is not correct because a deficit in both the current account and the capital account would require the use of some amount of official reserves.

27. **D** Exports are recorded as a positive and imports are recorded as a negative. Answer (a) is not correct because goods imports are recorded as a negative. Answer (b) is not correct because changes in foreign currency reserves are plus or minus depending on the amount necessary to bring the balance of payments to zero. Answer (c) is not correct because U. S. purchases of assets abroad are recorded as a negative to show an outflow.

28. **B** Alpha can produce more of X than Beta and Beta can produce more of Y than Alpha. Answer (a) is not correct because there are no amounts in the problem that would suggest such a relationship. Answer (c) is not correct because Alpha can produce more of X that Beta. Answer (d) is not correct because the amounts in the question suggest that specialization would be mutually beneficial.

29. **C** Direct investment by U. S. companies in foreign plants is included in the capital account, not the current account. Answer (a) is not correct because U. S. imports of foreign goods is included in the current account. Answer (b) is not correct because U. S. government spending in foreign countries is included in the current account. Answer (d) is not correct because U. S. purchases of services from foreigners are included in the current account.

30. **B** Negative balances in the current and capital accounts cause a loss of official reserves, here totaling $400 billion. Answer (a) is not correct because the negative balance in the capital account is not subtracted from the negative balance in the current account. Answer (c) is

Page 674   ©2007 Kaplan CPA Review

not correct because both the capital account and the current account indicate a reduction in official reserves. Answer (d) is not correct because both the capital account and the current account indicate a reduction in official reserves.

31. **A** When there is an external market, the appropriate transfer price is the market price at which the product is sold to the outsiders. Answer (b) is not correct because a cost-based transfer price would discourage the producer from controlling costs. Answer (c) is not correct because negotiated transfer prices are not appropriate if there is an independent source that would indicate the value of the product based on an arms- length transaction. Answer (d) is not correct because there is an independent source that would indicate the value of the product based on an arms-length transaction.

32. When the dollar depreciates, the opposing currency appreciates (inverse relationship). The depreciation of the dollar means that foreign goods become more expensive and import prices will increase. Conversely, as the value of the dollar decreases, our goods become cheaper to foreign customers and our export prices will decrease.

CRAM ESSENTIALS: CONTENTS

STUDY MANUAL – BUSINESS ENVIRONMENT & CONCEPTS

Business Structure 677
    Corporation 677
    Partnership 681

Financial Management 685
    Ratio Analysis 685
    Working Capital Management 688
    Capital Budgeting 694
    Risk 699
    Financial Models and Indices 699
    Derivatives 704

Quantitative Methods 708

Planning and Measurement 709
    Cost-Volume-Profit Analysis 709
    Cost Accounting 711
    Variance Analysis 714

Information Technology 716
    IT Fundamentals 716
    Business Information Systems 722
    Systems Operation 732
    IT Flowcharting and System Documentation 734
    Roles and Responsibilities of the IT Functions 737
    Disaster Recovery and Business Continuity 739
    Business Implications: Electronic Commerce 740
    IT Control 743

Economics 747
    Economics of the Firm 747
    Industry and Competitive Environment of the Firm 753
    Firm Performance and Sensitivity to the Economy 757
    Fiscal and Monetary Policies 763
    Global Currency Risks and Hedging 765

CRAM ESSENTIALS

STUDY MANUAL – BUSINESS ENVIRONMENT & CONCEPTS

BUSINESS STRUCTURE

A. Overview: From a legal perspective, there are three basic types of business structures, plus several hybrid types (such as limited liability companies).

1. A **sole proprietorship** is formed when an individual does business without incorporating or associating with a partner. The owner has unlimited liability.

2. A **partnership** is formed when two or more persons carry on, as co-owners, a business for profit. May be by formal agreement, informal agreement, or implied agreement.

    a. In a **general partnership**, all partners are general partners, which means that they each have unlimited liability for partnership liabilities (both contractual liabilities and tort obligations).

    b. In a **limited partnership**, some specific partners (the limited partners) enjoy limited liability for partnership debts, while the general partner(s) have unlimited liability. A limited partnership is formed only by following statutory requirements. Limited partners are investors but may participate in management without losing limited liability.

    c. **Limited liability partnerships** (LLPs) are a special form of partnership in which all partners have limited liability, but are otherwise treated as general partners.

    d. With LLCs (limited liability companies), like with LLPs, all "members" can participate in management but retain limited liability. Ownership interests are not as freely transferable as corporate stock.

3. A **corporation** is formed by following statutory state requirements. Unlike a partnership, a separate legal entity is formed.

B. A **corporation** is an artificial entity that comes into existence upon the proper filing of **articles of incorporation** and issuance by the state of a certificate of incorporation.

1. A number of different parties are involved with a corporation.

©2007 Kaplan CPA Review

Page 677

a. Shareholders are the owners of the corporation; shareholders elect **directors** to oversee the corporation. Shareholders are not agents of the corporation, but large shareholders may owe a fiduciary duty to other shareholders.

b. Directors are elected by shareholders to direct the main course of the corporation. The directors elect officers to run day-to-day business operations. The directors are agents of the corporation; directors declare dividends.

c. **Officers** are chosen by the directors to run the day-to-day business of the corporation as agents for the corporation.

2. A corporation has several general characteristics.

a. It is a separate legal entity; the corporation is a separate person. It is separate from the persons who formed the corporation or who currently own it.

b. The owners have **limited liability**. The shareholders can lose only what they invest in the corporation (what they pay or promise to pay for the stock of the corporation).

c. A corporation is taxed separately from its owners because the corporation is a new, separate entity in the eyes of the taxing authorities. When profits are paid to shareholders in the form of dividends the money is taxed again, resulting in **double taxation** of profits.

d. A corporation is able to have **continuous life**. The corporation continues in existence even after a shareholder dies. This is true even if there is only one shareholder.

e. A corporation allows its owners to transfer ownership. Stock, unless restricted at issuance, is freely transferable.

3. A corporation is created by following the process of incorporation.

a. Articles of incorporation must be filed with the corporation commission of the state in which incorporation is being sought. Articles of incorporation must include the following information:

- Name of corporation.
- Name of registered agent.
- Names of incorporators.
- Number of authorized shares.

b. **Registered agent** is appointed by the corporation to officially receive notice.

c. **Certificate of incorporation** is issued by the state upon proper filing of articles of incorporation and payment of all fees.

d. Organization meeting is the initial meeting to elect officers and directors.

e. By-laws are adopted by directors and officers to set structure of the corporation, to establish time and place of meetings, etc.

f. A **de jure corporation** is one that has been correctly formed.

g. A **de facto corporation** exists when the incorporators succeed in satisfying most requirements for incorporating but inadvertently fail to satisfy all. A corporation is still recognized.

h. **Promoters** are individuals who undertake to form a corporation and arrange its initial capitalization. They promote the sale of stock through subscriptions. A **subscription** is a written agreement to purchase stock; it is irrevocable for six months.

- Promoters have a fiduciary relationship with the not-yet-formed corporation. They must act in the best interest of the new corporation and not in their own interest.
- Since the corporation is not yet in existence, a promoter is not truly an agent of the corporation. Thus, pre-incorporation agreements are not binding on the corporation until adopted by it.

4. To raise capital, a corporation issues stock.

a. **Authorized stock** is the amount of stock that the articles of incorporation permit to be issued.

b. **Issued stock** is the amount of stock that has been delivered to the shareholders.

c. **Outstanding stock** is the amount of stock currently being held by the shareholders. It has been issued but not repurchased by the corporation as treasury stock.

d. A company will always have at least one class of stock but can also have a second class.

- **Common stock** usually has the most voting rights but the least rights to dividends and to assets upon liquidation of the corporation. A corporation must have common stock.
- **Preferred stock** usually has fewer (sometimes no) voting rights but greater rights to dividends and assets on liquidation. Many companies do not issue preferred stock.

e. In issuing stock, valid **consideration** must be received. Buyers must pay for stock in cash, property, or services that have already been rendered. Valid consideration does not include a promise to perform services, a promise to pay, or a promissory note.

f. If a **par value** is stated for the stock, the buyer must pay at least that amount or be liable to the corporation's creditors.

©2007 Kaplan CPA Review

5. According to the business judgment rule, officers and directors may be liable to shareholders for **negligence** committed in running the corporation, but not if they were acting in good faith in the exercise of business judgment. Corporation can indemnify officers and directors for damages suffered in such suits, including attorney's fees if approved by the court.

6. **Extraordinary transactions** such as merger, consolidation, or sale of all assets must have special approval.

   a. Directors meet and vote whether to recommend the action to the shareholders. Directors vote on and pass a resolution.

   b. Shareholders then meet to vote whether to adopt the resolution.

   c. If the resolution is approved by a majority of shareholders, dissenting shareholders have certain rights. A minority of shareholders cannot stop an extraordinary transaction, but they can insist on being paid fair market value for their stock. This is called "**dissenters**" **appraisal rights**.

7. Shareholders have the right to inspect corporate books.

   a. Includes minute books, stock certificate books, and general account books.

   b. Must have purpose that is reasonably related to interest as a shareholder.

   - It is okay to obtain information to try and gain control of corporation.
   - It is not okay to obtain information to compete with corporation.
   - Inspection may be refused if shareholder has misused information within the previous two years.

8. The validity of contracts between a corporation and its officers is based upon fairness and disclosure.

C. The directors of the company declare **dividends** that are to be paid to shareholders. Once declared, dividends are considered a debt of the corporation.

   1. Dividends are considered illegal if they render the corporation insolvent, so that is it is unable to pay debts as they come due.

D. A **dissolution** will terminate a corporation's existence. It is not complete until the winding up of affairs and distribution of assets have occurred.

   1. A dissolution can be voluntary: merger, consolidation, or the filing of articles of dissolution.

   2. A dissolution can be involuntary if it is caused either by the failure to pay the annual assessments to the state or if fraud occurred in the original articles of incorporation.

3. A **judicial dissolution** can also occur. When the directors are hopelessly deadlocked, shareholders can petition the court for dissolution.

E. A partnership can be formed in any one of several ways.

   1. There can be an explicit agreement. The agreement can be a formal document or simply an informal understanding.

   2. The formation of a partnership can be implied by operation of law. This occurs whenever the statutory definition of a partnership (two or more persons carry on, as co-owners, a business for profit) applies to the factual situation.

      a. For example, assume that two individuals together purchase a truck and contract to make deliveries. They then split the profits. Even if there is no partnership agreement of any type, the business will be considered a partnership by operation of law.

   3. A partnership can also be formed by **estoppel**. This situation arises where one person holds another individual out to be a partner and the latter fails to deny the partnership.

F. The authority that a partner has to bind a partnership to a contract is much like the authority found in agency law. Likewise, the responsibilities that each partner has to the other partners are also similar to those found in agency law.

   1. As to authority, the general rule is that a partner has actual (express) and apparent (ostensible) authority to bind other partners to a contract made in the ordinary course of business. The other partners are also able to ratify a contract that has been made.

   2. As to responsibilities, each partner has duties to every other partner that are similar to an agent's duties to a principal. These include fiduciary duties, duty to act in good faith, etc.

   3. Because of the relationship, notice to one partner is viewed as notice to all partners.

G. Partners can be liable for actions of other partners.

   1. For torts, the partners are jointly and severally liable. **Joint liability** means that all partners must be sued together. **Several liability** means that a party may sue any partner for the full amount of the claim. Thus, a partner in a general partnership who commits a tort in the ordinary course of partnership business has a personal liability and has created a liability for all other partners.

   2. Each partner is jointly liable with all other partners for the contracts of the partnership.

H. Partners are co-owners of the business. There are several separate aspects to this co-ownership.

©2007 Kaplan CPA Review

Page 681

STUDY MANUAL – BUSINESS ENVIRONMENT & CONCEPTS
CRAM ESSENTIALS

1. Each partner is entitled to share in the profits and surplus of the partnership.

   a. The right to profits and surplus can be transferred to a nonpartner, but the assignee does not become a partner unless admitted by unanimous vote of all partners. Profits are also subject to **attachment by creditors of the partner.**

   b. The right to profits and surplus can be passed to heirs at the partner's death. However, partnership property, such as buildings and equipment, passes to the other partners.

   c. There is no inherent right to a salary, only to a pro rata share of profits. A partnership agreement can specify the specific method by which profits (and losses) are to be allocated.

   d. Partners can agree to share profits in a different proportion to losses.

2. All partners have the right to participate in the management of the business. All partners must agree before a change can be made to this right.

3. Each partner has the right to use specific partnership property for partnership business only.

4. A new partner cannot be admitted without the unanimous consent of all partners unless the partnership agreement provides otherwise.

5. An incoming partner is liable only for future debts of the partnership, not for existing debts. Exception: money or property that the new partner puts into the partnership can be used to satisfy existing debts.

I. A partnership can dissolve and wind up its affairs for any of several reasons.

1. Dissolution of a **partnership at will** (usually a less formal partnership, one that is not formed for a stated time or particular undertaking) occurs when a partner withdraws.

2. Dissolution of the partnership which was formed for a stated time or particular undertaking *may* occur upon the **dissociation** of a partner, but only if, within 90 days, half or more of the remaining partners vote for dissolution. Dissociation of a partner occurs upon:

   a. Death of a partner (or termination of a corporate partner).

   b. Bankruptcy of a partner.

   c. Expulsion of a partner.

   d. Judicial order.

3. If a partner is dissociated from a partnership without resulting in a dissolution, the partnership must cause the dissociated partner's interest in the partnership to

Page 682   ©2007 Kaplan CPA Review

be purchased for a buyout price. The buyout price is a price equal to the greater of the liquidation value or the value based on a sale of the entire business as a going concern without the dissociated partner. Interest must be paid from the date of dissociation to the date of payment.

4. After dissolution, the partners have no authority to bind the partnership except as is necessary to wind up the partnership business.

5. If the business is not continued, the assets of the business must be distributed according to set guidelines.

    a. General creditors are paid in full first.

    b. Debts owed to individual partners are paid next.

    c. Any remainder is paid to the partners based on their final capital balances. If any of the final capital balances are negative, the partners must pay that much into the partnership to eliminate the deficit.

J. A **limited partnership** must comply with the requirements of state law for a limited partnership. There must be one or more general partners and one or more limited partners. Like a general partnership, no separate entity is formed. Like shareholders in a corporation, the limited partners have limited liability.

1. A certificate of limited partnership must be filed to meet statutory requirements.

2. A limited partner is primarily an investor, with no authority to bind the partnership. But under recent revisions in the law, limited partners do not lose their limited liability when they participate in management of the business or when their surname is used in the partnership name.

    a. Under the revised Uniform Limited Partnership Act, a limited partner may participate in managing the business without losing his/her limited liability status.

    b. A limited partner has no authority to bind the business.

    c. Under the revised Uniform Limited Partnership Act, a limited partnership may use the last name (surname) of a limited partner in the name of the partnership.

3. A number of events can lead to the **termination of a limited partnership.**

    a. A judicial order.

    b. Withdrawal, death, or insolvency of a general partner does not immediately terminate the limited partnership. If there are no remaining general partners, the limited partnership has 90 days to find a replacement general partner.

c. Termination does not result from the withdrawal, death, insolvency, or insanity of a limited partner.

d. Termination does not result from the transfer of a limited partner's interest to another party. The transfer by a limited partner of a partnership interest to a third party is treated as an assignment of the right to profits (if any are earned) unless the transferee is admitted as a limited partner by vote of the partners.

K. When starting a business, the individuals must decide what form of organization to employ (corporation, partnership, etc.). Advantages and disadvantages of various business forms and the advisability of certain forms under various circumstances involve three main considerations:

1. Forming a corporation will result in **double taxation** of profits, once when the corporation earns a profit and again when profits are distributed to shareholders or are paid to officers and other employees. A **subchapter S** selection with the IRS will avoid double taxation, but corporations with more than 100 shareholders are not permitted to make this election. A subchapter S Corporation is taxed much like a partnership. In addition, doing business as a partnership, limited partnership, and LLC can avoid double taxation.

2. General partners (including general partners in a limited partnership) are liable for all tort and contract (including loan) obligations of the business. Limited partners, shareholders in a corporation, and all partners (including general partners) in limited liability partnerships are insulated from such liability, although their investment in the business is at risk.

3. Corporations permit the free transferability of share ownership, whereas partnership interests and ownership interests in LLCs ("memberships") are not always freely transferable. This may be important to initial investors in a business.

L. Businesses can allocate profits and losses for distribution to owners by means of a partnership agreement. In general partnerships and limited partnerships, profits can be allocated in a different proportion than losses.

M. A business can be capitalized through debt or equity (or using hybrids which include characteristics of each). The implications of various capitalization options are that investors who extend loans to a business will be subject to less risk than equity investors but will realize far less potential reward should the business prosper. Equity investors assume more risk of loss but have greater control of the business and have greater potential for profit.

STUDY MANUAL – BUSINESS ENVIRONMENT & CONCEPTS
CRAM ESSENTIALS

FINANCIAL MANAGEMENT

A. Introduction

1. The goal of the financial function of an organization is to acquire and manage resources to maximize the value of the organization. Key activities include but are not limited to the following:

   a. Forecasting and planning.

   b. Financing (capital structure) and investment (capital budgeting) decisions.

   c. Coordination and control, breakeven analysis, and management of assets.

   d. Interaction with financial markets.

   e. Risk management.

2. Maximization of shareholders' wealth is the ultimate goal of management. This is not the same as maximizing profits. Increasing earnings per share (EPS) is usually correlated with increases in the value of the firm. However, if EPS are increased by taking substantially increased risks this may not be in the best interest of shareholders. Shareholders receive a stream of dividends (sometimes) and hopefully a capital gain when they sell their stock. Activities that increase the present value of the stream of dividends and the capital gain (stock price) increase shareholders' wealth.

3. Agency problem: how do shareholders get managers to act in the best interest of the shareholders rather than in the best interest of management?

   a. Compensation—stock options.

   b. Shareholder intervention—proxy fights.

   c. Threat of firing.

   d. Threat of a takeover.

B. **Ratio analysis.** Financial ratios are designed to help you evaluate financial statements. A ratio is one figure or balance divided by another. By dividing, we remove the issue of size and can compare firms of different size based on ratios. Ratios have acceptable ranges. The key is to be able to measure whether an organization's figures and balances fall within these acceptable ranges.

1. **Types of analysis.** In order for a ratio to provide information, it must be compared to a standard or **benchmark**. Common benchmarks or comparisons for ratios include:

©2007 Kaplan CPA Review

Page 685

a. **Time series** (trend analysis). Five years of data is desirable. Attempts to show how the firm is doing over time.

b. **Cross-section analysis.** In any given time period, tells how is the firm doing compared to:

- Industry average.
- Specific competitors.
- The overall economy.

2. Who uses ratios and why? Three major groups use ratio analysis.

a. **Creditors.** Can the firm repay its debts? Liquidity, debt, and coverage ratios are of most interest.

b. **Investors.** How much money is the firm making? Profitability is the key.

c. **Management.** Sets standards for each ratio and compares actual results to standards. Variances need to be investigated. **DuPont Analysis** breaks ratios into small pieces to determine what occurred to cause the ratio to change or be different than expected.

3. **Types of Ratios.** There are many different classification systems for ratios. One common approach is to divide ratios into five different types.

a. **Liquidity ratios.** These ratios help show the ability of the company to pay short-term obligations based on its balance sheet.

- **Current ratio.** Current assets (CA) divided by current liabilities (CL). CA/CL. Higher is generally better. A benchmark for a manufacturing company is 2.0; however, if the current ratio gets too high, the organization may be sacrificing profitability for liquidity.
- **Quick (asset test) ratio.** CA minus inventory divided by CL. Higher is normally better. A benchmark for a manufacturing organization is 1.0.
- **Net working capital** (NWC). CA – CL. NWC is measured in dollars. It is not a ratio. But it is a common loan covenant that the firm must maintain a minimum level of NWC.

b. **Debt ratios.** These ratios help show the ability of the company to pay long-term obligations based on its balance sheet.

- **Total debt to total asset ratio.** Total debt, both current and long-term, divided by total assets. Measure of leverage and risk. Manufacturing firm will generally be around 50 percent.
- **Debt to equity ratio.** Long-term debt (LTD) divided by stockholders' equity (SE): LTD/SE. An issue here is how to treat preferred stock. Is it debt or is it equity? Opinions differ on where preferred stock should be included.

Page 686   ©2007 Kaplan CPA Review

c. **Coverage ratios.** These ratios help show the ability of the company to pay short-term obligations based on its income statement.

- **Times interest earned ratio.** Earnings (net income) before interest and taxes (EBIT) divided by required interest payments. Higher is normally better. This is the simplest of the coverage ratios.

d. **Activity or efficiency ratios.** Output to input ratios. How effectively does the firm manage its assets?

- **Inventory turnover.** Defined as either sales or cost of goods sold divided by average inventory. A higher turnover is preferred. Average inventory should mean a weekly or monthly average rather than averaging the numbers of the two most recent balance sheets. If your sales figure or cost of goods sold is $1 million and inventory (or average inventory) is $100,000, turnover is 10 times (1million/100,000). Average age of inventory (number of days sales in inventory) is equal to 365/inventory turnover or 365/10 = 36.5 days in this example.
- **Average collection period** (days sales outstanding). Can be determined in different ways. One method is to divide total credit sales by 365 to get credit sales per day. That number is then divided into accounts receivable to determine the time that the average credit sale takes to be collected.
- **Total asset turnover.** Sales divided by total assets. Higher is normally better. This ratio measures the overall ability of the company's assets to generate sales.

e. **Profitability ratios.** Helps to measure the success of the company in generating net income.

- **Profit margins.** At least three profit margins can be calculated from an income statement. Higher is better for all margins.
  - **Gross margin.** Sales minus CGS divided by sales. Changes over time and comparison to competitors helps in evaluating the company.
  - **Operating margin.** EBIT divided by sales.
  - **Net margin.** Net income (NI) divided by sales. This measures the strength of the income statement.
- **Return on assets** (ROA). NI divided by total assets. Higher is better. DuPont ratio decomposition breaks ROA into two components: *net margin* times *total asset turnover*. Assume sales are $1million, total assets are $500,000, and NI is $50,000. ROA would be 50,000/500,000 = 10%. DuPont is 50,000/1million (NI/sales or net margin) *times* 1million/500,000 (total asset turnover). That comes out to be 5% × 2.0 = 10%. That shows the income statement impact times the balance sheet impact.
- **Return on equity** (ROE). NI divided by stockholders' equity. This is the return on the owners' capital. The greater the spread between ROA and ROE, the more leverage the firm has: in other words, the better use the company is making of the money that it receives by borrowing.

©2007 Kaplan CPA Review

STUDY MANUAL – BUSINESS ENVIRONMENT & CONCEPTS
CRAM ESSENTIALS

C. **Working capital management** refers to managing a company's current assets and current liabilities. Net working capital (NWC) = CA – CL. The higher the level of NWC, the greater the firm's liquidity and the safer the position of the firm's creditors.

1. **Managing current assets.** Current assets generally consist of cash, marketable securities, accounts receivable, and inventory. CA's provide liquidity. However, most firms face a sharply upward sloping yield curve for the asset side of their balance sheet (it is harder to make additional profits as the amount of current assets continues to rise). Fixed assets generally earn a substantially higher return than current assets. For that reason, increased liquidity comes at the cost of reduced profitability. Firms, therefore, generally try to minimize their current assets without jeopardizing their ability to pay their bills on a timely basis or adversely impacting their credit rating.

   a. **Cash.** There are a number of reasons to hold cash: transactions balance (bill payments), compensating balance (balances required by a bank in order to grant a loan), precautionary balance (unexpected expenses), and speculative balance (provides the ability to take advantage of opportunities). Firms want to generate positive cash flow but then want to invest as much of that cash as possible in income-generating assets because cash is an idle asset (non–income-producing). Consequently, companies attempt to keep low cash balances. Cash can be replaced by lines of credit—prearranged borrowing levels from a bank. Generally, if line of credit is not utilized there is no cost to the firm.

   b. Calculation of Minimum Cash Balance.

      - **Cash conversion cycle.** Time between payment for raw materials and receiving cash for your finished goods. Computed as the average age of inventory (assume 80 days) + average age of accounts receivable (40 days) minus average age of accounts payable (30 days). Therefore, 90 days is the cash conversion cycle in this example. Goal is to shorten the cycle.
      - **Cash turnover** = 365 days/cash cycle. 365/90 = 4.06 times.
      - **Minimum cash balance** (MCB) = annual cash expenditures (assume $10 million)/cash turnover. $10m/4.06 = $2,463,054.
      - **Opportunity cost.** Determined as the MCB × opportunity cost or cost of capital. Assume a 10 percent opportunity cost. Then there is $2,463,054 (0.10) or $246,305 in forgone revenue by holding $2,463,054 in a nonrevenue producing asset.

   c. **Cash management techniques. Float** is the difference between the balance shown in a checkbook and the balance on the banks' records. Net float is equal to disbursement float (the time between when you make a payment and your bank account is reduced) minus collections float (the time between when you make a collection and the your bank account is increased). The goal is to improve your collection and clearing process so that you limit the time when cash is not available to be used in generating revenues. Float has three components: mail float (the time the money being paid or received takes to get to or from the other party), processing float (the time the company takes to process payments and collections), and clearing (banking system) float (the time that it takes for money to get through the banking system). Methods available to speed up the process include the following:

- **Lockbox plan**. The system speeds up collections and reduces float by having customers send their payments to local area post office boxes. Several times a day, a bank (for a fee) opens the lockbox and deposits the checks in the bank. Lockboxes can make funds available two to five days faster.
- **Concentration banking**. Customers send their payment to a local branch office rather than to headquarters. This reduces float. For example, Sears would have customers send their payment to the closest office rather than to its headquarters in Chicago.
- **Wire payments or automatic debit**. Funds are automatically deducted from one account and deposited into another (electronic debits).
- **Depository Transfer Checks** (official bank check). Used to move funds from one account to another account of the same company without a signature being required.
- **Zero balance account**. A disbursement account on which a company writes checks, even though the balance is maintained at zero. When a check is written on the account, funds are automatically transferred into it by the bank from a master account held by the same company.

2. **Marketable securities**. Short-term (less than one year, mostly less than 270 days), highly liquid (easily converted into cash) securities that provide a positive (although usually low) rate of return. Treasury bills (U.S. government bonds), commercial paper (large corporate bonds), Certificates of Deposit (bank), and Bankers Acceptance (international trade) are examples of marketable securities. Marketable securities are sometimes referred to as money market securities.

3. **Inventory**. Rate of return on inventory is negative. Costs such as insurance, taxes, and rent must be paid while inventory is held, although they do not increase the value. In addition, funds must be borrowed to finance these assets with a resulting interest cost. Inventory is necessary to generate sales but can also be costly. Holding too little inventory may result in customer dissatisfaction and lost revenue. Holding too much inventory can result in increased carrying cost. Inventory costs fall into fixed (order costs) and variable (handling, insurance, storage) components. The goal is to minimize the total cost.

   a. **Economic order quantity** (EOQ) point. Formula to determine how many orders to place and how many units to order each time. EOQ is a function of order cost, the annual usage, and the variable cost of carrying a unit in inventory.

   b. **Reorder point**. Formula to determine when to place an order. Assume it takes a supplier five days to place an order and the company uses 1,600 units per day and works 365 days per year. Lead time (days it takes your supplier to fill your order, five days in this example) times daily usage (1,600/365 or 4.38) gives 5 × 4.38 or approximately 22 units to be used while the company awaits the delivery of the order. Company should place new order when 22 items of inventory remain.

©2007 Kaplan CPA Review

Page 689

STUDY MANUAL – BUSINESS ENVIRONMENT & CONCEPTS
CRAM ESSENTIALS

    c.   **Safety Stock.** Pure reorder point computed above assumes new order arrives just as inventory levels reach zero. A safety stock provides a cushion if shipment is delayed. In the previous example, if a safety stock of 10 is chosen, new order should be placed when current levels drop to 32 (22 reorder point plus the 10 safety stock).

    d.   **Just-in-time** (JIT). Attempt to keep inventory levels close to zero. Suppliers arrive each day with sufficient raw materials to complete the day's scheduled production needs. JIT lowers the firm's cost of carrying inventory. JIT requires reliable suppliers and defect-free raw materials. It also leaves you vulnerable to a supply disruption (e.g., a strike).

4. **Accounts receivable management.** Competitive forces require most firms to offer credit. Days sales outstanding (average collection period) is equal to annual sales/ 365. This measures collection performance and should be compared to the credit terms offered by the firm. An aging schedule breaks down the receivables by age of account. Credit terms involve stating the credit period and any discounts offered. The term 2/10 net 30 offers the buyer a 2 percent discount if invoice is paid by the tenth day. If not, the balance is due in 30 days. Credit standards determine the criteria for determining who gets credit and how much. Collection policy is the procedure the firm uses to collect its receivables. Accounts receivable can be used to obtain financing for the firm. **Pledging** involves using the firms' accounts receivable as collateral for a loan. **Factoring** is the sale of accounts receivable at a discount from face value.

5. **Managing current liabilities.** There are three advantages to using short-term liabilities rather than long-term liabilities: (1) lower cost, (2) flexibility, and (3) they can be obtained faster than long-term funds. The disadvantages are that the rates can change quickly, that the debt must be periodically refinanced, and that too much reliance of current liabilities may adversely impact liquidity and credit rating.

    a.   **Financing current and fixed assets.** Most businesses experience seasonal or cyclical variations in asset size. Several methods exist to finance a firm's assets. A matching maturity approach finances current assets with current liabilities and fixed assets with long-term funds. The advantage is that current liabilities are cheaper than long-term funds and cost would be lower. In an exact match there would be zero net working capital (NWC), which would adversely impact liquidity. A conservative approach would finance all anticipated assets with long-term liabilities, leaving current liabilities to cover unexpected financing needs. This policy results in maximum NWC and liquidity but a higher financing cost.

D. Bank Loans and Interest Notes

1. **Short-term bank loans. Promissory note** is a document that specifies the terms and conditions of a loan: the amount, interest rate, and repayment schedule. **Compensating balance** is a minimum amount the borrower must maintain in a checking account at the bank, usually a percentage of the loan amount. **Line of credit** is an agreement where the bank pre-approves the borrower up to a stated

maximum debt level. A revolving credit agreement is similar to a line of credit, but the bank has a legal obligation to make the funds available to the borrower in exchange for a commitment fee. Interest rates tend to be variable and tied to the **prime rate** (rate the banks charge their best business customers). Prime rate plus points is the standard format where 100 points = 1 percent. Prime plus 150 points is prime + 1.5 percent. Loans can be secured (with collateral) or unsecured. **LIBOR** (London Interbank Offered Rate) is often used to price loans outside the U.S. Increasingly, domestic loans are being priced at LIBOR plus points rather than prime plus points.

2. **Commercial Paper** (CP). Unsecured, short-term (less than 270 days) promissory note of a large corporation with very strong credit ratings. Denominations are for $100,000 and up. CP is sold at a discount from face value and pays face value at maturity. The discount equates to the interest earned/paid. The Commercial Paper interest rate tends to be below the prime rate but above the treasury bill rate.

3. **Loan covenants**. Requirements that the borrower must maintain or things they can not do as a condition of the loan. Covenants are designed to protect the lender and insure repayment of the loan. Common covenants include minimum levels of NWC and certain ratios such as the current ratio. There can also be limits on taking on additional debt without the permission of the existing debt holders. If a covenant is breached, the borrower is technically in default, and the entire loan amount becomes due immediately.

4. **Letter of credit** (LOC). A document issued by a bank (for a fee) guaranteeing the payment of a customer's draft up to a stated amount for a specified period. A LOC substitutes a bank's credit for that of the buyer, eliminating credit risk to the seller. Widely used in international trade transactions.

5. **Interest on loans**. Interest payments are tax-deductible expenses to a business. The after-tax cost of debt to a firm is the interest rate times (1-tax rate). Dividends are not deductible as expenses, so debt tends to have a lower after-tax cost to the firm than equity. Debt holders are paid before equity holders, so debt has less risk than equity. Other advantages of debt are the fact that it does not involve dilution in ownership, and that debt can create beneficial leverage if the company can make a higher return on the money borrowed than it pays in interest cost.

   a. **Fixed vs. variable rates**. Variable-rate debt has its interest rate tied to an index (such as the prime) and fluctuates over time. Generally, variable-rate debt has a lower rate than fixed-rate debt for the same maturity. Variable-rate debt is riskier to the borrower because the rate can escalate. Similarly, short-term debt costs less than long-term debt but is also riskier in regards to interest since rates can increase and the debt must be regularly refinanced because it comes due in a short period of time.

   b. Interest rates are expressed in *nominal* (stated rate to be paid on the contract) and *real* terms. Real interest rates are the rates being charged by lenders adjusted for inflation. If the bank charges 7 percent and inflation is 2 percent, the real interest rate is 5 percent. Historically, long-term real interest rates in the U.S. average around 4 percent. The *Fisher effect* states that nominal rates are comprised of the real rate demanded by investors increased by the expected rate of inflation.

c. **Term structure of interest rates.** The yield curve in Figure 1 diagrams the relationship between yields and maturity on U.S. government securities.

Figure 1: Yield Curve

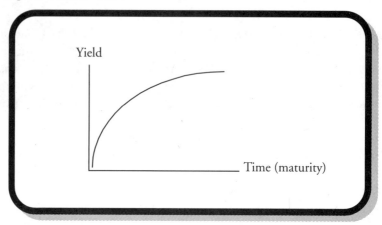

Yields on government bills (a term of less than one year), notes (one to ten years), and bonds (greater than ten years) are plotted on this curve. The normal yield curve is upward sloping as shown above. Longer-term debt typically has higher risk than short-term debt because so many circumstances can change over time. A normal yield curve offers investors a trade off between risk and return. Longer-term debt offers a higher return to offset the increased risk.

d. Three theories exist to explain the shape(s) of the yield curve:

- **Liquidity preference theory.** Investors prefer less risk to more and will only take an additional risk (longer maturity) if they are compensated with the additional return. Under this theory, the yield curve will always be upward sloping.
- **Market segmentation theory.** The term structure consists of multiple markets rather than a single market. There is a short-term, intermediate term, and a long-term market for government securities. Supply and demand in each market determines the shape of the yield curve.
- **Expectations theory.** Investors' expectations about future interest rates determine the shape of the yield curve. When rates are expected to rise, the yield curve is upward sloping. If rates are expected to decline, the curve will be inverted. When investors are undecided as to the direction of interest rates, it will be flat.
- **Stated (nominal) vs. effective interest rates.** The nominal rate is the rate to be paid that is stated on the loan, while the effective rate is the mathematical rate for both parties. (The mathematical rate depends upon

how the interest is actually paid and other characteristics of the loan agreement, as discussed below.)

e. **Discount interest.** A company borrows $10,000 for one year at 10 percent and makes only one payment at the end of the year of $11,000 ($10,000 principal + $1,000 interest). This is simple interest and the loan cost is 10 percent. However, if the bank requires the debtor to pay the interest in advance (discount interest), the interest payment is still $1,000 but the debtor only has $9,000 left to use after paying the interest. The effective cost is the interest paid divided by the money used or $1,000/$9,000 which is 11.11 percent even though the stated rate was 10 percent.

f. **Compensating balance.** If the bank charged 10 percent interest on a $10,000 loan at the end of the year but required the debtor to keep a compensating balance of 15 percent ($1,500). The debtor cannot use the $1,500, so the effective cost is $1,000/$8,500 or 11.764 percent. If the bank asks for interest in advance ($1,000) and a 15 percent compensating balance ($1,500), the effective cost is $1,000/$7,500 or 13.33 percent.

g. **Add-on interest (installment loans).** A debtor borrows $5,000 for one year at 10 percent to buy a used car. The 10 percent interest is add-on interest. You will make 12 equal monthly payments. Interest charged is $5,000 (original loan) × 0.10 (interest rate) or $500. $5,000 + $500 = $5,500 to be repaid divided by 12 gives a monthly payment of $458.33. However, the effective interest rate is 20 percent. The only time the debt was $5,000 was on day one. On the last day of the year the debt was zero. The average loan balance was $2,500 but the debtor paid $500 in interest, so that the rate is 20 percent ($500/$2,500).

h. **Annual percentage rate** (APR). Rate reported by lenders when the effective rate exceeds the nominal rate of interest. The reporting of this rate is required by the Truth in Lending Laws. APR = (periods per year) × (rate per period).

i. **Effective annual rate** (EAR). EAR is the rate of interest actually being earned (or paid). EAR = $(1 + Kd)n - 1$ where Kd is the rate compounded per period and n is the number of periods. Suppose $1,000 is put in a bank for one year. The bank pays 8 percent interest compounded annually. At the end of one year (future value or FV) how much money would be in this account? Future value is equal to present amount times one plus the interest rate (i) to the nth power (n being the number of periods). FV is the present amount times $(1 + i)n$ or FV = 1,000 (1.08) = $1,080. At the end of five years this same bank account would have 1,000(1.08)5 or $1,469.33 in the account. Suppose the bank paid 8 percent interest compounded semiannually. The formula is FV is the present amount multiplied by $(1 + i/m)(n \times m)$ where m is the number of times the interest is compounded per period. Because interest is compounded semiannually, m is two in this case. The future value after one year with semiannual compounding would be 1,000(1.04)2 or $1,081.60. The debtor pays one-half the interest but makes interest payments. The $1,081.60 is larger than the $1,080 for annual compounding because of the additional

STUDY MANUAL – BUSINESS ENVIRONMENT & CONCEPTS
CRAM ESSENTIALS

compounding. The EAR for semiannual compounding is $(1 + Kd)n - 1$ or $(1.04)2 - 1$ which is $1.0816 - 1 = 8.16\%$.

E. **Capital budgeting** involves generating, evaluating, selecting, and follow-up on capital expenditure alternatives. Usually this refers to acquisition, modernization, or replacement of plant, property, and equipment (PPE) financed with long-term funds. The process is utilized for decisions involving a long-term commitment of large sums of money. Step one is to calculate the net investment usually to be made at the current time. Then the benefits are calculated in terms of cash flow per period over the expected life of the project.

1. Terminology.

    a. **Sunk cost**—an outlay that has already been incurred and cannot be recovered, regardless of accepting or rejecting a proposed project. Sunk costs are *not* included in capital budgeting analysis. (In deciding whether to buy a new vehicle, the cost incurred for the old one you are getting rid of is a sunk cost.)

    b. **Opportunity cost**—the return that could be earned on the best alternative use of an asset. (A one-oven bakery that makes cookies cannot also make pies. An opportunity cost of the cookies is the pies that cannot be made and sold.) The cost of capital is used as an approximation of the opportunity cost.

    c. **Incremental cash flow.** The net cash flow from an investment project. If an old machine produces a cash flow of $20 and a new machine could generate $35, the incremental gain is $15.

    d. **Externalities.** Impact of a new project on the cash flows in other parts of the business. (A self-service postal machine may cut costs in the company's mail room, but it may cause inefficiencies in the sales department when the sales staff has to stand in line to post their own mail.)

    e. **Cannibalization.** A new product that causes sales of another (existing) product to decline. (A snack food company may introduce a new flavor of corn chips. Some customers will switch from the old flavor to the new flavor.)

2. **Alternative measures of cash flow** (CF). Numerous definitions of cash flow exist for capital budgeting.

    a. **Net income plus non-cash expenses.** Start with net income and add back depreciation, depletion, and amortization expenses to eliminate them. This is the most commonly used measure of CF.

    b. **Cash from operating activities from the statement of cash flows.** This is used when valuing an entire business entity.

    c. **Free cash flow** (FCF). Cash flow is defined as the amount available after any expenditures required to maintain the value of the entity. It is the cash from

Page 694   ©2007 Kaplan CPA Review

operations less any dividends and any required capital expenditures. Sometimes it also includes changes in working capital.

3. **Unsophisticated techniques.** Sophisticated methods are theoretically superior because they rely on cash flows and the time value of money. For all the techniques below, use the following example. Net investment is $100. The project will last for three years. The expected cash flows are $10 for the first year, $60 for the second, and $60 for the third. Cost of capital is 10 percent.

   a. **Payback**—measures the time that it takes to recoup the initial investment. Shorter payback is preferable. Companies may set a maximum acceptable time period. A project that costs $1 million and generates $300,000 in Cash Flows (CF) for 5 years has a payback of 3.33 years ($1 million/$300,000). Technique is simple to calculate and easy to understand. It does not take into account the time value of money (TVOM) and ignores all cash flows after payback is achieved. Payback for above example is 2.5 years because the $100 cost will be recovered half way through the third year ($10 plus $60 plus $30 [out of $60]).

   b. **Accounting rate of return** (ARR). Divide average net income or cash flow by the initial investment or the current year book value of the investment. A higher ARR is preferred. ARR here is (10 + 60 + 60)/3 for an average annual cash flow of $43.33 divided by either 50 (average investment over the period) or by 100, the initial investment.

4. **Sophisticated techniques.** These techniques use TVOM and the firm's cost of capital to discount future CFs and compare them to the project's net investment.

   a. **Net present value** (NPV) is the present value of the expected future CFs minus the project's net investment. If the NPV (expressed in dollars) is greater than or equal to zero, the project is acceptable. The discount rate of interest to be used is often referred to as the firm's opportunity cost, hurdle rate, required rate of return, or cost of capital. In the above example, the NPV = 10(0.909) + 60(0.826) + 60(0.751) − 100 = 18.73. This is an acceptable project because the net present value is positive (the present value of the future cash flows is greater than the project's cost).

      - **Internal rate of return** (IRR) **method.** For complex cash flows, this method usually requires the use of a financial calculator. For a single amount or for an annuity, the cost is divided by the cash flow (either the single amount or a single payment in the annuity). The resulting factor is looked up on a present value table to determine the exact rate of return being earned. If that rate is equal to or above the company's desired rate of return, the investment is viewed as a good project.
      - **Discounted payback.** Similar to payback, except the CFs are discounted at the cost of capital before the payback period is calculated. Once again, the length of time to receive cash equal to the investment is being calculated. Shorter is again preferred.
      - **Modified internal rate of return** (MIRR). The internal rate of return method (IRR) has some problems. If a project is expected to last five years

STUDY MANUAL – BUSINESS ENVIRONMENT & CONCEPTS
CRAM ESSENTIALS

and has an IRR of 12.87 percent, the project will only deliver that rate of return if each cash flow is reinvested at the IRR. This is called reinvestment rate risk. Conversely, the NPV method assumes reinvestment of CF's at the lower cost of capital. MIRR improves on IRR by altering the reinvestment rate assumption, usually to the cost of capital. Once computed, if MIRR is greater than or equal to the cost of capital, the project is acceptable. MIRR is equal to the value of the CFs at the end of year three. $10(1.10)2 + 60(1.10) + 60 = 138.10$. The accountant wants to know what rate of return causes $100.00 to become 138.10 in three years, which results in an MIRR of 11.5 percent.

- **Benefit to cost ratio.** NPV and IRR can be used as accept-reject and ranking tools. Ranking of the projects to indicate which is better is necessary if the projects are mutually exclusive (there are two or more ways to accomplish the same goal but only one can be accepted) or for capital rationing (there are more acceptable projects than the organization has funds). NPV can be converted to a ranking tool by calculating a **benefit cost ratio** (or profitability index), where you divide the present value of the cash inflows by the net investment that must be made. The decision rule is to accept a project if the benefit cost ratio is greater than or equal to one. The higher the number, the better the project. To rank projects when using IRR, start at the highest return and accept projects sequentially until all funds have been used.

- **Projects with unequal lives.** The above approaches work only on projects with the same expected lives. For example, a three-year project cannot be compared to a five-year project without making adjustments. Two options exist: (1) **replacement chain analysis**—the lowest common multiple of 3 and 5 is 15 so replicate both projects out to 15 years; (2) **equivalent annual annuity**—calculate the NPV for each project, and then convert the NPV into an annuity that will last the life expectancy on the project at the cost of capital. For example, assume that a 5-year project has a NPV of 15,500 and a cost of capital of 10 percent (PVA n = 5, i = 10% gives a present value factor of 3.7908). EAA = 15,500/3.7908 or $4,088.85. The project with the higher EAA is preferred.

5. **Cost of capital**—the cost of capital is normally the rate used to calculate NPV and as the benchmark in using IRR. Capital refers to the long-term financing of a company: long-term debt, preferred stock, retained earnings, and common stock. The weighted average cost of capital (WACC) is determined by calculating the after-tax cost of the four classes of capital and multiplying by a weighting system. Interest on debt is tax deductible, so the after-tax cost of a 10 percent long-term loan at a 35 percent tax bracket is 6.5 percent. Dividends paid are not deductible for tax purposes, so no adjustment is necessary for the other three capital classes. Four weighting systems exist: book value weights (balance sheet weights), market value weights (today's price in the newspaper), target weights (optimal capital structure), and marginal weights (how the money was actually raised). If the firm does not have preferred stock, there will only be three classes. As an alternative, some firms simply use two classes: debt and equity. Because interest is deductible for tax purposes, debt is generally the cheapest way to raise long-term funds. The desired rate for a project is usually set equal to the WACC. It can be set higher

Page 696

©2007 Kaplan CPA Review

but should never be set lower. For example, a firm can have a WACC of 8 percent and still set the hurdle rate (required rate) for a possible project at 15 percent.

a. **Cost of capital calculation.**

- **Cost of debt** is equal to the interest rate after adjustment for the tax effect of being able to deduct interest expense.
- **Cost of preferred stock** is usually the dividend divided by the current price of the preferred stock.
- **Cost of retained earnings.** Three alternative models exist to measure cost:
    - **Capital asset pricing model** (CAPM)

        K (cost) =
        RF (risk free rate) + beta (risk measure) [Km (return on the market) – RF].
        Therefore, if RF = 5%, B = 1.5, and Km = 10%, cost = 5 + 1.5[10 – 5] = 12.5%.
    - **Bond yield plus risk premium.** Cost of the firm's long-term bonds plus an equity risk premium.
    - **Dividend discount model** (DDM).
        Cost = (D1/market price) + g, where *D1* is the next period's forecasted dividend and *g* is the forecasted growth rate in dividends and earnings. For example, if D1 = 1.50, market price is $25 per share, and g = 6%, the cost of retained earnings is 1.50/25 + 0.06 = 12%.
- **Cost of new common stock.** Use the DDM but adjust current stock price downward by the amount of flotation costs that are necessary in order to sell new shares.
- **Calculation example of WACC.** Assume debt costs the firm 6 percent (Kd), preferred stock costs the firm 8 percent (Kp), retained earnings cost the firm 10 percent (Kr) and new common stock costs the firm 11 percent (Kc). The weights (based on balance sheet size) are assumed to be: debt 20 percent, preferred 20 percent, retained earnings 10 percent, and common stock 50 percent. WACC = 0.06(0.20) + 0.08(0.20) +0.10(0.10) + 0.50(11) = 9.3%.

6. **Hybrid financing alternatives.** Preferred stock is a hybrid security, sharing features of debt (fixed cost) and equity (no maturity). Two other hybrid securities that can be used for long-term financing are warrants and convertible bonds.

a. **Warrants** are long-term options to buy a fixed number of shares of common stock at a fixed price. Usually, warrants are attached to bonds to entice investors to either buy bonds they would otherwise avoid or to charge a lower interest rate to the firm. The warrants are generally detachable from the bond and can result in the owner eventually having a bond plus shares of stock. The value of a bond with warrants attached is equal to the value of the bond plus the value of the warrants. The value of the warrants is equal to the market price of the stock minus the exercise price plus a premium usually called time value. If the stock price is $25 and the warrants can be exercised

©2007 Kaplan CPA Review   Page 697

at $20 per share, the minimum value of each warrant is $5. Warrants like other options are valued using the Black-Scholes option pricing model.

b. **Convertible bonds** (or in some cases convertible preferred stock) allow the owner to exchange or convert the bond into a fixed number of shares of stock (conversion ratio). The owner must surrender the bond to get the stock. The conversion ratio times the conversion price is equal to the face value of the bond (usually $1,000). If a bond has a conversion ratio of 20, you can exchange the bond for 20 shares of stock at a conversion price of $50 (1,000/ 20 shares). A convertible bond has two values: the value as a straight bond (floor value) and the value as stock (conversion ratio × current stock price). The convertible bond will sell at the higher of the two values. A premium above the highest value may also be included (time value) in the market price.

- Example: A 10-year, 8 percent coupon bond (paying interest semiannually) is convertible into common stock with a conversion ratio of 25 and the current stock price of $42.50 per share. Similar bonds are paying a 10 percent interest rate. The value of the bond as a bond is equal to the PV of the future cash flows: the PV of the face amount ($1,000) plus the PV of the annuity interest ($80 a year paid semiannually or $40 for 20 periods) discounted at the market rate of interest (10 percent). The value as a straight bond is $1,000 (0.37695%, 20 periods) + $40 (12.4622) = $875.38. The value of the bond as stock is 25 shares × $42.50 = $1,062.50. The convertible will sell at $1,062.50 plus a time value premium since that is higher than $875.38.

7. **Economic value added** (EVA). Economic profit is income earned on capital minus the cost of capital. Accounting profit is different because it does not include a charge for capital. If the return on a project is greater than the cost of capital, value is created for stockholders. If a division of a company has $100 million in capital and a cost of capital of 10 percent, it must earn in excess of $10 million ($100 million × 0.10) to generate "value" to investors. EVA earnings are calculated in terms of net operating profits after taxes (NOPAT). NOPAT less [the total amount of capital in dollars multiplied by the cost of capital] equals EVA. Accepting projects with a positive NPV or IRR greater than cost of capital generates positive EVA. **Market value added** (MVA) is calculated as the market value of equity (price of the shares times the number of shares outstanding) minus the book value of stockholders' equity on the balance sheet. EVA stresses finding what a company does best and focusing solely on that aspect. Noncore businesses are spun off. EVA focuses on value drivers, return on invested capital (ROIC), and returns to "stakeholders" (shareholders, employees, society, etc.).

F. **Risk** is defined in finance as the chance or probability of an outcome other than one that is expected. We assume a normal distribution and measure risk as dispersion from the mean (expected outcome). Expected outcome is the measure of central tendency. It can be measured by mean, median, or mode. There are two types of means: arithmetic (add them up and divide by n or the number of items) and geometric (log function). In finance, expected return is used as the measure of central tendency. It is a mean weighted by probabilities. Dispersion is measured in terms of standard deviation and variance. These statistics measure the stand-alone risk of an investment. For a given level of return, the investment that offers the lowest risk is preferred. For projects with different expected returns, we calculate a coefficient of variation, which is standard deviation (risk) divided by expected return. The project with the lower coefficient of variation is preferred. There exists a positive linear relationship between risk and return in finance. You only earn higher returns if you are willing to bear increased risk.

1. Types of Risk.

   a. **Interest-rate risk.** A mathematical inverse relationship exists between the price of fixed-income securities (bonds, preferred stock, mortgages) and interest rates. If interest rates rise, the price of a fixed income security will fall; if rates fall, prices rise. Longer maturity securities will move a higher percentage in price for a given change in interest rates (duration) than shorter maturity securities. In exchange for the higher risk, longer maturity securities generally offer a higher return than shorter maturity securities.

   b. **Duration measures interest rate risk.** The higher a security's duration, the greater the interest rate risk.

   c. **Market risk.** The risk that the overall market you are investing in drops in value, adversely impacting your specific investment. If you own IBM stock and the NYSE drops 35 percent in value during the year, the probability is that IBM will also generate a negative return. It is very difficult for any stock to move counter to the overall market. Market risk for equities is measured by the Beta coefficient (used in the CAPM, discussed earlier). A Beta of one means average risk. The higher the Beta, the greater the market risk. Beta measures the risk of an asset within a diversified portfolio of assets rather than stand-alone risk.

   d. **Credit risk.** When borrowing from a lender or issuing debt instruments (bonds), a major determinant of the cost of borrowing is the credit worthiness of the borrower. Credit analysis is conducted to determine if the borrower can repay the debt.

   e. **Default risk.** The greater the likelihood of default, the higher the yield investors demand to compensate for the increased risk. U.S. Treasury securities are considered default risk-free. All other securities pay a risk premium to compensate investors. Bond rating agencies rate the default-risk of issuers. The highest rating is AAA, then AA, A, and BBB (triple B). A rating of BBB and above is considered investment grade. Below BBB is considered "junk" or high yield. The lower the rating, the higher the cost of borrowing.

G. **Financial models.** Finance, like many other disciplines, uses models to generate information used to make key decisions. All models are dependent on the quality of the data inputs and assumptions. Models provide guidance; they do not provide answers. The manager needs to add judgment. Finance uses models in many areas but mainly in the valuation area. Valuation models focus on three major types of securities: preferred stock, bonds, and common stock.

©2007 Kaplan CPA Review

STUDY MANUAL – BUSINESS ENVIRONMENT & CONCEPTS
CRAM ESSENTIALS

1. **Preferred stock** is a hybrid security that pays a fixed dividend forever. It is a **perpetuity**. A perpetuity is valued using a no growth dividend discount model (DDM). Value (V) is equal to the Dividend (D) divided by the required rate of return (K). V = D/K. For example, a $3 preferred stock pays a dividend of $3 a year forever. If the required rate of return of the investor is assumed to be 10 percent, the value of a share of the preferred stock is $30 ($3/0.10). The only thing that will change the value will be a change in the required rate of the investor (discount rate). If the discount rate increases (12%) the value will fall ($3/0.12 = $25). If the rate falls (8%) value will increase ($3/0.08 = $37.5).

2. **Bonds.** The value (price) of a bond is mathematically determined by taking the present value of both the stream of cash interest payments (often semiannual payments) and the return of face value (often $1,000) using the market rate of interest currently being paid by bonds of similar maturity and risk (bond rating). For example, AJAX has a 15-year (years remaining to maturity), AA-rated risk measure (AAA is the highest rating), 7.5 percent coupon (the bond pays 7.5 percent of its face value in interest each year) bond that pays interest semiannually (SA). The face value of the bond is $1,000. This bond pays investors $37.50 [0.075 × 1000)/2] twice a year for 15 years. The buyer will receive 30 payments of $37.50. At maturity, the company also repays the face value ($1,000). Assume the market rate of interest (the MRI) for similar bonds is currently 10 percent. Rates have apparently risen since this bond was issued (at only 7.5 percent) so the value of the bond has fallen. Since the coupon is less than the MRI, the bond will sell at a discount (less than face). The price of the bond is the present value (PV) of $37.50 for 30 periods at 5 percent (one-half of the MRI due to SA compounding) plus the PV of $1,000 (face) also for 30 periods at 5 percent. Using present value table factors, the price of the bond is 37.50 × 15.3725, (n = 30, l = 5%, PVA) which is equal to 576.47 plus 1,000 × 0.2314 or 231.40 for a total of $807.87. That price gives an effective interest rate of 10 percent annually. The current yield on this bond is calculated as the annual cash interest ($75) divided by the market price of the bond. 75/807.87 = 9.28%.

   a. Bond terminology.

   - **Debenture vs. a mortgage bond.** A debenture is unsecured (more risk) while a mortgage bond is backed by collateral.
   - **Senior vs. junior (subordinated) debt.** In the event that a firm cannot pay its obligations and must be liquidated, a priority of debtors exists. Secured debt (mortgage) gets paid before unsecured, and senior debt of the same level (first mortgage) gets paid before junior (second mortgage). Senior secured is the safest debt in terms of default risk.
   - **Bond indenture.** This is the contract between the issuer and bondholder that specifies the issuer's legal requirements. A trustee acts on behalf on the bondholders.
   - **Convertible bonds** can be exchanged by the bondholder into a fixed number of shares of common stock. If the bond is **callable** the issuer can force the holder to surrender the bond in exchange for a predetermined dollar amount prior to maturity. Bonds are often made callable to satisfy **sinking fund provisions.** Sinking funds provide for the systematic retirement of debt prior to maturity to reduce the risk to the bondholder.

Page 700   ©2007 Kaplan CPA Review

STUDY MANUAL – BUSINESS ENVIRONMENT & CONCEPTS
CRAM ESSENTIALS

- **Types of bonds.** U.S. Government (treasuries), agencies of the government, municipals (state and local government), and corporate bonds. International bonds are bonds sold outside the country of the borrower. **Foreign bonds** are bonds sold in another country denominated in that country's currency; for example, a German firm sells bonds in Japan denominated in yen. **Eurobonds** are bonds sold in a country other than the country in whose currency the bond is denominated. A German firm sells bonds in Japan denominated in dollars.
- **Bond maturity.** Debt with a maturity less than a year is referred to as a bill (treasury bill) while maturities of one to ten years are called notes. Maturities greater than ten years are referred to as bonds.
- **Interest payments.** Most bonds pay semiannual interest payments. Some bonds are sold at a significant discount from face value and, at their maturity, pay face value. They do not pay any interest payment. These bonds are referred to as **zero coupon bonds.** A 10 percent (semiannual) ten-year zero-coupon bond would sell for the present value of $1,000 based on 20 periods and an effective interest rate of 5 percent for each period or $376.90. It would not pay any interest and would mature at $1,000 in ten years.
- **Yield to maturity** (YTM) is the total return on the bond incorporating interest and capital gains (or losses) if the bond is held to maturity. YTM can only be calculated by using a financial calculator or computer.

3. **Common stock.** Valuing a bond is a mathematical science given the MRI (market rate of interest). Valuing a share of common stock (CS) is an "art form." For a bond, the timing and amount of the cash flows are givens; for stock, they are estimates. A holder of common stock receives a stream of dividends (maybe) plus a capital gain (maybe) when the stock is sold. The present value of the stream of estimated cash flows is the value of the stock. This approach to valuation utilizes the DDMs. There are three versions.

   a. **Dividend discount models.**

   - **No growth DDM.** We use this to value preferred stock.
   - **Constant growth DDM.** The assumption in this model is that the stream of earnings and dividends grows at a constant rate forever (unrealistic). If so, the value of a share of CS is equal to next period's forecasted dividend (D1) divided by [the required rate of return (K) of the investor minus the forecasted growth rate in earnings and dividends (G)]. $V = D1/(K - G)$. If $D1 = \$1.00$, $K = 10\%$, and $G = 8\%$, $V = 1/(0.10 - 0.08)$ or $50 per share. Remember, all the variables are estimates. This is considered to be a very volatile model. If you change your assumed growth rate from 8 percent to 9 percent, "value" doubles to $100 ($1/[0.10 - 0.09]$).
   - **Supernormal growth DDM.** Often firms can grow (G) at rates that exceed investors' required rate of return (K) for finite periods of time. In this case, the constant growth model will not produce a valuation. This is a very complex model for which we will not get into the details here. Examples of supernormal growth firms over time include IBM, Microsoft, CISCO, and Wal-Mart. Eventually, growth rates moderate to sustainable levels (G is less than K).

©2007 Kaplan CPA Review

Page 701

- **Limitations of DDMs.** Volatility of the model to changes in the inputs, especially K and G. All the inputs are estimates. Some (many) firms do not pay dividends. (If a firm does not pay a dividend, you can substitute free cash flow (FCF) for dividends in the three variations of the DDM.) Some firms do not generate positive FCF.
- **Inputs to DDM.** Where do we get the estimates for D, K, and G?
  - Growth rate estimate (G). Three approaches can be utilized to estimate G.
    - Calculate the historical growth rate in dividends and/or earnings per share, and forecast it to continue.
    - Determine the consensus of the stock analysts' forecasted growth rates.
    - Calculate the internal sustainable growth rate in EPS. G = ROE × retention rate. Retention rate is one minus the payout rate. If a firm has EPS of $1, an ROE of 10 percent, and pays a dividend of $0.40 (payout rate is 40 percent), the forecasted growth rate in EPS is 6 percent (ROE of 0.10 times the retention rate of 60 percent).
  - **Next period's dividend** (D1). The current dividend (D0) times 1 + G. In the example, 0.40 (1.06) = $0.424 per share.
  - The **required rate of return** (K). Two common methodologies exist to calculate (K).
    - You can build a K from three components: the real risk-free rate of return, the expected rate of inflation, and a risk premium that reflects the risk of owning equities in general and that firm in particular. Five types of risk are included in the risk premium: business risk, financial risk (leverage), liquidity risk, exchange rate risk (currency risk), and country risk.
    - The capital asset pricing model (CAPM). This is the equation for the security market line (SML). Expected return (K) is equal to the risk-free rate (RF) plus the firm's beta coefficient (B risk measure) times [the return on the overall equity market (RM) minus the risk-free rate]. K = RF + B[RM − RF]. If the RF rate (treasury securities) is 5 percent, the stock's beta is 1.5 [a risk measure, where an average risk stock has a beta = 1; a higher beta means more risk], and the return on the market (usually the S&P 500 index) is 10 percent. K = 5 + 1.5[10 − 5] = 12.5%.
- **Price to earnings multiple** (P/E) **valuation method.** If the DDM is not applicable to a firm or a second methodology is desired, the P/E model is the usual choice. Sustainable EPS levels are forecasted over the investors' time horizon, and the P/E is determined based on market, industry, and firm conditions. If a firm's EPS is estimated to be $3.00 and the proper P/E is judged to be 15 times earnings, then the stock is valued at $45 (15 × 3) a share.

◆ **Estimate of P/E multiple.** P/E = payout/(K – g). If EPS $1, dividend is $0.40, K = 10%, and G = 6% the multiple would be 0.40/(0.10 – 0.06), or ten times. These inputs are similar to those in the DDM. More firms have positive EPS than those that pay dividends, but many firms do not have positive EPS which limits the applicability of this approach.

- Other valuation techniques.
    ◆ **Price to cash flow** (P/CF). Value is a multiple of cash flow per share. It is usually a multiple of FCF.
    ◆ **Price to book value** (PBV). Value is a multiple of book value per share. It is often used instead of earnings power or cash flow when buying a firm's assets.
    ◆ **Price to sales** (P/S). Value is a multiple of sales per share. Some consider sales a "purer" number than EPS since it is harder to manipulate.
    ◆ **Liquidation value.** Value of the firm "dead" and the pieces sold off. The other techniques value the firm as an ongoing concern.

- **Valuation models**: summary. Numerous models exist to value securities and/or assets. All the approaches have advantages and limitations. No one model is best in all situations. Usually you use models in combination for a reality check on each other.

H. **Financial indices** (indexes). Security market indexes have several uses. They serve as benchmarks to measure the performance of fund managers. They are used to create and monitor index funds. In order to measure systematic risk (Beta), individual company returns are regressed against an index. The CAPM uses the return on an index as a proxy for the market rate of return.

1. **Factors in constructing indexes.** Three major factors come into play.

    a. **Sample size.** The Dow Jones Industrial Average (DJIA) uses a sample of 30 stocks. The Wilshire Index uses 5,000 stocks. The sample should be representative of the population.

    b. **Weighting system.** Three options exist: price weighted, market value weighted, and unweighted or equally weighted. In a price weighted index (the Dow Jones Industrial Average [DJIA] is an example) a $100 stock has more weight than a $10 stock. In a market value weighted index (S&P 500) larger firms (price x # of shares) have more weight.

    c. **Computational procedure.** Three options exist: calculate an arithmetic average (DJIA), calculate a geometric average (Value Line index), or compute an index and relate all changes to a base index level.

2. **Commonly used indexes.**

    a. **DJIA.** Price weighted arithmetic average of current prices using 30 large, well-known, industrial stocks as the sample. A divisor is used to account for stock splits and changes in sample composition over time.

©2007 Kaplan CPA Review

Page 703

b. **NIKKEI.** Japanese equivalent of the DJIA. Similar construction. 225 stocks traded on the Tokyo Stock Exchange.

c. **Standard & Poor's 500** (S&P 500). Market value weighted composite of 500 large cap firms. Most common benchmark for large cap equity managers. (Note: Large cap firms are companies having a market capitalization between $10 billion and $200 billion.)

d. **Russell 2000.** Market value weighted index of 2,000 small cap New York Stock Exchange (NYSE), American Stock Exchange (AMEX), and Over the Counter (OTC) stocks. Common benchmark for a small cap equity managers.

e. **Wilshire 5000.** Most comprehensive U.S. equity index. Market value of 5000 NYSE, AMEX, and OTC stocks.

f. **Composite indexes** cover the stocks listed on the major exchanges (NYSE composite, AMEX composite) and the OTC (NASDAQ composite) market.

g. **International indexes.** Morgan Stanley Capital International (MSCI) Indexes: 1,375 companies from 19 countries. Dow Jones World Stock Index.

I. **Derivatives**—a derivative security is an instrument whose value depends or derives from the value of an underlying asset or security. The primary derivative securities are options and futures.

1. **Options**—an option gives the owner the right (not the obligation) to purchase (call option) or sell (put option) the underlying security (e.g., 100 shares) at a fixed price (strike or exercise) for a fixed period of time (short-term, usually three months or less). A December 40 IBM call allows the owners to purchase 100 shares of IBM at a price of $40 per share until expiration in December (usually the third Friday of the month), regardless of the current market price of the stock.

   a. **American vs. European options.** American options can be exercised any time up to and including expiration. European options can only be exercised at expiration. Since American options are more flexible, their value is equal to or greater than similar European options.

   b. Stocks on which options trade. Options trade only on approximately 300 to 350 stocks.

   c. **Buyers vs. the writer of an option.** In order for someone to buy an option, someone must be willing to write (sell) one in exchange for a fee. The fee or price is determined by the marketplace. If a December 40 IBM call trades at $4, the buyer pays the writer $400 ($4 × 100 shares) for the right to buy one hundred shares of stock.

   d. **Exchanges** and the **option clearing corporation** (OCC). Options trade on an exchange. The OCC acts as middle person in the transaction. The buyer and writer have a contract with the OCC, not each other. There is no risk of

Page 704   ©2007 Kaplan CPA Review

nonperformance by the counterparty in the transaction. Counterparty risk is absorbed the OCC.

e. **Valuing an option**. Black-Scholes option pricing model. Value = in the money value (market price—exercise price for a call option) plus a premium. Four factors determine the size of the premium (if any): time to maturity, volatility of the underlying security, dividend yield, and interest rates. Time and volatility are the major components of the premium. Longer time to expiration results in a higher premium, as does increased volatility.

f. **In/at/out-of-the-money options**. If IBM's stock price is currently $40 per share and three option strike prices are traded at $45, $40, and $35, the $45 option is out of the money (the right to buy at $45 when the market price is $40 has no "value"), the $40 is at the money, and the $35 is in the money. The logic is reversed for a put option—the $35 is out, the $40 at, and the $45 option is in the money.

g. **Leaps** (long-term equity anticipation securities). Long-term call options with maturities up to 2.5 years. They trade on a limited number of stocks and indexes.

2. **Option strategies**.

a. **Purchase call options to create leverage**. Assume IBM currently trades at $40 per share. The December 40 IBM call at $4 allows the holder the ability to control 100 shares of IBM for a short period of time for $400. To purchase 100 shares of IBM would cost $4,000. If IBM moves to $48 per share by December, the stock has increased by 20 percent (8/40) but the call is worth at least $8 (plus premium) resulting in a gain of $4 (8 – 4) on an investment of $4 or 100 percent.

b. **Purchase a put to profit from a stock falling in value**. IBM currently trades at $40 and a December 40 put option trades at $2.75. If you pay $2.75 for the put option and IBM falls to $30, you have the right to sell 100 shares at $40 per share which is worth at least $10 per share.

c. **Writing covered calls to generate income**. You own 1,000 shares of IBM at $40 per share. You like the firm's long-run prospects but expect the stock to trade sideways (i.e., very little price change) for the next several months. If you write ten (1,000 shares/100) December 40 calls at $4 you get a check for $4,000 ($4 per share × 1,000 shares). If IBM stays at or under $40 per share, you keep your stock and the money. This is a conservative approach to generating income from your portfolio during periods when the market is flat.

d. **Purchasing protective puts**. You own 1,000 shares of IBM, and they are due to announce their quarterly earnings. If they beat analysts' expectations, you feel the stock will jump sharply. If not, you expect a sharp decline in price. You purchase ten December 40 puts at $2.75 or $2,750 as an "insurance policy." If the stock rises, you let the puts expire worthless. If the stock falls,

©2007 Kaplan CPA Review

STUDY MANUAL – BUSINESS ENVIRONMENT & CONCEPTS
CRAM ESSENTIALS

the gain on the puts will offset the loss on your portfolio. Here you are creating a **hedge**—a trading strategy that uses derivatives to reduce or offset an exposure to an underlying asset or liability.

e.   **Index puts**. Put options on stock indexes such as the DJIA (DJX), the S&P500 (SPX), and the Russell 2000 (small cap stocks, RUT). If you are a portfolio manager holding 60 different large cap stocks and you are uncertain of the direction the market will take, you can hold your portfolio, hoping for the market to move up, and purchase index options (puts) on the S&P 500 (large cap index) to protect your portfolio against a market decline.

3.   **Futures markets**. A *futures contract* is an agreement that provides for the exchange of an asset at a specified future date for a specified payment at delivery. Time and price are set today. A futures contract is a security itself and is traded on an exchange. It can be settled with the physical transfer of the actual asset or with a cash payment. A *forward contract* is an agreement between two counterparties that requires an exchange of a commodity or security at a fixed future date and fixed price. Forward contracts are generally an over the counter (OTC), *customized* transaction. The key difference between a forward and a futures contract is the fact that counterparty risk exists in forward market transactions. Forwards are *not* traded on an organized futures exchange.

   a.   **Markets futures** trade on commodities, metals, currencies, interest rates, and indexes.

   b.   **Long (buyer) vs. short (seller) positions**. Each transaction has a long and a short position. The long position gains when the price increases, and the short position gains when the price falls. Futures are a zero sum game. For someone to win, someone must lose.

   c.   Futures are an obligation, not a right; options are rights. Futures represent very large contract sizes and highly leveraged positions.

   d.   **Settlement procedures**. You can exit your position by taking a reversing trade or position (long cancels out short). At expiration, settlement involves delivery of a security or product. Index contracts settle in cash.

   e.   **Daily mark to market**. Daily settlement of winners and losers. If we are trading a December gold contract (100 oz) and the opening price was $380 per oz and the closing price was $384 per oz, the long position gained $400 (4 × 100 oz) and the short position lost $400. The losing position must pay up by the end of the day.

   f.   **Daily price change limits**. Some futures contracts have limits on the allowable price change (up or down) in a given day regardless of the change in the spot market. If gold had a $5 limit and opened at $380, the allowable range of trading that day would be $375 to $385.

4.   Futures strategies—speculators and hedgers participate in the futures markets. Speculators seek to profit from the tremendous leverage available in the market.

Page 706   ©2007 Kaplan CPA Review

a. **Currency hedge.** ALCAB, Inc. is competing for a contract to sell 1.5 million pounds of fabricated aluminum to ABC Aluminum in London. The price is $2 per pound, making the contract worth $3 million U.S. The credit terms are net 60. ALCAB's cost is $2.8 million U.S., resulting in a $200,000 profit. The current spot rate for the pound sterling is $1.50. ABC wants the contract denominated in pounds (£2 million = US$3 million/US$1.50 per pound sterling). In order to win the bid, ALCAB agrees. They are now subject to currency or exchange rate risk for the next 60 days. How do they hedge? They can sell pounds sterling (remember, they receive pounds sterling from ABC Aluminum) on the futures market for delivery in 60 days at a price specified today. Pounds trade on the Chicago Mercantile Exchange (CME) in contract sizes of 62,500 pounds.

b. **Commodities hedge.** Omega produces soybeans in Louisiana. The spot price for No. 1 yellow soybeans is $5.80 per bushel. Omega's cost is $4.60 a bushel. The crop will not be harvested for three months. Omega can wait to see what the spot price is in three months or sell their expected crop in the futures market for delivery in three months. General Foods uses soybeans to produce cereal and other products. They desire to secure a guaranteed cost for their raw materials. They will purchase soybeans for future delivery. Soybeans trade on the Chicago Board of Trade (CBT) in contract sizes of 5,000 bushels.

c. **Interest rate hedge.** AJAX plans to issue $10 million of five-year fixed-rate notes. The debt offering will come to the market in 90 days. The current interest rate on their debt would be 5 percent. AJAX is exposed to the risk that rates will move up in the next 90 days. AJAX can use treasury futures to hedge this risk. Five-year agency futures trade on the CBT in $100,000 contracts. AJAX would short (sell) 100 contracts ($10 million/$100,000 per contract). If rates rise, the firm will pay a higher interest rate on their debt but will gain on its short position in the futures market. If rates fall, they will pay less interest on their debt but lose money on the short position.

d. Uptown Bank specializes in making long-term (30-year) fixed-rate mortgages (its assets). Its liabilities (deposits) are short-term and variable rate. The bank has a **duration mismatch**. It can sell the mortgages on the secondary market or enter into an **interest rate swap**: an agreement for the periodic exchange of cash flows, one based on a fixed interest rate and the other linked to a variable rate index. Uptown would sell fixed and buy variable.

e. **Index futures hedge.** Between 1995 and 1998, CIGNA sold insurance promising to cover losses incurred by life insurance companies that sold variable annuities. The annuities functioned like mutual funds with the added feature that in the event of the owner's death, the heirs would receive at least the initial investment. CIGNA did not hedge this risk and took a $720 million charge to earnings. CIGNA could have hedged by selling (shorting) the market (indexes) or buying put options on the appropriate index(es).

STUDY MANUAL – BUSINESS ENVIRONMENT & CONCEPTS
CRAM ESSENTIALS

QUANTITATIVE METHODS

A. Determination of the **economic order quantity** (EOQ) is based on a formula that computes the number of inventory items that should be ordered (or produced) in each batch.

   1. Formula is complex but is based on (a) the cost of placing an order (the cost of setting up machinery is used if number of units to be produced is being computed), (b) annual demand for units, and (c) the cost of carrying a unit in inventory.

   2. A related figure is the **order point**. That is the number of units that should be held on the day that a new order is placed to avoid running out of inventory. It is computed by multiplying the number of units used each day by the maximum number of days needed to receive a new order.

   3. **Safety stock** is the amount of inventory that should still be on hand if an order is received in the normal number of days (rather than the maximum number of days). Maintaining a safety stock is designed to prevent a company from running out of units if an order takes longer than normal to be received.

B. **Regression analysis** is a mathematical measure of how one dependent variable is affected by another independent variable. It is an attempt to determine whether a cause and effect relationship exists so that future outcomes can be predicted.

   1. For example, a company might determine that each $1 increase in radio advertisement (the independent variable) will produce a $3 increase in sales revenue (the dependent variable).

C. **High-low method** can be used to approximate future outcomes. It is not nearly as accurate as regression analysis, but it is simpler and quicker to use.

   1. Past results are gathered, and only the highest and lowest outputs are selected. Both the monetary (cost) difference and the quantity difference between these two points are measured.

   2. Dividing the monetary difference by the quantity difference gives the variable cost per unit. Any amount spent at the lowest level that is not explained by this variable cost is assumed to be the associated fixed cost.

D. **Correlation analysis** measures how much of the change in one variable is caused by another variable (and not by other factors). A **coefficient of correlation** is computed for this purpose. If the coefficient is +1, it means that all movement in one variable is caused by the movement in the same direction of the other variable (for example, as a person's salary goes up, the amount that person pays for a car will go up). If the coefficient is −1, all movement in one variable is caused by the movement of the other variable in the opposite direction (for example, as the price of food rises, the amount of food purchased goes down). If the coefficient is zero, there is no relationship between the variables.

Page 708   ©2007 Kaplan CPA Review

E. **Probability analysis** is used to select one expected value based on several possibilities.

1. Expected value is determined based on a weighted-average calculation.

2. Each potential outcome is multiplied by its percentage of probability. For example, a potential outcome of $100 with a probability of 30 percent yields an EV of $30. All of the results are added to arrive at a single expected value.

F. A **just-in-time** (JIT) inventory system attempts to schedule all purchases and production so that inventory components will arrive both at the start of manufacturing and at each point in the system at the very moment they are needed. In the perfect system, employees never have to wait for goods and there is never a backlog at any point. A JIT system requires strong relationships with quality vendors. Benefits of a JIT system:

1. Attempts to reduce inventory levels to nearly zero to avoid both loss and breakage and to reduce funds tied up in inventory.

2. A JIT system is engineered to smooth out the process so that production takes less time.

COST-VOLUME-PROFIT ANALYSIS

A. All of the costs incurred by a company in producing a good or service for resale purposes can be divided into two categories.

1. **Fixed costs** such as rent, property taxes, depreciation, insurance, etc., do not change during a period unless the company's level of production goes outside of a *relevant range*.

   a. This total cost is assumed to be a set figure. However, if the number of units increases or decreases significantly, changes in the company can affect the amount. For example, if a new building has to be acquired to produce additional units, both depreciation and insurance will go up, even though they are viewed normally as fixed costs.

2. **Variable costs** such as direct materials, direct labor, electricity, etc., will change as production or sales change. The variable cost for an item might be $3.00 for every unit so that the total would depend on the number of units.

3. *Note*: Fixed costs remain the same in total, within the relevant range. Variable costs remain the same on a per unit basis.

B. **Direct (or variable) costing** can be used to compute projected net income when some type of change is being considered. It is used for internal decision-making purposes.

1. Direct costing is not recognized as a generally accepted accounting principle (GAAP) so it cannot be used for external reporting purposes.

©2007 Kaplan CPA Review

STUDY MANUAL – BUSINESS ENVIRONMENT & CONCEPTS
CRAM ESSENTIALS

2. Direct costing anticipates future net income by subtracting both variable costs and fixed costs from revenue.

   a. Sales minus variable costs is frequently referred to as the company's **contribution margin**.

   b. In order to make projections at different levels, variable cost is stated as a percentage of sales whereas fixed cost is a set figure. Thus, the impact on income created by changes in factors such as sales price or fixed cost can be measured.

3. A company's **breakeven point** is the amount of revenues that must be generated to exactly equal expenses so that neither a profit nor loss results.

4. **Margin of safety** is the amount by which current (or projected) revenues exceed revenues at the breakeven point.

C. For external reporting purposes, **absorption costing** is used.

   1. In absorption costing, the cost of manufactured inventory includes all direct material, direct labor, and factory overhead regardless of whether the cost is fixed or variable.

   2. Absorption costing will usually produce a different net income figure because fixed factory overhead is included as a cost of inventory (a product cost). Thus, this cost does not affect net income until the period in which the item is sold. (In direct or variable costing the fixed cost of the period is charged to cost of sales, so it is a period cost and not a product cost.)

   3. In contrast, direct costing views fixed-factory overhead as an expense (a period cost) so that it affects income immediately. In a period when inventories increase, absorption costing produces a lower net income because some of the fixed costs remain in inventory.

D. Variable and fixed-cost patterns can also be used to produce a **flexible budgeting system**.

   1. This budget is really a formula: any cost is anticipated as its fixed cost component plus its variable cost calculated as a percentage of revenues.

   2. A budgeted figure can be developed for costs based on any level of output so that comparisons of budgeted to actual figures are more realistic than with a static budget. In a static budget, only one level of output is assumed. Variances from a static budget are caused by both differences in the actual vs. the budgeted level of output as well as differences between the budgeted vs. actual costs.

Page 710   ©2007 Kaplan CPA Review

COST ACCOUNTING

A. Cost accounting refers to any accounting method by which costs are accumulated during production so that the cost of the finished goods can be determined.

1. During production, all costs are accumulated in a work-in-process (WIP) account. When units are completed, their cost (cost of goods manufactured) is transferred to a finished goods account. When items are sold, cost is transferred to a cost of goods sold account.

2. Three separate cost figures are accumulated in WIP account.

   a. **Direct material** is the cost of any materials that are traceable to the product being manufactured.

   b. **Direct labor** is the cost of labor that is used in the actual manufacturing process.

   c. **Factory overhead** is any manufacturing cost other than direct material and direct labor.

3. Direct labor and factory overhead are sometimes combined and called **conversion costs**. Direct materials and direct labor are sometimes combined and called **prime costs**.

4. The costs incurred for the various types of factory overhead can take a significant amount of time to accumulate. To get usable cost figures more quickly, factory overhead is often estimated (called "applied").

   a. A rate is determined based on some cause and effect relationship. A change in one item (the number of units, for example, or the direct labor cost) is identified that causes a change in factory overhead. The rate is determined at the beginning of the year based on estimated costs (numerator) divided by estimated quantity of the item (denominator).

   b. A factor (such as direct labor cost) that is believed to affect factory overhead is called a **cost driver**. As this factor increases during a period, more factory overhead cost is applied to the WIP account based on the rate in use. Example: if direct labor cost is the cost driver, the overhead application rate would be calculated at the beginning of the year as budgeted overhead cost/ budgeted direct labor cost. Assuming the rate is estimated to be $20.00 per direct labor dollar, then the overhead is applied at the rate of $20.00 per each dollar of direct labor cost that is incurred in the manufacture of the product.

   c. At the end of the year, the total applied overhead is compared to the actual overhead incurred. Any final difference between the amount of factory overhead applied to the WIP account and the actual amount incurred is usually recorded in the cost of goods sold account.

STUDY MANUAL – BUSINESS ENVIRONMENT & CONCEPTS
CRAM ESSENTIALS

B. **Job order cost accounting** is a system where a separate WIP account is maintained for each individual job. In this way, the resulting cost figures for a particular job should be very accurate. When the job is finished, its specific cost is transferred to finished goods. This method is used when the items being produced are individually unique, such as a custom house, a boat, or a printing job.

C. **Process cost accounting** is a system where a total cost is kept for a large number of similar items being mass produced. The average cost of the units is determined, but the cost of any specific item is unknown. Process cost accounting is used, for example, in food processing. If you manufacture canned green beans, the cost per can is simply the cost of all the cans, divided by the total cans. It is not possible to trace the exact cost of one specific can of beans.

   1. Usually the manufacturing process is divided into departments, and a separate WIP account is maintained for the items as they move through each department. (For canned green beans, it might be the washing department, the slicing department, the cooking department and the canning department.)

   2. An average cost is determined for each type of cost: direct materials, direct labor, and factory overhead. In addition, if a department is any but the first, costs transferred in from previous departments must also be monitored.

   3. For each separate type of cost, the cost is divided by the equivalent units of work done to get an average cost figure. However, the average cost per unit can be determined in either of two ways: FIFO or weighted average. These two methods compute both the costs to be included and the number of units in a different fashion.

   4. The difference in these two methods is in the handling of any beginning work-in-process, units which were started in the previous period but completed in the current period.

      a. In a **weighted average system**, costs include all current costs plus any costs brought into the period within the beginning work-in-process. The equivalent units of work is all work that has been done on the inventory by the end of the current period: 100 percent for the finished units plus the percentage completed to date on the ending work-in-process.

      b. In a **FIFO system**, costs include only current period costs. No cost from the previous period (i.e., beginning inventory) is included. The total units of work done is just the work done in the current period: 100 percent of the finished units plus the percentage completed for the ending work-in-process less any work done on beginning work-in-process during the previous period. Removing the beginning work-in-process leaves just the work done in the current period.

   5. Units can get spoiled or lost during production. These units can be viewed as an additional type of inventory (lost units). A cost figure can be determined in the same manner as for other inventory. The handling of that cost figure depends on the cause of the loss.

Page 712   ©2007 Kaplan CPA Review

a. If the loss is normal in the process, the cost of these lost units is viewed as a product cost. It is transferred to finished goods (if loss occurred at end of production) or allocated between finished goods and work-in-process if lost during production.

b. If the loss is abnormal, the cost of these lost units is a period cost. It is recorded as a loss in the current period.

6. Companies that have a very short production cycle will often use a **backflush system**. All costs are initially recorded as cost of goods sold. At the end of a period, the cost of ending inventory is determined and backed out of cost of goods sold and into inventory.

D. **Activity-based costing** (ABC) is a system for determining the cost of an output. It is often used where factory overhead is a major component of the cost (such as in an organization providing a service rather than a physical product).

1. Every separate activity from the inception of a product to its completion is identified. Overhead costs are assigned based on these activities rather than within departments (as with green beans, above). Assignment of costs is not limited to the manufacturing portion of the process but includes every activity.

2. For each activity, a **cost driver** is identified. That is the factor that is most responsible for the creation of factory overhead. Thus overhead should be assigned to each product in a much more accurate (and detailed) fashion. Rather than assigning overhead costs based on two or three departments, 20 or 30 separate cost drivers (activities) might be used. Activities utilizing the same cost driver can be grouped into cost pools to simplify the process. (Breaking down the cooking department for our green beans might result in *activities* of moving the beans to the cooking pot, starting the boiler, setting a timer, removing the beans from the boiler, cooling the beans, and moving the beans to the canning department.)

3. Activities are classified as either **value adding** (making the product better) or **nonvalue adding** (an activity such as storage that does not improve the product). Company should work to reduce or eliminate all nonvalue adding activities.

E. In a manufacturing process, two or more products will often be produced from one process. For example, crude oil is used to produce gasoline, kerosene, heating oil, plastics, etc.

1. The **joint costs** (the cost of the crude oil, for example) must be allocated to the various products in some logical fashion.

2. Many methods can be used to allocate such joint production costs. For example, costs can be assigned based on the number of units or the final sales value of each product. Probably the most common approach is the **relative sales value at split off method**.

©2007 Kaplan CPA Review

a. All joint costs are assigned to the individual products based on their relative sales value at the time the items are separated into their own production processes. (An item generating 35 percent of sales would be assigned 35 percent of the costs.)

b. A variation of this method is the **net realizable value method**. Costs required by a product after it is split off are determined and subtracted from the final sales value to get the net realizable value of the product at the point when it is divided from the other products. This net realizable value is then used to allocate the joint costs.

F. In manufacturing an item, a second product may be produced. If it is considered a joint product, the joint costs must be divided as indicated above. If the second product has only a minor sales value, it will be viewed as a **by-product**. The company may choose any of a number of different methods to account for the cost of a by-product and any eventual revenues generated from it.

1. One technique is to assign no portion of any joint product costs to the by-product. When it is sold, the entire amount received is reported as a miscellaneous revenue or as a reduction in cost of goods sold.

2. A second possibility is to assign a portion of any joint costs to the by-product equal to its net realizable value (eventual sales price less any costs necessary for the sale). When sold, this inventory balance is removed so that no revenue is recognized. Less cost remains to be assigned to any joint products.

VARIANCE ANALYSIS

A. In many manufacturing companies, a **standard cost** is determined for materials, labor, and overhead for each item being produced.

1. During production, standard (rather than actual) cost is recorded in work-in-process, finished goods, and cost of goods sold.

   a. In this manner, cost figures can be determined in a timely fashion.

   b. Differences between actual and standard figures can be determined and investigated, a process known as **variance analysis**. Remedial action can be taken quickly, if needed.

   c. For identification purposes, differences between standard and actual figures are recorded separately in variance accounts. At the end of the year, any balance in a variance account must be closed out. If the balance is small, it is reclassified to cost of goods sold. If the balance is large, it should be allocated among work-in-process, finished goods, and cost of goods sold.

B. In analyzing production costs, as many as eight separate variances can be calculated.

1. Four of these variances are **spending variances**. Too much (unfavorable) or too little (favorable) was spent for each element of cost. These are identified as a material price variance, labor rate variance, variable factory overhead spending variance, and fixed factory overhead spending variance.

2. Four of these variances are **quantity variances**. Too much or too little of a cost element was used in producing each unit. These are identified as a material quantity (or usage) variance, labor efficiency variance, variable factory overhead efficiency variance, and fixed factory overhead volume variance.

C. Each of the four spending variances can be computed using three steps.

1. First, the actual quantity of the cost element used during the period (such as actual pounds of material put into production or actual hours worked) is multiplied by the *actual unit cost* (price per pound or labor cost per hour).

2. Second, the actual quantity of the cost element used during the period is multiplied by the *standard unit cost*.

3. The difference in these two steps is the spending variance.

   a. For fixed factory overhead, the second computed figure (i.e., standard cost) is simply the single fixed overhead figure anticipated or planned for the period.

   b. For the material spending variance, the amount of material bought should be used if it is different than the amount of material put into production.

D. Each of the four quantity variances can be computed using three steps.

1. First, the actual quantity of the cost element used during the period is multiplied by the standard unit cost.

2. Second, the standard quantity of the cost element is multiplied by the standard unit cost. The standard quantity is the amount that should have been used based on the actual level of production.

3. The difference in these two steps is the quantity variance.

   a. For fixed factory overhead, the first computed figure is the single fixed overhead figure anticipated for the period.

E. Four **factory overhead variances** are computed as previously shown. Two spending variances are determined and two quantity variances.

1. There is also a three-variance method which is the same basic process except that the two fixed variances are combined into a single fixed overhead **volume variance**.

2. There is also a two-variance method, which is the same basic process except that the two variable overhead variances and the fixed overhead spending variance are

STUDY MANUAL – BUSINESS ENVIRONMENT & CONCEPTS
CRAM ESSENTIALS

all combined into a single variance, which is referred to as the **controllable factory overhead variance**. The remaining fixed factory overhead variance is still used but it is now called the **noncontrollable factory overhead variance**.

INFORMATION TECHNOLOGY

A. **IT fundamentals**

1. **Hardware:**

   a. **Input devices**—keyboard, mouse, trackball, track pads, light pens, audio/voice input devices, barcode scanners, optical character readers, point of sale devices, scanners.

   b. **Processors**—central processing unit (CPU) is the primary handler of processing information in a computer. Most processors require random access memory (RAM). The faster processor rating (in megahertz or clock speed or cycles per second) and higher amounts of RAM will make the overall system more efficient. Cache memory and read-only memory (ROM) are two other forms of physical memory. A CPU consists of an arithmetic/logic component, primary memory, and a control unit.

   c. **Storage**—tape, diskettes, zip drives, hard drives, floppy diskettes, CDs, DVDs. There are two methods of accessing digital or analog information within a storage device:

      • Random access—information directly accessed on storage device.
      • Sequential access—specific data must be processed in the order in which it is stored on the storage device.

   d. **Output devices**—printers (all types), hard copies and soft (screen) copies, sound cards, speakers, monitors.

   e. **Other hardware devices** to consider:

      • **Server**—a computer or software application that provides a specific kind of service to client software running on other computers. The term can refer to a particular piece of software, such as a Web server, or to the computer on which the software is running.
      • **Personal computer** (PC).
      • **Network computer** (NC).
      • **LAN** (local area network)—connects several computers within an organization's facility.
      • **WAN** (wide area network)—connects several or many computers to other facilities.
      • **PDAs** (personal digital assistants)—small compact mobile computers.

2. **Software:**

Page 716   ©2007 Kaplan CPA Review

a. **Systems software**—operating systems (Linux and Windows), utility programs (such as compilers, translators, debuggers, etc.), and software applications (ERP solutions, MS Office).

b. **Application software**—specific purpose software, controlled by systems software. Examples include spreadsheet and word processing applications.

3. **Networks**—communication networks come in several levels, varying from linking (networking) a couple of computers together to the Internet.

   a. Client server technology—the physical and logical division between user applications and the shared data that must be available to all users (such as databases and print queues).

      - **LANs** (local area networks)—link several different user machines, printers, and/or databases to other shared devices.
         - Three major component categories:
            - Computers with network adapters (NICs) and peripheral devices (printers, modems, etc.)
            - At least one server
            - A communications channel to connect them
         - A LAN will be connected using one of three common designs:
            - Bus
            - Ring
            - Star
      - **WANs** (wide area networks)—link distributed users and local area networks. Used to provide broad geographical coverage. Use currently existing phone lines to communicate.
      - **Internet**—provides a network that connects various secured WANs. Allows communication between dissimilar technology platforms. Web browsers are software programs that allow users access to browse various data sources on the Internet.
      - **Intranet**—link internal documents and databases using Web-based technology.

4. **Operating system** (OS)—the program that, after being initially loaded into the computer by a boot program, manages all the other programs in a computer. The other programs are called applications or application programs. The application programs make use of the operating system by making requests for services through a defined application program interface (API). In addition, users can interact directly with the operating system through a user interface, such as a command language or a graphical user interface (GUI).

   a. An operating system performs these services for applications:

      - In a multitasking operating system where multiple programs can be running at the same time, the operating system determines which

STUDY MANUAL – BUSINESS ENVIRONMENT & CONCEPTS
CRAM ESSENTIALS

applications should run in what order and how much time should be allowed for each application before giving another application a turn.

- It manages the sharing of internal memory among multiple applications.
- It handles input and output to and from attached hardware devices, such as hard disks, printers, and dial-up ports.
- It sends messages to each application or interactive user (or to a system operator) about the status of operation and any errors that may have occurred.
- It can offload the management of what are called batch jobs (for example, printing) so that the initiating application is freed from this work.
- On computers that can provide parallel processing, an operating system can manage how to divide the program so that it runs on more than one processor at a time.

b. Examples of operating systems include:

- Linux.
- Windows.
- VMS.
- Red Cap.
- AIX.
- DOS.

5. **Security**—developing and continuously updating a comprehensive security plan is one of the most important controls a company can identify. Authority and responsibility must be clearly divided among the following functions:

a. Systems analysis.

b. Programming.

c. Computer operations.

d. Users.

e. AIS library.

f. Data control.

6. **File organization**—the accounting records in an accounting information system fall into four main categories:

a. Source documents and other data capture records, such as customer order forms, sales invoices, journal vouchers, time cards, etc.

b. Data accumulation records (or journals), such as daily cash receipt summaries, weekly payroll summaries, monthly purchases journals, etc.

c. Subsidiary ledgers (or registers), such as accounts receivable ledger, plant and equipment register, etc.

Page 718 ©2007 Kaplan CPA Review

d. General ledger and financial statement records.

7. Database management systems:

   a. **Database management system** (DBMS)—a set of integrated programs and query instructions for creating, accessing, and managing data within databases. A DBMS translates a user's logical view into instructions for retrieving data from the physical storage. Examples of commercial DBMS include Oracle, Access, and Paradox. A database system is the combination of the database, the DBMS, and the application that uses the database.

   b. **Database:**

      - A set of files that accomplishes many processing and information needs.
        - Shared by multiple applications.
        - Data accessed through reports.
        - Data accessed through ad hoc queries.
        - Eliminates data redundancies.
        - Reduces storage costs.
        - Provides data integrity and data independence.
        - Ease of maintenance.
        - Provides data security.
      - The necessary information contained within a database shall be determined by data modeling. This data model shall identify an organization's logical and physical data. Types of data models to consider include:
        - Entity relationship modeling, with its two components: entities and relations.
        - REA data model [resources (funds), events (transactions), agents (people)]—used for developing accounting information systems.

   c. **Application data management**—prior to the development of the database concept, traditional "stovepipe" or stand-alone applications were utilized, each generating their own set of data. Data redundancies and multiple versions of information evolved along with extremely high storage costs. For example, the sales system and the credit system would each maintain their own mailing address for the same customer. Each set of files is distinguishable for each application.

   d. Types of processes:

      - **Transaction processing**—the main type of information system used for operational support in a business (an automated MIS). Four major functions:
        - **Input**—before transaction data can be brought into a system, it must be acquired from its source, called data capture (often captured from a source document). Data that is captured is put into the system, called data entry/data input. As more data is entered, the system must check for errors, called data validation.

- **Storage**—data is stored in two different types of data files or databases:
  - Master data files.
  - Transaction data files.
- **Process**—manipulation of data within a system. Two types of operations:
  - Computation.
  - Decision-making (built-in intelligence).
- **Output**—results (screen or paper or electronic).

- **Event data processing**—the collection and storage of activities that occur during the execution of business processes. This is usually performed by an organization's information system. In larger organizations, information systems will be comprised of subsystems. Subsystems process only a few closely related types of events. An example is the billing system, a subsystem to the accounting system. *Note*: *event-driven* data is at the original form, allowing users to customize their own queries.
- **Business event cycle**—a set of two or more closely related processes, such as the revenue cycle, the production cycle, and the expenditures cycle. These two or more cycles will have an iterative impact on the financial statements.
- **Distributed processing**—data processing in which some of the functions are performed in different places and connected by transmission facilities (physically separated devices). Also referred to as remote-access data processing or teleprocessing.

e. **Data hierarchy**—this hierarchy can also outline the hierarchy of a database.

- **Bit**—a binary digit, such as a 0 or 1.
- **Byte**—a group of bits. There are usually eight bits to one byte.
- **Character**—a basic unit of data, such as a letter, number, or symbol [3, J, #,), etc.].
- **Field**—a collection of "characters" that represent one attribute, such as a name or employee number (1001, Smith, VA, 23220, etc.).
- **Record**—a collection of related fields, such as address information or employee profiles (all information in the following table), that may be numbered and used as a Primary Key.
- **File**—a collection of related records, such as sales records or customer mailing addresses. (The following table depicts a basic file within a database.)
- **Database**—a collection of one or more interrelated files.
- **Array**—a collection of *ordered* values of a single data type, called elements. Useful for very large databases. Increases efficiency. Example would be an array that identified records #1 and #3 (as follows) as New York residents. This is different than a query.
- **Primary key**—an attribute that uniquely identifies any record within a file.

Record

#	ID	First Name	Middle Initial	Last Name	SSN#	Address	City	State	Zip	Phone
1	1001	John	J	Smith	123-45-6789	12 Main St.	New York	NY	11411	(516)555-1212
2	1002	Jane	S	Hall	987-65-4321	862 Pine St.	Richmond	VA	23220	(804)123-4567
3	1003	Paul	B	Adams	111-22-3333	1 N 5th Ave	New York	NY	10019	(212)666-3333

f. **Classification of data**—grouping data according to common and meaningful attributes or labels. Examples include job titles, tenure, and departments. Ways to classify data involve "coding" of data. Ways to code data (as each name implies):

- **Sequential/serial coding**—chronological sequence such as employee numbers. Limited functionality. Can only add at the end of the list.
- **Block coding**—groups of numbers are dedicated for certain attributes, such as UPC codes, where the first five digits represent the manufacturer and the last five digits represent the product number.
- **Significant digit coding**—specific digits represent specific meanings, such as a ball bearing part number #12-8, where the "1" defines the size, the "2" defines the material make-up, and the "8" defines the model it belongs to.
- **Hierarchical coding**—each digit is a sub-category of the digit to its immediate left, such as a facility number 1292A, where the "1" is the territory identifier, the "29" is the state, and the "2A" is the city within the state. Other examples include ZIP codes and internal routing numbers.
- **Self-checking digit coding**—the assignment of an extra character to check accuracy and validity. Examples include checking account numbers and credit card numbers.
- **Mnemonic coding**—an alphanumeric group of characters with specific/unique meanings, such as computer logon names or email addresses.

g. **Data warehousing and data mining**—data warehousing refers to the long-term storage of large amounts of data for an entire entity; data mining refers to the "exploration" and analysis of the large amounts of event-driven data within a data warehouse.

h. Types of data files for storage—two types:

- **Master data**—entity-type files. Main data used by a system. (employee ID numbers).
- **Business event data/transaction data**—files that are event driven; data about transactions that have occurred. (hours worked for April for each employee).

B. **Business Information Systems:**

1. **ERP systems: enterprise resource planning**—integrated software packages designed to provide complete integration of an organization's business information processing systems. ERP systems increase productivity, reduce lead-time and costs, and enhance product quality. Basic business information systems activities include:

   a. Entering data.

   b. Billing.

   c. Collections.

   d. Inventory management.

   e. Purchasing.

   f. Payments.

   g. Human resources and payroll.

   h. Financial reporting.

2. **Management information system (MIS)**—an integrated set of components to facilitate operational functions and management decision-making.

3. **Accounting information system (AIS)**—a specialized sub-system of the MIS related to the accounting aspects of the business events.

   a. Examples include:

      - Fixed asset accounting.
      - Budgeting.
      - Tax accounting.
      - Accounts payable.
      - Accounts receivable.

Figure 2: Automated Processing System

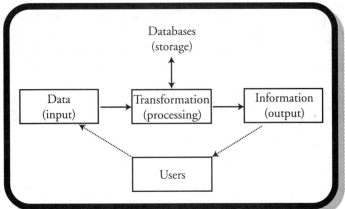

b. Manual AIS versus Automated AIS:

- Manual:
    - Journalize—record entries.
    - Post—to general ledger.
    - Summarize—prepare a trial balance.
- Automated:
    - Input—record event data in system (input to storage).
    - Process—update data storage.
    - Output—retrieve master data from storage.

4. **ERP modules**—components of an ERP system, named after the functions they support. Examples include:

   a. Accounting modules (such as finance, treasury).

   b. Human resources (HR) module.

   c. Planning module (such as budgeting).

   d. Production module.

   e. Logistics module (such as sales, distribution, material management).

   f. Purchases and payments module (for purchasing and paying vendors).

5. **Business**—the application of networks and business processes between individuals and organizations. Consider:

   a. Internet (external operation).

   b. Intranet (back office operations).

   c. Application processing modes—two types:

- Online real time—direct access processing. Transactions are processed in order of occurrence.
- Batch processing—transactions are processed in groups (batches) of similar transactions.

 d. Global marketing.

6. **Logical components of the business process:**

 a. **Management process**—consists of the people, authority, organization, policies, and procedures to plan and control the operations of the organization.

 b. **Operations process**—consists of the people, equipment, organization, policies, and procedures to accomplish the work of the organization.

7. **Certified information technology professional** (CITP)—recently developed by the AICPA to recognize CPAs who can provide skilled professional services on IT. This professional should be able to provide services on:

 a. Project management.

 b. Relationships between IT and the business processes.

 c. Competence in IT.

8. Two major functions of the accounting information system:

 a. Process, record, and report business events.

 b. Support management activities.

9. **Elements of the accounting information system:**

 a. **Data**—facts or figures in raw form. Data will be transformed into information.

 b. **Information**—data is information presented in a form that is useful in decision-making.

 c. **Quality of information**—recall the qualitative characteristics of accounting information, where materiality and understandability are attributes to relevance and reliability.

- Relevance—predictive value, feedback value, timeliness.
- Reliability—validity, accuracy, completeness, verifiability.

 d. **Decision-making**—the process of making choices.

- There are three levels of structured decision-making information (routine or repetitive):
  - Intelligence—such as environmental and organizational information.
  - Design—information related to different courses of action.
  - Choice—information about various outcomes and related courses of action.
- Unstructured decision-making is when none of the decision phases are routine or repetitive (such as making strategic planning decisions during next year's budgeting cycle).
- Iterative feedback is present among all steps of decision-making.

Attributes of Decisions	
Structured Decisions	*Unstructured Decisions*
well defined	undefined
internal	external
detailed	summarized
historical	future
frequent	infrequent
less accurate	more accurate
Note: Information systems focus on well-structured decision situations.	

- **Technology**—automated tools that can assist or replace the decision-maker.

10. **Reporting**—ad hoc and pre-defined reports. Information system must be able to generate the balance sheet, income statement, statement of cash flows, and statement of equity changes. Reports should depict accurate information and conform to GAAP. A "view" is an appearance of specific data pulled (or queried) from multiple tables. This view will often feed standardized report templates. There are three categories of reports:

    a. Detail reporting—lists detailed information.

    b. Summary report—outlines summarized information.

    c. Exception report—lists exception to norm.

11. **Balanced scorecard**—a methodology for assessing an organization's business performance via four major components of the organization. Along with standardized and ad-hoc reporting capabilities of ERP systems, business intelligence (or integrated analytical tools) is also integrated within an ERP

©2007 Kaplan CPA Review

STUDY MANUAL – BUSINESS ENVIRONMENT & CONCEPTS
CRAM ESSENTIALS

system to guide management. The four major components that are readily analyzed for relationships are:

a. Financial areas.

b. Internal business processes.

c. Customer characteristics and satisfaction.

d. Innovation and improvement activities.

12. **Management decision-making**—managers use information systems to:

a. Monitor current operations, such as levels of inventory or number of sales transactions.

b. Achieve satisfactory results for key stakeholders, such as monitor cash flows and timely deliveries.

c. Respond timely to favorable and/or unfavorable trends in the business environment.

d. Types of management decision systems:

- **Decision support system** (DSS):
  - Management will make decisions based on the outputs or results of the DSS.
  - Examples—spreadsheets, project planning software, databases, ad-hoc querying, etc.
- **Executive information system** (EIS) or executive support systems (ESS):
  - Preprogrammed executions or intelligence based on a set of outputs or results of the EIS or ESS. Implemented to support executive decision-making.
  - Examples—"red/yellow/green" or "traffic light" reports, sales/ marketing systems providing real time price quotes/trends of commodities to senior management.
- **Group support system** (GSS):
  - Collaborates many users' information and generates analyses, recommendations, or solutions.
  - Examples—company calendar or meeting scheduling system, document sharing.
- **Expert systems** (ES):
  - Extremely complex synthesis of data from many environments to emulate problem-solving techniques.
  - Examples—one complex company system monitoring the systems of H/R, accounting, sales/marketing, and corporate property to recommend optimal product mixes (modeling). Other examples include medical lab systems and engine diagnostic systems.

Page 726   ©2007 Kaplan CPA Review

- Intelligent agents:
  - A DSS with automated assistance and advice based on lessons learned from patterns.
  - Examples—spell and grammar checking, wizards, and auto-formatting.

13. **Systems development:**

  a. Four distinctive phases to system development:

  - **Analysis**—needs analysis, feasibility study, system survey, or initial requirements gathering, along with cost/benefit analysis of "status quo," "enhanced," and "new system." This first phase is often initiated after strategic management decisions request the analysis. Planned reviews are conducted in order to accomplish the following:
    - Determine if current system(s):
      - Yield problems (Does the system provide problems?).
      - Still satisfy user needs for information (different information, more information).
      - Should be changed due to higher levels of competition (faster processing, online, etc.).
      - Should be changed due to changing business needs and business focus (scope change).
    - Determine if new or additional business processes should be implemented (functionality).
    - Document current state processes. Define requirements and rank or classify into "critical" where the business stops, "important" where business would continue, and "nice to have."
  - **Design (blueprinting)**—convert logical solution into physical design; choose hardware and software; detail specifications; define fielding and training programs.
  - **Implementation (deployment or fielding)**—write, test, debug new program; train users.
  - **Operation (sustainment)**—includes systems maintenance and post-implementation review.

Figure 3: Systems Development Lifecycle: Cost of Errors and Changes

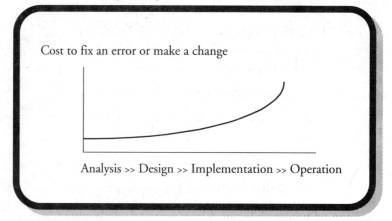

- System development also referred to as system life cycle or development life cycle.

Figure 4: Systems Development Lifecycle: Occurrence of Errors

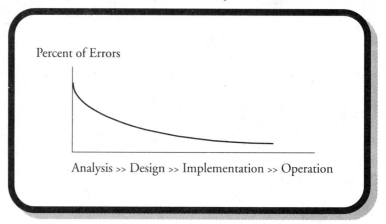

- The average company completes only 37 percent of large IT projects on time, and only 42 percent on budget. Many reasons occur to yield project failure, but the most summarized reasons are:
    - Lack of senior management support and involvement.
    - Shifting user needs.
    - Difficulty to identify specific requirements to a company-specific strategic environment.
    - Emerging technologies (hardware and software).
    - Lack of standardized project management and standardized methodologies.
    - Resistance to change; lack of proper "change management."
    - Size of project underestimated by entire organization.
    - Lack of user participation.
    - Inadequate testing and training.

- Poor project management—underestimation of time, resources, scope.
- To manage information systems development well, entities should adopt a framework of **"project management"** with the following attributes/conditions:
  - User participation early on and continuous.
  - Assignment of appropriate staff to tasks; outline clear responsibilities.
  - Clear scope of the project.
  - Feasibility study and management support/buy-in will feed a project plan development. (Economic feasibility—benefits exceed costs; costs are reasonable.) A feasibility study will contain certain key pieces of information:
    - An executive summary.
    - A detailed description of the problem (from interviews and surveys).
    - A detailed outline of objectives and goals.
    - Constraints (hardware, software, user, regulatory, etc.).
    - Statement of overall feasibility (including economic and technical feasibility).
    - Potential solutions (system-specific; large characteristics—i.e., Web-enabled).
    - Supporting documentation and attachments (minutes, flowcharts, manuals, etc.).
    - A detailed project plan, with manageable pieces identified (phases with tasks).
    - Each phase approved by management, before starting next phase.

e. **Accountant's involvement in information system development:**

- Possess accounting and auditing skills that can be applied to cost/benefit and life cycle cost analyses.
- Possess combined knowledge of IT, general business, accounting, and internal control along with communication skills to ensure new system(s) meet the needs of the users.
- Types of accountants that could be utilized during system development: System Specialist, Consultant, Staff Accountant, Internal or Independent Auditor.

STUDY MANUAL – BUSINESS ENVIRONMENT & CONCEPTS
CRAM ESSENTIALS

    f.   **Alternative system development processes:**

- **Prototyping**—an iterative development process focusing on user requirements and implementing portions of the proposed system. Prototypes are nothing more than "screen shots," which eventually are modeled into a portion of the functioning system.
- **Rapid application development** (RAD)—an iterative development process using prototypes and automated development tools (i.e., PowerBuilder and Visual Basic) to speed the development process.
- **Modular development**—development and installation of one sub-system (of an entire company system) at a time. Examples of modules include order entry, sales, and cash receipts.

    g.   **Business process reengineering**—more than just systems development, it includes all processes within an organization. A radical re-design of entire organization's processes.

    h.   **Change management**—an organization must be able to respond to change(s). Management must determine ways for users to overcome various dysfunctional behaviors towards a new system or process. Resistance to change is the foremost obstacle for a successful system implementation. The "human element." Change management must be an integral part of an implementation team.

    i.   **Project plan**—a mechanism for controlling a system development plan. Usually outlines a series of project work plans which define specific tasks. A project plan is a statement of a project's scope, timetable, resources needed, and costs. Usually consists of diagrams, schedules, analyses, and estimates of costs. Costs within a project plan are estimated, considering all necessary hardware and software costs, outside consultants' fees, fees for project teams, and life cycle costs. Project plans are usually depicted with project planning tools, such as Gantt charts or PERT (Program Evaluation Review Techniques) charts (see Figures 5 and 6). They identify interdependencies within the project.

Figure 5: Example of a Gantt Chart

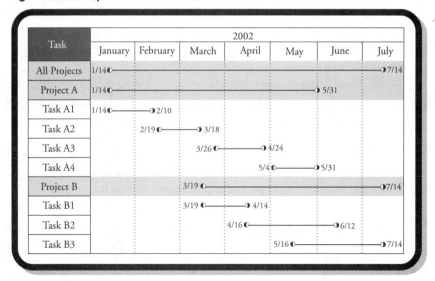

14. Some major challenges and opportunities for CPAs:

    a. Digital formats allow efficient monitoring.

    b. Integrated controls built into software packages.

    c. Ongoing training is necessary, in addition to accounting updates.

    d. Electronic reporting yields additional challenges for auditing.

    e. External systems integrated with client's systems (LANs, WANs, Internet).

    Figure 6: Example of a PERT Chart

    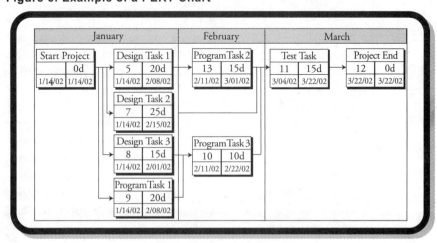

15. Reporting concepts and systems:

    a. **Customer relationship management systems (CRM)**—a customer service system designed to manage all data related to customers, such as marketing,

STUDY MANUAL – BUSINESS ENVIRONMENT & CONCEPTS
CRAM ESSENTIALS

field service, and contract management. CRM has become the primary focus of managers and CIOs for prioritizing new systems acquisitions. An example would be large customer service center phone banks.

b. **Management reporting systems (MRS)**—an accounting information subsystem that produces "special purpose" reports for internal purposes. These MRS generate financial statements and other financial reports. Not the same as a management information system (MIS).

C. **Systems operation**—an entity should examine the system in the production environment (from time to time) to determine whether the system is continuing to satisfy the users' needs. If the system can be made to work better for the user, the value to the user will increase. There are three different types of periodic examinations for a production environment:

a. **Post-implementation review**—a follow-up on a recently implemented system. Determines if requirements have been met. This should be brief and inexpensive. Evaluate quality of system. Recommend improvements if necessary.

b. **System maintenance**—performed in response to a request if the existing system has a minor defect or deficiency. Maintenance costs comprise over half the costs of a system's life cycle cost. Three types of maintenance costs:

   - **Corrective**—fix errors.
   - **Perfective**—improve performance.
   - **Adaptive**—adjust for changing business needs.

c. **System survey**—an overall system reevaluation. This reevaluation is performed when it is likely that the costs of the survey will be less than the cost of improvements discovered and suggested.

d. **Batch processing**—the aggregation of several business events over a set period of time with eventual processing of the related data (periodic processing). Typical batch processing is comprised of four characteristic steps with a delay between each step:

   - **Business event occurs**—such as sale of merchandise. Clerk prepares a sales receipt.
   - **Recordation of data in system**—data manually entered into system, such as a personal computer.
   - **Master files updated**—such as inventory, sales, and reordering.
   - **Output**—such as reports and automated reordering commands to supplier systems.

e. **Online transaction entry system**—data entry devices are used to enter information directly into the system, thereby merging the first two steps of the typical batch processing. Fairly efficient.

Page 732 ©2007 Kaplan CPA Review

f. **Real-time processing**—recordation of data occurs as the business event occurs, and the master file is updated immediately after recordation of the business event is completed. Updated information includes adding, deleting, and replacing master records and data. Up-to-date information available immediately. Very efficient.

Figure 7: Real-Time Processing Model

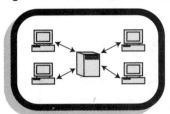

g. **Transaction processing system**—a real-time system that performs all or part of the processing activities at the data entry location. An example would be an ATM [updates all other ATMs afterwards].

Figure 8: Transaction Processing Model

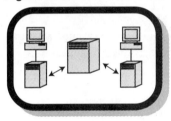

h. **Master file maintenance**—master files are repositories of relatively permanent data maintained over extended periods of time. Two types of master file updates are:

- **Information processing**—data processing of economic events, such as accounting or financial statement preparation.
- **Data maintenance**—adding, deleting, or updating standard or standing data (such as limits, prices, names, etc.).

i. **Data capture**—multiple techniques to collect or "capture" data. Includes manual (such as customer order forms, sales invoices, journal vouchers, time cards, etc.) and electronic (such as online screen entry, "cookies," auto-fill screens, etc.). Reduces the company's costs if properly done. Recall how accounting records are maintained in an information system.

j. **Ad hoc reporting**—"as needed" when information needs change on an ongoing basis. A "view" of selected data.

k. **Transaction/data flow**—auditors and analysts document information systems to understand, explain, and improve complex business processes and operations.

Three types of system documentation:

- Data flow diagrams (DFDs)—a graphical representation that depicts:
  - The system components and functions.
  - The data flows among the components.
  - The sources, destinations, and storage of the data.
  - There are only four symbols that depict a data flow diagram (DFD):

Figure 9: Symbols for Data Flow Diagram

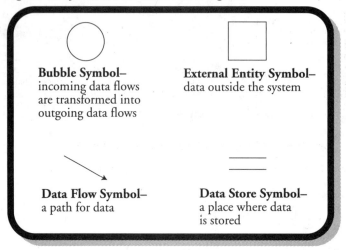

  - Examples of DFDs—context diagrams (high level), physical data flow diagrams (internal/external), and logical data flow diagrams (system processes).
- System flowcharts—a graphical representation that depicts:
  - Informational processes (such as logic flows, inputs, outputs, and data storage).
  - Operational processes (such as physical flows).
  - Many symbols are utilized to depict a system flowchart:

Figure 10: Flowchart Symbols

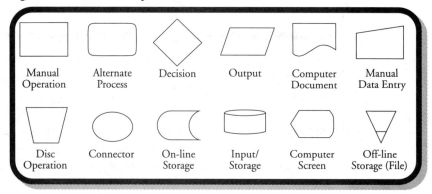

  - Basic guidelines for proper systems flowcharting:
    - Use columns and "swim lanes" for clarity of departments and functions and time periods.

- Connect all multi-page system flow diagrams with off-page connectors.
- Numerical sequencing of activities: summarized and detailed views of diagrams, reference numbers should be used to tie the summary to the detail. Example:

Figure 11: Systems Flowchart

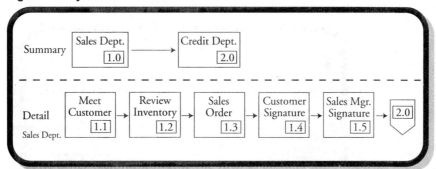

- **Entity relationship diagrams**—a graphical representation that reflects a system's key entities and the relationships among those entities. There are only two symbols that depict an entity relationship diagram:

Figure 12: Symbols for Entity Relationship Diagram

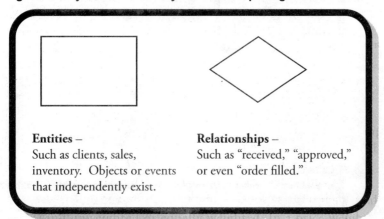

- Often used to depict high-level database requirements and referred to as a data model. The **data model** will evolve into a logical design that will ultimately transform into an actual database. There are four types of models that depict a logical view of a database:
    - **Relational**—the most popular. Data stored in two-dimensional tables. Multiple tables have a relationship or "link" with coding. Multiple tables give rise to a multi-dimensional environment. Relational databases allow for easy manipulation of data for ad-hoc (as-needed) reporting. An example would be the employee headcount tables linked to the financial planning tables. Entities are composed of attributes (characteristics); attributes are composed of composites. Every row is called a tuple; every column is called an *attribute*. Example of a relational database would be with related employee data:

Figure 13: Relational Database Data Model

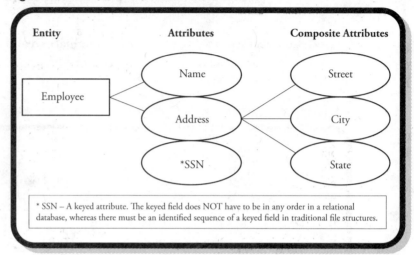

* SSN – A keyed attribute. The keyed field does NOT have to be in any order in a relational database, whereas there must be an identified sequence of a keyed field in traditional file structures.

- **Objected oriented**—data and non-data storage; text, audio, video storage. Procedures are "encapsulated" within the database. Encapsulated entities are depicted with rounded corners.

Figure 14: Object Oriented Database Data Model

- **Hierarchical**—the simplest. A parent/child (one/many) relationship: Examples include territory/salespersons or state/cities.
- **Network**—similar to hierarchical. Child can have more than one parent; many/one, one/many, one/one. Examples include customers/specific inventory items sold.
- **Normalization**—to detect and correct "gaps" between a logical design and the actual design of a database. Corrections due to oversight, misinterpretations, changing requirements, or needs.
- **Database mapping**—converting entity relationship diagrams into relational/logical database models. Five basic rules for mapping:
  - A separate relational table is created for each entity (a logical starting point).
  - Identify which relations will be "keyed."
  - Identify all of the attributes for each entity.
  - Implement all relationships among all entities.
  - Determine the attributes for each relationship table.
- **Structured query language** (SQL)—a powerful and common database language for design, query, reporting, and storage of data (a modern form of *Structured English Query Language* [SEQUEL]). Modern "wizards" are embedded with most database systems.
  - Three types of SQL to consider:

- Data definition language—used to identify and define a database.

- Data manipulation language—used for database maintenance and data retrieval.

- Data control language—control commands to secure a database.

- An example of creating a new/empty database with SQL by a corporate recruiter:

CREATE TABLE	(Phone Number	Char(10)	NOT NULL,
STUDENT	Social Number	Char(11)	NOT NULL,
	Name	VarChar(40)	NOT NULL);

- Three ways to update a database using SQL:

1. INSERT	INSERT	STUDENT
command	INTO	('2345685248', '123-45-6789', 'Jon Doe'
2. DELETE	DELETE	STUDENT
command	FROM	Name='John Doe'
3. UPDSATE	UPDATE	STUDENT
command	SET	Phone Number=9546789457
	WHERE	Social Number='111-11-9999'

D. **Roles and responsibilities of the IT functions:**

1. **Database administrators** (DBAs):

   a. The following attributes are common among DBAs:

   - Perform administrative and technical functions.
   - Maintain good people skills and are user-oriented.

   b. Roles and functions of a DBA:

   - Database designer and maintainer.
   - Policy setter.
   - Security control.
   - Consultant to users and programmers.
   - Contingency planning in the event of failure.
   - Performance evaluator (monitors the changing demands and resources of the database).

2. **Network administrators**—installs and supports the telecommunication hardware and software; helps users to acquire, setup, and properly utilize LANs and PCs.

3. **Systems analyst.**

a. Determines user requirements (through interviews and observations) and writes new system specifications.

b. Understands and prepares data flow diagrams (and other documentation) of systems.

c. Has some business skills/background.

d. Studies information-related problems and proposes solutions.

4. **Web administrators**—responsible for the operation and support of a Web server and for content hosted on that server (including updates and maintenance). A Web server is a *software* application that uses the hypertext transfer protocol (recognized as http://). A Web server is usually run on a computer that is connected to the Internet. There are many Web server software applications, including public domain software from Apache and commercial applications from Microsoft and Oracle.

5. **Computer operators**—provide efficient and effective operation of the computer equipment by loading tapes and disks, reloading paper, monitoring computer operations, responding to computer messages, etc.

6. **Librarians**—maintain custody of and control access to programs, files, and documents. Issue programs, data, and documentation to authorized users. Maintain record of data, programs, and document usage.

7. **Systems programmers**—convert a designer's specifications into systems, bringing multiple systems together to achieve a common purpose; modify and adapt system software [including operating system] and other utility software.

8. **Applications programmers**—convert a designer's specifications into applications programs; code, test, and debug applications programs; configure existing applications.

9. **Help desk**—answers help line calls and e-mails; resolves user problems; obtains technical support and vendor support when necessary.

10. **Chief information officer** (CIO)—also referred to as the vice president of the information system. Generally reports to the chief executive officer (CEO). Responsible for efficient and effective functions of existing systems. Plans for the development and technical resources for future systems. Controls hardware and software operations. Oversees the entire data center.

11. **Appropriate separation of duties of the various IT functions**—without proper segregation of duties, an organization may fail to achieve input accuracy or update accuracy; ultimately leading to misleading record keeping and management decisions. The general model for segregation of duties follows: authorization (approval), execution (physical activity such as pick, move, ship), recordation (record or post), and safeguarding resources (physically protect and maintain accountability of physical resources). The IT function will primarily

carry out control plans related to just recordation between the following specific areas:

   a. Users.

   b. AIS library.

   c. Data control.

   d. Computer operations.

   e. Programming.

   f. System analysis.

12. It will be the responsibility of management for the other areas to primarily ensure proper safeguard, authorization, and execution.

Figure 15: Control Plan

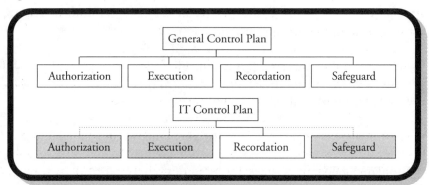

E. **Disaster recovery and business continuity**—management should establish a disaster recovery process coordinated with the overall business continuity strategy for all IT processes for internal and external functions. Process includes the organization and its partners. Contingency planning goes beyond just the backup of computer data and programs. Contingency planning includes backup and restoration of the physical computer facilities, supplies, key resources, and personnel. Modifications are necessary—Internet alternatives. There are many different data backup and recovery procedures (which should be part of the overall contingency plan):

1. **Mirror sites**—maintain copies of primary site's programs and data. Physically separate sites, updated simultaneously. Mirror sites can take over in a few seconds. Popular with e-business for seamless online commerce.

2. **Server clustering**—used to disperse processing load among several servers; if one server fails, another server can take over. Cluster servers are essentially mirror sites of each other.

3. **Alternate processing facilities**—for most companies, duplicate equipment is too costly. Therefore, arrangements with vendors and other external services for standby systems are preferred. Two types:

    a. **Hot sites**—a fully equipped data center in a bunker-like environment. Requires a subscriber's fee.

    b. **Cold site**—an air-conditioned space with necessary communications in which equipment can be moved (such as a mobile facility). Less expensive and less responsive than a Hot Site.

4. **Threat/risk assessment**—an entity's identification and analysis of relevant risks to achieve its objectives, forming a basis for determining how those risks should be managed.

F. **Business Implications: Electronic Commerce**—two or more individuals and/or organizations in the completion of electronic-based business events (back office processes); more than Internet businesses.

    a. Attributes:

- By-product is often the elimination of staff positions.
- Business processes are accelerated.
- Direct links to suppliers' systems and to other separate physical locations (ERP system).
- Price efficiency for buyers.
- Directly reach consumers via Internet commerce.

    b. Automated data entry—bar coding, optical character readers, scanners.

    c. Digital image processing system—systems for capture, storage retrieval and presentations of images. Usually for documents in business. Historically used for large mainframe computers; now seen on personal computers (scanners). Digital imaging takes a tremendous amount of storage space; therefore, "write once read many" (WORM) storage systems are less expensive and used.

    d. Four stages of e-commerce:

- Electronic mail (e-mail)—electronic transmission of non-standard messages between two parties. E-mail is a weak form of e-business because of the non-standard formats between parties. Freeform. Usually attachments within e-mail. E-mail lists with certain attributes are sold to vendors. Business recording activities still need to occur.
- Electronic document management (EDM)—the capturing, storage, management and control of electronic data images for supporting management decisions. Relies on digital image processing. Inexpensive alternative to a paper system. Two categories:

- Document storage and retrieval—such as for mortgages, certificates, public documents.
- Business event data processing—passing e-documents along at different stages of a process, such for approvals and feedback.
- Benefits of an EDM environment: reduction of paper costs and handling costs, improved staff productivity, better customer service, and faster processing.
  - Electronic data interchange (EDI)—computer to computer exchange of business data in a structured format that allows direct processing. Standardized EDI format: ANSI—American National Standards Institute.
  - Internet commerce—computer-to-computer exchange of business data in structured or semi-structured formats. Similar to EDI, but meant more for the individual-business relationship.

e. Client-server relationship—the connection between the client application and the vendor application.

f. Network providers—companies that provide a link to the Internet through their networks for a fee. Benefits include e-mail services, mailboxes, space allocation for Web development, and remote connection to other computer sites.

g. Security—over 90 percent of Internet users want more security for e-commerce related transactions. Internet assurance services provide limited assurance for vendors' Web sites (example is WebTrust). There is a need for anti-fraud software for credit card transactions to create a secure environment.

h. Electronic store fronts—Internet-created resources for displaying goods and services.

i. Electronic funds transfer (EFT), also referred to as the Automated Clearing House (ACH)—mostly used for direct deposit and automated deposits of funds between financial institutions. Reduces the problem of "float." Other technology advancements to reduce float include electronic checks and electronic lockboxes.

j. Point-of-sale transactions (POS)—an integrated transaction system that delivers information in real time. Immediate inventory, sales, and financial statement updates are made each time a POS transaction is completed. Usually the POS system is centralized so that secure data can be shared throughout the organization. Additionally, these POS systems integrate an entity's Web site, catalogues, and stores with the rest of the organization.

k. Internet-based transactions—benefits: improved competition, responsiveness, and global visibility; reduced costs; improved existing processes; ability to rethink controls. Risks include hackers, fraud.

©2007 Kaplan CPA Review

Page 741

STUDY MANUAL – BUSINESS ENVIRONMENT & CONCEPTS
CRAM ESSENTIALS

l.   Information systems function—the department that develops and operates an organization's information system. Comprised of people, equipment, and procedures. Usually centralized. Managed by the CIO.

m.   Issues and concerns in e-business:

- Mode of the payment.
- Security of the payment transaction.
- Privacy of individuals.
- Trust, authentication, and non-repudiation.
- Jurisdictional and legal issues.

Other key definitions:

1.   **Buffer**—a temporary storage medium to store a finite amount of data during computer operations.

2.   **Data dictionary**—contains information about the specific structure of a database. For each data element within a database, there is a corresponding record in the data dictionary describing the data element.

3.   **Domain**—a group of computers and devices on a network that are administered as a unit with common rules and procedures. Within the Internet, domains are defined by an IP address. All devices sharing a common part of the IP address are said to be in the same domain.

4.   **Domain name server** (DNS)—an Internet service that translates domain names into IP addresses. The domain name server is used to maintain records of the Web server aliases associated with the computer.

5.   **Home page**—a document in HTML format displayed as the initial document or page when a Web browser establishes a connection with a Web server.

6.   **HTML**—hypertext markup language (HTML) is the authoring language used to create documents accessed via the World Wide Web. HTML defines the structure and layout of all documents accessible via the World Wide Web by using a variety of tags and attributes. A document may contain textual content, images, and links to other documents (and possibly other applications), as well as formatting instructions for display on a screen.

7.   **Metadata**—data about data. The use of a structured set of elements to describe an information resource and its intellectual property rights. The elements used should assist in the identification, location, and retrieval of information resources by end-users.

8.   **MIPS**—a unit of measure: millions of instructions per second.

9.   **Peripheral equipment**—all non-CPU related hardware (for example, printers).

Page 742   ©2007 Kaplan CPA Review

10. **Secure server**—a server that uses secure sockets layer (SSL) technology to encrypt data during the transfer of data between a Web browser and a server. Secure servers have a digital certificate (or ID).

11. **Schema**—a schema describes the logical view of a database. There are three levels of schemas:

    a. **Conceptual**—an organization-wide view of the entire database.

    b. **External**—a set of individual user views of a database; also referred to as a subschema.

    c. **Internal**—a low level or detailed view of the database.

12. **Uniform resource locator** (URL)—a uniform resource locator or URL is the Internet address of a Web document or other Internet resource accessible via the World Wide Web. The first part of the address indicates what protocol is being used (for example FTP, HTTP), and the second part specifies the IP address or the domain name where the resource is located and may also include a directory name and a filename.

13. **World Wide Web**—The World Wide Web (also known as WWW, or the Web) is a hypermedia-based distributed information system based on the client/server communications model.

G. **Control**:

    a. Major reasons for control (an internal control system):

       • Provide reasonable assurance that the goals of each process are achieved (effective and efficient operations). Internal control is management's responsibility based on cost/benefit assessments.
       • Mitigate the risk that the enterprise will encounter some level of harm, danger, loss, or fraud (reliability of financial reporting).
       • Provide reasonable assurance (not absolute) that certain legal obligations are met (compliance).

    b. Major types of computer fraud (computer crimes) include deception, larceny, and embezzlement. The computer may be used as the tool to accomplish the illegal act, or the information actually stored on the computer is the target of the illegal act, including viruses. Insiders commit most computer crimes. System failure can be corrected by constant application of appropriate control plans.

    c. Controls must also be capable of minimizing simple innocent errors and omissions.

    d. **SAS No. 78: Consideration of Internal Control in a Financial Statement Audit**—identifies five components of internal control:

©2007 Kaplan CPA Review

Page 743

- **Control environment**—this is the foundation of all other components. It influences the "tone."
- **Risk assessment**—the identification and analysis of relevant risks to achieve the entity's objectives.
- **Control activities**—the policies and procedures to ensure management directives are carried out.
- **Information and communication**—identification, capture, and exchange of data in a format and time to allow proper tasks and responsibilities to be performed.
- **Monitor**—the process that assesses the quality of internal control performance over time.
- A possible sixth component would be "process," which is a series of actions leading to a specific and desirable result.

e. The desired internal control system model:

Figure 16: Internal Control System Model

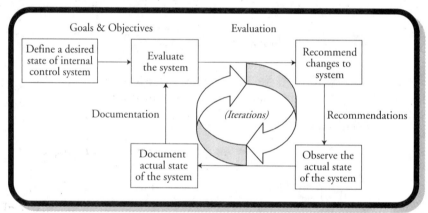

f. **Internal control system failure**—even the best-designed control systems are subject to failure due to:

- Human error.
- Faulty judgment.
- Collusion.
- Management override.

g. **Internal control goals**—process objectives that internal control systems are designed to achieve.

- Operations process goals should ensure:
  - **Effectiveness of operations**—strives to ensure than an intended process is fulfilling its intended purpose (such as proper management authorization for overrides).
  - **Efficient resources**—to have enough resources to ensure benefits exceed costs of controls.
  - **Security of resources**—protect all tangible and intangible resources.
- Information process control goals should ensure:

- Input validity—where input data approved to reflect accurate economic events.
- Input completeness—all valid events are captured.
- Input accuracy—all events are captured correctly.
- Update completeness—all events are reflected in respective master files.
- Update accuracy—all events are reflected correctly within master file.

h. **Control plans**—policies and procedures that assist in accomplishing control goals, mentioned in previous section. No control plan is 100 percent effective. A combination of plans must be used to maximize effectiveness. Three levels:

- **Control environment**—the top level. Many different attributes and factors that reinforce or mitigate the effectiveness of the *overall control plan*.
- **Pervasive control plans**—the middle level. Similar to control environment in regards to many different goals and objectives. Broad in scope. Applied equally across all AIS processes. Plans "pervade" all systems.
- **Application control plans**—the detailed level. Controls are specific to a particular process or subsystem.
- Another way to view control plans is in relation to the timing of their occurrence. Preventive control plans stop problems from occurring; detective control plans discover problems that have already occurred; corrective control plans correct problems that have already occurred.

i. **Control objectives for information and related technology** (cobiT)—developed by the Information Systems Audit and Control Foundation to provide guidance on best practices for management and information technology. Groups IT control processes into four domains:

- **Planning and organization**—establish strategic vision for the IT area; develop plan to achieve vision.
- **Acquisition and implementation**—identify automated and IT solutions; integrate the solutions; manage changes to existing systems; manage change with users (interacts with monitoring).
- **Delivery and support**—deliver required IT services; ensure security; provide on-going support.
- **Monitor**—monitor operations (interaction with acquisition and implementation).

j. Controls:

The CPA candidate should be able to discuss electronic controls regardless of system (billing, order entry, cash receipts, accounts receivable, etc.), including:

- Immediate recordation into electronic environment.

STUDY MANUAL – BUSINESS ENVIRONMENT & CONCEPTS
CRAM ESSENTIALS

- Validate security access.
- Constant reconciliation of balances.
- Unique transaction number.
- Transaction keyed to log file.
- Controls for rejecting specific transactions.
- Proper separation of duties for hardware and software.
- Communication to proper users and security.
- Check for authorized prices, part numbers, quantities, etc.
- Update inventory volumes and prices.
- Constant update of company financials.
- Automated batch totals.
- Automated/standardized reporting templates with proper security controls for changes to templates.
- Confirmation of customer account information.
- Automated acceptance/rejection ranges for any figure.
- Constant review of the acceptance and rejection ranges.
- Pre-formatted screens.
- Online prompting.
- Programmed edit checks.
- Compare new input to master data.
- Automated confirmation of changes before making changes.
- Allow users to cancel/logout at any time.
- Barcode scan check.
- Automated notification of external parties (banks, vendors, etc.).

k. **Management**—deliver cost-effective bug-free applications; advise systems development staff; implement, monitor, and control development standards.

l. **Audit trail**—the audit trail is a record left by the accounting information system of movements in individual transaction data. This record, in the form of references to the processing of the data, provides a trail of the processing of transactions and other events entered into by the entity. Note that while some accounting information systems provide a visible and complete audit trail, others may provide an invisible and/or incomplete trail. Depending on the accounting information system, the trail may start from the moment data about the event is first captured within the system to the time of its ultimate disposition in the financial statements. For example, the audit trail of a sales transaction may enable the tracing of the movement in data concerning the transaction from the time the order is placed by the customer until the time the transaction data is included in the appropriate general ledger accounts. An audit trail should allow for means to trace back to individual business events from the general ledger. An auditor may follow the audit trail of a transaction as part of a systems walk-through.

Page 746   ©2007 Kaplan CPA Review

ECONOMICS

A. Economics of the firm:

1. Prices and output of the firm are determined in a market through the interaction of supply and demand. When there is an excess supply, market prices fall. When there is excess demand, market prices rise.

    Figure 17: Demand Curve

    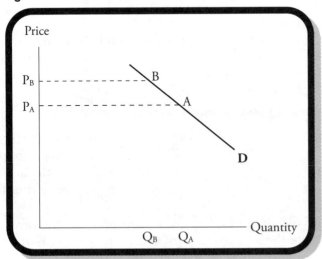

    a. The demand curve is a two-dimensional negative relationship between the quantity demanded and the price. According to the "law of demand," when the price goes up, the quantity demanded goes down. For example, in the following figure, when the price goes up from P^A to P^B, the quantity demanded goes down from Q^A to Q^B. Changes in price cause *movements along* the demand curve.

    The demand curve *shifts* due to changes in factors other than price, such as changes in income, consumer tastes and preferences; prices of other goods (substitutes and complements); and consumer expectations. Figure 18 is an illustration of a demand curve with shifts in demand.

    - An increase in consumer income will shift the demand curve upward from D1 to D2 (more demanded at every price) if the good is a normal good. If the demand for a good decreases from D1 to D3 (shift downward) when income goes up the good is an inferior good.

Figure 18: Shifts in Demand Curve

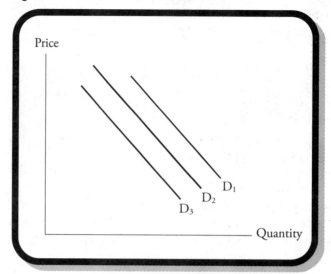

- If consumer tastes and preferences change so that the good is more attractive (less attractive) the demand curve will shift upward from D1 to D2 (downward from D1 to D3). Promotion strategies of the firm are partly designed to enhance the consumer's tastes and preferences for the product.
- Prices of goods that are substitutes for a firm's product will affect the demand curve for the firm. If prices of substitutes go up (down) consumer demand will increase from D1 to D2 (decrease from D1 to D3).
- Prices of complement goods also affect the firm's demand. If a complement good (a good used with the firm's product) has a price decrease (increase) the demand for the firm's product will increase from D1 to D2. A price increase in complement goods will cause a decrease in demand from D1 to D3. (Hamburger buns are complement goods to hamburgers.)
- Consumer expectations also affect the demand for a firm's product. For example, if consumers expect shortages or higher prices in the future, they may increase the demand for the product today, shown as a shift from D1 to D2.

Figure 19: Supply Curve

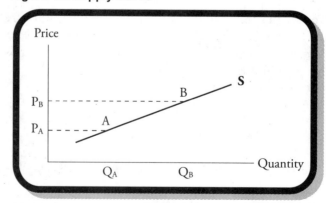

b. The supply curve is a two-dimensional positive relationship between price and quantity supplied. When the price goes up from P^A to P^B the quantity supplied goes up from Q^A to Q^B.

Shifts in the supply curve occur due to changes in factors other than price, such as technology, changes in input prices, and changes in trade relationships with other countries. Figure 20 is an illustration of a supply curve with shifts in supply.

- A change in technology that makes production costs lower will shift the supply curve outward from S1 to S2. Higher costs will shift the supply curve inward from S1 to S3.
- Changes in input prices will also shift the supply curve. Lower input prices make production costs lower, and the supply curve shifts outward from S1 to S2. Higher input prices cause a shift inward from S1 to S3. Bottlenecks and rigidities in input markets will also constrain supply, resulting in a shift from S1 to S3.

Figure 20: Shifts in Supply Curve

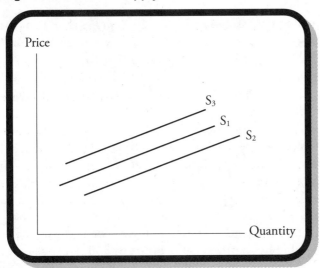

- Changes in trade relationships with other countries can either encourage or discourage foreign supply of a product. For example, trade barriers that reduce foreign supply will shift the supply curve inward from S1 to S3. Lower barriers or agreements that make it easier for foreign countries to sell products in the U.S. market will increase the market supply. Thus the shift occurs from S1 to S2.

c. Market equilibrium price and quantity occur where the supply curve and demand curve cross. The price at the point where the quantity demanded equals the quantity supplied is the market clearing price. There is no excess demand (occurs when the price is below the equilibrium price) or excess supply (occurs when the price is above the equilibrium price). Figure 21 illustrates a market equilibrium given demand curve D1 and supply curve S1. If there are shifts in the supply or demand curves, there will be a new market equilibrium price. For example, if there is an increase in demand (shift to the right) the market price goes up (assuming there is no change in supply). If there is no change in demand, but the supply curve shifts to the left, the market price falls.

Figure 21: Market Equilibrium

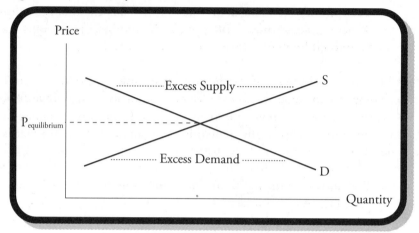

d. The price elasticity of demand is the percentage change in the quantity demanded given a percentage change in price: % change Q/% change P = $[(Q^1 - Q^0)/\text{avg. Q}] / [(P^1 - P^0)/\text{avg. P}]$.

For comparison purposes, the difference in elasticities between two demand curves is approximately given by differences in the slopes of the demand curves. Steeper demand curves are relatively more inelastic. Flat demand curves are very elastic, everything else equal. The elasticity of demand is always negative due to the law of demand. When prices go up, quantity demanded goes down.

Example: Assume you are thinking of changing your fees for tax accounting services from $50 an hour to $60 an hour. The higher price leads to a change in total billable hours from 1,000 hours to 800 hours as customers react to the higher fees.

What is the elasticity of demand for your services? The change in hours is –200 and the average number of hours is (1,000 + 800)/2 = 900. The change in price is 10 and the average price is 55. Answer: E = [(800 – 1,000)/900]/[60 – 50)/55] = –0.2222/0.1818 = –1.2222

We normally ignore the negative sign when interpreting the elasticity because we know price and quantity demanded go in opposite directions. We want to know about the relative sensitivities. In this case there is a larger percentage change in quantity than in price, so demand is price-elastic (sensitive to price changes).

- If the measure of price elasticity is greater than one (ignoring the negative sign), demand is elastic. When demand is elastic, an increase (decrease) in price will lead to lower (higher) total revenue. The drop in quantity demanded more than offsets the increase in price.

- If the measure of price elasticity is less than one, demand is inelastic and an increase (decrease) in price will lead to higher (lower) total revenue. Firms use advertising and differentiation strategies to make demand for their product relatively more inelastic. Demand is relatively more inelastic if there are few good substitutes, if the product is a small portion of the household budget, or if the product is a necessity.

e. The income elasticity of demand measures the sensitivity of demand given a change in consumer income: % change in quantity demanded/% change in income = $[(Q^1 - Q^0)/\text{avg. Q}]/[(\text{income}^1 - \text{income}^0)/\text{avg. income}]$. Changes in income cause shifts in the demand curve outward if the product is a normal good.

- The outward shift in the demand curve due to a change in income will be greater if the product has high income elasticity. Durable goods have high income elasticity because they do not need to be replaced every year and consumption is postponed when income falls. Luxury goods also tend to be income-elastic.
- A product is inferior if consumers demand less of the product when income goes up. For example, low quality/inexpensive goods with higher quality substitutes are often inferior goods. When income rises, consumers switch to a better quality brand.

2. Marginal analysis is the fundamental condition for optimal decisions in economics. The emphasis is on the last good consumed, last unit produced, etc. Fixed costs (sunk costs) are irrelevant in the decision process since fixed costs will be paid whether the decision is to go on or to stop.

a. Marginal utility is the satisfaction from the last unit consumed. An optimal situation occurs when the marginal utility per dollar paid for one product is equal to the marginal utility per dollar paid for another product.

b. Marginal propensity to consume is the change in consumption for a given change in disposable income. The average propensity to consume is total consumption divided by total income. Note the emphasis in marginal analysis is on what happens to consumption when disposable income *changes*. If a consumer is given one more dollar of disposable income, how much of that dollar is spent on consumption? The marginal propensity to save is the change in saving that occurs if a consumer is given an additional dollar of disposable income. Note that marginal propensity to consume + marginal propensity to save = 1.

c. Marginal product is a measure of the additional output provided by employing one more unit of a resource. The optimal decision would use inputs up to the point that the marginal product and the price of inputs are equal.

Example: A firm can hire either temporary workers or full-time workers. Full time workers are paid $20 per hour and part-time workers are paid $10 per hour. The following data are collected to show the relationship between the number of full time workers and hourly production and the number of part-time workers and hourly production:

# Full-Time Workers	Hourly Product	Marginal Product Per Worker	# Part-Time Workers	Hourly Product	Marginal Product Per Worker
10	100	—	5	40	—
12	140	20	7	64	12
14	170	15	9	84	10

The optimal mix of full-time and part-time workers would be 12 full-time and 9 part-time. Why? The addition of two more full time workers to get to 12 workers gives us a ratio of marginal product to wage of 20/$20 = 1. When we go from five to seven part-time workers we get a ratio of 12/$10 = 1.2. So we add more part-time. When we increase the part-time workers from seven to nine we get a marginal productivity to wage ratio of 10/$10 = 1. At this point the marginal productivity per wage ratio is the same for 12 full-time and nine part-time workers. Marginal productivity per dollar spent is the same at the optimal mix.

d. Marginal revenue is the additional revenue a firm receives from selling one more unit of output. Marginal revenue is not equal to the price if a firm must cut prices in order to sell more.

Example: A firm sells 100 units at a price of $10 and has total revenue of $1,000. In order to sell one more unit the firm must cut prices to $9.95 per unit (law of demand if the firm faces a downward sloping demand curve), but this is applied to all units sold unless the firm can separate customers (price discriminate). Total revenue at the price of $9.95 is 9.95 × 101 = $1.004.95. The marginal revenue of the last unit sold is $4.95. In order to sell the last unit the price had to go down by $.05 on 101 units.

e. Marginal cost is the additional cost a firm faces from the production of one more unit of output. Marginal cost falls in the early stages of production where there are increasing returns (producing more units costs less per unit, due to efficiencies), but when decreasing returns set in (volume of production is too high for the capacity and inefficiencies set in), marginal costs rise.

Example: A firm produces 100 units and has fixed costs of $40 and variable costs of $50. When one more unit is produced, the firm has fixed costs of $40 and variable costs of $55. The marginal cost is $5.

f. An equilibrium occurs when the marginal cost equals marginal revenue. The firm will produce and sell one more unit if the marginal revenue exceeds the marginal cost. Producing one more unit would require cutting price and a resulting lower marginal revenue. Inefficiencies occur in production as output is expanded so marginal cost rises eventually. The optimal output occurs where marginal revenue equals marginal cost.

Example: In the prior example, the firm could produce one more unit and sell all its units at $9.95. The marginal revenue was $4.95. The marginal cost of producing one more unit was $5. The firm would not try to sell beyond 100 units because the marginal cost would exceed the marginal revenue.

g. An optimal decision in economics will always be based on marginal analysis. Some examples follow:

- Optimal consumption: marginal utility of A/price of A = marginal utility of B/price of B.
- Optimal production: marginal product of input A/price of A = marginal product of input B/price of B.
- Profit maximization: marginal revenue = marginal cost.
- Investment decision: marginal benefits = marginal costs.

B. **Industry and Competitive Environment of the Firm:**

1. Firms face an external environment that affects the performance of the firm and introduces business risk, which is the sensitivity of the firm's operating income to the external environment. Optimal economic decisions within the firm are conditioned by the competitive environment and the larger macroeconomic environment. In this section, the objective is to outline the key forces in the competitive environment that shape the firm's strategic management decisions. A common framework for the analysis of the industry environment uses five key forces shown in Figure 22.

Figure 22: Economic Forces Affecting Competitive Environment

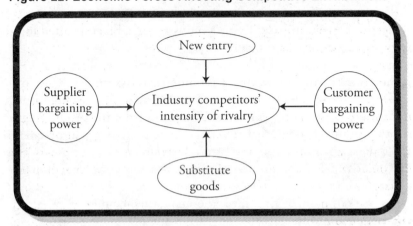

a. Industry competition is a key force affecting a firm's performance. The intensity of firm rivalry depends on the other four factors in the framework: threat of substitute goods, threat of new entrants into the market, bargaining power of customers, and bargaining power of suppliers.

b. Threats of substitute goods force the firm to work on differentiation strategies through either product design or promotional efforts. If there are a lot of good substitutes, the firm faces relatively higher price elasticity as customers shift to other products if prices are not in line.

c. Threats of new entrants keep existing firms from becoming inefficient. If entrants can do what existing firms are doing better, there is an incentive for the market to become more competitive as new firms enter. Barriers to new entrants may prevent increased competition from new competitors. Key barriers to entry include the following:

- Economies of scale—entry would require a firm to duplicate a large scale of production and immediately take a large part of the market.
- Patents or other forms of unique product attributes that cannot be duplicated.
- Brand or promotional identity makes it necessary for new entrants to spend large amounts for promotion to be competitive.
- Access to distribution channels may not be available to new entrants.
- Capital requirements may be too large for a new entrant to raise enough financing without a proven product or track record.
- Government policy or regulation may limit the number of competitors.
- Expected consequences of entry and forms of retaliation from firms already in the industry may discourage new entry.

d. Bargaining power of customers will limit the ability of firms in the industry to achieve favorable profit margins. Customer size and the concentration of buyers will play an important role. Other factors will be the degree of buyer information and perceptions of substitute goods.

e. Bargaining power of suppliers will affect the firm's costs and availability of inputs to continue production. The concentration of suppliers, differentiation of inputs provided by different suppliers, and threats of suppliers integrating into the firm's industry are all factors affecting the extent of supplier bargaining power.

2. Market structure represents the type of competitive environment the firm faces within the industry or relevant market. Market structure is heavily influenced by the size distribution and the number of competitors the firm faces. At the extreme, the firm may compete in a perfectly competitive environment where there are so many firms that no one firm affects the market supply. In this case, the firm is a price-taker and must accept the price set in the overall market through supply and demand. The other extreme occurs when there is only one firm in the market and that firm faces the market demand curve all alone. This later case is a monopoly.

a. In perfect competition, no one firm has an ability to influence price, and only a normal profit is possible. There are no barriers to entry or exit. If profits rise above a normal profit, other firms will enter, and competition will bring overall profits back to a normal profit. The firm faces a perfectly elastic (flat) demand curve in perfect competition because they are a price-taker and have virtually no influence on the total quantity supplied. Farm products tend to be sold in a perfectly competitive market. Farmers take the competitive market price set for their products and no single farmer's supply will be big enough to affect the market price.

b. Imperfect competition includes monopolistic competition and oligopoly. Both industry structures have some degree of product differentiation and price influence. This makes the demand faced by the firm relatively less elastic than for perfect competition. Firms try to make their products different and attract customers who do not see other goods as perfect substitutes. There are limits as to how far prices can go up before customers shift to other goods, but there is some degree of price discretion. The demand curve faced by the firm is downward sloping. Firms use product differentiation (fewer perceived substitutes) and merger/acquisition (fewer competitors) strategies to make their market less competitive and less like perfect competition. In oligopoly, there are only a few firms competing, and each firm tends to have a predictable reaction to price competition. As a result, non-price competition is more common in oligopolies.

c. Monopolies face the market demand curve, but they do not charge just any price they want. To maximize profit they must price so that marginal cost equals marginal revenue. They face the market demand alone, so there will be some reduction in quantity demanded as the price goes up and an increase in quantity demanded as price goes down. To preserve the monopoly, the firm must have some form of a barrier to entry due to patents, technology, etc. One form of a barrier to entry may be the optimal size of operation. If the optimal size of operation is close to the total market demand it only makes sense to have one producer. More than one producer would require each firm to operate at a less than optimal scale and have higher costs. To compete, a firm must enter at a large scale, but the market would not support another producer of such a size.

d. The table below shows the different pricing, number of firms, homogeneity of products, and barriers to entry for the four different market structures.

Industry Structure	Pricing	# of Firms	Product	Barriers
perfect competition	price taker	very many	homogeneous	none
monopolistic competition	price competition	many	differentiated	few
oligopoly	avoid competition	few	differentiated	many
monopoly	market demand	one	no substitutes	very many

3. Supply-chain management requires a sharing of information among suppliers, manufacturers, distributors, and retailers. For example, if retailers gather good information on consumer demand and share this information with the distributors and manufacturers, there will be a better flow of production and sales. In turn, if the manufacturer shares information with the suppliers, there will be even better information all along the supply chain. This improved flow of information or forecasts will reduce inventories and make the entire process more efficient. Supply-chain management is now more important as the markets have become more global and the relationships between initial suppliers, manufacturers, distributors, retailers, and customers have become more complex. The emphasis on supply-chain management also increased as a result of total quality management (TQM) applications and the increased use of outsourcing for inputs.

   a. Supply-chain management is the organization of activities between a company and its suppliers in an effort to provide for profitable development, production, and delivery of goods to customers. The goal is to focus on the entire supply chain to improve the levels of efficiencies at every level.

   b. Supply chains are sometimes called value chains to reflect value added as goods and services progress all the way to final delivery to the customer. An example of a typical supply chain follows:

   Supplier A   Storage → Manufacturing
   Supplier B   Storage → Distributor
   Supplier C   Retailer → Consumer

   c. There are a number of areas for analysis and information sharing in supply chain management to include the following:

   - Customers—what products/services are to be sold?
   - Forecasting—predict quantity and timing of what the consumer wants.
   - Design—consider the customers' wants, manufacturing capabilities, and timing to get to the market.
   - Purchasing—compare potential suppliers while meeting the needs of manufacturing operations. This is a link between an organization and its suppliers.
   - Inventory—balance the need to meet demands while managing the cost of holding inventory.
   - Suppliers—how will the quality of supplier goods be monitored while maintaining on-time delivery, flexibility, and good relations with suppliers?
   - Processing—how will quality be controlled, and how will work be scheduled?
   - Location—what is the best location of facilities along the supply chain?
   - Logistics—what is the best way to move and store materials?

4. Transfer prices are internal prices set by the parent company for transfers of goods and services *within* the company. If one subsidiary supplies an intermediate product for another subsidiary or for the parent company, the transaction is not a market sale. The firm must choose an appropriate transfer price to use to account for the sale by one subsidiary and the purchase by the other subsidiary. The transfer price may be set to approximate a market price if that information is available. In many cases it is impossible to apply the principles of market pricing to transfer prices.

   a. Transfer prices may be set too low. This hurts the accounting profits of the subsidiary supplying the product and helps the accounting profits of the subsidiary using the product as an input. If the transfer price is set too high, it helps the subsidiary supplying the product and hurts the subsidiary using the product as an input. If a subsidiary is judged as a profit center, the level of the transfer price is crucial to performance.

   b. The transfer price should be set to optimize the value of the firm. If market prices are not easily obtained, the firm may choose to lower taxes by setting a higher price for the subsidiary supplying the product if it is in a lower tax bracket than the subsidiary using the product.

C. **Firm performance and sensitivity to the economy:**

1. Accounting profits can be measured in different ways depending on the purpose. Operating profit is due to the operations of the firm without regard to financing and taxes. Operating profit is often called earnings before interest and taxes, or EBIT. Pre-tax profit is operating profit minus interest payments on debt financing (often called earnings before taxes, or EBT). Earnings or net income is the bottom line in the income statement. But we often add back in depreciation and other forms of non-cash charges and adjustments of working capital to get the annual cash flow. What is it about different firms that make their profits more or less volatile to changes in the overall market conditions? The answer is differences in sales elasticity, operating leverage, and financial leverage.

   a. Sales elasticity is a measure of how sensitive a firm's sales will be to a given change in the overall level of consumer disposable income in the economy. (We looked at income elasticity in a prior section.) Depending on the type of product the firm produces, a change in consumer disposable income will bring about a change in the firm's sales. For example, if goods are durable goods, the change in sales given a change in disposable income is relatively large. Some goods, like consumer staples, are not very sensitive to changes in disposable income. Sales elasticity is the first consideration in how the economy will affect the firm. Sales elasticity = % change in sales/% change in disposable income.

   b. Operating leverage is a measure of how sensitive the firm's operating income (EBIT) will be to a change in sales. A firm will have high or low operating leverage depending on the firm's combination of fixed costs relative to variable costs of production. If the firm has high operating leverage (high fixed costs), the firm will not be able to cut costs when sales fall, and the

©2007 Kaplan CPA Review

decline in sales will move right on to lower EBIT. If the firm has low fixed costs and high variable costs, a decline in sales can be met with cost-cutting measures that can keep EBIT from falling as far. Operating leverage = % change in EBIT/% change in sales.

- Operating leverage is not always bad. High fixed costs defend the company from rising input prices in periods of inflation. By fixing as many costs as possible, there are fewer variable costs that can be affected by inflation (overall increase in economic prices).
- Operating leverage is not all good because it also increases the firm's risk exposure to economic downturns or events that hurt the firm's sales. If the sales of the firm fall due to economic downturns (the firm's product is a normal good with income elasticity), the firm's operating income will fall more if costs are fixed. If costs were relatively more variable, the firm could cut per unit variable costs as sales fall and preserve more operating income.

c. Financial leverage is the use of debt financing to lever the firm's earnings for its stockholders. Operating income must be sufficient to cover the interest payments or the firm will be in bankruptcy. We can measure financial leverage as follows: financial leverage = % change in net income/% change in EBIT.

- If operating income covers interest payments, the firm's earnings per share will be higher under debt financing than if the firm had used equity financing. Debt makes it possible to lever earnings for shareholders.
- Higher financial leverage also increases the risk of bankruptcy, since higher interest payments create a higher hurdle that operating income must surpass.

d. Total leverage is the combined leverage due to relatively high fixed production costs *and* high fixed interest payments due to the use of debt. High total leverage increases the risk profile of the firm. A drop in sales due to an economic downturn or a competitive advantage of a competitor leaves the firm unable to cut costs to preserve operating income to meet the high level of fixed interest payments. This combination of potentially more volatile operating income and a higher interest payment presents a high risk of bankruptcy.

e. Accounting profit risks start with changes in the overall economy. The firm has no control of what happens at the overall economy level. But there are specific things about the firm that will make some firms more sensitive to the overall economy than others.

- Sensitivity of the firm's sales to economic events is the first level of accounting profit risk. Firms with high income elasticity will have high sales sensitivity to the ups and downs of the economy. Firms producing goods that are very interest rate sensitive will see sales go up and down with economic interest rate cycles. Firms facing relatively high price elasticity will be unable to increase prices as much as other firms in periods of inflation and will be at a competitive disadvantage to increased foreign competition in the domestic markets. Durable good producers tend to be good examples of firms facing high sales sensitivity to the economy's performance.

- Operating leverage is the next link in accounting profit risk. High sales sensitivity to the economy combined with high fixed costs relative to variable costs makes operating income volatile.

- Financial leverage adds the last link to accounting profit risk. High levels of debt financing relative to equity financing increases the chances that operating income will be insufficient to meet contractual obligations to debtors. (Note that bankruptcy is not an issue for equity financing since equity owners are residual claimants and are not guaranteed anything until all other stakeholders have been paid.)

D. **The Macroeconomy:**

1. The economy does not grow at an even rate over time. The up and down pattern of the economy over time is known as a business cycle. When the economy is at the bottom of the cycle, it is in the trough; when it is at the top of the cycle, it is at the peak. Business cycles have four stages that occur in order from peak to peak as follows:

   a. Contraction is the beginning of the economic downturn. Interest rates and inflation are at their peak and start to moderate as the rate of growth of the economy slows. Unemployment is low and begins to move up slowly. As sales slow, the inventory-to-sales ratio is high, causing firms to cut back on inventory orders. Manufacturing slows down, and excess capacity can be found in the economy.

   b. Recession is defined as two successive quarters of negative GDP growth. The economy is now shrinking. Inflation and interest rates hit low levels while unemployment reaches its highest level. Government policies to stimulate the economy are either already in place or are being implemented during this stage. Capacity utilization is very low.

   c. Expansion begins when spending picks up and businesses decide to replace depleted inventories. Manufacturing picks up and employment slowly begins to increase. Inflation and interest rates are low but begin to move up. Inventory is low, and businesses attempt to increase orders to keep up with rising sales. Capacity utilization starts to increase. GDP growth picks up quickly.

   d. The boom stage occurs when the rate of growth of GDP reaches a level that can not be sustained. Excess demand inflation becomes a problem. Supply bottlenecks occur, and capacity utilization is pushed to the limit. Government policies to "cool off" the economy are either in place or are being implemented to slow inflation. Interest rates hit a high, and the unemployment rate drops below a sustainable rate.

   e. The relationship between the four stages in the business cycle is shown in Figure 23.

©2007 Kaplan CPA Review

Figure 23: Stages of the Business Cycle

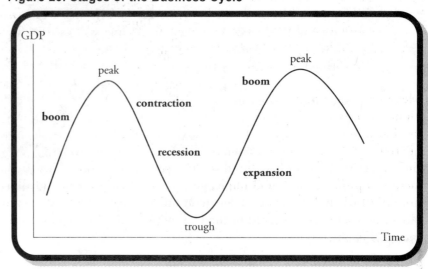

f. The different stages of the economy are associated with differences in GDP, unemployment, inflation, interest rates, and inventory-to-sales ratios. These relationships are outlined in the following table.

	Boom	Contraction	Recession	Expansion
GDP growth	peak	slowing	negative/low	growing
unemployment	lowest	rising	highest	falling
prices/inflation	rising	slowing	deflation	low
interest rates	peak	high/falling	low	low/rising
inventory/sales	high	falling	low	low/rising

2. Different sectors and industries in the economy perform best in different stages of the business cycle.

   a. Consumer staples and utilities are two sectors that continue to perform well in the contraction and recession phase. Examples would be food, drugs, cosmetics, tobacco, liquor, electric, gas, and water. These goods tend to be necessities or represent a low fraction of the consumer budget. Staples and utilities have very low income elasticity.

   b. Cyclicals and energy do well in the early expansion stage, and basic materials and technology sectors perform well as the expansion continues.

   • Examples of cyclicals are savings and loans, banking, advertising, apparel, retailers, and autos. The financial firms do well because interest rates are low and rising while business and consumer borrowing grows. Other sectors do well here if they have high income elasticity.
   • Basic materials and technology sectors include chemicals, plastics, paper, wood, metals, semiconductors, computer hardware, and communication equipment.

- In the late expansion and boom stage, the capital goods, financial firms, and transportation sectors do well. These sectors have high income elasticity and tend to do well when durable good replacement increases. Examples include machinery and equipment, manufacturers, airlines, trucking, railroad, and corporate/institutional banking.

3. Measures of economic growth are based on the rate of change in the Gross Domestic Product. The GDP is the market value of all goods and services produced *in the U.S.* over a given period. The GDP growth rate is measured quarterly. An alternative measure is the Gross National Product (GNP), which is the market value of all goods and services produced for a given period by U.S. factors of production. For example, goods and services *are* included in GNP (but not GDP) when U.S.-owned assets in another country are used for production. Goods and services produced in the U.S. with foreign-owned assets are *not* included in the GNP.

    a. The GDP is calculated by adding up all expenditures on goods and services produced in the U.S. by the consumer, business, government, and net international sectors. As a formula, this is $C + I + G + (X - M) = GDP$, where C is consumption, I is investment, G is government spending, and (X - M) is net exports. Most economists believe that a sustainable growth rate of GDP without inflation pressures is in the range of 2.5 to 3.5 percent. In the expansion phase, the rate of growth is higher than the sustainable rate, but excess capacity keeps inflation pressure low. In the boom phase, the rate of growth is higher than the sustainable rate, but there is little or no excess capacity. Thus inflation becomes a problem.

    b. It is always difficult to predict where the economy is going over the next year. An index of leading economic indicators is a composite of measures that tend to "lead" the economy. For example, the stock market index is one of the leading economic indicators that tends to turn down prior to an economic downturn and to turn up before an economic expansion. It normally takes several months of the index moving in a consistent direction to be considered a sign of an economic turn.

4. Inflation is an increase in overall prices, not just an increase in some prices. Inflation is measured by the percentage change in an inflation index, which is based on the prices of a set of goods in any year relative to the prices of those same goods in a base year.

    a. The consumer price index (CPI) uses a "market basket of goods" of a typical urban household to measure the index. A broader measure of inflation is the personal consumption expenditure index (PCE) because it uses a very broad range of consumer goods beyond the more narrow market basket used in the CPI. When wholesale prices of goods (normally intermediate goods used to produce other goods) are used to construct the index, we get the producer price index (PPI). The PPI is considered to be a leading indicator of what the CPI will be in the future, since final consumer goods are likely to move in the same direction as intermediate good prices.

STUDY MANUAL – BUSINESS ENVIRONMENT & CONCEPTS
CRAM ESSENTIALS

b. Deflation is a decrease in the *rate* of inflation. Most economists consider a trend of lower inflation rates to be deflation, rather than an actual decrease in prices. For example, if the inflation rate goes from 5 to 4 to 3 percent, we have a pattern of deflation.

c. The primary cause of inflation and deflation is movement of aggregate demand relative to aggregate supply in the economy. In the short run, aggregate supply tends to be fixed and is limited by the production capacity available. But, aggregate demand can continue to move up. During a boom, aggregate demand exceeds the ability of the economy to meet demand with supply. The result is excess demand inflation (too many dollars chasing too few goods). Deflation would be an excess aggregate supply phenomenon with weak aggregate demand. Deflation tends to occur in the contraction and recession phases of the economy.

d. Cost-push inflation is an alternative form of inflation that is *not* driven by excess aggregate demand. As the name implies, cost push inflation starts with rising costs of goods for which there are no good substitutes (price inelastic, like oil). If these costs are part of the costs of production, producers must try to raise output prices to maintain margins. But not all firms face markets where price increases are a good idea. If output markets are very price elastic, higher prices will cause a drop in total revenue due to a large drop in quantities sold. Overall prices rise, but some firms are hit hard by higher costs without an ability to increase prices. These firms have an inelastic demand for the inputs when costs are rising, but an elastic demand for their output prevents commensurate price increases.

5. Interest rates are the prices determined by the supply and demand for credit. Interest rates have a predictable relationship with the business cycle and with inflation.

a. Nominal interest rates are the market rates we see quoted. But the real rate of return to a lender is not the nominal rate. Part of the nominal rate of return just covers the reduction in purchasing power due to inflation. A lender must get the rate of inflation just to break even on a loan. A good approximation of the relationship between the nominal and real rates is given as follows: nominal interest rate = real interest rate + inflation premium + risk premium.

For example, if a lender expects inflation to be 3 percent, and the loan is risk-free, the lender would have a zero real rate of return if the nominal rate is 3 percent. The lender would need to charge 6 percent to have a 3 percent real increase in purchasing power from the money repaid at the end of the year. Of course, a risk premium would then be added depending on the risk presented by the borrower.

b. The real rate of interest tends to be about 3 percent in the long run. It goes up and down based on the supply and demand for credit. When the supply of credit increases (for example, more domestic savings, more foreign savings coming into the U.S. market, easier credit conditions by the Federal Reserve,

Page 762 ©2007 Kaplan CPA Review

etc.) relative to demand, real interest rates fall. When the demand for credit is high relative to the supply of credit, real interest rates rise.

c. The nominal interest rate cycle follows the business cycle. Rates go up in the expansion and boom as the demand for credit rises and as inflation rises. Rates go down in the contraction and recession as the demand for credit and inflation fall.

d. The interest rate cycle also affects business investment. As interest rates go up, businesses must be able to earn more on invested capital to cover interest rate costs. In the boom stage, firms are finding high return opportunities, but when rates get to a peak and sales growth slows, business investment really drops. The eventual slowing down of business investment at the peak of the business cycle is part of the reason a contraction takes shape.

e. Interest rates are quoted by lenders using the APR (annual percentage rate) as required by the truth-in-lending laws. But there is a difference between the APR and the effective annual yield (EAY) on an investment or loan.

For example, if a lender quotes a loan at 6 percent APR but payments are monthly, the borrower pays 0.5 percent per month in payments. Due to compounding, the effective annual rate on the loan would be $[1 + (0.06/12)]^{12} - 1 = (1.005)^{12} - 1 = 6.1678\%$. Note that the effective annual rate is higher due to compounding, and it represents what you really pay given the monthly payment period. APR is a simple interest rate where the annual rate is just the rate per period times the number of periods (in this case $0.005 \times 12 = 6\%$).

E. **Fiscal and monetary policies:**

1. Fiscal policy is based on government spending and taxing decisions directed at either stimulating or cooling off the economy. If the government runs a balanced budget, where spending equals tax revenues, it is playing a neutral role in the economy.

   a. Expansionary fiscal policies are designed to stimulate aggregate demand. Increased government spending and lower taxes are used to boost spending. Expansionary policies take the federal budget in the direction of deficits that are financed by the treasury through the issue of treasury bills, notes, and bonds. Expansionary policies tend to be implemented during the contraction and recession stages, but they take some time to work through the economy.

   b. Contractionary fiscal policies are designed to slow down the economy. Government spending is cut and taxes are increased. These moves are designed to reduce aggregate demand to take pressure off inflation and keep the economic growth within a low inflation but sustainable growth rate. Contractionary policies tend to be implemented during the boom stage.

©2007 Kaplan CPA Review

STUDY MANUAL – BUSINESS ENVIRONMENT & CONCEPTS
CRAM ESSENTIALS

    c.   The following table illustrates the different combinations of government spending and taxing policies for expansionary versus contractionary fiscal policies. The timing of fiscal policies can be difficult. For example, if contractionary policies are used during a boom to "cool off the economy," the policies can actually start a contraction if the policies are not timed correctly.

	Expansionary Fiscal Policy	Contractionary Fiscal Policy
Gov. spending (G)	increase	decrease
Taxes (T)	decrease	increase

2.   Monetary Policy is conducted by the Federal Reserve Bank through its ability to expand or contract member bank reserves, affect short-term interest rates, and affect expectations. The Fed is independent of both Congress and the president and is charged with managing stability of the banking system.

    a.   Open market operations (OMO) by the Fed either increase or decrease the overall money supply through purchases or sales of government securities.

- Expansionary open market operations are designed to increase the money supply and lower interest rates. When the Fed *buys* government securities, there will be an increase in bank reserves and a reduction in the amount of government securities in circulation. For example, when the Fed buys a security from a dealer or individual, the Fed credits the bank of the seller with a deposit that increases the bank's reserves. Since the bank must only keep a fraction of its deposits on reserve, it lends out the excess reserve. This process continues as the money supply is expanded. At the same time, the Fed's decision to buy government securities drives security prices up and yields down, thus contributing to lower interest rates.

- Contractionary open market operations call for selling government securities. The buyers of the government securities from the Fed will have their bank accounts charged, and banks in the system lose reserves. To regain the necessary reserves, banks cut back on loans and tighten credit conditions. At the same time, the selling of government securities by the Fed lowers bond prices and raises bond yields. The lower money supply and higher rates tend to cool off the economy.

    b.   The Fed can also change the discount rate to influence bank reserves and to alter short-term interest rates. The discount rate is the rate the Fed charges its member banks to borrow money. A higher discount rate is contractionary and makes it more expensive for banks to borrow reserves. A lower discount rate is expansionary, since it is cheaper for banks to borrow and increases bank reserves. The Fed also has influence over the federal funds rate, which is the short-term rate banks charge each other for loans and reserves. When the Fed cuts the fed fund rate, it is lowering short-term interest rates for banks. This will work its way through other short-term interest rates.

Page 764   ©2007 Kaplan CPA Review

c. The reserve requirement is the fraction of deposits that member banks must keep in reserve. When the Fed increases the reserve requirement, member banks must keep relatively more reserves and have less to lend. The higher reserve requirement is a contractionary move. A lower reserve requirement would give banks more loanable funds and would be expansionary.

d. The Fed can also use moral suasion to affect monetary conditions. With announcements and speeches, the Fed can signal information that will make banks and market participants act in a desired way. For example, the Fed chairman can simply make a speech that economic activity is getting too strong and the markets will anticipate a contractionary move by the Fed. The markets reaction will be pessimistic and expectations will be revised downward, all cooling off the economy without the Fed actually doing anything.

	Expansionary Monetary Policy	Contractionary Monetary Policy
OMO	buy gov. securities	sell gov. securities
Discount Rate (%)	lower	higher
Reserve Requirement	lower	higher
Moral Suasion	positive	negative

F. **Global currency risks and hedging.**

1. Currency risk occurs because exchange rates are not fixed, causing the future value of assets, liabilities, cash flows, and contracts to change as the exchange rate changes.

Figure 24: Equilibrium Exchange Rate

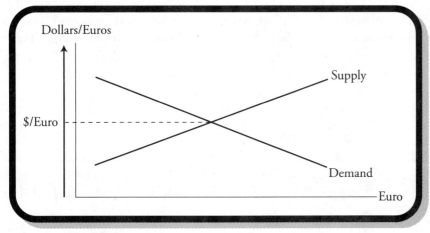

a. Exchange rates are simply prices of a currency (euros/dollar = price of a dollar in terms of euros). $1.20/euro = 0.8333 euros/$. If exchange rates are allowed

STUDY MANUAL – BUSINESS ENVIRONMENT & CONCEPTS
CRAM ESSENTIALS

to float, the exchange rate is determined by supply and demand conditions in a currency market. For example, the price of euros in terms of dollars is the equilibrium exchange rate, as illustrated in Figure 24.

2. Shifts in the demand and supply for a currency will cause the exchange rate to move up or down.

    a. Increases in the demand for euros occur due to an increase in demand for euro exports, euro securities, or expectations about the euro going stronger. The economic fundamentals behind such an increase in demand for the euro would be relatively lower inflation in the Euro zone, relatively higher real interest rates in the Euro zone, and/or relatively lower income in the Euro zone. This shift in demand is shown in Figure 25.

    Figure 25: Shifts in Demand for Foreign Currency

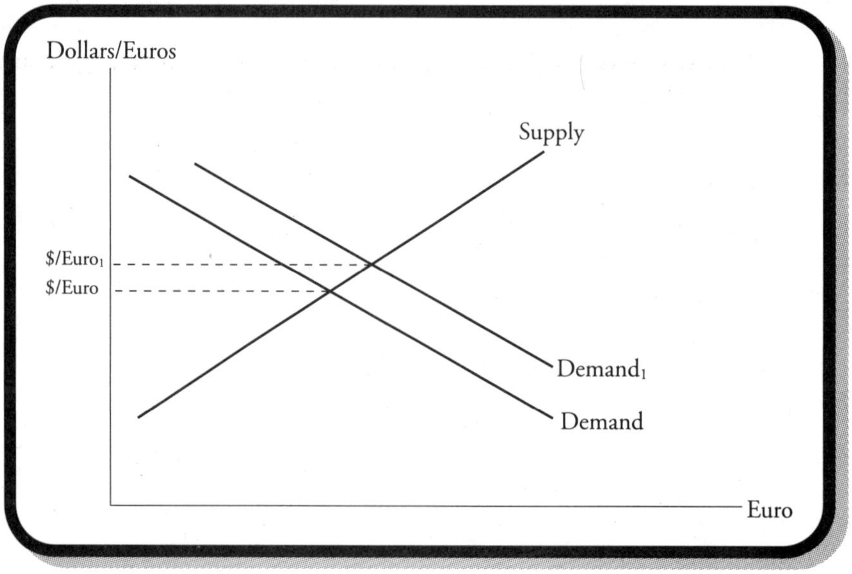

    b. Increases in the supply of euros occur due to increases in the demand for U.S. imports, relatively more attractive U.S. real interest rates, and/or relatively higher income in the Euro zone. The shift in supply is shown in Figure 26.

Page 766   ©2007 Kaplan CPA Review

Figure 26: Shifts in Supply of Foreign Currency

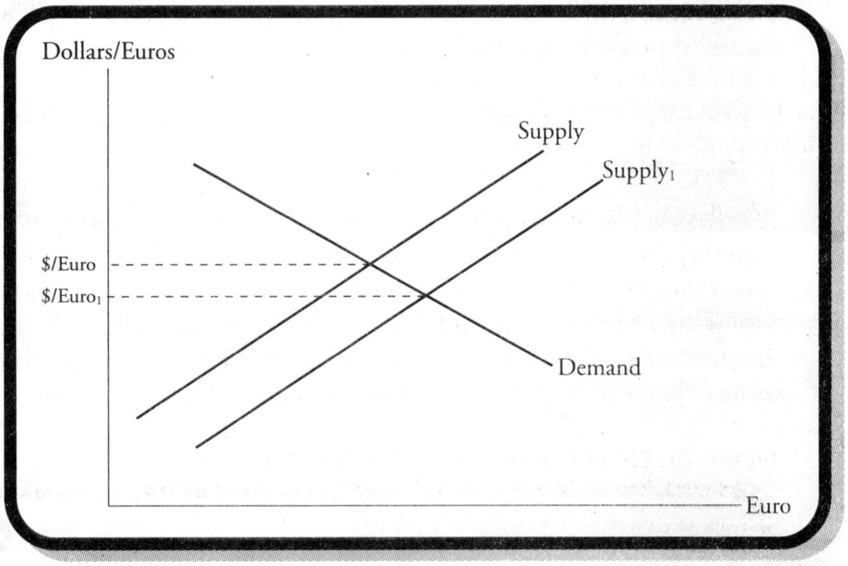

Dollars/Euros

Supply

Supply₁ → $Supply_1$

$/Euro

$/Euro₁ → $\$/Euro_1$

Demand

Euro

c. Fundamental factors that cause the dollar to be stronger are outlined in the following table.

Fundamental Factor	$ Stronger (euro/$ rate up or $/euro rate down)
inflation	relatively higher in the Euro zone
real interest rates	relatively higher in the U.S.
income	relatively higher in the Euro zone
expectations	favor holding dollars
central bank	buy dollars and sell euros in the currency market

3. A fixed exchange rate is not allowed to move in response to normal market shifts in supply or demand. The disequilibrium must be managed by either forcing an equilibrium with trade restrictions or through intervention in the currency market by central banks to buy or sell a currency until the fixed rate is achieved. For example, if the exchange rate is fixed above the equilibrium, the Euro zone countries could restrict purchases of U.S. goods and securities (quotas and trade restrictions). This would force the supply of euros to be reduced back to the point where the fixed rate is established. Another alternative is for the central bank to buy euros, shifting demand out to the point where the fixed rate is achieved.

a. When a country's currency falls in value, the country should see an improvement in its trade account. It will export relatively more and import relatively less. The example below illustrates why this is true, everything else equal.

©2007 Kaplan CPA Review

STUDY MANUAL – BUSINESS ENVIRONMENT & CONCEPTS
CRAM ESSENTIALS

Example: Assume the exchange rate is $1.20 per euro. Also, assume a U.S. product costs $48 in the U.S. and 40 euros in the Euro zone. The euro product costs 20 euros in the Euro zone and $24 in the U.S. Now assume the value of the dollar rises and the euro falls to 1 euro per dollar. The U.S. product would sell for 48 euros in the Euro zone, and U.S. exports will fall. The euro product would sell for $20 in the U.S., and U.S. imports would rise. The change in the exchange rate effectively changes the prices of goods for export and import. The country with the lower valued currency will export more and import less.

4. An exposure to a currency represents a potential gain or loss due to movement of the currency's exchange rate. For example, an account receivable invoiced in pounds will gain in dollar value if the $/pound exchange rate goes up. The account receivable will lose in dollar value if the $/pound rate goes down. The exposure is illustrated as:

AR exposure today... 1,000,000 pounds = $? depends on the $/pound exchange rate

a. Exposures to changes in an exchange rate can be managed by hedging. For example, an account receivable for pounds will gain in dollar value if the $/pound exchange rate goes up and will lose dollar value if the $/pound rate goes down. This can be hedged by an account payable of the same amount and same maturity, since the gain or loss on the payable is just the opposite of the gain or loss on a receivable. A hedge is created by having offsetting exposures to the same currency or to currencies that are very highly correlated with each other.

b. Most currencies (at least major currencies) are allowed to float in response to changes in supply and demand for the currency in the global currency market. Major drivers of the shifts in supply and demand for a currency are inflation, real interest rates, and income (frequently called the country's fundamentals). If two countries follow similar domestic policies and have similar fundamentals, their currencies will remain stable with each other. But most countries follow independent monetary and fiscal policies leading to different inflation rates, different real interest rates, and different rates of income growth. For this reason, exchange rates tend to be volatile, and currency risk must be managed.

- Countries with higher (lower) inflation will see the value of their currency fall (rise), everything else equal. If the U.S. has higher inflation than countries in the Euro zone, the euro/$ rate will fall. Higher inflation makes U.S. goods less attractive at the old exchange rate, so a reduction in demand for dollars results in a falling value of the dollar (depreciation).
- Countries with *higher (lower) real interest rates* will see the value of their *currency rise (fall)*. Demand for the currency with higher real rates shifts outward as investors seek the higher real rate of return. This makes the currency with the higher real rate go up (appreciate).
- Countries with *higher (lower) income growth* will see the value of their *currency fall (rise)*. This relationship is a little harder to see. If the U.S.

Page 768   ©2007 Kaplan CPA Review

economy has higher income growth than the Euro zone, the U.S. buys more from Euro countries than they buy from the U.S. This is especially true for income elastic exports and imports. The U.S. will have an increased demand for euros, but the demand for dollars will shift inward as less U.S. goods are bought, resulting in a lower euro/$ rate.

5. There are three types of currency risk exposures faced by the firm. Transactions exposures and operating exposures are real gains or losses. Translation exposure is an accounting exposure that is not realized unless the firm is liquidated.

   a. Transaction exposure occurs when a monetary amount of another currency is to be either paid or received at a future date. The risk is that the value of the monetary amount of the foreign currency in terms of the domestic currency depends on what happens to the exchange rate between now and maturity. For example, assume you have an account payable due in 60 days for one million euros. How many dollars will this payable cost? If the spot exchange rate in 60 days is $1.18 per euro, you will owe $1.18 million. But if the value of the euro drops to $1.10 you will only owe $1.1 million. This is the currency risk/uncertainty of not knowing what the exchange rate will be.

   b. Operating exposure occurs due to the effects unexpected changes in exchange rates have on non-monetary assets and future cash flows from operations. Operating exposure is normally an ongoing exposure without a specific maturity. For example, you own a ski resort in Aspen. When the value of the dollar appreciates relative to European currencies, more of your potential customers will choose to ski in the Swiss Alps or other European spots. The dollar will buy more Swiss Francs, making the trip to ski in Switzerland cheaper for U.S. skiers. This will hurt your operating cash flows, even though you do not have foreign currency assets, liabilities, or costs. Another example is a U.S. company producing in Canada but selling its products back in the U.S. If the $/C$ goes up, sales back in the U.S. will go down (it takes more $s to buy goods denominated in C$s).

   c. Translation exposure occurs because foreign currency accounts must be translated back into the home country's currency for consolidation. Depending on the translation method, some assets and liabilities are translated at the current exchange rate and some are translated at the old historic exchange rate. The imbalance that is created results in a translation gain or loss and is recorded in a cumulative translation adjustment account on the balance sheet (assuming FASB 52). There is no real loss, but there is an equity accounting entry to balance accounts.

   Example: A subsidiary uses the euro as its functional currency, and we must translate its balance sheet back into dollars. The firm has 20 million euros of exposed assets (exposed means it must be translated using the current spot rate) and 15 million of exposed liabilities. The net exposure is five million euros, since any movement of the euro that causes a gain or loss on assets will have the opposite effect on liabilities. If the spot rate ($/euro) used in translation falls by $0.07 then the translation gain or loss is equal to ($/euro 0.07)(5,000,000 euros) = $350,000. We had a translation gain of $350,000 due to the $0.07

appreciation per euro on our net exposure. We add this translation gain to the equity in a special cumulative account in the consolidated balance sheet.

6. Currency risk can be managed by using forward contracts, futures contracts, options, swaps, and internal balance sheet hedging to create offsetting exposures to whatever currency causes the currency risk. (Note that the financial contracts used for hedging are reviewed in the finance section.)

   a. Balance sheet hedging should be used first before contractual hedging with financial contracts is used. Balance sheet hedging simply requires netting out assets and liabilities with exposures to the same currency. For example, if we have ten million euros in assets and ten million euros in liabilities, there is a perfect balance sheet hedge. On the other hand, if we have 15 million euros in assets and ten million euros in liabilities, we have a five million euro *net* exposure to the $/euro rate. We would only use financial contracts to hedge the net exposure. We could also create a liability in euros for five million to achieve a hedge without using currency derivative contracts.

   b. Forward currency contracts are provided by dealers on a bid-ask spread basis. The dealer quotes forward prices that can be locked in today for delivery at a future date. For example, if a firm has a one million euro account receivable in 90 days, the firm loses if the $/euro rate falls. The exposure is hedged by selling the one million euros to a dealer in the forward contract. The dealer will give a $ quote for the euros today but with delivery in 90 days. Forwards are flexible and can be set for different amounts and different maturity dates. But forward contracts are not liquid and are difficult to change.

   c. Future currency contracts are much like forward contracts, but they are exchange traded. This makes futures much more liquid, but they are not very flexible. Contracts are in standard amounts with only four delivery dates a year. Also, margins are required. However, futures do not have the counterparty risk of forward contracts. For example, if a firm has a 70,000 pound account payable (owe pounds = short position) due in 90 days, it could get an offsetting future on pounds (long position = buy pounds). These two positions have opposite and offsetting exposures. But, there may be a mismatch of maturities and amounts. The pound future is for 62,500 pounds per contract, so a future for 70,000 pounds is not available. Also, the 90-day exposure of the account payable may not have the maturity date of the closest future contract.

   d. Currency options are also available for hedging purposes. Options are traded on exchanges and in dealer markets. The option hedge has a unique characteristic. Options can be allowed to expire if the exchange rate movement does not cause a loss in the underlying exposure. This allows option hedges aimed at hedging only the direction of an exchange rate movement that causes a loss. For example, if there is an account receivable exposure to pounds, the exposure loses if the value of a pound falls (fewer dollars for the pounds received). But if the value of the pound goes up, there is no need for a hedge. The option that gains when the value of a pound falls is a put on pounds. The pound put option matched with the pound account

Page 770   ©2007 Kaplan CPA Review

receivable hedges only falling pound values. If the pound goes up, the put will expire without being exercised, and the pounds received on the account receivable are sold at the market value. The premiums paid on the put are deducted from the pounds received, but upside potential for the exposure remains.

e. Swap contracts are also used to hedge currency exposure and are especially good for operating exposures. A currency swap is just an exchange of cash flows in one currency in exchange for cash flows in another currency. For example, assume a firm operates in the U.K. and earns pound cash flows over time. But the firm uses dollar financing and has to make dollar interest payments. The firm has risk because it doesn't know if the dollar value of the pounds in the future will be sufficient to pay the dollar interest payments.

Example: Firm 1 could enter into a swap of pounds for dollars over a relatively long time period, such as five years, with Firm 2. The current interest rate on pounds and the current interest rate on dollars will be used to set up the pound-for-dollar swap. A present value principal of pounds and dollars will be used based on the current spot rate, and cash flows will be set by taking the interest rates times the present value. For example, if the spot rate is $1.60 per pound, the annual interest rate on the dollar is 5 percent, and the rate on the pound is 6 percent, the annual cash flows for the next five years would be as shown in Figure 27 if the principal amount is one million pounds.

Figure 27: Swap Contract

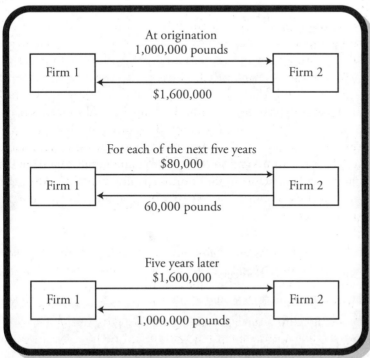

STUDY MANUAL – BUSINESS ENVIRONMENT & CONCEPTS
CRAM ESSENTIALS

Note that the swap is set up as two parallel loans. For example, one side gets $1,600,000 today and pays interest payments of $80,000 every year and a final repayment of the $1,600,000 principal at the end of five years.

- The following table provides a summary of hedging alternatives for different types of exposures.

Transaction Exposure	Hedging Alternatives
Accounts payable in euros	Buy euros forward
Buy euros in futures market (long position)	
Buy a call option on euros (long call)	
Match AP with AR in euros	
Accounts receivable in euros	Sell euros forward
Sell euros in futures market (short position)	
Match AR with AP in euros	

Operating Exposure	Hedging Alternatives
Assets in euros	Liabilities in euros
Cash flows in euros or $ cash flows fall if $/euro fall	Swap euros for dollars
Sell euro futures (short position)	
Buy puts on euros	
Sell euros forward	
Shift costs from $ to euros	

Translation Exposure	Hedging Alternatives
Exposed assets > exposed liabilities	Increase euro liabilities
Don't worry it will cancel out eventually	
Only in extreme cases we use:	
selling (short) euro futures	
buying (long) euro calls	
Exposed assets < exposed liabilities	Increase euro assets
Don't worry it will cancel out eventually	
Only in extreme cases would we use:	
buy (long) euro futures	
buy (long) euro calls	

EXAM STRATEGIES

STUDY MANUAL – BUSINESS ENVIRONMENT & CONCEPTS

OVERVIEW

Kaplan CPA Review applauds your desire to earn the CPA designation, one of the most prestigious and respected professional credentials in the world. Employing Kaplan's proven system for CPA examination preparation, you will be giving yourself a tremendous advantage in your efforts to join the more than 340,000 fellow CPAs and members of the American Institute of Certified Public Accountants (AICPA).

We have assembled some of the best minds in academia, along with a highly skilled professional staff, to develop a comprehensive review course for enhancing your chances of passing the CPA exam. We recommend that you follow the guidelines in this book and use the supporting course materials to ensure your success.

You should also be commended for working hard to complete your accounting degree. It is one of the most rigorous programs in business. With Kaplan's proven tools and CPA exam preparation formula, we can assist you with taking the knowledge you have acquired through the years and applying it to the CPA exam. Rigorous study alone will not ensure success. Your approach must focus your energy in a logical and organized manner, combining hard work with more effective and successful techniques. **Once you see that the "how" of studying is as crucial as the "what" to study, the effort and results will become readily apparent.**

This Tips and Techniques chapter will serve as a valuable tool to help you navigate the Kaplan course material, organize your study approach, and gain an understanding of the big picture regarding the CPA exam. We know that your chances for success will increase if you begin with this chapter and follow its recommendations, instructions, and advice.

The chapter is divided into six sections, which cover the following:

- Exam preparation.
- Strategy development.
- Multiple choice and simulation study strategies.
- Recommendations for exam day.
- Post-exam activities.

©2007 Kaplan CPA Review

Page 773

STUDY MANUAL – BUSINESS ENVIRONMENT & CONCEPTS
EXAM STRATEGIES

PLANNING TO TAKE THE EXAM

AICPA TESTING GOALS

You are taking the exam in a new era, one that will recognize the context of your current educational environment and work experience. The old, paper-based exam sought to test problem-solving skills and knowledge of financial literature. It required more memorization than demonstration of critical thinking and analytical and communication skills. Today's computerized exam focus requires more than a general familiarity with the material. It requires a complete grasp of the concepts and the ability to clearly communicate your knowledge to the graders. This reflects today's business environment, which requires more advanced skills in researching technical information; applying informed, sound judgment in decision making; and communicating more effectively with many different stakeholder groups.

What is the driving force behind all this change? Corporations and other organizations are demanding accounting professionals who possess skills in communication, critical thinking, and problem and opportunity definition and analysis to guide their institutions in the 21st century's global economy. Accountants have become business partners and not just "bean counters." In response to the growing need for CPAs to possess broader skills, curricula are changing at colleges and universities to promote more experiential and cooperative learning (e.g., group projects and class presentations). Likewise, the AICPA has incorporated the demands of the marketplace into the new CPA exam by transforming it from a paper-based to computer-based test and leveraging the benefits of a technology-based environment. Specifically, the computerized exam expands the learning goals and expectations beyond simply content and problem-solving skills. On the CBT exam, the candidate is expected to demonstrate mastery of the competencies listed below.

- *Research relevant financial literature.* The candidate should possess the ability to review current rules, regulations, and interpretations in a particular context, such as revenue recognition or impairment of goodwill. The CBT exam requires the candidate to demonstrate the ability to research an issue, identify the appropriate authoritative literature, understand its application to the issue, and offer an opinion or structure a transaction in compliance with the proper rules. This is now tested under the simulation dimension of the exam. The questions will require you to access, during the exam, an online database of literature from which you will retrieve your answer.
- *Communicate business information.* Through analysis, evaluation, and conclusion, a candidate should demonstrate the ability to conduct the appropriate research of financial literature. Findings must then be communicated in an effective, clear, and relevant manner. This part of the exam, requiring written communications, will be graded manually by the AICPA. Scoring will focus on your ability to write well— including developing, organizing, and expressing your ideas—as well as the technical content of your answer.
- *Analyze and interpret business information.* The candidate will review and evaluate information in context (e.g., business combinations), in order to offer opinions, conclusions, further discussions, or actions related to the analysis.

Page 774

©2007 Kaplan CPA Review

- *Render judgment based on available business information.* Traditional quantitative problems focus on generating an exact answer [e.g., net present value (NPV) of a proposed capital investment]. The computerized exam will test the candidate's ability to review the business context and relevant information, and offer an opinion beyond the formula. For example, while the NPV of a project may be positive, other risk factors, such as declining revenue and increasing expenses, may render the validity of the underlying assumptions (e.g., cash flow predictions) less reliable. Perhaps management should consider these issues prior to authorizing the investment.
- *Gain an understanding of key business terms, facts, and processes.* One major complaint by accounting firms and corporations has been that accounting graduates are not familiar with business in general, but know only how to record accounting entries. The pencil and paper CPA exam did not historically test for a breadth of understanding behind these entries. The paper-based exam assessed the candidate's proficiency in answering quantitative problems and memorizing rules. The essence of accounting is the interpretation of economic events and the translation of events into financial information. Therefore, it is critical for the candidate to understand the business environment and operations to ensure the proper evaluation of economic events along with their related recording and disclosure.

We feel confident that the knowledge gained from your college curriculum and current professional work experience, along with our guidance, will help you successfully demonstrate your mastery of these competencies.

So, yes, the CPA exam has entered the 21st century. It is more relevant than before. It is testing different skills, and testing the same skills in different ways. Does this make it more difficult to pass? Not really. Read on. There are actually some new features that will make you happy. This is not your grandfather's CPA exam!

ADVANTAGES OF THE COMPUTERIZED CPA EXAM

Probably the biggest advantage of the computerized exam is that you no longer have to prepare for all four parts of the exam at once. This is the best thing that has ever happened to a CPA exam candidate!

The CPA exam was changed from a paper-based test to a computer-based test (CBT) in April 2004. The CBT exam allows candidates to plan and schedule the time that they wish to take the exam, based on the following requirements:

- The exam is offered in more than 300 Prometric centers across the United States and its jurisdictions.
- Candidates can take the exam two months out of each quarter each year (January–February, April–May, July–August, and October–November).
- Candidates can take only one or as many as all four sections at a time and in any order desired.
- Each section is graded independently, and the outcome does not impact the other section results or qualification.
- Once you pass a section and earn credit, you have 18 months to pass the other three sections of the exam.
- There is no minimum score requirement for failed sections.

STUDY MANUAL – BUSINESS ENVIRONMENT & CONCEPTS
EXAM STRATEGIES

The new exam mirrors the flexibility that technology has brought to the workplace, most notably through telecommuting and flexible work arrangements. Candidates can now schedule sections within a testing window (i.e., 2-month period) and take the sections of the exam at a pace that meets their work schedule, study/readiness plan, and general preference.

Candidates should be careful to understand the rules imposed by the CBT exam. Under the paper-based method, there was a lack of uniformity among the jurisdictions in qualifying for sections as they were passed. For example, in some jurisdictions, you had to have a minimum score on all parts taken, or your passing grade on another part was not accepted. All jurisdictions now follow the same guidelines for granting credit. Each section is graded independently, without regard to your score on another section of the exam.

However, once you pass any section, your time clock begins, and you have 18 months from that passing notification to complete the remaining sections. It is imperative that you fully understand the time constraint that is imposed once a section is passed. Your professional career or personal demands could easily consume months, and before you know it, time has expired and you could be working under pressure to pass or face forfeiture of the sections for which you previously earned credit.

We will assist you in passing the exam as soon as possible to avoid this potential planning and scheduling challenge. We want you to be aware of the potential risk and avoid it with effective planning.

Do not procrastinate. Once you pass the first part of the exam, maintain your study schedule, with appropriate rest breaks, and keep going. Prepare for and pass sections on a time schedule that works for you, but just ensure that you pass all four sections before that 18-month period slips by!

CBT VS. PAPER-BASED EXAM

A CBT exam presents some unique advantages, which were noted above, along with some limitations listed below:

- The examination is linear; you must take each portion of an exam section (called a "testlet") in a series. You cannot start in the middle of the exam as you could do in the paper-based mode.
- Once you complete a portion (testlet) and exit from it, you cannot go back to review and/or change answers.
- The time limits are even more critical as the system will close the testlet once the time expires. There is no flexibility in allocating your time to portions or questions, which existed in the paper-based mode.

The candidate should visit the AICPA's Web site, *www.cpa-exam.org,* to become familiar with the CBT exam. The AICPA has developed and made available a free comprehensive tutorial, use of which is highly recommended. The tutorial provides examples of test questions and, more importantly, the technical mode of presentation and delivery. Utilizing these resources will ensure that you will be confident, prepared, and efficient

STUDY MANUAL – BUSINESS ENVIRONMENT & CONCEPTS
EXAM STRATEGIES

when the time comes. **We cannot overemphasize the importance of this step in your preparation.** The actual exam administration location (i.e., the Prometric Center) is not the place to learn what the new exam looks like!

Remember the last time you drove a car that you had never seen before? You had to get in, locate all the buttons and dials, adjust the seat, set the air conditioner and radio, etc. This is similar to how you will become familiar with the new exam experience. Do this on your own time with the tutorial, and our online materials, not at the exam, where your time is precious!

We recognize that you began your career in the information age, and you are probably quite adept at using technology. However, one aspect of technology is navigation, and it is essential that you gain an understanding of the software and mode of operation used for the CPA exam prior to exam day. Coaches and their players often visit a football field in advance of the game to ensure they know the stadium and the unique dimensions of the field, and to remove the fear of the unknown. Likewise, we want you to invest the necessary effort with the AICPA's tutorial and the Kaplan online materials. Take the opportunity to practice in a CBT environment similar to that where the test will be given. We want you to be free of exam-day jitters and be ready to pass.

EXAMINATION OVERVIEW

The CPA exam is prepared and administered by the AICPA for the 55 jurisdictions, including the District of Columbia, Virgin Islands, Puerto Rico, Guam, and the Commonwealth of the Northern Mariana Islands (CNMI). The AICPA is responsible for exam development, administration, and scoring. The AICPA has partnered with Prometrics Testing Services to administer the computerized examination at Prometric centers within the 55 jurisdictions.

Each state and jurisdiction has its own board of accountancy that administers the licensing function. For example, if you live, sit for, and pass the exam in Houston, Texas, the Texas State Board of Accountancy will issue your license to practice and your CPA certificate. The requirements for licensure vary from state to state. Be sure to check with your own state's board of accountancy for the requirements, both to sit for the exam and to become licensed after you pass.

©2007 Kaplan CPA Review

STUDY MANUAL – BUSINESS ENVIRONMENT & CONCEPTS
EXAM STRATEGIES

The CPA exam is given in four sections as follows:

Section	Test Format	Allowed Time
Auditing and Attestation	• Multiple choice given in three separate testlets of 24 to 30 questions each • 2 Simulation questions	4.5 hours
Financial Accounting and Reporting	• Multiple choice given in three separate testlets of 24 to 30 questions each • 2 Simulation questions	4.0 hours
Regulation	• Multiple choice given in three separate testlets of 24 to 30 questions each • 2 Simulation questions	3.0 hours
Business Environment and Concepts	• Multiple choice given in three separate testlets of 24 to 30 questions each (no sims)	2.5 hours
Total		14 hours

Topic coverage of CPA exam:

Section	Content Coverage Percent	Relevant Supporting Literature
Auditing and Attestation	• 100%	• Generally Accepted Auditing Standards • Standards for Attestation Engagements • Accounting and Review Services • Government Auditing Standards • Audit Risk Alerts • PCAOB Standards • For sims, a research database such as the AICPA Standards database

Financial Accounting and Reporting	• Business Enterprises—80%
	 • Government Entities—10%
	 • Not-for-Profits—10%
		• Generally Accepted Accounting Principles for:
		   - Business enterprises
		   - Not-for-profit organizations
		   - Government entities
		 • For sims, a research database such as FARS

Regulation	• Federal Taxation—60% • Law and Professional Responsibilities—40%	• Internal Revenue Code • Ethics pronouncements of AICPA • Sarbanes-Oxley Act of 2002 • PCAOB Pronouncements • Business Law textbook • For sims, a tax research database tool
Business Environment and Concepts	• Business Structures—20% • Economics—15% • Finance—20% • I.T.—25% • Planning & Measurement—25%	• Current textbooks and business periodicals provide good coverage for BEC • There are currently no plans to include sims on BEC

Page 778   ©2007 Kaplan CPA Review

Note: Because the ability to research technical questions is tested in the simulations, the AICPA makes a sample research database available to candidates for a period of time while they are preparing for the CPA exam. See *www.cpa-exam.org* for more details. Kaplan's simulations also provide a sample research tool for your use in practicing with simulations.

Your initial response could be "Wow! That is a lot of material to cover in such a short period of time," or "I have never had an exam that lasted more than three hours, even when I had back-to-back exams in college." Please relax. We will teach you how to navigate through the material, develop an effective study plan, and efficiently use your time to focus on the relevant topics required to successfully pass the exam.

Remember: You are *not* learning all these topics for the first time; you are learning how to pass the exam. There's a big difference. You are not trying to become an expert in all of these topical areas. What you need is a structured and focused review and a proper strategic approach. We will provide that, along with flexibility and content to support any areas where you have had little or no prior exposure.

Hopefully, after looking at this schedule, you can begin to see how this guide, along with other Kaplan materials, will assist you in using your time wisely. For example, you may not have taken a course in college; not everyone does. Since this is an important topic for the exam, you may want to spend a little more time to cover this topic well. Perhaps you took Individual Taxation in college, and you will be able to adequately cover this topic in less time than needed for the Corporation tax rules. This allows you to more effectively plan your time to properly manage the volume of material and breadth of topic coverage. With Kaplan materials, your focus can easily be tailored to reflect your particular background and you can efficiently and effectively prepare for the CPA exam.

BENEFITS OF THE KAPLAN CPA REVIEW MATERIALS

Kaplan has developed a comprehensive set of materials that will greatly assist candidates in their preparation to pass the CPA exam. The following is a guideline for each study aid and its recommended use and value:

Study Tool	Recommended Use	Benefit
Lesson Video	• Background material for a topic (e.g., basic auditing standards).	• Provides audio/visual lecture in a dynamic, interesting, and comprehensive manner.
Problems Video	• Demonstration of how to effectively solve problems in a specific content area (e.g., lease accounting).	• Provides a dynamic illustration of how to solve a problem.
Problems PDF	• Practice responding to problem-oriented questions within a topic area.	• Provides an opportunity for candidates to test their understanding and ability to complete CPA exam–like questions within a topic area.
Study Manuals	• Reference guides to support the review and study process for each topic.	• Provides a comprehensive resource for each topic area for ongoing reference and review.

STUDY MANUAL – BUSINESS ENVIRONMENT & CONCEPTS
EXAM STRATEGIES

	• Also includes essential outlines, exam strategy and technique, and a writing styles guide.	• Provides summary outlines for quick review. • Helps you understand the exam and the entire exam process. • Helps you structure your writing assignment in the sims to gain maximum points.
Kaplan Activity Planners	• Schedule the practice and review time in order to prepare for the CPA exam. • Impose discipline on your study schedule.	• Provides a terrific planning tool that integrates all of the Kaplan CPA Review materials by topic with a suggested study approach.
Kaplan Audio CDs	• A question/answer format to reinforce the content.	• Allows you to listen while you commute, go for a run or walk, or any other time it is appropriate for you to multi-task!
Kaplan Flashcards	• More than 2,000 cards organized by exam topic, in question-and- answer format.	• Provides additional reinforcement of the topics, in a format that is convenient to use and carry with you.
Kaplan Online Exam Testlets	• Evaluation mechanism to determine progress and areas where more work is required.	• Provides an opportunity for candidates to evaluate progress in an environment that simulates the actual CPA exam CBT format. This is an invaluable opportunity for candidates, not only to demonstrate their readiness in terms of the topic coverage, but also to increase their level of comfort with navigating the computerized exam environment.
Kaplan Online Exam Simulations	• Sims provide the opportunity to practice with exam-like case problems and with an online research database tool. • While simulations definitely give you the opportunity to reinforce content, the major benefit of using sims is to practice with the functionality of the software and the use of the research tool.	• Provides an opportunity for candidates to evaluate progress in an environment that simulates the actual CPA exam CBT format. Since the simulations are the newest component of the CPA exam, it is critical that the candidate understand the process and functionality of the software in this testing context. The simulations consist of multiple points and clicks, screen accesses, and other navigational requirements (e.g., professional literature review prior to responding to the specific questions). You should feel very comfortable with this process prior to exam day to ensure that you can maximize your available time to answer the questions, as opposed to being confused by the functions of the software. We want to minimize your stress on exam day by preparing you to anticipate every dimension of the exam, including content and operation.
Kaplan Online Question Bank	• True/False questions sequenced to develop your learning of the topics; multiple-choice questions that are similar to exam questions.	• Provides candidates with additional testing opportunities to identify strengths and weaknesses.

Page 780

©2007 Kaplan CPA Review

| E-mail a Kaplan Professor | • Resource for timely response to your questions. | • Provides candidates with a feedback mechanism to address issues and concerns as they arise. This is where our course becomes a personal tool, as this will complement any of our materials with the ability for you to ask specific questions. We also use this as a course material based on responses from candidates such as you. We want you to view this function as having access to a personal coach who will ensure that, as you practice, any issues or concerns you have will be addressed in a timely manner. We will be there for you and with you throughout this whole preparation period. You are not alone! |

KEY STEPS FOR PASSING THE EXAM

We recommend that you follow these guidelines to ensure that you maximize your time and appropriately utilize the resources made available through the Kaplan course.

1. **Visit the AICPA dedicated Web site for the CPA exam to gain a thorough understanding of the exam.** Take the tutorial, which gives you a sample of the test questions and mode of examination: *www.cpa-exam.org*. The AICPA has created for eligible candidates a wealth of free instructional information, such as tutorials, guides, and resources. This will allow you to be clear on the nature of the exam in terms of content and operation. It will also give you guidance on preparation and other critical information, such as scheduling the exam. **Be sure to obtain and read the Candidate Bulletin from that Web site.**

2. **Enroll in the following:** The AICPA is offering eligible candidates (refer to above Web site for more information) a 6-month free subscription to the AICPA Professional Standards, FASB Current Text, and FASB Original Pronouncements, which will provide students with a rich resource base to prepare for the research element of the simulation questions. Since the simulation questions will require research of the professional literature, the AICPA is offering a free subscription so you can practice conducting research prior to the exam. This will allow you to become familiar with both the content and the operation. This will greatly benefit you on exam day because you would have already mastered the research and the navigation effort. And it's free. What a great bargain!

3. **Determine when you plan to take the exam and contact your state board of accountancy and Prometric Center to apply and schedule a time.** As working professionals or students nearing graduation, your time is both limited and precious. Make sure you fully understand the "testing windows" concept and your availability prior to scheduling the exam. Keep in mind that you have new flexibility that was not previously available. But also note that you have an 18-month limitation once you pass a section to complete the rest of the exam. We want you to avoid the last-minute or "cram" approach to the exam. Your success depends on having sufficient time to study for and pass the exam.

STUDY MANUAL – BUSINESS ENVIRONMENT & CONCEPTS
EXAM STRATEGIES

4. **Use the Kaplan materials in conjunction with your study plan to ensure your readiness on exam day.** The Kaplan materials have been developed to support each section of the exam. The Kaplan materials also help prepare the candidate to perform effectively within the new computerized exam environment by providing CBT examples relevant to each topic and testing format (i.e., multiple choice or simulations). We strongly urge you to use these materials to prepare for the exam.

5. **Follow the suggestions in the Kaplan CPA Survival Guide (see** *www.kaplanCPAreview.com,* **under CPA Info and Resources).** This guide is a personal reminder to make sure you plan, prepare, relax, and succeed. Kaplan understands that you will work very hard to prepare for the exam. We will assist you in planning your time effectively so your preparation activities are efficient and effective. This should ensure that you can physically and mentally relax, both during your preparation and on exam day. We do encourage dedicated days off to refresh and rejuvenate during the practice period. Finally, we feel that if you are properly prepared, you can relax and minimize or even eliminate stress before and on exam day. We want you to just go out and do your very best. Remember: you practiced, practiced, and practiced; all you have to do now is demonstrate what you know. And, while there is no such thing as being overly prepared, you do want to reach your exam day in an optimistic frame of mind.

DEVELOPING A STUDY PLAN

Once you have determined that you are fully committed to taking the exam, we recommend you develop a careful, sensible, and comprehensive study plan. This will ensure that you use your time and Kaplan materials effectively and efficiently. This will help you manage the process of preparation and control the degree of stress that is often related to such endeavors. As you progress with your studies, you will also begin to see that, while this is a big effort, it is absolutely not an impossible effort. You will begin to develop the confidence needed to believe in yourself and to keep heading toward your goal.

The CBT exam is more focused on assessing the competencies previously noted in Chapter 1 than on the memorization of certain rules and techniques. A quote from a recent presentation by an AICPA representative, "More thought than rote," indicates a focus toward more critical thinking. It is essential that you invest the proper time to plan, because the process of demonstrating mastery of the five competencies is different from a cursory memorization process.

The paper-based exam emphasized the ability to recall facts and rules. Several review course providers recommended that candidates spend effort learning how to memorize certain facts (e.g., the four criteria for determining a lease) by using such aids as developing mnemonics. Preparing for the new exam requires effective application of the accounting foundation you acquired in college and/or work to the various contextual situations found throughout the exam.

Our review process focuses on providing you with adequate time to practice applying your knowledge, enhancing your knowledge in areas where you need support, and learning the testing environment. Therefore, you can relax and not be overwhelmed with

Page 782   ©2007 Kaplan CPA Review

the amount of material covered, or be concerned about your ability to memorize the complete set of GAAP and GAAS. We will help you prepare for this exam with proven methods that are relevant to the current expectations. We cannot emphasize enough that *how* you study is as important as *what* you study.

PREPARATION FRAMEWORK

When coaches prepare their teams for the forthcoming season, they develop a comprehensive plan that seeks to address every dimension of the competitive environment: game plan, winning strategy, physical component, and their team's mental readiness. Likewise, serving as your coach, Kaplan fully recognizes your world-class talent and capabilities and seeks to ensure that you walk away from the exam having given a winning effort.

We also want to address every key aspect of the CPA exam, relative to your strengths, talents, and professional, personal, and physical dimensions, so you are adequately prepared. Specifically, we will focus on strengthening and conditioning the following dimensions of your life related to preparing for the exam:

- Knowing the rules.
- Knowing how to implement the rules.
- Managing your emotional and mental energy while preparing.
- Maintaining your health and energy during the preparation period.

This chapter and our free weekly "CPA Exam Lesson" e-mails will provide you with a comprehensive and current review of the rules of the CPA exam (sign up for these lessons on our Web site under CPA Info and Resources). These Kaplan references provide a complete description of the exam and its objectives, explanation of its administration, registration information, and recommendations on how to leverage knowledge of the rules to your advantage. It is critical that you understand how the exam works. We go beyond the basics, giving you a background of the exam so you can fully appreciate why the current exam has been transformed from a paper-based, memorization-oriented test into a computerized exam that emphasizes critical thinking and analytical skills. We also feel it is important for you to know the registration process so you can make sure you are enrolled and eligible to sit for the exam when the time comes.

Kaplan will provide you with a rich set of tools that will assist in your preparation for the CPA exam. These tools include: lesson videos, problem videos, problems PDF, study manuals, Kaplan Activity Planner, Kaplan Online Test Bank and Testlets, research library, and simulation questions. Kaplan's tools are your manual for success, ensuring that your talents and mental attitude are ready to be put to the test.

We make an all-out effort to support your mental attitude by acting as your coach and cheerleader. This is especially true of our "E-mail Lessons" (mentioned above) and our interaction with you via our Web site announcements and our "e-mail the professor" feature. We know you have already worked hard to become eligible for the exam. We feel that our proven techniques will not only provide adequate preparation, but will instill the confidence needed to face the challenges of the CPA exam. In addition, if you ever feel an anxiety attack approaching, you can e-mail us via "E-mail a Kaplan Professor" and we will provide helpful feedback to resolve whatever issues are causing you stress. We will be there for you throughout the preparation period. Your coach will be on the sideline cheering, encouraging, and providing guidance right up to exam day.

The Kaplan Activity Planner, the "CPA Exam Lesson" e-mails, and the Kaplan CPA Survival Guide all encourage you to rest, relax, and refresh your energy throughout the preparation period. We recognize the fatigue that will arise from executing the recommended preparation schedule. We strongly encourage you to take periodic breaks at least once a week and also right before the exam. We want you to have the energy to rally all of your talents and knowledge to achieve peak performance. We want you to be as stress-free as possible during the preparation period. In fact, we want you to enjoy this process and anticipate and visualize your success. Most of all, we want you to enjoy the relief, satisfaction, and professional recognition that will come your way when you pass. So keeping healthy, alert, and confident is a very important part of this process.

DEVELOPING A STUDY PLAN AND SCHEDULE

Now that you fully understand the rules of the game, we need to focus on learning to play the game by practice, practice, and more practice. However, we want you to practice in an efficient, effective, and organized manner, and not just plunge into a set of materials. Besides not being very efficient, a haphazard approach may even lead to burnout.

We have developed a 4-step process for you to design a comprehensive study plan. This will prepare you for the planned "testing window" when you seek to take the exam. You must consider your level of knowledge section by section, your schedule, and the rules of your jurisdiction to outline a plan that will lead to successfully passing the exam.

Please review the following steps and begin to design your study plan.

Determine when you are going to take the exam and calculate how many weeks of study you have available. We recommend a minimum of 40 available days to study prior to taking the examination. Your schedule should also include planned days of NO study to provide balance and an opportunity to refresh and relax; this will help you avoid burnout and a negative attitude. We want you to be extremely realistic when considering your current responsibilities, and professional and personal commitments, and then, with our Kaplan Activity Planner, outline a study plan that you can fulfill. It is essential that you commit to the study days as well as to the days off. We want you to develop a balanced preparation approach that considers your intellectual efforts, as well as the need to maintain your mental and physical health. Another reason to be realistic in planning your study schedule is to ensure that you do not "over-schedule" yourself and then feel negative about yourself when you cannot meet that schedule. Set yourself up for success by being realistic from the beginning. Remember: this is really not a difficult exam, but it is a very long exam! Have someone who knows you well review your planned schedule and offer their opinion on whether you have a great chance of sticking with it.

Access the Kaplan CPA Review Kaplan Activity Planner that is available for each topic. Your Planner is a booklet that arrives in the box with all your other study materials. A video describing the Planner and the Kaplan approach to CPA Review can be viewed at

STUDY MANUAL – BUSINESS ENVIRONMENT & CONCEPTS
EXAM STRATEGIES

www.kaplanCPAreview under Online Lessons. We urge you to view this video as a part of your planning process.

- The planner provides a recommended schedule that offers a 40- or 70-day option for REG, AUD, and BEC, and a 50- or 80-day option for FAR.
- The appropriate Kaplan review course material is outlined within the topical study plan and schedule. For example, day one of the BEC requires the following action steps:
  - Read the introduction to the planner.
  - Watch an instructional video.
  - Activate your Kaplan e-mail accounts.
  - Read sections of the Study Manual.
  - Watch lesson videos.
  - Answer questions in software.

The nature of the planner makes it easy for the candidate to identify the course material required and the recommended use of that material for each topical area. The candidate needs to execute the first step, which is to identify an appropriate schedule and implement the planner accordingly. Once you determine the number of days to study, you can select the appropriate Kaplan Activity Planner. We have identified the specific course materials discussed earlier in this chapter and made recommendations for how to use them during the selected preparation period (e.g., 40 or 70 days for BEC). However, you can adjust this plan as you deem appropriate based on your unique schedule.

For example, alternative job schedules allow some people to be off every other Friday or Monday or to select a day off every week. Individuals who telecommute have the option of selecting schedules they prefer. This may impact your study schedule, however, and the Kaplan Activity Planner can be adjusted accordingly. This is your personal plan, and it should reflect your time availability and individual preparation needs. We have done the detailed work for you; all you need to do is adjust it to meet your personal circumstances.

UNDERSTAND THE "TESTING WINDOWS" FOR TAKING THE CPA EXAM AT THE PROMETRIC CENTERS

Testing Windows*	Closed Periods per Quarter
January and February	March
April and May	June
July and August	September
October and November	December

*A window is a consecutive 2-month period within a quarter that the exam is available via Prometric. Candidates can take one or all four parts or a combination thereof during a "window." Candidates cannot repeat a part during a window.

As noted earlier in this chapter, the CBT exam gives the candidate considerable flexibility. For example, during the January and February window, a candidate could elect to take Auditing and Attestation during the first week of January. This could be followed by

©2007 Kaplan CPA Review

Page 785

STUDY MANUAL – BUSINESS ENVIRONMENT & CONCEPTS
EXAM STRATEGIES

Regulation during the third week of January. They could then take Financial Accounting and Reporting during the second week of February and complete the exam with the Business Environment and Concepts section during the last week of February.

Another candidate might elect to take two of the sections during this period and defer the other two to the April and May window. Or another candidate might elect to take one section per window to complete the whole exam in a year. The number of sections you elect to take during a window is your choice. Just remember, you cannot repeat a section within a window. In other words, you cannot take Regulation twice in the January and February window.

The improved flexibility in the exam scheduling is a great benefit to candidates. Not only does it allow you to create your own schedule, but it also enables you to prepare for and take only one section at a time. Compared to the old exam requirement of sitting for all four sections at once, this is a huge stress reliever for you. If you have not experienced preparing for and sitting for all four sections over two days, just ask some of your colleagues at work how much fun that was!

Along with this great benefit from flexibility comes a huge responsibility. (There is no free lunch, right?) You have the responsibility to discipline yourself to begin the process. It is far too easy for some people to say, "Oh, well, I'll just take it next month." While it is much better for you to have this flexible scheduling, it is also easier for you to let yourself procrastinate. Think about this. Do not put it off. Get the process out of the way, and move on to other learning opportunities in your life and career. The hardest part of a difficult undertaking is just taking the first step.

Another scheduling consideration is when to schedule a re-take in the event something unexpected arises that prevents you from preparing sufficiently. You always want to get your scores on a section of the exam before you schedule a re-take. Realistically, you will probably not receive your grades in time to retake a section within the same window. Thus, the AICPA has a rule allowing you to take a section only once per window. In addition, we would want you to spend sufficient time addressing the weaknesses noted on any failed section so that we can assist you in avoiding the same mistakes. With adequate preparation, you can expect to pass. If something prevents you from preparing completely, we will help you assess what your next steps should be.

Here's another point to consider. Experience shows that few people leave the exam site saying, "Oh, great, I passed that with no problem." It just doesn't happen. Most candidates leave the exam with at least some doubt as to whether they passed. This is perfectly normal. Many of them find out their immediate assessment was wrong, and they did pass. So *always* know your score before scheduling another sitting of any part of the exam. In fact, the best thing to do after a part is over is to make note of any areas you felt very weak in while taking the exam, and then put away that note until you get your score. Next, go have some fun! You earned it. After a few days off, you can start preparing for the next section of the exam you plan to take.

Before going any further, take the time to review your plan. Consider whether the schedule you selected is realistic. For example, if you have just been promoted and your new position will require extensive travel, will you have online access to the Kaplan materials while you are on the road? Will you have the time to study adequately? We do

Page 786   ©2007 Kaplan CPA Review

not want you to design a plan that is not attainable. It is essential that you develop a program that makes sense for your professional and personal schedule, commitments, and responsibilities.

We want you to be committed to your schedule. Our tools, such as the Kaplan Activity Planner by section, are very useful. But these tools are only as good as how you use them to support your practice and preparation period. We recommend you document this plan in your PDA, online, or in the tool that best keeps you organized. This will provide an additional mechanism and the ability to track your progress, modify plans as your schedule changes, and ensure that you have considered all aspects of your professional and personal activities.

REGISTER TO TAKE THE EXAM

We want you to be mentally, physically, and emotionally ready for the exam. However, it will all be moot if you do not follow the process of enrollment and eligibility. We urge you to take sufficient time to understand the specific rules for registering to take the exam in your jurisdiction.

We have provided a list of steps for you to follow, which are relevant in each of the 55 jurisdictions.

Please note, these steps are general and you need to augment them after researching your respective jurisdiction.

Apply to your state board of accountancy. Your jurisdiction should have a Web site containing the registration information online. We recommend you pay particular attention to the eligibility rules (e.g., number of college credits and the lead time for filing). For example, if you seek to sit for the exam in the April through May "testing window," identify the deadline for registering for that time. This is critical, since missing the deadline to register for a desired testing window will impact your study plan.

Be sure to notice your jurisdictions's requirements for number of credits in accounting courses, number of credits in other business courses, rules for accepting online courses, and any requirement for courses specifically dedicated to Accounting Ethics (not general ethics). Some states are adopting new rules in these areas. Be sure you know exactly what is required to be eligible to sit for the exam. Don't make the assumption that because you hold an accounting degree, you have met all requirements. Do your research to be sure. We will assist you in this area if you have questions.

Obtain your Notice to Schedule (NTS). This is your confirmation of eligibility to sit for the exam. You will need to keep this in a safe place since it will be required for admission [along with the approved form(s) of identification] to the Prometric Center where you take the exam. The NTS also qualifies you for enrollment in the AICPA Professional Literature subscription, as noted previously.

©2007 Kaplan CPA Review

STUDY MANUAL – BUSINESS ENVIRONMENT & CONCEPTS
EXAM STRATEGIES

DETERMINE YOUR TESTING WINDOW SCHEDULE BASED ON THE STUDY PLAN YOU HAVE DEVELOPED

Again, you need to consider your professional and personal commitments. The rules for changing your testing window and any related refund for registration will vary by jurisdiction. We feel it is better to be certain and retain your scheduled testing window unless there is an emergency.

Schedule your examination appointment with Prometric. You can use the online or telephone contact information below. We recommend that you make your appointment as soon as you receive your NTS from your jurisdiction. This will ensure that your planned time and location are available.

- *www.prometric.com/cpa* (there is some very useful information on this site; visit it early in your planning).
- 800-580-9648.

We recommend you take the time to visit the Web site for the state board of accountancy in your jurisdiction to learn the process. Some states process applications directly, and some have delegated this function to the National Association of State Boards of Accountancy (NASBA). NASBA is the central organization that the AICPA works with to facilitate the grade distribution process. Some states have authorized NASBA to serve as the registration unit for their candidates. It is imperative that you know what organization is responsible for registration. This will allow you to determine their procedures, gather the appropriate information, and complete the application in a timely manner. Completion will include verification of your eligibility (i.e., sufficient hours in accounting and undergraduate coursework in compliance with your jurisdiction's requirements, which may be 150 hours).

AICPA GRADING PROCESS

We have given you information regarding the rules of the exam, which have included a comprehensive description of the how, what, when, and why of the exam's administration and delivery processes. It is important that you also know how your performance will be evaluated by the AICPA. Remember, we are concerned about you in every aspect and want to eliminate any ambiguity regarding the grading process. This will help eliminate any stress you may have over this particular issue.

The following table provides an outline of the process that occurs once you complete the exam, whether you take one section or all four sections. The table makes a distinction between the multiple-choice testlets and the simulation testlets, since the latter possess a written portion, which is manually, rather than electronically, graded.

Page 788   ©2007 Kaplan CPA Review

Function	Performer	Action
CPA exam	Candidate	Complete scheduled section(s) of exam. Once you finish a section, it is independently graded and processed. Each section is graded separately, based on its own merit. Multiple-choice testlets are graded electronically; simulations are graded both electronically (the objective questions) and manually (the writing assignment).
Exam distribution	Prometric Testing Services	Distributes candidate's electronic files to AICPA. The AICPA has the sole responsibility for grading, assembling the grades, and distributing the grades to NASBA and/or the candidate's jurisdiction.
Grading—multiple-choice testlets and objective portions of simulation testlets	AICPA	Conduct a sampling of answers to determine grading scales and any adjustments for defective questions with multiple answers. This allows the AICPA to calibrate the grading scales to reflect desired passing ranges and to consider overall candidate responses for each question. For example, if there is a noted trend on a multiple-choice question, it may indicate that the question is defective or that the intended clarity was not achieved, and consideration for an alternative answer may be valid. Review answers electronically and assign scores to candidates. Once the grading scales have been calibrated, the scoring process is electronically completed, summarized, and prepared for distribution.

STUDY MANUAL – BUSINESS ENVIRONMENT & CONCEPTS
EXAM STRATEGIES

Grading—written communications portion of simulation testlets	AICPA	Conduct a sampling of written questions to develop a grading guide for point assignment. This process mirrors the paper-based examination in regard to its manual nature in that it is still graded by humans rather than a computer. Fortunately, the graders do not have to navigate the various challenges of legibility issues that handwritten responses presented. However, they must read your response for both content and writing proficiency. The clarity, organization, accuracy, relevance, and content of your responses are critical because these characteristics will impact the graders' ability to determine your grade. If your response is not clear, then just as in the paper-based exam, the grader will make a quick determination that you are not worthy of passing the written portion of this simulation question. While the CBT exam spreads out the thousands of candidate responses throughout the year and within the window period, graders still have a large workload and have less than three minutes to look at your particular response. If in the first minute they feel you do not communicate effectively, they will suspend their effort and make a general assessment of failure.
		Execute manual review, evaluation, and grading of written communications. The written communication portion of the simulation questions is one of the reasons the exam is not like those of other professional certifications (e.g., Certified Management Accountant) that are also CBT and give immediate scoring. The written portion is still manually graded. In addition, the other professional accounting exams do not possess the public responsibility of a CPA. As a result, the AICPA and NASBA seek to control the grade distribution process, and, consequently, there will not be an immediate feedback mechanism used.
Grade distribution	NASBA/State Board of Accountancy	Distribute grades to candidate. You will receive a notice of your performance via the United States Post Office. You will not receive an e-mail or voice mail. You will receive the same paper-based notification that was used under the old exam. This is done for security and control purposes.

Now you have a customized study plan that reflects your practice and preparation needs and considers your professional and personal commitments. This plan will be your critical guide over the coming weeks to help you navigate the process of being prepared

STUDY MANUAL – BUSINESS ENVIRONMENT & CONCEPTS
EXAM STRATEGIES

for exam day. You should congratulate yourself for reaching this stage, because it reflects your commitment to investing the appropriate resources to pass the CPA exam.

TYPES OF QUESTIONS ON THE CPA EXAM

In order to prepare efficiently, you need to understand how the CPA exam questions are designed, the types of answers that are expected, and the recommended solution approach that will best help you achieve your goal of passing the CPA exam.

This chapter provides a guide based on the current approach the AICPA has developed for the CBT exam. We will discuss the multiple-choice question testlets for each section and address the different types of multiple-choice questions and recommended approaches to providing an answer. We will also do the same for the simulation questions that will be used on all of the sections except the Business Environment and Concepts.

PRESENTATION OF MULTIPLE-CHOICE QUESTIONS (MCQs)

In the rest of this chapter, you will see representative samples of every type of multiple-choice question from each of the four sections of the exam. It is key to your success that you become familiar with all the various types of questions, and that you practice with them in our materials and on the *www.cpa-exam.org* Web site. Strategy is undeniably important to your success on the exam. Take a look at the kinds of questions, and you will feel less like you are going into a mysterious event called the CPA exam. You will know what to expect, and that in itself is worth some points in your score!

We have selected multiple-choice questions (MCQs) and simulation questions from our online materials to help reinforce your study approach. This will allow you to refer to the actual section online for further review or to go back later to ensure that you understand both the question and the way it was presented.

SCREEN OUTLINE FOR MULTIPLE-CHOICE QUESTIONS

The screen for MCQs is outlined as follows for the CBT CPA exam. We feel it is important that through the AICPA tutorial and our online testlets and question bank, you become familiar and proficient with using this format and the related available tools, such as a calculator or review selection feature.

Top of Screen from Left to Right

- *AICPA logo.*
- *Testlet number* (e.g., Testlet 1 of 5).
- *Question number* (e.g., 1 of 25).
- *Time clock.* Shows remaining time for the total section, so it is counting down to zero.
- *Calculator.* You should use this online calculator for various exercises to ensure that you are comfortable with its operations. Yes, it looks and operates like the handheld calculators, as well as the one on your PC or laptop. However, we want you to feel confident with its operation so that on exam day you will not waste any unnecessary energy learning to use it.

©2007 Kaplan CPA Review

Page 791

STUDY MANUAL – BUSINESS ENVIRONMENT & CONCEPTS
EXAM STRATEGIES

- *Help.* Provides guidance on the CBT technical dimension, the MCQ aspect of the exam, and what to do if you need to ask a Prometric representative a question (does not provide help with correct answers! Sorry!).
- *Done.* Indicates that you have completed the section. Just as with most Windows-based operations, it will ask you to confirm (yes or no) your decision to leave the section through the appearance of a dialogue box.

Bottom of the Screen from Left to Right

- *Answer status.*
  - A check in one box indicates that you answered the question and are finished with that one.
  - A check in the other box indicates that you marked the question for another review. This is an important feature, whereby the question will be highlighted in a sequential list, allowing you to quickly determine which questions you need to complete prior to clicking the *Done* button.
- *Mark for review.* Allows you to mark an individual question for review, enabling a check mark to appear in the Status box.
- *Previous.* Allows you to return to the previous question when clicked.
- *Question sequence.* Indicates the answer status as follows:
  - Answered questions appear in a white box.
  - The current question appears in a black box.
  - Questions marked for review have a check that appears below the number. This allows you to identify the unanswered questions quickly so that they may be completed. We will discuss this in more detail at the end of this chapter.
- *Next.* Allows you to move to the next question.

The actual question appears in the middle of the screen in a format that you will see illustrated in the following sections. The MCQs operate in the manner of a traditional MCQ as you select your answer by clicking on a button next to one of the four answer choices. The answer status boxes will indicate your completion and election to mark for review.

It is critically important to become familiar with the screen design and the online practice tests so that you can position yourself to be successful on exam day and not be overwhelmed by the exam's method of delivery. We cannot overemphasize how important it is to be prepared for the "look and feel" of the screens.

TYPES OF MULTIPLE-CHOICE QUESTIONS

Let's first discuss the types of MCQs that exist. The two primary categories are *qualitative* and *quantitative*. *Qualitative* MCQs seek to determine your understanding of a principle and/or rule or its application, in view of a set of presented facts or procedures. In addition, some qualitative questions ask you to evaluate the four answer choices by selecting the "best," "least," or "most likely" answer. *Quantitative* questions require that you make a calculation based on a set of facts.

We have provided examples of both qualitative and quantitative MCQs with solutions from the online materials to get you familiar with both types. In addition, we have

Page 792 ©2007 Kaplan CPA Review

provided commentary regarding the type of information that was required to answer the question correctly, such as knowledge of a specific rule.

You have probably heard this advice before, but it bears repeating: Most MCQs will have a best answer, an almost correct answer, and two other answers that are much less correct! Be sure to read all the answers before making your choice. At least two of the distractors (wrong answers) are usually close to being correct. And, if you read the question too fast, or do not give adequate consideration to each answer, it will be easy for you to select the "almost" right answer. And never leave an answer blank. If you should run out of time, or have no idea, try to make an educated guess and record something. Even if you do not know the answer, you have a 25% chance of getting it correct by guessing!

BUSINESS ENVIRONMENTS AND CONCEPTS

The Business Environment and Concepts (BEC) section will test your understanding of key general business concepts, processes, practices, and emerging issues. The AICPA added the BEC section to further enhance its ability to test your proficiency in the real world of business. As we discussed earlier, the CPA exam was changed to ensure that CPAs were better educated, more well-rounded, and proficient in skills beyond the technical dimension of debits and credits. The AICPA also wanted to ensure that CPAs could effectively communicate, understand the impact of the business environment on their clients' organizations, and keep up to date with contemporary practices and emerging issues. This is reflective of a life-long learning environment, and the broadening of the role of the accounting profession and accounting professionals in business.

The specific areas of coverage consist of:

- Business Structures (corporations, partnerships, sole proprietorships).
- Economic Concepts (from your basic economics classes).
- Financial Management (from your basic finance course).
- Information Technology (basic concepts from Accounting Information Systems and Management Information Systems).
- Planning and Measurement (we used to call this Cost and Managerial accounting).

The five concepts noted above represent general knowledge categories that are not heavily rule-driven, but more factual (e.g., the types of legal entities, such as sole proprietorships, partnerships and corporations; or the key essence of the balanced scorecard). Of all parts of the CPA Exam, this is the one where frequent reading of the general business press will help you.

Remember, Finance, Economics and IT are fairly new topics for the CPA exam, and the AICPA has not yet developed simulation questions. Therefore, the BEC section consists of MCQs.

BUSINESS STRUCTURES

Business Structures is really a law topic. Most formation, operation and termination issues related to business forms derive from a law. You will see similarities between the

STUDY MANUAL – BUSINESS ENVIRONMENT & CONCEPTS
EXAM STRATEGIES

MCQs in BEC and in REG. This area will primarily test your understanding of current business structures and how they operate.

Let's review a few questions in this section so you can fully understand what to expect and will feel comfortable with your ability to successfully answer each MCQ.

> Grant and Ames are partners in a car repair business trading as G & A Services. Without authorization from Ames, Grant signed a contract for G & A Services to purchase an expensive automotive diagnostic machine from Harper Equipment, Inc. Harper Equipment, Inc., may pursue a claim for payment:
> A. against Grant and Ames.
> B. against Grant only.
> C. only against the partnership, G & A Services.
> D. against Grant, Ames or G & A Services, but only for what the cost of the equipment was to Harper Equipment, Inc.

The correct answer is A. Since G & A is a partnership, both Grant and Ames are liable, and G & A Services is liable as well, since every partner has the implied power to bind the partnership (and all partners) to contracts in the ordinary course of business. Once you understand partnerships, you will know that unless it is a limited partnership every partner is exposed to joint and several liability for activities of the entity.

Let's continue our review of business structures with a question that involves the sharing of profits.

> Lucy, Duff, and Gordon are general partners in a dress-making business. Lucy works full time in the business, while Duff and Gordon work only part-time. As a consequence of this, the partners have agreed that Lucy should receive one-half of the partnership profits. As a result:
> A. Lucy must be paid a salary.
> B. Lucy has greater voting rights than her partners.
> C. Lucy will be liable for half the losses, unless otherwise agreed.
> D. Duff and Gordon will have limited liability for partnership debts.

The correct answer is C. Unless specifically stated otherwise, profits and losses are shared equally by default. If a partnership has an agreement regarding the sharing of profits, but the agreement is silent with respect to losses, losses will be shared the same as profits. This is a fundamental concept of partnerships and is expected knowledge of anyone with a business degree, whether or not they are an accounting major. These concepts are not hard to grasp, rather they are simply general business knowledge. Much of the new material on BEC falls into the category of general business knowledge.

We should look at one more question just to make sure you see the nature and scope of the coverage in this area.

Page 794   ©2007 Kaplan CPA Review

Bernard, Chang, and Dorset are partners in a limited partnership, in which Bernard and Dorset are limited partners and Chang is the sole general partner. Chang withdraws from the partnership, but the business continues to operate. Which of the following statements is **TRUE**?
A. Withdrawal of one partner has no effect on the partnership's continued existence.
B. The partnership can avoid dissolution by replacing Chang within 90 days.
C. The limited partnership immediately dissolves.
D. The limited partnership immediately becomes a general partnership.

The correct answer is B. Under the latest version of the Uniform Limited Partnership Act, withdrawal of the sole general partner from a limited partnership no longer results in the automatic dissolution of the limited partnership. Partners have 90 days to find and replace a general partner. This question validates the importance of reviewing our online material for BEC since it represents the most current information for those sections. In this case, your old business law book or advanced accounting book may not contain the latest version of the Uniform Limited Partnership Act, and you should be careful when choosing additional materials for review.

We have covered three aspects of business structures: binding a partnership; sharing profits and losses; and what occurs when a partners leaves. We feel this is very representative of the MCQs that will be covered in the BEC section under the business structures area.

Now on to economics—the topic you enjoyed with a passion in college and hear about each day in the news. This area is tested to determine your ability to understand the macro and micro events surrounding your client.

ECONOMIC CONCEPTS

We believe that using the newspaper to stay current on the economy and reviewing our online material will provide sufficient preparation for this portion of BEC. We will provide some MCQs to demonstrate the nature of the coverage.

Economic activity does not occur at an even pace over time. An economic cycle occurs where the economy goes from a valley to a peak in activity and then repeats the cycle. Which of the following *best* describes the normal sequence of a business cycle?
A. Expansion, contraction, recession, boom.
B. Recession, contraction, boom, expansion.
C. Expansion, boom, contraction, recession.
D. Boom, contraction, expansion, recession.

The correct answer is C. This is general knowledge you would have obtained in your Economics 101 course. Now, just in case you have forgotten, here is a more detailed explanation. A series of short-term ups and downs in economic performance is a business cycle. Rather than moving along at a steady rate of growth, an economy goes through different stages of growth in production. The expansion phase is an early growth period, where: levels of income rise, unemployment remains flat or slowly begins to fall; interest

©2007 Kaplan CPA Review

STUDY MANUAL – BUSINESS ENVIRONMENT & CONCEPTS
EXAM STRATEGIES

rates are low and begin to rise; and inflation is low, but price pressure begins to build. From the expansion base the economy eventually reaches a boom phase, where: rates of production reach a peak; income growth is high; unemployment begins to reach a low; interest rates rise to high levels; and inflation becomes a problem due to excess demand as the economy reaches peak production. When the boom peaks, interest rates, inflation, and inventory levels are high. Businesses carry high inventories to accommodate strong sales. But when sales and expected sales slow due to higher interest rates, inflation, or any other factor, businesses cut investment and aggregate demand stalls or weakens. This is the start of a contraction phase. Economic performance levels are good, but the direction of growth begins to slow and ultimately reverse. Following a contraction, the economy enters a recession (defined as two successive quarters of negative growth in gross domestic product), where: unemployment rises; incomes fall; personal consumption begins to fall; business investment continues to fall; inflation rates fall; and interest rates fall. As the recession reaches its deepest point, we are in the valley of the cycle. The valley of the recession is the beginning of the next expansion phase and the cycle repeats.

Hopefully you get the point that this area is not hard; you just have to refresh your review of economic basics. Okay, let's cover one you hear in the news all the time: What makes our economy grow? You may have thought listening to the news would be of no value, but remember, the AICPA wants future CPAs to be well-informed about how the world businesses operate, which includes knowing about the economy.

> Which of the following should help promote expansion in the economy?
> A. Higher taxes.
> B. Increased imports.
> C. Falling inventory-to-sales ratio.
> D. Lower levels of government spending.

The correct answer is C. Falling inventories are an indication that consumers are buying and businesses will have to stock. The increase in production in turn means more jobs. The following answer is a bit more detailed and refers to the economic cycle discussed previously. Falling inventory-to-sales ratio will help promote an expansion. When the level of inventory is low relative to sales, businesses must increase production, bringing inventory levels back up to prevent stock-outs and lost sales. The increase in production stimulates job growth, income growth, and output growth which helps fuel an expansion. On the other hand, higher taxes take disposable income away from consumers. Lower consumer spending reduces aggregate demand and lowers economic growth. Imports are a "leakage" in that they are produced in other countries but take part of consumer disposable income. Net exports (exports – imports) contribute to higher gross domestic product (GDP), so higher imports will lower GDP. Government spending contributes to GDP, so lower spending slows down GDP growth.

Now let's look at a question with a quantitative requirement before we move on to the financial management area.

Page 796   ©2007 Kaplan CPA Review

STUDY MANUAL – BUSINESS ENVIRONMENT & CONCEPTS
EXAM STRATEGIES

If the nominal interest rate is 6% and the market expects inflation to be 2%, then the expected real interest rate must be:
A. 8%.
B. 6%.
C. 2%.
D. 4%.

The correct answer is D. You may remember this point from Economics 101. While this subject is discussed in the news, most of us have forgotten the detailed calculation. A nominal interest rate includes both the real rate and an inflation premium. It follows then that with a nominal rate of 6% and expected inflation of 2%, the difference—or real rate—must be 4%. This assumes a risk-free rate with no risk premium.

We can now proceed to the Planning and Measurement section where we expect to find a wide variety and greater number of quantitative questions.

PLANNING AND MEASUREMENT

In recent years, business leaders complained that our profession was weak in the area of planning and measurement during the 1980s and early 1990s. As a result, it is now tested on the CPA exam. Performance measurement is a major activity within management, and accounting is the key source of underlying information.

The area of Planning and Measurement covers an array of topics including cost-volume-profit analysis, planning and budgeting, cost measurement and performance measurement. We have selected both quantitative and qualitative questions so you can see the scope of coverage that we believe will be tested.

A company had sales of $2 million last year with variable costs of $1.2 million and fixed costs of $500,000. What was breakeven point?
A. $1.7 million.
B. $1.25 million.
C. $1.5 million.
D. $1.45 million.

The correct answer is B. This is a basic cost behavior analysis and cost-volume-profit question, where you must understand the cost relationships before you can calculate the breakeven point. Breakeven point (BEP) is the point where a company will make neither a profit nor a loss. So, the results of operations are set up as a formula, where:

Net income = sales – variable cost – fixed costs

Or: $NI = S - VC - FC$

And sales (S) is the unknown.

Variable costs "vary" with sales and can be expressed as a constant percentage of sales:
$VC / S = 1.2 / 2 = 0.6$

©2007 Kaplan CPA Review

Page 797

STUDY MANUAL – BUSINESS ENVIRONMENT & CONCEPTS
EXAM STRATEGIES

If variable costs are 60 percent of sales, then VC = 0.6S

Fixed costs (FC) = $500,000

Net Income (NI) = $0

Therefore: S – (0.6)S – 500,000 = 0

Solving the equation for S, we find sales at the break-even point = $1,250,000.

This is not a difficult question, and if you know the formula for calculating a BEP, you can easily answer a variety of BEP type questions.

The following question is a manipulation of the BEP equation since one of the variables, fixed costs, is missing. Once you know the formula for BEP, you will be prepared to respond to any version of MCQ.

Last year, a company had sales of $500,000, variable costs of $300,000, and a net loss of $40,000. How much must sales *increase* this year in order for the company to make a net income equal to 10% of sales?
A. $90,000.
B. $200,000.
C. $300,000.
D. $210,000.

The correct answer is C. Here fixed costs are not known, and the figure must be determined before the equation can be established to solve for sales (and the needed increase in sales). From last year we know:

S – VC – FC = NI, so: 500,000 – 300,000 – FC = (40,000)

So fixed costs must have been $240,000. That figure can then be used in making the computation for the current year, recognizing that "fixed" implies no change relative to changes in sales. Also notice in this problem that variable costs are again 60% of sales since 300,000 / 500,000 = 0.6. Finally, we would like to generate an income that is 10% of the current year's sales. So: S – 0.6S – 240,000 = 0.1S

Solving for S, we determine that sales must be $800,000 in order to meet the target net income.

Since the question asks about the increase in sales, the final answer is $300,000 or the difference between this year's and last year's sales. Once again this MCQ was not difficult and is similar to the last question, where it relies on the formula for BEP.

The following is a good example of a qualitative or conceptual MCQ.

Page 798   ©2007 Kaplan CPA Review

STUDY MANUAL – BUSINESS ENVIRONMENT & CONCEPTS
EXAM STRATEGIES

A balanced scorecard is a methodology for assessing an organization's business performance via four major components of the organization. Which of the following *most accurately* outlines those four major components?

A. Financial areas, internal business processes, employee characteristics and satisfaction, and innovation and improvement activities.
B. Marketing areas, internal business processes, customer characteristics and satisfaction, and innovation and improvement activities.
C. Financial areas, external business processes, customer characteristics and satisfaction, and innovation and improvement activities.
D. Financial areas, internal business processes, customer characteristics and satisfaction, and innovation and improvement activities.

The correct answer is D. The key here is to determine what has a direct impact on an organization's overall business performance. Management would certainly be concerned with employee concerns, characteristics, and job satisfaction, as well as external business processes. However, these are indirect business performance metrics on a balanced scorecard. Customer attributes and satisfaction are directly related to business performance. Marketing areas are also very important but would fall within the innovation and improvement activities.

These three MCQ examples demonstrate the level of coverage in the Planning and Measurement area. Let's now review the coverage under the Information Technology section.

INFORMATION TECHNOLOGY

This is a broad area within BEC. It's a lot of vocabulary and very basic concepts that you probably already know. The AICPA does not expect you to be a systems analyst, but you are expected to possess a general understanding of information technology, since it is a critical dimension of business and is especially relevant to the accounting profession.

Our first question is not difficult, and anyone who was in school or graduated around the era of Y2K should know about ERPs.

Enterprise Resource Planning (ERP) systems are integrated software applications designed to provide complete integration of an organization's business information processing systems. Certain activities within an ERP system, such as entering client data, managing different levels of inventory, and any specialized subsystem of the MIS related to accounting are all considered integral parts of the enterprise system. Which of the following specific systems is **NOT** considered part of the accounting information system of the ERP application?

A. Taxation.
B. Land, building, and equipment recordation.
C. Cash management.
D. Payroll.

The correct answer is C. This question required you to understand the components of an ERP system related to a particular function. Tax accounting, capital asset accounting, and payroll accounting are all integral parts of the accounting and reporting function, and

©2007 Kaplan CPA Review

Page 799

STUDY MANUAL – BUSINESS ENVIRONMENT & CONCEPTS
EXAM STRATEGIES

would be included in the accounting information system. Cash management, along with financial forecasting, portfolio management, and credit analysis, are all functions of the separate financial information systems. These are not difficult concepts, but they do require you to be current on the subject matter.

Let's look at one more question so we can see the diversity of coverage in this area.

> Which of the following types of reports are **NOT** considered a particular category of accounting information systems reports?
> A. Summary reports.
> B. Detail reports.
> C. Exception reports.
> D. Incremental reports.

The correct answer is D. The incremental report is not one of the normal outcomes of an accounting system. Accounting information systems must be able to generate summary reports, which include the balance sheet, income statement, statement of cash flows, and statement of equity changes. These reports should depict accurate information and conform to GAAP—at any level of detail. Three types of reporting are defined by accounting information systems: detail reports, which list detailed information, perhaps account balances; summary reports, which outline summarized information, such as balances summarized by geographic divisions; and exception reports, which list exceptions to normal reporting, such as a report on sales that do not meet a plan. You could at this point ask "what about the incremental report, which is not as common as the first two." This is why it is critical to practice taking MCQs in each of the areas within all of the sections to gain an understanding of the terminology used—so if there is something you are not familiar with, you can overcome this limitation prior to the exam.

The final area we will cover here, Financial Management, is one of the newest additions to the exam.

FINANCIAL MANAGEMENT

Financial Management topics include many from your basic finance course in college. There is some overlap between finance and accounting, so this is helpful here. Topics tested include financial models such as cash flow, net present value, internal rate of return, and payback, along with the tax considerations of these methods. Financing options, cost of capital, derivatives, and cash management are included. Financial statement analysis (ratios) is included here as well.

Let's review an example of what we might expect to find for MCQs in this area.

Page 800

©2007 Kaplan CPA Review

A BBB-rated Simpson Company bond pays a coupon rate of 6.5% (paid semiannually) and has a maturity of 10 years. The market rate of interest on bonds of similar risk (BBB) and maturity (10 years) is currently 7.5%. The price of this bond will be:

A. greater than face value.
B. equal to face value.
C. cannot be determined from the information given.
D. less than face value.

The correct answer is D. The Simpson bond pays $65 a year (6.5 percent of face value, which is by definition $1,000), while other bonds of the same maturity and risk are paying $75 in interest. Bonds of the same maturity and risk must provide the same total yield to maturity (YTM). Therefore, investors will bid down the price of this bond until its YTM is 7.5 percent. Rules of thumb: if the coupon rate is less than the market rate of interest (MRI) it will sell at a discount; if the coupon rate is greater than the MRI, it will sell at a premium; if the coupon equals the MRI, the bond will sell at face or par value. Here's a good example of a question that could easily be in BEC finance or FAR bonds.

Again, though not difficult, this section of the exam requires you to be current on a lot of material. We will help you review these concepts so that you are prepared for exam day.

FINAL COMMENTS ABOUT MCQs

The CBT CPA exam offers a valuable tool to assist you with executing your review process—*mark for review*. As described previously, this feature allows you to visually see all of the questions you have not completed. Once you have sequentially gone through a testlet and answered as many questions as possible, you should go back through and complete those that remain unanswered.

We want you to use your time wisely. When you approach a question, review the context of the question or its actual "question" prior to looking at the answer choices. Then apply the recommended approach to selecting an answer. If a question appears to be too difficult to resolve, continue on to the next question. Do not let a question frustrate you or cause any stress. Do not waste a lot of time on a question you do not know the answer to. The key is to remain positive and confident, so do what is necessary to maintain your composure and progress through the exam, knowing that you are managing your time toward a successful completion.

Once you have answered all of the questions you feel comfortable with, return to those you skipped. Perhaps by answering the other questions, your memory was jolted and/or your confidence has been boosted so that you can tackle these remaining questions effectively. Amazingly, sometimes you may "learn" an idea in a subsequent question that reminds you of the answer to a previous one.

It is critical that you complete every question. The CPA exam does not penalize guessing like some other exams you may have taken. While we want you to be prepared and minimize guessing—please do not leave any question blank. Your attempt will at least increase the possibility of receiving some points—and we hope we have prepared you to

STUDY MANUAL – BUSINESS ENVIRONMENT & CONCEPTS
EXAM STRATEGIES

take an educated guess on those questions where you are unclear of the approach. Never, never, never leave blanks.

Finally, time management is a required skill of CPAs; it was expected on the paper-based exam, and it is just as essential on the CBT exam. Always be aware of your time and keep an eye on the "remaining time" feature on your screens. You will actually have plenty of time, and many candidates will leave early. You will probably be surprised to learn that you do have sufficient time. But use that time wisely and maximize the amount of benefit in terms of points scored! Practice working with time constraints when you are preparing for the exam.

PREPARATION FOR THE EXAM

Now it's time to practice, and, as they say, practice makes perfect. You are now aware of how the exam is scheduled throughout the year, as well as what is required in terms of your eligibility to sit for the exam. Let's now concentrate on how to practice, so you will be prepared on exam day.

APPROACH

All work and no play will burn you out and result in fatigue, impairing your ability to be successful on exam day. To avoid this problem, we have developed a holistic approach to studying for the exam. Our Kaplan Activity Planner balances your preparation period by considering what it will take to pass the exam, while also recognizing that you have a full personal and professional life. We do not recommend that you put your personal life, including social and health management–related activities, completely on hold until you take the exam. In fact, we strongly encourage you to take time out, enjoy yourself, and relax periodically. This will allow you to return to your preparation activities with energy, enthusiasm, and clarity.

Now that you have elected to take the exam, you must look ahead at your schedule and consider your forthcoming personal and professional commitments. You may then make a realistic decision on how many sections of the exam you will take and when. You have 18 months to complete the entire exam successfully once you have passed any one of the four sections. For example, if you pass Auditing and Attestation in the January/February testing window, you have 18 months from that time forward to pass the other three sections. We feel confident that our process for exam preparation will enable you to complete the exam successfully within this time period.

PROGRESS EVALUATION

Kaplan has assembled an array of online materials to assist you with monitoring your preparation, as well as its quality and effectiveness. By using Kaplan's tools, you will always know how your study is progressing. The tools will indicate whether or not you have mastered a given subject matter and focus your attention on areas where you are not performing as well.

Page 802   ©2007 Kaplan CPA Review

So how can you measure your progress? Each time you take a test in a specific subject area, you receive a comprehensive view of where you stand. Testing also gives you the chance to see the actual testing condition. Once you complete the testlet, you can review your scores as well as an explanation for each answer to determine why you missed any particular question. This will provide you with a progress evaluation that should agree with what you have documented on your planner.

As you proceed through the practice season, the Planner will identify specific testlets for you to complete, which, as noted earlier, will serve as an ongoing evaluation of your performance. You will also receive daily progress reports as you complete each set of assigned problems. Our online material will allow you to score your performance immediately, with detailed results and answer solutions. In essence, our comprehensive program provides a continuous evaluation mechanism in the form of the assigned questions and problems, testlets, and simulation questions. In addition, you have the opportunity to go beyond the recommended questions for more practice in a particular subject area. Each of these additional tests operates in the same manner as the assigned problems, allowing you to obtain immediate feedback.

We hope this method of evaluation will serve as a source of encouragement. As you progress, we expect that your scores will improve. Use your improvement to boost your self esteem and confidence, and know that your hard work will pay off on exam day. Are you still visualizing that CPA certificate on your wall?

FINAL STRETCH

It's the fourth quarter and you have a comfortable lead. You have scheduled to take the exam on July 10, and it is now July 1. You may have told all of your friends and relatives that you cannot attend any of the Fourth of July festivities. Wrong! Now is just the time to take a break, and we will show you how to take a break and still be prepared. Having some fun in the final stretch is okay. After working so hard, you deserve a break!

We have outlined some key steps to follow during that final stretch period. Following, you will find a reference tool that you can use during the final few days before the exam to guide your activities effectively. Keep in mind, if you have consistently tested at a level of 80% or more, you are already testing at a level above the minimum passing rate of 75%. This fact should help keep your anxiety level down and enhance your confidence.

Also, understand there are certain things you should not do during the following few days. Do not try to learn new material. Doing so will cause unnecessary stress. Do not focus on areas of material that you don't know well or have consistently failed during the review period. Instead, focus on those areas where you have performed well and feel confident. Remember, you do not need to score 100%. Relax and look back at how well you have done during the practice period. You should review with a smile on your face, knowing that your hard work will allow you to take the exam with confidence.

©2007 Kaplan CPA Review

Page 803

STUDY MANUAL – BUSINESS ENVIRONMENT & CONCEPTS
EXAM STRATEGIES

FINAL STRETCH REFERENCE GUIDE

Use the following guide on July 1 to review your work during the practice season. The guide serves as a checklist and, hopefully, confirmation of your efforts to pass the CPA exam. We have listed seven questions, which we want you to answer.

Tip: Print this guide and place it on top of each of the planners that you have in use (e.g., Financial Accounting and Reporting).

Once you have completed your comments next to each question, step back and see where you stand. Answering yes to questions 1, 2, and 3 indicates that you have followed our recommendations for executing a structured process of exam preparation. It also shows that your hard work has consistently scored at 75% or better, which is what you need to pass the exam. Answering "no" to any of the seven questions is your indication of where to review during the coming days.

The remaining four questions will determine how you feel about navigating the exam (e.g., MCQ or simulation questions, or the specific CBT technology). If you have issues or concerns in this area, please feel free to e-mail us, or review the AICPA tutorial again to make sure you are comfortable with the technology. In terms of format issues, you can also go back to Chapter 3 in this chapter for additional review.

Assuming you launch the Final Stretch period on July 1, you have nine days to answer questions 1 through 7 in the Final Stretch Reference Guide. This will allow you time to review what you have covered, evaluate how well you performed, review the technology, and determine your proficiency in answering questions in a variety of formats. Hopefully, you will complete the guide and get the big picture! That is: you have read, reviewed, and completed a vast amount of material over the past 40 days; you were committed, faithful, and diligent; and you are ready to give your best on exam day.

It is critical that you do not allow the rigors of the preparation process to overwhelm, discourage, or distract you from the overall goal of becoming a CPA. Yes, it is a lot of work, but the rewards are outstanding, and you deserve to experience all of them. Therefore, we have developed a "CPA Survival Guide," which is a digital pocket guide of recommendations that we hope you will use to succeed in your goal of becoming a CPA.

Action Steps	Candidates Review Comments
1. Have you completed all key steps outlined in the Kaplan Activity Planner?	
2. Did you score at least 75% on all of the key topic areas?	
3. Did you review any area where you did not score 75%? If so, how did you do on the next test?	

4. Are there any areas where you still have trouble? What are they? What is the expected coverage on the exam?	
5. Overall, how do you feel about the qualitative multiple-choice questions?	
6. Overall, how do you feel about the qualitative/subjective simulation questions?	
7. Do you feel comfortable with the exam technology? Did you use the tutorial on the AICPA Web site? Have you used our testlets, which look just like the new CBT CPA exam technology? Did you have any trouble navigating through the technology?	

In the next section, we will continue with our review of preparation for the exam, but our focus will be on exam day. We will use the same example (i.e., sitting for the exam on July 10) to help illustrate our key points.

REST, REST, AND REST

It is the night before the exam, and all through the house not a soul is stirring, not even your computer mouse. That is exactly the atmosphere we want for you: peaceful and quiet the evening before the exam. The Final Stretch Reference Tool provided above will direct you to conduct a high-level review, but we don't want you to do anything on the day before the exam other than the following:

1. **Take the day of July 9 off from work; schedule a vacation or personal day, whatever is available.** If your family environment mandates, check into a hotel the night before the exam. Yes, that means in addition to the day(s) required to sit for two sections, you will also need a day of rest prior to the exam. Therefore, assuming you take one section per day, you will need a minimum of three days.

2. **Locate your Notice to Schedule (NTS).** Make sure you place the NTS next to your two forms of identification to ensure you will have it with you when you proceed to the exam on July 10.

3. **Go to the Internet and print out the directions to the testing site.** We actually recommend you do this when you first receive your NTS. Hopefully, you have physically visited the location and know all of the alternative routes in case of heavy traffic.

4. **Review the rules for Prometric Testing Centers.** The AICPA and NASBA, along with Prometric's standard policies, prohibit candidates from wearing certain articles of clothing without significant security reviews. This is intended to prevent the use of electronic devices such as hidden cameras or unauthorized transmitters.

STUDY MANUAL – BUSINESS ENVIRONMENT & CONCEPTS
EXAM STRATEGIES

We recommend that you go to *www.prometric.com/Sites/TestCenterTour.htm* and take the Test Center Tour. The tour will give you a feel for the site, your expected arrival time, a description of the process, and a list of "do's and don'ts."

5. **Look in your closet and locate comfortable clothes.** Remember to follow the instructions from the Prometric Web site, and adhere to the limitations of what you can wear and take to the exam.

6. **Go to your kitchen and identify what you will eat for breakfast.** Make sure the breakfast you select is something that will promote energy, rather than upset your stomach or cause any other unwanted side effects.

7. **Get a good night's sleep.** Now it is time to go to bed. If you have cable or satellite service, find a comedian, listen to a joke, and go to bed prepared to sleep and dream about the sweet success to come.

GUIDANCE ON EXAM DAY

Finally, it's July 10 and it's a beautiful morning. It is time to go outside and conquer the world of passing the CPA exam. This is the day we have been waiting for. Just like the Olympians who practice very hard in hopes of earning a gold medal, you have also worked very hard. Just remember, a bronze is good enough to pass the exam, but keep your eye on the gold medal.

So here we are. We have done what we promised. If you followed our steps, you should be prepared and ready to demonstrate just how well you know the underlying material. Before you leave for the Prometric Testing Center, please remember the following:

1. Be confident—you worked really hard to be prepared.

2. Do not forget your NTS and two forms of identification (e.g., driver's license and passport).

3. You will be provided with calculators, scratch paper, and pencils, along with lockers for small bags or wallets. Based on our discussions in Chapter 3, these are the only items you should bring to the exam. The only other thing to bring is the knowledge that you have acquired over the past few weeks and the confidence that you are prepared!

4. Remember to view the Prometric site at *www.prometric.com/cpa* or take the tour of the testing center at *www.prometric.com/Sites/TestCenterTour.htm* and make sure you follow their specific instructions.

5. Do not bring large bags, briefcases, or laptops, because they will not be allowed and they do not fit in the lockers. If you bring such items, you will have to go back to your car or even back home (if you did not drive), which could adversely impact your time.

Page 806   ©2007 Kaplan CPA Review

One last thing before you leave home: look in the mirror and what do you see? We see a CPA in the making, and the next step is successfully passing the sections you are taking today.

POST-EXAM ANALYSIS

You have just completed one of the most significant testing marathons of your life. How do you feel? You may be exhausted, but, hopefully, you feel relieved and confident. If you followed our program, you should have had some time to relax as you studied for the exam. Now you have to wait for the results. Even though the exam is computer-based, there are still portions that are manually graded the old-fashioned way. What should you do in the mean time? Do you wonder what you missed and think back about each question to see if you made a mistake? Certainly not! We want you to enjoy the break and think ahead to the remaining sections with optimism. Do not spend time reliving the exam you just completed. Most people who spend time trying to analyze their own results will underestimate how well they did. Move on. Have some fun. Don't try to mentally grade your own exam. Wait for the results before you even think about that section again.

The CBT is still too new to assess pass rates and trends. However, the AICPA has noted that the first CBT exam takers passed at a rate of around 45%. This rate is higher than the pass rate of the paper-based test. We sincerely hope that you are in that 45% group, and feel that we can make the difference when it comes to your success. We now recommend that you resume your regular schedule and not dwell on or worry about the results.

IT'S IN THE MAIL

The scores have finally arrived. Let's have a drum roll as you open the envelope. You open the envelope and find that you passed Financial Accounting and Reporting with a score of 76%, but failed to pass Auditing and Attestation at 65%. Congratulations, you deserve to celebrate! You have just passed part of the CPA exam, and you are on your way to earning one of the toughest professional certifications in the world.

What we need to do now is find out what happened with Auditing and Attestation. You did so well on the practice questions, testlets, and simulations that we were sure you would pass. Let's go back to the score reporting envelope and look at the diagnostic analysis of your score by each testlet, along with the additional analysis of your score by the AICPA Content Specification Outline (see the Appendix for further details). This analysis should tell you how you performed on the MCQs, and two simulation testlets by topic area. For example, you will know if you did well on the MCQs but performed poorly on the simulation tests. Use this information to direct your review for the next exam.

You should also review your score for the section that you passed to identify any trends (e.g., you performed marginally on the simulation questions in that section as well). Any such trends would suggest the need to work harder at becoming more proficient and comfortable with the simulation format questions.

©2007 Kaplan CPA Review

Page 807

STUDY MANUAL – BUSINESS ENVIRONMENT & CONCEPTS
EXAM STRATEGIES

So now you know your score. You passed one of the two sections and came very close to passing the other section. We still want you to celebrate and have some fun. When you return, we have more work to do; you now have 18 months remaining to become a CPA.

We hope you have found this chapter to be a beneficial preparation tool. As you continue preparing for the remainder of the CPA exam, be sure to use this chapter as one of your central resources for navigation and support.

INDEX

1st generation 426
2nd generation 426
3-factor analysis of factory overhead variances 391
3rd generation 426
4th generation 426
5th generation 427

A

absorption costing 710
absorption method 295
access control 483
access to partnership information 59
accountant's involvement in information system
    development 729
accounting costs 291, 606
accounting information system (AIS) 439, 722
accounting profit 578, 605, 757
accounting profit risks 758
accounting rate of return (ARR) 331, 695
accounts receivable management 134
acquisition & implementation 745
activity or efficiency ratios 687
activity-based costing 298, 713
actual authority 55, 66
actual cost system 298, 302
ad hoc reporting 733
adaptive 732
add-on interest (installment loans) 693
admission into an existing partnership 63
aggregate demand 511, 514, 762
aggregate supply 510, 762
AICPA testing goals 774
AIS and corporate strategy 452
alien corporation 9
alternate processing facilities 740
alternative measures of cash flow (CF) 694
amendments to the articles 31
American option 232
American options 234
American vs. European options 704
analysis 727
annual meetings 22

annual percentage rate (APR) 693
annual percentage yield (APY) 174
annual reports 95
annuity 208
apparent authority 55, 62, 66
application controls 480, 745
application data management 719
application processing modes 427
application software 425
applications programmers 458, 738
appraisal costs 386
array 720
articles of incorporation 9, 677
articles of organization 74
asset turnover 102
at-the-money 233
audit trail 746
authorized capital stock 17
authorized stock 679
automated 723
automated data entry 476, 740
availability 490
average age of inventory 687
average collection period 107, 687

B

backflush 713
balance of payments 663
balance sheet hedging 656, 770
bank loans and interest notes 690
bankruptcy 758
bargaining power of customers 754
bargaining power of suppliers 754
barriers to entry 560, 567, 570
basis risk 224
batch processing 430, 732
benchmark 685
benefit and cost ratio 696
block coding 721
blue-sky laws 11
board of directors 13, 24
bond 16

©2007 Kaplan CPA Review

Page 809

STUDY MANUAL – BUSINESS ENVIRONMENT & CONCEPTS
INDEX

bond indenture 700
bond maturity 701
bond terminology 700
bond yield plus risk premium 697
bonds 700
boom 759
brand or promotional identity 754
breach of fiduciary duty 24
breakeven 210
breakeven analysis 209
breakeven calculation 259
breakeven point 256, 710
breakeven sales 259
budget 330
budget variance 392
budgeting 328
budgets 329
buffer 742
business 723
business continuity 739
business continuity planning 469
business cycle 441, 509, 559, 759
business event cycle 720
business event data/transaction data 721
business event occurs 732
business information systems 722
business judgment rule 27
business process reengineering 730
business risk 222, 753
business structure 8, 677
buyers vs. the writer of an option 704
bylaws 13
by-product 327, 714

C

calculation example 697
call options 231
callable 700
calls 227, 233
cannibalization 172, 694
CAN-SPAM 488
capital asset pricing model (CAPM) 174, 178, 702
capital budgeting 164, 171, 331, 694
capital budgeting techniques 332
capital components 175
capital projects 164
capital rationing 174
capital requirements 754
capital structure 131, 137

capital structure policy 182
capital surplus 19
capitalization 16, 57
carrying costs 337
cash 688
cash budget 328
cash conversion cycle 688
cash flow 97, 757
cash flow for capital budgeting 171
cash from operations from the SCF 694
cash management 132
cash management techniques 688
cash turnover 688
centralized data storage 199
certificate of incorporation 9, 678
Certified Information Technology Professional (CITP) 427, 724
change in quantity demanded 516
change in technology 749
change management 457, 491, 730
changes in demand 516
changes in quantity supplied 518
changes in supply 654
changes in supply curves 518
character 720
charging order 58
Chief Information Officer (CIO) 738
chief security officer 487
classification of data 721
client-server relationship 741
close (or closely held) corporation 9
coefficient of correlation 293, 708
coefficient of determination 293
cold site 469, 740
collusion 569, 570
commercial paper (CP) 691
common shareholders 18
common stock 679, 701
commonly used indexes 703
common-size analysis 96
common-size financial statements 97
compensating balance 690
competition 556, 562, 570, 598, 631
competitive (price-taker) market 574
competitive advantage 561, 565
competitive environment of the firm 753
competitive strategy 561, 564
complement goods 748
component costs of capital 175
composite indexes 704

Page 810 ©2007 Kaplan CPA Review

compound interest 204
computational procedure 703
computer emergency response team (CERT) 487
computer fraud and abuse techniques 491, 493
computer operators 458, 738
computer-based storage 428
concentration banking 689
conceptual 743
confidentiality 487
consequences of entry and forms of retaliation 754
consideration 679
consolidation 32
constant growth DDM 701
constitutional rights 11
consumer choice 523, 527
consumer price index (CPI) 587, 621, 761
consumer staples 760
continuous life 678
contraction 759
contractionary fiscal policies 763
contractionary open market operations 764
contribution margin 257, 295, 710
control 743
control activities 495, 744
control environment 744, 745
control objectives 480
control objectives for information and related technology 745
control plans 745
controllable costs 291
controllable factory overhead variance 716
controls 745
conversion costs 298, 711
convertible bonds 698
convertible preferred stock 19
corporate charter 9
corporate risk 173
corporation 677, 678
corporation by estoppel 14
corporations 9
corrective 732
corrective control 480, 486
correlation analysis 292, 708
cost accounting 711
cost behavior 297, 308
cost categories 297
cost center 388
cost driver 299, 711, 713
cost drivers 299
cost flow for manufacturing 306

cost measurement 290
cost of capital 174, 182, 248, 331
cost of capital calculation 697
cost of debt 697
cost of goods manufactured 302
cost of goods sold 305
cost of new common stock 697
cost of preferred stock 697
cost of retained earning 697
cost pools 299
cost systems 302
cost/volume/profit 256
cost-push inflation 762
costs 605
cost-volume-profit analysis 255, 709
coverage ratios 687
CPA candidate bulletin 781
CPA exam 775
CPA website 781
credit risk 222, 699
credit spread risk 222
cross-section analysis 686
cumulative 25
cumulative preferred stock 18
currency exchange rate movements 651
currency exposure 649, 657, 664
currency fall 768
currency hedge 707
currency options 656, 770
currency rise 768
currency risk 648, 652, 664, 765
currency risk exposures 769
current ratio 106, 686
current yield 700
customer relationship management systems (CRM) 443, 731
cyclical unemployment 554, 590
cyclicals 760

D

daily mark to market 706
daily price change limits 706
data 422, 724
data capture 733
data control 459
data dictionary 742
data entry controls 489
data flow diagrams (DFDs) 734
data hierarchy 720

STUDY MANUAL – BUSINESS ENVIRONMENT & CONCEPTS
INDEX

data input 449
data maintenance 733
data model 735
data processing 449, 451
data storage 450
data transmission controls 489
data validation 427
data warehousing and data mining 721
database 719, 720
database administrators (DBAs) 459, 737
database management system (DBMS) 719
database mapping 736
database systems 428
de facto corporation 13, 679
de jure corporation 13, 679
debenture 17
debenture vs. a mortgage bond 700
debt 16
debt financing 248
debt ratios 686
debt to equity ratio 686
debt, cost of 176
debt-to-equity ratio 108
decision making 724
decision support systems (DSS) 443, 726
declaration date 20
default risk 206, 222, 699
defective incorporation 13
defense-in-depth 485
deflation 592, 762
delivery & support 745
demand curve 511, 516, 521, 550, 567, 599, 624, 747
demand for money 624
demand inflation 762
depository transfer checks 689
derivatives 221, 225, 704
detecting computer fraud 493
detective controls 480, 486
determinants of exchange rates 230
differentiation strategies 751
digital image processing systems 476, 740
direct (or variable) costing 709
direct labor 387, 711
direct labor budget 329
direct labor variance 388
direct material 290, 711
direct material variance 399
direct materials efficiency 388
direct materials price variance 387
direct or variable method 295

director's authority 25
directors 20, 678
director's duty of loyalty 27
disaster recovery 469, 491
disaster recovery and business continuity 739
discontinuing a segment 339
discount interest 693
discount rate 764
discounted cash flow analysis 175
discounted payback 695
discounted payback method 166
discounting 206
disposable income 589
dissociation 64, 682
dissolution 33, 64, 680
distributed processing 431, 720
distribution channels 754
dividend discount model (DDM) 697, 701
dividend in kind 20
dividend policy 144, 182
dividends 19, 680
DJIA 703
domain 478, 742
domain name server (DNS) 478, 742
domestic corporation 9, 14
DOS 718
double taxation 678, 684
downgrade risk 222
DuPont Analysis 686
DuPont system 99
durable goods 751
duration measures interest rate risk 699
duration mismatch 707
duties imposed upon partners 61
duty of care 61
duty of loyalty 61

E

early expansion 510
earned surplus 19
earnings or net income 757
earnings per share 758
ease of raising capital 10
EBIT 140
e-business 477
economic costs 606
economic measures 585
economic order quantity 337, 708
economic order quantity (EOQ) point 689

Page 812

©2007 Kaplan CPA Review

economic profit 212, 516, 567, 605

economic regulation 630

economic risk 665

economic value added (EVA) 213, 698

economics of the firm 747

economies of scale 558, 563, 754

effective annual rate (EAR) 174, 623, 693

effective annual yield (EAY) 763

effectiveness of operations 744

effects of monetary policy 627

effects of the business cycle 513

efficient resources 744

elastic 750

elastic demand curve 515

elasticity 522, 530, 594

elasticity of demand 529

electronic commerce 474, 740

electronic data interchange (EDI) 474, 741

electronic document management (EDM) 740

electronic funds transfer (EFT) 477, 741

electronic mail (e-mail) 476, 740

electronic store fronts 477, 741

elements of the accounting information system 724

eligibility requirements 10

embedded options 247

encryption 486, 487

enterprise resource planning systems (ERP Systems) 442

enterprise-wide risk management (ERM) 198

entity relationship diagrams 735

entry barriers 566

equation of exchange 625

equilibrium 519, 550, 574, 625, 630, 652, 663, 752

equilibrium adjustment process 520

equity insolvency test 19

equity risk 222

equity turnover 107

equivalent annual annuity 696

equivalent units (EU) of production 303

ERM system 199

ERP Modules 723

estimate of P/E multiple 703

estoppel 681

Eurobonds 701

European options 234, 235

event data processing 720

event risk 223

exam strategies 773

excess demand inflation 759

exchange rates 230

exchange risk 230

exchanges 704

executive information systems (EIS) or executive support systems (ESS) 443, 726

expansion 759

expansionary fiscal policies 763

expansionary open market operations 764

expectations 748

expectations theory 692

expenditure approach 620

expert systems (ES) 443, 726

explicit costs 605, 606

exposure to a currency 768

exposures 768

express powers 16

external 743

external failure costs 386

externalities 172, 694

extranets 426

extraordinary transactions 680

F

factoring 690

factors affecting business cycle 511

factors in constructing indexes 703

factory overhead 711

factory overhead applied 390

factory overhead budget 329

factory overhead control 300

factory overhead variance 390, 715

fiduciary duty 12, 66

field 720

FIFO system 712

file 720

file organization 718

filing 13

financial flexibility 139, 248

financial indices 703

financial leverage 102, 103, 140, 142, 223, 758

financial management 685

financial modeling 204

financial models 699

financial risk 223

financial statement analysis 92, 96, 114

financial statement analysis, steps of 97

financing current and fixed assets 690

finished goods account 305

finished goods inventory 306

firewall 485

firm performance and sensitivity to the economy 757

fiscal policy 763
fixed costs 209, 255, 290, 308, 531, 558, 600, 631, 709
fixed exchange rate 767
fixed vs. variable rates 691
flexible budgeting system 710
flexible budgets 330, 390
float 688, 766
floating-rate bonds 246
floating-rate securities 246
flowchart symbols 734
flowcharts 504
foreign bonds 701
foreign corporation 9, 14
Foreign Corrupt Practices Act 494
foreign currency 557, 598, 648, 655, 664
foreign exchange market 557, 598
foreign exchange quotations 664
foreign exchange risk 223, 229
forward contracts 235, 658
forward currency contracts 656, 770
forward exchange rate 236
forward interest rate 236
forward price 236
forwards 235, 660
free cash flow (FCF) 98, 694
free transferability of interests 10
frictional unemployment 553, 590
full employment 590
fundamental changes in structure 30
future currency contracts 656, 770
future margins 661
future value 204
futures 235, 241, 656
futures markets 706
futures price 236

G

Gantt charts or PERT (program evaluation review
    techniques) 730
general control issues 483
general controls 480
general partnership 53, 677
global currency risks and hedging 765
governance 20
government policy 570, 619, 754
grading process 788
gross domestic product (GDP) 509, 554, 585, 650, 761
gross margin 307, 687
gross national product (GNP) 586, 596, 761

gross profit 290
gross profit margin 107, 290
group support systems (GSS) 443, 726

H

hardware 423, 716
hedge 706, 768
hedging 239, 652, 664
hedging alternatives 657
help desk 459, 738
hierarchical 736
hierarchical coding 721
high income elasticity 758, 760
high price elasticity 758
high-availability clustering 471
higher income growth 768
higher inflation 768
higher real interest rates 768
high-low method 293, 294, 708
home page 478, 742
hot site 469, 740
hypertext markup language (HTML) 478, 742
hybrid financing alternatives 697

I

illegal dividends 23
imperfect competition 755
implementation (deployment or fielding) 727
implicit costs 605, 606
implied powers 16
in/at/out of the money options 705
income effect 534
income elasticity of demand 751
incorporation technicalities 12
incorporation, advantages of 10
incorporation, disadvantages of 11
incorporator 9
incremental analysis 341
incremental cash flows 171, 694
incremental costs 343
incremental or differential costs 339
index futures 236
index futures hedge 707
index of leading economic indicators 761
index puts 706
indifference curve analysis 533
indifference curves 532
industry comparison 104

Page 814   ©2007 Kaplan CPA Review

industry competition 753
industry life cycle 557, 565
industry pricing practices 560
industry profitability 561
inelastic demand curve 515
inferior 751
inflation 172, 554, 587, 621, 649, 663, 758
inflation premium 204
inflation risk 223
inflation, real interest rates, and income 768
information 422, 724
information and communication 441, 744
information output 451
information processing 733
information system librarian 458
information systems function 742
information technology (IT) 716
input 719
input devices 716
input prices 749
inputs to DDM 702
inside directors 25
integrated risk-analysis 200
integrity controls 489
intelligent agents 443, 727
interest coverage 108
interest expense rate 102
interest on loans 691
interest payments 701
interest rate cycle follows the business cycle 763
interest rate hedge 707
interest rate risk 223, 699
interest rate sensitive 758
interest rate swap 707
interest rates 622
internal 743
internal control 480
internal control goals 744
internal control system failure 744
internal failure costs 386
internal rate of return (IRR) method 168, 695
international indexes 704
international markets 517, 526, 648
Internet 426, 717
Internet based transactions 475, 741
Internet commerce 477, 741
in-the-money 233
intranet 717
intrinsic value 233
inventory 689

inventory accounts 305
inventory cost 295
inventory management 113, 336
inventory methods 112
inventory misstatements 111
inventory turnover 107, 687
investment center 291
investment decision 753
investment policy 182
investors 686
invisible hand 520, 552
issued 17, 23
issued stock 679
IT Control 479
IT Fundamentals 716
IT Roles and Responsibilities 457

J

JIT inventory 296
job order cost accounting 712
job order cost system 304
joint and several liability 63
joint costs 713
joint liability 681
joint product costs 326
joint products 326
joint venture 68
judicial dissolution 681
just-in-time 709

K

Kaplan Activity Planner 784

L

labor market 553, 556, 589, 597
late expansion 510
law of agency 54
law of diminishing marginal returns 522
law of diminishing marginal utility 524, 525
law of diminishing returns 536, 606
laws of supply and demand 515
leaps 705
leasing alternatives 115
legal and regulatory risk 224
letter of credit (LOC) 691
leverage 99, 113, 137
liabilities of a partner 63

STUDY MANUAL – BUSINESS ENVIRONMENT & CONCEPTS
INDEX

LIBOR 134, 246, 691
librarians 738
limitations of DDMs 702
limitations of GDP 588, 622
limited liability 10, 678
limited liability company 74
limited liability limited partnership 677
limited liability noncorporate entities 73
limited partnership 69, 677, 683
line of credit 690
liquidation 17, 34
liquidation value 703
liquidity analysis 98, 112
liquidity preference theory 692
liquidity ratios 686
liquidity risk 206, 224
load balancing 471
loan covenants 691
loanable funds market 556, 597
local area networks (LANs) 425, 716
lockbox plan 689
logical components of the business process 724
long 233, 237
long (buyer) vs. short (seller) positions 706
long hedge 239
long-arm statute 15
long-run equilibrium 518
low income elasticity 760
lower income growth 768
lower inflation 768
lower real interest rates 768
loyalty 61
luxury goods 751

M

M1 628, 630
M2 628, 630
macroeconomy 585, 759
make or buy decisions 343
management 686, 746
management decision-making 726
management process 724
management reporting systems (MRS) 443, 732
managing current assets 688
managing current liabilities 690
manual 723
manufacturing costs 297
manufacturing overhead 298
margin 237

margin of safety 258, 710
marginal 606
marginal analysis 751
marginal cost of capital (MCC) 181
marginal costs 605, 631, 752
marginal product 521, 537, 606, 751
marginal propensity 751
marginal propensity to consume 751
marginal revenue 752
marginal revenue product 521
marginal utility 525, 751
margins 556, 563, 656
mark for review 801
mark to market 661, 662
market (beta) risk 173
market equilibrium 518, 550
market equilibrium price and quantity 749
market influences on business strategies 520
market price 757
market risk 224, 699
market segmentation theory 692
market share 566
market structure 754
market value added (MVA) 213, 698
marketable securities (cash equivalents) 689
markets 517, 556, 571, 595, 627, 648, 660
marking to market 237, 661
master data 721
master file maintenance 733
master files updated 732
material account 305
maturity risk 206
member 75
merger 32
message acknowledgment techniques 490
metadata 742
michael porter 558
minimum cash balance (MCB) 688
minimum contact 14
minimum wage 576
MIPS 742
mirror sites 739
mirroring 471
mixed cost 309
mnemonic coding 721
modified internal rate of return (MIRR) 695
monetary policy 624, 763
money 627
money supply 510, 624, 630
monitor 744, 745

Page 816   ©2007 Kaplan CPA Review

monitoring 441
monopolist 567
monopoly 568, 630, 754
Monte Carlo simulation 174, 199
moral suasion 765
mortgage bonds 17
multiple-choice questions 791
multiplier effect 628, 629

N

national income 589
natural rate of unemployment 554, 590
necessity 751
negligence 680
net cash flow 171
net exposure 769
net income plus non cash expenses 694
net margin 687
net present value (NPV) 335, 695
net present value (NPV) method 167, 331
net profit margin 108
net realizable value method 714
net working capital (NWC) 172
network administrators 459, 737
network computer 716
network managers 457
network providers 741
networks 425, 717, 736
newly issued equity, cost of 180
next period's dividend (D1) 702
NIKKEI 704
no growth DDM 701
nominal GDP 587, 621, 625
nominal interest rates 622, 626, 762
nominal risk-free rate 206
noncontrollable factory overhead variance 716
nonvalue adding 713
no-par stock 18
NOPAT 213
normal cost system 298, 302
normal good 747, 751
normal profit 754
normalization 736
Notice to Schedule (NTS) 787
novation 12

O

objected oriented 736

off-balance-sheet financing 114
officers 13, 28, 678
official bank check 689
offsetting order 233
oligopolists 569
oligopoly 568, 569, 570
one-factor overhead variance 390
online batch processing 430
online transaction entry system 732
open market operations 629, 764
operating exposure 655, 769
operating leverage 139, 209, 248, 757
operating margin 102, 687
operating profit 757
operating system 424, 717
operation (sustainment) 727
operational risk 224
operations process 724
opportunity costs 172, 292, 339, 516, 550, 605, 688
optimal consumption 753
optimal decision 753
optimal production 753
option clearing corporation 704
option strategies 705
options 231, 704
options contracts 235
order costs (inventory) 337
order point 708
ordinary annuity 208
organizational meeting 13
other valuation techniques 703
out-of-the-money 234
output 720, 732
output controls 490
output devices 424, 716
outside directors 25
outstanding 17
outstanding stock 679
overall price level 511
over-applied overhead 301
overhead 299
overhead costs 302
overhead rate 299

P

par value 17, 23, 679
parity checking 490
participating preferred stock 19
partner, principal, and agent 54

STUDY MANUAL – BUSINESS ENVIRONMENT & CONCEPTS
INDEX

partnership 677, 681
partnership agreement 55
partnership at will 682
partnership by estoppel 57
partnership formation 55
partnership management 59
partnership property 60, 62
patents 754
payback 334, 695
payback method 331
payback period 165
payment date 20
perfect competition 754
perfective 732
perfectly competitive 754
period costs 297
peripheral equipment 742
perpetual life 10
perpetuity 700
personal computer 716
personal consumption expenditure index (PCE) 761
personal digital assitant (PDAs) 716
personal income 589
personal jurisdiction 14
personal liability 28
pervasive control plans 745
Phillips curve 554, 591
piercing the corporate veil 14
planning & organization 745
pledging 690
point of sale processing (POS) 430
point of sale transactions (POS) 477, 741
Porter's five competitive forces 558
post-implementation review 732
powers 61
powers of incorporation 15
preemptive rights 21
preferred shareholders 18
preferred stock 679, 700
preferred stock, cost of 177
pre-incorporation issues 11
premium 234
preparation framework 783
present value 166, 205
pre-tax profit 757
preventive controls 480
price ceiling 570, 574
price discrimination 572
price elasticity of demand 750
price floor 574

price searcher 572
price taker 573
price to book value (PBV) 703
price to cash flow (P/CF) 703
price to earnings multiple (P/E) valuation method 702
price to sales (P/S) 703
prices for resources 595
price-searcher 571
primary key 720
prime costs 298, 711
prime rate 691
privacy 488
probability analysis 709
process 720
process cost accounting 712
process cost system 302
processing controls 489
processing integrity 489
processors 716
producer price index (PPI) 761
product costs 297, 397
product development 565
product differentiation 755
product life cycle 555
production budget 329
production volume and fixed and variable costs 309
production volume variance 391
productivity 387
professional corporation 10
profit center 291
profit margins 687
profit maximization 753
profitability ratios 687
profit-volume graph 257
programmers 458
programming languages 426
project management 729
project plan 730
projects with unequal lives 696
Prometric Center 781, 788
Prometric website 788
promissory note 690
promoter 11, 679
prototyping 730
proxy 21
public corporation 9
purchase a put to profit from a stock falling in value 705
purchase call options to create leverage 705
purchasing power parity 662
purchasing protective puts 705

Page 818

©2007 Kaplan CPA Review

put options 231
puts 227

Q

quality control 386
quality of information 724
quantitative methods 708
quantity theory of money 626
quantity variances 715
quick (asset test) ratio 686
quick ratio 106
quorum 22

R

rate of return (interest rate) 204
ratio analysis 96, 685
raw materials purchase budget 329
real gdp 554, 559, 587, 621
real interest rates 514, 651
real rate 762
real rate of interest 762
real risk-free rate of interest 205
real-time processing 430, 733
reasonable care 26
recession 510, 556, 597, 624, 759
record 720
record date 20
recordation of data in system 732
recording variances 397
recovery 510
registered agent 12, 678
regression analysis 293, 708
regulation 560, 570, 598, 607, 628, 648
relational 735
relative sales value at split off method 713
relative sales value method 326
relevant costs 292, 339
relevant range 255, 290
reorder point 338, 689
replacement chain analysis 696
reporting 725
required interest rate on a security 206
required rate of return 702
required reserve ratio 629
reserve requirement 765
residual income 212, 346
resource cost/income approach 620
resource demand 521

resource supply and demand 594
responsibility centers 291
retention rate 109
return on capital 108
return on common equity 108
return on equity (ROE) 99, 109, 687
return on investment 331, 344
Revised Model Business Corporation Act
    (RMBCA) 12, 17, 21, 27, 31
Revised Uniform Partnership Act (RUPA) 53, 64
right to an accounting 60
right to choose associates 60
right to dissent 31
rights 59
risk 173, 198, 222, 698
risk assessment 494, 744
risk exposure 758
risk management 221
risk of bankruptcy 758
risk premium 204
risk, types of 699
risk-adjusted discount rate approach 174
risk-free rate 204
roles and responsibilities of the IT functions 737
Russell 2000 704

S

S corporation eligibility requirements 10
safety stock 338, 690, 708
sale of corporate assets 31
sales budget 329
sales elasticity 757
sample size 703
Sarbanes-Oxley Act of 2002 20, 29, 494
SAS No. 78 of Internal Control in a Financial Statement
    Audit 743
scatter diagram 293
scatter diagram approach 293
scenario analysis 173
schema 743
Secretary of State 12, 33
secure server 743
security 718, 741
security contols 484
security management 457
security of resources 744
segregation of duties in information technology
    functions 460
self-checking digit coding 721

STUDY MANUAL – BUSINESS ENVIRONMENT & CONCEPTS
INDEX

sell or process further 340
semi-variable cost 308
senior vs. junior (subordinated) debt 700
sensitivity analysis 173
separable cost 326
separation of duties of the various IT functions 738
separation of ownership from management 10
sequential/serial coding 721
server 424, 716
server clustering 739
setting standards 385
settlement price 237
settlement procedures 706
several liability 681
shareholder 10
shareholder agreements 24
shareholder derivative 23
shareholder liability 23
shareholders' equity 17
shareholders' rights 22
shift in demand 526
shifts in aggregate demand and aggregate supply 512
shifts in demand and supply 519
short 234, 237
short term bank loans 690
shortages 520
short-run equilibrium 518
short-term decision making 339
significant digit coding 721
sinking fund provisions 700
slowing (contraction) 510
small portion of the household budget 751
software 716
software languages 426
sole proprietorships 51, 677
solvency 114
sophisticated techniques 695
special orders, accept or reject 342
spending variance 392, 715
split-off point 326
spot contracts 235
spot price 237, 660
stagflation 593
stand-alone risk 173
Standard & Poor 500 (S&P 500) 704
standard costs 292, 385, 714
state board of accountancy 781, 787
stated (nominal) vs. effective interest rates 692
stated capital 19
statement of dissolution 66

statement of partnership authority 62
static budgets 330, 390
statutory merger 33
statutory powers 15
stock certificate 10
stock dividend 20
stock split 20
stock subscription 12
stock subscription agreements 23
stockout costs 336
stocks on which options trade 704
storage 424, 716, 720
strategic planning 565
strategy 561, 664
strike (exercise) price 233
structural unemployment 554, 590
structured query language (SQL) 736
subchapter S 684
subscription 679
substitutes 515, 748, 751
substitution effect 535
sum of least squares 293
sum of the least squares 294
sunk costs 291, 339, 605, 694
supernormal growth DDM 701
supply and demand 518, 550, 560, 574, 597, 652
supply and demand curves 515
supply chain 576, 577
supply chain management 576, 756
supply curve 512, 523, 556, 594, 625, 749
supply of money 625
supply shock 514
swap contracts 657, 771
swaps 226, 234, 244, 656
system 490
system maintenance 732
system survey 732
systems administrators 457
systems analyst 458, 737
systems concept 422
systems development 727
systems operation 732
systems programmers 458, 738
systems software 424

T

target profit 258
tastes and preferences 748
taxation 59

Page 820
©2007 Kaplan CPA Review

technology 725
tender offers 33
term structure of interest rates 136, 692
termination 64
termination of a limited partnership 683
testing windows 781, 785
threat/risk assessment 740
threats 480
threats of new entrants 754
threats of substitute goods 754
time series 686
time value 234
time value of money 166, 204
time-adjusted rate of return 331, 333
time-based model of security 485
times interest earned ratio 687
total asset turnover 107, 687
total debt to total asset ratio 686
total leverage 758
trade account 767
transaction exposure 655, 769
transaction processing 719
transaction processing system 733
transaction/data flow 733
transactions exposure 657
transfer prices 578, 757
translation 655
translation exposure 655, 769
translation risk 665
treasury stock 18, 679
trend analysis 96, 104
trust services 488
trust services framework 487

U

ultra vires 16
underapplied (underabsorbed) overhead 301
under-applied overhead 301
underlying 237
unemployment 509, 513, 553, 589, 626
unemployment rate 589
uniform resource locator (URL) 478, 743
units of output method 326
unsophisticated techniques 695
users of financial statements 93
usurpation 24

V

valuation models 703
value added network (VAN) 426
value adding 713
value at risk (VAR) methodologies 199
value chains 756
valuing an option 705
variable costs 209, 255, 291, 308, 606, 709
variable overhead 308
variance analysis 387, 714
variances 385
variances, disposition of 397
virtual private networks (VPNs) 426
volume variance 390, 715
voting agreement 21
voting for directors 21

W

warrant 697
watered stock 17, 23
web administrators 459, 738
weighted average cost of capital (WACC) 172, 180
weighted average system 712
weighting system 703
wide area networks (WANs) 426, 716
Wilshire 5000 704
winding up 64, 65, 66
Windows 718
wire payments or automatic debit 689
working capital management 131, 688
work-in-process account 305
work-in-process inventory 302
World Wide Web 743
writing covered calls to generate income 705

X

XBRL 478

Y

yield-curve risk 224

Z

zero balance account 689
zero coupon bonds 701

Notes